Murder in Dealey Plaza

Also by James H. Fetzer

Author

Scientific Knowledge: Causation, Explanation, and Corroboration

Artificial Intelligence: Its Scope and Limits

Philosophy and Cognitive Science

Computers and Cognition

Philosophy of Science

Co-Author

Glossary of Epistemology/Philosophy of Science

Glossary of Cognitive Science

Editor

Foundations of Philosophy of Science: Recent Developments

Science, Explanation, and Rationality

Principles of Philosophical Reasoning

The Philosophy of Carl G. Hempel

Sociobiology and Epistemology

Aspects of Artificial Intelligence

Epistemology and Cognition

Probability and Causality

Assassination Science

Co-Editor

Program Verification: Fundamental Issues in Computer Science

Philosophy, Language, and Artificial Intelligence

Philosophy, Mind, and Cognitive Inquiry

The New Theory of Reference

Definitions and Definability

MURDER IN DEALEY PLAZA

WHAT WE KNOW NOW THAT WE DIDN'T KNOW THEN ABOUT THE DEATH OF JFK

Edited by
James H. Fetzer, Ph.D.

CATFEET
PRESS
Chicago

This book and others from CATFEET PRESS™ and Open Court *may be ordered by calling* 1-800-815-2280 *or by visiting our website at* www.opencourtbooks.com.

CATFEET PRESS™ and the above logo are trademarks of Carus Publishing Company.

The front cover illustration is a frame from the fake Zapruder film featuring "the blob."
Back cover photograph of the editor by permission of Sarah M. Fetzer.

First printing 2000
Second printing 2001 (with corrections)
Third printing 2001 (with corrections)
Fourth printing 2001 (with corrections)
Fifth printing 2002 (with corrections)
Sixth printing 2003

Printed and bound in the United States of America.

Library of Congress Cataloging-in-Publication Data
Murder in Dealey Plaza : what we know now that we didn't know then about
   the death of JFK / edited by James H. Fetzer.
     p.   cm.
Includes bibliographical references and index.
ISBN: 0812694228 (pbk. : alk. paper)
  1. Kennedy, John F. (John Fitzgerald), 1917–1963—Assassination.
I. Fetzer, James H., 1940–
E842.9.M87 2000
364.15'24'092–dc21

                      12-035078
                      CIP

Robert B. Livingston, M.D.
with admiration

I know no safe depository of the ultimate powers of the society but the people themselves; and if we think them not enlightened enough to exercise their control with a wholesome discretion, the only remedy is not to take it from them but to inform their discretion.
                                                    —Thomas Jefferson

CONTENTS

Part V: The Zapruder Film

Part VI: Righting the Record

Epilogue

Appendices

Index

Acknowledgments

Contributors

Preface

Although you would not know from reading it in your daily newspaper, watching it on the evening news, or hearing it from the federal government, during the past decade—especially since 1992—enormous advances have been made in unraveling one of the greatest crimes of our time, the assassination of President John F. Kennedy. The murder was a state offense for which no one has ever been convicted. After more than 35 years, many Americans tend to think what happened will never be known and there is nothing new to learn. That opinion may be widely held, but it is also completely wrong. We know vastly more now than we ever have before, and we are learning more every day. What happened to this nation on 22 November 1963 occurred as a result of a meticulously executed conspiracy, whose character was concealed by a massive cover-up.

Indeed, unraveling the cover-up has provided an access route to understanding the conspiracy, which deprived the American people of their democratically-elected leader. A research group whose members came together in shared outrage over the blatant abuse of a leading medical journal in a crude but effective effort to perpetuate the cover-up—with the complicity of our nation's press—has discovered that JFK autopsy X-rays have been fabricated, autopsy photographs have been distorted or destroyed, the brain seen in official diagrams and photographs belonged to someone other than JFK, the autopsy report was a sham, and a great deal of the photographic record, including the Zapruder film of the assassination, has been edited by means of sophisticated techniques.

We have made strenuous efforts to bring these findings to the attention of the public, including repeated communications with *The New York Times*, ABC News, and the U.S. Department of Justice, but to no avail, as we have documented in *Assassination Science* (1998), a collection of studies devoted to placing research on the death of JFK upon an objective and scientific foundation (Appendix A).

The authors whose work appears there include a world authority on the human brain who is also an expert on wound ballistics (who has confirmed the substitution of someone else's brain for that of JFK); a Ph.D. in physics who is also board certified in radiation oncology (who has verified the fabrication of JFK autopsy X-rays); and several experts on various aspects of the photographic record (who have found detailed evidence of film and photo alteration).

As a professional philosopher and former Marine Corps officer, I have served as a catalytic agent by nurturing, promoting, and directing many of these efforts, such as by moderating a press conference in New York City on 18 November 1993, during which important medical findings were presented; by organizing a symposium on the alteration of the Zapruder film for a national convention on 21–22 November 1996; and by conducting the first professional conference on the death of JFK on a major campus at the University of Minnesota, Twin Cities, 14–16 May 1998. It has been my great pleasure to work with the most highly qualified individuals to ever study the assassination of JFK and I welcome the opportunity to advance their publication.

The present volume extends and deepens our past findings by taking advantage of new evidence provided by the release of more than 60,000 documents and records by the Assassination Records Review Board (ARRB), an entity of five persons created by Congress in the wake of the interest in this case rekindled by Oliver Stone's film, *JFK*, just as the House Select Committee on Assassinations' (HSCA) reinvestigation of 1977–78 had been incited by a television broadcast of the Zapruder film. The evidence to which we have now had access not only substantiates our previous findings but also enables us to understand in rather precise detail how the cover-up was conducted.

The fabrication of the X-rays, the substitution of someone else's brain, revision of the autopsy, photographic fakery, and the destruction and alteration of other crucial evidence—including the Presidential Lincoln limousine, which was "a crime scene on wheels"—was carried out by specific individuals who have specific names, including the autopsy physicians, James J. Humes and J. Thornton Boswell; John Ebersole, the officer in charge of radiology; Secret Service agents Roy Kellerman and William Greer, who were in charge of the limousine at the time of the assassination; and the President's personal physician, Admiral George G. Burkley, among others; but also unwitting employees of other government agencies, including two at the National Photographic Interpretation Center (NPIC), Homer McMahon and Bennett Hunter, who had a film of the crime in their hands the weekend it occurred.

Others at the Pentagon, the CIA, and the FBI may bear greater or lesser degrees of responsibility for the alteration and destruction of evidence. Homer McMahon and Bennett Hunter, for example, were paid by the CIA but were not agents of the CIA, and there appears to be no basis for suspecting their complicity in covering things up. Others, whose specific names and specific roles are explained and explored in various of the studies that follow, however, obviously assumed leading roles in managing the evidence whose alteration and destruction was ingeniously contrived. If one were to ask why officers of the Navy, agents of the Secret Service, and other persons associated with the FBI and the CIA should have assumed such roles, the answer is all too obvious.

While many theories have been advanced about who may have been responsible for the death of JFK, such as the Mafia, pro- or anti-Castro Cubans, or the KGB, it should be apparent that the Mafia, for example, could not have extended its reach into Bethesda Naval Hospital to fabricate X-rays under the control of officers of the Navy, agents of the Secret Service, and the President's personal physician. Neither pro- nor anti-Castro Cubans could have substituted diagrams and photographs of another brain—much less someone else's brain—for that of JFK. Nor could the KGB have had the opportunity to examine and reproduce an altered version of the Zapruder film, even though it may—like our CIA—have had the ability to do so. Nor could any of these things have been done by the alleged assassin, Lee Oswald, who was either in custody or already dead.

The principle of scientific reasoning known as *Occam's Razor* says that simpler theories should be preferred to more complex theories, provided that they are adequate to explain the evidence. What properly counts as "evidence" in this case, however, turns out to be a complicated question, where our most important contributions have involved discriminating between authentic and inauthentic evidence, where much of the evidence is a mixture or a blend of both original and artifical features to create deceptive composite fabrications. Most medical scientists, even forensic pathologists, are not accustomed to considering the possibility that their evidence may be fraudulent, which has contributed to the difficulty of finally securing a suitable foundation for differentiating between theories of the crime.

The greatest obstacle confronting the government account is to explain why so much of the evidence has been altered, created, or destroyed. The simplest explanation for government involvement in the cover-up, after all, is government involvement in the crime. It should not have been necessary to frame a guilty man. The studies published in this volume provide the simplest explanation for what happened to the evidence in this case. The conclusions they support afford understanding of the conspiracy itself, its scope and its duration. Unpacking the cover-up illuminates what has to be one the most extensive conspiracies of the 20th century. A judicial verdict may be said to be "beyond reasonable doubt" when no alternative explanation for the crime is reasonable. In this sense, the case has been settled beyond reasonable doubt.

Those who prefer to avoid unpleasant truths should proceed no further. Confronting what happened to the United States of America on 22 November 1963 is not for the fainthearted. One of the most perceptive critics of *The Warren Report* (1964), Harold Weisberg, shared the skepticism of Bertrand Russell about the investigation, but also proved that one did not have to be a genius to appreciate what was going on. Reading his observations for the first time, you may think they are exaggerations:

> [The Warren Commission and its *Report*] both ignored or suppressed what was opposed to the predetermined conclusion that Oswald alone was the assassin. This meant that the destruction, alteration and manipulation of evidence had to be "overlooked." It was. This meant that impossible testimony from preposterous witnesses had to be credited. It was. This meant that invalid reconstructions had to be made. They were. This meant that valuable evidence available to the Commission had to be avoided. It was.

> This meant that the incontrovertible proofs in the photographs had
> to be replaced by elaborate and and invalid reenactments which,
> in turn, had to be based upon inaccuracies, misinformation and
> misrepresentation, which is what was done. (Weisberg, *Whitewash*
> 1965, p. 51)

What we have found, alas, is that Russell and Weisberg were right, not simply about details, but about the heart of *The Warren Report*, which is corrupt to its core. What we know now differs only in quantity and quality from what they knew then.

It would be comforting to believe that discovering the truth, however bitter, about an event of this magnitude might lead to its dissemination to the American people by the American government. But, as recent developments clearly illustrate, that appears most unlikely. The Department of Justice has spent $16 million taxpayer dollars to take custody of the Zapruder film, in spite of repeated warnings that the film almost certainly was faked (Appendix B). The government went ahead with the purchase anyway. *The Washington Post* has now reported that, *prior* to the Bay of Pigs fiasco, the CIA—*our* CIA—had learned that the Soviet Union already knew the date of the planned attack, but went ahead anyway. Obviously, the Commander-in-Chief was not apprised, or he would have called it off. This was clearly an act of treason, if any acts are treasonous. At times, the President's ability to affect the government appears to be no greater than that of ordinary citizens.

J. H. F.

[I]t was a simple matter . . .
of a bullet right through the head.
—Malcolm Kilduff

Prologue

"Smoking Guns" in the Death of JFK

James H. Fetzer, Ph.D.

smoking gun [Colloq] *any conclusive evidence that proves guilt or fault.*
—Webster's New World Dictionary

During an interview shortly before a professional conference on "The Death of JFK" that would be held on the Twin Cities campus of The University of Minnesota on 14–16 May 1998, Federal Judge John R. Tunheim, who had served as Chair of the Assassination Records Review Board (ARRB), reported that no "smoking guns" had been discovered in the course of its efforts to declassify assassination records that had been secreted away for 50 years. The ARRB had come into existence as an effect of the passage of "The JFK Act" by Congress during the resurgence of interest in the assassination following the 1991 release of the Oliver Stone film, *JFK*.

The JFK Act had been passed over the intense opposition of President George Bush, a former Director of the CIA, perhaps in part because *JFK* implies that the CIA, the FBI, and the Pentagon played important roles in planning, executing, and covering up the death of our 35th President. Indeed, even after its passage, President Bush refused to appoint any members to the board, which had to await action by his successor, President Bill Clinton. As its own *Final Report* (*ARRB* 1998, p. xxiii) explains, this delay consumed the first 18 months of the existence of the ARRB, which began with a three-year mandate that later would be extended to four, during which it managed to declassify more than 60,000 records.

The ARRB

My concern, however, was less historical and more immediate. As the organizer and moderator of the Twin Cities conference, I had invited more than a dozen of the most accomplished students of JFK's assassination to serve as speakers and as commentators in an effort to broaden and deepen our understanding of this event by taking into account new findings, especially those of the ARRB.

1

It was my considered opinion—one I knew to be shared by virtually every other invited speaker, including Douglas Horne, Senior Military Analyst for the ARRB itself—that many records released by the ARRB not only substantiate previous conclusions about conspiracy and cover-up but clearly qualify as "smoking guns."

Judge Tunheim, whom I knew personally, was scheduled to speak at the opening banquet Friday evening, which meant his talk would be the very first presentation of the conference. I resolved to introduce him with a list of findings that, in my judgment, were on the order of "smoking guns," and drafted some notes as guidelines for my introduction. I thereby hoped to induce him to confront these issues directly. As luck would have it, he arrived nearly 45 minutes late, which made it impossible for me to present my list of discoveries and still keep the meeting on schedule. Although the opportunity was lost, I also resolved to pursue this issue in the belief that the American people should know at least as much as the Chair of the ARRB about its own findings. This book is meant to serve that purpose.

The Warren Report

John F. Kennedy, the 35th President of the United States, was murdered during a motorcade as it passed through Dealey Plaza in Dallas on 22 November 1963. The official government account of the crime, known as *The Warren Report* after its Chair, Chief Justice of the United States, Earl Warren—but technically entitled, *The Report of the President's Commission on the Assassination of President John F. Kennedy* (1964)—held that JFK was killed by a lone, demented assassin named Lee Harvey Oswald, who fired three shots with a high-velocity rifle from a sixth floor window of the nearby Texas School Book Depository, scoring two hits and one miss, which struck a distant concrete curb, ricocheted and slightly injured by-stander James Tague. (A photograph of the injury may be found in Robert Groden, *The Killing of a President* 1993, p. 41.)

The presumptive shots that hit, however, wreaked considerable damage. The first is alleged to have entered the President's back at the base of his neck, traversed his neck without impacting any bony structure, exited his throat at the level of his tie, entered the back of Texas Governor John Connally (riding in a jump seat in front of him), shattering a rib, exiting his chest, impacting his right wrist, and deflecting into his left thigh. The bullet supposed to have performed these remarkable feats, moreover, is alleged to have been recovered virtually undamaged from a stretcher at Parkland Hospital, where President Kennedy and Governor Connally were rushed for treatment, and has come to be known as "the magic bullet." The other struck JFK in the back of his head and killed him.

The HSCA

Indeed, these findings were reaffirmed and refined by the House Select Committee on Assassinations (HSCA) during its re-investigation of 1977–78 in its report of 1979, with the exception that—on the basis of disputed acoustical evidence, which it never adequately explored—it concluded that a fourth shot had been fired from "the grassy knoll," which made it probable that the President, after all, had been assassinated by a conspiracy, possibly one of small scale, a matter that the HSCA did not pursue. But, in relation to the major findings of the Warren Commission, the HSCA reaffirmed them. For the official government account of the death of JFK to be true, therefore, at least the following three conjectures—"hypotheses," let us call them, to avoid begging the question by taking for granted what needs to be established on independent grounds—have to be true:

(H1) *JFK was hit at the base of the back of his neck by a bullet that traversed his neck without hitting any bony structures and exited his throat at the level of his tie;*

(H2) *JFK was hit in the back of his head by a bullet fired from the sixth floor of the Texas School Book Depository, as its diagrams display, causing his death;* and,

(H3) *these bullets were fired by a sole assassin, Lee Harvey Oswald, using a high-powered rifle, which was identified as a 6.5 mm Italian Mannlicher-Carcano.*

As a point of deductive logic, if any of these hypotheses is false, then any account that entails them cannot be true. Yet it is surprisingly easy to show that all three are false.

Smoking Gun #1: *(H1) is an anatomical impossibility, because the bullet would have had to impact bony structures.*

Consider, for example, hypothesis (H1). David W. Mantik, M.D., Ph.D., who holds a Ph.D. in physics and is also board-certified in radiation oncology, has studied X-rays of the President's chest. He has used the cross-section of a body whose upper chest and neck dimensions were the same as those of JFK and performed a simple experiment. Taking the specific locations specified by the HSCA for the point of entry at the base of the back of the neck and the point of exit at the throat, he has drawn a straight line to represent the trajectory that any bullet would have to have taken from that point of entry to that point of exit. Any such trajectory would intersect cervical vertebrae. A CAT scan demonstrating Mantik's experiment has been published in a splendid study of some of the most basic evidence in this case by Stewart Galanor, *Cover-Up* (1998). Here is a visual representation of such a bullet's trajectory:

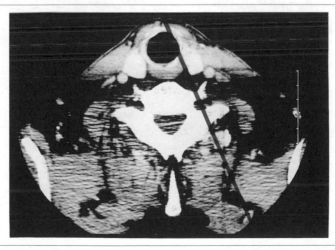

Mantik drew a line through a CAT scan

It would have been anatomically impossible for a bullet to have taken the trajectory specified by the official account. Hypothesis (H1) is not just false but cannot possibly be true. (Mantik's study may be found in *Assassination Science* 1998, pp. 157–58.)

Smoking Gun #2: *The head shot trajectory is inconsistent with the position of his head at the time of the shot, falsifying (H2).*

Consider (H2), the hypothesis that a bullet fired from the sixth floor of the Texas School Book Depository entered the back of JFK's head and killed him. The building in question was horizontally located to the President's rear, while the sixth floor of that building was vertically considerably above the President's head. Therefore, any such bullet must have entered the President's head from above and behind. That much is indisputable. No photographs of the President's injuries were published at the time, but *The Warren Report* (1964) did provide drawings (copies of which may be found in *Assassination Science* 1998, p. 438). The drawings of the head wound therefore appear to show a trajectory from above and behind, as the official account requires.

Stewart Galanor, *Cover-Up* (1998), however, has juxtaposed the official drawing with frame 312 of the Zapruder film, which the Warren Commission itself regarded as the moment before the fatal head shot incident to frame 313, with the following result:

The WC Drawing	*Zapruder Frame 312*

When the President's head is properly positioned, the Commission's own drawing displays an upward rather than a downward trajectory. If the official drawing of the injury to the head is correct, then the conjecture that the President was hit from above and behind cannot be true; and if the President was hit from above and behind, the official drawing of the injury must be false. Hypothesis (H2) cannot possibly be true.

Smoking Gun #3: *The weapon, which was not even a rifle, could not h*
bullets that killed the President, falsifying (H3).

Consider (H3), finally, which maintains that the bullets that hi
were fired by Lee Harvey Oswald using a high-powered rifle, which *The Warren
Report* (1964) also identified as a 6.5 mm Mannlicher-Carcano. As other authors,
including Harold Weisberg, *Whitewash* (1965), Peter Model and Robert Groden,
JKF: The Case for Conspiracy (1976), and Robert Groden and Harrison E.
Livingstone, *High Treason* (1989) have also observed, the Mannlicher-Carcano
that Oswald is supposed to have used is a 6.5 mm weapon, but it is not high
velocity. Its muzzle velocity of approximately 2,000 fps means that it qualifes as
a medium-to-low velocity weapon. [*Editor's note*: Indeed, the Mannlicher-Carcano
Oswald allegedly ordered is not a rifle but a carbine.]

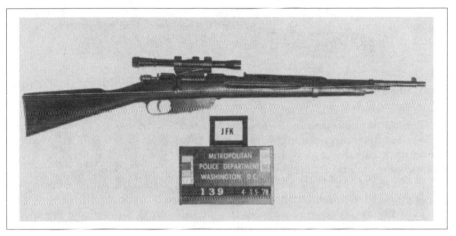

The 6.5 mm Mannlicher-Carcano, which is not a high-velocity weapon.

The death certificates, *The Warren Report*, articles in the *Journal of the AMA*,
and other sources state that the President was killed by wounds inflicted by high-
velocity missiles. (Some are reprinted in *Assassination Science* (1998).) The
Mannlicher-Carcano is the only weapon that Oswald is alleged to have used to kill
the President, but the Mannlicher-Carcano is not a high-velocity weapon; consequently, Lee Oswald could not have fired the bullets that killed the President. Thus,
hypothesis (H3) cannot be true. This discovery is especially important, because the
extensive damage sustained by JFK's skull and brain could not possibly have been
inflicted by a weapon of this kind. The major trauma the President endured had to
have been inflicted by one or more high-velocity weapons.

The Death of Deception

The hypotheses under consideration, (H1), (H2), and (H3), therefore, are not
merely false but are provably false. Moreover, these hypotheses are by no means
peripheral to the official account but the core of its conclusions. If (H1), (H2),
and (H3) are false, then *The Warren Report* (1964) cannot be salvaged, even in
spite of the best efforts of the Gerald Posners of the world. [*Editor's note*: Some
problems encountered by his popular attempt to revive it have been dissected in

Assassination Science (1998), pp. 145–152.] Among the central findings of *The Warren Report* (1964), therefore, the only one that appears to be true is the least important, namely: that bystander James Tague was hit by a bullet fragment that ricocheted from a distant curb and caused him minor injury.

There are many more, which may be found in this and other studies of the death of JFK. Since Bertrand Russell raised 16 "questions" about the investigation during 1964—even while it was still in progress—it seems appropriate to contrast what we know now with what Russell knew then by offering 16 "smoking guns" that complement his work. In some instances, these smoking guns overlap with Russell's questions, but discerning readers ought to have no difficulty discovering others in the course of study of this book. I have found that every access route to this subject—whether by means of the medical evidence, the physical evidence, the eyewitness evidence, the Dallas police, *The Warren Report*, the FBI, the CIA, the Pentagon, the Secret Service, or any other avenue of approach—leads to the same conclusions we have reached here and in *Assassination Science* (1998).

Other "Smoking Guns"

Smoking Gun #4: *The bullets, which were standard copper-jacketed World War II-vintage military ammunition, could not have caused the explosive damage.*

The ammunition that Oswald is alleged to have used was standard full-metal jacketed military ammunition, one round of which was supposed to have been found on a stretcher at Parkland Hospital, a photograph of which appears as Commission Exhibit 399 (elsewhere in this volume). This kind of ammunition conforms to Geneva Convention standards for humane conduct of warfare and is not intended to maim but, absent its impact with hard bodily features, to pass through a body. It does not explode. The lateral cranial X-ray of the President's head (the image of his head taken from the side), however, displays a pattern of metallic debris as effects of the impact of an exploding bullet, which could not have been caused by ammunition of the kind Oswald was alleged to have used, thereby exonerating him.

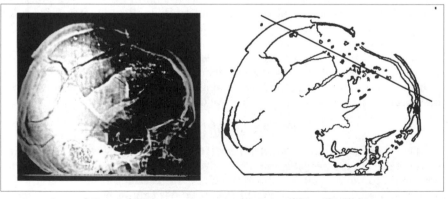

Lateral Cranial X-ray   *Axis of Metallic Debris*

Smoking Gun #5: *The axis of metallic debris is inconsistent with a shot from behind but consistent with a shot that entered the area of the right temple.*

The axis of debris appears to be consistent with a shot entering the area of the right temple rather than the back of the head. Studies of this issue are found in Joseph N. Riley, Ph.D., "The Head Wounds of John F. Kennedy: One Bullet Cannot Account for the Injuries," *The Third Decade* (March 1993), pp. 1–15, in Mantik's research on the X-rays published in *Assassination Science* (1998), in his comments on the recent deposition of James J. Humes, M.D., for the ARRB (Appendix G), and in his present study of the medical evidence. In the autopsy report, Humes had described this metallic trail as beginning low on the right rear of the skull. The actual trail, however, lies more than 4 inches higher, much closer to the top of the skull than to the bottom.

Confronted with this discrepancy, Humes concedes that the autopsy report was wrong by some 10 cm (Appendix G). Humes here faced an impossible paradox, which he could not honestly resolve. If he had described the trail correctly and simultaneously reported the low entry wound to the back of the head, then the only reasonable conclusion would have been two shots to the head—one from behind and one from in front—which, in turn, would have implied the existence of at least two gunmen. Humes had no choice but literally to move the trail of metallic debris downward by more than four inches (10 cm), which is precisely what he did. As Mantik explains, it took more than three decades for Humes to be asked to confront this important paradox, which falsifies the lone gunman theory.

Smoking Gun #6: *The official autopsy report was contradicted by more than 40 eyewitness reports and was inconsistent with HSCA diagrams and photographs.*

Gary Aguilar, M.D., has collated the testimony of more than 40 eyewitnesses, including spectators in Dealey Plaza, physicians and nurses at Parkland Hospital, Navy medical technicians and FBI agents at Bethesda Naval Hospital, who report a massive blow-out to the back of the head. Several physicians have diagrammed this blow-out as it was observed at Parkland, which had the general character of the wound depicted below. David Lifton, *Best Evidence* (1980), however, has diagrammed what the wound resembled based upon the official autopsy report from Bethesda. These may be labeled as "the heel" and "the footprint" due to their size and relationship. When the HSCA reinvestigated the crime in 1978–79, its diagrams and photographs now depicted a small entry wound, which is sometimes referred to as "the red spot".

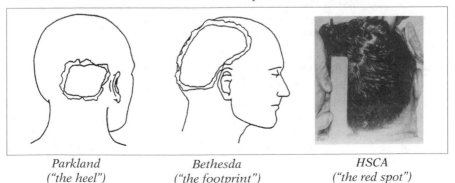

| Parkland | Bethesda | HSCA |
| ("the heel") | ("the footprint") | ("the red spot") |

Smoking Gun #7: *These eyewitness reports were rejected on the basis of the X-rays, which have been fabricated in at least two different ways.*

As Mantik has discovered through the employment of optical densitometry studies, the lateral cranial X-ray has been fabricated by imposing a patch over a massive defect to the back of the head, which corresponds to the eyewitness reports describing (what is called here) "the heel" shot. In effecting this deception, the perpetrators used material that was much too dense to be normal skull material, which enabled Mantik to discover what had been done. It turns out that, although not common knowledge at the time, instructions that could be followed to create composites were available in contemporary radiology publications. He has replicated these results in the radiology darkroom, as he explains here and in earlier studies in *Assassination Science* (1998).

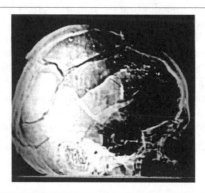 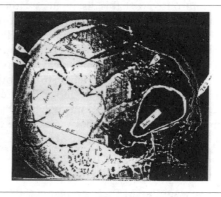

Lateral Cranial X-ray   *The Patch ("Area P")*

The anterior-posterior (front-to-rear) autopsy X-ray, moreover, has been fabricated by imposing a 6.5 mm "metal" object not present on the original, which Mantik has established on the basis of additional optical densitometry studies published in *Assassination Science* (1998). All three of the military pathologists who conducted the autopsy at Bethesda have now confirmed to the ARRB that they did not see this metallic object on the X-ray, no doubt because it was added after the autopsy was finished. The addition of this metallic object appears to have been done to implicate a 6.5 mm weapon, such as the Mannlicher-Carcano, in the assassination of President Kennedy. The conspirators made mistakes due to their lack of familiarity with this weapon, however, since it is not a high-velocity rifle and could not have inflicted the damage that caused the President's death.

Smoking Gun #8: *Diagrams and photos of a brain in the National Archives are of the brain of someone other than JFK.*

Robert B. Livingston, M.D., a world authority on the human brain, has concluded that credible reports of damage to the cerebrum and especially to the cerebellum—numerous and consistent from the physicians at Parkland, as Aguilar has explained—are incompatible with the diagrams and photographs that are alleged to be of the brain of President Kennedy. As he summarizes his findings, Livingston, who is also an expert on wound ballistics, states, "A conclusion is obligatorily forced that the photographs and drawings of the brain in the National Archives are those of some brain other than that of John Fitzgerald Kennedy" (*Assassination Science* 1998, p. 164). This stunning inference has been confirmed by new evidence released by the ARRB, which establishes the occurrence of two distinct post-autopsy brain examinations involving two distinct brains, as Douglas Horne, who was the Senior Analyst for Military Records of the ARRB, explains in a contribution to this volume.

Smoking Gun #9: *Those who took and processed the autopsy photographs claim that parts of the photographic record have been altered, created, or destroyed.*

As a consequence of depositions by the ARRB, we now also have extensive additional evidence that autopsy photographs have been altered, created, or destroyed. One of the fascinating discoveries that has emerged from its efforts are eyewitness reports from John Stringer, the offical autopsy photographer, that the photographs of the brain shown in the official set are not those that he took at the time; from Robert Knudsen, White House photographer, who has reported having in his possession—at one and the same time— photographs that displayed a major blow-out to the President's head and others that did not; and from Saundra Spencer, who processed the photographs, who explains that she knows they are not the same because they do not have the same physical markings as other photographs she processed using the same film, some of which she still possesses. The importance of these and related discoveries for understanding the medical evidence in this case is explored in studies by Aguilar and by Mantik elsewhere in this volume.

Smoking Gun #10: *The Zapruder film, among others, has been extensively edited using highly sophisticated techniques.*

Since *The Warren Report* (1964) published many of the frames of the Zapruder film and placed heavy reliance upon its authenticity in arriving at its conclusions about how many shots were fired and the time it took to fire them, if the photographic evidence is flawed, then the Commission's conclusions are equally in doubt. And, indeed, there are many reasons to question the authenticity of the Zapruder film as well as much of the other photographic evidence. In his major study of the assassination of JFK, *Bloody Treason* (1997), Noel Twyman reports consulting with Roderick Ryan, a leading technical expert on motion picture film. Twyman had been puzzled by the discovery of numerous anomalies in the film, including blurred stationary background figures but sharply focused limousine in frame 302 versus the sharp focus of both in frame 303.

Zapruder Frame 302   *Zapruder Frame 303*

When Twyman asked Ryan how this could be explained, he stated, *"the limousine is moving in 302 and standing still in 303"* (Twyman 1997, p. 150). And when Twyman asked him about the mysterious "blob" that seems to shift around from frame to frame immediately after the fatal head shot at frame 313, Ryan told him *"it looked as if the blobs had been painted in"* (Twyman 1997, p. 151). [*Editor's note:* The cover of this book highlights "the blob" and Jackie's face, which also seems to be painted in.] Ryan's opinions are all the more important insofar as they corroborate conclusions about film alteration that had been drawn independently by Jack White and by David Mantik, initially in Part IV of *Assassination Science* (1998) and now in Part V of the current volume. Dr. Ryan received an Oscar for his technical contributions to the motion picture industry during the April 2000 Academy Awards.

Among the most remarkable discoveries of the ARRB, moreover, was locating two persons who worked on evaluating a home movie of the assassination at the National Photographic Interpretation Center (NPIC) run by the CIA the weekend of the murder. This movie, which appears to have been the "out-of-camera" original of the Zapruder film, was studied by Homer McMahon, who was in charge of the color laboratory at the time. He has reported that, after viewing it at least 10 times, he had concluded that JFK was hit 6 or 8 times from at least three directions, a conclusion subsequently dismissed by Secret Service Agent William Smith, who declared that McMahon had to be mistaken because only three shots had been fired from above and behind, an opinion he had reached without studying the film at NPIC. This stunning episode was recorded in a series of interviews conducted for the ARRB by Douglas Horne and is published here.

Smoking Gun #11: *The official conclusion contradicts widely-broadcast reports on radio and television about two shots fired from the front.*

Descriptions of two wounds—a small wound to the throat as well as a massive blow-out of the back of the head caused by an entry wound to the right temple—were widely broadcast that afternoon. If you look at television coverage from that day, you will find that, at 1:35 PM, NBC reports both a shot to the throat and a shot through the right temple, findings attributed to Admiral George Burkley, the President's personal physician. At 1:45 PM, another network reports a shot through the head and a shot to the throat. Chet Huntley reports a shot through the right temple. Robert MacNeil says it is unclear to him how the President could have been shot through the throat and temple if the assassin was firing from above and behind. Frank McGee calls it "incongruous."

Malcolm Perry, M.D., who performed a tracheostomy in a vain attempt to save the life of the mortally injured President, was so certain that a small wound to the throat at the location of the tracheostomy had been fired from in front that—when told that the assassin had been above and behind the limousine—he concluded that JFK must have stood and turned to wave to spectators who were behind him. During a press conference held at Parkland that afternoon, he stated three times that the wound to the throat had been a wound of entry, not a wound of exit. Through deceptive use of a series of hypothetical questions—that *assumed* the bullet entered at the base of the neck, transited the neck without hitting any bony structures, and exited through the throat—the author of "the single bullet theory," Arlen Specter, was able to obfuscate these observations and thereby support the official account, in which the trajectories of these wounds were reversed.

Smoking Gun #12: *The (fabricated) X-rays, (altered) autopsy photographs, and even the (edited) Zapruder film were improperly used to discredit eyewitness reports.*

An important point of which most Americans are generally unaware is that legal procedure permits photographs and motion pictures to be used as evidence in courts of law only when a foundation for their introduction has been established by eyewitness testimony, as Milicent Cranor has observed. According to *McCormick on Evidence*, 3rd edition (1984), Section 214, for example, concerning photographs, movies, and sound recordings:

> The principle upon which photographs are most commonly admitted into evidence is the same as that underlying the admission of illustrative drawings, maps, and diagrams. Under this theory, a photograph is viewed merely as a graphic portrayal of oral testimony, and becomes admissible only when a witness has testified that it is a correct and accurate representation of the relevant facts personally observed by the witness.

The practice of the Warren Commission and apologists for its findings appears to be the exact opposite, where photographs and films—including X-rays—have been used to discount the testimony of eyewitnesses, which is not only the better evidence but is actually required to lay a foundation for the admissibility of evidence of those kinds.

Some defenders of the official account have maintained that the Warren Commission inquiry was not a legal proceeding but merely an advisory body offering its findings and its recommendations to the President, which is technically correct. The precise legal status of *The Warren Report* (1964) is therefore open to doubt. But how could the interests of the American people in truth, justice, and fairness—possibly be served by failing to adhere to clear and established principles for the admissibility of evidence? Alas, the question has only to be asked for the answer to be all too obvious. As Harold Weisberg and Bertrand Russell already understood, the Commission was not created to advance the interests of truth, justice, and fairness, but to convince the American people that a lone gunman had assassinated the 35th President of the United States, that the matter had been thoroughly investigated, and that there had been no conspiracy or cover-up.

Smoking Gun #13: *The motorcade route was changed at the last minute and yet the assassination occurred on the part that had been changed.*

Think about it. As Chief of Police Jesse Curry confirmed in his *JFK Assassination File* (1969), which I discuss elsewhere in this volume, it was not until 18 November 1963 that the final motorcade route was settled at a meeting between representatives of the Police Department and the Secret Service, when it was agreed that the motorcade would take a right off Main Street onto Houston and a very sharp left onto Elm en route to the Trade Mart, where JFK was scheduled to present a luncheon speech. At the turn from Houston onto Elm, remarkably, the motorcade was considered over and local security was no longer provided. This appears to be such a transparent pretext for disavowing responsibility for the President's security by the Dallas Police as to be indicative of what is known in the law as "consciousness of guilt" in failing to take or in taking measures that ordinarily would or would not be taken—save for knowledge of the circumstances of a crime.

The original motorcade route was even published in the morning newspaper, which raises a fascinating question, namely: How did the alleged assassin even know that the President would pass by the Texas School Book Depository in order for him to shoot him? In an interesting study, "The Mathematical Improbability of the Kennedy Assassination," *The Dealey Plaza Echo* (November 1999), pp. 2–6, Ed Dorsch, Jr., has calculated that the probability of Oswald and JFK coming within 100 yards of each other at random during his Presidency is approximately one in thirty-three billion! This suggests an encounter by the two was almost certainly no accident, yet Oswald had no reason to know he would only have to show up for work to have the chance to shoot JFK—and his wife even said that he had overslept! A more plausible explanation is that their proximity was not a matter of chance but was coordinated by plans about which Oswald had no knowledge and over which he had no control.

Smoking Gun #14: *Secret Service policies for the protection of the President were massively violated during the motorcade in Dallas.*

More than a dozen Secret Service policies for the protection of the President seem to have been violated during the motorcade in Dallas, including no protective military presence; no coverage of open windows; motorcycles out of position; agents not riding on the Presidential limousine; vehicles in improper sequence; utilization of an improper route, which included a turn of more than 90°; limousine slowed nearly to a halt at the corner of Houston and Elm; the limousine came to a halt after bullets began to be fired; agents were virtually unresponsive; brains and blood were washed from the limousine at Parkland, even before the President had been pronounced dead; the limousine was stripped down and being rebuilt by Monday, the day of the formal state funeral; a substitute windshield was later produced as evidence; and so on— discoveries that are strengthened and extended by Vincent Palamara and Douglas Weldon, J.D., in this book.

As an illustration, consider the sequence of vehicles. As the accompanying diagram displays (see Richard E. Sprague, *Computers and Automation* May 1970, pp. 48–49), the Presidential limousine was the lead vehicle in the motorcade, followed by the Secret Service "Queen Mary," the Vice-Presidential liousine, the Vice-President's security, then the Mayor, some dignitaries, Press

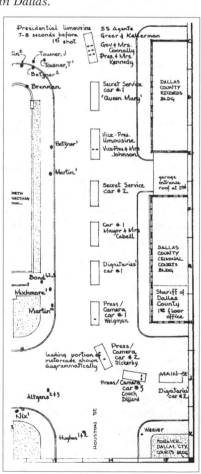

The Motorcade Sequence

Car #1, Press Car #2, and so on, which is completely absurd. A proper motorcade would have the lower-ranking dignitaries early on, then those in between, and finally the highest official, who would naturally be surrounded by the press, who were there, after all, to cover a political event! In this case, however, everything was wrong—even though, as Richard Trask, *Pictures of the Pain* (1994, p. 45), has observed, the vehicles were identified with numerals; the Mayor's car, for example, was marked with a number "**1**" on its windshield. Indeed, the President's personal physician, Admiral Burkley, was in the very last car!

This had to be deliberate, it had to be wrong, and everyone involved with security had to know that it was wrong. In this regard, one of the most remarkable paragraphs in the *Final Report of the Assassination Records Review Board* (1998) is the following:

> Congress passed the JFK Act of 1992. One month later, the Secret Service began its compliance efforts. However, in January 1995, the Secret Service destroyed presidential protection survey reports for some of President Kennedy's trips in the fall of 1963. The Review Board learned of the destruction approximately one week after the Secret Service destroyed them, when the Board was drafting its request for additional information. The Board believed that the Secret Service files on the President's travel in the weeks preceding his murder would be relevant.

From the ARRB Final Report *(1998), p. 149*

Here again we appear to be confronted with one more indication of consciousness of guilt, which we must add to other indications of Secret Service complicity in the death of JFK.

Smoking Gun #15: *Neither the Mafia nor pro- or anti-Castro Cubans nor the KGB could have done any of these things—much less Lee Oswald, who was either incarcerated or already dead.*

The complicity of medical officers of the United States Navy, agents of the Secret Service, the President's personal physician, and other representatives of the Pentagon, the FBI, and the CIA provides powerful evidence that can serve as a premise in the appraisal of alternative theories about the assassination of JFK. Neither the Mafia, pro- or anti-Castro Cubans, or the KGB could have fabricated autopsy X-rays; substituted the brain of someone else for the brain of JFK; created, altered, or destroyed autopsy photographs; or subjected motion pictures, such as the Zapruder film, to extensive editing using highly sophisticated techniques. Nor could any of these things have been done by the alleged assassin, Lee Oswald, who was either incarcerated or already dead.

The only theories that are remotely plausible, given these evidentiary findings, are those that implicate various elements of the government. It was a crime of such monstrous proportions and immense consequences that the clearly most reasonable explanation is that elements of the government covered up the crime because those same elements of the government committed the crime. For the CIA to have brought these effects about on its own, moreover, would have required medical officers of the U.S. Navy, agents of the Secret Service, and the President's personal physican, among many others, to have been working for or otherwise under its control. While the CIA has repeatedly demonstrated its abilities in bringing about changes in governments around the world—and no doubt elements of the CIA were involved in planning and covering up this crime—it looks as though it could not have done this one on its own.

Smoking Gun #16: *Many individuals knew details about the assassination before and after the fact, all of whom viewed Lee Oswald as no more than a patsy.*

One of the more amusing events involved in assassination studies occurred when Liz Smith, a syndicated columnist, apprised her readers that, although she had always taken for granted that *The Warren Report* (1964) was right and that Oswald had been a lone assassin, after reading Noel Twyman, *Bloody Treason* (1997), she was no longer sure. This provoked an outraged response from Jack Valenti, the Hollywood Czar and former aide to LBJ, who proclaimed that there was a simple way to know for sure no conspiracy had been involved, namely: that, if there had been a conspiracy, someone would have talked—*and no one has talked*! The possibility of a small scale conspiracy or that most of the conspirators might have been eliminated right away to keep things quiet may have escaped him, but for a conspiracy of any magnitude—involving dozens and dozens, if not hundreds of people—what Valenti said may have seemed to be right.

Of course, that presumes Valenti knew what he was talking about. On a single page of *Bloody Treason* (1997, p. 285), for example, Noel lists eight names of prominent persons who have talked, including Mafia Dons Carlos Marcello and Santo Trafficante, Jr.; right-wing extremist Joseph Milteer; mobster Johnny Roselli; high ranking CIA official David Atlee Phillips; his old boss, Lyndon Baines Johnson; CIA contract agent and professional anti-Communist Frank Sturgis; and Sam Giancana, who confessed the complicity of the mob in collusion with the CIA to his brother, Chuck. If Valenti cared about the truth in a matter of this kind, then he might have wanted to read Twyman's book before he set out to trash it, or visited his local book store and picked up a copy of *Double Cross* (1992).

Other Sources

These are hardly the only persons to have talked about the assassination. Jim Hicks, for example, who bears a striking resemblance to someone photographed outside of the Cuban Embassy in Mexico City impersonating Lee Oswald, was photographed in Dealey Plaza with an antenna hanging out of his pocket and claims to have been a communications coordinator for the killing. Charles Harrelson, serving a life term for the assassination of a federal judge with a high-powered rifle, once confessed to having killed Kennedy, by which I take it he meant he had fired the fatal shot. Chauncey Holt, a counterfeiter who worked as a contract agent for the CIA, has told me he was instructed to bring 15 sets of forged Secret Service credentials to Dealey Plaza, which he dutifully prepared, but that, in light of his extensive experience with the underworld, he thought it was not a mob hit but rather a military operation. I now suspect that Chauncey was correct. The role of the Pentagon in this affair certainly deserves further investigation, an opinion now dramatically confirmed by James Bamford, *Body of Secrets* (2001), pp. 78–91, which suggests that the assassination may have originated with the Joint Chiefs of Staff.

And there are others. Perhaps the most interesting is Madeleine Duncan Brown, a former mistress of LBJ by whom she had a son, who was not LBJ's only offspring out of wedlock but was his only son. Among the fascinating details she conveys in a book of their affair, *Texas in the Morning* (1997), is that Lyndon told her, at a social event the night before the murder at the home of oil baron Clint Murchison, that after tomorrow he would not have to put up with embarrassment from those Kennedy boys any longer. And that, during a New Year's Eve rendezvous at The Driskill Hotel in Austin, when she confronted him with rumors (rampant in Dallas at the time) that he had been involved (since no one stood to gain more personally), he blew up at her and told her that the CIA and the oil boys had decided that Jack had to be taken out—which is about as close as we are going to get to the font.

Then and Now

Having known Chauncey Holt and having talked with Madeleine Duncan Brown, no doubt I have cognitive advantages that Jack Valenti does not enjoy, simply because I know more about the case than he does. Although many Americans know that there are excellent books on the assassination—including Harold Weisberg, *Whitewash* (1965), Mark Lane, *Rush to Judgment* (1966), Josiah Thompson, *Six Seconds in Dallas* (1967), Sylvia Meagher, *Accessories After the Fact* (1967), James Hepburn, *Farewell America* (1968), George O'Toole, *The Assassination Tapes* (1975), Gary Shaw, *The Cover-Up* (1976), Peter Model and Robert Groden, *JFK: The Case for Conspiracy* (1976), David Lifton, *Best Evidence* (1980), Jim Garrison, *On the Trail of the Assassins* (1988), Jim Marrs, *Crossfire* (1989), Robert Groden and Harrison Livingstone, *High Treason* (1989), Charles Crenshaw, *JFK: Conspiracy of Silence* (1992), Harrison Livingstone, *High Treason 2* (1992), Robert Groden, *The Killing of a President* (1993), and Noel Twyman, *Bloody Treason* (1997)—to mention 16 of the best—they do not realize how much we know now on the basis of scientific findings.

In defense of Judge Tunheim, of course, the objection could be raised that he had his hands full with more than 60,000 records and might not have had any opportunity for reading other work on the assassination, even Stewart Galanor, *Cover-Up* (1998), a work of less than 200 pages that conclusively refutes Warren Commission and HSCA findings. Although he was Chair of the ARRB, it might be argued, he cannot be expected to have read everything ever written on this subject. And, indeed, that is not an unreasonable point to make for any American citizen. Let me therefore close with a recommendation. Start with Galanor's *Cover-Up* (1998), as I have done here; then read the book you have in your hands; and finally turn to *Assassination Science* (1998). You are entitled to know what happened to your country on 22 November 1963. As Charles Drago has eloquently observed, anyone sincerely interested in this case who does not conclude that JFK was murdered as the result of a conspiracy is either unfamiliar with the evidence or cognitively impaired.

APPENDIX A
THE MEMBERS OF THE ASSASSINATION RECORDS REVIEW BOARD

"The President, by and with the advice and consent of the Senate, shall appoint, without regard to political affiliation, five citizens to serve as members of the Review Board to ensure and facilitate the review, transmission to the Archivist, and public disclosure of Government records related to the assassination of President John F. Kennedy." JFK Act at § 7 (b)(1).

Although the Review Board members were Presidential appointees, the JFK Act recommended that the President select the Board members from lists of names submitted to the President by four professional associations—the American Historical Association, the Organization of American Historians, the Society of American Archivists, and the American Bar Association. The Review Board's biographies follow.

The Honorable John R. Tunheim. The American Bar Association recommended John R. Tunheim to the President. Judge Tunheim is currently a United States District Court Judge in the District of Minnesota, and, at the time of his nomination, was Chief Deputy Attorney General of the state of Minnesota. Judge Tunheim worked in the Office of the Attorney General for 11 years as the Solicitor General before his appointment as Chief Deputy. Earlier, he practiced law privately and served as Staff Assistant to U.S. Senator Hubert H. Humphrey. He received his J.D. from the University of Minnesota Law School, and his B.A. from Concordia College in Moorhead, Minnesota. The Review Board members elected Judge Tunheim to Chair the Review Board.

Henry F. Graff. Henry F. Graff was recommended to President Clinton by the White House staff. He is Professor Emeritus of History at Columbia University, where he held rank as Instructor to Full Professor from 1946-1991. He served as the Chairman of the History Department from 1961–1964. In the 1960s he served on the National Historical Publications Commission, having been appointed by President Lyndon B. Johnson. Dr. Graff was also a Senior Fellow of the Freedom Forum Media Studies Center from 1991-1992. He received his M.A. and his Ph.D. from Columbia University, and his B.S.S. from City College, New York.

Kermit L. Hall. The Organization of American Historians nominated Kermit L. Hall, Executive Dean of the Colleges of the Arts and Sciences, Dean of the College of Humanities, and Professor of History and Law at The Ohio State University. Dean Hall was appointed by Chief Justice William Rehnquist to the Historical Advisory Board of the Federal Judicial Center and is a director of the American Society for Legal History. Dean Hall received his Ph.D. from the University of Minnesota, a Master of Study of Law from Yale University Law School, received his M.A. from Syracuse University, and his B.A. from The University of Akron.

Final Report of the AARB (1998), p. 177

[Editor's note: *Shown are Chairman John R. Tunheim and two members of the board, Henry F. Graff and Kermit L. Hall, both of whom are former Army intelligence officers. Another member, Anna Kasten Nelson, asserts that the JFK Act "was designed to strip away theories that implicated federal agencies in a conspiracy to murder the young president" and that "assassination afficionados seeking the 'smoking gun' document(s) will be disappointed"* (Athan Theoharis, A Culture of Secrecy 1998, Chapter 10). *The language of the Act does not support her interpretation, however, and she does not explain how she could know in advance that the then-unfinished work of the Board would undermine conspiracy theories. Precisely the opposite has been the case. (See the chapter by Mantik on the medical evidence and the chapters by Horne on some of the most important ARRB discoveries.)*]

Part I

22 November 1963: A Chronology

Ira David Wood III

[*Editor's note*: Ira David Wood III began a chronology of events before, during, and after the murder of JFK as background for a dramatic work he planned to compose. A decade later, his massive undertaking remains incomplete. What he has done thus far affords a fascinating background for students of the assassination by providing a framework within which events may be temporally situated. This piece has been extracted from his *JFK Assassination Chronology*, which runs more than 400 pages in its current form. Like the other scholars contributing to this volume, he welcomes comments, corrections, and criticisms, which advance our efforts to understand what happened to our country on that fateful day.]

22 November 1963

12:00 AM   Nine Secret Service agents drinking at **Pat Kirkwood**'s bar the *"Cellar Door"* in Fort Worth, Texas. A sign on the wall of the nightclub reads: *"EVIL* SPELLED BACKWARDS IS *LIVE."* Several of the women serving liquor to the agents are strippers from **Jack Ruby**'s Carousel Club. (*Pat Kirkwood is a licensed pilot and owns a twin-engine plane. He will fly to Mexico hours after JFK's assassination.*)

In Madrid, Spain today—the CIA reports hearing from a Cuban journalist who claims to have received a letter stating that GPIDEAL [*President Kennedy*] will be killed today.

In today's issue of *Life* magazine, **Clint Murchison**'s lawyers, **Bedford Wynne** and **Thomas Webb**, are named as members of the "Bobby Baker Set." Wynne is already under federal investigation concerning government funds he is receiving through a Murchison family corporation, some of which have ended up as payoffs (*via Thomas Webb*) to the law firm of **Bobby Baker**. [Baker is LBJ's right hand man. Murchison's empire overlaps with that of Mafia financial wizard **Meyer Lansky** and Teamster leader **Jimmy Hoffa**.]

12:30 AM   **Marina Oswald** notices that her husband, LHO, is still awake.

12:50 AM   JFK reaches the Hotel Texas in Fort Worth.

2:00 AM   Seven Secret Service agents are still drinking at *"The Cellar."*

17

3:30 AM   The Secret Service men at *"The Cellar"* are joking about how several firemen are the only ones left guarding the President at the Hotel Texas, in Forth Worth.

5:00 AM   One Secret Service agent is still drinking at *"The Cellar."* **ALL AGENTS HAVE TO REPORT FOR DUTY AT 8:00 AM ON THE MORNING OF THE 22ND**—*three hours from now*.

Lee Harvey Oswald has been awake most of the night, not able to sleep, finally dozing off about this time. **Marina** avoided him last night—soaking in a bath for an hour before coming to bed.

6:30 AM   **Marina Oswald** awakens to feed her baby, **Rachel**, and checks on her other child, **June**.

7:00 AM   In Dallas, seventeen men line up before Deputy Chief **W. W. Stevenson**. The patrolmen are told that their function will be to "seal" the Trade Mart in preparation for JFK's visit. Two thousand, five hundred people are expected to attend this event which is scheduled for 12:30 PM.

Two Secret Service agents are at Fort Worth Police Headquarters examining two limousines which have been rented for the Kennedys and the Secret Service to use during the four-mile drive from the Hotel Texas to Carswell Air Force Base.

JFK's valet, **George Thomas**, awakens the President—who is asleep in Suite 850 of the Hotel Texas in Fort Worth.

7:08 AM   Dallas Police Chief **Jesse Curry** appears on local television and announces that the President will be in Dallas today and that Dallas wants no incidents. Curry concludes by asking all good citizens to please report to the Dallas Police Department anyone who has voiced violent opinions against the President or who has boasted, publicly or privately, of plans to demonstrate today.

7:10 AM   **Lee Harvey Oswald** is still asleep ten minutes after his alarm goes off. **Marina** wakes him. He rushes to dress in order to leave for work. He tells **Marina** that she should buy new shoes for baby **June**. He reportedly places his wallet in a dresser drawer. It contains $170. He keeps $13.87.

As JFK dresses this morning in Fort Worth, Texas, he dons his underwear and a surgical corset. He laces it tightly. He then pulls a long elastic bandage over his feet and twists it so that it forms a figure eight, then slips it up over both legs. It is finally adjusted over his hips where it supports the bottom of his torso, while the back brace holds the lower spine rigid.

7:15 AM   **Lee Harvey Oswald** leaves his home to go to work at the Texas Book Depository Building. (*The Dallas police will later claim they find a wallet on Oswald* <u>following</u> *the assassination. There is no indication that he used* <u>two</u> *wallets.*) He leaves his wedding ring in a cup on the top of Marina's dresser. This is cited by some as evidence that he intended to shoot JFK. He *does* leave home wearing his U.S.

Marine Corps signet ring and an identification bracelet with the name "Lee" inscribed on it. He will be wearing both of these items at the time of his arrest. LHO walks one block east from the Paine house and pokes his head into the back door of **Linnie Mae Randle**'s home, looking for her brother **Buell Frazier** for a ride to work.

Both Randle and Frazier will later agree that they observed LHO place a package in the backseat. Both are adamant that the package is far too small to be even a broken-down Mannlicher-Carcano rifle.

7:23 AM   LHO is driven to work by **Buell Wesley Frazier**. They don't talk very much during the trip. When asked what the package in the backseat is, Frazier testifies that Oswald answers: *"Curtain rods."* This is the package in which LHO supposedly carries the "broken down" assassination rifle. This bag is carried between his armpit and cupped hand into the TSBD. No one sees it come into the building. *The rifle, broken down, cannot fit under LHO's armpit and cupped hand—as Frazier testifies he carries it.* The "Bag" is homemade out of brown wrapping paper.

Frazier recalls that Oswald is wearing a *"gray, more or less flannel, wool-looking type of jacket."* **Linnie Mae Randle** says *"to the best of her recollection Oswald was wearing a tan shirt and gray jacket."*

7:55 AM.   Oswald and **Wesley Frazier** arrive at the parking lot next to the TSBD. It is raining. LHO leaves the car and walks ahead of Frazier into the building. LHO is out of Frazier's sight for a few moments before he enters the building. *Those who see LHO enter the TSBD will later say he does NOT enter the building carrying a package*

There are 13 employees working on the 6th floor of the TSBD building today, laying a tile floor. The floor crew starts work in the west end of the large room which constitutes the 6th floor—working eastward. Little by little, the cardboard boxes of school books are being inched toward the front windows of the building. LHO begins filling orders involving books published by *Scott Foresman & Company*.

NOTE: Two employees working on this floor have facial resemblances—**Billy Nolan Lovelady** and **Lee Harvey Oswald**.

8:01 AM   Dallas policeman **J.D. Tippit**, in police car #10, leaves the police station for patrol.

LHO is seen in the TSBD by **Wesley Frazier**, **Bonnie Ray Williams**, **Danny Arce**, **Roy Truly**, and **Jack Dougherty**.

8:30 AM   SS agent **Sorrels** meets Agent **Kinney** and Agent **George W. Hickey, Jr.** outside hotel in Dallas. They then drive out to Love Field.

LHO reportedly enters a Jiffy store located at 310 S. Industrial. **Fred Moore**, the store clerk says "identification of this individual arose when he asked him for identification as to proof of age for purchase of two bottles of beer. Moore said he figured the man was over 21 but the store frequently requires proof by reason of past difficulties with local authorities for serving beer to minors. This customer said, sure I got ID and pulled a Texas drivers license from his billfold. Moore said that he noted the name appeared as Lee Oswald or possibly as H. Lee Oswald. As Moore recalled, the birth date on the license was 1939 and he thought it to have been the 10th month."

8:45 AM   JFK emerges from his hotel in Fort Worth and strides across the street to greet a crowd waiting for him in a parking lot. Going downstairs, JFK sees his driver, **Muggsy O'Leary** and tells him: "**Mary Gallagher** *wasn't here last night to help Jackie. Mary hasn't any business in motorcades. She's supposed to reach hotels before we do, and so far she's batting zero. Get her on the ball.*" At **8:53**, he is telling the crowd that Jackie is *"organizing herself."* She hears him say this from her bed in the hotel.

While showering this morning, JFK takes off his Saint Jude and Saint Christopher medals and leaves them hanging on the shower head. When later "sweeping" the room, Secret Service agent **Ron Pontius** finds the medals and puts them in his pocket, with intentions of returning them to JFK after the Dallas motorcade. Pontius eventually gives the medals to **Marty Underwood** who, at last report, still retains them.

Desmond FitzGerald, a senior CIA officer, meets today with (**AM/LASH**) **Rolando Cubela** in Paris, France. FitzGerald delivers assurance of full support of the U.S. government in the overthrow of the Castro regime, which includes the murder of the highest officials. FitzGerald presents Cubela with a deadly pen which, when filled with poison, can be used to murder Castro. The pen is a hypodermic needle so thin that the victim will not feel its insertion. (*By March 1964, FitzGerald will have been promoted to chief of the CIA's Western Hemisphere Division.*)

9:00 AM   (*New Orleans*)—The last day of **Carlos Marcello**'s deportation trail begins in a packed courtroom.

(*Texas*) SS agents **Sorrels**, **Kinney**, and **Hickey** arrive at Love Field airport just outside of Dallas. They go directly to the garage and relieve the police of the security of the cars to be used in the motorcade. Both cars are washed, cleaned, and checked outside, inside, and underneath for security violations.

LHO reportedly returns to the Jiffy Store. Oswald returns "to buy two pieces of Peco Brittle at five cents each which he consumed on the premises. Moore remarked to him (Oswald) in the form of a question, "Candy and beer?," as he considered this to be an odd combination. The man seemed to be nervous while in the store, pacing the aisles as he ate the candy."

At the urging of his secretary, **Abraham Zapruder** goes home to get his new movie camera in order to film the JFK motorcade which he plans to see later in the day.

JFK enters the Grand Ballroom of the hotel in Fort Worth by going through the kitchen. He is to address the Fort Worth Chamber of Commerce and special, invited guests. He asks Agent **Duncan** where **Mrs. Kennedy** is. "*Call* **Clint Hill**," he says. "*I want her to come down to breakfast.*"

9:02 AM JFK confers with Governor **John Connally** about **Senator Yarborough's** refusal to ride with LBJ yesterday. (*It is Governor Connally who has postponed JFK's visit to Texas several times; it is Connally who feels that a Kennedy-Johnson ticket might be defeated in Texas in 1964, and there is considerable political risk in being seen with JFK.*)

9:05 AM According to **William Manchester**, this is the time **Richard Nixon** leaves Dallas on *AA Flight 82*. Nixon is legal counsel for Pepsico and has allegedly been in Dallas to attend a company meeting. (CIA agent **Russell Bintliff** will tell *The Washington Star* in 1976 that Pepsico had set up a bottling plant in Laos in the early 1960s that did not make Pepsi, but rather converted opium into heroin. One of the immediate consequences of the JFK assassination will be the escalation of American involvement in Vietnam, in theory providing the alleged Pepsico plant with a great deal more business.)

JFK is at a breakfast sponsored by the Fort Worth Chamber of Commerce.

9:22 AM Agent **Clint Hill** advises **Mrs. Kennedy** that JFK expects her downstairs in the Ballroom.

9:25 AM **Jackie Kennedy** appears at the breakfast wearing a pink suit and pill box hat. She is warmly received.

9:30–10 AM **Julius Hardee** is driving along towards the triple underpass on Elm St. He sees three men on top of the underpass. He states that two of the men he saw were carrying long guns.

9:55 AM At the Texas Hotel in Fort Worth, JFK and Jackie have returned to Suite 850. JFK informs **Kenny O'Donnell** that the Presidential party will leave at 10:40. Jackie asks: "*We have a whole hour?*" JFK asks her if she is enjoying the trip. "*Oh, Jack,*" she replies "*campaigning is so easy when you're President.*"

10:02 AM JFK confers with Governor **John Connally**.

At approximately ten o'clock this morning, **Harold Norman** (a worker in the Texas School Book Depository) will later testify: "**Junior Jarman** *and myself were on the first floor looking out towards Elm Street. Oswald walked up and asked us, 'What is everybody looking for? What is everybody waiting on?' So we told him we were waiting on the President to come by. He put his hand in his pocket and laughed and walked away. I thought maybe he's just been happy that morning or something.*"

10:00 AM   All traffic into the Dealey Plaza area, including the railroad yard, is supposedly cut off by the Dallas police.

Two Secret Service men leave the hotel in Fort Worth to drive to Dallas (*36 miles*) in order to set up the Presidential seal, flags, and JFK's prosthetic chair at the Trade Mart.

Three radio operators report for duty at Dallas Police Headquarters. Two of them man Channel One of KKB 364, and one mans Channel Two.

Of Historical Note: The official White House transcripts of what JFK said each day continue with this note:

"After the breakfast at the Texas Hotel in Fort Worth the President flew to Love Field in Dallas. There he acknowledged greeters for a brief period and then entered an open car. The motorcade traveled down a 10-mile route through downtown Dallas on its way to the Trade Mart, where the President planned to speak at a luncheon. At approximately 12:30 (CST) he was struck by two bullets fired by an assassin. The President was declared dead at 1 P.M. at the Parkland Hospital in Dallas."

10:30 AM   FBI informant, **William Augustus Somersett** receives a call in Miami from **Joseph Milteer** in Dallas stating that JFK will be there later that day and *will not be visiting Miami again*. Milteer then hangs up the phone and reportedly joins the crowd gathering near the corner of Elm Street in Dealey Plaza.

At his hotel suite in Fort Worth, JFK says *"You know, last night would have been a hell of a night to assassinate a President . . . There was the rain and the night, and we were all getting jostled. Suppose a man had a pistol in a briefcase."* He also sees a full-page advertisement in the *Dallas Morning News*: "**WELCOME MR. KENNEDY TO DALLAS**." It asks why he has allowed *"thousands of Cubans"* to be jailed and wheat sold to those who are killing Americans in Vietnam: "**Why have you scrapped the Monroe Doctrine in favor of the Spirit of Moscow? . . . Mr. Kennedy, we DEMAND answers to these questions and we want them now**." JFK says: *"We're heading into nut country today."*

The **112th Military Intelligence Group** at 4th Army Headquarters at Fort Sam Houston is told to *"stand down"* rather than report for duty in Dallas, over the protests of the unit commander, **Col. Maximillian Reich**. Nevertheless, **Lt. Colonel George Whitmeyer**, the commander of the local Army intelligence reserve, will be in the police pilot car which will precede the motorcade in Dallas, and an Army Intelligence officer is with FBI agent **James Hosty** 45 minutes *before* the parade, on Main Street.

Two important Secret Service reports regarding possible assassination attempts against JFK have now been transmitted to other field offices. <u>The only field office NOT to receive these two reports is the office in Dallas, Texas.</u>

Sheriff Bill Decker calls plainclothes men, detectives, and warrant men into his office, tells them that JFK is coming to Dallas and that the motorcade will come down Main St. Decker advises his employees to stand out in front of the building but <u>to take no part whatsoever in the security of the motorcade.</u> Uniformed policemen lining the motorcade route in downtown Dallas are instructed to stand with <u>their backs to the crowd</u> and to face the motorcade. <u>This order is not used in any other city and violates standard Presidential security measures</u> since it does not allow the police to watch either the crowds or the buildings along the route. Further, the Dallas Police have decided to *OFFICIALLY* end their security supervision for the motorcade one block short of the full route. **This unsupervised block includes Dealey Plaza**.

Also, this morning, hours *PRIOR* to the assassination of JFK, the CIA turns a photograph over to the FBI which purports to show **Lee Harvey Oswald** in Mexico City leaving a suspect embassy *(the CIA at one time implies it is the Cuban Embassy and at another time asserts it is the Soviet Embassy.)* The photo, as since proved, is **NOT** of Oswald.

10:32 AM   LBJ introduces his sister to JFK in the President's Texas Hotel suite.

10:40 AM   JFK's motorcade leaves the Texas Hotel for Carswell Air Force Base in Fort Worth in order to make the thirteen-minute flight to Dallas. There will be 36 people aboard *Air Force One*—not including the crew.

11:00 AM   **Julia Ann Mercer**, twenty-three years old, is driving west on Elm St. A few yards beyond the triple underpass, Miss Mercer's car is blocked from continuing by a green pickup truck parked partly on the curb. Mercer waits as long as three minutes during which a man removes a package that she believes is a rifle wrapped in paper. The young man walks up the embankment in the direction of the grassy knoll area in Dealey Plaza. This is the last time she sees him. She will later identify the driver of the truck as **Jack Ruby**. Two patrolmen—**E.V. Brown** and **Joe Murphy**—also observe this stalled pickup truck. According to them, it contains <u>three</u> construction workers. One of the patrolmen testifies that he assists in helping them get the truck moving again. *"There were three construction men in this truck, and he took one to the bank building to obtain another truck in order to assist in moving the stalled one. The other two men remained with the pickup truck along with two other officers. Shortly prior to the arrival of the motorcade, the man he had taken to the bank building returned with a second truck, and all three of the men left with the two trucks, one pushing the other."*

Author's Note: *Here we have a stalled truck on the motorcade route in the immediate vicinity of the assassination <u>as well as</u> an epileptic* *seizure which occurs minutes prior to the arrival of the President's car. <u>Two incidents</u> that prompt attention to events that necessitate the immediate involvement of police security along an eminently vital segment of the route. Eyes deflected from "above" in order to concentrate on seizure and stalled truck "below"? Major security attention is now on street level. Has this focus and attention been diverted on purpose or is this merely coincidence?*

Julius Hardee will tell *The Dallas Morning News* that he sees <u>three men</u> on top of the Triple underpass this morning carrying either shotguns or rifles. Whether these men are police officers or not will never be determined. Hardee claims he reported the incident to the FBI but <u>no report about the incident has yet surfaced</u>.

According to **Jack Ruby**, this is the time he goes to **Tony Zoppi**'s office to pick up Weimar brochure.

SS agents **Sorrels**, **Kinney**, and **Hickey** drive the motorcade cars *(this includes the Presidential limousine)* to the area at Love Field where the President is to be met when he arrives on *Air Force One*.

11:03 AM   Six members of the President's cabinet leave Honolulu for Japan by plane. Copies of their speeches have already been sent ahead. Some of these speeches will be printed in newspapers following the assassination as though nothing had occurred.

It is highly unusual, if not unheard of, for so many members of the Presidential cabinet to be away from the nation's capital at a given time.

11:10 AM   *According to* **Jack Ruby**, he is now talking to a salesman about the owner of the Castaway Club.

11:17 AM   *Air Force One* takes off from Fort Worth. The pilot, Colonel **James Swindal**, asks permission to fly at seven thousand feet and is permitted the request. During the flight to Dallas, JFK goes over the morning's *Intelligence Checklist*.

11:30 AM   **Jerry Coley**, a thirty-year old employee of the *Dallas Morning News*, and a friend, **Charlie Mulkey**, leave the *Morning News* building sometime before 11:30 AM and head toward Dealey Plaza, looking for a good vantage point to watch the motorcade. They finally take up a position near the entrance of the old county jail on Houston Street, a short distance from the TSBD.

At their home in Miami Beach, Florida **John Martino** and his wife **Robbyn** are talking about going to the Americana for lunch. An announcement comes over the radio concerning JFK's trip to Texas. According to Robbyn, John Martino then tells her: *"They're going to kill him. They're going to kill him when he gets to Dallas."* (Martino is a CIA-Mafia operative).

11:35 AM *Air Force Two* lands at Love Field. **Lyndon Johnson** and **Mrs. Johnson** are aboard this plane. They disembark and, as is the routine, prepare to greet JFK when his plane arrives.

For JFK, landing at Dallas completes 75,682 miles of travel in *Air Force One*—approximately three times around the world in one year. During the nine months prior to this day, the Secret Service has received more than *four hundred threats* on the President's life.

11:38 AM **J. Edgar Hoover** receives a telephone call from **Dwight D. Eisenhower** with news that he has heard from his friend **Fred Friendly** at CBS that *"a campaign to undermine the FBI and me is forming."* There is no further elaboration of this message, but Hoover urges Eisenhower to have Friendly call him for an interview so that Hoover can *"set the record straight."*

11:39 AM *Air Force One* lands at Love Field in Dallas—Runway 31. A Dallas resident will later be quoted as saying: *"President Kennedy should be awarded the Purple Heart just for coming to Dallas."*

11:40 AM Dallas Police Chief **Jesse Curry** meets President Kennedy at Love Field. JFK is impressed with the turnout and exclaims, *"This doesn't look like an anti-Kennedy crowd."*

Police Band (Channel 2): Curry asks for a weather report. Is told that it should be "fair" for most of the day. Reports of large crowds gathering along the route.

11:45 AM **Charles Givens**, an employee at the Texas Book Depository Building and a known narcotics user with a police record, later testifies that he works on the sixth floor until this time, then goes downstairs. As his elevator passes the fifth floor, he sees **Lee Harvey Oswald**. Givens, according to his testimony, then realizes he has left his cigarettes on the sixth floor and takes the elevator back upstairs to get his jacket with the cigarettes in it. He sees Oswald, clipboard in hand, walking from the southeast corner of the *sixth* floor toward the elevator.

(It is physically impossible for Givens to see Oswald, as he testifies he did, unless without any reason for doing so he walked far to the east of the elevator. It has been suggested that Givens, a black man with a drug record, was pressured into his story by the Dallas police. Givens, like Oswald, was missing from the Book Depository Building after the assassination.)

Bonnie Ray Williams and **Billy Lovelady** also testify that they see Oswald on the **fifth floor**, waiting impatiently for them to send one of the elevators back up <u>so he can come down</u>. The scenario is that the employees race the elevators to the first floor. **Charles Givens** sees LHO standing at the gate on the **fifth** floor as the elevator goes by.

11:50 AM **Charles Givens** now observes LHO reading a newspaper in the domino room where the employees eat lunch. This room is on the

first floor of the Book Depository Building. *(He will later deny testifying to this fact.)* **William Shelley** will testify that he sees Oswald when he [Shelley] "came down to eat lunch about ten to twelve."

11:55 AM JFK motorcade leaves Love Field for trip through downtown Dallas to the Trade Mart. **Marty Underwood** says: *"They had a hell of a fight there for about five minutes that day, before they started the motorcade. I don't mean a fight, but . . . ."* (**Concerning the bubble top for the Presidential limo**) *" . . . Jackie wanted it up and Kenny O'Donnell wanted it up, and Connally wanted it up. He (**JFK**) wanted people to see Jackie . . ."* *"We were getting ready to start the motorcade and **Connally**, **Kenny O'Donnell**, and **Dave Powers** and everybody talked to Kennedy and said, 'Look, let's put the bubble top up.' And he said, 'No this is Jackie's first trip and the people love her, and I'm going to keep it down.' It was his idea all the way."*

NOTE: As the motorcade begins, film footage from ABC television's Dallas/ Fort Worth affiliate WFAA shows SS agent **Henry J. Rybka** being recalled by shift leader (and commander of the follow-up car detail) **Emory P. Roberts**. As the limo begins leaving the area, Rybka's confusion is made clear as he throws his arms up several times before, during, and after the follow-up car passes him by, despite agent **Paul E. Landis** making room for Rybka on the running board of the car.

Additional Note: In 1991, **Marty Underwood** gives an interview to researcher **Vincent Palamara** in which he says that the CIA, the FBI, and the Mafia "knew (JFK) was going to be hit" on 11/22/63— this information came from his direct contacts with CIA officer **Win Scott**, the Mexico City Station Chief during Oswald's visit to that region. In addition, Underwood stated that, eighteen hours before Kennedy's murder, *"we were getting all sorts of rumors that the President was going to be assassinated in Dallas; there were no if's, and's, or but's about it."* When Underwood told JFK about these disturbing reports, the President merely said, *"Marty, you worry about me too much."*

The motorcade is spread over a half mile. Leading it is Deputy Chief **Lumpkin** in his "pilot car." In the motorcade's lead car are: Chief **Jesse Curry**, Sheriff **Bill Decker**, Special Agent **Forrest Sorrels** and Agent **Winston Lawson**. (*Chief Curry seems more talkative than usual.*) The lead car has four motorcycles in front of it to trim the curbside crowds. Three car lengths behind the lead car is the Presidential limo. Agent **William Greer** is driving. Sitting next to him is **Roy Kellerman**. Behind them in jump seats are **Governor** and **Mrs. Connally**—then **JFK** and **Mrs Kennedy**. Behind JFK's Lincoln are four motorcycles. They have been ordered not to pull up on the President unless he is endangered. Following JFK's limo is the Secret Service car—a 1955 Cadillac 9-passenger convertible. **Sam Kinney** drives; **Emory Roberts** mans the communications set. Mrs. Kennedy's guardian, **Clint Hill**, stands in the forward position of the left running board. **John Ready** has the opposite position on the right. Behind them stands **Bill McIntyre** and **Paul Landis**. **Glen Bennett** and **George Hickey** occupy two thirds of the back seat. Also riding with the Secret Service are **Kenneth O'Donnell** and **Dave Powers**. Next comes a rented 1964 Lincoln 4-door convertible, occupied by the **Lyndon Johnsons** and **Ralph Yarborough**. In the front seat is **Rufus Youngblood**, LBJ's agent. **Hurchel Jacks** of the Texas Highway Patrol is driving LBJ. This car is followed by another Secret Service car called *Varsity*. Next, comes a Mercury with **Mayor** and **Mrs. Earle Cabell**. Behind them is the press pool car consisting of four men who, if a news story breaks, will get it on the wires as a *"flash."*

12:00 PM   **Bonnie Ray Williams** returns to the **sixth** floor to eat his lunch. He has brought fried chicken in a paper bag. He does NOT see LHO or **Douglas Givens** on the sixth floor.

Eddie Piper, an employee at the Texas Book Depository, sees Oswald on the **first** floor of the building. According to Piper, Oswald tells him *"I'm going up to eat."* Oswald then goes to the **second** floor and buys his lunch from one of the vending machines.

Richard Carr, a steelworker, notices a man in a window on the **seventh** floor of the Book Depository Building . The man is wearing a brown suit coat.

12:14 PM   **Police Band (Channel 2):** Curry reports that motorcade is just turning on to Turtle Creek. The speed of the motorcade is 12 MPH. Officers check in on radio, reporting that crowds are good and everything is in good shape along the way.

12:15 PM   **Arnold Rowland**, a bystander in the Plaza, asks his wife if she would like to see a Secret Service agent. He points to a window on the sixth floor where he has noticed *"a man back from the window—he was standing and holding a rifle . . . we thought momentarily that maybe we should tell someone, but then the thought came to us that it is a security agent."* The man Rowland sees is *not* stationed in the now famous sixth floor window, but in the far *left*-hand window. Rowland also spots a **second** figure at the famous *right*-hand window. This second man is dark complexioned, and Rowland thinks he is a Negro.

NOTE: Windows along the motorcade are not systematically being watched by law enforcement personnel since no order has been given (*as eventually confirmed by Dallas policeman* **Perdue Lawrence**), although it was agent Lawson's "usual instructions" to do so. The Dealey Plaza triple underpass will not be cleared of spectators (as Lawson himself later testifies that he was trying to wave them off shortly before the shooting begins). In addition, ambulances (*such as the one on standby for JFK that was called to Dealey Plaza five minutes before Kennedy arrived to pick up an alleged "epileptic seizure" victim*) have been called to this same area on false alarms in the days and weeks before 22 November, as ambulance driver **Aubrey Rike** will eventually testify.

Carolyn Arnold, secretary to the Vice-President of the Book Depository, goes into the lunchroom on the **second** floor and sees Oswald sitting in one of the booth seats on the right hand side of the room. He is alone and appears to be having lunch. **The motorcade will pass the building in just fifteen minutes**.

NOTE: The FBI alters Arnold's report to say that she merely *glimpsed* LHO in the hallway.

John Powell, one of many inmates housed on the sixth floor of the Dallas County Jail, watches **two** men with a gun in the **sixth floor** window of the Book Depository Building. He claims he can see them so clearly that he even recalls them *"fooling with the scope"* on the gun. Powell says, *"Quite a few of us saw 'em. Everybody was trying to watch the parade and all that. We were looking across the street because it was directly straight across. The first thing I thought is, it was security guards . . . I remember the guys."*

Mrs. **Carolyn Walther** notices **two** men with a gun in an open window at the extreme right-hand end of the Depository on the **fifth** floor. One of the men is wearing a brown suit coat. *"It startled me, then I thought, 'Well, they probably have guards, possibly in all the buildings,' so I didn't say anything."*

Ruby Henderson sees **two** men standing back from a window on one of the upper floors of the Book Depository. She particularly notices that one of the men *"had dark hair . . . a darker complexion than the other."*

Lee E. Bowers, Jr., a railroad employee who is perched in a fourteen-foot railroad switching tower overlooking the parking lot *behind* the stockade fence, sees a black 1957 *Ford* enter the lot. Bowers believes the driver is holding a microphone or perhaps a mobile telephone. The car leaves the lot around 12:20.

Gordon Arnold, a young army soldier, wants to get a good view of the motorcade in order to use his movie camera. As he approaches the overpass bridge, he is rebuffed by a plainclothes man identifying himself as Secret Service. Arnold then moves off to a spot near the grassy knoll where he will watch the motorcade. *(AP photographer James Altgens is also denied permission to be on the bridge.)* And yet, thirteen railroad employees of the Union Terminal are allowed on the bridge. Police officers **White** and **Foster**, are assigned places at the East and West sides of a bridge than runs North-South. *Access to the overpass bridge may have been limited to those with photography equipment*.

THE MOTORCADE IS NOW PASSING CEDAR SPRINGS ROAD

A young man described as wearing green Army fatigues suddenly collapses at 100 N. Houston, near the front door of the Texas School

Book Depository. He apparently is suffering some sort of seizure. An ambulance is called at **12:19 P.M.** to take him to Parkland Hospital. Parkland never records a patient registering at this time. This *"emergency"* results in the opening of a route directly and exactly to Parkland Hospital (*"cut all traffic for the ambulance going to Parkland"*)—not for the President, who will be shot only midway through this "emergency," but for the man with the *"epileptic seizure." "Patient"* is later identified as **Jerry B. Belknap**. He dies in 1986. *(It has been suggested the seizure was staged to distract attention from windows of surrounding buildings and to open route to hospital prior to JFK's arrival in Dealey Plaza.)*

In the motorcade, SS agent **Clint Hill** moves four times from the forward position of the left running board of the follow-up car to the rear step of the Presidential automobile and back again—due to crowd surges along the route.

12:20 PM   **Bonnie Ray Williams** testifies that, at this time, the **sixth** floor of the Book Depository Building is apparently **vacant** as he leaves it to go downstairs. Williams has gone to the **sixth** floor to eat his lunch. (*The Warren Commission will later say that Oswald is on the* **sixth** *floor from 11:55 AM until 12:30 P.M.*)

Railroad worker, **Lee E. Bowers, Jr.** sees *another* unfamiliar vehicle, a 1961 *Chevrolet*, enter the parking lot behind the stockade fence. The car circles around and leaves about 12:25. In addition to the strange cars circling the lot, Bowers also notices **two men** standing behind the stockade fence. They remain there until *after* shots are fired at the motorcade.

Police Band (Channel 2): Reports crowd along motorcade spilling into street from Harwood to Ross

12:23 PM   From his office on the 7th floor of the Mercantile Building, **H.L. Hunt** reportedly watches JFK ride towards Dealey Plaza. A few moments later, escorted by six men in two cars, Hunt leaves the center of Dallas without even stopping by his house. He eventually flies to Mexico where he remains for one month. He will also be eventually joined by **General Edwin Walker**. He does not return until Christmas. (According to a research paper now known as **The Torbitt Document**—H.L. Hunt and his family are flown to New York on orders from **J. Edgar Hoover**. Five FBI agents keep the Hunts at a hotel in New York for three weeks until it is determined that Hunt's alleged part in the assassination is going to be kept from public knowledge. Other reports actually place H.L. Hunt in Washington following the assassination. Supposedly it was there that J. Edgar Hoover could better protect the Texas oilman and his interests.)

12:24 PM   The Presidential motorcade passes FBI agent **James Hosty**.

12:25 PM   Depository employee **Carolyn Arnold** sees Oswald on the **first** floor near the front door of the building.

The Presidential motorcade is preceded by a *pilot car*. In this car are: **B.L. Senkel**, **F. P. Turner**, Deputy Chief **George Lumpkin** (*also a member of the Army Intelligence Reserve*), Lieutenant Colonel **George Whitmeyer** (*a local army-reserve commander*) and **Jack Puterbaugh**, the local advance man for the Democratic National Committee who was present when the parade route in front of the TSBD was set. This pilot car makes only one recorded stop along the parade route today—*exactly in front of the TSBD*. (*"Deputy Chief G. L. Lumpkin . . . stopped momentarily at the corner of Houston and Elm" and spoke to the policeman "working traffic at that corner."*) None of the three policemen assigned to that corner will report this conversation in their later affidavits.

12:26 PM   **Police Band (Channel 2):** #158 (rear car) reports that everything is okay.

12:28 PM   **Police Band (Channel 2):** Size of crowd noted on radio—"Big crowd."

12:29 PM   The police radio, **Channel 1**, goes dead for at least 4 minutes, rendering communication in the motorcade impossible. (*It has been established that one of the motorcycle escorts in the motorcade had a microphone that was "stuck" open, thus rendering communication impossible. For a long time, researchers identified a motorcycle policeman,* **H.B. McLain**, *as the man with the microphone in question. McLain will later admit to having many open mike problems in the past. Recent evidence suggests that the open microphone might not have even been in the motorcade but at the Trade Mart. Eventually, spectrograms will show that there were possibly as many as four other microphones on, or attempting to get on, the radio channel during this time.*)

On Houston Street, waiting to see the President are two county clerks, **Ronald Fischer** and **Robert Edwards**. According to their affidavits, they see a man through the window on the **fifth** floor of the School Book Depository Building at this time.

THE MOTORCADE TURNS ONTO HOUSTON FROM MAIN (*The motorcade is now five minutes behind schedule.*)

Dealey Plaza, named after George Bannerman Dealey, a pioneer Dallas civic leader and founder of *The Dallas Morning News*. The 3.07-acre plaza, the site of the first home in Dallas as well as the first courthouse, post office, store, fraternal lodge and hotel, has been called the "Birthplace of Dallas." It was acquired by the city for the construction of the Triple Underpass which allows railroad traffic to pass over Commerce, Main and Elm Streets. The property was christened "Dealey Plaza" in 1935 and placed under the authority of the city's Park Board in 1936 with the official opening of the underpass. Both incoming and outgoing traffic between downtown Dallas and the major freeway systems to the west is channeled through Dealey Plaza. It is bounded on the east by Houston Street.

Facing onto Houston are the new County Court House (still under construction that day), the historic old County Court House, the Criminal Courts Building containing the County Jail and the Sheriff's Office, the Dallas County Records Building and the Dal-Tex office building. Just west of the Dal-Tex building, across Houston, is the red-brick building which in 1963 contained the Texas School Book Depository and publishers' offices. Bisecting Dealey Plaza is Main Street, with Commerce Street branching off to the south and Elm Street curving in on the north. These three main arteries converge on the west side of the plaza at the railroad bridge known as the Triple Underpass. Facing Houston Street on the west are fountains and monuments to Dealey. On the north and south sides of the plaza are two small arbors or pergolas, flanked on the east by a line of trees and shrubs and on the west by a wooden stockade fence about five feet high.

The seven-story, red-brick Texas School Book Depository building now comes into view of those in the motorcade. The motorcade is proceeding directly towards the building prior to making a left turn onto Elm St.

Of the 69 people who work in this building, only 33 are employees of the company that owns the building. Prior to this past summer, the building had been occupied by a wholesale grocery company engaged in supplying restaurants and institutions. Since the year it was built in 1903, this building located at 411 Elm Street has primarily functioned as a warehouse. In order to make it more suitable as an office building, extensive and very costly modifications are now underway inside. Though the building is seven stories tall, the inside passenger elevator, recently installed, only goes as high as the *fourth* floor. The machinery for lifting it is on the *fifth* floor. When the passenger elevator became operational, the stairway in the northwest corner was closed off because of "repairs." No one is allowed to use it. The nature of the repairs on the stairway remains unknown, although they are not the kind that will prevent heavy use of the stairs later this day. **The installation of a elevator which only goes up to the fourth floor, followed by the closure of the northwest stairway, creates a situation which makes the upper floors effectively off-limits to everyone except those who are assigned warehouse duties**. Several witnesses will see a gunman on the *fifth* floor of this building; also on the **fifth** floor at the time of the shooting are **four** warehouse men. **Six** warehouse workers have spent the entire morning on the sixth floor covering the old floor with new sheets of plywood. Unlike the office workers of the Book Depository, these warehouse men do *not* receive standard payroll checks; instead they are paid in cash. There will also be eventual evidence that **three** employee time charts for this day, later printed in the Warren Commission Exhibits, show signs of fraudulent fabrication.

NOTE: Advance agent **Winston G. Lawson** informed Committee investigators that he had nothing to do with the selection of the Main-Houston-Elm turn before 14 November. **Forrest Sorrel's** WC Exhibit No. 4 suggests that both men drove the entire route on 18 November. It is not certain that both men knew about the turn earlier than this date. Besides limiting motorcycle protection, Lawson prevented the Dallas Police Department from inserting into the motorcade, behind the Vice-Presidential car, a Dallas Police Department squad car. Lawson was asked by the Committee why he made no mention of the Dallas Police Department homicide car that **Jesse Curry** believed on 14 November to have been included and whose absence Curry protested at the meeting of 21 November. He answered that '*the Dallas Police Department could have put it (*a Dallas Police Department car) *in on their own,*' that '*he could not recall who took it out,* '*that he was not sure it was scheduled to be there;*' and that '*he didn't know who concealed the Dallas Police Department car because he didn't know who decided to include it.*'

As the motorcade passes, **Joseph Milteer** is reportedly photographed and filmed on the eastern curb of Houston Street, diagonally across Dealey Plaza. If these reports are true, he will witness the assassination.

Jack Ruby sits in a nearby newspaper office with a view of Dealey Plaza. (***This is one account**. However, considering the **Dallas Morning News** is only two blocks from Dealey Plaza, it is also possible that Ruby could have been there—as claimed by **Julia Ann Mercer**, **Jean Hill**, **Phil Willis**, and Policeman **Tom Tilson**—and still hurried back to the paper before 1:00*)

JFK's limo passes almost twenty sheriff's deputies standing at the intersection of Main and Houston in front of the Sheriff's Office. (Later, the deputies will almost unanimously agree that they believe the shots came from the railroad yards located just behind the grassy knoll.)

In the motorcade's Vice Presidential limousine, **Lyndon Johnson** is later described as having his ear up against a small walkie-talkie held over the back seat, listening to the device which is turned low. (This description comes from **Sen. Ralph Yarborough** who is riding with Johnson.)

Lyndon Johnson's Secret Service detail is already "*on the alert.*" Photographic evidence reveals that the left side rear door to Johnson's Secret Service back-up car is already being held open—the agents inside seem poised for immediate action.

Local Dallas newspaper reporters have been joking all morning about when and where "*the shooting will start.*"

Geneva Hine, the only employee in the Depository's second floor offices, observes the *electrical power* and *telephone system* go dead.

Nellie Connally, sitting in the Presidential Limousine, turns and remarks to JFK: *"Mr. Kennedy, you can't say that Dallas doesn't love you."*

12:30 PM   THE MOTORCADE TURNS ONTO ELM FROM HOUSTON

<u>SPEED OF LIMOUSINE:</u> Secret Service Agent, **William Greer**, driver of the Presidential limousine, estimated the car's speed at the time of the first shot as 12 to 15 miles per hour. Other witnesses in the motorcade estimated the speed of the President's limousine from 7 to 22 miles per hour. A more precise determination has been made from motion pictures taken on the scene by an amateur photographer, Abraham Zapruder. Based on these films, the speed of the President's automobile is computed at an average speed of 11.2 miles per hour. The car maintained this average speed over a distance of approximately 186 feet immediately preceding the shot which struck the President in the head. While the car traveled this distance, the Zapruder camera ran 152 frames. Since the camera operates at a speed of 18.3 frames per second, it was calculated that the car required 8.3 seconds to cover the 136 feet. This represents a speed of 11.2 miles per hour—*if the Zapruder film is indeed an accurate measurement of true elapsed time.*

William Greer, driver of the limousine, seems to have difficulty making this turn—nearly hitting a curb outcropping in front of the TSBD. He then begins to slow the limousine—*perhaps* to let those vehicles behind the Presidential limo catch up. Greer will later testify that, in such parades, the limo is driven in *"low gear"* for greater control. A lower gear can also enhance a vehicle's ability to accelerate quickly .

A strong wind begins to blow into the plaza from the North. Patrolman **M. L. Baker** rounds the corner from Main onto Houston and the gust of wind almost unseats him from his two-wheeled motorcycle which is behind the last press car of the motorcade. (*Baker will be the first man to see LHO immediately following the assassination.*)

Abraham Zapruder, a Dallas dress manufacturer, begins to film the motorcade with his new 8mm camera. He is filming from the President's right as the limousine moves along Elm St. [*Editor's note*: New studies of the Zapruder film by Jack White and by David W. Mantik, M.D., Ph.D., may be found elsewhere in this volume.]

Harrison Edward Livingstone, *Killing The Truth*, reports that once Zapruder turns his undeveloped movie film over to the printing lab, copies are immediately duplicated and distributed as follows:

1. FBI lab
2. Dallas FBI office
3. Washington, DC, FBI office
4. Henry Wade
5. Dallas Police
6. **and 7:** Two copies for the two couples who owned the film lab
8. Secret Service copy
9. Somewhere along the line, **H.L. Hunt** had his copy from the start.

Thomas Atkins, an official photographer for the Kennedy White House has also been photographing the motorcade with a quality camera, a 16 mm Arriflex S. He is riding six cars behind Kennedy and filming the motorcade as it moves through Dealey Plaza. *(Atkins will eventually assemble his film footage into a movie entitled **The Last Two Days**. The film will be described as "terribly damaging to the Warren Commission finding that Lee Harvey Oswald was the lone assassin." Neither Atkins's testimony nor his film will be studied by either of the federal panels investigating the assassination.)*

In the motorcade's lead car which is almost beneath the overpass, **Forrest V**. **Sorrels** says to Chief **Jesse Curry**: *"Five more minutes and we'll have him there."* **Winston G**. **Lawson** calls the Trade Mart, giving them a five minute warning.

Rose Cheramie, now convalescing at a state hospital in Jackson, Louisiana, is watching television with several nurses when a spot report about JFK's motorcade comes on. Cheramie says *"This is when it is going to happen!"* The nurses dismiss her remarks—until moments later. Cheramie has also told one of the hospital interns *". . . that one of the men involved in the plot was a man named* **Jack Rubinstein**."

Positioned in the front doorway of the Texas School Book Depository, watching the motorcade are: **Wesley Buell Frazier**, **Danny Arce**, **Billy Lovelady** and—fifteen feet away, near a lone v-shaped oak tree—**Mr**. **Roy Truly** and **Mr**. **Ochus Campbell**.

Army Intelligence officer, **James Powell**, is now in the Dal Tex building. This is the building that **Jim Braden** will be found coming out of in a matter of minutes and will be arrested. Braden has an office in New Orleans: Room 1701 in the Pere Marquette Building. During this same period in late 1963, **David Ferrie** is working for **Carlos Marcello** on the same floor. . . in the same building. . . just down the hall from Braden—in Room 1707.

Dallas Deputy **Harry Weatherford**, a crackshot rifleman, is now on the roof of the Dallas County Records Building with a high powered rifle.

An Associated Press photographer, **James Altgens**, has stationed himself at a vantage point on Elm Street across from the Texas School Book Depository Building to photograph the Presidential motorcade as it passes through Dealey Plaza and heads onto the Stemmons Freeway.

Altgens captures the President on film in a now-famous shot taken within two seconds of the impact of the bullet that strikes JFK's head. For a while, controversy rages around a figure visible in the background of the photograph. A man many people think strongly resembles Lee Harvey Oswald is pictured standing in the front entrance of the Book Depository Building. If it is, in fact, Oswald, he could not have been on the sixth floor of the building when the shots were fired. The Warren Commission will discount any possibility that the figure is Oswald, and instead identifies the man as **Billy Nolan Lovelady**, another building employee. The man in the photo is wearing a dark, heavy-textured shirt open halfway to the waist over a white undershirt. Lovelady later tells reporters that he was wearing a red-and-white-striped sport shirt that day. The identity of the man in the photo has never been clearly established. James Altgens will tell Commission investigators that he raced up the grassy knoll immediately after the President was hit because several uniformed Dallas police officers ran in that direction with weapons drawn, apparently in response to the sound of gunfire from that direction. Altgens' testimony that "flesh particles flew out of the side of his [Kennedy's] head in my direction from where I was standing . . . " has been cited by many investigators to support the conclusion that the President's head wound was caused by a bullet fired from the grassy knoll, which was to Kennedy's right and front, not from the Texas School Book Depository Building, which was to his rear.

The President is in an open, unarmored car.

The route chosen is along busy streets with many overlooking high buildings on each side.

Windows in these buildings (estimated: 20,000 along the route) have not been closed, sealed, or put under surveillance.

Secret Service units and trained military units that are required by regulations to be there are not in place. As a result there is limited ground and building surveillance.

Sewer covers along the way have not been welded shut.

The route is particularly hazardous, with sharp turns requiring slow speeds, in violation of protection regulations.

NOTE Beyond the triple overpass, the "barricade" suggested by the Warren Commission is a three-inch curb, which could have been easily navigated by every vehicle in the motorcade, with discomfort to none. [*Editor's note:* Studies of the conduct of the Secret Service on this occasion by Douglas Weldon, J.D., and by Vincent Palamara may be found elsewhere in this volume.]

A total of 178 officers, including reserves, are assigned to the motorcade route today. Captain of the Dallas reserves, **Charles Arnett**, will later tell the Warren Commission that the reserves were ordered to take no action if spectators booed the President, but if there was a threat of bodily harm, they were to report their concerns to the nearest "regular officer."

SS agent **Winston Lawson**, riding in the motorcade's lead car, tries to wave onlookers off the triple underpass. The Dallas police officer, standing with the railroad employees on the overpass, does not notice the signaling.

Arnold Rowland notices a Dallas police officer on the sidewalk in front of the TSBD.

Police Band (Channel 2): Curry, in the lead car, reports that his car has just reached the underpass. Eight seconds later, the police dispatcher announces the time: "12:30:18 PM CST".

ASSASSINATION SCENARIO as postulated by **Craig Roberts**, author of ***Kill Zone***. *Roberts is a former U.S. Marine sniper and veteran of the Vietnam War.*

"As the Lincoln enters the kill zone—the section of street where the firing trajectories of all sniper positions intersect—the order is given to commence firing. "

The President's limo is just passing a "Stemmons Freeway" sign.

SHOTS ARE FIRED AT THE MOTORCADE

At approximately Zapruder frame 200, Kennedy's movements suddenly freeze; his right hand abruptly stops in the midst of a waving motion and his head moves rapidly from right to his left in the direction of his wife. Based on these movements, it appears that by the time the President goes behind the sign at frame 207 he is evidencing some kind of reaction to a severe external stimulus.

On hearing the first burst of firing, **Sheriff Decker** glances back and thinks he sees a bullet bouncing off the street pavement. Motorcycle officer, **Stavis Ellis** also will testify he sees a bullet hit the pavement. (*Neither Decker nor Ellis will ever be questioned about this by the Warren Commission.*) Motorcycle officer **James Chaney** will also tell newsmen this day that *the first shot missed*. It is suggested that JFK is hit by small pieces of the street pavement and stops waving for a moment.

Governor Connally recognizes the first noise as a rifle shot and the thought immediately crosses his mind that it is an assassination attempt. From his position in the right jump seat immediately in front of JFK, he instinctively turns to his right because, to him, the shot seems to have come from over his right shoulder.

James T. Tague, standing near the concrete abutment of the triple underpass, about 260 feet downhill from the President's position, is hit on his cheek by a piece of concrete blown off the street curb when it is hit by one of the bullets fired at the President. Tague is standing on a curb on Main Street, not Elm Street. He is more than one full block away from the President's car. Tague will not be questioned by the Warren Commission and his existence is not even publicly announced for seven months following the assassination.

NOTE: If one draws a line from the point of impact on the curbstone (*where Tague was standing*) back to a position within a circle with an eighteen-inch diameter around the President's head and shoulders and then project that line back to some firing point, the gunman is placed in **a window on the second floor of the Dal-Tex building, behind the President's car**. On the other hand, if a line is drawn from that same point of contact with the curbstone back to the alleged lone gunman's lair on the sixth floor of the Book Depository building, the bullet would have traveled about twenty-two feet to its right.

Tague will later say: *"J. Edgar Hoover didn't want me to exist. I was the only proof that there were more shots fired. I didn't see anything to shed any light on the assassination. I was just one man slightly injured. I was ignored."*

Patrolman **M.L. Baker** is regaining control of his motorcycle after the strong gust of wind from the North when he hears the sound of gunfire. He is riding a two-wheeled motorcycle behind the last press car of the motorcade.

Mrs. Cabell turns to her husband and says: *"Earle, it is a shot."*

All of the following incidents occur at approximately the same time:

JFK is wounded. He clutches for his neck.

Governor Connally is also hit by a bullet.

Secret Service agent **Clint Hill** realizes immediately that something is wrong and jumps off the SS follow-up car. He sprints towards the President's limousine.

Rufus Youngblood, LBJ's SS bodyguard—yelling *"Get down!"*—immediately jumps on top of Vice-President **Johnson** and pushes him down in the car. Youngblood then practically sits on top of the prone VP, an account disputed by **Senator Yarborough**.

Motorcycle policeman **Marrion L. Baker** immediately glances up and sees pigeons fluttering off the Depository's roof. He believes the shots have come from either the Depository or the Dal-Tex building. He dismounts from his motorcycle and, gun in hand, rushes towards the TSBD building.

Jack Dougherty, an employee in the TSBD, is working on the fifth floor. He hears a noise that sounds to him like a backfire. (*Dougherty will later testify that he takes the West elevator from the fifth to the first floor where* **Eddie Piper** *will tell him that JFK has been shot.*)

Harold Norman, Junior Jarman and **B.R. Williams** are watching to motorcade from a **fifth floor** window in the Texas Book Depository building. This window is directly under the "sniper's nest" window on the **sixth floor**. Norman will later testify that he can hear: *"Boom, Click-Click, Boom, Click-Click, Boom."* (*Norman will continue to work at the TSBD for over 30 more years and will disavow some of the reports in his Warren Commission testimony.*)

Secret Service agent **Glen Bennett** sees a shot *"hit the Boss about four inches down from the right shoulder . . . "*

Senator Yarborough says: "*My God, they've shot the President!*"

Lady Bird Johnson says: "*Oh, no. That can't be.*"

Kenneth O'Donnell begins to bless himself. **Dave Powers** murmurs: "*Jesus, Mary, and Joseph . . . .*"

SS agent **Roy Kellerman**, sitting next to the driver of JFK's limo *(William Greer)*, testifies that he hears JFK call out: "*My God! I'm hit!*" JFK, who is wearing a rigid back brace does not slump, but is held erect by the device. Kellerman also says he hears Mrs. Kennedy say to JFK: "*What are they doing to you?*"

(There is speculation that the first shot fired misses JFK and actually slams into the pavement some twenty feet behind the car. There is evidence that JFK receives a superficial wound in his scalp from a piece of pavement that is blown away by the bullet and that this wound is what he initially reacts to in the Zapruder film. **Note also** that Kellerman never moves toward JFK in order to shield him. The SS manual in 1963 plainly states that "*the first duty of the agents in the motorcade is to attempt to cover the President as closely as possible and practicable to shield him by attempting to place themselves between the President and any source of danger.*" Is it just possible that Kellerman does not move to the rear in order to shield JFK because he considers the source of danger lies in front and ahead of the limo?)

Later, it will be said of **William Greer**, JFK's driver: "*It is absolutely incredible that a trained Secret Service agent, whose critical responsibility is to protect the President, and after hearing two gunshots, the panic of his passenger's exclaiming "My God, I am hit," and "Oh, no, no, they're going to kill us all," and after turning his head to verify "something was wrong" would not have immediately accelerated out of trouble. Instead, in that remaining critical five to six seconds before the fatal bullet to the President's head, the driver turns to look again, the limousine slows down, and the driver does not turn back around again until after the President's head has exploded.*"

Roy Kellerman, turning to driver **Greer**, mutters: "*We are hit!*" (Kellerman will later tell the Warren Commission: "*If President Kennedy had from all reports four wounds, Governor Connally three, there have got to be more than three shots, gentlemen.*")

Greer ignores Kellerman's warning. The Presidential limousine, which has been moving at about eleven miles an hour, slows down perceptibly. *The brake lights go on.* Greer turns around in his seat to look directly at JFK. (*Later, the Zapruder film will be closely studied and it will be determined that frames showing Greer's head turn have been altered.*) Next to the Stemmons Freeway sign, at curbside, stands a man holding an open umbrella—*the only open umbrella in the area.* After the first shot, the "**umbrella man**" pumps the umbrella up and down. This action (and the umbrella man) is filmed by **Abraham Zapruder**.

Agent **John D. Ready** jumps off SS follow-up car to dash to JFK's limo. He is *recalled* by special Agent-in-Charge **Emory Roberts**.

In her open convertible, **Mrs. Earle Cabell** smells the unmistakable odor of gunpowder in the air. **Ralph Yarborough** also smells gunpowder. He will eventually say: *"I always thought that was strange because, being familiar with firearms, I never could see how I could smell the powder from a rifle high in that building."*

Mary Moorman has fallen on the grass after taking a Polaroid photograph of JFK in his limo. She pulls at the leg of **Jean Hill**, screaming: *"Get down! They're shooting!"*

Five seconds after JFK has first clutched his neck, the limousine still seems to be in its stultifying pause, the driver (**Greer**, *fifty-five years old)* looking over his shoulder into the back seat).

In the motorcade press buses, men are asking each other if what they've just heard could be rifle fire. A driver says: *"They're giving him a twenty-one-gun salute."*

Mrs. Earle Cabell, wife of the Dallas mayor, is riding in an open convertible six cars back from the motorcade's lead car. At this moment, her car is just passing the Depository building. She jerks her head up on hearing the first shot because *"I heard the direction from which the shot came . . . ."* Looking up, she sees an object projecting from one of the top windows of the Depository building.

Another series of shots rings out.

While still sprinting toward the Presidential limousine, **Clint Hill** hears more shots.

At the sound of the second shot, the driver, **William Greer,** will testify, he realizes that something is wrong, and he presses down on the accelerator as **Roy Kellerman** yells, *"Get out of here fast."* As he issues his instructions to Greer and to the lead car, Kellerman hears a "flurry of shots" within 5 seconds of the first noise.

Mr. and **Mrs. John Chism**, and their three-year-old son are standing along the curb with their backs to the grassy knoll near the Stemmons Freeway sign. John Chism and his wife look behind them to see exactly where the shots are coming from, believing the shooter is somewhere on the knoll.

Hugh Betzner, Jr., witnesses the assassination almost immediately after snapping three photographs of the scene near the intersection of Houston and Elm streets. He runs through Dealey Plaza in an effort to keep pace with the President's limousine while taking several more pictures. Betzner allegedly tells a sheriff's deputy that he believes at least some of the shots were fired from the area of the picket fence on the grassy knoll. He surrenders his camera and film to **Deputy Eugene L. Boone**, who has the film developed and returns both the camera and the negatives to Betzner.

NOTE: <u>DID THE PRESIDENT'S CAR COME TO A STOP?</u>

NBC reporter **Robert MacNeil** (rode in White House Press Bus)—
"The President's driver **slammed on the brakes** —after the third
shot."

DPD **James Chaney** (one of the four Presidential motorcyclists)—
stated that the Presidential limousine **stopped momentarily** after
the first shot (according to the testimony of **Mark Lane**;
corroborated by the testimony of fellow DPD motorcycle officer
Marrion Baker: Chaney told him that " at the time, after the
shooting, from the time the first shot rang out, the car stopped
completely, pulled to the left and stopped. Now I have heard several
of them say that, **Mr. Truly** was standing out there, he said it stopped.
Several officers said **it stopped completely**."

Mrs. Earle ("Dearie") Cabell (rode in the Mayor's car)—the
motorcade "**stopped dead still** when the noise of the shot was
heard."

TSBD Supervisor **Roy Truly**—after the first shot, "I saw the
President's car swerve to the left **and stop** somewheres down in the
area. . . [It stopped] for a second or two or something like that. . . I
just saw it stop."

[Editor's note: 59 eyewitness reports concerning the limo stop
collated by Vincent Palamara may be found elsewhere in this
volume.]

JFK IS FATALLY HIT IN THE HEAD BY GUNFIRE

**The right side of the President's head explodes in a shower of
blood and brain tissue. In the Zapruder film, JFK is slammed
backwards and to the left with violent force**. This reaction is
filmed by **Abraham Zapruder** and will be the subject of considerable
discussion in years to come. [*Editor's note:* as will the wound itself.]

At first **Mrs. Connally** thinks that her husband has been killed, but
then she notices an almost imperceptible movement and realizes
that he is still alive. She says, "*It's all right. Be still.*" The Governor is
lying with his head on his wife's lap when he hears a shot hit JFK.
At this point, both Governor and Mrs. Connally observe brain tissue
splatter over the interior of the car. According to Governor and Mrs.
Connally, it is <u>after this shot</u> that **Roy Kellerman** issues his
emergency instructions and the car accelerates.

Escort motorcycle officers, **Bobby W. Hargis** and **B. J. Martin** are
splattered by blood and brain matter. Martin, who has looked to his
right after the first shots, will later find bloodstains on the left side
of his helmet. Hargis, who is riding nearest the limousine about six
to eight feet from the left rear fender, sees Kennedy's head explode
and is hit by bits of flesh and bone with such impact that he will tell
reporters he thought *he* had been shot. The motorcycle policemen
to the right rear of the President's limousine are not struck with any

debris. A piece of bone will later be found by **Billy Harper** (later identified as occipital bone by the Chief Pathologist at Methodist Hospital) twenty-five feet <u>behind and to the left</u> of the car's position when the President was hit in the head, according to the Secret Service.

Gordon Arnold, on leave following his Army basic training, is an amateur cinematographer anxious to film the Presidential motorcade from the best possible angle. Dressed in his Army uniform, Arnold first chooses as his site the railroad overpass at the western end of Dealey Plaza, which offers a clear, unobstructed view of the plaza, through which the motorcade is to pass. Arnold is prevented from entering the overpass by a well-dressed man who shows him a Secret Service badge and ID. Official records indicate that no Secret Service agents are assigned to patrol the area on foot today. However, a Dallas police officer and a county deputy sheriff reportedly encounter a second such "agent" on the grassy knoll immediately after the shooting. Arnold then finds a suitable vantage point from which to shoot his movie film, only a few feet in front of the stockade fence on the grassy knoll. Suddenly he feels a shot whiz past his left ear. He throws himself to the ground in an involuntary reaction, probably due to his recent training. Questioned by a uniformed police officer a few seconds later, Arnold insists that the shots came from behind him. The officer confiscates Arnold's film. Arnold will recount the experience in a 1978 interview published in *The Dallas Morning News*. While some people discount his story, it receives tacit corroboration from Senator Ralph Yarborough, who is riding with Vice President Lyndon B. Johnson two cars behind Kennedy's. Yarborough will write the *Morning News* that he recalls that when the first shot was fired he saw a uniformed figure immediately "hit the dirt" at the spot where Arnold said he was filming. The senator remembers thinking to himself that the man's quick reaction suggested he must be a "combat veteran." Nothing more has ever been heard of Arnold's confiscated film, and the police officer who took it. The Secret Service agent who prevented Arnold from going onto the overpass has never been identified.

Jacqueline Kennedy will later recall that she had been presented yellow roses in every Texas stop with the exception of Dallas—where she was presented red roses. Of the fatal shot, she will later recall: " *. . . his last expression was so neat; he had his hand out, I could see a piece of his skull coming off; it was flesh colored not white—he was holding out his hand—and I can see this perfectly clean piece detaching itself from his head; then he slumped in my lap . . . . his head was so beautiful. I'd tried to hold the top of his head down, maybe I could keep it in . . . I knew he was dead."*

NOTE: Jack Ruby telephones a friend on 22 November and asks if he would *"like to watch the fireworks."* Unknown to Ruby, his friend is an informant for the criminal intelligence division of the Internal

Revenue Service. He and Ruby are allegedly standing at the corner of the Postal Annex Building at the time of the shooting. Minutes after the shooting **Phil Willis**, who knows Jack Ruby, sees and photographs a man who looks like Ruby near the front of the School Book Depository.

Jim Bishop, *The Day Kennedy Was Shot*, writes of the fatal head wound: *"This one the President did not feel. The light had gone out with no memories, no regrets. After forty-six and a half years, he was again engulfed by the dark eternity from which he had come. For good or evil, his work, his joys, his responsibilities were complete."*

Special Agent **William Greer** will testify that *"the last two shots seemed to be just simultaneously, one behind the other."*

Forrest V. Sorrels, head of the Dallas office of the Secret Service, certain there are gunshots, shouts to Curry: *"Let's get out of here!"*

Senator **Ralph Yarborough**, a few cars behind JFK's, will remember: *"All of the Secret Service men seemed to me to respond very slowly, with no more than a puzzled look. Knowing something of the training that combat infantrymen and Marines receive, I am amazed at the lack of instantaneous response by the Secret Service when the rifle fire began."*

The assassination occurred during a twenty-six-second period from 12:29:52 to 12:30:18 PM CST.

Police Band (Channel 2): Order to get to Parkland Hospital. 12:30:18 PM CST. Curry says to get someone to go up to the overpass and see what happened up there. Have Parkland Hospital stand by. Get men into the railroad yard. Hold everything up there 'til homicide and investigators get there. When asked if he can give any more information, Curry says that it appears Kennedy's been hit.

Sixty-four seconds after Curry orders the motorcade to the hospital, at 12:31:22, Sheriff Deckers says, "Hold everything secure until the homicide and other investigators can get there."

THE DEALEY PLAZA "*MARKSMANSHIP*": Gunnery Sergeant **Carlos Hathcock**, former senior instructor for the U.S. Marine Corps Sniper Instructor School at Quantico, Virginia eventually says: "Let me tell you what we did at Quantico. We reconstructed the whole thing: the angle, the range, the moving target, the time limit, the obstacles, everything. I don't know how many times we tried it, but we couldn't duplicate what the Warren Commission said Oswald did. Now if I can't do it, how in the world could a guy who was a non-qualified on the rifle range and later only qualified 'marksman' do it?' "

According to **Victor Ostrovsky**, an Israeli Mossad agent, the Mossad also reenact the shooting: "To test their theory, they did a simulation exercise of the Presidential cavalcade to see if expert marksmen with far better equipment than Oswald's could hit a moving target from the recorded distance of 88 yards. They couldn't . . . The Mossad had every available film of the Dallas assassination. Pictures of the area, the topography, aerial photographs, everything. Using mannequins, they duplicated the Presidential cavalcade over and over again. Professionals will do a job in the same way. If I'm going to use a high powered rifle, there are very few places I'd work from, and ideally I'd want a place where I held the target for the longest possible time, where I could get closest to it . . . we picked a few likely places, and we had more than one person doing the shooting from more than one angle . . . . The Mossad, using better, more powerful equipment, would aim their rifles, they'd say *"bang"* over the loudspeakers and a laser direction-finder would show where people in the car would have been hit and the bullet exits. It was just an an exercise which showed that it was impossible to do what Oswald was supposed to have done."

In the Secret Service car immediately behind the Presidential limousine, SS agent **George W. Hickey, Jr.**, reaches down and picks up an **AR-15** *(an automatic rifle)* which has been kept *"locked and loaded"* in the car. Releasing the safety on the weapon, Hickey stands up in the rear car seat of the convertible and looks around to find the source of the shots. In a moment, the car will lurch forward, knocking him backward. *(The book **MORTAL ERROR** suggests that Hickey accidentally fires his AR-15, and thereby inflicts JFK's mortal head wound.)*

Lumpkin, now on Stemmons Freeway in the motorcade's pilot car, using motorcycle policemen to divert traffic, speaks into the microphone to **Chief Curry**: *"What do you want with these men out here with me?"* Curry: *"Just go on to Parkland Hospital with me."* Patrolman **R.L. Gross**: *"Dispatcher on Channel One seems to have his mike stuck."* Curry: *"Get those trucks out of the way. Hold everything. Get out of the way!"*

Agent-in-Charge **Emory Roberts**, in the follow-up car, picks up the phone: *"Escort us to the nearest hospital—fast but at a safe speed."*

The twenty sheriff's deputies who have just watched JFK's motorcade pass the Sheriff's Office at the intersection of Main and Houston begin running in the direction of the grassy knoll.

Richard Carr, on the seventh floor of the new courthouse watches as **two** men run from behind the Texas School Book Depository. The men enter a waiting **station wagon** and speed off north on Houston Street.

NOTE: Richard Carr described the man he saw as "heavy set, wearing a hat, tan sport coat and horn rimmed glasses." Minutes after the shooting, **James Worrell** saw a person described as "5'10" and wearing some sort of coat" leave the rear of the Depository heading south on Houston Street. Carr saw the same man and recognized him as the man he had seen on the 6th floor of the Book Depository.

The man walked south on Houston, turned east on Commerce, and got into a **Nash Rambler station wagon** parked on the corner of Commerce and Record. The Rambler was next seen in front of the Book Depository by Deputy Sheriff **Roger Craig**. Craig saw a person wearing a light-colored, short-sleeved shirt, who he later identified as Oswald, get into the station wagon and then travel under the triple overpass towards Oak Cliff. **Marvin Robinson** was driving his Cadillac when the **station wagon** in front of him abruptly stopped in front of the Book Depository. A young man walked down the grassy incline and got into the **station wagon** which subsequently sped away under the triple overpass. A third witness, **Roy Cooper**, was behind Marvin Robinson's Cadillac. He observed a white male wave at, enter, and leave in the **station wagon**. A photograph, taken by **Jim Murray**, shows a man wearing a light-colored short-sleeved shirt headed toward the **station wagon** in front of the Book Depository. Deputy Sheriff Roger Craig, also in the photo, is pictured looking at the man and the **station wagon**. The Hertz sign, on top of the Book Depository, shows the time as 12:40 PM. The man in the white shirt, possibly **Lee Oswald**, left Dealey Plaza in the **station wagon** and was last seen heading toward Oak Cliff.

Avery Davis, an employee in the Texas School Book Depository Building, is standing in front of the building entrance. It is her impression the shots are coming from the overpass in *front* of the motorcade.

Teacher **Jean Hill**, who has just seen the President's head explode a few feet in front of her, notices a man running from the area of the wooden fence.

SS agent **Clint Hill** who has rushed from the SS back-up car to JFK limo, has just secured a grip on a handhold when the car begins accelerating. Looking into the back seat of the limousine, Hill sees that the right *rear* portion of the President's head is missing. He protects President and Mrs. Kennedy with his body all the way to Parkland Hospital. While protecting the Presidential party, Hill looks back at the agents in the Secret Service car immediately behind the JFK limo and shakes his head. In the Secret Service car agent **Emory Roberts** then tells the other agents that they have to take care of LBJ.

Witnesses testify that, in the shadows of the overpass, there comes a cacophony of screeching tires and swerving vehicles.

About this time, **Victoria Adams**, an TSBD employee goes down the stairs from the fourth floor to the first. She will later testify that she never saw LHO descending the stairs. If LHO is at the sixth floor window within seconds of the final head shot, he is wiping away finger prints and preparing to hide his rifle as he crosses the sixth floor—through stacks of boxes—to the northeast corner in order to descend the stairs. (*Tests will establish that LHO* **could** *have reached the second floor vestibule in 1 minute 14 seconds*.) *Miss Adams will testify that she watched the motorcade from an open window on the fourth floor (the third set of double windows from the southeast corner), in company with other employees in the Scott, Foresman Co. publishing office where she worked.* After the last shot, she and **Sandra Styles** immediately run down the back stairs to the first floor, where she sees **Billy Lovelady** and **William Shelley** standing near the elevator.

In a session with the Warren Commission counsel, **Victoria Adams** will volunteer the opinion that the shots she heard came from below her fourth-floor window and to the right, not from above and the left, where Oswald allegedly fired the fatal bullet. Adams will offer another unsolicited piece of information that will fuel the controversies surrounding the shooting scene. She will recall that when she reached the street minutes after the assassination, she and coworker **Mrs. Avery Davis** see a man at the corner of Houston and Elm streets questioning people much in the manner of a police officer. Later, after viewing Jack Ruby on television, she will say he "looked very similar" to the man at Houston and Elm. However, other persuasive testimony places Ruby at *The Dallas Morning News* offices at the time.

Outside—**James Worrell, Jr.**, a twenty-year-old witness to the assassination, races northward, up Houston Street, where he sees **a man** exit from the back door of the Depository and walk quickly south on Houston. The man is wearing a brown suit coat. (*This man is next seen by* **Richard Carr**; *a steelworker at the corner of Houston and Commerce. Carr remembers seeing this same man around noon at a window on the seventh floor of the Book Depository Building.*)

Nightclub singer **Beverly Oliver** is standing on the south side of Elm Street across from the wooden fence and films the entire assassination with her 8-millimeter camera. She observes a puff of smoke from the fence on the knoll. Her film is confiscated within a week by men identifying themselves as government agents. (*This film has never been seen since.*) Oliver later identifies the FBI man who confiscated her film as **Regis Kennedy**. *Some researchers will later take issue with Oliver's statements and the fact that she claims to be the "Babushka lady."*

Ed Hoffman, a deaf-mute on the overpass, has witnessed **two men** behind the picket fence—one has a rifle. After the assassination, he sees one man toss the rifle to the other who then takes it to a spot near the railroad tracks and "breaks it down" and then puts it in a box which resembles a tool kit. Hoffman, being deaf and mute, has a very frantic and difficult time trying to communicate this information to the authorities. (***Once Oswald is in custody*, *Hoffman is told by an FBI agent to keep quiet or "you might get***

killed." Reports of his sighting are hidden from the public for twenty-two years.) Hoffman also watches the President's car as it moves toward the freeway entrance. The car stops there for about 30 seconds to receive directions from the lead car, which they have passed moments earlier. While **William Greer** waits for the lead car to catch up, Hoffman looks into the Presidential limousine. He sees that the entire *rear* of JFK's head is gone.

Emory Roberts waves LBJ's car closer to his follow-up car and yells, pointing ahead: *"They got him. They got him."* He then points to Agent **McIntyre**: *"You and Bennett take over Johnson as soon as we stop."*

Victoria Adams and **Sandra Styles** have been on the fourth floor of the TSBD, watching the motorcade from one of the windows. They hear gunfire as JFK's car disappears behind a tree. To learn what has happened, they run down the back stairs and go out the back door. (Adams estimates that she and her friend were going outside about a minute after the shooting.) They are stopped by a policeman. *"Get back into the building,"* he says. *"But I work here,"* Adams pleads.

"That is tough, get back." "Well, was the President shot?" "I don't know. Go back." The two women obey, yet they do not return the way they came, but rather by going all the way around the west side to reenter the TSBD through the front entrance—talking to people along the way.

12:32 PM   Dashing into the Book Depository Building, **Officer Baker** and **Roy Truly** see and identify Oswald on the **second floor**. Oswald is also seen on the **second floor** by Depository employee **Mrs. Robert Reid** as she returns to her desk. Oswald calmly walks east and south to the second floor stairway and descends to the **first floor** of the building and exits the TSBD from the main entrance—before the building is effectively sealed off by police.

Postal Inspector **Harry Holmes**, viewing the assassination through binoculars from the window of the Terminal Annex Building overlooking Dealey Plaza from the south, observes a man in the grassy knoll area "trying to take a gun away" from a woman. (*Holmes will later explain that "it later developed that he was trying to protect her from the shots." How the postal inspector came to "know" this later is unknown. He was never asked to describe her or her male companion.*)

Howard Brennan jumps off the wall where he has been sitting and is frightened enough to run to the Houston Street side of his position and crouch for protection.

Richard Randolph Carr notices a man wearing a brown suit coat walking very fast, proceeding south on Houston Street and then turning left on Commerce. In addition to his brown suit coat, Carr also says he is now wearing a hat and has on horn-rimmed glasses.

He steps into a 1961 or 1962 gray Nash **Rambler station wagon** parked along the street. The driver is a young Negro. The brown suit coat man is last seen as a passenger of this car going north on Record Street. (*Carr is never called upon to testify. Still, police and other officials repeatedly come to his house outside Dallas to intimidate him into silence. He suffers death threats and coercion at the hands of the FBI who tell him, "If you didn't see Lee Harvey Oswald in the School Book Depository with a rifle, then you didn't see anything."* **Jim Garrison** *secures Carr to testify at the* **Clay Shaw** *trial. The day before his testimony, Carr finds dynamite wired to the ignition of his car; however, he does testify. Carr will receive numerous threats and will suffer attacks on his life. He even shoots and kills one of his attackers. He will eventually be stabbed to death in Atlanta in the 1970s.*)

Further details on Carr: Just prior to the sound of shots, **Richard R. Carr** has been looking for work at the site of the new courthouse on Houston St. He is seeking out the foreman on the ninth floor, and as he ascends, he stops at the **sixth floor**, from which he can view the top floor of the Depository. He notes a heavy-set man looking out a window next to the one on the far east end. This man is wearing a hat, glasses, and, according to Carr, a tan sportcoat. For a short time, Carr studies the man, and then he continues his ascent. About a minute or two later, he hears a loud noise that sounds like a firecracker. He turns his eyes toward the triple underpass, which is where he thinks the shots have come from. In the grassy area between Elm and Main he can see several individuals falling to the ground. To learn more, he immediately begins to descend the stairs. After Carr reaches the ground, he again sees the man whom he has previously seen on the sixth floor of the Book Depository. He is rapidly approaching Carr at a very fast walking pace. When he gets to the corner of Commerce, he turns left. On the next street over is a 1961 or 1962 Nash Rambler **station wagon**, parked facing north. It has a luggage rack on top and Texas plates. In the driver's seat is a young black man. The heavy-set man opens the rear door and gets in. The car is last seen heading north on Record Street. [This momentary sighting dovetails with the observation of sheriff's deputy **Roger Craig**, who also sees a Nash Rambler **station wagon**, also driven by a dark-complected man, about <u>fifteen minutes</u> after the shooting, heading west on Elm. It stops in front of the TSBD and a man later identified by Craig as Lee Harvey Oswald gets inside. The car is last seen going under the triple under-pass in a direction that could have taken it toward Oak Cliff.]

Police Band (Channel 2): "There is a motorcycle officer up on Stemmons with his mike stuck open on Channel 1. Could you send someone up there to tell him to shut it off?" Report that Parkland has been notified.

Panic and confusion erupt in Dealey Plaza, yet the *"umbrella man"* calmly lowers his umbrella and gazes around. He then has a brief conference with another man who approaches him with what appears to be *a two-way radio*. After talking briefly together, the *two men calmly leave the Plaza*. Researcher **Penn Jones** will later locate the Umbrella Man. When questioned, the Umbrella Man, **Mr. Witt**, shows the HSCA an umbrella that has a different number of "ribs" than the one in the Zapruder film. His testimony about his actions during and after the shooting will be disproved by films and photos.

Abraham Zapruder, according to his secretary, shakily puts down his camera and starts screaming *"They killed him! They killed him! They killed him!"* He is so stricken by the experience that he never quite gets over it. His own is the last film or news report about Kennedy he will ever watch.

NOTE: Author **Doug Mizzer** will eventually point out an apparent discrepancy between the Zapruder and Nix films. **Clint Hill** testifies that he grabbed **Jackie Kennedy** and put her back into her seat. In the Nix film, Hill gets both feet onto the limousine and puts one hand on each of Jackie's shoulders. He even seems to be hugging her head and shoulders as he pushes her back into the seat. But the Zapruder film shows that he only reaches out and perhaps barely touches her outstretched hand when she turns and climbs back into the seat.

Jim Hicks, an eyewitness in Dealey Plaza, walks toward the knoll as the motorcade's press bus speeds by on its way to Parkland hospital. Photographs of Hicks, taken from the rear, show something in his back pocket resembling a radio with an antenna. (*Hicks will later tell New Orleans District Attorney Jim Garrison that he was the radio coordinator for the assassination team. Shortly after admitting this to Garrison, Hicks is beaten up, kidnapped, and taken to an Air Force mental institution in Oklahoma, where he will be incarcerated until 1988. A few days after his release, Hicks will be murdered in Oklahoma.*) It will later be suggested that Jim Hicks is possibly the man photographed in the Cuban and Soviet Embassies in Mexico by the CIA. He is identified incorrectly as Oswald in those photographs.

Jerry Coley (*a thirty-year old employee of the Dallas Morning News*) and his friend, **Charlie Mulkey**, cross Houston St. from their vantage point near the old county jail. They circle behind the TSBD and cross a dirt field to reach the knoll. Heading to the TSBD from the knoll they notice a pool of red liquid on the steps leading down to Elm St. Mulkey touches the liquid with his finger, tastes it and says: *"My God, Jerry, that's blood."* Both men return to the *Morning News* building and get photographer **Jim Hood**. Returning to the scene Hood takes several pictures of the red liquid from different angles. Both men then hurry back to the newspaper offices to develop the photographs.

Building engineer **J. C. Price** is on the roof of the Terminal Annex Building on the south side of Dealey Plaza. He sees a man run from the area behind the wooden fence. Price states that the man has something in his right hand and *"was running very fast, which gave me the suspicion that he was doing the shooting."*

Dallas Police Officer **Joe Marshall Smith** has drawn his pistol and is checking out the parking lot directly behind the fence on the grassy knoll. He encounters a man behind the stockade fence on the grassy knoll who produces Secret Service credentials. He is allowed to continue on his way.

Crossing Elm Street to the area of the wooden fence, **Malcolm Summers** is stopped by a man in a suit with an overcoat over his arm. The man reveals a small automatic weapon under the overcoat and tells Summers, *"Don't you'all come up here any further. You could get shot."*

Sergeant D. V. Harkness goes to rear of the Book Depository Building where he encounters **several "well armed" men** dressed in suits. They tell Sergeant Harkness they are with the Secret Service.

NOTE: OF THE TWENTY-EIGHT SECRET SERVICE AGENTS PRESENT IN DALLAS THIS DAY, NOT A SINGLE ONE WAS EVER IN THE GRASSY KNOLL AREA OR THE PARKING AREA BEHIND IT. NO AGENT WAS ON FOOT IN THE AREA BEFORE OR AFTER THE SHOOTING.

One secret service agent is momentarily stranded in Dealey Plaza when he leaves a Secret Service follow-up car, but is quickly picked up by another passing motorcade car and taken immediately to Parkland Hospital.

Deputy Constable **Seymour Weitzman**, standing at the corner of Main and Houston Streets, has heard the shots. He immediately runs toward the underpass and to the stockade fence atop the knoll. There, Deputy Weitzman is informed by a bystander that the *"firecracker or shot had come from the other side of the fence."* During the time Weitzman is running from the intersection of Main and Houston, he observes **a blonde woman**, 20 to 25 years old, drop **a lunch sack** at a point about half a block west of the Texas School Book Depository building. He thinks nothing of it at the time. Only later will Weitzman determine that this lunch sack was very similar to the lunch sack found at the sixth floor window where the assassin apparently stationed himself. **He will bring this information to the attention of the Dallas Police Department.** Weitzman subsequently picks up a piece of JFK's skull, which he finds near the curb on the south side of Elm Street, and turns it over to authorities. (*Later, when Weitzman tells the Warren Commission about this piece of skull, he is suddenly taken "off the record."*)

Nearly a *dozen* people are taken into custody at various times and places following the shots. **Larry Florer** is arrested coming out of the Dal-Tex building, reportedly drunk; he is held for questioning and later released.

NOTE: Several people in Dealey Plaza (*including* **Phil Willis** *and his family*) witness the arrest of a young man wearing a black leather jacket and black gloves. He is ushered out of the Dal-Tex building by two uniformed policemen, who put him in a police car and drive away from the crime scene as the crowd curses and jeers him. There is no official record of this arrest.

Approximately fifteen minutes from now, the elevator operator in the Dal-Tex Building notices an unknown man inside the building. Feeling that the man doesn't belong in the building, the elevator operator seeks out a policeman, who detains the suspicious man, bringing him to the sheriff's office for questioning. They hold him for nearly three hours. He tells police that his name is **Jim Braden**, and that he is in Dallas on oil business. He shows them identification, and explains that he had entered the building in hopes of finding a telephone to call his mother. Braden further asserts that he entered the building only after the assassination occurred, although eyewitnesses place him in the building at the time the shots were actually fired. Eventually, the police accept his explanation and release him. Jim Braden is actually **Eugene Hale Brading**, an ex-con from Southern California with reputed underworld ties.

On **10 September**, just two months before the assassination, Brading had his name legally changed to Braden. Had Dallas police known his actual name, they would have learned that he was a parolee with thirty-five arrests on his record.

Brading had told his parole officer that he was going to Dallas on oil business, and his parole records indicate that he planned to meet with **Lamar Hunt**. Although he later denied meeting with Hunt, a witness (Hunt's chief of security **Paul Rothermel**) placed Brading and three friends at the offices of Lamar Hunt on the afternoon before the assassination. Brading's presence at Hunt's office was also confirmed in an FBI report. Coincidentally, **Jack Ruby** accompanied a young woman to the Hunts' office that same afternoon. And on the twenty-first (*last night*), Brading checked into the Cabana Hotel in Dallas, where Jack Ruby just happened to visit sometime around midnight that same evening.

During the months preceding the assassination, Brading kept an office in the Pete Marquette Building in New Orleans. Also occupying an office in that building, on the same floor and just down the hall, was **G. Wray Gill**, a lawyer for New Orleans crime boss **Carlos Marcello**. One of Gill's detectives is **David Ferrie**, who has been in and out of Gill's office many times during the time Brading keeps an office there. Ferrie later became the focus of New Orleans District Attorney Jim Garrison's investigation into the President's assassination.

On the evening of 4 June 1968, Brading will check in to the Century Plaza Hotel in Los Angeles, more than a hundred miles from his home. Just a few minutes away at the Ambassador Hotel, Robert Kennedy will be murdered in the hotel pantry after winning the California primary. Upon learning of Brading's close proximity to the Ambassador Hotel that evening, the Los Angeles Police Department will be concerned enough to question Brading about his possible role in both assassinations.

12: 33 PM **Warren Commission states:** This is the earliest time Oswald could have left the Texas Book Depository Building after shooting the President. He departs the building from the main entrance. Oswald will later testify that **a Secret Service agent** stops him in front of the Book Depository to ask where the nearest telephone is located. The man Oswald meets leaving the Texas School Book Depository is also claimed to be **Pierce Allman**, a crew cut reporter who enters the TSBD to telephone a report to WFAA radio. [*Editor's note:* It may have been reporter Robert MacNeil.] (*After Oswald's eventual arrest,* **Captain Fritz** *and the other interrogators of Oswald will <u>never</u> ask him which exit he used or whether a policeman had been stationed at the door, and if so, whether he had tried to prevent him from leaving or had checked his credentials.*)

(12:35 pm) When interviewed by **Captain Fritz** on 22 November 1963, Oswald said "as he was leaving the TSBD building, two men (one with a crew cut) had intercepted him at the front door; identified themselves as Secret Service Agents and asked for the location of a telephone." Oswald was probably mistaken as to the identity of these men. **Mr. Pierce Allman**, who had brown crew cut hair, and **Terrence Ford**, of WFAA TV, ran into the TSBD a few minutes after the shooting. They entered the front door of the building, emerged into a hallway and there met a white male who they could not further identify. Allman asked this person for the location of a telephone. Oswald watched as Allman used the phone and Oswald then left the TSBD and walked east on Elm.

A KBOX news car arrives on the scene—near the rear of the TSBD.

The interference on police **Channel 1** stops. (*The microphone has been "stuck" open for at least **four** minutes total*). But first there is an electronic beeping in precisely the Morse code signal for "**Victory**."

The telephone system in Washington, D.C. is interrupted and, in some areas, goes dead and *remains out of service for an hour*.

12:34 PM <u>**FIRST UPI NEWS FLASH**</u>. The radio telephone in a press car carrying representatives of the wire services is rendered inoperative immediately after **Merriman Smith** gets out the first utterance of the shooting. (*The press pool car contains Merriman Smith, Jack Bell, Marty Underwood, Bob Clark of ABC, and Bob Bascomb of* The Dallas Morning News, *plus the driver who is an employee of Southwest Bell Telephone.*)

NOTE: (Death of Secret Service Agent) Eddie Barker, KRLD-TV, a CBS affiliate, will note, "The word is that the President was killed, one of his agents is dead, and Governor Connally was wounded." ABC News in Washington will report, "A Secret Service agent apparently was shot by one of the assassin's bullets." ABC's **Bill Lord** report includes, "Did confirm the death of the Secret Service agent. . . one of the Secret Service agents was killed. . . Secret Service agents usually walk right beside the car." ABC Washington will also note, "One of the Secret Service agents traveling with the President was killed today." The Associated Press (AP) is quoted on WFAA (ABC):"A Secret Service agent and a Dallas policeman were shot and killed some distance from where the President was shot."

Police Band (Channel 2): Orders to keep everything out of the emergency entrance to Parkland Hospital. Get all of the traffic out of the way. An officer in Dealey Plaza radios that he has a witness who saw a man with a gun in the TSBD. Curry tells officer get name, address, phone number and all information. Cut traffic on Hines and Industrial Boulevard.

12:35 PM   **J. Edgar Hoover** calls Attorney General RFK at home. *"The President's been shot. I think it is serious. I'll call you back when I find out more."* **Robert Morganthau** watches as RFK turns away, a look of horror on his face, clapping his hand to his mouth. He turns to his aides and screams *"Jack's been shot! It might be fatal."* RFK then goes back to the main house, walking around in a state of shock. Later, followed by **Ethel**, he goes up to their bedroom to try calling Dallas. He is also simultaneously preparing to pack for an emergency flight to Texas.

Eventually, RFK's call to Parkland is put through. He isn't sure to whom, though he believes it is to Secret Service agent **Clint Hill**. Later, RFK recalls: *"They said that it was very serious. And I asked if he was conscious, and they said he wasn't, and I asked if they'd gotten a priest, and they said they had . . . Then, I said, will you call me back, and he said yes, and then he—Clint Hill called me back, and I think it was about thirty minutes after I talked to Hoover . . . and he said, "The President's dead."*

Tom Dillard snaps two photographs in the rail yard next to the TSBD parking area which show a 1959 Rambler **station wagon**.

Sergeant Tom Tilson, an off-duty Dallas policeman, and his daughter are in his car just west of the triple underpass. They watch as a man in dark clothing comes down the railroad embankment to a black automobile. He throws something into the backseat, hurries around to the front, gets into the car, and speeds off westward. Thinking this suspicious, they pursue the vehicle but lose it in the traffic. The man, Tilson later says, looked and dressed like **Jack Ruby**.

Of the **twenty** sheriff's deputies watching the motorcade from in front of the Sheriff's Office, **sixteen** place the origin of the shots near the Triple Underpass, **three** give no opinion, and **one** implies the Book Depository Building. Of the Dallas policemen interviewed, **four** place shots from the grassy knoll, **four** say shots came from the Depository, and **four** give no opinion.

NOTE: The Warren Commission will eventually question **126** of the **266** known witnesses either by testimony or affidavit. Regarding the source of the shots, **thirty-eight gave no opinion**—most are not asked—**thirty two indicate the TSBD**, and *fifty-one place the shots in the vicinity of the grassy knoll*. Several believe shots were fired from *two* different locations.

Police Band (Channel 2)—"Do not move on Industrial Blvd. Keep all traffic out of that area."

A police sergeant radios headquarters that he has a witness who says shots came from the **fifth** floor.

S. M. Holland, who hurries to the spot behind the fence where he thinks one shot has been fired, finds a number of Dallas police officers already there, in the area behind the picket fence reserved for parking for the sheriff's department and others who work at the courthouse.

In New Orleans, at the trial of **Carlos Marcello**, **Judge Herbert W. Christenberry** has just delivered his fifteen minute charge to the jury. A bailiff suddenly strides into the courtroom and, going up to the bench, hands the judge a note. As Judge Christenberry reads it, a look of shock and consternation spreads over his face. Recovering quickly, he stands up and announces that President JFK has just been shot in Dallas and is feared dead. Carlos Marcello and his brother Joe file out of the courtroom for an hour's recess showing absolutely no emotion. Also leaving the federal courthouse is **David Ferrie**. Shortly thereafter, Ferrie telephones a motel Carlos Marcello owns in Houston and makes a reservation for this night for himself and two young male companions, **Alvin Beauboeuf** and **Melvin Coffey**. He then places a call to the owner and operator of the Winterland Skating Rink in Houston, inquiring about the rink's skating schedule. *(Three days later, he will lie to the FBI about the nature of the call.)*

12:36 PM Marsalis Bus No. 1213 leaves the intersection of St. Paul and Elm, going west on Elm Street—bound for Oak Cliff. Behind it is another city bus also bound for Oak Cliff—the Beckley bus. These two buses will travel together down Elm Street through dense city traffic. At Dealey Plaza their routes will diverge, the Marsalis bus turning south on Houston Street, and the Beckley bus continuing westward past the Texas School Book Depository. *LHO will supposedly board the Marsalis bus in a matter of minutes.*

Mary Bledsoe boards the bus at at St. Paul and Elm and sits across the aisle from the driver. This bus, identified as the "Marsalis-Ramona-Elwood," is driven by **Cecil McWatters** . A few blocks later the bus stops to pick up a passenger. Bledsoe recognizes the passenger as Oswald when he boards the bus. He passes by her while walking toward the rear of the bus. When the bus becomes stalled in traffic, Oswald again passes by Bledsoe, this time while walking toward the front of the bus. Oswald obtains a transfer from McWatters and exits through the front door.

When interviewed on 23 November 1963, Bledsoe remembered that Oswald wore "a brown shirt with holes in the elbows and "ragged gray work pants." Bledsoe was the only witness on the bus who paid any attention to Oswald, probably because she knew him, and thus was able to identify the clothing he wore.

Before her WC testimony Bledsoe prepared notes, at the suggestion of SS Agent **Forrest Sorrels**, in order to refresh her memory. Reading from notes to refresh a witnesses testimony is, as any lawyer knows, not uncommon in courtroom proceedings. It is allowed in all state and federal court proceedings (*Federal Rules of Evidence*— Rule 612 and Rule 803-S).

Cecil McWatters was interviewed on 22 and 23 November. On 22 November, McWatters was driving the "Marsalis, Ramona, Elwood, Munger" bus run, known as run 1213. McWatters, with his time checked by the company dispatcher, arrived on schedule at St. Paul and Elm at 12:36 pm. At Elm and Griffin "I come to a complete stop, and when I did, someone come up and beat on the door of the bus, and that is about even with Griffin St." The man boarded the bus, paid his 23 cent fare, and "he took the third chair back on the right." Mary Bledsoe, sitting across from McWatters, identified the man as her former tenant—Lee Harvey Oswald.

Near Poydrus, when the bus becomes tied up in traffic, a man gets out of the car in front of the bus, walks back to the bus and tells Whaley the President has been shot. An unknown woman and Oswald get up from their seats, ask for and obtain bus transfers from McWatters and leave the bus. McWatters told the Warren Commission, "Yes, sir; I gave him one (bus transfer) about two blocks from where he got on. . . the reason I recall the incident, I had— there was a lady that when I stopped in this traffic, there was a lady who had a suitcase and she said, I have got to make a 1 o'clock train at Union Station . . . so I gave her a transfer and opened the door and as she was going out the gentlemen I had picked up about 2 blocks asked for a transfer and got off at the same place in the middle of the block where the lady did. . . it was the intersection near Lamar St.." Oswald's transfer is valid for 15 minutes or until the next scheduled bus after the time of issue.

After departing McWatters bus, Oswald walks two blocks south on Lamar St. and says to **William Whaley**, "May I have this cab?." After Oswald leaves the bus, two policemen board the bus and inform

McWatters and passengers of the assassination. They question each passenger to see if they are carrying weapons.

Interviewed on 22 November, McWatters did not mention or identify the clothing worn by Oswald. Before the Warren Commission McWatters said, "To me he had on just work clothes, he didn't have on a suit of clothes, and some type of jacket. I would say a cloth jacket." When taken to the DPD that evening for a lineup, McWatters picked a man "whom he said is the only one in the lineup who resembles the man who had ridden on his bus on 22 November 1963. He emphasized that he cannot specifically identify him (Oswald) as being on his bus or as being the person who made the remark to the effect that the President was shot in the temple".

Roy Milton Jones was not interviewed until 30 March 1964. Jones said that a "blond woman and a dark haired man" boarded the bus approximately six blocks before Houston Street. The man sat in the seat behind him and the woman occupied a seat further to the rear of the bus. When the bus was stopped in traffic, and prior to the appearance of the police, the woman left the bus by the rear door to catch a train at the depot and the man who was sitting behind him (Oswald) left the bus by the front door while the bus was in the middle of the block. Jones "emphasized he did not have a good view of this man at any time and could not positively identify him as being identical with Lee Harvey Oswald. He said he was inclined to think it might have been Oswald only because the bus driver told him so."

When interviewed four months later by the FBI, Jones said the man sitting behind him was wearing a "light blue jacket and gray khaki trousers." Jones had seen this nondescript and unknown man, who sat behind him four months earlier, for a brief few seconds. (Mr. Jones should be commended for remembering anything at all about this man.)

McWatters picked up a passenger "between the corner of Poydras and Elm and the corner of Commerce and Houston." McWatters said after turning onto Houston Street, he proceeded across the Houston Street viaduct to Oak Cliff, and then turned south on Marsalis Street. After McWatters turned south on Marsalis Street he said to a male passenger, "I wonder where they shot the President." The man replied, "They shot him in the temple."

McWatters continued south on Marsalis and "picked up an old lady at the corner of Vermont and Marsalis." McWatters, who stated "she was at least 55 or 60 years of age," did not recall ever seeing her before. He asks her if she "had heard that the President had been shot. She tells McWatters not to joke about such a matter, and he tells her that if she does not believe him to ask the man sitting behind him. She looks at this man, who is the one who had told McWatters that the President had been shot in the temple, and says "why he's smiling; you're joking!"

McWatters continues south on Marsalis and remembers letting the smiling man off the bus "south of Saner Avenue." The smiling man, described by McWatters as a "teenager, about 5'8," 155 lbs, medium build, slim faced," is later identified as Roy Milton Jones, who regularly rides McWatters bus. In fact, McWatters said "the man rode with me the next day," 23 November. McWatters' memory of where the young man got off the bus proves correct. Jones lives one block south of Saner Avenue at 512 E Brownlee Avenue.

In Washington, **Desmond FitzGerald** is at lunch at the City Tavern Club in Georgetown when a telephone call comes in for him. His executive assistant, **Sam Halpern**, sees FitzGerald emerge from the call "white as a ghost." FitzGerald says: *"The President's been shot."* "Halpern replies, *"I hope this has nothing to do with the Cubans."* The two men then race across the Potomac to CIA headquarters.

12:37 PM   The telephone rings at Parkland's emergency room nurse's station. Head nurse **Doris Nelson** is advised by The Dallas Police Department that JFK has been shot and is en route to the hospital.

When Parkland Hospital receives the notification, the staff in the emergency area is alerted and trauma rooms 1 and 2 are prepared. These rooms are for the emergency treatment of acutely ill or injured patients. Although the first message mentions an injury only to JFK, two rooms are prepared. As the President's limousine speeds toward the hospital, 12 doctors rush to the emergency area: surgeons, **Drs. Malcolm O. Perry, Charles R. Baxter, Robert N. McClelland, Ronald C. Jones;** the chief neurologist, **Dr. William Kemp Clark;** 4 anesthesiologists, **Drs. Marion T. Jenkins, Adolph H. Gieseeke, Jr., Jackie H. Hunt, Gene C. Akin;** urological surgeon, **Dr. Paul C. Peters;** an oral surgeon, **Dr. Don T. Curtis;** and a heart specialist, **Dr. Fouad A. Bashour.** [*Editor's note:* And **Dr. Charles Crenshaw.**]

Dallas police Inspector **Herbert Sawyer** orders two guards posted at the front door of the TSBD building and guards at the loading platform behind the building. Their orders: "No one is to enter; nobody is allowed to leave." Without orders, Sawyer inches down through the crowds until he parks his car in front of the TSBD.

12:38 PM   Parkland Hospital prepares to admit JFK, case *"24740,"* white male, suffering from *"gunshot wound."*

Agent **Rufus Youngblood**, protecting LBJ with his body, says to the Vice President: *"When we get where we're going, you and me are going to move off and not tie in with other people."* Johnson replies: *"O.K. O.K., partner."*

ABC interrupts its radio broadcasting with news of the shooting. The flash is relayed by **Don Gardiner**. UPI says JFK has been wounded *"perhaps fatally."*

Around this time, **James Underwood**, assistant news director at KRLD-TV in Dallas hears **Amos L. Euins**, a 15-year-old boy, tell a motorcycle officer he *"had seen a colored man lean out of the window upstairs and he had a rifle."* Underwood interviews Euins on the spot, asking the boy if the man he saw was *"white or black."* Euins replies, *"It was a colored man." "Are you sure it was a colored man?"* Underwood asks. Euins answers, *"Yes sir."* Euins is taken to the Dallas Sheriff's office, where an affidavit is prepared for him. The affidavit states that the man Euins has seen is *"a **white** man."*

Dallas police detain **a Latin man** whom they have seized on Elm Street. *(**Deputy Sheriff Roger Craig** states that this is the same man he will see driving a Rambler **station wagon** that picks up a man in front of the TSBD a few minutes later.)* The Latin man is released when he indicates he can not speak English.

Police Band (Channel 2): Report of a witness to the shooting who has been hit by a ricochet. "Has the TSBD been sealed off?" Someone asks what has happened. Curry replies that there's been an accident. The President is involved. Report that officers are now surrounding and searching TSBD building. Six or 7 more people may have been shot.

12:40 PM Deputy **Sheriff Roger Craig** meets **E.R. Walthers** on the south side of Elm Street where several officers and bystanders are looking at the curb on Elm St. where a nick caused by a bullet is reported to have hit. Craig hears a shrill whistle and turns to see a white male running down the hill from the Texas School Book Depository Bldg. He sees a light-colored *Rambler station wagon* pull over to the curb, driven by **a dark-complected white male**. According to Craig, the man running from the building, gets into the station wagon and the car drives away. Later in the day, Craig identifies the man fleeing the building as **Lee Harvey Oswald**. He makes a positive ID at police headquarters.

A *Nash Rambler station wagon* is also seen by **Marvin Robinson**, who notices no passenger. The vehicle stops on Elm Street and a white male comes down the grassy incline and enters the station wagon. The car speeds away towards the Oak Cliff section of Dallas. *(This is the same incident witnessed by **Roger Craig and Helen Forrest**.)* An additional witness, **Roy Cooper**, also observes "a white male somewhere between 20 and 30 years of age wave at a Nash Rambler station wagon, light colored, as it pulled out and was ready to leave from Elm and Houston." Once the man got into the car, Cooper says "They drove off at a rather fast rate of speed and went down toward the overpass toward Oak Cliff."

NOTE: On **29 May 1989**, researcher **Richard Bartholomew** locates what he believes to be the Rambler **station wagon** on the campus of University of Texas at Austin (UT). The Rambler is found bearing a 1964 Mexico Federal Turista window sticker and displaying at least two magazines published in 1963 on its rear seat. The car is owned by a Spanish professor who had bought it from a very close friend of Lyndon Johnson in April 1963. The used car lot's sales manager who signed the car's warranty died of a heart attack after feeling a sharp pain in his back while sitting in a dark movie theater. He died only seven weeks after the assassination. If this UT Rambler *WAS* the one used by the conspirators in the JFK assassination, then it was in Mexico in 1964, ended up back in the United States as some sort of souvenir, and stayed near a circle of friends that included **Lyndon Johnson**, his close adviser **Walt Rostow**, UT adjunct professor **Jack Dulles**, former UT President and chancellor **Harry Ransom**, Lyndon Johnson's friend **C. B. Smith**, and two professors of Spanish and Portuguese at the University of Texas at Austin.

According to **Harrison Edward Livingston**, *Killing The Truth*: *"Then there was the getaway of the shooters. There are repeated reports that cars were changed in Temple or Paris, Texas, and that a man recognized* **Mac (Malcolm) Wallace** *there. He is believed by* **Madeleine Brown** *and others of being one of the shooters."*

According to the Warren Commission: This is the time **Oswald** boards a bus at a point on Elm St. seven short blocks east of the Depository Building. The bus is traveling west toward the very building from which Oswald has come. *To do this, LHO has had to have walked, at a brisk pace, seven blocks from Dealey Plaza. The bus he supposedly boards is headed <u>back</u> towards Dealey Plaza, which at this time is a scene of convulsive activity. JFK has been shot there only ten minutes earlier.* The Warren commission's only witness for substantiating LHO's presence on the bus is **Mary Bledsoe**, an elderly widow who lives at 621 N. Marsalis St. (*Bledsoe first met LHO in early October 1963 when he had rented a room in her house. He stayed there for only a week. This is the first time she has supposedly seen him since then.*) Her account, however, differs from two other witnesses on the bus: the bus driver, **Cecil J. McWatters** and **Milton Jones** (*a part-time student attending the morning classes at Crozier Technical High School*) who is sitting near the front of the bus. McWatters and Jones agree that **(1)** The man who boards the bus is wearing a jacket. Bledsoe testifies that he is in shirtsleeves and **(2)** the man who boards the bus takes a seat near the <u>front</u> of the bus—immediately behind Jones. Bledsoe says the man sits in the <u>back</u> of the bus. Bledsoe's testimony is accepted by the Commission over that of McWatters and Jones.

CBS interrupts *"As The World Turns"* and **Walter Cronkite** announces the first reports of the shooting.

Patrolman J.W. Foster leaves his station atop the triple underpass in Dealey Plaza and hurries to the area behind the wooden fence. There he discovers footprints and cigarette butts near the spot where witnesses observed a puff of smoke during the shooting.

Emmett Hudson, who was standing directly in front of the picket fence at the time of the shots will testify that he does not see any guns except in the possession of the police.

Mrs. **Donald Baker** runs quickly to the knoll and sees only policemen and those working around the tracks.

Police Band (Channel 2): Curry says it appears to him that the President's head was practically blown off.

Aboard the military aircraft carrying six members of the President's cabinet to Japan, a Teletype message reports that shots have been fired at the President. With specific procedures for such an emergency, officials attempt to reach the White House Situation Room. They are prevented from doing so because *the official code book is missing from its special place aboard the plane*.

General **Edwin Walker**, aboard a Braniff flight from New Orleans, reportedly becomes upset when word of the assassination is broadcast over the plane's loudspeaker. He roams up and down the aisle telling fellow passengers to remember that he is on that flight at the time of JFK's death.

Norman Similas, of Toronto, also witnesses the assassination of JFK and promptly leaves town.

In Washington, **McGeorge Bundy** and **Commander Oliver Hallet** man the Situation Room in the White House. Much of their information is coming from the *Defense Intelligence Agency (DIA)* in the Pentagon. Officials in the Pentagon are calling the White House switchboard at the Dallas-Sheraton Hotel asking who is now in command. An officer—a member of the Presidential party—will eventually grab the microphone and assure the Pentagon that Secretary of Defense **Robert McNamara** and the **Joint Chiefs of Staff** are now the President.

12:43 PM   The motorcade arrives at Parkland Hospital. **Emory Roberts** rushes up to the Presidential limo. Roberts turns to **Kellerman**, saying: *"You stay with the President. I'm taking some of my men to Johnson."* **Jacqueline Kennedy** at first refuses to get out of the car. She has been holding the President's head in her lap. **Clint Hill**, realizing she doesn't want JFK to be seen like he is, takes his coat off and drapes it over JFK's head. Only then does Mrs. Kennedy allow JFK's body to be removed from the automobile. *Jesse Curry testifies: "Agent Hill finally convinced her to let go of the President. Apparently she didn't want anyone to see that the back of the President's head was partially blown off. He gave her his coat which she used to carefully wrap the President's head and neck as five or six Secret Service men lifted him toward the stretcher. His body was limp like a dead man's; they struggled to get him on the stretcher."*

Parkland nurse **Diana Bowron** first sees JFK in the limousine, and helps wheel him into the Emergency Room. Describing JFK's condition, she will testify to the Warren commission that "*He was moribund. He was lying across Mrs. Kennedy's knee and there seemed to be blood everywhere. When I went around to the other side of the car, I saw the condition of his head . . . the back of his head . . . it was very bad . . . I just saw one large hole.*"

Nurse **Patricia (Hutton) Gustafson** testifies that there was ". . . *a massive opening in the back of the head.*" She goes out to the limousine and helps wheel President Kennedy to the Emergency Room where she is asked to put a pressure bandage on the head wound. "*I tried to do so but there was really nothing to put a pressure bandage on. It was too massive. So he told me just to leave it be.*"

Dr. **Ronald Coy Jones** testifies: "*There was a large defect in the back side of the head as the President lay on the cart with what appeared to be some brain hanging out of this wound with multiple pieces of skull noted next with the brain and with a tremendous amount of clot and blood.*"

Dr. **Gene Akin**, an Anesthesiologist at Parkland, testifies that "*the back of the right occipital-parietal portion of (JFK's) head was shattered, with brain substance extruding.*"

Dr. **Charles Baxter** testifies that there is "*a large gaping wound in the back of the skull.*" Baxter will also insist that the wound in the throat was "*no more than a pinpoint. It was made by a small caliber weapons. And it was an entry wound.*"

[*Editor's note:* See the discussions of the medical evidence by Gary Aguilar, M.D., and by David Mantik, M.D., Ph.D., elsewhere in this volume.]

Governor Connally, who has lost consciousness on the ride to the hospital, regains consciousness when the limousine stops abruptly at the emergency entrance. Despite his serious wounds, Governor Connally tries to get out of the way so that medical help can reach the President. Although he is reclining in his wife's arms, he lurches forward in an effort to stand upright and get out of the car, but he collapses again. Then he experiences his first sensation of pain, which becomes excruciating. The Governor is then lifted onto a stretcher and taken into Trauma Room #2.

At almost the same time, three agents—**McIntyre, Bennett and Youngblood**—hustle Vice-President LBJ inside the hospital through the emergency door. JFK is immediately wheeled into *Trauma Room #1*. **SA Taylor** follows LBJ with **Mrs. Johnson**. They place the Johnsons in an isolated room and draw the shades. **SA Emory Roberts** tells LBJ that, at the moment, no one knows whether this is a widespread plot to assassinate the leading men in the United States government. He also informs LBJ that he doesn't think the President will make it. Youngblood asks LBJ to "*think it over. We may have to swear you in.*" LBJ asks for Congressman **Homer Thornberry** and Congressman **Jack Brooks** to join him. He also asks that someone go to get coffee for him and Mrs. Johnson. **Cliff Carter** does so.

Dr. **George G. Burkley**, JFK's personal physician who is riding in the motorcade, will not arrive at the hospital for another ten crucial minutes.

A Secret Service agent is stationed at the entrance of the Vice President's room to stop anyone who is not a member of the Presidential party. U.S. Representatives **Henry B. Gonzalez, Jack Brooks, Homer Thornberry**, and **Albert Thomas** join **Clifton C. Carter** and the group of special agents protecting the Vice President. *(On one occasion Mrs. Johnson, accompanied by two Secret Service agents, leaves the room to see Mrs. Kennedy and Mrs. Connally.)*

Miss **Doris Nelson** asks Mrs. Kennedy to leave Trauma Room #1. **Diana Bowron, S.R.N.** and **Margaret Hinchcliffe, R.N.**, undress JFK swiftly, removing all his clothes except his undershorts and brace and fold them on a corner shelf. The first physician to arrive, **Charles J. Carrico**, a second-year surgical resident, examines JFK quickly. There is no pulse, no blood pressure at all. Yet, JFK is making slow, agonizing efforts to breathe, and an occasional heart beat can be detected. Blood is caked on JFK's steel-gray suit, and his shirt is the same crimson color. **Dr. Charles A. Crenshaw** notices that the entire right hemisphere of his brain is missing, beginning at his hairline and extending all the way behind his right ear. Pieces of skull that haven't been blown away are hanging by blood-matted hair. Part of his brain, the cerebellum, is dangling from the back of his head by a single strand of tissue. It is reported that someone in the Trauma Room orders the medical team to *"Get him (JFK) some steroids."* This order refers to JFK's secret Addison's disease and that it created the life-or-death urgency of an immediate infusion of cortical hormones in order to treat JFK's shock. Testimony reveals that *"some admiral"* behind **Dr. Paul Peters** gives this order. Some researchers credit the order to Dr. **George G. Burkley**. This, however, is impossible, since evidence points to the fact that Burkley did not arrive until around 12:53 PM. The late arrival by Burkley at Parkland Hospital is documented on film and corroborated by other photographs and testimony. It has also been suggested that Burkley's late arrival could have been innocent and covered up to protect his reputation or it could have been planned. *Trauma to someone with an adrenal deficiency will result in death if hydrocortisone is not administered immediately.*

Other doctors rush into Trauma Room #1 to help. SS agent, **Clint Hill**, is rambling around the room in wild-eyed, disoriented fashion, waving a cocked and ready-to-fire .38 caliber pistol. **Doris Nelson**, supervisor of the emergency room turns to Hill and snaps: *"Whoever shot the President is not in this room."* Hill leaves. Dr. Crenshaw removes the President's shoes and right sock and begins cutting off his suit trousers, with nurses **Diana Bowron** and **Margaret**

Hinchcliffe assisting. **Don Curtis**, an oral surgery resident, is doing the same thing to the left limb. Dr. Crenshaw notices that one of the Oxford shoes that he has tossed to the side of the room has a lift in the sole. The President's right leg is three-quarters of an inch longer than his left leg. As the doctors cut away JFK's suit pants, they also unstrap his back brace and sling it to the wall and out of the way. Admiral **George Burkley**, JFK's personal physician, traveling with the Presidential party, arrives and gives **Dr**. **Carrico** three 100-mg vials of Solu-Cortef from the medical bag he carries which contains JFK's personal medication. (*As a matter of policy, the government has not furnished the President's blood type or medical history to Parkland prior to the President's arrival. This has to be determined on the spot.*) JFK's blood type is O, RH positive. Everyone in the emergency room remains in utter bewilderment. FBI and Secret Service agents, as well as the Dallas police, are rushing around, trying to identify one another and secure the hospital.

Police Band (Channel 2): Move police from Main St. to secure the area and the TSBD. More men needed in that area. Trying to seal off building.

Dr. **Charles Crenshaw**, observing JFK's head wound in Trauma Room #1, considers it a *four-plus* injury, which no one survives. Still, the medical team does everything it can to save the President.

12:44 PM This is the time **Oswald**, as his bus approaches the congestion of Dealey Plaza, supposedly gets off the bus and walks south to the Greyhound bus station in search of a taxicab.

The Presidential limousine is at least partially cleaned as it is parked at Parkland Hospital's emergency entrance. The bubble-top is put on. (*There is no record of any evidence found at this time. The car will eventually be driven to Love Field and placed aboard a plane by Secret Service Agent Kinney.*) Several people examine what is later described as a bullet hole in the front windshield of the car while it is parked at the hospital.

Inside Parkland Hospital, SS agent **Kellerman** tells agent **Clint Hill** to establish continual telephone contact with **Gerald A. Behn**, Secret Service, White House. Telephone contact is made. Kellerman tells Behn there's been a double tragedy, that the President and Governor Connally have been shot. Hill takes over the telephone conversation and tells Behn the situation looks critical. Suddenly, the operator cuts in and says the Attorney General wants to speak to Hill. RFK comes on the line and asks Hill what the situation is. Hill advises him that JFK has been injured very seriously. Hill says he will keep RFK informed. Kellerman, who has gone into Trauma Room #1 to check on JFK, comes back and tells Hill: "*Clint, tell Gerry that this is not for release and not official, but **the man is dead**.*"

NOTE: Gerald A. Behn has not only broken precedent by not coming to Texas with the Secret Service detail, he has left his men without a leader. In Parkland, **Kellerman** and **Youngblood** sometimes act independently of each other. For instance, when LBJ is taken to Air Force One, Kellerman will **not** be informed of the move. The power base has been shifted.

When he sees Mrs. Kennedy at Parkland Hospital, limousine driver **William Robert Greer** breaks down and says, *"Oh, Mrs. Kennedy, oh my God! Oh my God! I didn't mean to do it, I didn't hear, I should have swerved the car, I couldn't help it! Oh, Mrs. Kennedy, as soon as I saw it I swerved the car. If only I'd seen it in time!"* He then weeps on the former First Lady's shoulder.

12:45 PM **Police broadcast description of suspect**. *(The possibility that suspect may be using a **Winchester rifle** is broadcast on Police Band, Channel 2.)* The source of the suspect description has never been clear, but it may have been based on information provided by a witness on the ground who said he saw a man with a rifle in a sixth-floor window of the TSBD Building. How this witness could have determined height and weight is unclear, since the partial view of the shooter in the window would have revealed the subject only from chest level upward. The description is for *"an unknown white male, approximately thirty, slender build, height five feet ten inches, weight one hundred sixty-five pounds, reported to be armed with what is believed to be a .30-caliber rifle."*

Police Band (Channel 2)—TSBD should be saturated by now. Unknown if suspect is still inside. All information we have indicates the shot came from the 4th or 5th floor of the TSBD.

In Parkland Hospital's Trauma Room #1, **Dr. Kemp Clark** notes that the President's eyes are fixed and dilated. Glancing at the other doctors in the room, he shakes his head, indicating that it is too late. Still determined to continue, **Dr. Perry** begins closed-chest cardiac massage. **Dr. Jenkins** continues to administer pure oxygen. None of the doctors wants to quit. Finally, there is nothing left to do and the medical team steps away from the table in silent surrender. The President's eyes are closed and Drs. Jenkins and **Crenshaw** cover JFK's body with *a sheet*.

NOTE: Another Dallas doctor, **Dr. McClelland** will be interviewed in 1989. He will explain that when he saw the President in the emergency room, a great flap of scalp and hair had been *"split and thrown backwards, so we had looked down into the hole."* Dr. McClelland will go on to say that the *"great defect in the back"* **is** visible on some photographs amongst the *full* set of some fifty pictures he will eventually see at the National Archives—pictures in which the torn scalp has been allowed to fall back on the President's neck. *None of the other doctors who will, over twenty-five years from now, inspect the autopsy evidence will refer to such photographs. On* Inside Edition, *a nationally syndicated television program, Dr. McClelland will, in 1989, say that "the X-rays do not show the same*

*injuries to the President's head that he saw in the emergency room."
"There is an inconsistency. Some of the skull X-rays show only the
back part of the head missing, with a fracture of the anterior part of
the skull on the right. Others, on the other hand, show what appears
to be the entire right side on the skull gone, with a portion of the
orbit—that's the skull around the eye—missing too. That to me is an
inconsistent finding. I don't understand that, unless there has been
some attempt to cover up the nature of the wound."* [*Editor's note*:
Studies of the medical evidence by Gary Aguilar, M.D. , and by David
W. Mantik, M.D., Ph.D., are found in this volume.']

Within the next hour, Dallas police sergeant **D.V. Harkness**, along
with several other officers, rousts *three* "**tramps**" from a railroad
car in the train yard just behind the Texas School Book Depository.
The men have been spotted by Union Pacific Railroad dispatcher
Lee Bowers and he orders the train stopped, then summons the
Dallas Police. Once in the sheriff's custody, the three "**tramps**" officially disappear. (The House Subcommittee on Government Information and Individual Rights discovered in 1975 that Dallas police
arrest records for 22 November 1963, compiled for the Warren Commission, are missing.) [*Editor's note*: The "Three Tramps," who
were photographed as they were being "escorted" through Dealey
Plaza, have been identified as **Charles Rogers** (a.k.a. **Richard Mon-
toya**), **Charles Harrelson**, and **Chauncey Holt** by Lois Gibson, a
forensic artist for the Houston Police Department. *(See* John Craig
and Philip Rogers, *The Man on the Grassy Knoll* 1992, and *Assassination Science* 1998, p. 368.)]

Tramp 1	Tramp 2	Tramp 3
Charles Rogers	*Charles Harrelson*	*Chauncey Holt*

After requesting orders, Officer **J.D. Tippit** in car #10 is ordered by radio to proceed to the central Oak Cliff and to stand by for any emergency. Oak Cliff is about four miles from Dealey Plaza.

NOTE: The previous statement is based on a transcript of the Dallas Police dictabelt recording. There is some question about whether or not this particular order was dubbed onto the tape at a later date by (*police*) friends of **J. D. Tippit**. Not only is such an inexplicable instruction believed to be unique in the Dallas Police Department, it also was **NOT** included in the first transcript supplied to the Warren Commission. The speculation derives from the fact that, at the height of the turbulence and confusion surrounding the shooting of the President, when the police switchboard is constantly jammed with incoming and outgoing messages of utmost importance, someone still has time to order J.D. Tippit into central Oak Cliff, where at this time, **there is not a single significant crime that requires police attention**.

NOTE: On the Oak Cliff side of the Houston Street viaduct is the Good Luck Oil Company service station (GLOCO). Five witnesses see **J.D. Tippit** arrive at the GLOCO station at 12:45 PM. He sits in his car and watches traffic cross the bridge from Dallas for about 10 minutes. There are no police dispatches ordering Tippit to this location. Within a minute of the cab passing the GLOCO station, Tippit leaves and speeds south on Lancaster. Two minutes later, at 12:54 PM, Tippit answers his dispatcher and says he is at "8th and Lancaster"—a mile south of the GLOCO Station. He turns right on Jefferson Blvd. and stops at the Top Ten Record Store a few minutes before 1:00 PM. Store owner **Dub Stark** and clerk **Louis Cortinas** watch Tippit rush into the store and use the telephone. Without completing his call or speaking to store personnel Tippit leaves, jumps into his squad car, and speeds north across Jefferson Blvd. He runs a stop sign, turns right on Sunset and is last seen speeding east—one block from N. Beckley. Tippit is now two minutes (*at 45 mph*) from Oswald's rooming house. **Tippit's whereabouts for the next 8-10 minutes remain unknown**.

At CBS, while taking a momentary break, **Walter Cronkite** numbly answers a studio telephone. A woman complains that it is in poor taste to have Cronkite broadcasting the news of the shooting because, as she says: " . . . *everybody knows that Cronkite spent all his time trying to get the President*." "*This IS Walter Cronkite*," the anchorman replies. "*And you are a goddamned idiot*."

Eugene Brading is arrested in the Dal-Tex Building across the street from the Texas School Book Depository. He is arrested for acting suspicious in the building, but is released after he uses a fictitious name (*James Braden*) and convinces the authorities he is only making a phone call. (*Brading stayed at the Cabana Motel in Dallas on the evening of 21 November. The Cabana is owned by **Joe Campisi** who has strong ties with **Carlos Marcello**.*) Brading has only recently been released from prison and has a rap sheet of 35 arrests and possible links to the underworld. *One theory suggests that Brading actually directed the assassination.*

12:48 PM   (*The Warren Commission says:*) **Oswald** gets into a taxicab that is parked in front of the Greyhound bus station about five blocks away from Dealey Plaza. The cab is driven by **William Whaley**. Whaley's log for 22 November records a trip for a single passenger from the Greyhound Bus Station to 500 North Beckley. It shows that the trip lasted from **12:30** PM to 12:45 PM If his time records are correct, it means that <u>Oswald boards the cab at the exact time JFK is being shot in Dealey Plaza</u>. The Warren Commission will later try to explain this away by saying that Whaley recorded his trips by *quarter-hour intervals* regardless of their actual length. But Whaley's log proves this theory to be in error. Further, Whaley testifies that, just as he was about to drive off, an old lady who sees his passenger enter the cab, tells Whaley she wants a cab too. Whaley's passenger opens the cab door and tells the lady that she can have Whaley's cab. The lady then says that Whaley can easily call another cab for her. *Some researchers do not think the chivalrous passenger's behavior in this instance is that of a fugitive who has just assassinated the President of the United States.* Relying solely on Whaley's testimony, the Warren Commission will eventually conclude that Oswald was unquestionably the man driven from the Greyhound Bus Station to North Beckley on the afternoon of 22 November. To reach this finding, however, it has first to disprove almost *every* statement ***initially*** made by Whaley.

Police Band (Channel 2): Someone remarks about an "interesting seizure" that someone had in the crowd prior to the motorcade's arrival in the Plaza. Instructions are given to check it out.

12:49 PM   **Captain Talbert** is giving orders to seal the TSBD: *"have that cut off on the back side, will you? Make sure nobody leaves there."*

Police Band (Channel 2): Was Governor Connally hit? No information. What to do at the Trade Mart?

12:51 PM   **Police Band (Channel 2):** Homicide Chief **Will Fritz** (from his post at the Trade Mart): "Can we tell the crowd at the Trade Mart anything?" Governor Connally and the President have been shot. "Is President going to appear at Trade Mart?" "Very doubtful." Request for additional help at Main and Houston. Fire Dept. and rescue equipment are being dispatched to the location. Again, a request for a report on the extent of injuries. Was the Governor hit? Reply is that Governor Connally was hit. Injuries to JFK unknown.

Dallas police radio now indicates that the suspect is still believed to be in the TSBD and armed.

12:52 PM   An emergency telephone call is made from a Riverside 8 exchange in Dallas to a **Pablo Brenner** or **Bruner** in Mexico City. The caller states, *"**He's dead**, **he's dead**."* The news of the President's death has not yet been publicly announced.

12:54 PM   Officer **J.D. Tippit**, Car #10, radios that he has moved as directed and will be available for any emergency. By this time the police radio has broadcast several messages alerting the police to the suspect described by **Howard Brennan** at the scene of the assassination—*a slender white male, about 30 years old, 5 feet 10 inches and weighing about 165 pounds.*

12:55 PM   For almost twenty minutes the emergency room crew in Parkland Hospital's Trauma Room #1 has been working to revive JFK. **Drs. James "Red" Duke** and **David Mebane** are stabilizing **Governor Connally** in Trauma Room #2 by inserting a chest tube and starting intravenous infusion of Ringer's lactate before taking him to x-ray and surgery.

Under heavy guard, **Lyndon Johnson** remains hidden behind a curtain in the minor medicine room just across the hall from the President. Present in the room with LBJ are **Mrs Johnson**, Congressman **Homer Thornberry**, ASAIC **Youngblood**, and most of the time, Congressman **Jack Brooks** and Special Agents **Jerry Kivett** and **Warren Taylor**. SS agent **Kellerman** discusses JFK's condition with LBJ. LBJ requests coffee for himself and Mrs. Johnson. SS agent **Youngblood** tells **Kivett** to contact Austin and Washington and have agents assigned to the Vice President's daughters. Youngblood tells SS agent **Thomas L. Johns** (*at the request of LBJ*) to ask Kellerman for a report on the condition of JFK.

Jacqueline Kennedy remains just outside of Trauma Room #1. In shock, she sits down in a chair and asks a passing aide for a cigarette.

SS Agent Roberts tells LBJ: *"The President won't make it. Let's get out of here."* **Youngblood** concurs: *"We don't know know the scope of this thing. We should get away from here immediately. **We don't know what type of conspiracy this is, or who else is marked**. The only place we can be sure you are safe is Washington."*

Ken O'Donnell to **Marty Underwood** (*advance man for JFK*): *"Marty, we don't know whether this is a plot—maybe they're after Johnson, maybe they're not. We don't know. Get the vice President, and get them back to the plane."*

T. F. Bowley picks up his daughter at the R.L. Thornton School in Singing Hills. He then leaves the school to pick up his wife at the telephone company at Ninth Street and Zangs. He drives west on Tenth Street.

12:57 PM   Last rites are administered to JFK in Trauma Room #1 by **Father Huber**. JFK's clothes are now neatly folded and placed at one end of the room.

12:58 PM   Dallas Police Capt. **Will Fritz** arrives at the Texas School Book
Depository and gives orders to seal the building. There has been no
effective containment of the crime scene for at least 10 minutes <u>and
possibly as long as twenty-eight minute</u>s.

James Powell, Special Agent with the *112th Military Intelligence
Group* at *4th* Army Headquarters at Fort Sam Houston—carrying a
35mm Minolta camera enters the Texas School Book Depository
and is forced to show his identification after Dallas police seal the
building. **Powell has been taking photographs in Dealey Plaza
prior to the assassination**. No meaningful investigation is made
by the government to determine what intelligence agent Powell is
doing in Dealey Plaza at the time of the assassination.

According to **William C. Bishop**, a CIA contract agent, U.S. Army
colonel and confessed political assassin, he is awaiting JFK's arrival
at the Trade Mart. He further states that his job this day is to make
sure the press at the Trade Mart have proper credentials. He hears
that shots have been fired in Dealey Plaza. He commandeers a police
car and orders the driver to take him directly to Parkland Hospital.
There, the SS instruct him to secure the area outside the Trauma
Room and to make himself available to the First Lady or medical
staff.

*Bishop will assert to assassination researchers in 1990 that one of his
CIA assignments was the assassination of Dominican Republic
dictator* **Rafael Trujillo** *in 1961.*

1:00 PM   **Dr**. **Kemp Clark**, Parkland's director of neurological surgery, tells
Jacqueline Kennedy : *"Your husband has sustained a fatal wound."*
She replies: *"I know."* **Dr. Clark pronounces JFK dead**. There are
approximately 19 doctors and nurses present during JFK's final
agony—plus other witnesses such as the President's wife, Secret
Service men, the Dallas Chief of Police, and Congressman **Henry
Gonzalez**—who years from now will briefly serve as Chairman of
the Assassinations committee.

Police officers are filmed by **Ernest Charles Mentesana** removing
a rifle from the roof of the TSBD. The rifle has no sling, no scope
and protrudes at least 7-8 inches past the stock. In the film two
police officers are standing on a fire escape at the seventh floor of
the Depository gesturing to the roof. In the next sequence the rifle
is being examined. When Fort Worth *Star-Telegram* reporter **Thayer
Waldo** questions a secretary who is privy to the officers'
conversations, she tells Waldo that police officers found the rifle on
the *"roof of the School Book Depository."* There is no official record
of this rifle. **Frank Ellsworth**, an agent of the Alcohol, Tobacco,
and Firearms agency assists in the TSBD search. He will testify that
the *"gun was not found on the same floor as the cartridges, but on a
lower floor by a couple of city detectives . . . I think the rifle was found
on the fourth floor."*

Henry Gonzales, in the halls of Parkland Hospital, overhears a man talking on the telephone saying: *"Yes, yes, yes, I saw him. It's all over with, I tell you, I saw the body! It's over!"*

NOTE: All of the doctors and nurses who see JFK's body at Parkland hospital in Dallas describe a large exit wound at the back of JFK's head. They also describe a small entry wound in the front of the throat. Neither of these wounds appear to be present at the Bethesda autopsy. (It is generally accepted that the neck entry wound was partially obscured by the tracheotomy performed in Parkland.) But nothing accounts for the drastic changes in the appearance of the President's head wounds from Dallas to Maryland. As an example of the contradictory evidence researchers have had to contend with, a piece of the President's occipital bone is discovered in Dealey Plaza and is subsequently examined and photographed in Dallas.

In Washington, **J. Edgar Hoover** places a second call to **RFK**. His terse words are *"The President is dead."* He hangs up. RFK notes that the Director's voice appears very calm, as if he were reporting some minor incident. From this moment on, Hoover rarely speaks to the attorney general while he is in office. According to another source, it is RFK who tells Hoover that JFK is dead. According to this source, Hoover is still talking about critical wounds. RFK snaps: *"You may be interested to know that my brother is dead."*

NOTE: By 1:00 PM, Dallas time, according to a University of Chicago study, 68 percent of all adults in the United States—over 75 million people—know about the shooting in Dallas.

Also at this time, a Dallas police car pulls up in front of Oswald's rooming house, toots its horn, then drives off. Oswald is still inside. *(Exhaustive investigations have virtually established that the ONLY police car officially in the vicinity was that of Officer J.D. Tippit.)* It has also been suggested that the person who stopped and sounded his car horn in front of Oswald's rooming house was actually Assistant D. A. **William Alexander**—who was also a Right-Wing extremist. Alexander will be at The Texas Theater minutes later when Oswald is arrested there.

Alexander rides in a car with Officer **Gerald Hill**, another Right Wing activist and friend of Jack Ruby. *Hill was in command of the search that found the cartridge cases on the sixth floor of the TSBD. The discovery is actually credited in official reports to Deputy Sheriff* ***Luke Mooney****. Researchers have since become interested in the fact that Hill seems to be in quite a few important locations this day: present at TSBD and finds empty rifle cartridges; in the second squad car to arrive at scene of Tippit murder; at the Texas Theater to assist in Oswald's arrest; and in photo of Will Fritz's office—famous for finally proving Roger Craig's presence.*

FBI SAC **J. Gordon Shanklin** orders SA **J. Doyle Williams** to go to Parkland Hospital, locate the SS agent in charge, and inform him that Hoover has ordered all bureau resources to be at the ready to assist. Williams speeds to hospital, finds **Roy Kellerman** and relays message. He then offers J. Edgar Hoover's condolences to Mrs. Kennedy. He then asks one of the nurses to help him find a telephone so that he can report to his superiors. When he returns from making this telephone call, reports of what happens next are confusing. Williams testifies that he is grabbed from behind by two SS agents and wrestled to the hall floor. **Roy Kellerman** steps in and asks Williams to leave. He does so and returns to FBI office.

NOTE: Hoover will eventually demote Williams for this incident

SS agent **Jerry D. Kivett**, on orders from SS agent **Youngblood**, radios Love Field and speaks to someone aboard *Air Force One*. He orders them to refuel and be prepared for take-off and to move the plane to another section of the airport. Kivett is advised that the plane is already refueled and that they are in the process of trying to locate another location at the airport.

Jack Lawrence, a salesman from the Downtown Lincoln-Mercury dealership (*two blocks west of Dealey Plaza*) hurries into the dealership showroom with mud on his clothes. Pale and sweating profusely, he runs into the restroom and throws up. He tells co-workers that he has been ill and tried to drive a car (*borrowed the day before from the dealership*) back to the showroom but finally had to leave it parked some distance away because the traffic was so heavy. Two employees go to pick up the car and find it parked behind the wooden fence on the grassy knoll. The car salesman is arrested and soon released. He leaves Dallas immediately and is never questioned by the Warren Commission. An Air Force veteran, Lawrence has been qualified as an expert marksman. (*It is interesting to note that* **Carlos Marcello** *had an interest in car dealerships in Dallas and his son,* **Carlos, Jr.**, *settled in Highland Park, the ritzy suburb of Dallas.*) **Sam Giancana** will later reportedly allege that Lawrence was sent along with **Charles Harrelson** by Carlos Marcello to take part in the assassination.

Also at **about 1:00 PM**, neighbors who live along the road running by the little Redbird private airport between Dallas and Fort Worth begin calling the police. A twin-engine plane, they report, is out there behaving very peculiarly. For an hour it has been revving its engines, not on the runway but parked at the end of the airstrip on a grassy area next to the fence. The noise has prevented nearby residents from hearing their TV's, as news comes over about the terrible events in downtown Dallas. But the police are too busy to check it out, and shortly thereafter the plane takes off.

Officers are also searching the bus that LHO has reportedly boarded. This search may suggest that someone other than Marina and Ruth

Paine knows that LHO can not operate an automobile and has supposedly chosen to travel by bus.

Also of possible interest is the fact that no individual employed at the TSBD comes forward to police to indicate they are afraid to reenter the building. This may tell us that either all seventy-three known employees are convinced that shots have come from elsewhere, or that they know, or suspect, the depository as a location for shots, but now that JFK's car has passed, there is no further threat to human life.

Among his many telephone calls early this afternoon, RFK contacts **McGeorge Bundy**, JFK's national security adviser, and tells him to protect JFK's papers. Bundy, after checking with the State Department, orders that the combinations to JFK's locked files be changed at once—before LBJ's men can begin rummaging through them.

NOTE: Butch Burroughs, an employee of the Texas Theater, hears someone enter the Texas Theater shortly after 1:00 PM and go to the balcony. **Lee Harvey Oswald** has apparently entered the theater and gone to the balcony without being seen by Burroughs. About 1:15 PM Harvey comes down from the balcony and buys popcorn from Burroughs. Burroughs watches him walk down the aisle and take a seat on the main floor. He sits next to **Jack Davis** during the opening credits of the first movie, several minutes before 1:20 PM. Oswald then moves across the aisle and sits next to another man. A few minutes later Davis notices he moves again and sits next to a pregnant woman. Just before the police arrive, the pregnant woman goes to the balcony and is never seen again. In addition to Harvey there are seven people watching the movie on the main level (*six after the pregnant woman left*). Within 10 minutes, LHO has sat next to half of them. Note that at this time, J.D. Tippit has not yet been shot.

Bricklayer **William Lawrence Smith** leaves his Dallas construction job for lunch at the Town and Country Cafe—two doors west of the 10th Street Barber Shop. While walking east to the cafe a man, whom Smith later identifies as Oswald, walks past him heading west—toward 10th and Patton.

1:01 PM   Oswald is seen by **Jimmy Burt** and **William. A. Smith** walking west. (The WC says he is walking east.)

1:03 PM   **Oswald** leaves his rooming house. He is last seen by the housekeeper, standing at the bus stop a short distance away. (This is when LHO supposedly retrieves his pistol.)

1:04 PM   **Helen Markham** leaves the washateria of her apartment house near the corner of 9th and Patton. While walking south on Patton she notices a police car driving slowly east on 10th Street. One half block in front of Markham, on the opposite side of Patton, cab driver **William Scoggins** is eating lunch in his cab. Scoggins notices a man walking <u>west</u> as **J. D. Tippit**'s patrol car passes slowly in front of him. **Jack Tatum**, sitting in his red 1964 Ford Galaxie a block east, notices the same man turn and walk toward the police car. Tatum turns left onto 10th street and drives slowly west past Tippit's car.

1:10 PM   Officer **J. D. Tippit** in car #10 now supposedly spots a man walking <u>east</u> along Tenth Street *(Oswald)* who seems to fit the description of the suspected assailant in Dealey Plaza. Tippit then supposedly stops and calls the man over to his car. The man walks over to the car, leans down, and speaks to Tippit through the window on the passenger's side. There is no indication that Tippit is at all concerned about the possibility of danger. Then, according to the Warren Commission report, Tippit gets out and starts to walk around the front of the car. As Tippit reaches the left front wheel, the man pulls out a revolver and fires several shots.

NOTE: Earlier this morning, Tippit hugged his oldest son **Allen** and said, "*no matter what happens today, I want you to know that I love you.*" Such overt signs of affection toward his son are uncharacteristic of Tippit. This is the last time young Allen Tippit sees his father alive.

When **Jack Tatum** hears shots, he stops his car, looks over his shoulder and sees Tippit lying on the ground. He sees the gunman walk around the rear of the police car, then turn and walk along the driver's side of the car to where Tippit has fallen. The man then shoots Tippit in the head. Tatum says "*whoever shot Tippit was determined that he shouldn't live and he was determined to finish the job.*" The committee will eventually conclude that "*This action, which is often encountered in gangland murders and is commonly described as a coup de grace, is more indicative of an execution than an act of defense intended to allow escape or prevent apprehension.*"

Four bullets hit **J. D. Tippit** and kill him instantly. The gunman starts back toward Patton Avenue, allegedly ejecting the empty cartridge cases before reloading with fresh bullets. *(George DeMohrenschildt will write in his manuscript that Oswald owns a Beretta.)*

Police will find a set of fingerprints on Tippit's car, and *they are not Oswald's*. Officer **Paul Bentley** gives conflicting stories on the fingerprints, but told **George O'Toole** that "*we do know that his [Oswald's] fingerprints were taken off the passenger side of Tippit's car.*" Yet Sergeant **W.E. Barnes** (who dusted Tippit's car for prints) told the Warren Commission, "*There were several smear prints. None of value . . . No legible prints were found.*"

When Tippit's cruiser is found, a police shirt is also found on the rear seat, and <u>it does not belong to Tippit</u>.

(When LHO is eventually arrested at The Texas Theatre, he will be wearing a <u>rust brown</u> salt-and-pepper shirt. Tippit witnesses describe

Tippit's killer as wearing a <u>white</u> shirt underneath a tannish gray jacket, both of which are lighter in color than the rust brown shirt.)

NOTE: Only two of the 13 witnesses testifying to Tippit's murder will be able to reconstruct it: **Helen Markham** and **Domingo Benavides**. Markham will not describe any physical characteristics of the assassin when the police arrive at the scene. At the police station, Markham is shown a lineup which includes Oswald. At first she will not recognize any of them as the man who had killed the policeman. According to **Mark Lane**, the Dallas prosecutor makes <u>five</u> attempts. Since he needs a quick identification, he presses for a positive response on Oswald, contrary to the norms of the penal process. Markham, nervous, under pressure, and hesitant, will finally agree to the identification. Domingo Benavides, whose declaration will be taken by the Warren Commission lawyer, will <u>not</u> identify Oswald. **Helen Markham's will be the only testimony upon which the Warren Commission can accuse Oswald of the death of Tippit**. But days before testifying before the Commission, she will tell Mark Lane that the killer of the policeman was short and fat.

By now it is *at least* 1:07 PM.

Domingo Benavides, driving by the scene, watches as the gunman empties his revolver, reloads, and moves from the scene. Benavides waits "*a few minutes*" until the gunman is gone and then runs to Tippit's car. Unfamiliar with the police radio, Benavides fumbles with the microphone unsuccessfully. *(Benavides, who has perhaps the best view of Tippit's murder, can not identify Oswald as the killer and will not be called to testify before the Warren Commission.)*

A medical technician for Baylor Hospital, **Jack Tatum**, is driving a red 1964 Ford Galaxie down Tenth St. When the shooting occurs, he pulls over and looks through his rear view mirror. A man with a gun is firing into the head of a prone police officer by the side of a squad car. When the gunman starts moving in a direction that is toward Tatum's car, Tatum puts his car in gear and speeds away.

Aquilla Clemons, another eyewitness, sees *two* men at the scene. These men, she reports, converse with hand signals and then depart in different directions.

When news comes over the police radio that a police officer has been shot, Deputy **Roger Craig**, searching the sixth floor of the TSBD, looks at his watch and notes that the time is 1:06 PM.

Wes Wise, a reporter with KRLD-TV in Dallas *(and later mayor of Dallas)* says he receives information that a car near the scene of the Tippit shooting was traced to **Carl Mather**, a close friend of Tippit's.

Tippit has also worked part-time at Austin's Barbecue. The owner, **Austin Cook**, is a member of the John Birch Society.

NOTE: Despite a preponderance of evidence that the killer and Tippit's car were moving <u>toward</u> each other, the Warren Report will conclude that the killer was walking in the opposite direction. This will be necessary for the Warren Commission's tenuous version to work at all. If he is Oswald, the killer has to be walking *EAST*, in the same direction as the police car is moving when it overtakes the killer. Otherwise, Oswald, on his exceedingly tight time schedule, would have had to move from the rooming house to a point *BEYOND* the scene of the shooting and then to have turned and been heading *BACK* to reach the location of the murder.

Of the four bullets eventually extracted from Tippit's body, three are Winchester-Western brand, and one is Remington-Peters. Of the four shells found at the scene of the crime, two are Winchester, and two Remington.

The .38 revolver eventually taken from Oswald in the Texas Theater had been rechambered (slightly enlarged) to accept .38 Special cartridges. When discharged through a rechambered weapon, .38 Special cartridges "bulge" in the middle and are noticeably "fatter" than cartridges fired in an unchambered revolver. The empty cartridges, found in the National Archives, appear normal in size, indicating that they were fired in an original .38 revolver—not in a rechambered revolver such as the one taken from Lee Harvey Oswald at the Texas Theater.

Witness, **Helen Markham**, rushes over to the fatally wounded Tippit. She will testify that he tries to say something to her, but she can not understand his words. He quickly expires after this.

NOTE: In order for the Warren Commission to assert that Oswald killed Tippit, there has to be enough time for him to walk from his rooming house to 10th and Patton—over a mile away. The Warren Commission and HSCA will ignore Markham's time of 1:06 PM, will not interview Bowley (1:10 PM), will not ask Roger Craig (1:06 PM) and will not use the time shown on original Dallas police logs. Instead, the Warren Commission (1964) will conclude that Oswald walks that distance in 13 minutes. The House Select Committee on Assassinations (1979) will determine the time was 14 minutes, 30 seconds. Both will conclude that Oswald was last seen at the corner of Beckley and Zang at 1:03 PM. Either of their times, 13 minutes or 14 minutes and 30 seconds, would place Oswald at 10th and Patton at 1:16 PM or later. The time of the Tippit shooting as placed by the Commission, 1:16 PM, contradicts the testimony of Markham, Bowley, Craig and the Dallas Police log. Another problem for the Warren Commission to overcome is the direction in which Oswald is supposedly walking. If he was walking west, as all of the evidence suggests, he would have had to cover even more ground in the same unreasonably short period of time. The Dallas Police record that the defendant was walking "west in the 400 block of East 10th." The Commission will ignore the evidence—5 witnesses and the official Dallas Police report of the event—and will state that he was walking east, away from the Texas Theatre.

A few miles south of Dallas, on Interstate 45, Texas Highway patrolmen stop a black automobile for speeding. Witnesses to the incident observe at least three men in suits in the car. One of the three men identifies himself to the officer as a Secret Service agent and states, *"We're in a hurry to get to New Orleans to investigate part of the shooting."* **There is no record of Secret Service personnel being dispatched to New Orleans on the day of the assassination**.

Also during the day, Dallas police receive reports of a man seen with a rifle near Cobb Stadium, located on the Stemmons Freeway route from downtown to the Trade Mart. Nothing comes of this report.

1:10 PM   **Police Band (Channel 2):** Report that Secret Service are coming downtown. Request made for K9 squad to help search TSBD.

Barely an hour after the news from Dallas breaks, RFK is called by **Haynes Johnson** of the Washington *Evening Star*, who is on leave from the paper to write a book on the Bay of Pigs invasion. Johnson is in **Harry William**'s room at the Ebbitt Hotel in Washington, the CIA's lodging of choice for visiting operatives precisely because it is so nondescript. Williams, who has just arrived from his penultimate meeting with CIA officials on *"the problem of Cuba,"* is Johnson's prime source among the Bay of Pigs veterans. He is also RFK's best-and-brightest choice to lead a renewed effort to get rid of Castro. As Bobby well knows, the CIA agenda has included assassination. *"One of your guys did it,"* RFK tells Johnson in a flat, unemotional voice.

1:12 PM   **Police Band (Channel 2):** Rifle hulls found in TSBD on sixth floor. Obvious that "the man" had been there for some time. A drunk has been spotted wandering on the railroad tracks. Ordered to be taken to #9 at Elm and Houston. Someone questions whether we should hold all men presently on duty. The answer is "Yes."

A police inspector reports that empty shells have been found on the **fifth** floor, as well as evidence indicating that a man has been there for some time. A number of people come to the same inspector to tell him they saw a rifle or part of a rifle projecting from a window which the inspector thinks is the **fifth** floor.

Two lawmen on the **sixth** floor at the time—deputy sheriffs **Roger Craig** and **Luke Mooney**—tell researchers they see the **three** hulls lying side by side only inches apart under the window, all pointing in the same direction. This position would be impossible if the shells had been normally ejected from a rifle. A rifle is also found and initially identified as a '7.65' Mauser. It also seems incredible that the assassin in the Depository would go to the trouble of trying to hide the rifle behind boxes on the opposite side of the sixth floor from the southeast window and then leave incriminating shells lying on the floor—unless, of course, the hulls are deliberately left behind to incriminate Oswald. Officer **Gerald Hill** is in command of the search that finds the cartidge cases.

NOTE: The unfired cartridge represented as Item-6 of Exhibit CE-738 more closely resembles an L.B.C.936, 6.5x52mm MC Italian GI cartridge, then it does an American made WCC 6.5x52mm MC Cartridge. Virtually all American bullets are jacketed with Gilders Metal which is an alloy of copper and zinc, with a distinct brassy appearance. The color photos of the unfired cartridge show a bullet that is distinctly silver in color consistent with the copper-nickle alloy used by European bullet makers.

The MC cartridge possesses a shoulder width of .160" and a shoulder bevel of 25 degrees. This is an extremely critical point as measurement of the spent cases show a shoulder width of .186" and a shoulder bevel of 24 degrees, for a difference of .026" in shoulder width and 1 degree of angle in the bevel.

Conclusion: The spent cases more closely resemble a 6.5x54mm Mannlicher-Schoenauer (MS) Cartridge then they do a 6.5x52mm MC cartridge. The distinction made in the above conclusion, if it holds up, is an important one as the Austrian designed MS rifle is prized for its smooth action, magazine efficiency, chambering characteristics and accuracy as opposed to the dismal performance of the MC rifle. [*Editor's note:* Those attempting to implicate Oswald may have planted the wrong Mannlicher, the wrong shells, or both.]

Additional Bullets found:

1) **The Barbee Specimen:** This intact bullet was found embedded in the roof of a building located at 1615 Stemmons Freeway by **William Barbee** in the summer of 1966. The building, which was located about a 1/4 mile from the TSBD, happened to be in the line of fire from where Oswald allegedly shot. Mr. Barbee turned the bullet over to the FBI for analysis in December 1967, when current publicity about the assassination caused him to wonder if this bullet might be relevant evidence. The FBI lab determined the bullet to be a .30 caliber full metal jacketed military bullet. Its rifling pattern of 4 grooves, right hand twist was the same as that produced by the U.S. government .30 carbine. The FBI took little interest in this bullet once having determined that it came from a weapon other than Oswald's rifle. Apparently, the thought of a second gunmen was never entertained. Yet this bullet is consistent with that which could be shot from the CIA's silenced M-1 .30 caliber carbine. One can speculate that this bullet was shot out in the suburbs by a hunter engaged in target practice. Consider, however, that M-1 .30 caliber carbines were not prevalent amongst the civilian population as they had only been released by the government for civilian use in mid-1963. Furthermore, it was and continues to be illegal to use full metal jacketed military ammunition for hunting purposes.

2) **The Haythorne Specimen:** The second piece of evidence was a bullet found in 1967 on top of the Massey building by **Rich Haythorne**, a roofer doing work on the building. The Massey Building was located about 8 blocks away from the TSBD in the 1200 block of Elm Street. It has since been torn down. The bullet remained in the possession of Haythorne's attorney, until it was delivered to the HSCA for examination. The HSCA utilized the services of the Washington, D.C. police department, where it was determined that the bullet was a jacketed, soft-point .30 caliber bullet, weighing 149 grains which was consistent with the .30 caliber ammunition produced by Remington-Peters. Such ammunition was a popular hunting load and many gun manufacturers chambered their rifles to accommodate this ammunition. The 6 groove, right hand twist rifling marks on the bullet indicated that the bullet was not shot from Oswald's purported Mannlicher-Carcano.

3) **The Lester Specimen:** The third specimen was a bullet fragment found in Dealey Plaza by **Richard Lester** in 1974. Its precise location was reported to be 500 yards from the TSBD and 61 paces east of the triple overpass abutment. Mr. Lester turned the fragment over to the FBI for analysis in December 1976. The FBI reported its findings in July 1977, and concluded that the fragment, which consisted of the base portion of a bullet and weighed 52.7 grains, was consistent with the diameter of a 6.5 mm bullet. It was also determined that the fragment came from a metal jacketed soft point or hollow point sporting bullet. The rifling characteristics did not match those of a Mannlicher-Carcano. Even though the bullet exhibited the same 4 grooves, right hand twist pattern as Oswald's purported Mannlicher-Carcano, the lands between the grooves were spaced further apart than his Carcano. Once again, no one ventured to suggest that the fragment might represent the work of a second gunman.

4) **The Dal-Tex Specimen:** The fourth piece of firearm evidence consists of a rusted shell casing found on the rooftop of the Dal-Tex Building in 1977 by an air-conditioning repair man. The Dal-Tex Building is just east of the TSBD, across Houston Street. Assassination researchers have long speculated that a second gunman was positioned at that building. Judging by the rusted condition of the shell case, it had been there for quite some time. What was unique about this case was the crimped edges along the neck suggesting that either the shell had been handloaded or had been used in conjunction with a sabot, by means of which a smaller caliber slug can be fired from a higher caliber weapon. Specimens 1), 2) and 3) could conceivably have been shot from locations other than Dealey Plaza by some careless hunter. However, this shell casing meant that the rifle was shot where the shell was expended and it is unlikely that deer hunters ever had occasion to position themselves on a rooftop in downtown Dallas.

Also, at least three Warren Commission photographs of the sixth floor *"sniper's nest"*—Commission Exhibits 509, 724, and 733—Show **three different versions** of the boxes stacked near the sixth-floor window.

T. F. Bowley, driving west on Tenth street sees a group of by-standers gathered around a fallen policeman. As Bowley gets out of his car to lend assistance, he looks at his watch and notes the time to be 1:10 PM.

1:13 PM   In Parkland Hospital, **Agent Emory Roberts** tells LBJ that JFK is dead. Johnson immediately looks at his watch and then turns to his wife and tells her to *"make a note of the time."*

1:15 PM   *Warren Commission states:* Officer **J. D. Tippit** is driving slowly in an easterly direction on East 10th St. in Oak Cliff.

1:16 PM   In the Oak Cliff area of Dallas, **T. F. Bowley** runs up to police car #10, grabs the microphone from **Benavides** and radios the dispatcher that an officer *(Tippit)* has been shot. *"We've had a shooting here . . . it's a police officer, somebody shot him!"* This is the first report of the murder of Officer J.D. Tippit. *(**The bullets in Tippit's body are never linked ballistically to Oswald's revolver. Because of alterations that had been done on the gun, a routine ballistics matching proves impossible. No fingerprints are found on the gun.**)*

NOTE: It seems virtually impossible for Oswald to have <u>walked</u> nearly a mile in **twelve** minutes, murdered Tippit, and lingered long enough to reload his pistol before leaving the murder scene. Still, this becomes the official version as presented by the Warren Commission.

1:20 PM   **Police Band (Channel 2):** Need extra officers at Parkland Hospital As the killer leaves the Tippit murder scene, he discards his light jacket on the street a few blocks away. A patrolman later examines the jacket and radios his colleagues: *"The jacket the suspect was wearing . . . bears a laundry tag with the letter **B 9738**. See if there is any way you can check this laundry tag."*

NOTE: Eventually, *every* laundry and dry-cleaning establishment in the Dallas-Fort Worth area is checked—424 of them in all—with no success. Knowing that Oswald has lived in New Orleans, the FBI checks 293 establishments in that area with similarly negative results. Further, the FBI's eventual examination of all of Oswald's clothing shows not a single laundry or dry-cleaning mark. The FBI will also learn that while the jacket is size *medium*, all of Oswald's other clothing is size *small*.

OF HISTORICAL NOTE:

According to Anthony Summers, *Conspiracy*: "For Officer Tippit, it now appears, 22 November 1963 began as a day of marital drama, a sad suburban soap opera that became by chance a sideshow of national tragedy. A Dallas citizen, **Larry Harris**—along with a friend in law enforcement, **Ken Holmes Jr.**—has spent much time investigating the background of the dead policeman. He discovered that Tippit, a married man with three children, had been having a long affair with a blonde waitress at *Austin's Barbecue Drive-In*, where he moonlighted as a security man on weekends. The waitress, too, was married. Harris and Holmes traced Tippit's former mistress, who admitted that she and the policeman were lovers for some two years. According to the mistress' husband, whom she divorced in August 1963, Tippit's murder led directly to their reconciliation. He and his former wife went together, he says, to view the policeman's body at the funeral home, before the widow and her family arrived. The experience greatly upset the mistress, and she confessed that **she was pregnant by Tippit**. A child was indeed born seven months later. Tippit's mistress, though, claims it was her former husband's child, and that it was reared accordingly. After JFK's assassination—and Officer Tippit's murder—the couple stayed together for several years, then parted finally in 1968. According to one source, Tippit's wife visited a neighbor on the morning of 22 November in tears, because "on that morning Officer Tippit has told her he wanted a divorce to marry some else. . . . By the mistress' account, her husband—though a drinker and womanizer himself—had been greatly upset by her affair with Tippit. Several times he had followed her and Tippit late at night, trailing them in his car."

An ambulance is dispatched from Dudley Hughes Funeral Home (*allegedly at 1:18 PM*) and arrives at the Tippet murder scene within a minute. Tippit's body is quickly loaded into the ambulance by **Clayton Butler**, **Eddie Kinsley** (*both Dudley Hughes employees*) and **Mr. Bowley**. Tippit's body is en route to the Parkland Hospital by the time the Police arrive. Dallas Police Officer **Westbrook** finds a brown wallet next to where Tippit had fallen. He shows the wallet to FBI **Agent Barrett**. The wallet contains identification, including a driver's license, for **Lee Harvey Oswald**. *It seems unbelievable that anyone would leave a wallet, containing identification, next to a policeman he has just shot. But Barrett insists Oswald's wallet was found at the Tippit murder scene. Supposedly, LHO does not drive— and yet a driver's license is also reportedly found in this wallet.*

NOTE: A Texas driver's license belonging to Lee Oswald will turn up at the Department of Public Safety the following week. **Aletha Frair**, and 6 employees of the DPS will see and handle Oswald's driver's license. It is dirty and worn as though it has been carried in a billfold. **Mrs. Lee Bozarth** (*employee of DPS*) states that she knows from direct personal experience there was a Texas driver's license file for Lee Harvey Oswald. The DPS file is pulled shortly after the assassination.

The *second* police car to arrive at the scene where Tippit was murdered is driven by **Officer Gerald Hill**. Riding with Hill is

William Alexander. *(Officer Hill testifies that he is given custody of the .38 revolver supposedly found on Oswald when he is arrested a few moments later.)*

NOTE: In 1978, author and researcher **Anthony Summers** retraces the route LHO took to the scene of the Tippit murder with **William Alexander**, who in 1963 was assistant district attorney in Dallas. Alexander says: *"One of the questions that I would like to have answered is why Oswald was where he was when he shot Tippit . . . Along with the police, we measured the route, all the conceivable routes he could have taken to that place. We interrogated bus drivers, we checked the cab-company records, but we still do not know how he got to where he was, or why he was where he was. I feel like if we could ever find out why he was there, then maybe some of the other mysteries would be solved. Was he supposed to meet someone? Was he trying to make a getaway? Did he miss a connection? Was there a connection? If you look at Oswald's behavior, he made very few nonpurposeful motions, very seldom did he do anything that did not serve a purpose to him. People who've studied his behavior feel there was a purpose in his being where he was. I, for one, would like to know what that was."*

1:20 PM   Presidential aide **Kenneth O'Donnell** informs LBJ that JFK is dead. O'Donnell advises LBJ to return to Washington ASAP.

1:21 PM   **Police Band (Channel 2):** Get me 20 more uniformed officers to Parkland entrance immediately. This is a precautionary move.

1:22 PM   The alleged murder rifle is discovered in the TSBD. *(This is less than one hour after the shooting.)* The rifle found is initially described as a **7.65 mm German Mauser**. It is so described by Deputy Sheriff **E. L. Boone**, discoverer of the rifle, in his report of this day. Boone's report is supported by that of Deputy Constable **Seymour Weitzman**. Both lawmen reportedly have more than an average knowledge of weapons. This account is further confirmed by **Deputy Craig**, who will tell Texas researchers that he actually sees the word Mauser stamped on the weapon's receiver. *(When asked about the make of rifle shortly after midnight this day, Dallas District Attorney **Henry Wade** replies: "It's a Mauser, I believe.")* The Warren Commission will eventually indicate that *Weitzman is simply mistaken* in his identification of the rifle and that the others, including Wade, probably repeated this mistaken identification. However, Wade never gives any indication as to the source of his idea that the rifle is a Mauser. Boone tells the Commission he thinks it was **Captain Fritz** who termed it a Mauser. Even the CIA has doubts as to the true identity of the assassination rifle. Five days after the assassination, in an internal report transmitted from Italy to Langley headquarters, CIA officials note that two different kinds of Italian-made carbines are being identified as the single murder weapon. The CIA document states: *"The weapon which appears to have been employed in this criminal attack is a Model 91 rifle, 7.35* *caliber, 1938 modification . . . The description of a 'Mannlicher-Carcano' rifle in the Italian and foreign press **is in error**."* **No special precautions are taken to isolate the weapon as historic evidence**. In tests of the rifle, <u>metal shims have to be placed under the telescopic sight before the Army laboratory can test the accuracy of it</u>. This evidence is known to both the FBI and the Warren Commission, but is never adequately relayed to the public.

No prints are initially found on the rifle. LHO's palm print will eventually be discovered on the Mannlicher-Carcano. DPD Crime Scene Search division lieutenant **Carl Day** will note, in an October 1993 interview, *"The prints on the rifle weren't made the day of the assassination—or the day before that, or the day before that. The prints were at least weeks, if not months, old."* <u>It remains to be explained how the gun was fired on this day without fresh prints, but with the old prints left intact.</u>

The original inventory of articles found in what becomes known as "the sniper's nest," where **Lee Harvey Oswald** allegedly fired at JFK, does **not** list an ammunition clip despite an otherwise meticulous detailing of every item recovered along with the rifle. According to assassination researcher **Sylvia Meagher**, the first reference to a clip surfaces in the Warren Report, published in September 1964. Prior to this, <u>no mention of an ammunition clip appears anywhere</u>. Some researchers, seeking to explain the apparent absence of a clip, have advanced the theory that Oswald reloaded the rifle manually and that someone later added the clip to the inventory. Most experts agree that without using a clip Oswald could not possibly have fired more than one round before the President's car sped from the scene, indicating that the additional shots had to have come from a second source. The gun found in the TSBD building has a difficult bolt, eccentric trigger, maladjusted scope, and disintegrating firing pin. Despite this impressive list of disabilities, the WC will conclude that it is the rifle that, in three shots, felled JFK and the Governor.

NOTE: Ten days will pass before Lee Harvey Oswald's clipboard is discovered on the sixth floor. His jacket is not found until **late November**. This seems to demonstrate that there is no real systematic search of the building once the Mannlicher-Carcano rifle is discovered there—OR evidence is planted <u>after the fact</u> to shore up the attempt to place Oswald on the sixth floor at the time of the shooting.

The Warren Report will also eventually state that *"when the rifle was found in the Texas School book Depository Building <u>it contained a clip</u>."* The assertion that the rifle contained a clip is absolutely unsupported by direct evidence or testimony. No witness who gave testimony about the search of the TSBD or the discovery of the rifle mentions an ammunition clip, either in the rifle or elsewhere on the sixth floor—*assuming this was the floor the rifle was actually* *found on*. FBI expert Latona will later specifically refer to the clip by stating that no prints were found on the ammunition clip. The WC will state that *"there is no evidence that Oswald wore gloves or that he wiped prints off the rifle."* The clip should have been ejected from the rifle, falling on the floor somewhere near the southeast corner window. If it was not ejected, it may have been defective or deformed in such a way that it remained stuck in the weapon—and that in itself should have been the subject of comment by Frazier or other witnesses. No such comment was made. The fact is that the rifle had not been fully loaded at the time of the assassination but had held only four cartridges instead of seven. If an ammunition clip was used in firing the rifle found in the Book Depository, it must have been empty, since the single, live round was ejected from the chamber and no other unexpended ammunition was found in the Book Depository. The clip should therefore have been ejected, falling on the floor somewhere near the southeast corner window. Such an assassin would have had to be certain that he would hit his victim or victims without missing, and that his escape was guaranteed, so that there would be no need to shoot his way out of the Book Depository. The Warren Commission scenario, based upon available evidence, indicates that the rifle had not been fully loaded at the time of the assassination but held only four cartridges instead of seven. Thus, it conjures up a picture of a rather implausible assassin, who set out to kill the President *armed with only four bullets*, his last and only ones

Further adding to the mystery of the rifle, ATF agent **Frank Ellsworth**, who participates in a second search of the book depository conducted after 1:30 PM on this date, according to a Secret Service document, confirms that the Mannlicher-Carcano was found by a DPD detective on the fourth or fifth floor of the building, "not on the same floor as the cartridges [the sixth floor]." He adds: *"I remember we talked about it, and figured that he [LHO] must have run out from the stairwell [to the lower floor] and dropped it [the Mannlicher] as he was running downstairs."*

DPD dispatch describing suspect: "Last seen about the 300 block East Jefferson. He's a white male about 30, 5'8." Black hair, slender, wearing a white jacket, white shirt and dark slacks."

1:23 PM   CBS's **Walter Cronkite** reports, *"A Secret Service man was also killed in the fusillade of shots."* **Seth Kantor**, a reporter for Scripps-Howard, will write in his notebook, which is published by the Warren Commission, *"They even have to die in secret."*

(*Sardinia, Italy*) When he hears the news of JFK's death, **William Harvey**, the CIA's former Mongoose coordinator says: *"This was bound to happen, and it's probably good that it did."* When Harvey eventually discovers that his deputy is spending time helping local officials with condolences, he sends the deputy packing for the U.S. saying: *"I haven't got time for this kind of crap."*

1:25 PM   Justice of the Peace **Theron Ward** is escorted to the door of Trauma Room #1 at Parkland Hospital by Secret Service Agent **Roy Kellerman**. Viewing the President's body from the doorway, he never enters the room. Kellerman requests Ward to release the body into Secret Service custody. The judge replies, "*I will have to consult with Dallas District Attorney Henry Wade.*" Advice from **Henry Wade** and Chief **Jesse Curry** is not to release the body until the "*missile*" *(bullet)* is taken into evidence. CE-399 isn't discovered until 1:45 PM. The obvious question is how Wade even knows that a bullet <u>will be</u> discovered. *(Texas law is breached and a critical link in the investigative process is violated. The President's body is taken illegally by force from the proper Texas state authorities by Secret Service agents. Technically, the Federal Government does not have any jurisdiction in the case, and does not have the authority to take the body or to perform an autopsy.)*

1:26 PM   With heavy guard, **Police Chief Curry** drives **Lyndon Johnson** to Love Field, where he boards *Air Force One*. On the way to Love Field, Johnson crouches down in the backseat of the station wagon. Secret Service agents sit in the front seat. Also traveling with LBJ are: Congressman **Homer Thornberry** and Congressman **Albert Thomas**. **Mrs. Johnson**, sitting upright, is driven in a second car. **Youngblood** radios ahead to LBJ's valet, **Paul Glynn**, and tells him to transfer all of LBJ's luggage to *Air Force One*.

Kenneth O'Donnell, JFK's special assistant, writes: "*I distinctly remember that when Johnson and I talked at the hospital there was no mention of which of the two planes he should use. Nor was there any mention that he was considering waiting for Jackie and the President's casket to be on the same plane with him before he left Dallas. Later a lawyer for the Warren Commission, **Arlen Specter**, pointed out to me that according to Johnson's testimony, I had told him to board Air Force One.*" "*Specter asked me, to my amazement, if I would change my testimony so that it would agree with the President's. 'Was I under oath?' I asked Specter, as, of course, I was. 'Certainly I wouldn't change anything I said under oath.*"

1:30 PM   Veteran newsman **Seth Kantor** encounters **Jack Ruby** at Parkland Hospital. They share a brief conversation. **Mrs. Wilma Tice** also testifies that she sees Ruby at Parkland.

<u>A second search of the TSBD begins sometime after 1:30 PM.</u> Law enforcement agents will warn everyone who works in the building not to discuss the case, even with members of their own families.

Press Secretary **Malcolm Kilduff** announces JFK's death to the press. It immediately goes out on the news wires.

Marina Oswald is in the backyard at 2515 West Fifth Street, Irving, Texas, hanging clothes on a clothesline. **Ruth Paine** comes out and says: "*Kennedy is dead.*" There is no response from Marina. Mrs. Paine also informs Marina that the news reports say that the shots came from the School Book Depository on Elm Street—where LHO works.

1:33 PM   **Lyndon Johnson**, under heavy guard, hurriedly boards *Air Force One* and tells Colonel **James B. Swindal** that the aircraft will not leave for Washington without JFK's body. All window shades aboard Air Force One are drawn and a television is turned on in order for them to get the news reports. LBJ will soon change his shirt and comb his hair. For a time, he actually hides in the restroom of the President's private bedroom aboard the plane. When **Kenny O'Donnell** asks LBJ about the plane's departure, LBJ says: "I talked to **Bobby** [Kennedy]. They think I should be sworn in right here. Judge Hughes is on her way—should be here any minute."

After allegedly shooting Officer Tippit, the assassin goes south on Patton Street and turns west on Jefferson. Two used car lot workers named **Warren Reynolds** and **B.M.** **Patterson** see him and start to chase him. The gunman realizes that he is being followed and dashes behind a Texaco gas station, hiding among the cars of a parking lot. The parking lot behind the gas station is quickly becoming an inescapable trap, as police come swarming into the area. The capture of the gunman quickly becomes a foregone conclusion.

A Dallas police radio dispatch reports, "*He* [the suspect] *is in the library, Jefferson, East 500 block, Marsalis and Jefferson.*" Minutes later, a follow-up dispatch says, "*We are all at the library.*"

This radio dispatch immediately pulls the police out of the parking lot behind the gas station where the supposed assassin of Tippit is hiding. The police, some researchers speculate, are pulled out and sent to the library on a "wild goose chase" in order to allow the gunman to escape capture. LHO is actually making his appearance in front of The Texas Theater around this time.

Again, minutes later, the police at the library broadcast: "*It was the wrong man.*"

The Marsalis city bus LHO *supposedly* boarded and briefly rode passes this library at about this same time. It was due at 12:50—but has been slowed down by the traffic on Elm St.

NOTE: Who is this suspect, described as "*the wrong man*"? At this early stage, the only way they could have known it is the wrong man would be for them to know the *right* man. The library, located at the intersection of East Jefferson Street and Marsalis Avenue, is six blocks from Oswald's rooming house and within only one block of Ruby's apartment. Oswald is known to have frequented this library at least three to four times in a week.

By this time, **Alan Belmont** at FBI headquarters has prepared a Teletype to all offices to:

"immediately contact all informants and sources to immediately establish the whereabouts of bombing suspects, Klan and other racial group members, racial extremists, and any other individuals who on the basis of information in the files might have been involved."

Later today, Secret Service Chief **James Rowley** will tell RFK that his agency believes JFK has been the victim of a powerful organization. The book *Farewell America* asserts that "Ten hours after the assassination Rowley knew that there had been three gunmen, and perhaps four, at Dallas that day, and later on the telephone **Jerry Behn** [head of the White House detail] remarks to **Forrest Sorrels** [head of the Dallas Secret Service], *"It's a plot."* *"Of course,"* is Sorrel's reply.

1:35 PM   A man is noticed slipping into **The Texas Theater** at 231 W. Jefferson. Concession stand operator, **Butch Burroughs** says that it could not have been Oswald because Oswald entered the theater shortly after 1 PM. If this testimony is correct, Oswald could **not** have shot officer J.D. Tippit. **Julia Postal**, the theater cashier, has been alerted to the fact that LHO slipped into the theatre without paying. She calls the police and tells them she thinks *"we have your man."* The voice on the other end of the phone says: *"Why do you think it's our man?"* She gives them a description of the suspect. *"Every time the sirens go by,"* she continues, *"he ducks."* Postal has been informed of LHO's presence in the theatre by **Johnny Calvin Brewer**, the manager of nearby Hardy's Shoe Shop. He is twenty-three years old and noticed LHO seemingly attempting to duck out of sight of police cars as they passed by on the street.

Johnny C. Brewer claims that on the day of the assassination, he sees a man standing in the lobby of his shoe store at about 1:30 PM. He watches the man walk west on Jefferson and thinks (Brewer says he is not positive) that he ducks into the Texas Theater. It is not until 6 December, two weeks after Lee Harvey Oswald's arrest, that Brewer describes the man he saw as wearing a brown shirt. He asks theater cashier **Julia Postal** if she has sold the man a ticket. Postal replies *"she did not think so, but she had been listening to the radio and did not remember."* She does remember, when testifying before the Warren Commission, that she sold 24 tickets that day.

The police, meanwhile, having received a tip indirectly from an out-of-town caller, broadcast the description of a car that has allegedly been used in the assassination. It was seen parked on Commerce St. The car and driver are picked up in Fort Worth, eight miles away. The man is taken to jail and kept there until FBI agents arrive. The suspect explains that he has driven 100 miles from his home in Ranger, Texas to Dallas hoping to visit an old friend. When he is unsuccessful, he decided that since he was downtown and traffic was heavy, he would stay there and see the Presidential parade. **The suspect is released as soon as Oswald's arrest is announced**.

The TSBD is mentioned on **Police Channel 2**: "*It's being secured now.*" This is an hour and five minutes after the shots, twenty-one minutes after the death of Officer Tippit, sixteen minutes before the arrest of LHO, and long after the departure of any or all who had anything to do with the shots fired from the TSBD.

1:36 PM   A policeman at the scene of the Tippit shooting radioes a description: "*I got an eyeball witness to the getaway man—that suspect in this shooting. He is a white male . . . apparently armed with a .32, dark finish, automatic pistol.*" A few minutes from now, Sergeant **Gerald Hill** will send a similar message: "*The shells at the scene indicate that the suspect is armed with an automatic .38 rather than a pistol.*" (Hill has years of army experience and police work behind him, a background which affords him a certain expertise.)

The autopsy report on Tippit is not found in the 26 volumes of Hearings and Exhibits of the WC Report.

1:40 PM   Undertaker **Vernon O'Neal** arrives at Parkland Hospital in a hearse with *a four-hundred-pound Elgin Brittania casket*. When Kennedy's body is placed in the casket, it is *wrapped in sheets* .

In Tampa, Florida, this afternoon **Frank Ragano** is about to leave his office to give a lecture at a legal seminar at the Tampa County Courthouse when a lawyer bursts in and tells him about the assassination of JFK. A few minutes later, **Jimmy Hoffa** calls Ragano. "*Have you heard the good news?*" Hoffa begins. "*They killed the sonofabitch. This means Bobby is out as attorney general. Lyndon will get rid of him.*" When a reporter later asks Jimmy Hoffa about RFK, his reply is: "*Bobby Kennedy is just another lawyer now.*" Hoffa also chides his secretary for crying over JFK's death.

1:43 PM   A memo from **J. Edgar Hoover**: "*. . . got first news flash from Dallas that Kennedy and Connally had been shot; called the Attorney General (RFK) to advise him of this; was told by RFK to do whatever we could and told RFK I would get in touch with Secret Service.*"

In the Texas Theater, LHO has bought popcorn, walks to the main floor and reportedly takes a seat next to a pregnant woman. Minutes before police arrive, this woman disappears into the balcony and is never seen again. She is not one of the seven patrons counted by **Officer Hutson**. *Captain Westbrook and FBI Agent Barrett come into the theater from the rear entrance minutes later. Westbrook may be looking for "Lee Harvey Oswald"—identified from the contents of the wallet he found at the scene of Tippit's murder.*

The Texas Theater has a main floor level and a balcony. Upon entering the theater from the "outside doors," there are stairs leading to the balcony on the right. Straight ahead are a second set of "inside doors" leading to the concession stand and the main floor. It is possible to go directly to the balcony, without being seen by people at the concession stand, by climbing the stairs to the right. **Johnny Brewer** walks through the first and second set of double doors to the concession stand. He asks **Butch Burroughs**, who operates the concession stand, if he has seen the man come in. Burroughs says that he has been busy and has not noticed. Brewer checks the darkened balcony but does not see the man he has followed. Brewer and Burroughs then check and made sure the exits have not been opened. Brewer then goes back to the box office and tells **Julia Postal** he thinks the man is still in the theater and to call the police. Julia then calls the police.

1:45 PM   A report comes into Dallas Police headquarters alerting them to the fact that a man fitting the suspect's description has entered The Texas Theater without paying. Cars are immediately dispatched. Police broadcasts at 1:45 PM report, *"Have information a suspect just went into the Texas Theater. . .. Supposed to be hiding in the balcony."* When the police arrive, they are told by a "young female," probably **Julia Postal**, that the man is in the balcony. The police who enter the front of the theater go to the balcony. They are questioning a young man when Officers **Walker**, **McDonald** and **Hutson** enter the rear of the theater. Hutson counts seven theater patrons on the main level. From the record, these seven break down as follows:

- 2 boys (half way down center section searched by Walker and McDonald while Hutson look on)
- 1 Oswald (3rd row from back center section)
- 1 Jack Davis (right rear section-Oswald first sat next to him)
- 1 Unknown person (across the aisle from Davis—Oswald left his seat next to Davis and moved to a seat next to this person; Oswald then got up and walked into the theater lobby)
- 1 George Applin (6 rows from back-center section)
- 1 John Gibson (1st seat from the back on the far right side)

KRLD-TV, a CBS affiliate, reports that a Secret Service agent has been killed along with JFK.

Jack Ruby arrives at his *Carousel Club* and instructs **Andrew Armstrong**, the bartender, to notify employees that the club will be closed that night. During the next hour, Ruby speaks by telephone to several persons who are or have been especially close to him, and the remainder of the time he watches television and speaks with Armstrong and **Larry Crafard** about the assassination.

A bullet—eventually to be known as **CE-399**—is discovered on a Parkland hospital stretcher by **Darrell Tomlinson**. It is reported to be in almost pristine condition.

NOTE: Tapes of the telephone conversations of President LBJ show that he was told by FBI Director **J. Edgar Hoover** within a week of the assassination that the bullet tagged as CE-399 was found on the *President's* stretcher, and was dislodged as emergency procedures were performed. If CE-399 came from the President's stretcher, it could not have been the magic bullet, which could only have fallen out of **Governor Connally**.

The whole argument about the number of grains missing from the bullet in terms of its pristine weight is inconclusive so long as the pristine weight is unknown, and there is considerable evidence to suggest that the fragments exceeded the maximum decrease in the original weight of the stretcher bullet.

No attempt is made to determine what happened to the President's stretcher once it was placed in trauma room No. 2. It is impossible to account for one of the two stretchers involved in the discovery of the bullet.

In June 1964 the WC will request the FBI to establish the chain of possession of the stretcher bullet, but the engineer, the chief of personnel at the hospital, the Secret Service agent, and Chief Rowley will be unable to make a positive identification of the stretcher bullet (CE-399) as the bullet found on the day of the assassination.

Night has descended on Munich, Germany when, at 7:44 PM, a news flash arrives. *Radio Free Europe* beams the news of the assassination to Poland, Czechoslovakia, Hungary, Rumania, and Bulgaria in several languages.

1:46 PM   Inspector **J. Herbert Sawyer** calls the dispatcher saying: *We have a man that we would like to have you pass this on to CID* [Criminal Investigation Division] *to see if we can pick this man up. Charles Douglas Givens. . . . He is a colored male . . . a porter that worked on this floor up here. He has a police record and he left.*

1:51 PM   In the Texas Theatre, **Johnny Brewer** has finished checking all the exits except the door behind the stage. He opens it and finds himself facing four policemen with guns drawn. **Nick McDonald** is one of the police officers. Brewer identifies himself and he and the policemen then reenter the theatre. McDonald approaches LHO and orders him to his feet. (*There are sixteen policemen now in the theatre.*) LHO rises, draws his pistol. A scuffle breaks out between LHO and McDonald. LHO is subdued. Officers in Oak Cliff radio headquarters that they have seized the man who had entered the Texas Theater and they believe him to be the killer of the police officer (*J.D. Tippit*). LHO is taken from the theater to police headquarters under heavy guard. When he is taken inside the headquarters, a human shield of policemen move ahead of him. He is taken to the third-floor office of **Captain Will Fritz** and placed in a seat in the hallway. *It is perhaps worth noting that Oswald is described as nervous and fearful by those who supposedly see him <u>prior</u> to his arrest. Once he is placed in the* *police car at the Texas Theater his entire demeanor seems to change. He becomes calm—even smug.*

NOTE: From police broadcasts, the police are supposedly looking for a suspect wearing a white shirt, white jacket, with dark brown or black hair, and hiding in the balcony. But their attention quickly focuses on a man wearing a brown shirt with medium brown hair, on the main floor. When this man is approached by **Officer McDonald**, he allegedly hits McDonald and then tries to fire his .38 revolver. Several police officers and theater patrons hear the "snap" of a pistol trying to fire. A cartridge is later removed from the .38 and found to have an indentation on the primer. An FBI report describes the firing pin as "bent." The man in the brown shirt, **Lee Harvey Oswald**, is subdued by Officers Hawkins, Hutson, Walker, Carroll and Hill, and then handcuffed. Captain Westbrook orders the officers to *"get him out of here as fast as you can and don't let anybody see him."* As he is taken out the front, **Johnny Brewer** hears an officer remark *"Kill the President, will you!"* [*Editor's note:* See the original arrest report on Oswald in my chapter on Jesse Curry's *JFK Assassination File* elsewhere in this volume.]

Bernard J. Haire, owner of *Bernie's Hobby House*, located two doors east of the Texas Theater, walks through his store and out into the back alley when he sees police cars arrive. Haire is unaware of the assassination news. In the **back** alley, he sees police bring out a young white man dressed in a pullover shirt and slacks. The man appears flushed as if having been in a struggle. Although Haire is unable to see if the man is handcuffed, he is certainly under the impression that the man is under arrest. Haire watches as police put the man in a police car and drive off. Haire is under the impression that he has witnessed the arrest of Lee Harvey Oswald. Twenty-five years later, Haire is shocked to discover that Oswald was **handcuffed** and brought out of the **front** door of the theater.

George Applin is a patron in the Texas Theater when LHO is arrested there for the murder of Police Officer **J. D. Tippit**. Applin will tell the Warren Commission that during Oswald's arrest, he observed a man sitting in the rear of the theater who not only appeared uninterested in the film but also quietly watched over the arrest while other patrons were ducking for cover. In 1979, Applin admits to the *Dallas Morning News* that he later recognized **Jack Ruby** as the man he had seen in the movie house. He said he was afraid to tell the police or the Commission what he knew in 1964 because he had read an article about the deaths of people who were witnesses to the assassination or connected in some way to the incident.

NOTE: There are no reports that anyone has checked Oswald's identification at this time. Yet as they take LHO out the front of the theater, a DPD officer tells **Julia Postal** *"we have our man on both* *counts.*" She says this is the first time she hears of Tippit's death and the officers arresting LHO identify him to her by calling his name—"Oswald." It is surmised that some of the Dallas police officers at the Texas Theatre have arrived from the Tippit murder scene. WFAA news film shows Dallas police officers looking through LHO's wallet which was reportedly found at the scene.

FBI Agent **Bardwell Odum**, who observes Oswald as he is being brought out the front of the Texas Theater, says Oswald is wearing a "brown jacket." Other witnesses mistakenly identify Oswald as wearing a "brown jacket" at the time of his arrest. Oswald is actually wearing a "brown shirt" (*not a brown jacket*) over a "white t-shirt."

During his first interview today, Oswald tells Captain Fritz that he had arrived at N. Beckley and changed his trousers. The following day he tells Fritz he had changed both his trousers and shirt. Oswald described his dirty clothes as being a reddish colored, long sleeved shirt with a button down collar and gray colored trousers. He indicated that he placed these clothes in the lower drawer of his dresser. One "brown shirt with button down collar" and "one pair of gray trousers" were found at Oswald's N. Beckley address by Dallas Detective Fay M. Turner. Both articles of clothing were inventoried by Dallas Police and listed as "1 brown shirt with button-down collar and 1 pair gray trousers and other miscellaneous men's clothing"

The gray pants, remembered by **Bledsoe** and **Jones** from the bus and by cab driver **William Whaley**, were also found at N. Beckley— exactly where Oswald had told Fritz he had placed them. They were inventoried by Dallas Police Detective **Fay M. Turner**. The gray jacket worn by Oswald the morning of 22 November as remembered by **Linnie Mae Randle** and **Wesley Frazier**, may have been found by the Dallas Police at the TSBD. They found a heavy, blue colored, "Sir Jac" brand jacket at the TSBD. This jacket is never claimed by anyone.

NOTE: Marina Oswald will testify that her husband owned only two jackets, one blue and the other gray. The blue jacket was found in the TSBD and was identified by Marina as her husband's. Marina also identified Commission Exhibit No. 162, the jacket found by Captain **Westbrook**, as her husband's second jacket. **Sylvia Meagher** maintains, in *Accessories After The Fact*, that the jacket was NOT found by Westbrook. According to the list of items of evidence turned over to the FBI by the Dallas police on 28 November 1963, the gray zipper jacket which bears a laundry tag with the number "**B 9738**." When Captain **Will Fritz** interrogates LHO about his visit to his rented room at one o'clock, LHO will state that he had "changed both his shirt and trousers before going to the show. Fritz. with the gray zipper jacket (or a white jacket) already presumably in his possession, will not even ask LHO if he had put on any garment over his shirt. In short, both at the line-ups and the interrogations, the police will act as though there is NO jacket, gray or white. The police never confront LHO with the jacket or give him the opportunity to confirm or deny that it is his property. *"Oswald complained of a line-up wherein he had not been granted a request to put on a jacket"* like the other men in the line-up. If the police really had in their hands a gray zipper jacket which they believed belonged to LHO and which they thought he had worn at the Tippit scene, why didn't they let him wear that jacket in the sight of witnesses for whose benefit LHO will soon be displayed in line-ups?

COMMISSION EXHIBIT 162 IS A LIGHT-WEIGHT GRAY ZIPPER JACKET.

Domingo Benavides says LHO was wearing a light beige zipper-type jacket. **Helen Markham** says it was "a short jacket, open in the front, kind of grayish tan." (*When LHO's jacket was shown to her she said that she had never seen it before..* **William Scoggins** does not give an independent description of the killer's jacket. (*When LHO's jacket is shown to him, he fails to identify it.*) **Barbara Jeanette Davis** says the suspect wore "a dark coat." **William Arthur Smith** thinks that the killer wore "a sport coat of some kind." **Virginia Davis** testifies that the killer "had on a light-brown-tan jacket." **Ted Callaway** describes it as "a light tannish gray windbreaker jacket. (When shown LHO's jacket, he says that it is the same type jacket but "**actually, I thought it had a little more tan to it.**") **Earlene Roberts** fails to identify the jacket. **Wesley Frazier** is unable to recognize the gray zipper jacket. **Sam Guinyard** is the only witness who describes the gray zipper jacket accurately and then identifies it without qualification. The other seven witnesses either do not describe the gray zipper jacket accurately, or fail to identify it as the one worn by the suspect, or identified the wrong jacket. The WC does not call attention to the fact that the same group of witnesses fail to identify the brown long-sleeved shirt which LHO supposedly was wearing under his jacket—not because they could not see the shirt but because they did not recognize it.

As LHO is being driven to the police station, the detectives who are with him in the car note his behavior. **C.T. Walker** says, "*He was real calm. He was extra calm. He wasn't a bit excited or nervous or anything.*" Sgt. **Gerald Hill** says, "*He gave the appearance of arrogance, but he did not talk boastfully. In fact, he talked very little. This was one of the things that stuck out most about him in my mind, was how quiet he did keep.*" LHO does, however, protest his arrest. He says, "*I don't know why you are treating me like this. The only thing I have done was carry a pistol in a movie.*" "*Yes, sir, you have done a lot more. You have killed a policeman.*" With absolutely no emotion, he replies, "*Well, you can only fry for that.*" "*Maybe you will get a chance to find out.* "*Well, I understand it only takes a minute.*" Someone asks, "*Why did you kill the officer?*" LHO does not answer. He is asked other questions, but he refuses to respond to any of them. He just sits in silence for the rest of the way to the police station.

Officer **Gerald Hill** testifies that he has custody of the .38 revolver found on Oswald. He says that **Bob Carroll**, driver of the car, gets in and hands the gun to him. He breaks it open and purportedly finds six shells in the chambers of the gun: 3 Western .38 Specials and 3 Remington-Peters .38 Specials. Five live cartridges are found in LHO's pocket, 3 Western .38s and 2 Remington-Peters .38s. Four bullets are recovered from Tippit's body—3 Western-Winchesters and 1 Remington-Peters. NO bullets of either kind are found in LHO's room in Dallas or in the Paine home at Irving. If LHO did NOT purchase two boxes of ammunition, how did he acquire the 11 Western and the 4 Remington-Peter's 38s? If he DID purchase supplies of each brand, there is no evidence of the transaction, no evidence of use, and no left-over ammunition among his possessions.

LHO is wearing an identification bracelet on his left wrist at the time of his arrest. Sergeant **Gerald Hill** will testify that when Oswald is asked his name in the car, he makes no reply. Hill says that he then suggests that Detective **Paul Bentley** should see if the suspect had identification on his person. Bently reportedly takes LHO's wallet from his left hip pocket and, in it, finds a selective service card bearing the name "**Alek J. Hidell**." LHO also has, among other ID cards, a social security card in the name of Lee Harvey Oswald. Bentley will fail to mention the Hidell card in his report dated 3 December 1963. The Secret Service will ask **Marina Oswald** on 10 December 1963, if LHO had used the name "Hidell" as an alias. She will reply in the negative. Her testimony will have changed by 4 February 1964—when she will tell the Warren Commission that LHO used the name in New Orleans. There is immediate publicity on this day about the alias "**O.H. Lee**," which becomes known after the investigation, but NOT about Hidell, supposedly discovered at once in a search of Oswald's person.

NOTE: As **Lieutenant Martello** reports, LHO did carries a Fair Play for Cuba Committee membership card in his own name when he is arrested and also a New Orleans FPCC chapter card in his own name, signed by "A.J. Hidell, Chapter President." The Warren Commission's handwriting experts will conclude that the Hidell signature on that card is not in LHO's hand. Subsequently **Marina Oswald**, under duress, will testify that she had signed the name "Hidell" on the card. The Commission will make no attempt to elucidate LHO's rationale in coercing his wife to forge the name on an innocuous FPCC membership card, while writing the name in his own hand on other documents, including such incriminating papers as the mail orders for the revolver and the rifle. In reports filed in December 1963 by both Hill and Bentley, NO mention of the Hidell card is made. Exactly the same silence about the Hidell card is seen in the reports submitted to the police chief during the first week of December 1963 by other arresting officers—**Bob Carroll**, **K.E. Lyons**, and **C. T. Walker**.

Sometime between 1:00 and 2:00, at Parkland Hospital, **SS Agent Johnsen** hands over bullet *(CE-399)* supposedly found on the stretcher which carried Governor **Connally** into the hospital. This eventually becomes the *"magic"* bullet CE-399. **Darrell Tomlinson**, *the man who finds the original bullet, will later say that it looked entirely different than the present and "official" bullet CE-399.*

Of interest is the surface condition of the stretcher bullet when it is delivered to FBI Expert **Robert Frazier** for examination within hours of its discovery. Frazier testifies that the bullet is **clean** and has **no blood or tissue** on it. Yet, asked later about the bullet **fragments** which have been recovered from inside the Presidential car, Frazier indicates that *"there was a very slight residue of blood or some other material adhering"* which was wiped off to clean up the fragments for examination. Even more extraordinary than the absence of blood and tissue on the stretcher bullet is the **absence of fabric threads** or impression. **Dr. Cyril H**. **Wecht**, chief forensic pathologist of Allegheny County, says that it is tantamount to impossible that a bullet could have emerged from such contacts without readily apparent traces of threads. While it is possible that blood and tissue might have been shed from the stretcher bullet, leaving only microscopic traces, it is inconceivable that the missile should be barren of thread from the several fabrics it supposedly penetrated.

In 1993, **Wallace Milam**, a highly respected researcher, interviews **Elizabeth Goode Wright**, the director of nursing at Parkland in 1963. Ms. Wright reveals for the first time that two bullets had been found at the hospital on 22 November 1963, both by her husband, **O.P. Wright** *(now deceased)*, who was then director of Parkland security. Mr. Wright is widely known as one of the handlers of the "magic bullet" prior to its receipt by the Secret Service. But according to Mrs. Wright, her husband also found an unfired "whole" bullet that same day on a hospital gurney. This one was not turned over to authorities, as Ms. Wright had kept it all these years and displayed it to Milam. The bullet is an unfired, "whole" .38 with manufacturer's case markings ".38 SP WCC"—the very same markings as 2 of the 4 shell casings allegedly retrieved from the Tippit scene and supposedly matched to the pistol taken from Oswald at the time of his arrest.

1:58 PM JFK's bronze casket is being wheeled from the emergency room to be placed aboard the O'Neal hearse for the trip to the airport *(Love Field)*.

2:00 PM LBJ telephones RFK from *Air Force One. (The records of this call remain secret.)* LBJ also telephones **Abe Fortas** to ask about **Don Reynolds** and his testimony yesterday before the Senate Rules Committee. LBJ wants to know if Reynolds linked him to the **Bobby Baker** scandal. LBJ then calls **J. W. "Waddie" Bullion**, a Dallas lawyer and Johnson business crony. LBJ calls, in part, for advice on what to do with his stocks in light of the market's almost certain plunge on news of the assassination.

Observing LBJ's behavior, **Kenney O'Donnell** is heard to say, *"He's got what he wants now. But we take it back in '68."* RFK dispatches **Jack Miller** to Dallas to be his eyes and ears and to determine what has happened. Miller is an Assistant Attorney General in the Justice Department's Criminal Division.

Capt. **Fritz** arrives back at Dallas police headquarters. One of the things he comments on is the fact that LHO was the only employee not accounted for following the assassination. History will prove this statement incorrect. The Dallas Police Department's own list of employees shows that *four* employees did not return to the book depository until three in the afternoon (or later).

When the police car, carrying LHO, arrives at the police station, the detectives get the suspect out of the car and form a wedge around him, guiding him through the crowded basement. **Sgt**. **Hill** suggests to him that he could hide his face if he wants to. LHO says, *"Why should I hide my face? I haven't done anything to be ashamed of."*

Also, about this time—and according to films taken by what is now known as **The Dallas Cinema Associates**—*another* rifle is shown being brought down the east-side fire escape of the TSBD. Lieutenant **Carl Day** has already brought the Oswald rifle outside at 1:30 PM; there are photographs of Day quickly carrying this rifle away, holding it by its strap. In the DCA film, the policeman holds the rifle up as a crowd gathers to inspect it. This particular rifle has a fairly short stock, a heavy barrel, and a different action from the so-called Oswald rifle. Questioned about this rifle in 1967, authorities said <u>it was a security man's rifle accidentally left there</u>. (*The Dallas police all carried shotguns. The sheriff's office had rifles, but they were of American manufacture. The rifle in the DCA photographs appears to be a British Enfield rifle*.) Deputy Sheriff and crack shot **Harry Weatherford** *was* on the roof of the Dallas County Jail (*Records Building*) ***with a rifle*** during the assassination. Weatherford received a custom-made silencer for his rifle several weeks before the assassination. He is ordered to the roof of the building by Dallas sheriff **Bill Decker**. (*When Decker dies in 1970, Weatherford is at his bedside*.) A researcher once asks him if he shot JFK. Weatherford replies, *"You little son of a bitch, I shoot lots of people."* Dallas Police Department photographs show **Lt**. **Day** dusting a rifle for prints while in the Texas School Book Depository. The photograph shows that the rifle <u>has no ammunition clip</u>. However, another picture of Lt. Day carrying the rifle from the Depository <u>shows a rifle with an ammunition clip clearly visible and protruding from the bottom of the magazine of the rifle</u>. The photo also shows a rifle with sling swivels mounted on the *left side* of the weapon, while CE-746B (*a Warren Commission enlargement of CE-133A, which is a photo of*

Oswald with rifle) clearly shows that LHO's rifle had the sling swivels on the *bottom*.

Lieutenant **Carl Day** will also testify that he examines the outside of the paper bag LHO supposedly carried the broken down rifle in and finds no prints at all. This "bag" was never photographed as part of the crime scene. **Luke Mooney**, who stumbles on the "*sniper's nest*" first and might have been expected to see this long paper bag in his inventory of the scene, does *not* see it.

2:07 PM **The N.Y. Stock Exchange closes after the market falls 24 points. Certain individuals make over $500 million selling short.**

Memo from **J. Edgar Hoover** at this time: Shanklin called to report JFK "*in very poor condition but not dead*," that shots came from 4th floor of an unnamed building from a Winchester rifle; asked if RFK would be coming to Dallas, Hoover does not know.

Mr. T. F. White observes a man sitting in a 1961 red Ford Falcon, with the engine running, in the El Chico parking lot behind his garage. *This is five blocks north of the Texas Theater.* As Mr. White approaches the car, the driver turns and looks at him. The driver then speeds off in a westerly direction on Davis Street. Mr. White, who will later see Oswald's picture on TV, says the man in the Falcon was identical to Oswald and wore a "white T-shirt." When eventually told by the FBI that Oswald was in jail at 2:00 PM, White will still maintain that the man he saw driving the red Falcon was "possibly identical" to the Oswald he had seen on TV after the assassination. Mr. White writes down the vehicle's license plate number. The plates belong to a blue 1957 Plymouth 4 door sedan—not a 1961 red Ford Falcon. The Plymouth belongs to **Carl Mather**, a long time employee of Collins Radio and close friend of **J.D. Tippit**. (*Mather is later interviewed by the HSCA, but most of the documents relating to that interview remain classified in the National Archives.*)

NOTE: Oswald's prior connection to Collins Radio: Oswald, in the company of **George De Mohrenschildt**, had once visited the home of retired Admiral **Henry Bruton**, who was an executive of Collins Radio. Bruton had been a lawyer in Virginia before becoming a Navy intelligence officer. Bruton's specialty was electronic surveillance and this is what he was bringing to Collins Radio. In **April of 1963**, the Wall Street Journal announced that Collins would construct a modern radio communications system linking Laos, Thailand, and South Vietnam. On **1 November 1963**, the New York Times reported that **Fidel Castro** had captured a large boat called the Rex which was being leased to Collins Radio at the time. The next day, one of the captured Cuban exiles aboard the Rex confessed that the boat had been used to ferry arms into Cuba and that "the CIA organized all arms shipments." The Rex reportedly was the flagship of the JM/WAVE fleet, the CIA's super station in Miami.

Castro announced that the arms shipments were meant for an assassination attempt on top Cuban leaders.

Scenario: five blocks from where Oswald was arrested we have an Oswald double in a car traced to Tippit's friend and the friend works for a CIA associated company that plays a role in the plots against Cuba and Castro.

2:08 PM   After a heated argument between Dallas officials and Secret Service men, the body of JFK is removed from Parkland Hospital almost at gun point. ***By law***, ***it should have remained in Texas for autopsy***. Dr. **Earl Rose** warns the Secret Service agents that they are breaking the chain of evidence. **Roy Kellerman** suggests that Rose might like to come along to Washington, watching the casket all the way to make certain that the chain of evidence was not broken. Rose replies: *"There is nothing that would allow me to do it under our law. The autopsy will be performed here."* Kellerman counters: *"The family doesn't have to go through this . We will take care of the matter when we get back to Washington."* A Dallas policeman, wearing a helmet and a revolver, now stands at Dr. Rose's side. *"These people say you can't go,"* the policeman says. **Larry O'Brien** snaps: *"One side!"* **Kenny O'Donnell** says: *"We're leaving."* Dr. **George Burkley** raises his voice: *"We are removing it! This is the President of the United States; you can waive your local laws."* Moments later, Judge **Theron Ward** is stunned to hear District Attorney **Wade** state, over the phone, that he has no objection whatever to the removal of the President's body. None at all. The casket is wheeled through the hospital doors.

Outside the hospital, the bronze casket is quickly loaded into an ambulance. **Roy Kellerman** orders Agent **Andy Berger** to get behind the wheel of the ambulance and drive immediately to Love Field. Kellerman radios ahead telling his agents at Love Field to permit an ambulance and one following car through the fence. **Kenny O'Donnell** is also radioing identical instructions from the second car. He also says to tell Colonel Swindal, the pilot of *Air Force One*, to get ready for takeoff at once.

2:10 PM   From **J. Edgar Hoover** memo: called RFK to advise him of President's condition and was told by RFK that JFK was dead; repeated all information from phone calls from **Shanklin**.

2:14 PM   The O'Neal hearse, carrying the bronze casket containing JFK's body, arrives at the plane *(Air Force One)*. It is hastily loaded. **Clint Hill** sees a photographer taking pictures. *"I'll get him,"* he says to **Jacqueline Kennedy**. *"No,"* she replies. *"I want them to see what they have done."*

AP again makes note that: *"A Secret Service Agent and a Dallas policeman were shot and killed today."*

About this time, Senator **Edward Kennedy** and **Eunice Kennedy Shriver** arrive at the White House.

2:15 PM *NBC News* reports that a rifle has been found on the **fifth** floor of the Book Depository Building. Newspaper reports indicate that the rifle is a **Mauser**. Also reported is the discovery of the remains of a chicken lunch left by the assassin on the **fifth** floor.

2:17 PM J. **Edgar Hoover** memo: Shanklin called and said local agents had learned that JFK wad dead. Shanklin said "they had located 3 or 4 shells in the building and the Sheriff's office had picked up one man." Shanklin said Dallas police had informed him that a Secret Service agent had been killed.

2:18 PM Seats have been removed in the rear section of *Air Force One*. JFK's casket is placed inside. The casket is secured on the left side of the plane barely inside the rear door. General **Godfrey McHugh** announces that *"The President is aboard."* He is referring to JFK. **Kenny O'Donnell** tells McHugh to *"Run forward and tell Colonel Swindal to get the plane out of here."* It is at this point that the Kennedy entourage is shocked to realize that the Johnson entourage is also aboard *Air Force One*. There is a feeling of awkward friction and tension. **Mrs. Johnson**, seeing that **Mrs. Kennedy**'s dress is soaked in blood, suggests that she get someone to help her change. Mrs. Kennedy replies: *"Oh, no. Perhaps later I'll ask **Mary Gallagher**. But not right now."* LBJ and Mrs. Johnson retire from the aft compartment, and LBJ goes into the private bedroom to make certain that **Marie Fehmer** has the oath of office typewritten correctly. He barely sits down when the compartment door opens revealing Jacqueline Kennedy. LBJ rises immediately, asks Miss Fehmer to leave and apologizes to Mrs. Kennedy. He leaves the room and Mrs. Kennedy goes into the lavatory.

2:20 PM Dallas doctors' press conference. **Dr. Perry** says throat wound is an *entry* wound.

2:21 PM J. **Edgar Hoover** makes note of his conversation with **James Rowley**, chief of the Secret Service, repeating the "information" from his calls from Shanklin. Rowley is unaware that one of his agents has been killed. *"Mr. Rowley stated he was also thinking of subversive elements—Mexico and Cuba. I then mentioned the Klan element."* Hoover has apparently received some further information after Shanklin's 1:48 statement about a witness seeing a "Negro" shooter: *"They do not know whether it was a white or a black."*

2:30 PM A plane takes off from Redbird Airport [*a private airstrip located four miles to the south of LHO's Beckley Street address*]—as witnessed by **Louis D. Gaudin**, the air traffic controller. It is a green and white Comanche-type aircraft Gaudin speaks with the planes three well-dressed occupants. Forty minutes later, the plane returns to the airport with only two occupants. It is met by a part-time employee who is moonlighting from the Dallas Police Department. The plane then takes off again. According to CIA documents released in 1977, two Cuban men arrived at the Mexico City airport from Dallas, via

Tijuana, on a twin-engine aircraft. The CIA receives "highly reliable" information that the men were met at the Mexico airport by Cuban diplomatic personnel from the Cuban embassy. One of the men then boarded either a FAR or Cubana Airlines plane, avoiding customs, and traveled to Cuba in the cockpit so as to avoid mixing with the passengers.

Judge Sarah Hughes arrives at Love Field, boards *Air Force One*. LBJ is to be sworn in. He requests that **Jacqueline Kennedy** come into the stateroom and stand with him while the oath is being administered. Mrs. Kennedy is found by **Evelyn Lincoln** in the lavatory on the airplane. When Mrs. Kennedy steps into the stateroom, LBJ grasps both her hands and whispers, *"Thank you."* General **Godfrey McHugh** is demanding to know why the plane has not taken off as he has ordered. **Malcolm Kilduff**, passing the communications shack, hears the voices and tells the plane's pilot, Colonel **Swindal**, not to take off. Judge Hughes administers oath of office to LBJ. He is now—officially—President of the United States. His first order is *"Let's get airborne."*

NOTE: This is the critical time period that author/researcher **David Lifton** theorizes that the body of JFK is left unguarded and could have been removed from the bronze casket aboard Air Force One during LBJ's swearing in.

During the swearing in of LBJ as President, only General **Godfrey McHugh** remains with the casket. *Godfrey McHugh was listed in* **Who's Who in the CIA***, a book confirmed by the Pentagon Papers as being accurate. McHugh's home of record is Fort Worth, although he was born in Belgium and educated in Paris. Jackie had known and dated McHugh during her "Paris days."* **Penn Jones, Jr.***—an assassination researcher who also retired from the military a brigadier general says:* **"Since the assassination was planned and executed by the military of the United States, we feel now that General McHugh was a high-ranking traitor for the military inside the Kennedy camp. We hope we are wrong, and we hope McHugh will defend himself, but the evidence so far indicates treachery."**

NOTE: David Lifton puts forward in his book, *BEST EVIDENCE*, the theory that JFK's body was stolen from its coffin in the rear of the plane in the first few minutes directly after it was brought on board in Dallas. *"The critical period was 2:18 to 2:32 PM (CST). It appeared, from the public record, that the coffin was then unattended."*

2:40 PM   The Dallas Police radio, channel two, reports that: *"One of the Secret Service men on the field—Elm and Houston, said that it came over his Teletype that one of the Secret Service men has been killed."*

2:45 PM   **John Franklin Elrod i**s arrested in Dallas. (*During the assassination, Elrod had been about two and one half miles from the scene at Lemon and Oaklawn Streets in Dallas.*) Before the end of the day, Elrod will later say that his cell mate is **Lee Harvey Oswald**—who will speak to him, while in jail, of a gun deal involving a man with a *"smashed-up"* face, a Thunderbird loaded with guns—and of **Jack Ruby**. One other person also held in the Dallas jail today is a man named "**Daniel Wayne Douglas**" who is held in either cell F-1 or F-4. Douglas is described as 19 years old, from Memphis and a confessed car thief. Elrod will not recount the story of his conversation with LHO until August 1964. The driver of the Thunderbird mentioned by LHO is later determined to be **Donnell Whitter**, Jack Ruby's mechanic. The man with the *smashed up face* is later determined to be **Lawrence Reginald Miller**—a passenger in the Thunderbird. His face hit the windshield when the car crashed on 18 November 1963 after a high speed chase with police. The car contained a large quantity of guns. Miller was treated at the emergency room of Parkland Hospital and charged with multiple criminal violations arising out of the incident. After having his face stitched up, he was remanded to the Dallas city jail. Miller and Whitter were hired to run guns by **John Thomas Masen**—a right-wing gun shop owner. (*Masen is one of only two dealers in Dallas selling 6.5mm Mannlicher-Carcano ammunition.*) *(The information on Elrod's arrest and conversations with LHO will not surface until 1992. A book on Elrod and this incident will finally appear in 1996.)*

2:47 PM   *Air Force One* is now airborne and climbs to 40,000 feet over a storm. LBJ orders soup and crackers. He will shortly talk to both **Rose Kennedy** and **Mrs. Connally** by phone from the plane. LBJ, while talking to Rose Kennedy, puts Mrs. Johnson on the telephone. Rose Kennedy does not ask Mrs. Johnson to switch her to **Jacqueline Kennedy**, who is sitting fifty feet behind the Johnsons. Nor does Mrs. John F. Kennedy phone her mother in law. (Four months after the assassination, Rose Kennedy will tell author **Jim Bishop**: "*I have not heard from 'Mrs. Kennedy' since the funeral.*") General **Godfrey McHugh** notices **Merriman Smith** and other news writers aboard the plane and reminds them that "*throughout this trip I remained back there with the President.*" **Jim Bishop** will write that LBJ seems to be telephoning **McGeorge Bundy** in the White House Situation Room every few minutes.

NOTE: McGeorge Bundy will be quite busy on 22 November 1963. After having spent a good deal of time on the telephone with President Johnson, he manages to be at the new President's side when Air Force One lands. He is seen with Lyndon B. Johnson when the President emerges from the South Lawn of the White House. Bundy will remain with President Johnson to be designated by him as one of the leading hawkish advisers of the Johnson Administration. McGeorge Bundy and his brother, William, will continue to help shape the foreign policy of the Johnson Administration. McGeorge Bundy becomes part of Johnson's Tuesday lunch arrangement which will be in fact the National Security Council, Johnson style. Bundy will do most of the foreign policy coordinating for Johnson in the early part of his administration. It is McGeorge Bundy who by happenstance will be in South Vietnam when Pleiku is shelled. After an inspection of the Pleiku base, he will recommend to President Johnson instant retaliation. He will urge upon the President a steady program of bombing the North, which recommendation will be followed with horrendous consequences to peace. In the Gulf of Tonkin farce, Bundy will be full of admiration for Johnson's decisiveness. Bundy will say to friends that he has ". . . never seen a man who knew so clearly what he wanted to do or so exactly how to go about it."

The communications crew at the forward end of *Air Force One* cannot handle the traffic. The outgoing calls are heavy. Mrs. Kennedy is not accepting any incoming calls unless they are from her brother-in-law RFK. Other calls are referred to her secretary, **Pamela Turnure**. **General Clifton** asks Andrews Air Force Base to have a forklift ready to carry the casket down the rear exit. He also phones the Army's <u>Walter Reed Hospital</u> and says that the autopsy will be performed *there*.

WASHINGTON, DC—While *Air Force One* is airborne, a senior Secret Service agent, **Robert I. Bouck**, begins disassembling the Tandberg tape-recording systems JFK had secretly ordered to be installed in the Oval Office, Cabinet Room, and in the President's living quarters on the second floor of the White House. There is also a separate Dictabelt recording system for use on the telephone lines in the President's office and his upstairs bedroom. Bouck has apparently told only two people of the system's existence—his immediate superior, **James J. Rowley**, chief of the Secret Service, and a subordinate who helps him monitor the equipment. It is Bouck's understanding that only two others know of the system while JFK was alive—**Bobby Kennedy** and **Evelyn Lincoln**, the President's longtime personal secretary. During its sixteen months of operation, Bouck will later say that the taping system produced *"at least two hundred"* reels of tapes. *"They never told me why they wanted the tapes and I never had possession of any of the used tapes."* *"I didn't want Lyndon Johnson to get to listen to them."*

The tape recordings remain in direct control of the Kennedy family until May 1976 when they are deeded to the John F. Kennedy Library in Boston. In a report issued in 1985, the library acknowledges that it is "impossible to establish with any certainty how much might have been removed" from the collection prior to 1975. "That at least some items were removed cannot be doubted." Some Dictabelt tapes of telephone conversations were also discovered to be in the possession of Evelyn Lincoln after her death in 1995. The tapes made after 8 November 1963 are now missing.

RFK places a call to Presidential aide **McGeorge Bundy**, directing him to change the combinations on White House safes containing JFK's personal files.

Today, Patrolman **J**. **Raz** brings into the Homicide and Robbery Bureau, Dallas PD, a brown paper sack which contains a snub-nosed .38 caliber Smith & Wesson, SN 893265 . . . has been found . . . near the curb at the corner of Ross and Lamar Streets and is turned in by one **Willie Flat**.

2:50 PM   Dallas police take a paraffin test of Oswald's hands and right cheek. Test is positive for hands; negative for the face. His interrogation continues.

Captain **Will Fritz** wrote the following remarks concerning Oswald's knowledge of police interrogation methods: "*I noted that in questioning him that he did answer very quickly, and I asked him if he had ever been questioned before, and he told me that he had. He was questioned one time for a long time by the FBI after he returned from Russia. He said they used different methods, they tried the hard and soft, and the buddy method and said he was very familiar with interrogation.*" Former Police Chief **Jesse Curry** told author **Anthony Summers** in 1977, "*One would think Oswald had been trained in interrogation techniques and resisting interrogation techniques.*" To the same author, **D.A. William Alexander** had this to say: "*I was amazed that a person so young would have had the self-control he had. It was almost as if he had been rehearsed or programmed to meet the situation he found himself in.*" Detective **Boyd** said, "*I never saw another man just exactly like him. . . just as soon as you would ask him a question, he would just give you the answer right back—he didn't hesitate about his answers. I mean as soon as you would pop him a question, he would shoot you an answer right back and like I said, I never saw a man that could answer questions like he did.*" According to **L.C.Graves**, "*He was quick to answer and quick to make a remark when he was spoken to or asked a question. . . He is sharp when it comes to talking to the men. He listened to everything, everybody he saw, and he had an answer by the time you got through asking him. . . He didn't hung for words, didn't hesitate at all.*" **Leavelle** said, "*He did always smile and never hesitated for an answer, always had an answer.*" And **Sims** said, "*He had the answers ready when you got through with the questions.*" According to FBI **Agent Bookhout**, "*Anytime you asked a question that would be pertinent to the investigation, that would be the type of question he would refuse to discuss.*" And **Capt**. **Fritz** concluded, "*Every time I asked him a question that meant something, that would produce evidence, he immediately told me he wouldn't tell me about it and he seemed to anticipate what I was going to ask.*"

Chief of Police **Jesse Curry** will eventually say: "*We don't have any proof that Oswald fired the rifle, and never did. Nobody's yet been able to put him in that building with a gun in his hand.*"

"Sir:

On November 22, 1963, at approximately 2:50 P.M., the undersigned officer met Special Agent James Hosty of the Federal bureau of Investigation in the basement of the City Hall.

At that time Special Agent Hosty related to this officer that the Subject was a member of the Communist Party, and that he was residing in Dallas.

The Subject was arrested for the murder of Officer J. D. Tippit and is a prime suspect in the assassination of President Kennedy.

The information regarding the Subject's affiliation with the Communist Party is the first information this officer has received from the Federal Bureau of Investigation regarding same.

Agent Hosty further stated that the Federal Bureau of Investigation was aware of the Subject and that they had information that this Subject was capable of committing the assassination of President Kennedy.

Respectfully submitted,

Jack Revill, Lieutenant

Criminal Intelligence Section"

When Dallas Police Chief **J. E. Curry** subsequently reports this information to the press, he receives a telephone call from the FBI agent-in-charge in Dallas, **Gordon Shanklin**, saying that *"the bureau was extremely desirous that I retract my statement to the press. I then appeared before the press again and retracted my statement."*

Jim Bishop reports that a Dallas policeman whispers to Captain **Will Fritz**: *"I hear this Oswald has a furnished room on Beckley."* (*It has been suggested that the policeman who gave Fritz this information could have been* **Roscoe White**.)

2:55 PM   A printed list of Texas School Book Depository employees shows that FOUR employees (**L.R. Viles**, **Mrs. William Parker**, **Dolores Koonas**, and **Virgie Rackley**) are still out of the TSBD building.

3:00 PM   Word reaches LBJ aboard *Air Force One* (through Major General **Chester Clifton** who is sorting messages in the communications shack) that LHO has a dossier in the State Department. LBJ asks for a quick check to find out if the State Department has erred in permitting LHO to return to the USA from Russia. **Jacqueline Kennedy** is offered a Scotch by **Kenny O'Donnell**. *"I've never had a Scotch in my life,"* she replies. O'Donnell says: *"Now is as good a time to start as any."*

A Dallas police dispatcher, speaking to Captain **C. E. Talbert** on Channel Two says: *"A Mr.* **Bill Moyers** *is on his way to swear in Mr. Johnson as President and he will need an escort, but we don't know when he is going to get here."*

3:15 PM   **Lee Harvey Oswald's arrest is broadcast by news media. Jack Ruby** leaves The Carousel Club and drives to **Eva Grant**'s house but leaves soon after he arrives, to obtain some weekend food for his sister and himself.

3:20 PM In New Orleans, **Carlos Marcello** is acquitted. He walks from courtroom showing no emotion.

3:30 PM Deputy sheriffs arrive at the Paine residence in Irving, Texas. Detective **Gus Rose** of **Captain Fritz**'s staff is asked by **Ruth Paine** if he has a search warrant. He says no *"but I can get the sheriff out here with one if you want."* Paine says: *"No, that's all right. Be my guests."* Ruth retranslates her opinions back to Russian for **Marina Oswald**'s benefit and it becomes obvious that Mrs. Oswald is not happy with her friend's show of initiative. Paine answers what questions she can, without translating for Marina. **Linnie Mae Randle**, who is also present, tells the sheriffs that LHO rode with her brother, **Wesley Frazier**, to work this morning and that LHO put something long on the back seat of Wes's car. It was, she recalls, wrapped in paper or maybe a box.

3:40 PM Assistant Secretary of the Treasury **Robert A. Wallace** reports, *"No Secret Service man was injured in the attack on President Kennedy."*

4:00 PM Somewhere, high over the United States in *Air Force One*, the new President, **Lyndon Johnson**, receives news that the assassination is the act of <u>one lone individual</u> and that <u>no conspiracy exists</u>. The information comes from the nation's capitol. Specifically, it comes from either **McGeorge Bundy** or **Commander Oliver Hallet** in the Situation Room of the White House Communications Center. LBJ tells McGeorge Bundy that he wants to call a series of meetings tonight and tomorrow morning. "Bipartisan," LBJ adds.

In Texas, Chief **Jesse Curry** arrives back at Dallas police headquarters from Love Field where he drove LBJ to board *Air Force One*.

4-4:30 PM **Jack Ruby** is reported seen in the crowded Dallas Police Headquarters.

Oswald places a telephone call to Mrs. **Ruth Paine** from the Dallas City Hall. The call concerns his search for legal assistance. His first interrogation begins at 4:20 PM.

Regarding the assassination, the afternoon edition of *The Dallas Times Herald* states: "Witnesses said six or seven shots were fired."

Around this time, **Abram Chayez**, the Legal Counsel to the State Department in Washington receives a call from Acting Secretary of State **George Ball** (Secretary **Rusk** being away on the trip to the Honolulu conference) with the direction to *"gather together the files in the Department on Oswald, and to prepare a report to be available to him the first thing in the morning, covering as best we could within that time span the contacts that Oswald had with the Department."* **Consider:** LHO was arrested and only brought to headquarters about two hours earlier. There have been no line-ups in which LHO has been identified even as Tippit's killer, no confession or any *"connections to the rifle."* Researchers have posed the question as to what available facts could have possibly prompted Under-Secretary Ball to commit so much manpower to a report on LHO—*and* to further order that the report be ready by the following morning. LBJ is *just* receiving a telephone call aboard Air Force One from the White House Situation Room that the assassination has been the work of one lone individual. LHO is being rapidly identified as *the* lone suspect to the exclusion of all other potential leads.

An initial search of the garage of the Paine home in Irving, Texas— where Oswald has stored belongings—reveals **NO** backyard photographs. The Dallas Police list of property that is seized contains the following item: "four 3 x 5 cards bearing respectively names **G. Hall; A. J. Hidell; B. Davis;** and **V.T. Lee**." Hall, Davis and Lee are real persons of some prominence in political movements of the Left.

NOTE: There is immediate publicity on 22 November 1963 about the alias "**O.H. Lee**," which becomes known after investigation, but **NOT** about **Hidell**, supposedly discovered at once in a search of Oswald's person.

When Dallas police officers arrive to search the Paine residence, they are met by sheriff's officers (*including Sheriff's Officer* **Harry Weatherford**) who have the jurisdiction but choose to leave the search to the locals. At quitting time, not much beyond a blanket has been found officially. Yet, <u>tomorrow</u>, the now-famous *"backyard photos"* will be "found" at the Paine residence—another "backyard" photograph will eventually turn up in the possession of **Roscoe White**.

Robert Hester, a commercial photographer in Dallas, is called from home to help process assassination-related photographs of Oswald holding a rifle and pistol, sees an FBI agent with a color transparency of one of those pictures and one of the backyard photos he processes <u>shows no figure in the picture</u>. This claim is corroborated by Hester's wife. The photographs in question are not *"officially"* discovered until *twelve hours later* in the Paine's garage after an initial search reveals nothing.

4:01 PM   (2:01 CST) **J. Edgar Hoover** calls RFK to say he thinks we have *"the man who killed the President down in Dallas."*

4:35 PM   **Oswald** is taken by officers to the show-up room for the first of several line ups. Though he has been searched at the time of his arrest, Detectives **Boyd** and **Sims** decide to search him again. In Oswald's pockets they find five live rounds of .38 ammunition and a bus transfer slip. Tippit-shooting-witness **Helen Markham** views the lineup of Oswald and three others and gives a very shaky identification.

5:00 PM   According to **Cecil Hamlin**, **Jack Ruby** telephones him at this time and weeps freely during the call. He tells Hamlin that he has closed both of his clubs for the weekend and expresses his sorrow for the Kennedy *"kids."*

5:05 PM   *Air Force One* lands at Andrews with LBJ and the body of JFK. Bronze casket unloaded. <u>A helicopter immediately takes off from the opposite</u>

side of the aircraft. Its function and destination—unknown. LBJ makes brief public statement, then boards a helicopter for the White House.

Controversy has surrounded this flight of *Air Force One* almost from the moment it touches down at Andrews Air Force Base. The fact that it arrives one-half hour late leads to speculation that the President's body was either tampered with during the flight or was removed from the coffin, spirited from the plane at Andrews, secretly placed aboard a nearby Army helicopter, and flown somewhere else to afford members of the conspiracy an opportunity to alter Kennedy's wounds before the autopsy. A second possibility is that the President's body was removed from *Air Force One* while it was still at Love Field before departing Dallas.

5:10 PM　**Jacqueline** and **Robert Kennedy** depart in a *GRAY* navy ambulance for Bethesda Naval Hospital with bronze casket. **William Greer** drives the ambulance carrying the President's official coffin from Andrews Air Force Base to Bethesda Naval Hospital.

5:15 PM　In an FBI memo, **J. Edgar Hoover** describes Oswald to RFK as being *"in the category of a nut and the extremist pro-Castro crowd . . . an extreme radical of the left."* Further, to RFK Hoover says that LHO was said to have fled the building and a *"block or two away"* shot at two policemen trying to apprehend him, killing one. RFK asks Hoover if Oswald is a communist and Hoover says no, but that he has *"communist leanings"* and is a *"very mean-minded individual."* He also says that LHO had been eating fried chicken sandwiches prior to the shooting in the TSBD and *"we have to check this out and find where he obtained the chicken."*

　Dr. James Humes, lab director at the Bethesda Naval Hospital, receives a telephone call from Admiral **Edward Kenney**, the Surgeon General of the Navy, who says: *"Jim, you'd better hurry over to the hospital."*

5:26 PM　Chopper lands on White House lawn with LBJ.

5:30 PM　Texas Deputy Sheriff **Roger Craig** is taken by **Will Fritz** into an office where the suspect, **Lee Harvey Oswald**, is being held. Craig positively identifies Oswald as the man he saw fleeing the Texas School Book Depository and get into the Rambler Station wagon. Oswald tells them that the station wagon belongs to **Mrs. Paine**. *"Don't try to tie her into this."* Oswald says, *"She had nothing to do with it."* Then he continues by saying: *"Everybody will know who I am now."* It is not noted that LHO denies getting into the Rambler Station wagon. (*Will Fritz decides that he does not want a stenographer to take notes while he questions LHO. Nor does he desire a tape recorder.*)

　Jack Ruby, according to one report, arrives again at his sister's home and remains there for two hours. He continues his rapid rate of telephone calls, eats sparingly, becomes ill, and attempts to get some rest. He decides to close his club for three days. However, according to Detective **August Eberhardt**, who has known Ruby for five years, he speaks with Ruby between 6 and 7 o'clock in the third-floor hallway of the Dallas police building.

Felipe Vidal Santiago arrives back in Miami from Dallas, Texas by 5:30 pm EST. It is suggested that he is flown on a private or military jet.

This afternoon, according to his wife, **David Atlee Phillips** comes home and says nothing at all. He shows neither sadness, nor pleasure, nor interest. He simply has nothing to say.

Also, during the afternoon of Nov. 22nd, **Gilberto Policarpo Lopez** crosses into Mexico from Nuevo Laredo. It is only hours after this border is reopened following its closure in the wake of the assassination. (*By March 1964, Policarpo's name will be put forward by the CIA as having been involved in the Kennedy assassination. The CIA, however, will never inform the Warren Commission of Policarpo's activities.*)

5:45 PM	**Dennis David** observes arrival of *BLACK* hearse at the rear entrance of Bethesda with plain metal casket, accompanied by 6—7 men in plain clothes. He is told it is body of JFK. Plain metal casket brought into Bethesda morgue. **Paul O'Connor** reports JFK's body wrapped in *BODY BAG*; with no brain inside head.
5:55 PM (CST)	*GRAY* Navy ambulance, driven by **William Greer**, arrives at Bethesda front entrance. **Jacqueline Kennedy** enters hospital.
6:00 PM	Ambulance drives off. Casket team loses ambulance; chase according to Clark and Felder; two fruitless round trips to rear of hospital, according to Barnum; confusion caused by *TWO* ambulances. FBI accompanies bronze Dallas casket to Bethesda morgue entrance. FBI prevented from entering morgue.

Erwin Swartz and **Abraham Zapruder** take the original positive copy of the assassination film footage to Jamison Film, in Dallas, and have three reversal duplicates made. They have a Jamison representative sign a statement that they will make no more than the three reversal duplicates. Swartz and Zapruder then take the three reversal duplicates to Eastman Kodak where three additional positive prints are made.

Army Sergeant **James Felder** is a member of the Casket Team charged with transporting the President's coffin. Felder will be eventually interviewed by researcher **David S. Lifton**. According to Lifton, Felder substantiates reports of confusion at Bethesda Naval Hospital involving the use of two Navy ambulances and the team's difficulty locating Kennedy's coffin during a *thirty-minute interval* following its arrival at the hospital.

When Air Force One landed at Andrews Air Force Base, the President's coffin was removed from the craft and placed inside a Navy ambulance for the trip to Bethesda Naval Hospital. Jacqueline Kennedy and Attorney General Robert F. Kennedy, who had met the plane, also rode in the ambulance. A second ambulance reportedly joined the motorcade from the air base to the hospital to serve as a decoy, drawing the crowd of curiosity seekers away from the ambulance bearing the President's coffin. The motorcade reached Bethesda at approximately 6:55 PM, Friday, 22 November 1963. Mrs. Kennedy and the President's brother alighted and entered the front door of the hospital, leaving the ambulance containing the coffin outside under guard by a group of sailors hand-picked specifically for this duty. The Military District of Washington, D.C., Casket Team had flown by helicopter from Andrews to Bethesda, where the members loaded into a pickup truck. They waited near the front entrance to the hospital until the ambulance pulled away to drive around back to the loading dock. The truck attempted to keep pace with the ambulance, which reportedly drove at high speed, but lost sight of it and then lost its bearings. Returning to the hospital's main entrance, the truck started again for the rear of the building, where the ambulance was found waiting. The coffin was finally removed by the Casket Team. Although Bureau records purportedly indicate that FBI agents accompanied the coffin from the ambulance to the autopsy room at 7:17 PM (EST), the Casket Team case report puts the time the coffin was transferred at 8:00 PM (EST) According to a statement that researcher David S. Lifton attributed to Petty Officer Dennis David, who was chief of the day for the medical school when Kennedy's body arrived, David brought with him to the loading platform "seven or eight sailors" who unloaded the coffin and brought it into the autopsy room. This does not correspond with either of the two reports, one by the FBI men at the scene (the O'Neill and Sibert report) and the other by the Casket Team, concerning who unloaded the coffin. Adding to the controversy is a statement Lifton attributed to X-ray technician Jerrol F. Custer that Custer witnessed Mrs. Kennedy's arrival through the front entrance of the hospital while he was carrying X-rays of her husband's head to be developed. If the President's body was still in the coffin inside the ambulance in which Mrs. Kennedy arrived, it was impossible for Custer to be arranging to develop X-rays of his wounds.

6:10 PM   The Marsalis City bus driven by **Cecil McWatters** comes to the bus stop at Dallas police headquarters. Two men get on board and identify themselves as police detectives. They ask McWatters to come inside for questioning. They take him in through the main entrance and up to the third floor. When shown bus transfer No. 4459 McWatters says *"Yes, that is the transfer I issued because it had my punch mark on it . . . I only gave two transfers going through town on that trip* (from North Dallas south to Oak Cliff) *and that was at the one stop of where I gave the lady and the gentlemen that got off the bus, I issued two transfers. But that was the only two transfers were issued."*

6:17 PM (CST)   Time of preparation for Bethesda autopsy, according to FBI

6:20 PM   Oswald's second interrogation begins.

6:30 PM   WFAA radio and television reporter **Victor Robertson, Jr**. stands in the hall near the entrance to **Captain Fritz**'s third-floor office in Dallas. Two police officers are guarding the door. Robertson sees **Jack Ruby** approach and attempt to enter the office. He is prevented from doing so by one of the officers who says: *"You can't go in there Jack."* Ruby makes a joking remark and heads back down the hall toward the elevator.

At some point during this early evening, CIA agent **Gary Underhill** drives out of Washington, DC and heads for New York—and the home of **Robert Fitzsimmons** on Long Island. (*Fitzsimmons and his wife* **Charlene**, *are longtime friends whom Underhill feels he can trust.*) Bob is sleeping; Charlene is awake. Underhill tells Charlene that he fears for his life and plans on leaving the country. *"I've got to get out of the country . . . This country is too dangerous for me now. I've got to get on a boat . . . I'm really afraid for my life."* Upon questing by Charlene, Underhill goes on to explain that he has information about the Kennedy assassination and that *"Oswald is a patsy. They set him up. It's too much. The bastards have done something outrageous. They've killed the President! I've been listening and hearing things. I couldn't believe they'd get away with it, but they did!"* Underhill, emotionally distraught, continues to explain *"They've gone mad! They're a bunch of drug runners and gun runners—a real violence group. God, the CIA is under enough pressure already without that bunch in Southeast Asia . . . . I know who they are. That's the problem. They know I know. That's why I'm here."* Underhill begs Charlene to help hide him, and she consents to let him stay a few hours until Bob awakens—then possibly Bob will leave Gary a key while the couple vacations in Spain, a trip they have previously planned on taking with departure, ironically, taking place this very day. *"No, that's all right,"* says Underhill. *"Maybe I shouldn't leave the country."* Underhill turns toward the door. *"I'll be back in a couple of hours."* He does not come back. Underhill returns quietly to Washington and begins investigating JFK's assassination on his own. He mentions his efforts to another friend, **Asher Brynes**, of *The New Republic*, but probably no one else. (*In six months, Underhill will be dead—"suicide." He will be shot behind his left ear. Yet, Underhill is right-handed.*)

7:00 PM   Oswald is formally charged with the murder of J.D. Tippit.

Jack Ruby is seen at the Dallas police station. He is carrying a loaded gun, to which he later admits in his testimonies to the Warren Commission.

Marina Oswald and Mr. and **Mrs. Paine** are brought into police headquarters in Dallas. Shown the rifle allegedly found on the sixth floor of the TSBD, Marina states that it is *"like"* her husband's but that she is *"not sure."* Officers take her affidavit.

In Washington, LBJ has his first appointment as President with CIA director **John McCone**. What they discuss remains unknown.

Also this evening, **Santos Trafficante** meets **Frank Ragano** and his nineteen-year-old fiancee, **Nancy**, at Tampa, Florida's *International Inn*. He has invited them to supper and meets them in a jubilant mood. He embraces both of them warmly. *"Our problems are over,"* he tells Ragano. *"I hope Jimmy [Hoffa] is happy now. We will build hotels again. We'll get back into Cuba now."* Once at the table, Trafficante launches into a tirade against the slain President, then proposes a toast. Turning to Ragano and his future bride, he raises a glass and says: *"To your health and John Kennedy's death."* Nancy, a college student, is horrified at what Trafficante has just said. She has only just come from her campus where the students are still crying over what has happened in Dallas. Unable to take it, she runs out of the restaurant, leaving Frank and Santos alone.

7:10 PM   The New Orleans FBI Bureau chief, **Harry Maynor**, contacts SAC **Shanklin** in Dallas *"to determine if he could supply information that might make it unnecessary to determine the whereabouts of all Klan members, etc. and to determine if sufficient information was then available to definitely tie Oswald into the assassination of the President."* Shanklin replies that *"Oswald was probably a good suspect but they have been unable to develop information connecting the rifle with Oswald."*

7:29 PM   LBJ writes **John** and **Caroline Kennedy** a letter in the Executive Office Building in Washington, DC.

7:30 PM   SS Agent **Richard Johnsen** of the White House Detail gives bullet **399** to SS Chief **James Rowley** at the Executive Office building in Washington. The bullet has traveled, in Johnsen's coat pocket, to Washington from Dallas.

Detective **Roy Standifer**, an acquaintance of **Jack Ruby** will later testify that they exchange greetings in the third floor hallway of the Dallas police building during this time period.

7:40 PM   **Lee Harvey Oswald**'s third interrogation session begins. No notes or recordings are made. Oswald is still not represented by counsel. Six Secret Service agents and four FBI agents who are present at the interrogations of Oswald will never be questioned by the Warren Commission.

7:56 PM   In Washington, the Kennedy children are returned to the White House.

8:00 PM   Oswald places a telephone call to **Ruth Paine** *(his second call to her today.)*

8:15 PM   FBI agents **James W. Sibert** and **Francis X. O'Neill** note that the first incision is made on the body of JFK, thus officially beginning the Bethesda autopsy. *(This time notation is seriously questioned by some researchers.)* Sibert and O'Neill also indicate in their report that some type of surgery has already been performed on JFK's head area. No surgery on his head has been performed at Parkland Hospital.

8:50 PM   (*Washington*) SS Chief **Rowley** sends bullet CE-399 to the FBI laboratory.

8:55 PM   Detectives **J. B. Hicks** and **Robert Studebaker** take Lee Harvey Oswald to the Homicide and Robbery Office for fingerprinting. A few minutes later, Detective **Pete Barnes** comes in and the three crime lab men make paraffin casts of Oswald's hands and right cheek. The tests come back positive for his hands and negative for his right cheek, indicating that Lee Harvey Oswald *may* have fired a pistol but *NOT* a rifle.

This evening, a man identifying himself as **Jim Rizzuto** calls a New York City radio station to report that LHO had been seen in Greenwich village in 1962 in the company of **Steve L'Eandes**, a Nazi sympathizer and right-wing agitator from Wiggins, Mississippi. The FBI will ultimately determine that Rizzuto's story is a hoax and the Rizzuto's real name is **Stephen Harris Landesberg**. *"Rizzuto"* goes on to claim that he served in the Marine Corps with both LHO and L'Eandes in the Marine Corps at Camp LeJeune, North Carolina during the summer of 1956. (*Landesberg is eventually charged with providing false information to the FBI and is committed by Federal Judge* **John Cannella** *to 10 days of psychiatric observation at Bellevue Hospital.*)

9:00 PM   From New Orleans, **David Ferrie** and two young male friends, set off by car on a seven-hour drive through a storm to Houston, Texas—a distance of 364 miles. The purpose of the trip, as Ferrie will later explain, is to look over an ice skating rink and to do some skating. Ferrie describes the trip as a *"whim."* While at the rink, Ferrie never puts on a pair of skates. He stays instead beside a public telephone for two hours, until he receives a call.

9:10 PM   LBJ confers by telephone for fifteen minutes with **J. Edgar Hoover**.

10:45 PM   Oswald, installed in a cell on the fifth floor of the Dallas City Hall, places a long distance call to **Raleigh**, **North Carolina**. According to one of the switchboard operators, **Mrs. Troon**, she and a co-worker (**Mrs. Swinney**) have been alerted that law enforcement officers—she thinks they might be Secret Service men—will be arriving to listen in on an Oswald telephone call. *Two men* arrive, show identification and are shown into a room next to the switchboard. When Oswald places the call, at about **10:45 PM** this evening, Mrs. Swinney handles the call with Mrs. Troon listening in. Oswald is told by Mrs. Swinney, as per her instructions, that the number doesn't answer. The call is then disconnected without ever really going through. A few moments later, Mrs. Swinney tears the page off her notation pad and throws it into the wastepaper basket. Mrs. Troon later retrieves the note and keeps it as a souvenir. (*That slip of paper, which will turn up seven years from now in a Freedom of Information suit brought by Chicago researcher* **Sherman H. Skolnick** *(a civil action filed in Federal District Court in Chicago, April 6, 1970, No. 70C 790), contains some startling things. It purports to show a collect call attempted from the jail by Lee Harvey Oswald to a John Hurt at 919-834-7430 and it gives another telephone number in* *the 919 Area Code, 833-1253*.) The call is made to ***Raleigh, North Carolina*** to a man named **John Hurt**. The note lists *two* alternative numbers, which do relate to listed subscribers of that name. One of the two John D. Hurts served in U.S. Military Intelligence during World War II. The Chief Counsel of Congress' Assassinations Committee, **Professor Blakey**, will eventually conclude: *"It was an outgoing call, and therefore I consider it very troublesome material. The direction in which it went was deeply disturbing."*

NOTE: Victor Marchetti, author of *THE CIA AND THE CULT OF INTELLIGENCE*, alleges that Oswald's attempted call to Raleigh is an effort to contact a *"fake cutout."* He explains that all intelligence agents work through *"cutouts,"* middlemen who are called if an agent is in a scrape. Therefore, according to Marchetti, Oswald thought he was working for a spy agency, most probably the CIA.

The House Assassinations Committee gave one of its staffers, **Surell Brady**, responsibility for investigating the "Raleigh Call." Though the committee's final report did not mention the call, Brady wrote a 28-page internal memorandum outlining the results of their investigation of the incident.

In an insert after page 15 of the document, it is incorrectly reported that the two numbers listed on the telephone slip "were unpublished in 1963." This information was reported as having been supplied by **Carolyn Rabon** of Southern Bell Telephone Co. in 1978. However, a simple check of the December 1962 Southern Bell telephone directory for Raleigh, North Carolina (which would have been current at the time of the assassination) and the December 1963 directory (which would contain any new information and reflect any changes of listing status) shows that both numbers were published.

Thus, both of these numbers would have been available to anyone calling "Information" in Raleigh, asking for a John Hurt. This is the way the listings appear in those directories:

DECEMBER, 1962

Hurt John D 415 New Bern Av	TE4-7430
Hurt John W Old Wake Forest Rd	833-1253

DECEMBER, 1963

Hurt John D 201 Hillsbro	834-7430
Hurt John W Old Wake Forest Rd	833-1253

Why Southern Bell would have provided incorrect information, or how they could have made such a gross mistake, is uncertain. Other than identifying the second telephone number as belonging to one "John W. Hurt of [Old Wake] Forest Road in Raleigh, North Carolina," the Brady report does not supply any information about that number. Subsequent attempts to trace John W. Hurt have proven fruitless.

The first number, however, presents less of a mystery. I dialed the number and spoke at some length with a man who identified himself as **John David Hurt**. The most tantalizing aspect of this Mr. Hurt is that he was a U.S. Army Counterintelligence officer during World War II. Mr. Hurt acknowledged this wartime service, but denied ever having been anything other than an insurance investigator and an employee of the State of North Carolina since the war.

Hurt denied that he made or received a call to or from the Dallas jail or Lee Harvey Oswald. When asked if he knew of any reason why Lee Harvey Oswald would wish to call him, he said, "I do not. I never heard of the man before President Kennedy's death." Mr. Hurt professed to having been a "great Kennedyphile," and said he "would have been more inclined to kill" Oswald than anything else. Asked if he had any explanation as to why his name and telephone number should turn up this way, he said, "None whatever."

The Secret Service took an interest in someone named Hurt on 23 November 1963. In a statement from former agent **Abraham Bolden**, who was duty officer for the Secret Service's Chicago office that weekend, he claims that the Dallas Secret Service office called him late on the 23rd and asked for a rundown on any phonetic spelling of "Hurt" or "Heard." Obviously, something happened in Dallas that day to cause such a far-flung investigation all the way to Chicago. Whether this was because of Oswald's interest in a party named "Hurt" or because of a crank call into the Dallas jail is still unknown."

General Time Shift in Listing from CST to EST

8:15 PM   **Autopsy on JFK at Bethesda Hospital.** Among those who participate in or witness the autopsy of President Kennedy's body are the following individuals: Dr. **Thornton Boswell**, Bethesda's chief of pathology; Dr. **George Burkley**, chief medical officer of the White House and President Kennedy's personal physician; Dr. **Robert Canada**; **Jerrol F. Custer; Dennis David; Dr. John Ebersole; Dr. Pierre Finck; Dr. Calvin Galloway; Dr. James J. Humes; James E. Metzler; Paul K. O'Connor; Edward Reed; Floyd A. Riebe**; and **Jan Gail Rudnicki**. Many researchers believe that many more people were in the autopsy room, including a number of civilians who sat in the gallery overlooking it, than have been identified in official reports. A Dr. **George Bakeman** is listed in the autopsy report as being among those present in the room when the President's body is examined, but no information exists regarding who he is.

AUTOPSY—The three military physicians who perform JFK's autopsy are clinical pathologists with little experience in gunshot wounds. Neither Navy Cdr. **James J. Humes** nor Navy Cdr. **J. Thornton Boswell** has practical, firsthand experience with bullet wounds. Army Lt. Col. **Pierre Finck** does have some such experience, but he later says he was hampered in his autopsy procedures by officials in the room. The military autopsy doctors apparently are surrounded by both military and civilian superiors who direct much of the autopsy— some of this direction going against normal autopsy procedures.

Additionally chief pathologist, Dr. **James Humes**, said (*in 1964, in 1978, and again in 1996*) that photographs were taken of the interior of JFK's chest during the autopsy. Agreeing with this statement are **Drs. J. Thornton Boswell** and **Robert Karnei—also John Stringer and Floyd Riebe**) There are no such images listed in the official inventory at the National Archives. Pierre Finck swore to the HSCA in 1978, and to the Assassination Records Review Board in 1996, that photographs he took of JFK's skull wound—showing the characteristic features of cratering, or "beveling," that demonstrate direction of the bullet's path in bone—also never made it to the official National Archives inventory.

Review Board documents additionally reveal that the HSCA misstated the opinions of the autopsy witnesses it interviewed. These witnesses never endorsed the wounds as depicted in the autopsy photographs. By both word and by hand-prepared diagrams, the autopsy witnesses independently, and overwhelmingly, corroborate the Dallas physicians' claims that JFK's skull defect was rearward.

Editors of the quarterly *Current Medicine for Attorneys* will write: "The question is, was President Kennedy 'impaired for public life' when he ran for office—by reason of adrenal pathology? Certainly the absence of findings in the autopsy on this point suggest that he was." Obviously an autopsy report which has been influenced by political considerations and about which officials responsible refuse to provide clarification requested by reputable sources cannot be regarded as an authoritative document in the reconstruction of the crime.

Dr. John Walsh, Jackie Kennedy's obstetrician, arrives at Bethesda and quickly notices the unmistakable signs of nervous exhaustion in the widow. Jackie says *"Maybe you could give me something so I could have a little nap."* Walsh proceeds to inject her with 100 milligrams of Visatril. The dose has no effect. Walsh thinks *"I might just as well have given her a shot of Coca-Cola."*

NOTE: Prior to the beginning of the autopsy, **Dr. Robert B. Livingston** telephones **Dr. Humes** and informs him that JFK's front neck wound is probably an entry wound. Dr. Humes, however, does not probe or dissect the neck wound to determine its nature or direction. Humes tells Livingston that he has to terminate the telephone conversation because FBI agents will not let him continue.

8:50 PM   Secret Service gives bullet **CE-399** to FBI lab.

9:00 PM   **Jack Ruby** is reported to be back at his apartment.

9:10 PM   **Oswald** is formally advised that he has been charged with the murder of Patrolman J. D. Tippit.

9:30 PM   New Orleans FBI chief, **Harry Maynor**, contacts **Alan Belmont** at FBI headquarters about how much he should continue to persist in efforts to locate Klan members who might possibly have been involved with the assassination. Belmont gives a somewhat ambivalent answer, being *"somewhat reluctant"* to authorize direct interviews with such suspects, unless their *"whereabouts"* can not be determined by other means, and unless such interviews can be done without *"any repercussions from such contact."* It is perhaps noteworthy that **J. Edgar Hoover** has already identified LHO as being the sole assassination suspect [lone nut]. There is <u>great</u> reluctance on the part of agents to go against Hoover's assumption. Any leads or revelations to the contrary can now only embarrass the FBI Director.

10:00 PM   **Jack Ruby** visits a Dallas synagogue for religious services.

Two bullet *fragments* are found in JFK limo.

10:30 PM   A *Cubana Airlines* flight from Mexico City to Cuba has been delayed for *four hours and ten minutes*, awaiting a passenger. The airfield at Mexico City has been particularly clogged with Cuban diplomatic personnel. The passenger arrives and boards the private twin-engine plane. He gets onto the flight directly without having to go through customs. Once aboard, he enters the cockpit of the aircraft and remains there during the entire flight to Havana. No other passengers see him well enough to be able later to identify him. He is believed to be one **Miguel Casas Saez**. According to the CIA, Casas was born in Cuba, is either twenty-one or twenty-seven, 5'5" in height, weighs 155 lbs., speaks Russian and is an ardent admirer of **Raul Castro**, the brother of the Cuban premier. He is also believed to be part of the Cuban intelligence service. Using the name of **Angel Dominiguez Martinez**, Casas is believed to have entered the USA in early November in Miami. (*One source in a CIA document reports that Casas was on "**a sabotage and espionage mission**" in the United States. Further CIA sources in Cuba report that Casas was in Dallas, Texas on the day of the assassination.*)

The HSCA will later conclude that it had been alleged that the flight was delayed 5 hours, awaiting the arrival at 9:30 PM of a private twin-engine aircraft. The aircraft was supposed to have deposited an unidentified passenger who boarded the Cubans flight without clearing customs and traveled to Havana in the pilot's cabin. The Senate committee reported that the Cubana flight departed at 10 PM This committee checked the times of key events that night by reviewing extensive investigative agency documents. It found the following facts: The Cubana flight was on the ground in Mexico City for a total of only about 4 hours and 10 minutes and thus could not have been delayed five hours. The Cubana flight had departed for Havana at 8:30 PM, about an hour before the arrival of the private aircraft reportedly carrying a mysterious passenger, so he could not have taken the flight. The committee found that extensive records of flight arrivals and departures at the Mexico City airport were available and deemed it doubtful that the alleged transfer of a passenger from a private aircraft to the Cubana flight could have gone unnoticed, had it occurred. The committee concluded, therefore, that the transfer did not occur.

Jack Ruby has the Nichols parking garage attendant sign a receipt that **Karen Carlin** was given $5 at 9:30 PM.

11:00 PM   **Jack Ruby** is back at Dallas Police Headquarters armed with about a dozen sandwiches he has bought to give to officers.

In Washington, **Arthur Schlesinger, Jr.** comes into the White House to join others who are now gathering there. *"What kind of country is this?"* Schlesinger asks through his tears. *"Those who preached hate and violence, the far right. This was their doing. Our fault was that we had never taken them seriously."*

11:45 PM   The supposed assassination rifle is released to the FBI by the Dallas Police. On Saturday morning (*tomorrow*) it will be examined at the FBI Laboratory in Washington, D.C., by FBI fingerprint expert **Sebastian F. Latona.**

12:00 PM   **Dr. Humes** states autopsy results—*two shots from the rear*.

NOTE: Of the **26** people present at the JFK autopsy in Bethesda, Maryland, **22** were never shown the resulting X-rays or autopsy photographs. No one saw the photographs at the autopsy. In fact, *NONE* of the doctors even remotely agreed with the photographs when they were later viewed. According to **Jerrol Custer**, the hospital technician who made the X-rays of JFK:

"The next day I was placed in a room in the X-ray department with a portable X-ray machine and films, and was told to take X-ray films of bones of the skull with bullet fragments on them. I was ordered by **Dr. Ebersole** to complete this duty—so that a bust of the President's head could be made. These fragments were brought to me the next day by Dr. Ebersole."

Following JFK's autopsy, **Robert Bouck**, an employee of the Protective Research Section of the Treasury Department, signs a receipt that reads *"One receipt from FBI for a missile removed during the examination of the body."* This corroborates the memo written by FBI agents **Francis O'Neill** and **James Sibert** that a bullet was removed from JFK's body during the autopsy. *Officially, no such bullet exists*.

NOTE: Secret Service agent **Elmer Moore** will later tell one **Jim Gochenaur** how he was in charge of the Dallas doctors eventual testimony in the JFK case. One of his assignments, as liaison for the Warren Commission, seems to have been talking **Dr. Malcolm Perry** out of his original statement that JFK's throat wound was one of entry, which would have indicated an assassin in front of Kennedy. But another thing Gouchenaur related in his Church Committee interview, Gouchenaur also described the tirade SS Agent Moore went into the longer he talked to him: how Kennedy was a pinko who was selling us out to the communists. This went on for hours. Gochenaur was actually frightened by the time Moore drove him home.

Within the next few minutes tonight, Dallas District Attorney **Henry Wade** replies to a reporter who asks the make of the rifle supposedly used to murder the President. Wade answers: *"It's a **Mauser**, I believe."* Wade later admits that he publicly identified the rifle as a Mauser, on the basis of secondhand information from someone. The Warren Commission will never ask who that *"someone"* was.

23 November 1963

12:01 AM   Pertinent physical evidence in the case involving Oswald and the slaying of JFK is turned over to **Mr. Vince Drain** of the FBI to be delivered in person to the FBI laboratory in Washington, D.C. for processing.

Death certificate drafted for JFK by **Dr. George Burkley**. This is one day before Burkley verifies the autopsy face sheet (*Boswell's drawings*).

A <u>second</u> search of Oswald's belongings in a garage of the Paine home in Irving, Texas reveals **two** prints and **one** negative of pictures showing Lee Harvey Oswald standing in his backyard wearing a holstered pistol and holding a rifle and some communist literature. These eventually become known as the *"backyard photographs."* <u>It is interesting to continually note that the chain of possession of evidence in this case, so vital to any possible court proceeding, is broken in virtually every instance.</u>

Shortly after midnight, **Lee Harvey Oswald** faces the press for the first time in a basement assembly room at police headquarters. **Jack Ruby** mingles in the crowd, correcting District Attorney **Henry Wade**'s explanation that Oswald is a member of the *"Free Cuba Committee"* by shouting out: *"Henry, that's the Fair Play for Cuba Committee."*

Ronald Jenkins testifies that no identifications are checked for the midnight press conference and that press cards are lying on the table for anyone's access. **Thayer Waldo**, the first journalist to arrive at headquarters, agrees with Jenkins' assessment that anyone could have wandered into the press conference, which **Seth Kantor** describes as *"something akin, I guess, to something you might conjure up for the Middle Ages."*

12:20 AM   **(23 November) Lee Harvey Oswald** is placed in a maximum-security cell on the fifth floor of the Dallas jail.

12:35 AM   **(23 November)** Cabinet's plane lands at Andrews Air Force Base.

At a motel in Irving, Texas (*about fifteen miles away from Dallas*) **Marina** and **Marguerite Oswald** seek refuge from the hundreds of reporters assigned to the story.

Also on this date, **William Somersett** and **Joseph Milteer** meet at Union Station in Jacksonville, Florida. Milteer has just come from Dallas and is jubilant over the assassination. He brags to

Somersett that *"everything ran true to form. I guess you thought I was kidding when I said he would be killed from a window with a high-powered rifle."*

At around 1:30 AM, Lee Harvey Oswald is formally charged with murdering President John F. Kennedy. LHO is awakened in his cell and brought before the judge. Judge **J. P. Johnson** pens across the bottom of statement charging LHO: **"1:35 AM 11-23-63. Bond hearing—defendant remanded to Sheriff, Dallas County, Texas. No Bond—Capital offense**." (LHO had the legal right to be transferred *"forthwith."*) LHO listens, and says: *"I don't know what you're talking about."* Johnson tells him: *"You will be given the opportunity to contact the lawyer of your choice."* LHO has asked for **John Abt** of New York almost all day. LHO adds that if Abt is unavailable he will accept the services of a Dallas American Civil Liberties Union lawyer. LHO is irritated. He has pleaded for legal assistance for the past eight hours. He has begged for it at a press conference. He has phoned for it. He is still unrepresented. Judge Johnson will swear before the Commission on the Assassination of President Kennedy that he apprised LHO of his constitutional right *"again."* Chief **Jesse Curry**, a witness, will eventually swear: *"I do not recall whether he did or not."* The American Civil Liberties Union has earlier contacted the police in an attempt to protect LHO's rights. They have been told by the police that LHO has declined the services of a lawyer.

At the Navy Hospital, the body of JFK is now ready for burial. It has been prepared by employees of Gawler's funeral home. The morticians are certain that the only scalp missing on the corpse was in the back of the head. The gap was just about the size of an orange. Eventually, in at least one autopsy photograph, the scalp will appear in place—seemingly intact. **Tom Robinson**, one of the morticians, will also eventually say that there is a small hole in JFK's right forehead that he filled with wax. He will also testify that there are three small holes in JFK's cheek, which he also plugged to prevent leakage of the embalming fluid. The description of the hole in the back of JFK's head will be repeated by **John Van Hoesen**, another of the undertakers, who will say that the hole was the size of an orange in *". . . the centerline of the back of the head, and its location was in the upper posterior of the skull. . . at or just below the cowlick area."*

3:30 AM   **(23 November)** (*Washington*) President LBJ goes to bed.

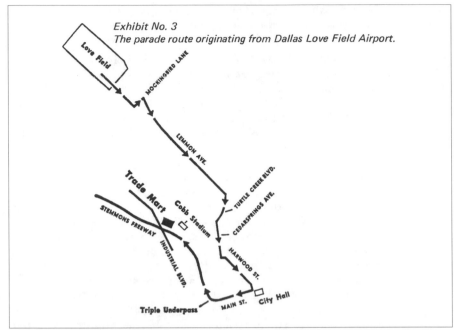

Exhibit No. 3
The parade route originating from Dallas Love Field Airport.

The published motorcade route, which does not include the turn from Main to Houston and from Houston to Elm. [Editor's note: *From Jesse Curry,* JFK Assassination File *(1969), which is discussed elsewhere in this volume.*]

James H. Fetzer, Ph.D., and Chauncey Holt
near San Diego, California, on 13 June 1997.
[Editor's note: *See* Newsweek *(23 December 1991), pp. 52-54.]*

59 Witnesses:
Delay on Elm Street

Vincent Palamara

[*Editor's note*: Vincent Palamara has been immersed in the study of the assassination since his youth, but became a serious student of the case in 1988, the 25th observance of the death of JFK. He has undertaken extensive research on at least three aspects of the case, including the role of the Secret Service, the medical evidence, and eyewitness reports of events in Dealey Plaza. In this study, Palamara summarizes the reports of 59 witnesses who reported observing the Presidential limousine either slowing dramatically or coming to a complete halt after bullets began to be fired. This supports allegations that photographic evidence, including the Zapruder film, has been subjected to extensive alteration, and also reflects the level of protection that the Secret Service provided JFK that day. Specifically, if the eyewitnesses are correct, then, since the Zapruder film does not include frames that correspond to their reports, those frames—at the very least—must have been excised from the film. Moreover, since eyewitness testimony is required in courts of law to establish the admissability of photographs and films, as the Prologue explains, conflicts between them are to be resolved in favor of the eyewitnesses.]

> *"In the right hand picture* (a frame from the Muchmore film),
> *the driver slams on the brakes and the police escort pulls up."*
> — UPI's *Four Days* (1964), p. 17

> *"For a chaotic moment, the motorcade*
> *ground to an uncertain halt."*
> — *Newsweek* (12/2/63), p. 2

> *"There was a shocking momentary*
> *stillness, a frozen tableau."*
> — *Time* (11/29/63), p. 23

> *"Incredibly, SA Greer, sensing that something was wrong in*
> *the back of the car, slowed the vehicle to almost a standstill."*
> — Gerald Posner, *Case Closed* (1993), p. 234

> *By turning around the second time and looking at JFK as the*
> *Car slows down, Posner says that "What he [Greer] has done is*
> *inadvertently given Oswald the easiest of the three shots."*
> — *Final Chapter?* (CBS), 11/19/93

119

1. Houston Chronicle reporter **Bo Byers** (riding in the White House Press Bus) twice stated that the Presidential limousine *"almost came to a stop, almost to a dead stop."* In fact he has had nightmares about this [C-SPAN, 11/20/93, Laura Hlavach and Darwin Payne, eds., *Journalists Remember The Kennedy Assassination*; see also *Reporting the Kennedy Assassination*, (1996), p. 34. This book contains transcripts of the same journalists' reunion covered by the C-SPAN program.]

2. ABC reporter **Bob Clark** (riding in the National Press Pool Car) reported on the air that the limousine stopped on Elm Street during the shooting [WFAA-ABC, 11/22/63]

3. UPI White House reporter **Merriman Smith** (riding in the same car as Clark, above): *"The President's car, possibly as much as 150 or 222 yards ahead, seemed to falter briefly"* [UPI story, 11/23/63, as reported in UPI's *Four Days* (1964), p. 32]

4. DPD motorcycle officer **James W. Courson** (one of two mid-motorcade motorcyclists): *"The limousine came to a stop and Mrs. Kennedy was on the back. I noticed that as I came round the corner of Elm. Then the Secret Service agent (Clint Hill) helped push her back in the car, and the motorcade took off at a high rate of speed."* [Larry Sneed, *No More Silence* (1998), p. 129]

5. DPD motorcycle officer **Bobby Joe Dale** (one of two rear mid-motorcade motorcyclists): *"After the shots were fired, the whole motorcade came to a stop. I stood and looked through the plaza noticed there was commotion, and saw people running around his* (JFK's) *car. It started to move, then it slowed again; that's when I saw Mrs. Kennedy coming back on the trunk and another guy (Clint Hill) pushing her back into the car."* [Sneed 1998, p. 134]

6. **Clemon Earl Johnson** (standing on the Triple Overpass above Elm Street): *"You could see it* (the limo) *speed up and then stop, then speed up, and you could see it stop while they* (that is, Clint Hill) *threw Mrs. Kennedy back in the car. Then they just left out of there like a bat of the eye and were just gone."* [Sneed 1998, p. 80]

7. **Malcolm Summers** (standing on the grass on the south side of Elm Street, directly opposite the limo at the time of the head shot): *"There was some hesitation in the caravan itself, a momentary halt, to give the Secret Service man* (Clint Hill) *a chance to catch up with the car and jump on. It seems to me that it started back up by the time he got to the car."* [Sneed 1998, p. 103]

8. NBC reporter **Robert MacNeil** (riding in White House Press Bus): *"The President's driver slammed on the brakes - after the third shot."* [Robert MacNeil, *The Way We Were, 1963: The Year Kennedy Was Shot* (1988), p. 193]

9. AP photographer **Henry Burroughs** (riding in Camera Car #2, the seventh car behind the limo): *"We heard the shots and the motorcade stopped."* [Letter, Burroughs to Palamara, dated 10/14/98]

10. DPD Patrolman **Earle Brown** (standing at the northern end of the Triple Underpass): *"The first I noticed the* (JFK's) *car was when it stopped ... after it made the turn and when the shots were fired, it stopped."* [6H233]

11. DPD motorcycle Officer **Bobby Hargis** (riding inboard to the left rear of the Presidential limo): *"At that time* (immediately before the head shot) *the Presidential car slowed down. I heard somebody say 'Get going.' I felt blood hit me in the face and the Presidential car stopped almost immediately after that."* [6H 294; Fred Newcomb and Perry Adams, *Murder From Within* (1974), p. 71. Also *"That guy* (Greer) *slowed down, maybe his orders was to slow down, slowed down almost to a stop."* Videotaped interview with Mark Oakes, and Ian Griggs, 6/26/95. Like Posner, Hargis feels Greer gave Oswald the chance to kill Kennedy].

12. DPD Sergeant **D. V. Harkness** (standing at the north west corner of the Houston and Main intersection): *"I saw the first shot and the President's car slow(ed) down to almost a stop...I heard the first shot and saw the President's car almost come to a stop and some of the agents (were) piling off the car."* (6H 309]

13. DPD motorcycle Officer **James Chaney** (riding inboard at the right rear of the Presidential limo) stated that the Presidential limousine stopped momentarily after the first shot (according to the testimony of **Mark Lane**; corroborated by the testimony of Chaney's fellow DPD motorcycle Officer **Marrion Baker**). Chaney told Baker that *"at the time, after the shooting, from the time the shot first rang out, the car stopped completely, pulled to the left and stopped...Now I have heard several of them say that Mr. Truly was standing out there, he said it stopped. Several officers said it stopped completely."* [3H266; also 2H44-45 (Lane), referring to Chaney's statement as reported in *The Houston Chronicle*, 11/24/63]

14. DPD motorcycle Officer **Billy Joe Martin** (riding outboard to the left rear of the limo, alongside Hargis) saw JFK's car stop *"just for a moment."* [Newcomb and Adams 1974, p. 71]

15. DPD motorcycle Officer **Douglas L. Jackson** (riding outboard to the right rear of the Presidential limo, alongside Chaney) stated that *"the car just all but stopped just a moment ."* [Newcomb and Adams 1974, p. 71]

16. Texas Highway Patrolman **Joe Henry Rich** (driver of LBJ's Secret Service car, three cars behind the Presidential limo) stated that *"the motorcade came to a stop momentarily."* [Newcomb and Adams 1974, p. 71]

17. DPD Patrolmen **J. W. Foster** (standing on the Triple Underpass above Elm Street) stated that *"immediately after President Kennedy was struck, the car in which he was riding pulled to the kerb"* [CD-897, pp. 20-21; Newcomb and Adams 1974, p. 97]

18. Secret Service Agent **Sam Kinney** (driver of the follow-up car behind JFK's limo) indicates, via his report to Chief Rowley, that Greer hit the gas after the fatal head shot to JFK and after the President's slump to the left towards Jackie [18H 731-732]. From the HSCA's 2/26/78 interview of Kinney: "He

also remarked that "*when Greer* (the driver of the Presidential limousine) *looked back, his foot must have come off the accelerator.*" Kinney observed that at the time of the first shot, the speed of the motorcade was "*3 to 5 miles an hour.*" [RIF#180-10078-10493; author's interviews with Kinney, 1992-94]

19. Secret Service Agent **Clint Hill** (standing on the left running board of follow-up car, rear of limo): *"I jumped from the follow-up car and ran toward the Presidential automobile. I heard a second firecracker type noise. SA Greer had, as I jumped on to the Presidential automobile, accelerated the Presidential automobile forward.*" [18H 742; Nix film; "The Secret Service" and "Inside the Secret Service" videos from 1995]

20. Secret Service Agent **John Ready** (standing on the right running board of follow-up car): *"I heard what sounded like firecrackers going off from my post on the right front running board. The President's car slowed.*" [18H750]

21. Secret Service Agent **Glen Bennett** (riding in follow-up car): after the fatal head shot "*the President's car immediately kicked into high gear.*" [18H 760; 24H 541-542] During his 1/30/78 HSCA interview, Bennett said that the follow-up car was moving at "*10-12 mph*"—an indication of the pace of the motorcade on Elm Street. [RIF#180-10082-10452]

22. Secret Service Agent **Thomas "Lem" Johns** (riding in Vice-Presidential follow-up car): *"I felt that if there was a danger (it was) due to the slow speed of the automobile.*" [18H 774] During his 8/8/78 HSCA interview, Johns said that "*our car was moving very slowly*"—a similar indication to SA Bennett's of the pace of the motorcade on Elm Street. [RIF#180-10074-10079; Altgens photograph]

23. Secret Service Agent **Winston Lawson** (riding in the lead car, immediately in front of the Presidential limousine): *"I think it* (the lead car on Elm Street) *was a little further ahead* (of JFK's limo) *than it had been in the motorcade, because when I looked back we were further ahead.*" [4H352]--an indication of the lag in the limo during the assassination.

24. Secret Service Agent **William "Tim" McIntyre** (standing on left running board of the follow-up car immediately behind SA Hill) stated that "*Greer, driver of the Presidential limousine, accelerated after the third shot.*" [RIF#18010082-10454; 1/31/78 HSCA interview]

25. **Mrs. Earle ("Dearie") Cabell** (riding in the Mayor's car, four cars behind JFK): *"I was aware that the motorcade stopped dead still...when the sound of the shot was heard."* [7H 487; Sylvia Meagher, *Accessories After The Fact* (1967), p. 4; Newcomb and Adams 1974, p. 71]

26. **Phil Willis** (standing at the southwest corner of Elm and Houston, opposite the TSBD): "*The* (Presidential) *party had come to a temporary halt before proceeding on to the underpass.*" [7H 497; Jim Marrs, *Crossfire* (1989), p. 24]

27. **Mrs. Phil (Marilyn) Willis** (standing close to her husband, Phil Willis): after the fatal head shot she stated *"the Presidential limousine momentarily paused and then sped away under the Triple Underpass."* [FBI report dated 6/19/64; Harold Weisberg, *Photographic Whitewash* (1967), p. 179]

28. **Mrs. John (Nellie) Connally** (riding in JFK's limo): stated that JFK's car did not accelerate until after the fatal head shot [4H 11147; *The Warren Report* (1964), p. 50; David Lifton, *Best Evidence* (1988), p. 122]

29. **Texas Governor John Connally** (riding in JFK's limo and was himself a victim of the shooting): *"After the third shot, I heard Roy Kellerman tell the driver 'Bill, get out of line.' And then I saw him move, and I assumed he was moving a button or something on the panel of the automobile, and he said 'Get us to a hospital quick.' At about this time we began to pull out of the cavalcade, out of line."* [4H 133; *The Warren Report* (1964), p. 50; Marrs 1989, p. 13]

30. *Dallas Morning News* reporter **Robert Baskin** (riding in the National Press Pool Car) stated that *"the motorcade ground to a halt."* [*The Dallas Morning News* (11/23/63), p. 2; Newcomb and Adams (1974), p. 71]

31. *Dallas Morning News* reporter **Mary Woodward** (standing on the north side of Elm, a few yards east of the Stemmons sign): *"Instead of speeding up the car, the car came to a halt."* She saw the car come to a halt after the first shot. Then, after hearing two more shots, close together, the car sped up. [2H43 (Lane); *The Dallas Morning News* (11/23/63); 24H 520; "The Men Who Killed Kennedy" (1988 video)] She spoke forcefully about the car almost coming to a stop and the lack of proper reaction by the Secret Service in 1993. [C-SPAN, 11/20/93, "Journalists Remember The Kennedy Assassination"; see also *Reporting the Kennedy Assassination*, p. 42]

32. AP photographer **James Altgens**: *"He said the President's car was proceeding at about ten miles per hour at the time* (of the shooting). *Altgens stated the driver of the Presidential limousine apparently realized what had happened and speeded up toward the Stemmons Expressway."* [FBI report dated 6/5/64; Weisberg 1967, p. 203; *"The car's driver realized what had happened and almost by reflex speeded up toward the Stemmons Expressway."* [AP dispatch, 11/22/63; Stewart Galanor, *Cover Up* (1998), Document 28]

33. **Alan Smith** (according to a man claiming to be "Alan Smith", interviewed by Ian Griggs in 1992, he was standing inside the northern pergola, close to the Hesters): *"The car was ten feet from me when a bullet hit the President in the forehead...the car went about five feet and stopped."* [*The Chicago Tribune* (11/23/63), p. 9; Newcomb and Adams (1974), p. 71]

34. **Mrs. Ruth M. Smith** (watching from a window on the 2nd floor of the Old Court House): confirmed that the Presidential limousine had come to a stop. [CD 206, p. 9; Newcomb and Adams (1974), p. 97]

35. TSBD supervisor **Roy Truly** (standing in front of the TSBD) said that after the first shot *"I saw the President's car swerve to the left and stop*

somewheres down in this area." [3H 221 (Truly)]; also *"Mr. Truly was stand-ing out there, he said it stopped."* [3H266 (**Marrion Baker**)]

36. **L. R. Terry** (standing on north side of Elm, midway between the TSBD and the Stemmons sign): *"The parade stopped right in front of the building (TSBD)."* [Marrs 1998, p. 26]

37. **Ochus V. Campbell** (standing in front of TSBD): after hearing shots *"he then observed the car bearing President Kennedy to slow down, a near stop, and a motorcycle policeman rushed up. Immediately following this, he observed the car rush away from the scene."* [22H845 (FBI report)]

38. **Peggy Joyce Hawkins** (standing on the front steps of the TSBD) *"estimated that the President's car was less than fifty feet away from her when he was shot, that the car slowed down, almost coming to a stop."* [Newcomb and Adams 1974, p. 97]

39. **Billy Lovelady** (standing on the front steps of the TSBD): *"I recall that following the shooting, I ran toward the spot where President Kennedy's car had stopped.""* [22H662]

40. **An unnamed witness** (from his vantage point in the Courthouse building): stated that *"The cavalcade stopped there and there was bedlam."* [*The Dallas Times Herald* (11/24/63); Newcomb and Adams (1974), p. 97]

41. Postal Inspector **Harry D. Holmes** (from a window on the top floor of the Post Office Annex, while viewing through binoculars): *"The car almost came to a stop, and Mrs. Kennedy pulled loose of him and crawled out over the turtleback of this Presidential car."* [7H291] He noticed the car pull to a halt, and Holmes thought: *"They are dodging something being thrown."* [Jim Bishop, *The Day Kennedy Was Shot* (1967), p. 176]

42. Jennifer Junior (Zapruder) employee **Peggy Burney** (standing on north side of Elm, exact location not certain) stated that *"JFK's car had come to a stop."* [*The Dallas Times Herald*, 11/24/63; Newcomb and Adams 1974, p. 97. Interestingly, during the C-SPAN "Journalists Remember" conference (11/20/93), Vivian Castleberry of *The Dallas Times Herald* made the claim that her first cousin, Peggy Burney, had been Abraham Zapruder's direct assis-tant and was standing next to him when he shot the famous film and was holding some of his photographic equipment even while he shot it. [See Sheldon Inkol's article, *The Fourth Decade* (January 1994); see also *Report-ing the Kennedy Assassination*, pp. 55-56]

43. *Washington Evening Star* reporter **David Broden** (in one of the White House press buses): *"The President's car paused momentarily, then on orders from a Secret Service agent, spurted ahead."* [*The Washington Evening Star* (11/23/63), p. 8]

44. **Sam Holland** (standing on Triple Underpass above Elm Street): stated that *"the Presidential limousine slowed down on Elm Street."* [taped interview with Holland, April 1965]

45. **Maurice Orr** (standing on north side of Elm; exact position uncertain; possibly on the concrete steps?) noted that *"the motorcade stopped."* [Arch Kimbrough, Mary Ferrell, and Sue Fitch Chronology, unpublished manuscript; see also Anthony Summers, *Conspiracy* (1989), p. 20 and 23]

46. TSBD employee **Mrs. Herman (Billie P.) Clay** (standing on north side of Elm 50 yards west of TSBD): *"When I heard the second and third shots I knew someone was shooting at the President. I did not know if the President had been hit, but I knew something was wrong. At this point the car President Kennedy was in slowed, and I along with others, moved toward the President's car. As we neared the car it sped off."* [22H641 (FBI report)]

47. Deputy District Court Clerk **Rose Clark** (watching from second-floor window in the Dallas County Courts Building): *"She noticed that the President's automobile came almost to a halt following the three shots, before it picked up speed and drove away."* [24H533 (FBI report)]

48. **Hugh Betzner** (running down Elm from Houston, just behind and to the left of the Presidential follow-up car): *"I looked down the street and could see the President's scar and another one and they looked like the cars were stopped...Then the President's car sped on under the underpass."* [24H467 (statement, 11/22/63)]

49. **John Chism** (standing on north side of Elm, by Stemmons sign): after the shots he saw *"the motorcade beginning to speed up."* [Marrs 1989, p. 29]

50. **Bill Newman** (standing on the north side of Elm, a few yards west of Stemmons sign): *"the car momentarily stopped and the driver seemed to have a radio or phone up to his ear and he seemed to be waiting on some word. Some Secret Service men reached into their car and came out with some sort of machine gun. Then the cars roared off."* [Marrs 1989, p. 70]; *"I believe Kennedy's car came to a full stop after the final shot."* [Bill Sloan, *JFK: Breaking The Silence* (1993), p. 169; *"I believe it was the passenger in the front seat* (SA Roy Kellerman)—*there were two men in the front seat—had a telephone or something to his ear and the car momentarily stopped. Now everywhere that you read about it, you don't read anything about the car stopping. And when I say 'stopped' I mean very momentarily, like they hit the brakes and just a few seconds passed and then they floorboarded and accelerated on."* [11/12/97 videotaped interview with William Law, Mark Rowe, and Ian Griggs, as transcribed in Connie Kritzberg and Larry Hancock, *November Patriots* (1998), p. 362, and also in *The Dealey Plaza Echo* (March 1998), p. 7] **"One of the two men in the front seat of the car had a telephone in his hand, and as I was looking back at the car, covering my son, I can remember seeing the tail lights of the car, and just for a moment they hesitated and stopped, and then they floorboarded the car and shot off."** [Sneed 1998, p. 96]

51. **Charles Brehm** (standing on the south side of Elm, opposite Zapruder): *"Brehm expressed his opinion that between the first and third shots, the President's car only seemed to move some ten or twelve feet. It seemed to*

him that the automobile almost came to a halt after the first shot. After the third shot, the car in which the President was riding increased its speed and went under the freeway overpass and out of sight." [22H837-838 (FBI report)]

52. **Mary Moorman** (standing on the south side of Elm, 3 yards west of Brehm): *"She recalls that the President's automobile was moving at the time she took the second picture, and when she heard the shots, and has the impression that the car either stopped momentarily or hesitated and then drove off in a hurry."* [22H838-839 (FBI report)]

53. **Jean Hill** (standing on the south side of Elm Street, just to the right of Moorman): *"The motorcade came to almost a halt at the time the shots rang out and I would say it* (JFK's limo) *was just approximately, if not—it couldn't have been in the same position, I'm sure it wasn't, but just a very, very short distance from where it had been. It was just almost stunned."* [6H 208-209] Hill's testimony on this matter was dramatized in the Oliver Stone movie *JFK* (1991) when she said *"The driver had stopped— I don't know what was wrong with that driver."* See also Oliver Stone and Zachary Sklar, *JFK: The Book of the Film* (1992), p. 122, wherein is referenced a 1991 conversation with Jean Hill.

54. Railroad Inspector **James Leon Simmons** (standing on the Triple Underpass above center of Elm Street): *"The car stopped or almost stopped."* [2/15/69 Clay Shaw trial testimony; Penn Jones, *Forgive My Grief*, Vol. III (1969), p. 53; Robert Groden and Harrison Livingstone, *High Treason* (1990), p. 22.]

55. **Norman Similas** (claimed to be standing on north side of Elm Street 'less than seven feet (from) the assassination): *"The Presidential limousine had passed me and slowed down slightly."* [*Liberty Magazine* (7/15/64), p. 13; Weisberg (1967), p. 233]

56. Presidential Aide **Ken O'Donnell** (riding in the Presidential follow-up car): *"If the Secret Service men in the front had reacted quicker to the first two shots at the President's car, if the driver had stepped on the gas before instead of after the fatal third shot was fired, would President Kennedy be alive today?"* [as quoted in Marrs 1989, p. 248, based on a passage from Ken O'Donnell and David Powers, *Johnny, We Hardly Knew Ye* (1972), where O'Donnell also reports that *"Greer had been remorseful all day, feeling that he could have saved President Kennedy's life by swerving the car or speeding suddenly after the first shots."* (O'Donnell and Powers 1972, p. 44). Indeed, William E. Sale, an Airman First Class aircraft mechanic assigned to Carswell AFB, who was stationed at Love Field before, during, and after the assassination, stated that *"when the agent who was driving JFK's car came back to Air Force One he was as white as a ghost and had to be helped back to the plane."* [Undated letter by Sale, provided to the author by researcher Martin Shackelford.]

57. Presidential Aide **Dave Powers** (riding next to O'Donnell in the follow-up car): *"At that time we were travelling very slowly. At about the time of the*

third shot, the President's car accelerated sharply." [7H473-475. On 11/22/88, Powers was interviewed by CBS' Charles Kuralt. Powers remarked about the remorse Greer felt about not speeding up in time to save JFK's life and agreed with Kuralt that if Greer had sped up before the fatal head shot instead of afterwards, JFK might still be alive today (CBS, 11/22/88—a very dramatic and compelling short interview). If that were not enough, the ARRB's Thomas Samoluk told me that during the course of an interview he conducted in 1996, in which the Board was in the process of obtaining Powers' film, Powers said that he agreed with my take on the Secret Service!]

58. Texas Senator **Ralph Yarborough** (riding in LBJ's car, two cards behind JFK): *"When the noise of the shot was heard, the motorcade slowed to what seemed to me a complete stop (though it could have been a near stop). After the third shot was fired, but only after the third shot was fired, the cavalcade speeded up, gained speed rapidly, and roared away to the Parkland Hospital."* [7H440— Affidavit of 7/10/64] *"The cars all stopped. I put in there* (the Affidavit) *'I don't want to hurt anyone's feelings but for the protection of future Presidents, they (the Secret Service) should be trained to take off when a shot is fired."* [Marrs 1989, p. 482. See also the 1988 video *The Men Who Killed Kennedy,* wherein Yarborough states: "The Secret Service in the car in front of us kind of casually looked around and were rather slow to react."]

59. First Lady **Jacqueline Kennedy** (riding beside JFK in the limo): *"We could see a tunnel in front of us. Everything was really slow then (immediately after the shooting) . . . and just being down in the car with his head in my lap. And it just seemed an eternity. . . And finally I remember a voice behind me, or something, and then I remember the people in the front seat, or somebody, finally knew something was wrong, and a voice yelling, which must have been Mr. Hill, 'Get to the hospital,' or maybe it was Mr. Kellerman, in the front seat . . . We were really slowing turning the corner (Houston on to Elm) . . .I remember a sensation of enormous speed, which must have been when we took off . . . . those poor men in the front"* [5H179-181]. Mary Gallagher reported in her book: *"She mentioned one Secret Service man who had not acted during the crucial moment, and said bitterly to me 'He might just as well have been Miss Shaw!'"* [Mary Barelli Gallagher, *My Life with Jacqueline Kennedy* (1969), p. 342]. Secret Service Agent Marty Venker, *Confessions of an Ex-Secret Agent* (1986), p. 15; and and C. David Heymann, *A Woman Called Jackie* (1991), p. 41, confirm that this unnamed agent was indeed William Greer. Jackie also told Gallagher that *"You should get yourself a good driver so that nothing ever happens to you."* [Gallagher 1969, p. 351]. William Manchester, who interviewed Greer, tells us that the driver told Jackie at Parkland Hospital: *"Oh, Mrs. Kennedy, oh my God, oh my God, I didn't mean to do it. I didn't hear. I should have swerved the car. I couldn't help it. Oh, Mrs. Kennedy, as soon as I saw it, I swerved. If only I'd seen it in time! Oh!"* [Willam Manchester, *The Death of a President* (1967), p. 290].

The Summary

Fifty nine witnesses (ten police officers, seven Secret Service Agents, thirty-seven spectators, two Presidential aides, one Senator, one State Governor, and the First Lady of the United States) as well as the Zapruder film [*Editor's note*: An extensive discussion of the Zapruder film and its possible alteration may be found elsewhere in this volume.] document Secret Service Agent William Greer's deceleration of the Presidential limousine, as well as his two separate looks back at JFK during the assassination. (Greer denied all this to the Warren Commission [see his entire testimony at 2H 112-132].)

By decelerating from an already slow 11.2 mph, Greer greatly endangered the President's life and as even Gerald Posner admitted, Greer contributed greatly to the success of the assassination. When we consider that Greer disobeyed a direct order from his superior, Roy Kellerman, to get out of line before the fatal shot struck the President's head, it is hard to give Agent Greer the benefit of the doubt. As ASAIC Roy H. Kellerman said: *"Greer then looked in the back of the car. Maybe he didn't believe me."* [Manchester 1967, p. 160] Clearly, Greer was responsible, at fault, and felt remorse. In short, Greer had survivor's guilt.

Then, however, stories and feelings changed.

* From an FBI report dated 11/22/63: "Greer stated that they (the Secret Service) have always been instructed to keep the motorcade moving at a considerable speed inasmuch as a moving car offers a much more difficult target than a car travelling at a very slow speed" [James Siebert and Francis O'Neill, FBI Report dated 11/22/63].

* From *The Warren Report*: "The Presidential car did not stop or almost come to a halt after the firing of the first shot or any other shots. The driver, Special Agent William R. Greer, has testified that he accelerated the car after what was probably the second shot." [*The Warren Report* (1964), p. 641] [*Editor's note:* But, of course, if the eyewitnesses are correct, the vehicle did come to a halt, the film has been edited, and Greer's testimony is false.]

* From an 11/19/64 interview with William Manchester, who quoted Greer: "After the second shot I glanced back. I saw blood on the Governor's white shirt and I knew we were in trouble. The blood was coming out of his right breast. When I heard the first shot, I thought it was a backfire. I was tramping on the accelerator and at the same time Roy Kellerman was saying, 'Let's get out of here fast.'" [RIF#180-10116-10119]. Remember what SA Roy Kellerman said, however: "Greer then looked in the back of the car. Maybe he didn't believe me." [Manchester 1967, p. 160]

* From a 2/28/78 HSCA interview: "The first shot sounded to him like a backfire. He did not react to it. After the second shot he turned to his right and saw blood on Governor Connally's shirt. At the same time, he heard Kellerman say 'We're hit. Let's get out of here' or words to that effect. He said he immediately accelerated and followed the pilot car to Parkland Hospital. However, DNC Advance man Jack Puterbaugh, who rode in the pilot car, said they "pulled over and let the motorcade pass.'" [HSCA interview, 4/14/78]

Part II

The Kennedy Limousine: Dallas 1963

Douglas Weldon, J.D.

[*Editor's note*: Douglas Weldon, J.D., a Michigan attorney with extensive experience in the investigation of crime, has focused his attention on the Presidential Lincoln limousine as an access route toward understanding the assassination of JFK. Secret Service agents began washing blood and brains from the limousine even before the President had been pronounced dead and, by Monday, 25 November 1963, even though it was a crime scene on wheels that belonged in the Smithsonian, it had been stripped clean of virtually every remnant of the crime. This study vividly displays the kind of knowledge that can be acquired concerning a complex event through the pursuit of a specific line of inquiry by employing intelligence, perseverance, and discipline.]

For those of us who were alive on 22 November 1963, it remains forever a current event embedded in our memories. I was a 10-year-old boy at the time. That fall day defined the beginning of a turbulent era whose ripples continue to be felt today throughout our government and the nation's psyche. A faith and trust in government was lost that only truth can possibly restore.

The Premise

I have studied the assassination of John Fitzgerald Kennedy since 1978. Like anyone who has engaged in a serious examination of the event, I have experienced a mixture of emotions ranging the full gamut from hope to frustration. There is a basic premise that must be the foundation for anyone who pursues the study of those events from 1963. That premise is that if we are to be a democracy then our history deserves truth. It has been stated that history is the myth that people choose to believe. It is time that the myth about what occurred on 22 November 1963 be removed from the folklore of our history.

Most research on the assassination of John F. Kennedy is not new, but rather is an affirmation and corroboration of findings that many dedicated researchers have addressed over the years. The study of the assassination is best analogized by comparing it to a puzzle. If people are willing to critically examine the evidence that exists today and treat each piece of credible evidence as a piece of a puzzle then we, as a nation, would have enough pieces to see a picture emerge from that puzzle. That picture would conclusively show that John Fitzgerald Kennedy, the 35th President of the United States, died as a result of a conspiracy. That conspiracy continues to cast a cloud over the official response of our government and its apologists.

Martin Luther King, Jr., when asked about his lack of patriotism in criticizing the Vietnam War, once responded that he only criticized those things that he cared about and that he loved his country. He criticized his government because he loved his country and knew what it could be. Our country today collectively shares shame by allowing myths to perpetuate and thrive about the events of 22 November 1963. I, like Martin Luther King, Jr., also criticize my government, because I, too, care about my country.

This account will include excerpts from an interview I conducted in 1993. Candidly, I did not appreciate the significance of the information conveyed to me at the time of the interview. Today, I equate what I then thought was an interesting, small piece of the puzzle of the assassination as comparable to what people thought was a small scrape on the side of the *Titanic*. The information obtained that day, combined with an examination of the totality of the evidence, should cause each one of us to reevaluate our thoughts about what happened to our nation with the death of John Fitzgerald Kennedy.

I have personally interviewed many people with connections to the assassination, including a number of members of the Dallas Police Department who played an important role in the events that day. Many members of the Dallas Police Department of 1963 have been unfairly criticized over the ensuing years. We will never know what kind of investigation they would have conducted because they were deprived of the opportunity to examine much of the evidence.

Though I believe it is possible, and perhaps even probable, that some members of the Dallas police may have cooperated with the falsification of evidence or perhaps in a more sinister fashion, the officers I have spoken with were committed to the service of justice. Unfortunately, some members of another group, who also were sworn to have been committed to the same standards of justice and who also had members of their group in Dallas that day, did not permit the legally proper handling of evidence by the Dallas police. The members of that group worked for the United States Secret Service.

Few people would argue against the position that the most important piece of evidence of the crime in Dallas was the President's body. It is well documented that the body was illegally removed by force from Parkland Hospital by the U.S. Secret Service. However, another piece of evidence was also removed that day. That evidence was second in importance only to the body because at the time, despite efforts to do so, it was evidence that could not be altered at the scene in Dallas. [*Editor's note*: An agent was photographed taking a bucket of water and a sponge to wash blood and brains from the back seat as the limousine sat at Parkland. See, for example, Richard Trask, *Pictures of the Pain* (1994), p. 41.] That evidence was also removed illegally from Parkland Hospital. It was also removed by the Secret Service of the United States. That evidence would perhaps have told a different story from what we later heard as the official explanation from our government. I am, of course, referring to the Presidential limousine. That limousine may yet tell us a story today.

The story of the limousine in the aftermath of the assassination is information that has been chronicled in many speeches, books, and articles. It is time to take a fresh look at credible evidence that should cause everyone to consider the evidence presented by the government about the assassination of John Fitzgerald Kennedy in a different light. Two questions need to be addressed. The first question, What happened to the limousine after the assassination and why? Once that question is answered the second question becomes, Can we now provide a reasonable explanation for the origin of the shot that caused the entrance wound to the throat of the President?

The focus of this paper will concentrate on damage done to the windshield. of the Presidential limousine. It will not explore the questions raised by another hole that was alleged to have been in the floor pan or the damage done to the chrome stripping by the windshield. However, these are issues that merit further attention and provide their own questions to be answered.

Background of the Limousine

It is important to understand aspects of the historical background of the limousine that played such an important role in Dallas. Work began on the ill-fated limousine the day before Kennedy's inauguration. Until it was completed, Kennedy used a 1950 Lincoln "bubble-top," which had been used by President Truman and President Eisenhower. Over 21 feet long, this new vehicle was an elongated version of the 1961 Lincoln Continental convertible. It was a result of four years of planning and discussion with the Secret Service and had more specially designed innovations than any automobile ever used by a President.

These features included various roof combinations and a hydraulically controlled rear seat that could be raised and lowered up to 10 inches. It provided a railing to assist the President in standing upright during a parade. The completed limousine also had another unique feature. That feature has been unknown to the public. That feature was a throttle that, when opened, would allow the limousine to maintain a "parade speed" of 10-12 miles per hour.

A standard Lincoln Continental 430-cubic-inch engine provided the power for the new limousine. When completed, it was 3 feet longer than when it left the Lincoln assembly plant in Wixom, Michigan. The original stock vehicle weighed 5,215 pounds and retailed for sale at a price of $7,347. When the modification was completed, it had entailed expenditures of over $200,000, was 3 feet longer and now weighed over 7,800 pounds. Ford Motor Company technicians designed the vehicle in cooperation with Hess & Eisenhardt, one of the oldest custom car body firms in the United States.

Hess & Eisenhardt was located in Cincinnati, Ohio. (In 1980, Hess & Eisenhardt changed its name to Ogara, Hess & Eisenhardt following the retirement of Willard Hess.) Hess & Eisenhardt began work on modifying the automobile in December 1960 and completed their complicated work to the specifications of the Secret Service and the Ford Motor Company in May 1961. The limousine was then returned to the Ford Motor Company in Michigan and, after some additional mechanical modifications, was delivered to the White House in early June 1961 for use by the new President, John F. Kennedy.

The limousine was dubbed the "X-100" by the Secret Service. It is important to note that the limousine was always the property of the Ford Motor Company, which entered into an agreement to lease it to the Secret Service for $500.00 a year. The Ford Motor Company leased the vehicle for such a token amount because of the positive publicity that would be generated by the President using the vehicle in parades and other ceremonial events. It is also very important to observe that this leasing arrangement established a close relationship between the Ford Motor Company and the Secret Service.

The Limousine in Dallas, Texas: November 1963 and After

The vehicle was flown into Texas on a C-130 cargo plane one day prior to Kennedy's arrival for the Texas trip. After President Kennedy was pronounced dead at Parkland Hospital and his body was removed by the Secret Service, the limousine was hurriedly taken away and flown back to Washington D.C. [*Editor's note*: As will become apparent, one of the objectives of this study is to establish the precise disposition of the limousine.]

It is critical to understand that in 1963 there was no federal statute that made it a crime to kill the President of the United States. Legally, this was simply a murder that should have been governed by the statutes of the state of Texas. Texas had the sole authority to investigate the crime, to take evidence into its custody, to perform the autopsy on the deceased President, and to pursue any criminal prosecution that might result therefrom.

The FBI and the Secret Service usurped that Texas authority. Reports surfaced that the President's body was taken by the Secret Service with guns drawn and the exercise of force. Most state statutes today would hold the individuals involved in such actions criminally responsible for obstruction of justice. Furthermore, there exists compelling evidence that certain members of those government agencies engaged in the destruction and fabrication of evidence in a capital crime. Under statutes today, conduct of this kind could carry a sanction of long-term incarceration.

Stories about the Limousine

The government's official version of what happened to the limousine after the assassination appears very simple if one conducts a cursory examination. That "story" alleges that the limousine was flown to Washington D.C. on the evening of 22 November 1963. It then remained in the White House Garage under the supervision of the Secret Service until, according to James Rowley, Chief of the Secret Service, it was *driven* to Dearborn, Michigan—approximately 500 miles—on 20 December 1963 to design a new bubble-top. The vehicle was then supposed to have been driven from Dearborn, Michigan to Hess & Eisenhardt in Cincinnati, Ohio, on 24 December 1963, for the manufacture and installation of the new bullet resistant bubble-top. (*See Appendix C.*)

This was the official account James Rowley provided to Mr. J. Lee Rankin, General Counsel to the Warren Commission in a letter dated 6 January 1964, a version of events which has been suspect for many years, even though proofs to the contrary have not previously emerged in any substantive or detailed form. Other reports have suggested different scenarios as to what happened to the limousine after the assassination. It is important to examine some of these different versions of what allegedly happened to the limousine in the aftermath of the assassination. The fact that such numerous and varying stories exist should by itself cause researchers to scrutinize the reasons why there are such varying accounts for what should be an easily documented history.

The House Select Committee on Assassinations (HSCA), during its tenure from 1976 to 1978, became confused about what happened to the limousine in the aftermath of the assassination. In an examination of 11 specific dates regarding the limousine after the assassination beginning with 22 November 1963, the HSCA noted conspicuous discrepancies in testimony about 4 of those dates as it developed its chronology of the movements of the limousine.

An article published in *Car Exchange* (December 1983) reported that the limousine was delivered to Hess & Eisenhardt around the date of 12 December 1963. In addition, however, the HSCA, in referring to the records of Hess & Eisenhardt, also noted that the vehicle was delivered to Hess & Eisenhardt on 13 December 1963. This date was confirmed to me personally by Willard Hess, one of the owners of the company. Notice that both of these dates drastically contradict the information provided by the Chief of the Secret Service to Mr. Rankin in his letter of 6 January 1964.

Further examination of this issue demonstrates that no record exists anywhere, apart from James Rowley's written assertion to Rankin—and a memorandum by F. Vaughn Ferguson, a Ford employee—that the limousine was driven anywhere immediately after the assassination. (See Appendix D.) Not one newspaper article or radio or television report mentioned the limousine being driven hundreds of miles in the harsh winters of Michigan and Ohio.

Common sense dictates that the Secret Service would not have wanted to chance a breakdown, a flat tire, or even the obvious necessity of refueling it by driving the bloody limousine on the highways or back roads of this country with the risk of inclement weather. An examination of the weather reports reveals that the road conditions were quite treacherous during that period of time. The Chief of the Secret Service, James Rowley, apparently was not telling the truth.

Dr. Charles Crenshaw, a physician present at Parkland Hospital in 1963 when the President was brought in, mortally wounded, advanced another version in his book JFK, *Conspiracy of Silence* (1992). He wrote that:

> three days after the assassination, Carl Renas, head of security for the Dearborn Division of the Ford Motor Company, drives the limousine, helicopters hovering overhead, from Washington to Cincinnati. In doing so, he noted several bullet holes, the most notable being the one on the windshield's chrome molding strip, which he said was clearly "a primary strike" and not a fragment." The limousine was driven by Renas to Hess & Eisenhardt, where the chrome molding was replaced. The Secret Service told Renas to "Keep your mouth shut." Renas recalls thinking at the time, "Something is wrong" (1992, p. 106).

Though again there is no record in any form of media that would support this story, Carl Renas, in this interesting account, should certainly be given credit for being perceptive enough to recognize that something was wrong.

Indeed, in his book, *Cover-Up* (1976), author Gary Shaw had previously observed, "Within 48 hours of the shots in Dealey Plaza the Kennedy death car was shipped to the Ford Motor Company in Detroit and completely destroyed as far as evidence was concerned" (Shaw 1976, p. 59). The late journalist and author Penn Jones, Jr., had documented similar information. And, of course, as F. Vaughn Ferguson's statement conveyed and as the creation of the vehicle itself implied, there was a close connection noted between the Secret Service and the Ford Motor Company.

F. Vaughn Ferguson, a Ford Motor Company employee, has provided one of the most intriguing accounts about the limousine at the White House garage. In a declassified Ford Motor Company interoffice memorandum dated 18 December 1963, Ferguson described the vehicle's presence and work performed on it in the White House Garage from 23 November through 27 November 1963 (Appendix D). His memorandum further implied that he was also there for some days after the 27 November date. He offers specific and sometimes graphic details, such as cleaning blood from the vehicle and actually removing and installing new carpeting.

He subsequently testified that he was the individual that actually drove the limousine to Dearborn, Michigan on 20 December 1963. This story was fairly consistent with what Secret Service Chief James Rowley conveyed to the Warren Commission in his letter to Rankin. However, in one of my interviews with Willard Hess, Hess indicated that this could not have happened and did not happen. Mr. Hess was also shocked that he was only contacted one time by the Warren Commission and only asked a very innocuous question. That contact was the extent of official communications ever made with him by anyone associated with the Warren Commission.

Ferguson's account of his involvement with the limousine also appears to be suspect on other grounds. Two of the four discrepancies noted by the HSCA in relation to its attempted chronology concerned Ferguson's testimony. Indeed, a close examination of the memorandum also reveals some curious findings. Mr. Ferguson described the windshield as he observed it on 23 November 1963 as follows: "Examination of the windshield disclosed no perforation, but substantial cracks radiating a couple of inches from the center of the windshield at a point *directly* (emphasis added) beneath the mirror." I extend an open invitation to anyone to produce a diagram, a report, or a picture showing a crack or other damage at a point directly beneath the mirror. The questions have to be asked: Did Ferguson really see the windshield? Could this be an example of evidence of the cooperation and complicity between the Ford Motor Company and the United States Secret Service to distort the actual record as to what really happened to the limousine upon its return to Washington D.C.?

The White House Garage Logs

The Ferguson memorandum raises other questions. An examination of the White House Garage logs is revealing. Mr. Ferguson's name, for example, does not appear on the logs until 26 November 1963. While this admittedly may not be conclusive of sinister actions, the question must be answered as to what unique status did Ferguson have that it was not required that he be logged in upon his entry to the White House Garage. Did Mr. Ferguson have open access to the White House Garage? It appears that such a procedure of logging in was carefully documented for anyone entering the White House Garage. This documentation would be especially important for 23 November 1963, the date that he first claimed that he examined the vehicle in the White House Garage.

The logs also reveal more critical information. The most significant aspect of the White House Garage logs is the absence of even one person logging in to see the limousine on 25 November 1963. This critical observation becomes of paramount importance when the statement of a witness from the Ford Motor Company, who asserts that he worked on the windshield at Ford on 25 November, is scrutinized. Was the vehicle in the White House Garage on 25 November 1963? Why are there two conflicting stories, with one Ford employee, Carl Renas, alleging that he was driving the car three days after the assassination while another Ford employee, F. Vaughn Ferguson, alleges something totally contradictory?

Ferguson's account is also confusing in light of James Rowley's 6 January 1964 memorandum to Rankin. In that memorandum, Rowley wrote that Secret Service Agent Morgan Geis of the White House Garage detail requested permission to clean the blood from the back seat on 23 November 1963. The reason given was that the odor was bothersome to him. According to Rowley, permission was given to Geis, Special Officer (William) Davis, and White House Police Officer (Andrew) Hutch to remove these bloodstains on late Sunday evening, 24 November 1963 (CD-80). But where was Ferguson at this time? Why did Ferguson document in his memorandum that it was he who cleaned the vehicle? Why did Chief Rowley fail to mention that Ferguson had done anything to clean the limousine? This is another conflict in the record that disturbed the HSCA regarding its chronology of the limousine.

Ferguson's memorandum maintains that the Secret Service cleaned the upholstery on 23 November, not on 24 November, as conveyed by Rowley. Why do Rowley and Ferguson's stories conflict? Ferguson also asserts in his memorandum that the Arlington Glass Company replaced the windshield on the limousine on 25 November 1963. And yet the White House Garage Logs indicate that that was done on 26 November 1963. Was this another error by Ferguson? Why is it that almost every statement in the memorandum contradicts other evidence? Was the 25 November 1963 date used in the memorandum intended to provide a cover for what occurred in Dearborn, Michigan on that same date?

Further Problems with the Evidence

A further review of the evidence is also revealing. Even the Warren Commission in 1964 was again provided with contradictory stories by the Secret Service and the FBI. The confusion they generated was never resolved.

What is clear is that, after the limousine arrived in Washington D.C. on 22 November 1963, the FBI conducted an examination of the vehicle sometime after 1:00 a.m. on 23 November. The FBI team was composed of agents Orrin H. Bartlett, Charles L. Killiam, Cortland Cunningham, Robert A. Frazier, and Walter E. Thomas. The FBI specifically noted in their report of the examination that no bullet holes were found.

Significantly, there were a couple of Secret Service agents who also were part of a report regarding that examination of the windshield. The limousine had departed Parkland Hospital at approximately 2:04 p.m. on 22 November 1963 driven by Secret Service Agent George W. Hickey, Jr. and a Dallas police officer.

It was placed aboard a cargo plane—an Air Force C-130—and flown to Washington. The plane arrived at Andrews Air Force Base at 8:00 p.m. Special Agent Samuel Kinney, accompanied by Agent Charles Taylor, Jr., drove the vehicle under police escort to the White House Garage.

Mr. Taylor would have been in an ideal position to carefully observe any windshield damage. In the report of Secret Service agents Charles Taylor, Jr. and Harry Geiglin, Mr. Taylor, who was present at the same time as the FBI agents, specifically wrote upon observing the windshield that "of particular note was the small hole just left of center from which what appeared to be bullet fragments were removed." Did someone fail to instruct Taylor and Geiglin about what they were to place in their reports? How could Charles Taylor have examined the windshield at the same time as the FBI team and noted startling evidence that is totally opposite to the observations of the FBI team?

Further controversy emerged. A week after the windshield was examined in Washington D. C. on 22 November, the evening of the assassination, a windshield—which might or might not have been the same—was removed from the automobile and stored in the White House garage. Subsequently, in March 1964, at the request of the Warren Commission, the Secret Service would sent a windshield to the FBI laboratory, which determined that it contained no hole but only damage to the outside surface. The inside surface was smooth.

James Rowley, however, in the aforementioned 6 January 1964 letter to the Warren Commission, referred to two other agents who were present when the limousine arrived. It is now believed that the agents he was making reference to were Special Officer William Davis and Special Agent Morgan Geis. It was claimed that they ran their hands over the windshield and the outside surface was "smooth and unbroken." However, neither the report completed by the FBI agents nor Charles Taylor, Jr., makes any mention of these two Secret Service agents! Rowley also omitted in his letter any reference to the hole noted in the report of Charles Taylor, Jr.

Furthermore, Secret Service Agent Roy Kellerman claimed that he examined the windshield on 27 November 1963, allegedly a short time before it was removed from the limousine. Agent Kellerman had been an occupant in the front passenger seat of the Kennedy limousine during the assassination. His examination of the surface of the windshield was consistent with Rowley's assertions about the two other Secret Service agents examination of the windshield (Davis and Geis). Kellerman noted that he ran his hand over the outside of the windshield and found it to be smooth, the opposite of what the later FBI report would show. Kellerman stated that the damage was on the inside surface of the windshield. In Kellerman's mind, such an observation logically indicated a shot from the rear.

Under normal circumstances, such an inference would be correct, had the windshield been constructed with ordinary glass. However, the windshield in the Kennedy limousine on the day of the assassination was made of safety glass. Safety glass responds to an object striking its surface in the opposite way of regular glass. A nontransiting shot at safety glass will leave the outside surface smooth while the inside surface will fragment. Indeed, why would so many individuals run their hands over the windshield, if there clearly was no damage on the outside? If there was damage to the outside, then the obeservations of Agents Kellerman, Geis, and Davis were actually consistent with a shot from the front.

Agent Morgan Geis, on the White House Detail, apparently made the same error after the vehicle had been placed in the White House Garage. According to Jim Bishop, *The Day Kennedy Was Shot* (1968): "When the vehicle was being stored there he [Geis] claimed that he looked across the hood of the car stating, 'Whatever it is, the crack isn't on the outside. This side is smooth'" (Bishop 1968, p. 511)

To further complicate matters, F. Vaughn Ferguson, as noted, wrote in his 18 December 1963 memorandum that personnel from Arlington Glass had removed the windshield from the vehicle on 25 November 1963. His memorandum specifically reports that the windshield was placed in a stockroom under lock and key at the White House Garage. Mr. Ferguson is unequivocal in stating in his memorandum that he had not seen the windshield since 25 November 1963. If this is accurate, however, then how could Agent Roy Kellerman have seen a windshield on 27 November, two days after Ferguson noted that it was placed under lock and key? If Mr. Ferguson's memorandum is accurate in noting that he was at the White House Garage on 27 November and the windshield was locked away, then what windshield did Kellerman see? What was really going on? It is obvious that Ferguson and Kellerman cannot both be right. Who was not telling the truth and why? Is it possible that neither was telling the truth?

When Kellerman testified before the Warren Commission in March 1964, he was asked to run his hand over the *inside* (emphasis added) of the windshield. Incredibly, he then testified to the exact opposite of his original statement, remarking ". . . it feels rather smooth today." This changed statement was now consistent with an object striking the windshield from the rear. Also, it is quite clear that the windshield presented to the Warren Commission did not have any hole going through it (CE-350 and CE-351).

Researcher Robert P. Smith interviewed Bill Ashby, the crew leader of the Arlington Glass Company team. In the interview Mr. Ashby claimed that he removed the windshield from the limousine on 27 November 1963 at the White House Garage. Ashby recalled that the inside surface of the windshield was damaged. What windshield did he remove if Ferguson was correct in noting that the windshield had been already removed and stored on November 25th? And, again, if Mr. Ferguson is credible, why is there no record of anyone, including people from the Arlington Glass Company, coming into the White House garage on that date? Mr. Ashby's story of the Arlington Glass Company is incompatible with Ferguson's memorandum. The White House Garage logs indicate that Ashby came in on November 26, 1963, a date that contradicts both Ferguson and Ashby. How can one make sense of Kellerman's story given all of these contradictions?

Mr. Ferguson also made yet another extremely interesting notation in his memorandum. Coincidentally, just as the FBI agents reported the absence of any holes during their examination, Ferguson made the same observation in his memorandum. Ferguson, for some reason, also made a special effort to note something that he did not see rather than only describe what he did observe. He remarked, "Examination of the windshield disclosed no perforation, but substantial cracks radiating a couple of inches from the center of the windshield at a point directly below the mirror." But there are several problems with Mr. Ferguson's statement. If no perforation existed, why would he even mention such a possibility? In addition, his description of the location of the damage is inconsistent with every other witness, reports done by the FBI and by Charles Taylor, Jr., and Commission Exhibits 350 and 351. In fact, there is no record that tends to corroborate such an observation.

There have been rumors for many years that the Secret Service ordered up to twenty-one windshields for the limousine soon after the assassination. Dr. Robert B. Livingston, M.D., for example, then the Scientific Director of the National Institute for Mental Health and of the National Institute for Neurological Diseases and Blindness, had learned that the Secret Service had obtained a dozen windshields from the Ford Motor Company, allegedly for "target practice." [Editor's note: Dr. Livingston's personal account may be found in Assassination Science (1998), pp. 161–166.] Could this be significant in light of all of these differing stories? Was it necessary to have a number of windshields on hand in an effort to duplicate the approximate damage that was evident in the windshield? It is likely that it would have taken a number of careful efforts to closely duplicate the damage if that was indeed their intent. Indeed, Dr. Livingston has speculated that the number of windshields raises doubt as to whether the windshield in the National Archives was the same windshield on the limousine in Dallas.

Did the Secret Service substitute a windshield with a crack they fabricated and was that the windshield Ashby and Kellerman examined on November 27, 1963? Is that why they describe a windshield with inside damage indicating a shot from the front? Did the Secret Service then realize that safety glass shatters in the opposite direction of regular glass, thus forcing them to again substitute another windshield? Is this why the glass had been described in various ways and why Kellerman's testimony changed? Kellerman could not lie before the Warren Commission about the then-present state of the the windshield, because by that time the Commission members could verify the condition of the then-present glass for themselves.

As an inexplicable irony, William Greer, the driver of the fateful limousine, years and years later, continued to tell some researchers and friends that there had been no damage to the windshield! This is contrary to virtually every piece of evidence that has been proffered by everyone else who was in a position to make observations of its condition.

In an undated letter, but which was apparently mailed in March 1964, J. Lee Rankin, Chief Counsel for the Warren Commission, informed J. Edgar Hoover, Director of the FBI, that the windshield has a "marking which was apparently caused by a hard object hitting the windshield. At this point, the windshield appears to be smooth on both sides." This suggests the possibility that the windshield might have been changed yet again.

There is a picture of the windshield that currently resides in the National Archives in College Park, Maryland, a copy of which appears in the re-release of the Harrison Edward Livingstone's book, High Treason (1998). Do those cracks appear to be the same as those recorded in Warren Commission Exhibits 350 and 351? Generally speaking, it would be virtually impossible to exactly duplicate damage to a windshield each time a windshield is changed, which may account for these apparent discrepancies.

Evidence of a Hole in the Windshield

One of the tests of veracity in our legal system when physical evidence is not available or questionable is independent corroboration. Such corroboration exists here. There are many people who witnessed a hole in the limousine windshield on 22 November 1963 at Parkland Hospital. I consider some of these people heroic because considerable pressure was placed upon them to retract their observations. Several of these people, with whom I have talked directly, remain hesitant to this day to discuss their observations and continue to fear for their personal safety.

Richard Dudman, a reporter for *The St. Louis Post Dispatch*, for example, wrote in an article entitled "Commentary of an Eyewitness" that appeared in *The New Republic* (21 December 1963): "A few of us noticed the hole in the windshield when the limousine was standing at the emergency entrance after the President had been carried inside. I could not approach close enough to see which side was the cup-shaped spot that indicates a bullet had pierced the glass from the opposite side." [*Editor's note*: A copy of Dudman's article appears in *Assassination Science* (1998), p. 167.]

Dudman told interviewers that a Secret Service agent shoved him and the other reporters away when he tried to examine the hole to determine the direction from which it had been fired (Mark Lane, Amherst speech, 1964). It is interesting to note that Dudman became aware of no less than five bullets that were fired in Dealey Plaza that day. Dudman was also critical of the lack of security on the top of the triple overpass, noting that the standing Secret Service orders were to keep the overpass clear. That order was violated that day. He also wrote that: "The south end of the viaduct is four short blocks from the office of *The Dallas Morning News*, where Jack Ruby was seen before and after the shooting. . . . No one remembered for sure seeing Ruby between 12:15 and 12:45. The shooting was at 12:30." Mr. Dudman has declined to discuss the assassination with anyone for many years, while his earlier commentary bears mute witness to his present silence.

Former Dallas Police Officer H.R. Freeman, who rode in the motorcade, noted in a 1971 interview by Gil Toff of his observation of the limousine at Parkland Hospital immediately after the shooting, "I was right beside it. I could have touched it. It was a bullet hole. You could tell what it was." And he was not the only police officer—a type of witness usually prized for his accurate and reliable observations—who saw similar damage to the glass.

Dallas Police Officer Stavis Ellis, who was in charge of the motorcade escort through Dallas, remarked, in later interviews to reporters and on radio programs, "You could put a pencil through it." Over extensive interviews with this author, Mr. Ellis was unequivocal about observing the hole. His recollection was that the hole was lower in the windshield, but he is absolutely certain of its existence. He did describe the hole as being on the driver's side of the rearview mirror, which is consistent with other observations and the photographic evidence. He recalls actually placing a pencil in the hole. He recounted that there were numerous people and police officers at Parkland Hospital who viewed the hole. He vividly remembers that while he was observing the hole a Secret Service agent came up to him and tried to persuade him that he was seeing a "fragment" and not a hole.

Mr. Ellis noted: "It wasn't a damn fragment. It was a hole." Mr. Ellis has been totally consistent with this statement over the years and has not wavered in his insistence that he saw a hole in the windshield immediately after the assassination. Ellis, moreover, had a distinguished career with the United States Army and the Dallas Police.

Stavis Ellis also distinctly recalled another incident at Parkland Memorial Hospital that also occurred outside the hospital on that day, which he found disturbing. When a young boy, who had taken photographs along the motorcade route, took pictures of the limousine at Parkland Hospital, a Secret Service agent grabbed the boy's camera and exposed his film by rolling it out of the camera. Dallas Police Officer James W. Courson, another motorcade officer, corroborated this account of the Secret Service agent destroying the film.

It should be observed that the Secret Service destroyed this evidence when the identity of one or more assassins was officially unknown and at a time when it was also uncertain what pictures may have been taken by the boy in Dealey Plaza. The evidentiary value of the pictures was potentially considerable. Both Ellis and Courson were shocked and remember the boy as being extremely upset that he had been treated in such a hostile manner by a member of the President's protective service. Frank Cormier, another reporter for *The St. Louis Post Dispatch*, also observed the hole.

One of the most intriguing witnesses, however, was Dr. Evalea Glanges, then a second year medical student at Southwestern, next to Parkland Hospital. When it was reported in class that the President had been shot, she inferred the President would be taken to Parkland Hospital and went to the outside of the emergency room. By circumstance, she found herself standing next to the limousine. She leaned against the fender and viewed the hole in the windshield. Looking from the outside she noted "It was a real clean hole." A friend, also a physician, was with Dr. Glanges at Parkland Hospital and refuses to speak to this date about the incident. Dr. Glanges did not disclose the name of that person in an interview conducted by this author in January 1999. Apparently there was concern that disclosure might jeopardize her friend's employment or otherwise be hazardous to his health.

Glanges told me that, when she talked about the hole in a loud voice at Parkland, someone got into the vehicle and sped away, "almost taking my arm off." Dr. Glanges was Chairperson of the Department of Surgery at John Peter Smith Hospital in Fort Worth, Texas at the time of the interview. She stated she felt she "needed to keep her mouth shut." She was insistent that the official story was "phony." When I interviewed her, she was anticipating retirement in the near future. She confirmed that she was 100% certain that there was a hole in the windshield in the limousine at Parkland hospital. I am sorry to report that Dr. Glanges was unable to enjoy her retirement. A most credible witness, she died on 27 February 1999, one month after our interview.

In January 1992, an unidentified caller to the *Larry King* television show stated that he had viewed the hole in the windshield. And Chicago Special Agent Abraham W. Bolden Sr., in an interview conducted by researcher Vince Palamara, indicated that he had been aware of the existence of a hole in the windshield. As he then remarked to Mr. Palamara "I heard about that [the hole in the windshield] when I was in the Secret Service...the limousine was parked on the South Lawn of the White House...they did change the windshield."

Interestingly, Michael Paine, husband of Ruth Paine, the woman whom Marina Oswald was residing with at the time of the assassination, indicated that he was aware of a possible hole during his Warren Commission testimony: "Somebody else said there was a shot through the windshield of the car. We went down to the place (Dealey Plaza) and looked around, and he thought that—he had a theory that the man had been shot from a manhole in the street, so I recognized that my views could change with evidence" (2H 423).

As an experienced attorney, I should point out that none of those persons I have identified as having observing the hole knew more than a single one of the others who had made similar observations. This makes their testimony collectively a powerful statement with independent corroboration.

Willard Hess and the Secret Service

I have personally interviewed Willard Hess on numerous occasions. Mr. Hess is a remarkable man at 93 years of age. He continues to give occasional talks about his company. He informed me that he was certain that the limousine had been *flown* (emphasis added) to Dayton, Ohio for delivery to his company. He recalled seeing a windshield and clearly remembers that he did not observe any damage to it. He also remembers allegations of a hole in the floor pan, but that his employees had found no evidence of such a hole.

I inquired as to whether the windshield was changed while in his company's possession. He responded in the affirmative, noting that the Pittsburgh Glass Company was involved. He indicated that this was done in order to install bullet resistant glass. He volunteered to me that this was necessary because the windshield that arrived at his company was *standard safety glass* (emphasis added). This is highly significant in examining the credibility of the man whom I interviewed from the Ford Motor Company. It is also important to recall that Hess & E Eisenhardt's official records show that the limousine arrived at his company on 13 December 1963. This was days before the vehicle left the White House Garage, according to James Rowley and F. Vaughn Ferguson.

Mr. Hess also made another statement that I have found puzzling. He informed me that the Secret Service had told him that the limousine had remained in Dallas for several days after the assassination. This is to be false; and it is difficult to discern the motive for the Secret Service to have provided him such information, unless it was to mislead about the actual whereabouts of the vehicle and to imply that it had not been subject to any previous body work.

Mr. Hess recalled that there was continual contact with the Secret Service and that a man named John Morgan, who was connected to the Secret Service as a technical advisor and in Ohio at least on a weekly basis. He also noted that Mr. Morgan's expertise was in explosives and he thought that Mr. Morgan would assist in preparation for parade routes by examining sewers and drains as a security concern. He ended our conversation one day with the comment that he believes the "full story has not been told."

In one of our conversations, Mr. Hess recalled that the Secret Service informed him that the limousine should maintain a consistent "parade speed" of 10–12 miles per hour. This was important for many reasons. The Secret Service had informed him that studies showed that this speed would make the President a difficult, moving target for a potential assassin. It was a speed that would allow the President to stand up during a parade but still afford Secret Service agents a reasonable opportunity to run along the side of the President's vehicle when such security was necessary. He has confirmed that the limousine was equipped with a throttle that would maintain the limousine at this specific "parade speed."

On 22 November 1963, there was a very sparse crowd on Elm Street when the President was shot. People were not in the street creating safety hazards that would necessitate that Kennedy's vehicle be driven at a slower speed than 10-12 mph. The lead vehicle in front of the Kennedy limousine was a significant distance from the front of Kennedy's vehicle. Though experts have determined that Kennedy's vehicle had an average speed of 11-12 mph on Elm Street at the time of the assassination, there has not been any disagreement that the vehicle was traveling at varying speeds and slowed down significantly while on Elm Street.

There has been a vigorous debate by researchers as to whether the limousine actually stopped during the shooting sequence. [*Editor's note*: A summary of eyewitness testimony on this point by Vincent Palamara appears elsewhere in this volume.] The brake lights of the limousine were clearly activated. Whether the vehicle came to a complete stop or not, the question remains as to why the vehicle was not traveling at the constant "parade speed" on Elm Street. It was actually the easiest portion of the whole route to comply with the Secret Service's own protocol. I am unaware that this issue has ever been discussed in any investigation of the assassination.

A Witness from the Ford Motor Company

On 15 August 1993, I was able to conduct an interview that answered many of the questions raised by the windshield controversy. Awareness of the existence of this individual came to me purely by circumstance and not through any investigative efforts for which I can take credit. I am not revealing the identity of the individual at this time. A number of trusted researchers have been provided this information with an unedited copy of the full interview between us as a verification of its legitimacy. As I write today, this individual is still living but in poor health.

Having been an attorney since 1978, I have literally seen thousands of people testify in the courtroom. While serving as a hearing official for a number of those years, it has been my duty to weigh the credibility of witnesses. This individual was as credible a witness as I had ever observed in any courtroom. I had promised him that I would not reveal the contents of the interview during his lifetime and I do so now after a successful appeal to his family as to the urgency of the information being provided to the American public.

He had worked for the Ford Motor Company for forty years, starting in 1934. He has never forgotten what occurred on 25 November 1963. The two lab men to whom he makes reference are now deceased. These are some important excerpts from my interview:

> Around noon, we got it around 2:00 that he had been killed. So, right away they called meetings to find out what we were going to do. Are we gonna run Monday morning with the President being killed? We didn't decide on anything at that meeting, and being that I had charge of all power service, I was in charge of getting that plant ready

to run or to shut it down and everything. So, they decided that they would let everything ride and they would call me on Sunday. So, on Sunday, around noon—I had just finished dinner—they called me up and told me to go in and make arrangements to start the plant up. Cause we would have to start that plant up around midnight to get it going for the day shift and number two shift. So, that I did, but then I arrived my normal time on Monday and they had me on a two-way radio and they had me on a Cushman scooter because I was covering a large plant. So I got a call from the Vice President of the division, and he told me on the radio that I was wanted in the glass plant lab, *now*! So I went down to the lab and the door was locked. . . .

I knocked on the door and they let me in. There were two of the lab men in there and they had the windshield there. And they told me that we were to use that to—see now the car was a special built car. We were to use that windshield as a template to make a new windshield. And the windshield had a bullet hole in it, coming from the outside through. You could see it, from the way it was broken. . . .

But the car was in the B building, where we had a repair garage. And they had taken the windshield out, it was back in the glass plant, we were using it as a template. And to make a windshield, and we were told to follow it right straight through until it was a finished product and get it back to the B building. We were told if anybody asked us what we were doing, we were running a template for a prototype. . . .

After describing the process for making a new windshield he noted,

We laminated it, when we took it out of there, it was a finished windshield. We took it to the B building; it was put in that limousine. Now that limousine had the entire interior completely stripped out. . . . The carpeting and everything was gone. . . .

It was gone, it was nothing, it was down to metal, and they restored the whole interior." When asked if the limousine had been "stripped" at the plant, he replied, ". . . I assumed it was there, that's what they did. . . .

Later on that day, I met the Vice President of the division and I said to him, 'Bob', I said, 'do you know what they were doing down there in that lab this morning?' He said, "I don't know what was happening.' He evidently knew, but he didn't want me to know he knew. That's the whole story. . . .

It was a good clean bullet hole, right straight through, from the front. And you can tell, when the bullet hits the windshield, like when you hit a rock or anything, what happens? The back chips out and the front may just have a pinhole in it. . . . This had a clean round hole in the front and fragmented in the back. . . .

I went on from there and I became superintendent of the division and I had the whole five plant divisions.

The following exchange then occurred:

Question: "Do you know what ever happened to the window?"
Answer: "As far as I know it's sitting out in Dearborn, in Greenfield Village."
Question: "The original windshield, with the bullet [hole]?"
Answer: "No, no, [the windshield with the] bullet, we scrapped it. We broke it up and scrapped it."
Question: "Were you told to scrap it?"
Answer: "That's right!"
Question: "Who told you to scrap it?"
Answer: "That was the orders the two lab man had. They got the initial instructions and I was called in after they had got their instructions."
Question: "Do you have any idea who gave them those orders?"
Answer: "I assume that it came from the Vice President of the division, I would assume. . . . All I know is that somebody told me is that we want you down there now! "

He then described how he and his wife went to view the limousine at Greenfield Village in Dearborn, Michigan, years later. He found it covered up and sitting out in a barn. He recounted seeing the car, "So, I stepped over the rope they had around it. I went in and looked at it. My wife said, 'You're going to get in trouble for getting in.' So I went right up to it. The windshield is the windshield we put in there. It's a regular standard laminated window."

This statement may appear puzzling at first impression. Some records indicate that the refurbished vehicle should have had bullet resistant glass in the windshield. But when the final project—called "project D-2" or "quick fix"—involving the glass was complete, it was reported to be a major engineering feat by a company called Pittsburg Plate Glass, at a cost rumored to be $125,000. (This is the change in the windshield described by Willard Hess.) The glass was a very expensive "water white" glass that provided minimum distortion to the onlooker. The result was achieved by constructing the window in the same manner as safety glass except that a polycarbonate vinyl was sandwiched between the plate glass, as Randy Mason has explained, "Three Special Lincolns," *The Herald*, Vol. 11/No .1 (1982). (*The Herald* is a joint publication of the Henry Ford Museum and Greenfield Village.)

There may have been further layers of glass but it is difficult for the casual observer to discern. Willard Hess informed me that one would have to flash a light on the glass in order to tell the difference. It should also be remembered that the witness from the Ford Motor Company only took a quick look at the windshield. The vehicle was not on public display at the time he saw it. Under these circumstances, it is probable that there would not appear to be anything unique about the windshield in comparison to regular safety glass in which vinyl is inserted in the same way between the glass.

I concluded the interview by asking how certain he was that the bullet hole he saw in the windshield came from the front? Was he 100%, 90%, etc.?

Answer: "I worked in the industry for forty years and I've seen all kinds of testing on glass and I know it came from the front."

Question: "So you're 100% certain."

Answer: "I'm 100% positive that it came from the front!"

As I have already affirmed, I found this witness to be completely credible. The question for others, however, may become: Why should anyone else believe this man's recollections? It may therefore be important to enumerate some of the grounds that support his credibility:

(1) He stated that this occurred on 25 November 1963. This was the only date in the White House Garage log that doesn't show anyone checking in to see the limousine.

(2) He does not know, nor has he ever had contact with, anyone I have named as seeing the windshield at Parkland Hospital.

(3) He spoke with me only with great reluctance. His son had to encourage him to speak with me. His wife was very fearful. She can be heard in the background urging him to leave. Her final statement to me was one of utter fear stating, "We have family, you know."

(4) He has never researched or read a book on the assassination. During the interview he made mistakes that would be expected of someone who had never studied the case. He thought the limousine had been flown in from Houston, not Washington D.C. He thought the Ford Motor Company leased the vehicle to the federal government for $1.00 per year. The correct amount was $500.00 per year. If he had studied the assassination he would not have erred on these basic facts. He has never been to Dealey Plaza. He was only certain of what he had personally witnessed. He would have no way of knowing whether his observations would be corroborated by other evidence, especially the discovery that there turns out to be a unique geographical location in Dealey Plaza that would confirm the origin of a shot causing the hole that he observed in the windshield.

(5) It was obvious that he was deeply troubled by what he saw. He was concerned that this information could lead back to him. He must have reflected on what he did that day very much since 1963. He was remarkably clear about his recall. He realized that something was not in order with what occurred that day. He did not try to fill in details about what others did but only made assumptions based upon what he knew at the time.

(6) He does not seek nor has he ever sought any attention or publicity. I had promised not to use the information during his lifetime and do so only now with consent obtained via his son and the urgency that exists in solving this murder.

(7) I verified that he talked about this within his family since 1963. He had two sons. One is now deceased. The other son was a high school student in 1963 who had, purely by coincidence, noticed that I was reading a book on the assassination. He informed me that his father had worked at the Ford Motor Plant in 1963 and was often talking at the dinner table about a personal incident that concerned the assassination.

This information was, until now, never shared outside his immediate family. He wants nothing tangible or intangible for this information. He did not want to name his superior, the Vice President of the division at that time. He was continuing to protect that name during the interview in 1993. I have subsequently

discovered the name through another source. The name of the Vice President
that he would not reveal to me was "Bob Miller." Mr. Miller has reportedly retired in Colorado. I do not know if he is still alive.

I believe that the witness from Ford regretted being interviewed. He was very
hesitant and appeared apprehensive when he saw that I had a tape recorder. It
was only after the urging of his son that he did consent to have our interview on
tape. He has resisted any opportunity to talk with me since that time. After a
stroke and heart attack subsequent to the interview, his health and memories
have probably suffered. It was only by virtue of circumstance that he was in this
unique position at the Ford Motor Company in 1963.

(8) The most important verification of the legitimacy of his disclosure is that,
at the time the interview occurred, he was unaware that there was any
other windshield in existence for the vehicle apart from the one he helped
to build on 25 November 1963. He was not aware that Warren Commission
exhibits 350 and 351 even existed. He was not aware that a cracked windshield was presented to the Warren Commission. He is not aware to this
day that there is a windshield in the National Archives that was purported
to be from the limousine at the time Kennedy was killed. When he went to
the Henry Ford Museum and Greenfield Village years later, he was satisfied that the flawless windshield he observed was the same windshield he
made on 25 November 1963.

The information provided by Willard Hess does not contradict the recollection
of this gentleman working at the Ford Motor Company. On the contrary, their
two recollections are entirely consistent with each other. The statement from the
gentleman at the Ford even explains why Mr. Hess saw an undamaged standard
laminated windshield and may also explain why no hole in the floor pan was
discovered in Cincinnati.

Further evidence exists that something unusual was happening with the limousine and the windshield. Gary Shaw and Penn Jones, Jr. wrote about the removal of the limousine from Washington D.C. within the first few days (Shaw
1976). It was evident to them that information about the movement of the limousine was being leaked very soon after the assassination. Long time researcher
and author Mark Lane gave a speech in Amherst, Massachusetts on 12 March
1964. He stated: ". . .they [the Secret Service] flew the car immediately to Washington where the windshield was removed and the car was then flown to Dearborn
where the entire interior was refurbished probably forever destroying a good
portion of the physical evidence."

One of the most startling discoveries is a UPI report that was released on
Wednesday, 18 December 1963:

Detroit, Dec. 18. The car in which President Kennedy was assassinated is
being refitted with bulletproof glass and armor plate for use by President
Johnson. The work on the famous "bubbletop," Presidential Continental is
being done at a *Ford Motor Co. Experimental Garage in suburban Dearborn,
But Ford officials and the Secret Service declined to comment.* (Emphasis added)

However, sources said, the limousine in which Mr. Kennedy was killed and
Texas Gov. John Connally was wounded in Dallas was brought to Dearborn un-

der a cloak of secrecy Saturday night. The article later made two other important observations: "It was learned that the following work is being done: *one*—A new windshield has been installed, lending credence to reports the old one was damaged in the shooting." And, at the conclusion of the article it stated: "New trim and carpeting have been installed in the back seat where Mr. Kennedy was riding when he was shot." This article corroborates exactly what the gentleman from the Ford Motor Company said during our interview, though he described the scenario as occuring in B Building.

The date referred to therefore would have been 14 December 1963. As aforenoted, according to James Rowley, Chief of the Secret Service, which was in charge of the limousine at the White House Garage, the limousine was there until 20 December 1963. Hess & Eisenhardt in Cinncinnati allegedly came into the limousine's possession either 12 or 13 December 1963. The official records of Hess & Eisenhardt presented to the House Select Committee indicate that the vehicle was received by them on 13 December 1963.

It has often been stated that secrets cannot be kept. It is clear that information was leaking out soon after the assassination. The Ferguson memorandum, allegedly written on 18 December 1963, has only recently been released. Was this an effort by the Ford Motor Company in cooperation with the Secret Service to purposely distort the record of what really happened? In reviewing the UPI article, is it merely a coincidence that the garage being described in Dearborn and the work done to the limousine is exactly what the witness I interviewed in 1993 asserted, but that the correct date was not being obtained from their "sources"? Did the government's position become entangled in its own lies and distortions?

Who Was Responsible?

The significance of all of this is overwhelming. First, it reveals a link of complicity between James Rowley, Chief of the Secret Service, and Lyndon Johnson, the new President of the United States, the only two people in the United States with the power and authority to approve of the movement of this vehicle from Washington to Dearborn. It also demonstrates a sinister complicity by the Ford Motor Company in cooperating with the deception and criminal destruction of evidence. Further evidence of complicity between Johnson and the Secret Service of which I am aware will have to be addressed at another time. (But it is curious to note that Rowley was the first person to shake Johnson's hand as Johnson arrived at Andrews Air Force Base on the evening of the assassination.) I would, however, like to explore yet another dimension of the implications of this information.

The available evidence suggests that it was the second shot that caused the hole in the windshield. Motorcade officer James Chaney, in an interview on 22 November 1963 told a reporter that the second shot hit Kennedy in the face. Dallas Motorcade Officer Stavis Ellis saw what he believed to be a shot hit the ground shortly after the Elm Street turn. He has diagrammed for me exactly where he viewed this. He was on a motorcycle approximately 100 to 125 feet in front of the Kennedy limousine. He discussed this with Officer James Chaney after the assassination. He had noticed debris from the ground kick up consistent with the impact of a shot. The location was across the depository on the south side of Elm Street. Later, FBI agents investigating the crime for the Warren Commission told him that he could not have seen such an effect. He nevertheless restated his observations for HSCA investigators (12H23, JFK Document No. 013841).

Royce G. Skelton, a private citizen, noted in his statement: "I saw a bullet, or I guess it was a bullet—I take it for granted that it was—hit in the left front of the President's car on the cement, and when it did, the smoke carried with it—away from the building" (6H238).

People have argued that such an early shot would not have occurred because of the barrier caused by a tree would have obstructed the view from the 6th floor of the depository for any shooter aiming at the President. It appears possible that this shot described by Stavis Ellis could have happened before the tree became an obstruction. [Editor's note: But of course this presumes that the shot was fired from the 6th floor.] If the major purpose of the shot was to create a diversion that would draw the attention of spectators, however, it did not matter where the shot hit or if a tree was in the way.

Any person present in Dealey Plaza would have had his attention drawn to the nearest sound. It is of interest that some of the witnesses believed that the first shot sounded like a firecracker. Some thought the firecracker sound appeared to be in the limousine itself. In a personal interview, for example, witness Bill Newman reported that the firecracker sound appeared to be "by the limousine." One phenomenon that certainly could have sounded like a firecracker in the vicinity of the limousine would have been a bullet hitting the windshield. Mr. Newman is one of many witnesses who further maintains to this date the belief that the limousine came to a stop or near stop during the shooting on Elm Street.

If the witness from Ford is to have credibility, it is important to discern a location from where the shot to the windshield would have originated. The best evidence of damage to the windshield is seen in the famous James Altgens photograph that has been shown to correspond to Zapruder frame number 255. There appears to be clear evidence of a crack and hole in the windshield. However, at least two other versions of that photograph exist, which depict the area of damage in the windshield in a different manner. One photograph portrays the dot—corresponding to descriptions of the hole, in the center of the nebulae— as a diagonal line instead of a dot. A photograph published in newspapers on 23 November 1963 has the portion of the windshield that showed the defect removed altogether. It is not too difficult to imagine that these photographs were tampered with in the exact location of the windshield because they displayed evidence of a bullet hole.

Looking at the area in the Altgens photograph that the witness from Ford described, evidence of the hole can be discerned in the area corresponding to Kennedy's left ear. [Editor's note: The presence of this indication in the Altgens photograph was discovered by Roy Schaeffer of Dayton, Ohio, as Assassination Science (1998), pp. 143–144, explains.]

There is only one location in Dealey Plaza from which someone shooting at the President could have been in a concealed location, fired a rifle, and caused damage to this area of the windshield by the time the Altgens photograph was taken. This is a crucial question to which I shall shortly return. As we shall see, there is simply no other place from which the damage described by the Ford witness could have originated.

The Altgens photograph. Circle 1. The apparent through-and-through hole in the windshield. Circle 2. An alleged Oswald look-alike. Circle 3. A probable assassin's location. Circle 4. The door of the Vice President's Secret Service vehicle is already open.

The Throat Wound: Entrance or Exit?

First, it is critical to weigh the possibility that Kennedy had suffered an entry wound to the throat at the time of the Altgens photograph. At the time of the Altgens photograph, it is obvious that Kennedy's arms are both lifted towards his throat. Not surprisingly, the initial observations made by the physicians and medical personnel at Parkland Hospital are very important in determining this issue.

The evidence that the wound to the throat of President Kennedy was in fact a wound of entrance is powerful. Dr. Malcom Perry, who performed the tracheotomy on the President, referred to the wound as "an entrance wound" on several occasions on 22 November 1963. *Life Magazine* quoted him as stating that, if the shots had come from behind, as officials were then claiming, then, in his opinion, Kennedy must have turned around and waved at the crowd in order to have exposed his throat to the shooter's nest. The transcript of a press conference at Parkland Hospital that very afternoon is completely unambiguous.

Question: Where was the entrance wound?
Dr. Perry: There was an entrance wound in the neck, in regards to the one in the head, I cannot say.
Question: Which way was the bullet coming on the neck wound? At him?
Dr. Perry: It appeared to be coming at him. . . . [and subsequently]
Dr. Perry: The wound appeared to be an entrance wound in the front of the throat; yes, that is correct.

[*Editor's note*: The complete transcript of the Parkland press conference has been published in *Assassination Science* (1998), pp. 419–427.]

In 1979, Dr. Charles Baxter described the wound as an entry wound and during a 1992 interview stated, "Looking at the hole, one would have to [think]— and my immediate thought was that this was an entry wound because it was so small. The hole was only the size of a pencil eraser, about 2 or 2.5 mm across. . ." (Harrison Livingstone, *Killing the Truth* (1993), p. 718).

Dr. Robert McClelland noted that the throat wound "had the appearance of the usual entrance wound of a bullet" (6H36-37). Dr. Charles Carrico from Parkland Hospital confirmed that the wound was "a small penetrating wound" (CE-392). Dr. Gene Akin testified: "...this must have been an entrance wound. . ." (6H65,67). During an interview with Harrison Livingstone, nurse Diana Bowron replied, "Well, that looked like an entry wound" (Livingstone 1993, p. 718).

There is much more evidence on this point. Dr. Perry reevaluated his statement only after pressure from the Secret Service. Dr. Perry later testified that the wound would have been one of exit, if it had occurred as a Warren Commission staff attorney, Arlen Specter, asked him to take for granted, namely: that the bullet entered the base of the back of his neck, passed through the neck without hitting any bony structures, and exited his throat.

Other sophisticated research by such people as researcher Milicent Cranor also provides persuasive evidence that the wound to the throat was one of entry. [*Editor's note*: This point is discussed in *Assassination Science* (1998), p. 58, for example.]

It is very evident from the Altgens photograph and the Abraham Zapruder film that Kennedy appears to be clutching his throat. There is apparent damage to the windshield and, as *Assassination Science* (1998, p. 143), has explained, there is strong evidence of a hole. Coincidentally, the location of this hole is in the identical location that the witness from the Ford Motor Plant described. Because the only physical reaction from President Kennedy is the motion of raising his arms to the area of his throat, it is obvious that this had to be the result of one of the first shots.

If one can accept the persuasive evidence of the hole in the windshield and believes that the witness from the Ford Motor Company is credible in describing the bullet hole as striking from the front, then one further—reasonably, if not completely self-evident—assumption should be made. That assumption is that any shooter causing that damage to the windshield was attempting to strike President Kennedy.

Again, as remarked, one can observe in the Altgens photograph that there is damage to the windshield and that the President is clutching his hands towards his throat. The logical question then becomes: Is there a location in Dealey Plaza that could account for the origin of such a shot? With the patently justified assumption that the shooter was trying to hit the President, that question can be answered in the affirmative.

The Origin of the Shot through the Windshield

From a careful study of Dealey Plaza, there is only one area that can account for such a shot. There is one location that logically works to perfection to the exclusion of any other location. Because of the limousine disappearing momentarily behind the Stemmons Freeway sign, it can be discerned that the shot to the windshield occurred in the time frame equivalent to that depicted between Z-frames 185–235. [*Editor's note*: Frames of the Zapruder film are referred to as "Z-frames" by their number (out of 486 frames in total).]

It is not necessary to debate Zapruder film alteration to conservatively determine the locations on Elm Street where the limousine had to have been. The location from which the shot had to have originated was from the south side of the underpass near the top of the Stemmons Freeway. The exact location could vary depending on precisely where the limousine was on Elm Street. This, however, is the only location that could work and that does work perfectly.

The highest standard of proof in the American system of justice is "beyond a reasonable doubt." [*Editor's note*: This phrase implies the conclusion that no alternative explanation of the evidence is reasonable.] In some states the term equates to moral certainty. Neither a shot from this area, the hole in the windshield, an entrance wound to the throat of the President, or the location of the limousine when the President reaches for his throat can work independently without these several variables being systematically coordinated.

Though it is conclusive that if the hole entered the front of the windshield with the intent to shoot Kennedy it must have originated from the south side of the underpass, it would be important to determine whether there is corroboration for such a shot. Such corroboration would certainly enhance the validity of such a conclusion. An extensive review of the literature on the assassination does yield some specific positive results.

(a) There was early speculation about a shot from the south grassy knoll area. Witnesses described a sidewalk scar on the sidewalk on the north side of Elm Street. A local newsman, who called it a bullet mark, pointed it out to them. This story allegedly was broadcast on the 6 o'clock news on the evening of 22 November 1963.

(b) When the Warren Commission report failed to mention the sidewalk scar, Eugene Aldredge, a private citizen, discussed the matter with Chas Freund, a reporter for *The Dallas Morning News*. Both men thought the scar on the sidewalk was the result of a bullet. Mr. Aldredge, who did not want to become involved with the matter, reported it to the FBI. The FBI came out two days later and scraped some material from the sidewalk for analysis, apparently to appease public relations concerns.

(c) The House Select Committee also failed to address evidence of a shot from the south knoll area including a close examination of the photograph of that area taken within one minute of the shooting by UPI photographer Frank Cancellare.

(d) Moreover, Dr. Robert McClelland, Dr. Marion Jenkins, and Dr. Adolph Giesecke testified to seeing a wound of the left temporal region of President Kennedy. [*Editor's note*: Studies of the medical evidence by Gary Aguilar, M.D., and David W. Mantik, M.D., Ph.D., may be found elsewhere in this volume.]

(e) Photographers James Altgens and Norman Similas likewise claimed there was a left-sided head wound. Researcher Edgar F. Tatro has discussed this issue extensively. (See *The Quincy Sun*, 11/21/84, pp. 1--17.)

(f) Researcher Milicent Cranor has advised me that she spoke with a gentleman in 1991 who pointed to the area of the south underpass and he had told her that he had heard a shot come from that location. He identified himself by the name of Johnny Brown.

(g) Another individual provides further support of a shooter from the south side of the underpass. His name is Tosh Plumlee. He has disclosed to several researchers that he was a CIA pilot and was in Dealey Plaza on the day of the assassination to abort an assassination attempt on the President. He claimed that he was standing on the south knoll during the assassination. After the assassination, he went to the top of the south overpass area. He and another individual with him distinctly smelled the odor of gunpowder.

What makes this latter recollection so significant is that this information was revealed prior to any release of the interview of the witness from the Ford Motor Company or other factors that would point to a shooter from that area. I was provided this information in December 1998. I am confident that this individual could not have been aware of the other facts I have presented. There is also photographic evidence in one of the Cancellare photographs of what appears to be a person holding a rifle standing in the area where the aforementioned individual claimed to have gone soon after the time of the assassination.

(h) Finally, in Penn Jones, Jr's *Forgive My Grief IV* (1974) there is further striking corroboration:

One witness to the assassination of President Kennedy told this writer that shortly after the shooting he observed a woman being taped by a TV camera. He heard her say that she saw a shot fired from the south side of the railroad overpass as the President was killed. To our knowledge, there is no record that this tape was ever shown on TV. In fact, we have never learned the identity of the woman. The witness did not get her name: but he stayed up all night hoping to see himself on TV (Jones, Jr., 1974, p. 132).

This one unidentified woman closes the loop. A shot fired from the South side of the underpass provides the most practical and reasonable explanation for a shot that would have caused the wound to the President's throat.

Why a Shot through the Windshield?

A reasonable question could be raised as to why a shooter would fire a shot through the windshield of the limousine from such a relatively great distance in order to hit President Kennedy. The approximate distance from the top of the south side of the underpass to Kennedy turns out to be 225 yards. But there are some logical answers to that question.

The logistics of the south side of the underpass must be understood. Researcher Jack Brazil has raised the issue of shots being fired from the storm drain on the north side of the underpass at the intersection of the underpass with the picket fence on the grassy knoll. He revealed that a shooter could stand upright in the storm drain and then have been in position to brace a rifle for a perfect shot. With the grate removed from the drain, a vehicle could be parked over the drain, providing total concealment for the shooter.

The storm drains were also part of an intricate network that could also have provided an escape route, if necessary, or to allow the shooter to abandon the weapon inside a drain opening. The storm drain on the north side of the underpass can still be examined today by anyone disposed to do so. But the situation on the south side of the underpass does not afford that luxury.

Most people do not realize or appreciate the symmetry that existed on top of the Stemmons overpass in 1963. In addition to the storm drain on the north side of the underpass that exists today, there was a counterpart storm drain on the south side of the underpass. That site would have been a perfect location for a shooter and is a possible location for the shooter who caused the hole in the windshield of the limousine.

The area of the south storm drain also was concealed from anyone who would have been standing on the main section of the underpass. There is a picket fence that attaches and veers off at an angle of about 45 degrees. The storm drain is not visible to anyone from the main underpass. It is documented from photographs that there were police officers and spectators on the main portion of the underpass, though as noted this was not the standard security measure that should have been implemented by the Secret Service.

Depending on when the shot occurred, the shooter could have been concealed from the spectators and police officers on the main portion of the underpass over a distance of approximately 15 feet. Besides standing in the storm drain and bracing a rifle on the ground, a shooter could also have fired from a prone position, a position ensuring great accuracy and have been beside, beneath, or between vehicles. A spotter or accomplice could have also provided assistance and ensured concealment.

The storm drain on the south side of the underpass is now paved over and is not visible anymore. An electrical box is also on the south knoll obstructing views of certain possible trajectories. The only explanation I have obtained for the reason for paving over the drain is that, because of the walkways on the underpass, it may have been a safety issue. The reasoning fails to explain why such remedial procedures were not implemented for the north storm drain. Could this occurrence be innocent? Perhaps, but perhaps not.

In 1963, the area of the south storm drain not only provided excellent concealment but afforded an unobstructed trajectory to the limousine. It was also very isolated. Spectators positioned themselves much closer to the passing motorcade. Dealey Plaza, as opposed to the rest of the motorcade, was occupied by a very sparse crowd. This was the end of the parade route. The attention of everyone was focused on the motorcade, the crowd, and the immediate surroundings. There was no reason for anyone to look at this desolate area up on the south side of the underpass.

The windshield shot offered a perfect trajectory for a sniper firing from the top of the south side of the underpass. Because of the unique downward slope of Elm Street, it is only a slight downward trajectory as a vehicle approached the overpass on Elm Street after the turn from Houston Street. Also, the angle of Elm Street, as one turns from Houston Street, points a vehicle almost directly at the area of the south underpass. It is, for all practical purposes, not even a moving target, since for a couple of seconds the vehicle is virtually approaching the area head on.

A serious sniper would have practiced such a shot for accuracy, trajectory, and to determine what ammunition could penetrate the safety glass with the desired effect. The one factor that could not be planned was the weather. Inclement weather could have compelled the use of the bubbletop for weather protection. In fact, it appeared earlier in the morning on 22 November 1963 that the use of the bubbletop on Kennedy's vehicle might be necessary. The bubbletop would have created a multitude of problems for any shooter. However, reasonable variations in the weather would not have affected a sniper shooting from the vicinity of the south underpass aiming a rifle through the windshield.

Unusual Circumstances in Dallas

Other curious situations existed that day. It is important to chronicle a few of them. Dallas, Texas was known to be a hostile environment in November 1963. United Nations Ambassador and former Presidential candidate Adlai Stevenson was hit with a sign and spat upon in a highly publicized incident in Dallas in October 1963. Consider the following:

(i) It was standard practice that someone occupy the front seat of Kennedy's limousine during motorcades. Major General Ted Clifton was one such person. Another person was Presidential aide General Godfrey McHugh. Both of these persons were in Dallas during the assassination. On this date, Godfrey McHugh was placed in the back of the motorcade. He later acknowledged that this was unusual. This was the first time he was advised not to ride in the car, "so that attention would be focused on the President." Obviously, if anyone had occupied such a position in the front seat, a shot at Kennedy through the windshield would have been an impossibility.

(ii) It is well chronicled that after the initial shots rang out that the driver of the limousine, Secret Service Agent William Greer, at a minimum, decelerated the vehicle, though many witnesses stated that the vehicle actually stopped. [*Editor's note*: A summary of eyewitness testimony on this point by Vincent Palamara appears elsewhere in this volume.] Certainly, the vehicle did not move at a consistent "parade speed."

(iii) There were no Secret Service agents on the Kennedy limousine. This was attributed to Kennedy's orders, even though there appears not to be any support for such a conclusion. Indeed, earlier in the motorcade Agent Clint Hill rode on the bumper of Kennedy's vehicle. In fact, he even did so on Main Street, a brief interval before the assassination.

(iv) The overpasses had been cleared except for Dealey Plaza. No precautions had been taken by the Secret Service for the open windows in buildings. No action was taken nor a report filed on the man standing with an open umbrella in Dealey Plaza on a sunny day. Not one agent mentioned this incident in their reports of that day.

(v) Dallas Police Chief Jesse Curry noted that security was relatively light in the area of Elm Street. He made some revealing statements to the Warren Commission:

Curry: In the planning of this motorcade, we had more motorcycles lined up to be with the President's car, but the Secret Service didn't want that many.

Question: Did they tell you why?

Curry: We actually had two on each side but we wanted four on each side and they asked us to drop out some of them and back down the motorcade, along the motorcade, which we did (4H171).

(vi) Secret Service Agent Emory Roberts was in command of the agents in the follow-up car to the Kennedy vehicle. He ordered the agents not to move after the sound of the first shot. Agent John Ready had even begun to move towards Kennedy and was called back by Roberts. It was Agent Roberts who appeared to take command of the situation at Parkland Hospital, exercising an authority he did not possess.

(vii) Billy Joe Martin, another motorcade officer, reported that the four motorcycle officers covering the Presidential limousine were ordered that under no circumstances were they to leave their positions "regardless of what happened." Martin explained to the Warren Commission that the Secret Service told them that they didn't want anyone riding past the President's car and that they were to ride to the rear (6H293). Martin allegedly told his girlfriend, Jean Hill: "Johnson's Secret Service people came over to the motorcycle cops and gave us a bunch of instructions. . . . They also ordered us into the damndest escort formation I've ever seen. Ordinarily, you bracket the car with four motorcycles, one on each fender. But this time, they told the four of us assigned to the President's car there'd be no forward escorts. We were to stay well in back and not let ourselves get ahead of the car's rear wheels under any circumstances.

I'd never heard of a formation like that, much less ridden in one, but they said they wanted the crowds to get an unrestricted view of the President. Well, I guess somebody got an 'unrestricted' view of him, all right."

Conclusions

These are only a few of many suspicious examples of the conduct of the Secret Service that day. If people are willing to be objective and find only one witness that I have presented to be credible, then there is powerful evidence that a shooter fired a shot through the windshield of the Kennedy limousine from the south side of the underpass. The likely result is that this shot caused an entrance wound to Kennedy's throat. The security that existed in Dealey Plaza was the responsibility of the United States Secret Service. Their actions, of which only a few have been chronicled, can only lead to the conclusion that certain members of that group participated in the killing of President Kennedy and/or the cover-up. [*Editor's note*: Studies of the conduct of key members of the Secret Service by Vincent Palamara may be found elsewhere in this volume.]

It is clear that not one observation by any witness, evidence of the hole in the windshield, or statements of people who saw a shooter on the south underpass are consistant with any other explanation. The available evidence passes the tests of independent corroboration, geographical limitations and necessity, and time constraints. It is also supported by the photographic evidence. [*Editor's note*: It thus appears to satisfy the conditions for an inference to the best explanation, as *Assassination Science* (1998), p. 210 and pp. 345–348, define them.] And it can be demonstrated beyond any reasonable doubt that, unlike the windshield, there is evidence that was not destroyed. That evidence remains alive in testimony, independent corroboration, photographic evidence, and Dealey Plaza itself.

The final question is to ascertain the difficulty of the shot. It is conceded that only certain ammunition could result in the clean hole to the windshield and cause the wound to Kennedy's throat. One expert wrote me that the throat wound was too small to have been made by a 6.5mm projectile. The wound appears to be more consistent with 5–6mm caliber ammunition. There were many highly accurate cartridges in 1963 that could perform accurately from the distance of the south underpass. He further noted that for a bullet to penetrate automobile safety glass and inflict a uniform wound, it would have to have been a non-frangible or full metal-jacketed projectile. [*Editor's note*: This issue is addressed by David W. Mantik, M.D., Ph.D., in his study of the medical evidence elsewhere in this volume.]

I further consulted with a number of experts about the feasibility of a shot originating from the south side of the underpass. All responded that it was not a difficult shot for a world-class sniper. One such expert is John Ritchson, formerly of the U.S. Army and now a gunsmith and ballistics expert. Though the actual distance from the south side of the underpass to the furthest distance the shot could have struck Kennedy would not have exceeded 225 yards, my inquiry was of a conservative nature. I was also concerned that a sniper might have possibly used a silencer from such a location to further minimize being detected. (It is known that silencers were available in 1963 that could have been utilized.)

When I inquired about the accuracy of a shot from 300 yards and the possible effect of a silencer on a rifle Mr. Ritchson replied:

A world class shooter could easily shoot one inch groupings at the range you specify. A sniper will always maximize the range out to 1000 yards, and some even beyond in order to minimize detection and location. A silencer will not adversely affect accuracy and, while it will not muffle the crack of a supersonic bullet, it will, however, silence the muzzle crack, confusing people as to the location of the shooter.

That helped to explain what popular opinion might not understand, namely: that shooting from a distance can be considered to be an advantage under certain types of conditions.

The conclusions that I have been forced to reach in light of compelling evidence are not only disturbing but leave me with both emptiness and sadness. I was 10 years old on 22 November 1963. Over one-half of the people alive in the United States today had yet to be born on that date. People ask: What difference does it make what happened over thirty-five years ago? And that is a legitimate question. For any American who was alive on that day, it will always remain a current event. It is a date forever frozen in our memories. As a 10-year-old boy I saw the world as frightening but full of promise. John F. Kennedy was the President of the United States. It meant something in a way that it never has since.

People have become very cynical about our leaders. Whether Kennedy was liked or not, or was good or bad, something changed that day. A faith and trust in government was lost that can only be cleansed by the truth. History deserves that truth. Those alive now as well as future generations also deserve that truth. I hope that everyone can recapture the promise that we should have. Walter Lippman once asked the rhetorical question as to why old men plant trees that they will never see grow. The answer is obvious. To survive as a people we must be concerned for our children, our grandchildren, and beyond. People need to remember the promise that they once had. History not only deserves truth, *it demands truth*. Only when that happens can we truly be a nation of, by, and for the people.

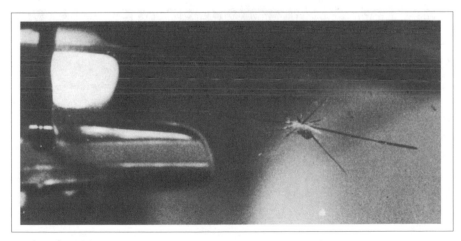

Windshield produced by the Secret Service the week after the assassination
[Editor's note: *See Robert Groden,* The Killing of a President *(1993), p. 36.*]

```
            MAY 1993                                           PAGE    1
                             Report Format: $OBJECT

        -------------------------------------------------------------------

        ID:       78.4.1                   Other Num:VIN.1Y86H405950
        Object(s):Lincoln Automobile; X-100; Presidential Lincoln Limousine
        Maker/Loc:  Ford Motor Co.
        Date:     1961
        Descr.:   Steel; MN.74.A
        Subject:  John F. Kennedy
        Used:     John F. Kennedy
        Photo:    B.90245
        Remarks:  VIN. 1Y86H405950-revised 4 door convertible sedan.  Model
                  74A.  OHV, V8, 430 C.I.D., approx. 350 B.H.P., twin range
                  turbo drive automatic transmission.  Black exterior.
                  Color: medium blue and dark blue leather interior.  Has
                  heavy duty transmission, suspension, steering, brakes,
                  axle and tires to accommodate added weight.  Steps and
                  grab handles provided sides and rear for secret service
                  guards.  Original cost $195,000.  Total cost after rebuilt
                  $1,029,600.00.  Actual mileage 55,332.

                             Modified by the addition of armor plate,
                  bullet proof glass and bullet resistant transparent top
                  after the Kennedy assassination in Nov.1963.  Front
                  license plate 1776 Bicentennial 1976/227-100/Washington
                  D.C. Assigned code number X-100 by the Secret Service.
                                     DIMENSIONS: OAL: 21'; WB:
                  156"; H. 61"; W:80" add 12" for steps; Wgt.: 9800
                  lbs(orig. wgt. 5157 lbs.).
        Roll.Shot   Video
        331.13      01.31714
        Cond                       Dim
        EX                         Length          21.00000 ft    ( 22.4 ft wrong )
                                   Wheelbase      156.00000 in
                                   Height           5.08330 ft    5.9' .
                                   Width            6.66670 ft
                                   Weight        9800.0000 lb


                   Henry Ford Museum & Greenfield Village
```

Ford Motor Company internal document concerning the limousine

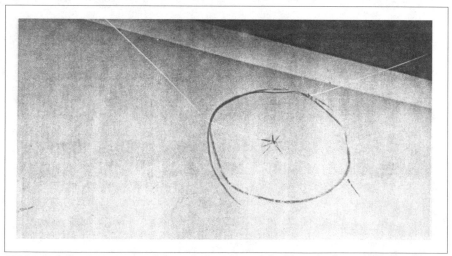

HSCA Exhibit 351 is one of the substitute windshields, which not only appears to be inconsistent with the Altgens photograph but also with the windshield originally produced by the Secret Service.

The Secret Service: On the Job in Dallas

Vincent Palamara

[*Editor's note*: Vincent Palamara, the leading student of the involvement of the Secret Service in the assassination, has been immersed in the study of the assassination since his youth, but became a serious student of the case in 1988, the 25th observance of the death of JFK. He has undertaken extensive research on at least three aspects of the case: the role of the Secret Service, the medical evidence, and eyewitness reports of events in Dealey Plaza. This article consists of three studies of members of the Secret Service with crucial responsibilities in relation to Presidential security: (1) Floyd M. Boring, Assistant Special Agent in Charge of the White House Detail; (2) Emory Roberts, Agent in Charge of the Secret Service Detail in Dallas; and (3) William Greer, the driver of the Presidential Lincoln limousine during the motorcade.]

Part I. Boring is Interesting

Without question, Secret Service agent Floyd M. Boring, the Assistant Special Agent in Charge (ASAIC) of the White House Detail during the Kennedy Administration (SAIC Behn's direct assistant), bears a heavy burden in any analysis of JFK's mortal trip to the Lone Star state of Texas in November 1963, whether we view the President's murder as the act of a lone nut (Oswald) or as the result of a deadly conspiracy. Boring, who was not physically present in Texas with the President (that honor went to a third-stringer, ASAIC Roy H. Kellerman), had just recently been with the President in Florida (11/18/63), where JFK visited Tampa, Miami, and Palm Beach. According to Agent Sam Kinney, SAIC Jerry Behn was finally able to take a vacation coinciding with the time period of JFK's Texas trip, which left ASAIC Boring able to oversee things from his home in Washington, D. C. (You don't always have to be physically present to be in charge of things. A case in point is when the SAIC of the Protective Research Section, Robert Bouck, monitored the 11/9/63 Joseph Milteer threats made in Miami from the Executive Office Building in Washington.) In other words, Floyd Boring was in charge of *planning* the Texas trip (based upon my two interviews with Mr. Boring, 9/22/93 and 3/4/94, as well as an important reference in Jim Bishop, *The Day Kennedy was Shot* [1992, p. 558], not to mention several conversations with Sam Kinney).

159

It was during the President's last trip before the Texas tour, in Tampa, Florida, where Boring took it upon himself to order the agents who were riding in protective positions on the rear of JFK's limo to dismount and return to the follow-up car. He attributed this to the President's instructions, despite 5 April 1964 reports to the contrary [1], Sam Kinney, Dave Powers, Rufus Youngblood, Gerald Behn (author of a report), Robert Bouck, John Norris, Abraham Bolden, Bob Lilley, Art Godfrey, Don Lawton, Cecil Stoughton, Maurice Martineau, Marty Underwood, and, suprisingly, *Floyd Boring* himself (author of a report and the primary sources for the other 4 reports; Clint Hill named him as the source during his Warren Commission testimony [2]) told me that JFK did not prevent the agents from doing anything! By blaming JFK for this action, however, Boring was able to keep the attention away from himself. In addition, by his absence from the Texas trip, Boring was kept out of the swirling controversies involving what should-and-should-not-have-happened in regard to security matters. Behn was interviewed in Executive session of the HSCA, while Roy Kellerman, Chief James Rowley, and Inspector Kelley testified to both the Warren Commission and the HSCA. *Why*, after-the-fact, did Boring (and the others after him) blame JFK for this order? I was unable to get a definitive answer, but one thing is for certain: if John Ready and Clint Hill had *already* been stationed on the rear of the limo in Dallas during the shooting on Elm Street, then these men would have been able to protect JFK from, at the very least, the fatal head shot that ultimately killed him, inactions by Greer and by Roberts—see below—notwithstanding.

So, is that it? Is that all Boring is responsible for (although quite important, nonetheless)? Far from it. Consider:

(1)   Boring gave Advance Agent Winston Lawson the Dallas assignment on 11/4/63, coinciding with Behn's—or *someone's*—call to Sorrels. [*Editor's note*: Lawson was the advance man for planning the Dallas trip, while Forrest V. Sorrels was the Agent in Charge of the Dallas office of the Secret Service.]

(2)   Several days later, Lawson phoned Behn's office about the critical Trade Mart decision—Lawson wasn't sure he actually spoke to Behn [4]. In light of the fact that Behn was dead set against going to the Trade Mart after seeing pictures of the catwalks, an excellent perch for snipers ("We'll *never* go there," he said [5]. Along with Jerry Bruno and Ken O'Donnell, he wanted the Women's Building, which the Secret Service conceded was the better choice from a security standpoint [6]). Insofar as Kellerman did not become involved with any planning until four days later (11/8/63), it appears quite likely that Lawson spoke to Boring and received information that was conducive to some kind of approval for this site as a suitable spot for JFK's speech, which, in turn, had a direct bearing on the potential route choices, the speed of the limousine, and the security of the building!

(3)   Of the three known PRS checks of potential threats to the President in Texas, with the particular focus on Dallas, Boring was involved in at least two, all three of which yielded NO information at all, which Roy Kellerman (to the WC [7]) and Abe Bolden (to me) both said was very unusual. Lawson inquired into the first check on 11/8/63, but Boring told him there wouldn't be any information of any consequence until this date. Kellerman inquired into the second check on 11/10/63—he even said Boring was probably involved

with this particular inquiry. Youngblood inquired into the third known check on the morning of 11/22/63 through an *unnamed* agent [8] .What makes this even more unbelievable is the following.

(4) As the agent in charge of Kennedy's trip to Florida, Boring had to have been much aware of Joseph Milteer's threats, as well as the anti-Castro Cuban Community's threats *and* the organized crime threat, which, according to Sam Kinney, gave the agents a scare down there [9]. A motorcade in Miami was deemed unwise (it was not just canceled, it was nipped in the bud), as the Secret Service (including Bouck in Washington and the agents from the Miami field office) believed via their knowledge of the aforementioned threats. However, although Advance Agent David Grant came from Florida to assist in motorcade security in Dallas on the evening of 11/18/63 (along with, among others, Donald Lawton, Sam Kinney, Emory Roberts, and later on Bert deFreese [10]), and Boring was in charge of planning the Texas trip, knowledge of the threat was *not* relayed to the advance team in Dallas! Perhaps this is why Jerry Behn told me that he was asked about the Florida trip in Executive Session of the HSCA—Behn wasn't on this trip either, and none of his testimony was published.

(5) David Grant was a key player in the planning of the motorcade route (which was *changed* shortly after his arrival on 11/18/63 [11]. Prior to this date, only Main Street was mentioned, although, as Sam Kinney and Win Lawson told me, there were *alternative* routes [12]. Behn told me the route was indeed changed, yet another matter the HSCA brought up in its private forum [13]). This included the "uniquely insecure" removal of flanking motorcycles in direct contrast to prior Texas motorcades in San Antonio, Houston, and Fort Worth on 11/21/63 and 11/22/63! [14], the deletion of the Dallas police squad car [15] (Chief Curry wanted this car there), the reshuffling of the motorcade order (with Lawson [16]), and the placement of the press, Dr. Burkley, Godfrey McHugh and Ted Clifton to the *rear* of the motorcade procession. Burkley protested about this, McHugh told CFTR radio this was "unusual," and photographer Tom Dillard said this effectively and uniquely took them out of the picture, as the press usually rode on a flatbed truck directly in front of JFK's limo, not to mention the press bus which usually follows the follow-up car [17]). Grant (who was involved in the drinking incident [18]) had worked hand-in-glove with Boring in Florida, too.

(6) On 11/21/63, Dallas Sheriff Bill Decker agreed to offer Dallas Agent Forrest Sorrels his "full support" to motorcade security for 11/22/63 (as verified in Sorrel's report published in the WC volumes [19]). Yet, on the morning of 11/22/63, according to Roger Craig (and as verified in several films/photos), Decker had his men standing idly on the corner of Main and Houston as "spectators" and nothing more [20]. According to author/ researcher Gary Shaw [21] and Dr. Grant Leitma [22] (a Maryland researcher), these unusual standdown orders came to Decker via a call from a still unknown source in the nation's capitol (recall that Chief Curry stated in his book that the security arrangements were directed from Washington [23])! If true, it is quite possible that Mr. Boring, stationed in Washington and in charge of planning the Texas trip, gave these orders.

Boring has a diverse background—he was President Truman's temporary chauffeur (Bill Greer drove Truman, as well) and, on 11/1/50, while Truman was sleeping in Blair House during the renovation of the White House, two Puerto Rican Nationalists began their assassination attempt with guns ablaze while Boring was *temporarily* in charge of the White House Detail for that day (see Baughman's book and McCullough's book on Truman) and guarding Blair House (with agents Vincent Mroz and several White House policeman). As it turned out, Boring fired the only official bullets ever fired by a Secret Service agent in its long history of protecting the nation's presidents [24]. One was killed, Grisselia Torreselo, while the other, Oscar Collazo, was wounded but survived. (Sam Kinney later guarded him in the hospital; Collazo, who was later inexplicably pardoned by Jimmy Carter, passed away in 1994 [25])! Interestingly, another agent, Stu Stout, was guarding Truman inside Blair House, fending off the many shouts of angry housekeepers with his Thompson submachine gun, refusing to budge from his assigned position on the chance that the assassins made their way past Boring. (Stout was later commended by Secret Service officials for his action, the housekeepers notwithstanding [26].) Ironically, on 11/22/63, while President Kennedy was the victim of a successful assassination, Stout assumed the very same position—tucked safely away inside a building (the Trade Mart). Sam Kinney, Rex Scouten, and Boring himself told me that Stout died not long after 11/22/63, the first agent to die after the assassination (this is a matter of some dispute—others have claimed that Stout actually passed away in 1976).

Boring, whose code name was "Deacon" (later used by Jimmy Carter [27]), served in the Secret Service from FDR's administration until 1967, when he retired as an Inspector during the Johnson administration. Although Youngblood's ghost-written book states that both Boring and Behn became Inspectors—a highly coveted position of power—after the assassination, Behn told me emphatically that he did *not* become an Inspector, although Floyd Boring did. (Behn considered his January 1965 transfer out of the White House Detail a "demotion," as he went with another former SAIC, Stu Knight, from LBJ's detail, to a division known as "Special Investigations," which was a non-protective function. Its goal was to investigate violations of the Gold Act, among others [28]). In fact, it is ironic that Boring appears to have been the only agent in a supervisory capacity in JFK's detail to have benefited after the murder. (Chief Rowley took much heat, before, during, and after both his Warren Commission and HSCA testimony, and was later replaced as Chief in 1973 during the Watergate crisis by none other than Stu Knight. Behn retired in 1967 and went to the Post Office Department. His boss was JFK Aide Bill Hartigan, the same man who would later interview Behn for an extremely tight-lipped JFK Library Oral History in 1976. Roy Kellerman's power was usurped at Parkland Hospital by his deputy, Emory Roberts, and he would later become an Assistant Administrator in charge of payroll—a desk job. He retired in 1968. Although ASAIC of V.P. Detail, Rufus Youngblood, who was to become the SAIC of this particular detail on 11/25/63, advancing ahead of the equally-absent Stu Knight, went on to become one of the ASAIC's of LBJ's Presidential Detail (due to LBJ's call to Rowley), he was, of course, already an "LBJ man." [*Editor's note*: In contrast to the lack of security provided to JFK, Rufus Youngblood threw his body on top of LBJ's immediately upon the sound of rifle shots, an account denied by Senator Yarborough.]

Youngblood became one of the ASAICs of the White House Detail immediately after the murder. Behn, Boring, and Kellerman temporarily kept their nominal positions until January 1965, when Youngblood became the SAIC of the White House Detail (we already know what happened to Behn and Knight) with Kellerman now his deputy along with a new deputy ASAIC, Thomas "Lem" Johns, another Dealey Plaza veteran [29]. According to Sam Kinney, Emory Roberts became the Appointment Secretary to LBJ, and Sam assisted Emory. Emory Roberts was the other agent to die from the Texas trip detail between the WC and HSCA inquiries. Interestingly, an unknown agent took his own life with a handgun, according to Agent Marty Venker [30]. Nevertheless, it was Boring who immediately advanced the highest and the fastest after the tragedy. Knight became the Chief nine years later, while Agent Clint Hill was SAIC of the White House Detail during the Ford administration, some 10–12 years later.

Boring, now 84 years old and a partial stroke victim, still has an agile mind. It is unfortunate that he was not interviewed by either the Warren Commission or the HSCA—of the books he was interviewed for (former Chief Baughman's *Secret Service Chief* and McCullough's *Truman*), there is nothing but fodder for Truman historians. The only Kennedy book that quotes him, Manchester's *The Death of a President* [31], is a true enigma. Boring was not interviewed for this book (see the book's endnotes) as Boring confirmed this to me on two occasions. Alas, the story is not over just yet: in regard to another author who is known for his errors and *alleged* interviews, Gerald Posner, during the course of my research, I attempted to find out if Posner's claims at the end of his book were true—that, via Hamilton Brown, the Executive Secretary of the Former Agents of the Secret Service (formerly on Joseph Kennedy's Detail on 11/22/63, first name actually "Percy"), Posner was able to locate and speak with several former agents [32].

Since none were credited in the text or his endnotes, I began to get suspicious. This was heightened when Ann Eisele of *The Washington Post* called me in November 1993 and wanted to get in touch with Brown. Along with some Italian and English journalists, I was contacted a lot that fall in regard to the Secret Service. I gave her the number after I received confirmation that a) she was who she said she was and b) that she would NOT let Brown know I gave her the number (as readers may be aware, Brown told me angrily to "cease and desist from contacting any more of my associates," and I did not want to incur his wrath again! [33]). Even under these circumstances, with her impeccable credentials and no cause for alarm, Brown would not communicate with her or give her any information on how to get in touch with former agents (although that was his job, and she was working with *Newsweek* and CBS for an Oswald-did-it piece for TV and print)! So I wondered why Brown would help this relative nobody named Gerald Posner out unless—just as Posner received exclusive access to Nosenko from the CIA in exchange for a book to their "liking"—Brown was somehow assured by Posner (and by Random House) of the same thing.

However, there is one little wrinkle in this story—I confirmed that there was one agent who was contacted by Posner, and it was this agent that referred him to Brown for reasons that remain unclear: Floyd M. Boring [34].

Boring is interesting.

[*Editor's note:* Originally written March 1995 but updated in February 1999, this study first appeared in *The Forth Decade* in 1995. Here are some comments on this 1999 update by Vincent M. Palamara in February 1999.]

A lot has happened since this article first appeared in May 1995, especially in regard to agent Floyd Boring:

(a) 1995. In the fall of 1995 the Discovery Channel aired the program "Inside The Secret Service" (later a home video; since rebroadcast) which featured, among other former agents, none other than Floyd Boring himself (this was his very first television interview). While interesting, the program only interviewed Boring regarding his role in protecting former Presidents Truman and Eisenhower.

(b) 1996. I received Boring's heretofore unknown Truman Library Oral History, dated 9/21/88, in 1996. The agent defined his role during JFK's term to the Truman Library in 1988: "I was on all the advance work out of there. I was assigned all the advance work, sort of an administrator. . ... I was second in charge [behind Special Agent in Charge Jerry Behn]." Also, by request, I donated all of my audio-taped interviews, including all of my correspondence, to the ARRB for inclusion in the National Archives (my two interviews with Boring mentioned in the above article were included). In fact, I am cited on pages xvii and 138 of ARRB's Final Report!

(c) 1997. Floyd Boring appeared on the PBS program "Truman" in 1997 (along with former Truman-era agent Rex Scouten), based on David McCullough's book of the same name. In addition, I wrote to Mr. Boring and received a prompt reply, ironically, on 11/22/97. The former #2 ASAIC of Kennedy's WHD confirmed what he had previously told me on 9/22/93 and 3/4/94 when he wrote that "President Kennedy was a very congenial man knowing most agents by their first name. He was very cooperative with the Secret Service, and well liked and admired by all of us."

(d) 1998. As a result of my efforts, Boring's oral history was finally released by the JFK Library (January 1998).

My thanks go to researcher Bill Adams for letting me know of this development. I recently ordered the document and have it in hand now. Although this Oral History was made on 2/25/76, the day after SAIC Gerald A. Behn's was made, and with the very same interviewer from the JFK Library (Bill Hartigan, former JFK aide), it has only recently surfaced, although the Behn Oral History has been available for many years as one of the many items listed in the Library's catalogue. There is one reason for this: on 9/22/93, Boring told me that he did an Oral History for the JFK Library, but both himself and Hartigan "sounded like a bunch of sopranos" when they listened back to the tape (unavailable); this is duly noted at the end of the transcript, as well. It seems that, despite being able to transcribe the faulty tape (the transcript is typewritten and appears contemporaneous), the Library decided not to release it until just early in 1998, after I brought Floyd Boring's name to the attention of the JFK Library (and a score of other prominent people, including the ARRB)! There is much of value in these 29 pages, especially for someone like me (!).

Boring confirms what he told the Truman Library in his Oral History on 9/21/88 (76 pages) by stating that "part of my job at the White House during the entire President Kennedy administration was to be in charge of the advance work." Importantly, Boring makes absolutely NO mention of any alleged JFK "desires" to limit any form of security (in Dallas or elsewhere), confirming what he told me emphatically and unequivocally on two different occasions: JFK did not interfere with the Secret Service at all and did NOT tell the agents to remove themselves from the rear of the limousine, thus debunking Manchester, Bishop, and a whole host of others. Boring is strongly corroborated by many of his colleagues whom I interviewed.

In the second major development, Floyd Boring's 9/19/96 ARRB interview (MD 259) was released and referred to in Livingstone and Groden's updated *High Treason* (1998), pp. 432-433. The relevant passages:

"When shown the HSCA summary of its interview with Miami SAIC John Marshall (specifically, Marshall's twice expressed opinion that there may have been a Secret Service conspiracy [RIF#180-10074-10393: 2/22/78 HSCA interview of Marshall]), Mr. Boring expressed surprise at those sentiments and said he had never heard that opinion expressed by SAIC Marshall, a personal friend of his. When shown the HSCA interview summary of its interview with Miami field office SA Ernest Aragon (specifically, Aragon's allegations of Secret Service security lapses [RIF#10078-10450: 3/25/78 HSCA interview of Aragon]), he said he would not agree with that statement, and expressed the opinion that SA Aragon may not have known what he was talking about."

Mr. Boring was asked to read and comment on several pages of the HSCA 6/1/77 interview transcript [RIF#180-10109-10310] of its interview with former graduate student James Gouchenaur, in which Gouchenaur recounted a very long conversation with SA Elmer Moore in 1970. Mr. Boring examined the portions of the transcript in which Gouchenaur quoted Moore as saying that Kennedy was a traitor for giving things away to the Russians; that it was a shame people had to die, but maybe it was a good thing; that the Secret Service personnel had to go along with the way the assassination was being investigated ("I did everything I was told, we all did everything we were told, or we'd get our heads cut off"); and that he felt remorse for the way he (Moore) had badgered Dr. Perry into changing his testimony to the effect that there was not, after all, an entrance wound in the front of the president's neck. Mr. Boring made clear during the interview that he felt Lee Harvey Oswald had shot President Kennedy acting alone, and that there was no shot from the grassy knoll."

Notes

1. 18H803-809. 2. 2H136-137. 3. 4H342. 4. 4H337. 5. *The Lone Star—The Life of John Connally*, James Reston, Jr. (New York: Harper and Row, 1989), p. 258; 11HSCA516; 12/13/77 HSCA interview with DNC advance man Jerry Bruno. 6. 21H546; 11HSCA516. 7. 2H107-108; 11HSCA523. 8. *The Third Alternative—Survivor's Guilt: The Secret Service and the JFK Murder*, Vince Palamara (Texas: Lancer, 1997), pp. 9–10, 57. 9. Author's interview with Sam Kinney 4/15/94. [Kinney passed away 7/21/97]. 10. WR 445; 18H789; 17H 601; author's interviews with Winston Lawson (9/27/92) and Sam Kinney (1992-1994). 11. Author's interview with Gerald Behn 9/27/92. [Behn passed away 4/93]. 12. See also 4H326. 13. Author's interview with Gerald Behn 9/27/92. 14. 11HSCA 527-529; NBC video of Houston motorcade 11/21/63; still photo provided to the author by Russ Shearer.

15. 11HSCA530. 16. 25H786; author's interview with Winston Lawson 9/27/92; *The Third Alternative*, pp. 13 and 35. 17. *The Third Alternative*, pp. 35 and 58. 18. 18H684. 19. 21H547. 20. "Two Men In Dallas" video; see also the Hughes film. 21. Author's phone conversation with author Gary Shaw 8/23/93 22. Letter to author 12/14/93. 23. *JFK Assassination File*, Jesse Curry, p. 9. [*Editor's note*: An analysis of Curry's book may be found elsewhere in this volume.] 24. Author's interviews with Floyd Boring, 9/22/93 and 3/4/94; Truman Library Oral History 1988; JFK Library Oral History 1976 [released 1998]. 25. Author's interview with Sam Kinney 3/5/94; *Confessions of an Ex-Secret Service Agent*, George Rush (New York: Pocket Books, 1988), p. 133. 26. *The Secret Service Story*, Michael Dorman (New York: Dell, 1967), p. 69. 27. *The Death of a President*, William Manchester (New York: Harper and Row, 1988 edition), p. xxi; "Air Force One: The Planes and the Presidents—Flight II" video (1991). 28. Author's interview with Rufus Youngblood 2/8/94 [Youngblood passed away 10/96]; author's interview with Stu Knight 10/22/92. 29. Author's interviews with Rufus Youngblood, 10/22/92 and 2/89/94. 30. Rush, pp. 216–217 31. Manchester (1988), p. 37; the author contacted Manchester about this dramatic contradiction in August 1993, but he refused to show me his notes or any other means with which to back up his published claim. 32. *Case Closed*, Gerald Posner (New York: Random House, 1993), p. 503. 33. Author's interview with Hamilton Brown 9/30/92 (former agents' Bob Lilley and Sam Kinney were offended at Brown's conduct, but the Secret Service has traditionally advised against any interviews other than those channeled through the "official" Public Affairs Department). 34. Boring told me that he did not tell Posner anything other than Brown's phone number and that he did not know if Posner followed through with the call. It is very interesting that Posner picked up on Boring's importance to the assassination.

Part II. The Strange Actions (and Inaction) of Agent Emory Roberts

During the last five years or so, I have often been asked, "What agent or agents are you most suspicious of?" in relation to the tragic events of 22 November 1963. I have always answered: "There are three agents at the top of my list: Bill Greer, Floyd Boring, and Emory Roberts." My research into Bill Greer [1] and Floyd Boring [2] has been well covered in the pages of several journals and in my manuscript, *The Third Alternative—Survivor's Guilt: The Secret Service and the JFK Murder*. However, Emory P. Roberts merits the same scrutiny, if not more so; a look at his role is now in order.

Secret Service agent Emory P. Roberts was a former Baltimore policeman [3] (and high school colleague of author Howard Donahue of *Mortal Error* fame) [4] who had recently been on President Kennedy's trip to Florida on 18 November 1963. As he was later to do on the fateful Texas trip, Roberts served as the commander of the agents in the follow-up car, one of two well-used 1956 Cadillac convertibles that sometimes served as the Presidential limousine (an example is provided by JFK's summer 1963 Ireland trip) [5]. On both trips, Sam Kinney served as the driver of this car [6]. As one of three Shift Leaders of the White House Detail (the other two were Stewart G. Stout, Jr. and Arthur L. Godfrey, both also on the Texas trip with Roberts) [7], Emory was a stern and forceful agent who took and gave out orders in a serious manner while working on President Kennedy's trips.

It was during the Florida trip that some interesting things involving Agent Roberts occurred which would have a direct bearing on 22 November 1963. The President visited Palm Beach, Miami, and Tampa on 18 November 1963; however, only the beautiful city of Tampa involved a motorcade, and quite an eventful one at that. As agents Chuck Zboril and Don Lawton were riding on the rear of the limousine, someone from the crowd threw a red Powerhouse candy bar at the motorcade, and the confection landed with a "thud" on the hood of the Secret Service follow-up car. Thinking it could be a lethal stick of dynamite, Agent Roberts pushed the object forcefully off the hood. Realizing what the object was, Roberts and the other agents shared a laugh about it [8].

But they had had good reason to be jumpy: the atmosphere in Tampa was one that gave the agents cause for concern—hostility from the anti-Castro Cuban community [9], the Joseph Milteer threat [10], and an organized crime related-scare [11]. As he had done countless times before, Mr. Roberts had the two agents that were riding on the rear of the presidential limousine "fall back" from time to time (sometimes based on Special Agent in Charge Jerry Behn's suggestion; in this case it was the number two agent, Assistant Special Agent in Charge Floyd Boring). This was quite often a spur-of-the-moment decision based on the speed of the cars, the size and proximity of the crowd, and the potential for threats at the moment [12]. Often, the two agents to the rear of JFK's limousine took their own initiative in going between the two cars, as agent Clint Hill did several times in Dallas. (This will become important later.)

In Dallas on 22 November 1963 (after friendly, enthusiastic, and uneventful motorcades in San Antonio, Houston, and Fort Worth on 21–22 November 1963), Agent Roberts assigned the other seven agents on his particular shift to the follow-up car: Sam Kinney, Clint Hill, Paul Landis, William "Tim" McIntyre, Glen Bennett, George Hickey, and John Ready [13]—four of whom had only hours before participated in the infamous drinking incident in Ft. Worth. Roberts' shift was the worst offender of the three shifts [14]! What makes this tragic is that Roberts had the most important shift of all: the 8:00 a.m. to 4:00 p.m. shift—the Fort Worth/Dallas part of the Texas trip (the other two shifts, Agent Stout's 4:00 P.M. to midnight detail and Agent Godfrey's midnight to 8:00 A.M. shift were not actively protecting JFK during the Dallas motorcade. They were all waiting for JFK to complete the motorcade—Stout's detail at the Trade Mart, Godfrey's detail in Austin with Bob Burke and Bill Payne at both the Commodore-Perry Hotel and at the LBJ Ranch).

Cover-Up Number One.

Agent Roberts would later write (28 April 1964) that "there was no question in my mind as to (the agents') physical and mental capacity to function effectively in their assigned duties" [15]. Like Chief Rowley and Inspector Kelley before both the WC and the HSCA, Agent Roberts covered up the drinking incident, despite Secret Service regulations which stated that this was grounds for removal from the agency [16]. Sleep deprivation and alcohol consumption wreak havoc on even the best trained reflexes. While leaving Love Field, Agent Roberts rose from his seat and, using his voice and several hand gestures, forced agent

Henry J. Rybka fall back from the rear area of JFK's limousine, causing a perplexed Rybka to stop and raise his arms several times in disgust. Rybka would then remain at the airport during the murder, having been effectively neutralized. Although Paul Landis made room for him on the right running board of the follow-up car, Agent Rybka did not budge [17]. Although Rybka worked the follow-up in Houston the day before [18] and was a gun-carrying protective agent, he was not allowed to do his job on 22 November 1963. (Rybka has since died.)

Cover-Up Number Two.

Both Emory Roberts and Winston Lawson placed Agent Rybka in the follow-up car in their initial reports, only to "correct" the record later, after 22 November, although Rybka was not even mentioned anywhere in Agent Lawson's Preliminary Survey Report—making it seem obvious that he was covering for Emory Roberts [19]. As the cars approached the Main and Houston Street intersection, Clint Hill fell back to the follow-up car. Agent Hill was the only agent to ride on the rear of the limousine in Dallas and he was not even assigned to JFK. (As a last-minute addition to the trip, Agent Hill was, like Paul Landis, part of Jackie's detail, and came at the First Lady's personal request.) John Ready, a relatively new agent, never approached JFK's side of the limousine. Why not? Emory Roberts explained: "SA Ready would have done the same thing (as Agent Hill did) if a motorcycle was not at President's corner of car" [20]. Strange, since this had posed no problem at all for Agent Don Lawton on 18 November 1963, in Tampa [21]. (Unfortunately, like Rybka, Lawton was left at Love Field and was not in the motorcade detail in Dallas [22].) In any event, there was always cooperation between the motorcycles and the agents; they maneuvered around each other countless times, including on 22 November.

Cover-Up Number Three.

The 22 April 1964 reports from Agents Behn, Boring, Ready, Hill, and Emory Roberts, alleging, after-the-fact, that President Kennedy had ordered agents off the rear of the limousine on 18 November 1963 in Tampa, and in other cities [23]. It should be stated again, and with some new corroboration to boot: JFK never ordered the agents to do anything, let alone telling the men to get off the rear of the limousine (or to take off the bubbletop, reduce the number of motorcycles, etc.). Agents Behn and Boring totally refuted their own (alleged) reports in conversations with me, while agents Kinney, Youngblood, Bouck, Norris, Bolden, Lilley, Martineau, plus two recently-interviewed agents, Don Lawton and Art Godfrey, confirmed the fact that JFK never ordered the agents to do anything. He was "very cooperative," they told me. Kenny O'Donnell did not "relay" any orders either and, in addition, Dave Powers, Marty Underwood, and a new contact, White House photographer Cecil Stoughton, confirmed to me what all the agents have told me to date [24]!

During the critical time frame in which these "presidential orders" allegedly occurred, 18–21 November 1963, the peril they caused in Dallas is obvious: no protection—as "requested"—on JFK's side of the car, including no bubbletop, partial or full, nor the usual number of motorcycles riding next to JFK, something that occurred everywhere except Dallas [25]. When I mentioned this to Agent Chuck Zboril (who was in Tampa with Agent Lawton on 11/18/63), he nervously said: "Where did you read that (JFK's alleged orders)? Do you want me commenting officially? I'm. . .speaking to someone I don't even know. . .you see. . . someone else testified about what happened in Tampa [Clint Hill]. . .(pause). . . can you. . . send me what you have on this matter?" After I sent Mr. Zboril a video and a contents sheet, he declined to respond as promised [26]. I have since learned that many former agents now have "caller I.D." on their phones and have been warned not to speak to me. (On 6/7/96, I called the home of Winston Lawson. After asking for him, his wife called him by name and he then got on the phone and told me I had the wrong number!)

Although Agent Roberts admitted recognizing "Oswald's" first shot as a rifle blast [27], as the Altgens photo confirms, he made a mysterious transmission via radio microphone that is not accounted for in his reports or in the official record [28]. Instead of offering a shout of alarm, alert, or orders to his agents to do something that their own initiative lacked for some reason, i.e., protective action, he did nothing to help the wounded President. Roberts' recall of Agent Ready is well documented [29], although we still have one more cover-up.

Cover-Up Number Four.

The alleged speed of the limousine, 9–11 mph, and the alleged five foot distance between the two cars not the 20–25 mph and 20–25 feet stated in both SAs Roberts and Agent Ready's reports were used as the pretext for the recall of Ready [30]. Taking everything cited on this point into account, there is still another factor that has escaped virtually everyone, which came about quite accidentally. Groden and Livingstone (High Treason 1998, pp. 16 and 487 of the Berkley edition, respectively), noted that "Emory Roberts ordered the agents not to move." I took this to be an unintended overstatement at the time. So, I decided to read the passage to Sam Kinney who told me, "Exactly right, and I'm involved in that, too!" Besides the Love Field recall of Agent Rybka and Dealey Plaza recall of Ready, Roberts also immobilized the other agents at a critical juncture in the shooting, causing a non-JFK agent (Clint Hill) to react too late to do anything but cover the corpse of the President [31]. I believe aides Ken O'Donnell and Dave Powers best summed up the situation when they wrote:

"Roberts, one of President Kennedy's agents. . .had decided to switch to Johnson as soon as Kennedy was shot" (emphasis added [32]). In addition, four other authors have noted Agent Roberts' "switch of allegiance," including Chief Curry [33]! Once at Parkland Hospital, SA Robert totally usurped his superior, number three man Roy Kellerman (on his first major trip on his own for the first-time vacationing Gerry Behn, leaving Floyd Boring in charge of the Texas trip back in Washington, DC [34]); Emory gave orders to Kellerman's agents and confided in Rufus Youngblood, the soon-to-be SAIC, replacing the absent Behn, just as ASAIC Youngblood replaced SAIC Stu Knight in Dallas, and Henry Fowler replaced the absent Treasury Secretary C. Douglas Dillon. (For his part, Youngblood was to become the SAIC of the Vice-Presidential Detail on 25 November 1963, a move planned before Dallas, but he rose much higher after Dallas.)

William Manchester reports as having occurred at Parkland on page 170 of his book makes one both sick and repulsed: "Powers and O'Donnell bounded toward the Lincoln. Powers heard Emory Roberts shouting at him to stop but disregarded him; a second might save Kennedy's life [Dave, too bad you weren't on the running board of the follow-up car. . . !] . . . Emory Roberts brushed past O'Donnell, determined to make sure that Kennedy was dead. 'Get up,' he said to Jacqueline Kennedy. there was no reply. She was crooning faintly. From his side Roberts could see the President's face, so he lifted her elbow for a close look. He dropped it. To Kellerman, his superior, he said tersely, 'You stay with Kennedy. I'm going to Johnson.'" [35].

It is a shame that Emory Roberts cannot tell us more: having never been questioned by the WC or the FBI; he died in the late 1960s, the same time an unnamed agent took his life with his own weapon in Washington (he showed signs he was beginning to buckle) [36]—was this Roberts? LBJ's chief private secretary was Mrs. Juanita Roberts [37]—was Emory her husband?

Notes

1. "47 Witnesses: Delay on Elm Street" *The Third Decade*, January /March 1992. [Editor's note: An updated version of this study appears elsewhere in this volume.] *The Third Alternative* pp. 22-33. 2. "Boring is Interesting," *The Forth Decade*, May 1995; "More Boring Details," op.cit., November 1995. 3. Manchester, *The Death of a President* 1988 (Perennial Library edition), p.165. 4. Author's interview with Howard Donahue, 23 September 1992. 5. From the videotape presentations "Kennedy's Ireland" and "JFK: A Celebration of his Life and Times" (the vehicle had the D.C. license plate number GG678). 6. Author's interviews with Sam Kinney during October 1992, March–April 1994. 7. Author's interview with Art Godfrey (who guarded JFK at the Hotel Texas in Ft. Worth on the evening of November 21, 1963, and was waiting for the President in Austin when the assassination occurred; for his part, Agent Stout also protected President Truman during the assassination attempt at Blair House in 1950—along with Floyd Boring). Their designation was "ATSAIC"— Assistant to the Special Agent in Charge, a position right below ASAIC.

8. Author's interviews with Kinney and Agent Don Lawton. 9. Peter Dale Scott, *Deep Politics and the Death of JFK* (Berkeley: University of California Press, 1993); see also Gaeton Fonzi, *The Last Investigation* (New York: Thunder's Mouth, 1993) 10. Author's interviews with Robert Bouck, September 27, 1992; HSCA document 180-10074-10394, an interview with agent Robert J. Jamison states that "the threat of November 18, 1963 was posed by a mobile, unidentified rifleman with a high-powered rifle fitted with a scope." In addition, HSCA document 180-10083-10419, an interview with Lubert F. deFrees, states that "a threat did surface in connection with the Miami trip," the stop right after the trip to Tampa. 11. See Note 6. 12. Author's interviews with Jerry Behn (9/27/92), Robert Bouck (9/27/92) and Bob Lilly (three). 13. 18H738. Agent John Ready may have also been mentally occupied: an unidentified "emergency leave" took Ready out of the White house detail from15–19 November 1963, missing the entire Florida trip. Although he went back on duty 21 November, he did not ride in the follow up car in San Antonio, Houston or Fort Worth on 21 November 1963.

14. 18H665-702; Agents Hill, Ready, Landis, and Bennett were the guilty parties in Roberts' shift. 15.18H679. 16. 18H665. 17.WFAA-TV (ABC's Dallas affiliate) on 11/22/63; 25H 787. 18. Advance man Jerry Bruno's notes from the JFK Library in Boston. Agent Henry Rybka was also on the follow-up car team in San

Antonio on 11/21/63. In addition, the newly-released Cooper film depicts Rybka jumping out of the follow-up car in Fort Worth on 11/22/63—he was the first agent out of the car. In neither case was Rybka the driver. 19. 18H739, Lawson's final Survey Report. Incredibly, Emory Roberts made the same "mistake" twice: In the shift report of 11/22/63 (separate from the one depicted in 18H739), Roberts placed Rybka in the "center rear seat" between Hickey and Bennett! Oddly, this was not the first time Rybka was "mistakenly" replaced in the follow-up car during November 1963. The shift report of 11/9/63, written by agent David Grant, stated that Rybka drove the follow-up car in New York. The problem lies in the fact that Rybka was actually left behind in Washington, D.C., at the time, as the November 8 and 9 shift reports make abundantly clear—bizarre indeed!

20. 18H738. 21. Cecil Stoughton photos from John F. Kennedy Library in Boston; interviews with agents Don Lawton and Chuck Zboril (November 1995). 22.25H786. 23.18H803–809. 24. Author's interviews 1992–1996, also *The Third Alternative*. 25. Hill: 18H809 and 2H136-137; Hill even reported the 11/18/63 episode on the 1995 Discovery cable channel program "Inside the Secret Service." In fact, so did William Manchester back in 1967, allegedly quoting Agent Floyd Boring as hearing President Kennedy tell him to "keep those Ivy League charlatans off the back of the car" (*The Death of a President*, pp. 37-38). However, Boring told me quite emphatically on more than one occasion that he never spoke to Manchester (as pp. 660-669 indicates) and that this was totally false! Interestingly, Manchester did interview Emory Roberts twice (p. 667). 26. Author's interviews with Chuck Zboril during November 1995. 27. 18H734–735, Manchester, p. 155.

28. 18H735–739—the first transmission was made a full minute before the shooting, while the other was made after the shooting (see also *The Third Alternative*, pp. 27-28). 29. 18H749–750; also 734. 30. See Note 29. 31. Hill described the President's skull defect as located in the "right rear" with an actual missing piece of skull lying in the back of the car. This was confirmed to me by Agent Sam Kinney on two occasions. 32. Kenny O'Donnell, Dave Powers and Joe McCarthy, *Johnny We Hardly Knew Ye* (Boston: Little, Brown and Company, 1970), p. 32. 33. Manchester, p. 165, Curry, pp. 36–37, Hepburn, p. 229, Jerry ter Horst, *The Flying White House*, p. 215

34. Manchester 232-233; interviews with Kinney and Boring in March and April 1994. The Texas trip was apparently Kellerman's first major trip on his own in a supervisory capacity, for the 8th and 9th November shift reports place Kellerman in New York (without Agents Behn or Boring). This was not the more publicized trip which JFK made to the same city a few days later (11/14 and 15 with Floyd Boring). Evidently, the president made a low-key trip to New York before the NYC trip that was well-covered in the media. As for Floyd Boring, the agent defined his role during JFK's term to the Truman Library in 1988: "I was on all the advance work out of there. I was assigned all the advance work, sort of an administrator. . ... I was second in charge [behind Special Agent in Charge Jerry Behn]." 35. Manchester, p. 170. 36. *Confessions of an Ex-Secret Service Agent*, pp. 216–217. 37. Manchester, p. 403; Jim Bishop, *The Day Kennedy was Shot* (Harper Perennial Edition, 1992), pp. 430 and 528.

Part III. Notes on Secret Service Agent Bill Greer: The Tale of the Tapes

Authors Fred Newcomb and the late Perry Adams interviewed Bill Greer for their unpublished manuscript, entitled *Murder from Within* (1974), which took five years to research and write. The authors' only TV appearance was on the now-defunct "Inside Report" on NBC in May 1990. Their voluminous tome first introduced everyone to body alteration, Zapruder film tampering (as acknowledged by Harrison Livingstone in *Killing Kennedy* and in several chapters of Fetzer's *Assassination Science*), Oswald backyard photo fakery (even acknowledged by Jack White in his video "The Many Faces of Lee Harvey Oswald" and in Jim Marrs' book, *Crossfire*), Dodd Committee/Seaport Traders/LHO theory (see pps. 300 and 528 of Henry Hurt's *Reasonable Doubt*), and, last but not least, the inane Greer-shooting-JFK [years before Bill Cooper!] theory (which, like Hickey-shooting-JFK in *Mortal Error*, greatly damaged the good work in the rest of the book). Fred Newcomb was also the first to track down the Air Force One transcripts at the LBJ Library in 1975 (*Best Evidence*, p. 681) and the first to show that one of the Willis photos had possibly been retouched by the FBI (see *Who's Who in the JFK Assassination* by Michael Benson, p. 310). Newcomb and Adams accomplished much.

They also interviewed the following members of the Dallas Police: Chief Jesse Curry, B.J. Martin, Douglas Jackson, James Chaney, Stavis Ellis, Marrion Baker, Joe M. Smith, and Earle V. Brown. Also interviewed were Jean Hill, Bill Newman, Charles Brehm, Ralph Yarborough, Joe H. Rich, Henry Gonzalez, Dean Andrews, Harry Holmes, Roy Kellerman, and, of course, Bill Greer.

Although Greer was interviewed informally by the FBI at the Bethesda morgue on the night of the assassination [RIF#124-10012-10239] and formally on 27 November 1963 at the White House [CD7/ RIF#180-10004-10466]; submitted a Secret Service report of his own [18H723]; testified before the Warren Commission on 9 March 1964 [2H112–132]; was interviewed by William Manchester on 19 Novemeber 1964 [*The Death of a President*, p. 671; RIF#180-10116–10119]; interviewed by Jim Bishop for *The Day Kennedy Was Shot* [p. 684]; interviewed 20 November 1967 and 18 January 1971 by David Lifton [*Best Evidence*, pp. 401 and 448]; interviewed in 1970 by Walt Brown [*Treachery in Dallas*, pp. 50–51]; interviewed 28 February 1978 and 4 December 1978 by the HSCA [RIF#180-10099-10491; HSCA Record Number 1211021]; interviewed informally several times by researcher Robert Milner from 1978 until 1985 [author correspondence with Milner 1998]; and by *The Asheville (NC) Citizen-Times*, 6 November 1983, the only known audio records to survive to date are the tape recordings form phone calls made from 6 December 1970 and 26 June 1971 for Newcomb and Adams' project, courtesy of researcher Gary Murr. Bill Greer passed away in February 1985 [*The Washington Post*, 28 February 1985; this author interviewed Greer's son Richard on 17 September 1991, 7 October 1991, and 23 September 1992. An audio tape does exist of the 7 October 1991 interview]. As someone fascinated by the Secret Service, especially in the context of JFK, it is interesting to finally be able to hear the voice of a man long studied and since deceased. The total running time of the tape, including both telephonic interviews, is about 45 minutes. A lengthy, word-for-word transcript is beyond the scope of this short piece (and much of it is familiar anyway), but I have decided to point out some of the highlights from this rare recording herein as follows:

(a)   Greer retired in July 1966 after having undergone a stomach operation. Jackie Kennedy sent him a letter thanking him for being with the President until the end.

(b)   He said he "saw blood on Connally's shirt" and looked back only "one time," in direct contrast to the Zapruder film. He went on to say that he "didn't really see the President at all."

(c)   He said the Zapruder film "was proven legitimate."

(d)   He claimed to have not seen anyone on the triple overpass.

(e)   Regarding the assassination itself, Greer claimed that "we never stopped. . .there was no reason to stop. . .no need to stop." In regard to the direction of the shots, he said that "everyone was hit from the rear. . .my back was covered with it [debris from head shot]." When told that Connally has always insisted that he was hit with a different bullet than had hit JFK, Greer said, "I feel that way, too. They [the Warren Commission] had lawyers working on it. . .these lawyers had already made up their mind." Greer also believed that the back wound [which he referred to as being in the "back of the shoulder"] did not go through and that that was also the first thought of the autopsy doctors in attendance.

(f)   Greer claimed he was "in the *operating room* at Parkland" (emphasis added) and stated that JFK's clothes "were in my custody from Parkland to Washington."

(g)   Greer denied that there was a hole in the limousine's windshield. He said there was only a "star," a spidering crack.

(h)   Greer did not know why the photographers were out of their usual position in front of and close to JFK's limousine, but did not seem to regard this as suspicious.

(i)   Regarding agent Roy Kellerman, Greer said twice that he was "a very fine gentleman." Regarding President Kennedy, Greer said "He and I were pretty close friends. He treated me just wonderful."

(j)   Regarding William Manchester and his book *The Death of a President*, Greer said harshly "He's garbage. . .didn't like it at all," further commenting on Manchester's criticism concerning his age and reflexes behind the wheel [Greer thought that his expertise, coming from "years of experience," was an advantage, and certainly not a disadvantage]. He went on to say that he thought that Jim Bishop's book (*The Day Kennedy Was Shot*) was the best book of all regarding the events of 22 November 1963. (However, his comments were made in 1970.)

(k)   Greer said, somewhat cryptically, "there's a lot of things I know that no one else knows."

(l)   Finally, Greer said that the Warren Commission closed up shop too soon and that "there might have been a conspiracy in another part of the country."

[Editor's note:
*Secret Service agents (L–R)
Clint Hill, Roy Kellerman, and
William Greer are photo-
graphed as they emerge from
presenting their testimony to
the Warren Commission.
See, for example, Josiah
Thompson,* Six Seconds in
Dallas *1967, pp. 95–98.*]

Beverly Oliver:
"The whole back of his head went flying out the back of the car."

Phillip Willis:
"It took the back of his head off."

Marilyn Willis:
"A red 'halo' [was] coming out the back of his head."

Ed Hoffman:
"The rear of his head was gone, blasted outward."

Dr. Robert McClelland:
"It was in the right back part of the head—very large . . . a portion of the cerebellum fell out on the table while we were doing the tracheotomy."

Dr. Paul Peters:
". . . right there, occipital parietal."

Dr. Kenneth Salyer:
"This wound extended into the parietal area."

Dr. Charles Carrico:
"There was a large—quite a large—defect about here [pointing] on his skull."

Dr. Rirchard Delaney:
"It was up in this area."

Dr. Charles Crenshaw:
"The wound was the size of a baseball."

Dr. Ronald Jones:
"My impression was there was a wound in this area of the head." When shown the faked autopsy X-ray, Parkland Hospital's Dr. Jones said, "There was no damage to the face that was visible. . . . The X-rays are incompatible with the photographs, which show no injury to the face."

Nurse Audrey Bell:
"There was a massive wound at the back of his head."

Theron Ward:
"It was right back here."

Aubrey Rike:
"You could feel the sharp edges of the bone at the edge of the hole in the back of his head."

Frank O'Neill:
". . . a massive wound in the right rear."

Jarrol Custer:
"From the top of his head, almost to the base of the skull, you could see where that part was gone."

Paul O'Connor:
"[There was] an open area all the way across into the rear of the brain."

Floyd Reibe:
". . . a big gaping hole in the back of the head."

Eyewitnesses from Parkland and Bethesda identify the location where they observed a massive blowout to the back of the President's head. (*See* Robert Groden, *The Killing of a President* (1963), pp. 86–88.)

Part III

The Converging Medical Case for Conspiracy in the Death of JFK

Gary Aguilar, M.D.

[*Editor's note*: After more than a dozen years of study, Gary L. Aguilar, M.D., has become a leading expert on medical aspects of the assassination of JFK. He has lectured widely on the subject and has conducted many inquiries and interviews with physicians and other witnesses to the crime. Among his more important contributions have been severe critiques of the abuse of *JAMA* by its then Editor-in-Chief, George Lundberg, M.D., his sustained criticism of Gerald Posner's *Case Closed* (1993), and his efforts to clarify differences in observations of the wounds by the physicians at Parkland Memorial Hospital and by the pathologists at Bethesda Naval Hospital. This study provides an integrated presentation of his important work in all three of these areas.]

Part I: Coping with Contradictions

Perhaps the most favorable outcome of the public reaction to Oliver Stone's film, *JFK,* was the creation of a federal panel of five civilians charged with the task of identifying and releasing long-suppressed documents pertaining to John F. Kennedy's assassination. By the time it ceased operations after a three-year stint in the fall of 1998, the Assassinations Records Review Board (ARRB) had done what the government should have done much earlier but didn't: It declassified mountains of suppressed documents in what the government had claimed for 35-years was an "open and shut" case for the sole guilt of Lee Harvey Oswald. It also conducted long overdue interviews with key witnesses to JFK's failed resuscitation effort at Parkland Hospital in Dallas, as well as with witnesses to JFK's autopsy at the Naval Hospital in Bethesda, Maryland. Stone's controversial film attracted largely favorable comment in the peer-reviewed academic history literature.[1] However, it was blistered in the peer-reviewed journal run by the American Medical Association, *JAMA,* for the film's depiction of JFK's autopsy. With respect to whose depiction of the conduct of JFK's autopsy is more accurate—Stone's or *JAMA*'s—in light of the ARRB's contributions, it appears that Oliver Stone has won another round.

175

Nowhere is that more evident than when one compares the revelations from the ARRB with the second of two articles published on 27 May 1992 by an in-house *JAMA* writer, Mr. Dennis Breo, titled *"JFK's Death, Part II—Dallas M.D.s Recall Their Memories."* Working under *JAMA* editor George D. Lundberg, M.D.'s close supervision, and seeking to shore up the Warren Commission by demolishing a vocal physician skeptic, Breo presented interviews that he had conducted with six physicians who had treated JFK in Dallas: Malcolm Perry, M.D., James Carrico, M.D., Charles Baxter, M.D., M. T. "Pepper" Jenkins, M.D., Robert McClelland, M.D. and Earl Rose, M.D. Proclaiming, "This special report is our attempt to confront the defamers of the truth," Breo and Lundberg had lofty ambitions for the piece.

Explaining the purpose of his interviews, Breo wrote, "Previously, the four (Perry, Carrico, Baxter, and Jenkins) have kept their memories private but they agreed to be interviewed by *JAMA* in the wake of a new book written by one of their former Parkland Hospital colleagues, Charles Crenshaw, M.D., that has bolstered conspiracy theorists because of Crenshaw's incredible 1992 claim that the bullets 'struck (President John F.) Kennedy from the front,' and the autopsy photos must have been altered, proving 'there was something rotten in America in 1963' . . . ."[2] The physicians Breo chose were indeed some of the key treating physicians, who apparently willingly signed on to Breo's campaign to undermine Crenshaw's then best-selling book, *JFK—Conspiracy of Silence*.[3] Unfortunately, what Breo wrote proved that *The New York Times* was right when it reported on 26 May 1992 that "the Journal's research was less than thorough." It also proved that Breo's sources left a lot to be desired.

It was not true, for example, that his interviewees had previously kept their memories private. The available, public record, unacknowledged by *JAMA*, is littered with their comments over the years. They had testified to the Warren Commission in 1964, some to the House Select Committee on Assassinations (HSCA) in 1978 (Perrry, Jenkins, and McClelland). Some had given interviews in 1963 to the *Texas State Journal of Medicine* (see January, 1964 issue: Carrico, Perry, McClelland and Baxter), and to the *Boston Globe* (6/21/81, p. A-23), to journalist Jimmy Breslin (Perry), to *The Baltimore Sun* (Perry, 11/28/79), and even to *The AMA News* (Jenkins).[4]

But there were greater ironies. Had Breo bothered to read what his witnesses had previously said at times under oath, when *not* keeping their memories private, he might have felt constrained to endorse Crenshaw on the grounds Crenshaw's claims had greater credibility than his detractors did. Breo probably also would have concluded that, by the contemporaneous medical records and early sworn testimonies of his own interviewees, which often flatly contradicted the statements attributed to them in *JAMA*, there was ample reason to suspect that there had indeed *been* a conspiracy!

But Breo made no reference to this inconvenient evidence. His business was only about savaging the author of a then best-selling conspiracy book. The result was a small disaster for the American Medical Association and its journal. The day *JAMA*'s JFK articles appeared, *The New York Times* said, "The merit of (Crenshaw's) book aside, it turns out that the (AMA) journal's research was less than thorough." In 1993 the articles were slammed in the October and November issues of the prestigious *Columbia Journalism Review*. Following that, the

AMA quietly paid Crenshaw almost a quarter of a million dollars to settle his suit for defamation out of court. Nevertheless, the AMA's foray into the Kennedy case was a fortuitous effort. For it is hard to imagine a better starting point than those articles for exploring the fascinating new JFK medical/autopsy evidence, and also for exploring how writers with an agenda can influence the memories of witnesses who wish to please, and, in doing so, pollute an otherwise credible *peer-reviewed* publication.

The Irresponsible Critic

Breo began his assault by broadly hinting that Crenshaw was a fraud who had never witnessed the events described in his book. Breo wrote: ". . .the other four Parkland physicians have some doubt about whether Dr. Crenshaw wrote most of the sensationalistic book or deferred to his two co-authors, both of whom are conspiracy theorists . . . . Since it is hard to prove a negative, no one can say with certainty what some suspect—that Crenshaw was *not even in* the trauma room; none of the four recalls ever seeing him at the scene,"[5] and, "Most of those who know the facts express disgust at Crenshaw's actions and question if he was involved in the care of the President at all . . .".[6] (author's emphasis) Breo's was a serious charge, but he was not the only writer to claim Parkland physicians were skeptical about Crenshaw's presence. Controversial anti-conspiracy author Gerald Posner reported that Parkland's Ronald Jones, M.D. had told him, "I don't remember (Crenshaw) in there (JFK's trauma room) at any time," and Charles Baxter, M.D. allegedly chimed in, "Neither do I!"[7]

Besides suggesting Crenshaw was a fraud who had not seen what he reported, Crenshaw's colleagues employed extraordinarily harsh language in *JAMA* to ridicule several claims in *JFK—Conspiracy of Silence:* that Crenshaw had been in the forefront of the resuscitation effort; that JFK's throat wound had been tampered with after he left Parkland; and that perhaps the autopsy photographs had been falsified. His book was dismissed as "bogus stuff" and "pathetic," and *JAMA* attributed to Baxter the opinion that Crenshaw's motivation for writing the book was "a desire for personal recognition and monetary gain."[8]

JAMA was right, at least about one of the charges. But it was one that Crenshaw had acknowledged in *The New York Times* the moment Breo's articles were publicized: Crenshaw's book *had* exaggerated his own role. The *Times* reported: "Dr. Crenshaw . . . admitted in an interview that the role he played in Kennedy's case was minor . . . Dr. Crenshaw said that he relied on his co-authors . . . for the facts of the assassination and that they took 'poetic license' in describing his role . . . 'I am sorry that image came through,' Dr. Crenshaw said, but 'it's the way they edited it' after he last saw the material."[9] The other charges Breo's interviewees leveled, however, were less well founded.

For example, though Baxter had apparently expressed doubt Crenshaw had treated JFK in 1992, in 1964, when his memory was fresh, Warren Commission counsel Arlen Specter asked Baxter under oath, "Can you identify any other doctors who were there at that time?" Baxter answered, "There was Crenshaw, Peters, and Kemp Clark, Dr Bashour finally came . . .".[10] Besides being named as a participant by Baxter, the *UPI*'s Bryce Miller named him in a story on 11/29/63. In all, Warren Commission testimony from five witnesses placed Crenshaw at the scene.[11] This included the testimony of another witness whom Breo had interviewed besides Baxter: Robert McClelland, M.D.

JAMA'S Dubious Sources

But having forgotten his own testimony about Crenshaw was not the only problem Baxter had with his memory. More embarrassingly for the AMA, there were unrecognized problems with the memories of Breo's other accusing interviewees, too. Breo presented all the Parkland doctors save McClelland as convinced the Warren Commission was right. Breo witness Charles Carrico, M.D.'s comment, "Nothing we observed contradicts the autopsy finding that the bullets were fired from above and behind by a high-velocity rifle,"[12] summed up the views of *JAMA*'s sources. But as we will see, the observations these same men made literally from the day of the assassination up until the early 1990s often contradicted the official verdict that JFK's wounds had been inflicted from above and behind—that is, from Oswald's supposed 6th floor sniper's nest in the Texas School Book Depository.

For example, to refute Crenshaw's claim that JFK had a large rearward skull defect—which supported Crenshaw's frontal-entry-rearward-exit trajectory—controversial author Gerald Posner, who wrote the recent anti-conspiracy book, *Case Closed*, claimed Baxter had told him: "I never even saw the back of (JFK's) head. The wound was on the right side, not the back."[13] (Posner did not explain how Baxter could have known JFK's skull wound was *not* in a location he'd never seen.) This recent description of Baxter's fits with anti-conspiracists, who hold that Oswald's fatal bullet hit JFK in the "occiput," the back of the head, leaving the only mark that can be seen behind JFK's right ear in the autopsy photographs: a tiny wound toward the top rear of what otherwise appears to be undamaged rear scalp (Figure 1).

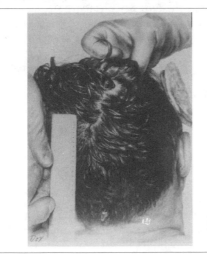

Figure 1. Ida Dox's rendition of original autopsy photograph showing the back of JFK's head (left). The small spot toward the top of the skull, which appears red in color photographs, was said to be the entrance location for the fatal bullet. The wound described is not evident in the actual photo (right).

The bullet then supposedly broke apart into a cloud of fragments, the largest of which exploded out through an exit wound on the right side. This wound appears in autopsy photographs as a large wound in front of JFK's right ear, and it involves the top and side of his skull as well.

But Baxter's comment that JFK's skull wound was on the side does not square well with what one of his colleagues, Marion Jenkins, M.D., told *JAMA*: "(T)he President's great shock of hair and the location of the head wound were such that it was not visible to those standing down each side of the gurney where they were carrying out their resuscitative maneuvers . . .".[14] While the premortem and autopsy photographs show no "great shock of hair" on the side of JFK's head that would have hidden a blow-out side wound, Jenkins wasn't the only witness who said the wound could not be seen from the side.

Author David Lifton reported that Parkland emergency nurse Audrey Bell claimed JFK's skull wound "was so localized at the rear of JFK's skull that, from her position on the right hand side, with Kennedy lying face up, she couldn't see any damage."[15] It is certainly likely that a blow-out skull wound on the right side would have been visible to witnesses standing on that side. But had the skull defect been more on the back of JFK's head, rather than on the side—which, as we'll see, is what virtually all the witness first reported—then some sense can be made of Jenkins' and Bell's comments that the wound was not visible to side witnesses. It also would help explain the similar, previously suppressed, report from a witness who was present at JFK's autopsy—General Philip C. Wehle, commanding officer of the military District of Washington, D. C. After interviewing Wehle in 1978, House Select Committee on Assassinations (HSCA) counsel D. Andy Purdy, J.D., reported that, "(Wehle) noted that the wound was in the back of the head so he would not see it because the President was lying face up . . . ."[16]

According to another Parkland witness, Ronald Jones, M.D., whom Breo did not interview, Jenkins may have been right about the invisibility of JFK's skull wound to side witnesses. Filmed by Sylvia Chase for a 1982 KRON television interview, Jones placed his right hand over the right side of his own head, between his right ear and the edge of his forehead—exactly where JFK's skull wound appears in some autopsy photographs—and he said, "I can tell you this, the wound was *not* here."[17] Under oath to the Warren Commission in 1964, Jones said that JFK had "large defect in the back side of the head,"[18] which he said, "appeared to be an exit wound in the posterior portion of the skull".[19] Author David Lifton reported that Jones had told him in 1983, "If you brought (JFK) in here today, *I'd still say he was shot from the front*"[20] (author's emphasis).

Numerous other credible witnesses at Parkland Hospital told the Warren Commission that the gaping skull wound was in the back of JFK's head:

Kemp Clark, M.D. was a professor of neurosurgery at Parkland. He was JFK's senior treating physician, and the man who, after examining JFK's skull, pronounced the President dead and signed the death certificate. On the day of the murder, Clark wrote that the skull wound was, "in the occipital region of the skull. . . . There was a large wound in the right occipitoparietal region. . . . Both cerebral and cerebellar tissue were extruding from the wound."[21] Under oath to the Warren Commission, Clark reported that JFK's skull wound was, "in the right occipital region of the President's skull."[22] Typically, neurosurgery professors are not careless in describing the head wounds of their patients.

Gene Akin, M.D., an anesthesiologist, echoing Dr. Jones, told the Warren Commission JFK's skull wound was in "The back of the right occipitalparietal portion of his head,"[23] adding that, "I assume the right occipitalparietal region was the exit . . .".[24]

Paul Peters, M.D., a resident surgeon, told the Warren Commission, "I noticed that there was a large defect in the occiput "It seemed to me that in the right occipitalparietal area that there was a large defect."[25]

Robert McClelland, M.D., whom Breo reluctantly acknowledged believed JFK had been shot from the front, told the Warren Commission, "I could very closely examine the head wound, and I noted that the right posterior portion of the skull had been extremely blasted. It had been shattered"so that the parietal bone was protruded up through the scalp and seemed to be fractured almost along its right posterior half, as well as some of the occipital bone being fractured in its lateral half, and this sprung open the bones that I mentioned in such a way that you could actually look down into the skull cavity itself and see that probably a third or so, at least, of the brain tissue, posterior cerebral tissue and some of the cerebellar tissue had been blasted out."[26]

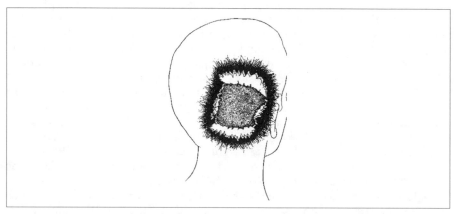

Figure 2. Pictorial representation of President Kennedy's head wound as endorsed by Robert McClelland, MD, one of the treating Dallas surgeons.

These independent and consistent assertions that JFK had a gaping rearward skull defect contradict Baxter's confident assertion that the skull defect was on the side. A gaping skull wound in the rear of the head, of course, suggests a shot from the front. Thus, Carrico's comment, "Nothing we observed contradicts the autopsy finding that the bullets were fired from above and behind by a high-velocity rifle," *has been* contradicted by other, credible witnesses from Parkland, including, ironically, one of *JAMA's* own star witnesses, Charles Baxter himself!

On the day Baxter attended JFK in the emergency room—30 years before he knew there was no wound on the back of JFK's head—Baxter wrote a note by hand that was published by the Warren Commission. Baxter wrote: ". . . the right temporal and occipital bones were missing and the brain was lying on the table. . . "[27] A few months later, Baxter swore to the Warren Commission that a portion of the back of JFK's brains had been blown out, saying, "the right side of his head had been blown off. . . [and] cerebellum was present."[28] As we will see, the early descriptions of Breo's other interviewees echoed Baxter's description of JFK's head wound as being toward the back and side. But before exploring them, a little background discussion may help make the various medical descriptions, and the contradictions they entail, comprehensible to non-physicians.

The Autopsy Controversies

Elements of Anatomy

The skull is comprised of bones that develop before birth. During childhood, these bones fuse with one another to create a continuous bony case that protects the two major portions of the brain: the cerebrum and cerebellum. The cerebrum is comprised of a pair of large lobes that fill the top of the brain case from the front to the back, the right and left "cerebral lobes." The "cerebellum" is made up of the small, paired lobes that lie under the rear, or "occipital," portion of the cerebral lobes.

The occipital bone is the lowest portion of the rear of the skull. It overlies the cerebellum. A small elevation in the middle of the occipital bone, the "external occipital protuberance" (EOP), overlies the upper margin of the cerebellum which lies beneath it. In the upright position, the EOP, an important landmark in the Kennedy case, can be felt as a small bump at the very bottom of the skull. The soft tissues of the neck and the bony spinal column can be felt immediately below it. About two inches above the EOP, the occipital bone stops and the parietal bone begins. It extends from the upper rear skull area forward to the edge of the frontal bone, which it meets at a point above the anterior edge of the ear, but well behind the hairline.

The side of the skull, referred to by laymen as the "temple," is comprised of the temporal bone. A large rearward skull defect would likely extend beyond the confines of the low occipital bone. If it included the top of the rear of the head, it would properly be described as "occipitoparietal." If such a defect also involved the side of the skull as well as the rear, "occipitoparietotemporal" would describe it, which in fact is the way JFK's skull wound was described in the autopsy report and by many witnesses. The frontal bone, which begins above the anterior edge of the ear, continues forward under the hairline and makes up the bone of the forehead and that of the tops of the bony eye sockets.

Two Different Head Wounds

The Warren Commission said that JFK was wounded by two—and only two—bullets fired from above and behind. The first is supposed to have struck the President in the upper back and exited his throat, and then, improbably, gone on to cause five wounds in Governor John Connally, who was sitting in front of JFK. The second, and fatal, bullet has two different "official" paths: one determined by the examining pathologists on the night of the autopsy and accepted by the Warren Commission, and a second path determined by a panel of civilian experts chosen by the U.S. Justice Department in 1968, the so-called "Clark Panel."

Citing the autopsy report, the Warren Commission concluded, "The fatal missile entered the skull above and to the right of the external occipital protuberance. A portion of the projectile traversed the cranial cavity in a posterior-anterior direction " A portion of the projectile made its exit through the parietal bone on the right carrying with it portions of cerebrum, skull and scalp."[29] After examining JFK's autopsy photographs and X-rays in 1968, the Clark Panel decided that JFK's pathologists—James H. Humes, M.D., J. Thornton Boswell, M.D. and Pierre Finck, M.D.—had been mistaken about where the fatal bullet entered JFK's skull. And on the basis, again, of photographs and X-rays, in 1978 the HSCA's panel of forensic experts, under the direction of New York coroner Michael Baden, sided with the Clark Panel.

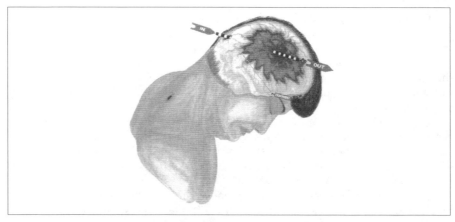

Figure 3. Rydberg Diagram. Published by the Warren Commission (CE–388), this diagram of JFK's head wound was said to be accurate by JFK's pathologists, who worked with the artist who prepared it.

Both the Clark and HSCA consultants decided that the fatal bullet did not enter "just above" the EOP, as the autopsy report said, but 100-mm above it—more than 4 inches! While JFK's autopsy report says that the fatal bullet entered "just above" the EOP, the autopsists didn't mean more than 4 inches above. They depicted JFK's wounds on three different occasions: on the night of the autopsy in Boswell's face sheet diagram, in diagrams prepared for their Warren Commission testimony (Figure 3),[30] and then in 1977, to remove any confusion, they labeled a skull for the HSCA.[31] In all cases they depicted the skull entrance wound as no higher than 1 cm above the EOP.

The Experts' Opinions

The HSCA's forensic consultants encouraged JFK's autopsists to come around to the Clark Panel's conclusion that the autopsy photographs and X-rays proved the wound was higher. They wouldn't budge, not even when confronted with the autopsy evidence.[32] Gazing at the autopsy photographs with the HSCA's forensics panel (see Figure 1), both Drs. James Humes and J. Thornton Boswell scoffed at the notion the high spot on the back of JFK's otherwise unblemished head was where the bullet entered. "I can assure you," Humes said, "that as we reflected the scalp to get to this point, there was no defect corresponding to this in the skull at any point. I don't know what that is. It could be to me clotted blood. I don't, I just don't know what it is, but it certainly was not a wound of entrance."[33]

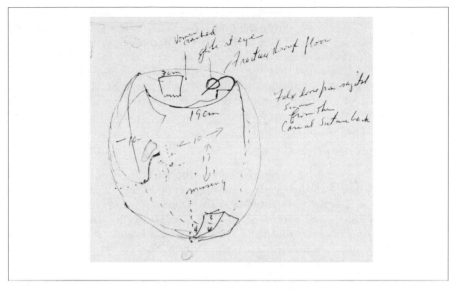

Figure 4. Dr. Boswell's "face sheet" diagram. This Commission-published diagram (CE-397) was prepared on the night of JFK's autopsy. It presumably depicts the top of JFK's skull.

But after continued pestering, the HSCA managed to get Humes to make a second appearance before the committee, this time in front of klieg lights and rolling cameras.

Suddenly, Humes appeared to agree the wound was high, if with artfully chosen words. The HSCA reported that Humes ultimately had changed his mind.[34] Behind the scenes the HSCA used Humes' apparent turnabout to lean on Boswell and Finck. ARRB-declassified letters reveal that the HSCA pursued Boswell and Finck, requesting they reconsider their placement of the skull wound in light of Humes' new opinion. They balked. Leaving a divided opinion in the record, the HSCA wrote, "Finck believed strongly that the observations of the autopsy pathologists were more valid than individuals (meaning the Clark Panel and HSCA's forensic consultants) who might subsequently examine photographs."[35] But despite Humes' equivocation during his second HSCA interview, it appears that he never really changed his mind. In 1992 Humes told *JAMA* the wound was low, and in 1997 he swore to the ARRB (as did Finck and Boswell), that he had never wavered from his certainty that JFK's skull wound was low.

Before a committee conducted by Congressman John Conyers on 11/17/93, author Gerald Posner testified that Humes and Boswell had told him they had changed their minds, that they now agreed JFK's skull wound was high. But as I first reported in the *Federal Bar News and Journal* 41 (1994), p.388), both physicians denied Posner's assertions in recorded conversations I've since made available at the National Archives. Just as they told *JAMA* and the ARRB, they told me that they had *not* changed their minds. And Boswell twice told me that he had never ever spoken with Posner. Alerted by my tape recording, the ARRB asked Posner for his information. And, as the ARRB noted in its *Final Report* (1998),

Posner stonewalled, refusing to respond to their inquiries. Similarly, although he is a lawyer, Posner never wrote the *FBNJ* to rebut my charges and defend his reputation in a law journal. There is therefore little reason to suppose Posner's congressional claims were true.

It is the high likelihood that JFK's 'professor pathologists'—they were then active in teaching resident physicians—did *not* make the colossal mistake others have assumed about the simple matter of where JFK's skull wound was that has continued to inspire skepticism about the official conclusions that JFK's autopsy evidence points to Oswald.

JFK's Autopsy Report

Because if the pathologists are right about there having been a wound as low in the skull as noted in the original autopsy report, Oswald didn't do it. Any bullet striking JFK at the base of his skull from Oswald's supposed perch would have created a "blow-out" exit wound in JFK's face. This is not mere speculation. The Warren Commission published photographs of a human skull test-fired to simulate JFK's skull wounding. Dr. Alfred Olivier, who performed the simulation, explained the photograph to the Commission: "This particular skull blew out the right side in a manner very similar to the wounds of the President . . . We found that this bullet could do exactly—could make the type of wound that the President received,"[36] The images show a bullet entrance just above the EOP, with the exit wound involving virtually the entire right side of the skull, including a good portion of the right forehead, the entire right eye socket and part of the cheekbone.[37] By contrast, no damage was reported to JFK's face in the autopsy report. Nor was it depicted in the Warren Commission's autopsy diagrams. Nor is any such damage visible in the autopsy photographs. [Though Olivier's experimental "duplication" of JFK's wounds resulted in skull injuries vastly different than JFK's skull wounds as documented in original physician notes, in Commission diagrams (Figures 2 and 3), and in several sworn statements before the Commission, none of the Commissioners or staff members took any notice of the marked discrepancies.]

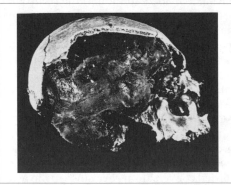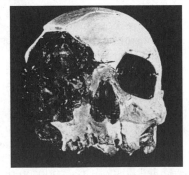

Figure 5. Shooting experiments done to duplicate JFK's skull wound for the Warren Commission in 1964 resulted in "wounds" vastly different from JFK's, as shown in these Warren Commission photographs—CE-861 and CE-862 (Compare with Figure 3).

What about the higher entrance location selected by the Clark Panel and the HSCA? Could a match be created by shooting at skulls a little higher? While the match is better, it is by no means good. To test the higher entrance site favored by the HSCA, urologist John Lattimer, M.D. test-fired skulls, striking them from the rear at the higher location, in parietal bone rather than occipital bone. On page 254 of his book, *Kennedy and Lincoln*, Lattimer reproduced a photograph of his results.[38] Claiming "(t)he skull wounds produced were strikingly similar to Kennedy's," the image shows a skull with extensive portions of both the right and left frontal and anterior parietal bones blown out, but no damage to the posterior parietal, temporal, or occipital bones, except for cracks.

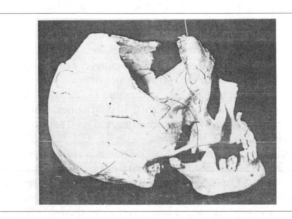

Figure 6. John Lattimer, M.D.'s test-fired skull. Although he adjusted his firing upward to correct for Dr. Olivier's assumed error in the correct location of JFK's fatal wound, the injury to Lattimer's target skull was still unlike that of JFK's. Lattimer described his results as "strikingly similar" to JFK's skull injury.

Yet the autopsy report, Warren Commission diagrams, and numerous witness accounts disclose *no* damage to the frontal or *anterior* parietal bones; instead, the damage was in the *posterior* parietal, temporal and occipital regions.[39] Had JFK taken the shot Lattimer's skull took, it would have blown off the entire top of the President's forehead just above the eyebrows, leaving undamaged the very area described by the autopsists and witnesses as destroyed. Lattimer's experiments, of course, don't prove exactly how a shot would affect a living head. They do, however, reveal a greater similarity to Olivier's results than they do to the wounds described by JFK's pathologists and credible witnesses, including experienced neurosurgeons and other physicians.

The X-rays and Photographs

JFK's autopsy photographs show that the portion of JFK's scalp behind the right ear is fully intact, lacking any depression on the right rear side that might suggest there was underlying bone loss or damage. (See Figure 1.) The only visible blemish is a small red spot, believed by some to be a bullet wound, near the top rear of the skull. The apparent blow-out exit wound is on the right side of

JFK's skull. It includes the side and top of JFK's skull in front of his ear. This right-forward damage implies damage to the frontal and temporal bones underneath it. The X-rays, similarly, show the skull defect toward the front of JFK's skull, not the back.

With the compelling "hard" evidence of mutually corroborating autopsy photographs, and X-rays that seem to be consistent with the photographs—both proving the skull defect was more toward the front than the back—one might expect it would be sheer folly to carry on a dispute. The dispute, nevertheless, lingers. It lingers, as we will see, because there is overwhelming, contrary evidence from credible witnesses who dispute not only the kind of wounds we see in autopsy photographs and X-rays, but also the bona fides of the photographs and X-rays themselves.

The autopsy report, for example, contradicts *both* JFK's photographs and X-rays. It describes the skull defect as a continuous, bony right parietal-temporal-occipital defect. The only place in the skull a single, continuous defect could encompass all three regions is in the right rear quadrant of the skull—just where over 40 witnesses from Parkland and the morgue said it was! (Tables I and II) Was the defect *only* in the rear of JFK's skull? Probably not. Compelling autopsy and witness evidence suggests it probably extended well forward of the occiput along the right side and top of JFK's skull.

Otherwise, little sense can be made of the only surviving document from the night of autopsy that was not needlessly destroyed by the pathologists: a blood-stained, "face sheet" diagram prepared by the second in command that night, J. Thornton Boswell, M.D. On that face sheet, Boswell drew a diagram of JFK's skull as seen from the top. Marked plainly were the terms "17" and "missing," with arrows pointing from fore to aft. (See Fgure 4.) Boswell told the HSCA that when they first examined JFK's skull wound, 17 cm of bone was missing, measured from back to front.[40]

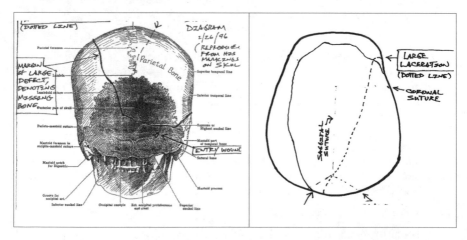

*Figure 7. Based on the markings Dr. Boswell made on a three-dimensional
human skull model for the ARRB in 1997, this two-dimensional
diagram of JFK's skull damage was drawn by the ARRB in 1997.
Note the similarities to his original "face sheet" diagram (Figure 4).*

If one grants that the pathologists knew how to use a ruler, and from measurements made on human skulls (by the author), for there to have been 17 cm of bone missing, the rearward defect described both in Dallas and at the autopsy would also have had to have extended far forward. (Though the autopsy report says that 13 cm of skull was missing, Boswell explained that the "13 cm" represented how much of the skull defect was left after a late-arriving fragment had been put back into the 17 cm defect that was present when the head was first examined.[41] During sworn testimony Boswell gave before the ARRB, he labeled a human skull, marking the size of the defect. Drawn images based on Boswell's markings reveal a large skull defect that indeed *does* go from fore to aft, and which is consistent with his 11/22/63 measurement of 17 cm, as well as the "face sheet" diagram he prepared while he worked on the slain President. (See Figure 7.)

Whether 13 cm or 17 cm, one thing is certain: the skull wound in the morgue was described as larger than the one described at Parkland Hospital. Author David Lifton contends the skull wound was enlarged when JFK's body was intercepted en route to the morgue so as to falsify the autopsy findings and prove a shot from Oswald's position.[42] But that the wound was described as larger at autopsy than noted by emergency personnel is not proof it was surgically enlarged. Wounds picked apart during an autopsy examination are often found to be larger than they first appeared to emergency personnel. In Kennedy's case, moreover, Jackie Kennedy testified that she tried to hold the top of JFK's head down while they raced from Dealey Plaza to Parkland Hospital. It is not hard to imagine the possibility that during the time it took the Presidential limousine to get to Parkland Hospital, clot had formed gluing a portion of disrupted scalp down making JFK's skull defect appear smaller to treating surgeons than it later would to autopsy surgeons.

In sum, on the location of, if not the exact size of, the major portion of JFK's skull defect—right rearward—there is no disagreement between the autopsy report and both the Dallas witnesses and the autopsy witnesses. Neither group, however, agrees with the autopsy photographs and X-rays, a baffling discrepancy. Because even if one were to argue witness error, had someone truly blown out the right front part of JFK's skull, one would expect that of the 40+ witnesses who described JFK's skull wound, some of them would have reported that that is what they saw. But not one of them did, at least not when his memory was fresh. And time hasn't helped resolve the conflict. Today, in the wake of the ARRB's depositions and declassifications, there are even more witnesses who have described, and diagrammed, a visible rearward defect in the stricken President's skull. But few have ever described it more clearly than the Parkland witnesses *JAMA* cited—that is, when they originally described JFK's fatal wound right after they first saw it. In fact the Dallas doctors' early descriptions posed a considerable problem for the HSCA, leading to another fascinating part of the story.

The Parkland Observations

The gaping, rearward wound in JFK's skull that Dallas physicians described troubled the HSCA investigators for at least two reasons. First, such an injury is all but incompatible with any shot Oswald could have fired. A bullet from Oswald's perch would have entered the rear of JFK's skull and left a gaping wound toward the front as it exited, just as Olivier's and Lattimer's tests had shown. (Figures 5 and 6) It would not have left the noticeable rearward wound the Dallas doctors had described. Second, JFK's autopsy photographs show no such wound in the back of JFK's skull.

The HSCA reported it had found a simple solution to the conflict: the Dallas doctors were wrong. And on what basis did the HSCA argue they were wrong? It said that 26 witnesses present at JFK's autopsy were interviewed, and that they had all refuted the Dallas doctors. The HSCA thus concluded, "(I)t appears more probable that the observations of the Parkland doctors are incorrect."[43] (author's emphasis) Had the HSCA's statement about the autopsy witnesses been true, it would have been a powerful refutation of the Dallas doctors.

But as will be explored below (in Part II), declassified files reveal that the autopsy witnesses did not endorse the autopsy photographs. Like the Parkland doctors before them, the autopsy witnesses refuted the pictures. (See Table I and Table II.) And we learned in 1995 that the HSCA's forensic panel was kept in the dark by HSCA investigators about the fact that autopsy witnesses had refuted the autopsy photographs. When I showed showed HSCA consultants Michael Baden, M.D. and Cyril Wecht, M.D., J.D. the autopsy witness statements and diagrams at a public Coalition on Political Assassinations conference in 1995, both claimed they had never seen them before. HSCA counsel. D. Andy Purdy, J.D., who had conducted most of the interviews and who was on the podium with Baden and Wecht, explained why this pertinent evidence was withheld from the HSCA's own experts: it was thought best to compartmentalize the evidence so as to keep the forensic consultants free from bias. So the HSCA's consultants, who were charged with assessing the autopsy evidence, were not advised about this highly relevant evidence from witnesses who were present at the autopsy.

Given the strenuous efforts the HSCA undertook to refute the Dallas doctors, one is constrained to wonder if perhaps the unidentified writer of the HSCA's false passage was himself also "compartmentalized away" from the HSCA interviews with autopsy witnesses. (This will be further discussed in Part II.) But whatever the truth, the seemingly unimpeachable autopsy photographs gave the HSCA a solid anchor for the single bullet theory (SBT) in the stormy evidentiary sea. While the images can't prove the single bullet theory, or Oswald's guilt, they can be cited to support it. They show a back wound and a red spot high in the rear of JFK's skull, said by some, but not JFK's pathologists, to be a bullet hole. (See Figure 1.) There also appears to be what looks like a blowout exit wound toward the right front of JFK's skull, which fits with the HSCA's conclusion that the shots were probably fired from Oswald's supposed perch.

More on the Autopsy Photographs

Declassified files and new evidence have thrown a spanner into the works. All three of JFK's pathologists, both autopsy photographers, a White House photographer (Robert Knudsen) and a Naval Photographic Center (NPC) photo technician, Saundra Spencer, have testified that some of JFK's autopsy photographs are missing.[44 45 46 47 48 49 50 51] Both Knudsen and Spencer claimed that they developed color negative film, but no such film currently exists in the "authentic" inventory.[52] Spencer claimed, from NPC film she has kept in her personal possession since the time of JFK's murder, that the current film on which JFK's images appear was *not* in use at the NPC when she developed JFK's autopsy photographs there in 1963.[53] FBI agents who saw the autopsy images of JFK's skull wound testified under oath to the ARRB that JFK's fatal skull wound looked nothing at all like the photographs that showed the backside of JFK's skull and scalp intact. Instead, they claimed a sizable rearward skull defect was present, [54][55] a defect that was corroborated by numerous witnesses from both Dallas and the autopsy, including neurosurgeons and pathologists. [56][57][58][59][60][61][62][63][64][65][66][67][68][69][70] John Stringer, the autopsy photographer of record, denied that he had taken the photographs of JFK's brain that survive in the current inventory.[71]

Nevertheless, it was precisely this set of apparently compromised autopsy images that formed a significant basis for the HSCA's determination that Oswald was probably responsible for JFK's wounds. But whether the images accurately reflect JFK's skull damage is another question altogether. Just as multiple, independent sources have cast doubts on the bona fides of JFK's autopsy photographs, overwhelming witness evidence suggests that the autopsy photographs do *not* accurately reflect JFK's actual skull injuries.

What about witness reliability? Though sometimes dismissed as unreliable, the reigning authority on eyewitness testimony, Elizabeth Loftus, claims witnesses are not always *unreliable*. There are circumstances in which they are *very* reliable.[72] Relevant to the Kennedy case, Loftus has identified the factors that degrade witness accuracy. Principal among them are: poor lighting, short duration of event or long duration between the event and questions about it, unimportance of event to the witness, violence, witness stress or drug/alcohol influence, and the absence of specialized training on the witness's part.[73] Absent these factors, Loftus's work shows that witnesses are very reliable.

With respect to JFK's skull damage, none of Loftus's adverse circumstances were present that would explain how both the witnesses in Dallas and in the morgue might have erred. Both groups were working as highly trained experts in their usual capacity and in their usual circumstances and setting. Moreover, both groups had more than ample time to make accurate observations, many of which were recorded immediately. The overwhelming odds are that they were right.

It seems, therefore, that only two possibilities exist: either 40+ witnesses from two different locations were wrong about JFK's rearward skull injury, or JFK's autopsy photographs have were falsified in some manner to mask the rearward skull damage that these credible witnesses described. Besides doubts that arise from conflicting witness accounts, the autopsy pictures are also under siege on multiple other fronts: from credible witnesses who deny they show JFK's real head injury; from all three of JFK's pathologists and both autopsy photographers, who insist images they took are missing; and from government photo technicians, who claim they saw images in 1963 are no longer in the current inventory.

There remained, however, a compelling reason for accepting the photographs, at least until the ARRB finished its work: the HSCA's assertion that it had authenticated JFK's autopsy images. But as we will see in Part II, the HSCA did *not* authenticate the images: it was unable to match JFK's autopsy photographs with the camera that took them.

JAMA'S Prosecuting Witnesses

Getting back to *JAMA*, Drs. Baxter and McClelland, ironically, were not the only *JAMA* interviewees to give unambiguous, early evidence about JFK's skull wound that supported Crenshaw's account and Oswald's innocence. So also did *all* of *JAMA*'s other anti-conspiracy sources: Malcolm Perry, M.D., James Carrico, M.D., and Marion Thomas ("Pepper") Jenkins, M.D.! And they didn't give this evidence just once, but over and over again, often over many years.

Malcolm Perry, M.D., was the surgeon who performed a tracheostomy on the dying president to help his breathing. In a television interview on the day of the assassination Perry said, "There was . . . a large wound in his head in the right rear area."[74] In a note written at Parkland Hospital and dated 11-22-63, Perry described the head wound as, "A large wound of the right posterior cranium. . ."[75] In the 12/14/63 issue of the *Saturday Evening Post*, journalist Jimmy Breslin said that Perry had told him, "The occipitoparietal (skull) had a huge flap . . . (t)he second bullet tore through his cerebellum, the lower part of the brain."

Describing Kennedy's appearance to the Warren Commission, Perry stated, "there was a large avulsive wound on the right posterior cranium", "[76] and, "I noted a large avulsive wound of the right parietal occipital area . . .".[77] After interviewing Parry on 1/11/78, the HSCA's D. Andy Purdy, J.D. reported that, "Dr. Perry"believed the head wound was located on the 'occipital parietal' (sic) region of the skull and that the right posterior aspect of the skull was missing"[78] Purdy also claimed that Parry had said, "I looked at the head wound briefly by leaning over the table and noticed that the parietal occipital head wound was largely avulsive and there was visible brain tissue in the macard (sic) and some cerebellum seen."[79]

However, when interviewed in 1992 by author Gerald Posner, apparently Perry's recollection suddenly changed. Posner reported that Perry told him, "I did not see any cerebellum."[80] In 1998, after ARRB counsel T. Jeremy Gunn quoted Perry's own Warren Commission description of JFK's "right posterior cranium" skull injury,[81] Perry quickly retreated, lamely declaring, "I made only a cursory examination of the head . . . I didn't look at it. I was in some kind of a hurry."[82] While Perry apparently didn't recall that early on he himself had described seeing cerebellum, he was quick to mock those who did.

Told by author Gerald Posner that his Parkland colleague, Robert McClelland, M.D., had claimed "I saw cerebellum fall out on the stretcher," Posner reported Perry had remarked, "I am astonished that Bob [McClelland] would say that. It shows such poor judgment, and usually he has such good judgment." By criticizing his Parkland colleague, Perry proved he was not exclusively reserving disapproval for Crenshaw. Unfairly chastising others, unfortunately, was a side of Perry that was not without precedent. It is a history, as we will explore below, that involves sworn statements he made to the Warren Commission, statements made when his contemporaneous news conference comments that JFK's throat wound was a wound of entrance caused problems for the Warren Commission's single bullet theory. [*Editor's note*: The transcript of the Parkland press conference appears in *Assassination Science* (1998), p. 419—427.] Nonetheless, the point to be made here is that Perry was oblivious to his own early, sworn statements. So also, apparently, were Breo, *JAMA*'s fact-checkers, and Posner. This, despite *JAMA*'s legendary research capabilities, and Posner's having advised readers of his book: "Testimony closer to the event must be given greater weight than changes or additions made years later, when the witnesses's own memory is often muddied."[83]

James Carrico, M.D.: Under oath to the Warren Commission, Carrico described JFK's skull wound as, "This was a 5 by 71 cm (sic—the author feels certain that Dr. Carrico must have said 5 by 7 cm) defect in the posterior skull, the occipital region . . . ."[84] After interviewing Carrico in 1978, HSCA staff investigator D. Andy Purdy, J.D. reported Carrico had said, "(The skull wound) was a fairly large wound in the right side of the head, in the parietal, occipital area. (sic) One could see blood and brains, both cerebellum/and cerebrum fragments in that wound." (sic)[85]

Despite having told the same story over a 15-year time span, Dr. Carrico's memory seemed to undergo a sudden improvement when confronted by Gerald Posner. In his book *Case Closed*, Posner reported Carrico had said, "We saw a large hole on the right side of his head. I don't believe we saw any occipital bone. It was not there. It (the location of the skull defect) was parietal bone. . . ". [86] (Carrico's inconstant memory seems to have also affected his recollection of JFK's other wound—the throat wound. See below.)

Marion Thomas, ("Pepper") Jenkins, M.D.: In a Warren Commission-published hospital note, dated 11/22/63, Jenkins wrote that there was "a great laceration on the right side of the head (temporal and occipital) (sic), causing a great defect in the skull plate so that there was herniation and laceration of great areas of the brain, even to the extent that the cerebellum had protruded from the wound."[87] [*Editor's note*: A copy of Jenkin's statement appears elsewhere in this volume.] Testifying to the Warren Commission, Jenkins said, "Part of the brain was herniated; I really think part of the cerebellum, as I recognized it, was herniated from the wound. . . "[88] Jenkins added that he believed that the cerebellum-exuding wound was a wound of exit, saying, "the wound with the exploded area of the scalp, as I interpreted it being exploded, I would interpret it being a wound of exit. . . ."[89]

Reporting on an 11 October 1977 interview with Jenkins, the HSCA's Purdy wrote, "Regarding the head wound, Dr. Jenkins said that only one segment of bone was blown out—it was a segment of occipital or temporal bone. He noted that a portion of the cerebellum (lower rear brain) (sic) was hanging out from a hole in the right—rear of the head.'[90]

In an interview with the *American Medical News* published on 24 November 1978, Jenkins was quoted to say, "(Kennedy) had part of his head blown away and part of his cerebellum was hanging out."

Almost certainly oblivious to all of Jenkins' prior descriptions, Gerald Posner reported that in a 1992 interview, Jenkins claimed, "The description of the cerebellum was my fault. When I read my report over I realized there could not be any cerebellum. The autopsy photo, with the rear of the head intact and a protrusion in the parietal region, is the way I remember it. I never did say occipital."[91] When Posner told him that McClelland had said, "I saw a piece of cerebellum fall out on the stretcher." Jenkins responded, "Bob (McClelland) is an excellent surgeon. He knows anatomy. I hate to say Bob is mistaken, but that is clearly not right . . .".[92]

On 27 August 1998 ARRB counsel, T. Jeremy Gunn, M.D., Ph.D., conducted sworn interviews of several Parkland physician witnesses: Charles Baxter, Ronald C. Jones, Robert McClelland, Malcolm O. Perry, and Paul Peters. At the outset of the group interview, Gunn reviewed how similarly these men had described JFK's skull wound to the Warren Commission. Gunn commented, "In my very lay sense—and I am not a doctor—there seems to be a fair degree of coherence among the testimony that you offered about the (rearward) location of the (skull) wound."[93] Confronted with so many unambiguous and complementary accounts, including his own, Charles Baxter, M.D. sought to refute his own earliest statements, as well as those of his mates: "None of us at that time, I don't think, were in any position to view the head injury. And, in fact, I never saw anything above the scalpline, forehead line that I could comment on."[94] The "temporal and occipital" skull bones Baxter mentioned on the day of the assassination, of course, are well above the scalp line. The "cerebellum" he originally described seeing, an organ that resides exclusively in the rear, reinforces that the wound he saw involved the very rear of the skull.

While one is tempted to fault Breo and Posner (and fact-checkers at *JAMA* and Random House) for having neglected the early, contrary statements of this key witness, in fairness it must be said that Breo and Posner were not selective—neither made any mention of *any* Parkland witness's early statements. It was apparently not important for either to assess the credibility of witnesses who were willing to contradict themselves by saying what was desired. Moreover, Breo's supervising editor, *JAMA*'s editor-in-chief George D. Lundberg, M.D., had a related agenda. In an accompanying article in the same issue of *JAMA*, Breo and Lundberg interviewed JFK's pathologists as part of a transparent crusade to bash Oliver Stone's film, *JFK*. Only later did it emerge that JFK's pathologists just happened to be among Lundberg's personal acquaintances.

Before he became *JAMA*'s editor, Lundberg had himself been a military pathologist. Lundberg's motivation for producing the JFK articles was at least partly revealed during Crenshaw's victorious libel suit against the American Medical Association. Court documents proved that Lundberg was incensed at the unflattering, but almost certainly at least partly accurate, depiction of JFK's autopsy in Oliver Stone's film, *JFK*, an exam performed by men working under intense and meddlesome military pressure. Lundberg set out to repair the Oliver Stone-sullied reputations of his friends and military colleagues. Lundberg's disinterest in the real conundrums in the medical autopsy evidence is perhaps best illustrated by the fact that nowhere in Breo's articles did he or Lundberg raise a single question about one of the central controversies: Where did the fatal bullet enter JFK's skull—high or low? (In *JAMA*, the autopsists claimed it was low.)

That task was left to me, in a letter I wrote that *JAMA* published on 14 October 1992. In all, eight physician letters, selected by *JAMA*'s editors as deserving an answer, were published in that issue, asking JFK's pathologists numerous questions about their published claims. But by that time the bold spirit that had impelled them to declare on *JAMA*'s pages that they had nothing to hide had departed. The pathologists stonewalled every colleague letter that *JAMA*'s editors had chosen. And then they tried to stonewall the American public, too. When the civilian ARRB invited Humes, Boswell and Finck to come in voluntarily to help resolve discrepancies in the autopsy evidence, they refused. They did finally appear, but only after the *ARRB* slapped them with subpoenas. It was a fitting end to articles that have, for good reason, been all but forgotten. What continues after them are the medical mysteries, such as: What kind of skull damage did JFK sustain?

Examining JFK"s Skull Wound

Because the autopsy photographs show no wound in the rear of JFK's skull, there has been speculation to explain how Parkland physicians, including neurosurgeons, could have believed they saw one there. The *Boston Globe* reported that, "some (Parkland) doctors doubted the extent to which a wound to the rear of the head would have been visible since the President was lying supine with the back of his head on a hospital cart."

The *Globe* immediately refuted that speculation, reporting: "But others, like (Dr. Richard) Dulaney and (neurosurgeon Dr. Robert) Grossman, said the head at some point was lifted up, thereby exposing the rear wound."[95] Similarly, author David Lifton reported that Parkland emergency nurse Audrey Bell, who couldn't see JFK's head wound, though she was standing on the right side, asked Dr. Perry, "'Where was the wound?' Perry pointed to the back of the President's head and moved the head slightly in order to show her the wound."[96] During sworn interviews with the ARRB in 1998, Dr. Paul Peters reported, "(anesthesiologist Dr. Marion T.) Jenkins said, 'Boys, before you think about opening the chest, you'd better step up here and look at this brain.' And so at that point I did step around Dr. Baxter and looked in the President's head . . . ."[97] The ARRB's Gunn interviewed neurosurgeon Robert Grossman, M.D. on March 21, 1997, reporting, "(H)e (Grossman) and Kemp Clark (Chairman of Neurosurgery at Parkland) (sic) together lifted President Kennedy's head so as to be able to observe the damage to the President's head."[98]

The Throat Wound

JFK's non-fatal wound, his throat wound, was discussed in depth in *JAMA*. It has been a source of continuing controversy among students of the Kennedy case for the last 35 years. It has encouraged conspiracists, in no small measure, because of early evidence from two of the men *JAMA* featured to refute conspiracy: Carrico and Perry.

James Carrico, M.D.: In a hand-written note prepared on 11-22-63, Carrico, described the throat wound as, "One small penetrating wound of anterior neck in lower 1/3."[99] In common medical parlance, the word "penetrating" carries the same meaning it would to a layman: entrance. So it seems that on the day of the murder Carrico—like many other Parkland doctors—believed JFK's throat wound was an entrance wound.

When the Parkland doctors, including Carrico, appeared a few months later to testify, the Warren Commissioners made it clear to them that the throat wound was the exit site for a bullet that had entered JFK's back. Nonetheless, Carrico offered the Warren Commission pro-conspiracy evidence about the throat wound that *JAMA* did not cite or refer to:

Arlen Specter asked Carrico: "Will you describe, as specifically as you can then, the neck wounds which you heretofore mentioned briefly?"

Carrico: "There was a small wound, 5- to 8-mm in size, located in the lower third of the neck, below the thyroid cartilage, the Adams apple."

Dulles: "Will you show us about where it was?"

Carrico: "Just about where your tie would be."

Dulles: "Where did it enter?"

Carrico: "It entered?"

Dulles: "Yes."

Carrico: "At the time we did not know—"

Dulles: "I see."

Carrico: "The entrance. All we knew this was a small wound here."

Dulles: "I see. And you put your hand *right above where your tie is*? (author's emphasis)

Carrico: "Yes, sir; just where the tie—"

Dulles: "A little bit to the left."

Carrico: "To the right."

Dulles: "Yes; to the right."[100]

Carrico told the Commission that the bullet penetrated JFK's throat right above where the tie is, and one must assume he meant above the knot in JFK's tie. Therefore it was just above the upper edge of JFK's shirt collar. Author Harold Weisberg reported in 1975 that Carrico corroborated this claim to him: "Carrico was the first doctor to see the President. He saw the anterior neck wound immediately. *It was above the shirt collar.* Carrico was definite on this . . . He does remember confirming (to the Commission) that the hole *was* above the collar"[101] (emphasis in original).

The official explanation, however, has the bullet emerging through the front of JFK's shirt, below the top button, and below the top of JFK's tie. It supposedly then nicked the left side of JFK's tie, leaving vertical slits in the shirt below the collar band, as well as a nick in the knot of JFK's tie, to mark its passing. Weisberg reported that Carrico told him he didn't accept this scenario. Carrico believed the nick in the tie and the holes in the shirt were due to a nurse's scalpel, which had inadvertently cut the fabric while they were removing JFK's clothing. "He (Carrico) saw neither the nick in the tie nor the cuts in the shirt before the nurses started cutting."[102] Besides Carrico, another key *JAMA* witness gave pro-conspiracy evidence early on about JFK's throat wound: Malcolm Perry, M.D.

Malcom Perry, M.D.: When he arrived at Parkland, it was apparent to the emergency crew that a wound in JFK's throat was impairing his ability to breathe. Malcolm Perry, M.D. performed a "tracheostomy" on JFK to help. This procedure involves the creation of a surgical incision in the front of the throat. Through the incision a tube is inserted into the windpipe that allows oxygen to pass directly to the lungs, bypassing the injured segment of the airway. Perry reported that to create the tracheostomy, and to get air to the President, he had to cut through a bleeding wound that was present on Kennedy's throat when he arrived.

Two hours after JFK died, Perry answered questions at a press conference. A newsman asked Perry: "Where was the entrance wound?"

Perry: "There was an entrance wound in the neck . . .".
Question: "Which way was the bullet coming on the neck wound? At him?".
Perry: "It appeared to be coming at him."
Question: "Doctor, describe the entrance wound. You think from the front in the throat?"
Perry: "The wound appeared to be an entrance wound in the front of the throat; yes, that is correct. The exit wound, I don't know. It could have been the head or there could have been a second wound of the head. There was not time to determine this at the particular instant."[103]

While Perry's contemporaneous and unrehearsed responses are not proof that JFK's throat wound was in fact an entrance wound, as opposed to an exit wound, his verbatim comments on the day of the murder are unambiguous. Perry offered the press no opinion other than that a bullet had entered the front of JFK's throat. [*Editor's note:* The origin of this shot receives considerable attention in a study of the Presidential limousine by Douglas Weldon, J.D., elsewhere in this volume.]

On 11/22/63 *UPI* reported that Perry said, "There was an entrance wound below the Adam's apple."[104] The *New York Times* reported, "Dr. Malcolm Perry, an attending surgeon, and Dr. Kemp Clark, chief of neurosurgery at Parkland Hospital, gave more details. Mr. Kennedy was hit by a bullet in the throat, just below the Adam's apple, they said. This wound had the appearance of a bullet's entry."[105] [*Editor's note*: The relevant portion of the newspaper appears in *Assassination Science* (1998), p. 15.] On 11/23/63, the *Dallas Morning News* reported, "The front neck hole was described as an entrance wound," and it quoted Perry to say, "It did however appear to be the entrance wound at the front of the throat."

Several months later, the Warren Commission's Arlen Specter was eager to prove that JFK's throat wound was not an entrance wound, but instead the exit site for the first bullet that had hit JFK, the so-called "magic bullet." Specter was understandably concerned about the published reports of the "entrance" throat wound from Perry's press conference. Specter took the unusual step of contacting Perry before his testimony to the Warren Commission. He indicated that he would, as Specter advised the Commission, obtain recordings of Perry's public comments for Perry to review "prior to his appearance, before deposition or before the Commission." [106] Specter apparently never produced the recording; however. Perry was apparently also visited more than once by the Secret Service prior to testifying, although no records have surfaced revealing what was discussed during those visits.

Speaking under oath, Perry gave the Warren Commission ambiguous, though apparently acceptable, descriptions of JFK's throat wound. He allowed that such a wound could have been either an entrance or exit wound. Perry testified that he had told newsmen he had no way of knowing which way the bullets were going when they struck JFK. Perry also, unfortunately, blamed newsmen for mistakenly reporting that he had said JFK's throat wound was an entrance wound.

Arlen Specter asked: "What responses did you give to [reporters'] questions relating to the source (entrance or exit) of the bullets, if such questions were asked?"

Perry: "I could not. I pointed out that both Dr. Clark and I had no way of
              knowing from whence the bullets came."
Warren Commissioner Allen Dulles followed-up with: "Was there any rea-
              sonably good account in any of the press of this interview?"
Perry: "No, sir."[107]
Then Representative Gerald Ford followed with: "Were those reportings by
              the news media accurate or inaccurate as to what you and others
              said?"
Perry.   "In general, they were inaccurate."[108]

The Warren Commissioners subsequently reported, "Dr. Perry stated to the
press that a variety of possibilities could account for the President's wounds."[109]
Perry, however, did *not* offer the press a variety of possibilities. The Commission
took Perry's inaccurate testimony at face value and ignored the verbatim transcript from Perry's news conference. The press accounts Perry repudiated under
oath were more faithful to the original than Perry's own testimony, and they
were more accurate than the Warren Commission's account of this incident. This
episode also proves that Perry's memory, even in 1964, could be influenced.

Ironically, despite Perry's Warren Commission-extracted equivocation, Perry
apparently privately continued to believe the throat wound was an entrance
wound, at least until the mid 1980s. On 2-14-92 Robert Artwohl, M.D., then an
emergency room physician in Baltimore, wrote in a *Prodigy* computer bulletin
board news group message that he had had a private conversation with Perry in
1986. Artwohl wrote that Perry had confided, "(O)ne of the biggest regrets in his
life was having to make the incision for the emergency tracheostomy through
the bullet wound, because he was certain that it was an entrance wound. He
remembered making a very good mental note of the wound since he was cutting
through it. Speaking with Dr. Perry that night, one physician to another in (sic)
Dr Perry stated he firmly believed the wound to be an entrance wound."[110] (After
he appeared with *JAMA* editor George Lundberg, M.D., to defend the Warren
Commission in a public debate in 1993, Artwohl retracted this anecdote about
Perry.)

Summary

In sum, *JAMA*'s dispute with Crenshaw permits a dissection of the mysteries
that still lie at the heart of the JFK medical/autopsy evidence. Though reversing
themselves only in 1992, apparently to please *JAMA*, the very Dallas doctors *JAMA*
cited to rebut Crenshaw (and conspiracy) gave (to both the Warren Commission
and the HSCA) accounts of JFK's wounds that tended to exculpate Oswald and
support conspiracy. Those early accounts were one with the reports of over 40
witnesses who saw JFK both at Parkland Hospital in Dallas and in the morgue at
Bethesda.

Two different shooting tests have demonstrated that had JFK in fact suffered
skull damage from shots fired from Oswald's alleged perch, the most visible blow-
out wound would have been toward the front of his skull, perhaps involving
JFK's forehead and eye socket. There is no evidence of any such wounds. Thus
neither witnesses nor JFK's autopsy photographs give evidence that JFK had
skull damage that fits well with the experiments that were performed to duplicate JFK's wounds by firing at skulls from Oswald's alleged feat.

Part II: Convergence Toward Conspiracy

Introduction

Over twenty Parkland witnesses repeated neurosurgery professor Kemp Clark's description of a right-rearward, "occipital," skull defect. (See Table I.)[111] Among the Parkland witnesses who described JFK's skull defect as rearward, eight participating physicians used the term "occipital" in documents published by the Warren Commission: Drs. Kemp Clark, Robert McClelland, Marion Thomas Jenkins, Charles J. Carrico, Malcolm Perry, Gene Akin, Paul Peters, and Charles R. Baxter. Seven of them described having seen cerebellum, a very different-looking portion of brain only found at the rear. The autopsy photographs, which show a large blow-out wound in the front of the right ear, apparently prove them all wrong. Could so many good witnesses indeed have been in agreement, and yet so wrong?

A 1971 *Harvard Law Review* study demonstrating that in some circumstances witnesses tended to be more often right than wrong deepens the mystery. Marshall, Marquis and Oskamp found that when test subjects were asked about "salient" details of a complex, two-minute film clip they were shown, their accuracy rate was high: 78% to 98%. Even when a detail was *not* considered salient, as judged by the witnesses themselves, they were still accurate 60% of the time.[112] While it is hard to imagine that the location of JFK's fatal wound would not have been a "salient" detail to the experienced medical witnesses involved in JFK's "routine" emergency resuscitation, if the autopsy photographs are right they prove that virtually all the witnesses were wrong. Yet these were highly trained, experienced witnesses who were performing a familiar procedure in familiar surroundings. And they had a 30-minute opportunity to observe JFK's wounds with little to distract them because so many people were helping with an effort that is often comfortably handled by one-fourth of the number of people who were on hand. Only a few Parkland witnesses—witnesses who played a minor role in JFK's care—gave vague descriptions. And it is only these who, while they don't reflect what is visible in the autopsy photographs, don't flatly contradict them.[113] So even if one were to accept witness error as an explanation, one has still to explain how so many of experienced witnesses made the exact same mistake by agreeing with the same wrong location.

The HSCA vs. Parkland Witnesses

The controversy over Parkland witnesses' descriptions of JFK's skull wound is over twenty years old. In fact, as noted in Part I, the HSCA, which in 1978 reversed the Warren Commission's 1964 verdict by concluding that a conspiracy was "probable" in JFK's death, made a specific point of refuting Parkland witnesses on the appearance of JFK's skull wound. The HSCA wrote, "Critics of the Warren Commission's medical evidence findings have found (sic) on the observations recorded by the Parkland Hospital doctors. They believe it is unlikely that trained medical personnel could be so consistently in error regarding the nature of the wound, even though their recollections were not based on careful examinations of the wounds . . . In disagreement with the observations of the Parkland doctors are the 26 people present at the autopsy. *All of those interviewed* who attended the autopsy corroborated the general location of the wounds as depicted in the photographs; *none had differing accounts* . . . it appears more probable that the observations of the Parkland doctors are incorrect."[114] (author's emphasis.)

The HSCA said its statement was supported by "Staff interviews with persons present at the autopsy." The HSCA's finding was devastating to skeptics who believed that Parkland witnesses proved a different wound, a different bullet trajectory, and, most importantly, a different gunman than Oswald. In *JAMA* Breo tried to put the "mistake" in perspective, explaining that Parkland witnesses were more concerned with saving JFK's life in an emergency situation than accurately observing his wounds.[115] By contrast, the refuting autopsy witnesses, some of whom were physicians, calmly watched the pathologists explore JFK's wounds over a period of several hours. They were certainly in a better position than the emergency personnel to accurately observe JFK's wounds. But the proof—the autopsy witnesses' actual interviews—did not appear anywhere in the 12 volumes the HSCA published. And they were also withheld from public inspection. Had it not been for the ARRB, access to these non-sensitive interviews would have been restricted until 2029.

ARRB-released documents have revealed for the first time that the HSCA misrepresented the statements of its own Bethesda autopsy witnesses on the location of JFK's skull defect. The HSCA also misrepresented the Warren Commission statements of the autopsy witnesses as well, that is, assuming the HSCA author was aware of them It was not true, as the HSCA reported, that it had 26 autopsy witnesses who disagreed with the Dallas doctors. The HSCA had interviewed perhaps 13 autopsy witnesses. None of them disagreed with the descriptions given by the Dallas doctors. Whereas over 20 witnesses at Parkland described JFK's skull defect as rearward, the HSCA's autopsy witnesses said the same thing, whether in public Warren Commission documents, or in the suppressed HSCA interviews. In fact, not a single one of the autopsy witnesses described the right-front skull wound that appears in the photographs. (See Table I: Observations at Parkland, and Table II: Observations at Bethesda.) Assuming the photographs were accurate representations of JFK's wounds, the mystery suddenly doubled. Not only were all the witnesses' descriptions wrong, not one of them—of over 40 from two different locations—got it right!

For example, in his Warren Commission testimony Secret Service agent, Clinton J. Hill, said, "When I arrived the autopsy had been completed and I observed . . . (a) wound on the right rear portion of the skull."[116] Hill's recollections, as well as other, similar autopsy witness descriptions of JFK's rearward skull defect, have been available in the Warren Commission volumes since 1964. But what of the HSCA's suppressed autopsy witnesses?

Jan Gail Rudnicki, a lab assistant on the night of the autopsy, was interviewed on 5/2/78 by the HSCA. Although no verbatim transcript survives, the interviewer, Mark Flanagan, J.D., reported Rudnicki told him, the *"back-right quadrant of the head was missin."*[117](author's emphasis). Philip C. Wehle, Commanding officer of the military District of Washington, D. C., was interviewed by HSCA counsel, D. Andy Purdy, J.D. on 8-19-77. Purdy's recently released memo, released with no transcript, states, "(Wehle) noted that the wound was in the *back of the head* so he would not see it because the President was lying face up"[118] (author's emphasis). Several of the autopsy witnesses, including two FBI agents, prepared diagrams for the HSCA that depicted JFK's skull defect as rearward. These diagrams were also suppressed.

	RIGHT REAR	RIGHT SIDE	RIGHT ANTERIOR
1. WILLIAM KEMP CLARK, MD	X		
2. ROBERT McCLELLAND, MD	X		
3 MARION T. JENKINS, MD	X		
4. CHARLES J. CARRICO, MD	X		
5. MALCOLM PERRY, MD	X		
6. RONALD COY JONES, MD	X		
7. GENE AKIN, MD	X		
8. PAUL PETERS, MD	X		
9. CHARLES CRENSHAW, MD	X		
10. CHARLES R. BAXTER, MD	X		
11. ROBERT GROSSMAN, MD	X	X	
12. RICHARD B. DULANY, MD	X		
13. ADOLPHE GIESECKE, MD*	X	X	X
14. FOUAD BASHOUR, MD	X		
15. KENNETH E. SALYER, MD	X	X	X
16. PAT HUTTON, RN	Z		
17. DORIS NELSON, RN	X		
18. WILLIAM GREER	X		
19. CLINTON J. HILL	X		
20. DIANA HAMILTON BOWRON	X		
21. WILLIAM MIDGETT	X	X	

Table I: Observations at Parkland (earliest statements)

	RIGHT REAR	RIGHT ONLY	RIGHT ANTERIOR
1. GODFREY McHUGH	X		
2. JOHN STRINGER	X		
3. WILLIAM GREER	X		
4. ROY KELLERMAN	X		
5. CLINTON J. HILL	X		
6. FRANCIS O'NEILL	X		
7. JAMES W. SIBERT	X		
8. TOM ROBINSON	X		
9. ROBERT KARNEI, MD	X		
10. PAUL O'CONNOR	X		X
11. JAMES C. JENKINS	X		
12. EDWARD REED	X		
13. JERROL CUSTER	X		
14. JAN GAIL RUDNICKI	X		
15 JAMES E. METZLER	X		
16. DAVID OSBORNE, MD	X		
17. JOHN EBERSOLE, MD	X		
18. RICHARD LIPSEY	X		
19. CAPT. JOHN STOVER	(? – "TOP OF HEAD")		
20. CHESTER BOYERS	X		X
21. JAMES HUMES, MD	X		X
22. J T BOSWELL, MD	X		X

Table II: Observations at Bethesda (earliest statements)

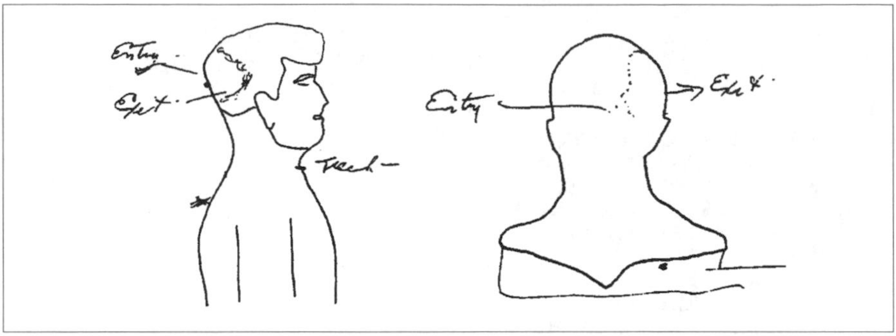

Figure 8. This diagram of JFK's skull wound was prepared by
FBI Agent Francis O'Neill for the HSCA in 1978.

I searched for the author of the HSCA's inaccurate summary, and the identity of the person who had decided to keep the interviews and diagrams from the public. I wrote HSCA counsel, Mark Flanagan, J.D., who had conducted a number of the interviews. He never answered. HSCA counsel, D. Andy Purdy, J.D., who conducted many of the interviews, and the former HSCA chief counsel, Robert Blakey, now a Notre Dame law professor, both denied any knowledge of the author of the inaccurate passage. Purdy did concede, however, that he was "not happy" with the wording of the passage.

As previously noted, the public was not the only group that was kept in the dark about the HSCA's autopsy witnesses. So too were the HSCA's own expert forensic consultants. In 1995, I showed both the head of the HSCA's forensic panel, Michael Baden, M.D., and one of the panelists, Cyril Wecht, M.D., J.D., the current coroner of Pittsburgh, the suppressed autopsy interviews and diagrams.[119] Neither had ever seen them before, despite the fact it was their responsibility to assess this evidence for the HSCA. Had this knowledge of the vast discrepancies between myriad witnesses and the photographs been shared with the HSCA's forensics consultants, it might have led the HSCA investigators toward evidence only finally unearthed by the ARRB twenty years later: the likelihood autopsy photographs are missing, and the possibility that some of those that remain have been tampered with.

Tampering with Photographs

While the HSCA claimed the autopsy photographs were "authenticated," there are problems with the extant photographic record:

- All three of JFK's pathologists, Bethesda pathologist-witness, Robert Karnei, M.D., and both autopsy photographers recalled that specific photographs were taken during the President's autopsy that do not now exist.
- Chief White House photographer, Robert Knudsen told the HSCA (in formerly suppressed interviews conducted in 1978) that right after the assassination he developed images that do not now exist. In 1997 former government photographer Joe O'Donnell told the ARRB that in 1963 his friend, Robert Knudsen, showed him a photograph of JFK's head that revealed a large hole in the backside of the skull. No such image can now be found in the official inventory.

- Naval Photographic Center employee Saundra Spencer told the ARRB that while developing JFK's autopsy photographs shortly after the assassination she, like Joseph O'Donnell, also saw an image revealing a hole in the back of JFK's skull. She also claimed that the film on which current autopsy photographs appear was *not* available in the lab where it is supposed to have developed in November 1963.

- Chief autopsy photographer John Stringer disavowed the extant autopsy photographs of JFK's brain. Though Stringer was the photographer of record, he swore to the ARRB that he did not take the extant images. Moreover, he said that the current images were taken on film he is certain he did not use in 1963.

- Robert Grossman, M.D., a neurosurgeon who attended JFK at Parkland hospital in Dallas, was shown an image of the back of JFK's head taken from the autopsy. As investigator Doug Horne put it in an ARRB memo, "When shown the Ida Dox drawing of the back of the head autopsy image found on page 104 of HSCA Volume 7 (Figure 1), Dr. Grossman immediately opined, 'that's completely incorrect.'"[120] Dr. Grossman then drew on a diagram of a human skull a defect square in the occiput that coincided with his clear recollection of the size and location of a defect in the back of JFK's skull (Figure 9).

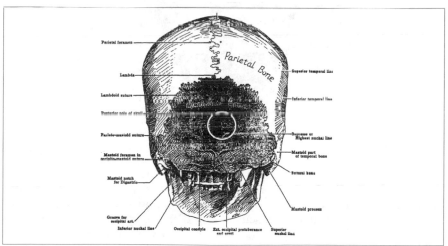

Figure 9 Diagram of JFK's rearward skull wound according to Robert Grossman, M.D., one of JFK's treating neurosurgeons. [Author's note: Dr. Grossman also recalled that in addition to this rearward wound, JFK also had a distinct and separate wound on the right side of his skull.]

- Upon being shown the autopsy photographs for the first time in 1997, the two FBI agents who witnessed the autopsy, Francis X. O'Neill and James Sibert, told the ARRB the image showing the backside of JFK's skull intact had been, as agent O'Neill initially put it, "doctored." Both agents claimed there was a sizable defect in the rear of JFK's skull. Sibert indicated the size and location of JFK's right-rearward skull defect on a diagram he prepared for the ARRB (Figure 10).

The Photographic Inventory

But as with so much else in the Kennedy case, the photographic record of the autopsy is also paradoxical. There is, in fact, some evidence that the photographic file *is* complete. That evidence consists of an inventory signed by pathologists James H. Humes, M.D. and J. Thornton Boswell, M.D., radiologist John Ebersole, and autopsy photographer, John Stringer. Signed on 11/1/66 after they had examined the autopsy photographs for the first time, the inventory includes a sentence that reads, "The X-rays and photographs described and listed above include all the X-rays and photographs taken by us during the autopsy, and we have no reason to believe that any other photographs or X-rays were made during the autopsy."[121]

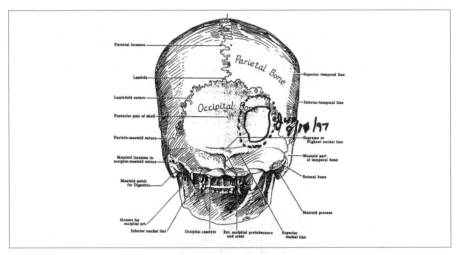

Figure 10. Diagram of skull wound by FBI agent James Sibert for the ARRB

This attestation is not truthful, and it was not written by the men who signed it. Instead, it is likely that someone at the U. S. Justice Department—the agency under whose authority the FBI investigated the JFK murder for the Warren Commission in 1964—prepared this document for them to sign. This was shown by a recently declassified document that was signed by Carl W. Belcher of the U.S. Justice Department. The document reads, "On the afternoon of November 10, 1966, I took the original and one carbon copy of the document entitled 'Report of Inspection by Naval Medical Staff on November 1, 1966 at National Archives of X-Rays and Photographs of Autopsy of President John F. Kennedy' to the Naval Medical Center, Bethesda, M.D., where it was read and signed by Captain Humes, Dr. Boswell, Captain Ebersole and Mr. John T. Stringer. Certain ink corrections were made in the document before they signed it." [122]

This memo probably reflects the importance that Attorney General Ramsey Clark attached to getting additional corroboration for the Warren Commission's autopsy findings, even if only self-affirmations from JFK's original pathologists. For after LBJ spoke with Ramsey Clark on 26 January 1967, the President wrote a once-secret memo which includes the comment: "On the other matter, I think we have the three pathologists and the photographer signed up now on the autopsy review and their conclusion is that the autopsy photos and x-rays [sic] conclusively support the autopsy report rendered by them to the Warren Commission *though we were not able to tie down the question of the missing photo entirely* but we feel much better about it and we have three of the four sign an affidavit that says these are all the photos that they took and they do not believe anybody else took any others. *There is this unfortunate reference in the Warren Commission report by Dr. Hinn* [sic—almost certainly "Dr. Humes," for the name "Dr. Hinn" or "Mr. Hinn" appears nowhere else in the Kennedy saga] *to a picture that just does not exist as far as we know"*[123] (author's emphasis).

This self-affirmation appears to have been judged insufficient. Afterward— and at least as far as the public was concerned—JFK pathologist J. Thornton Boswell *apparently* took it upon himself to write the Justice Department to request an independent reexamination of JFK's autopsy evidence. In response, Ramsey Clark convened a civilian panel to do just that: the so-called "Clark Panel." Though Boswell wrote up the request, behind him, again, was the Justice Department at play. Under oath, Boswell told the ARRB, "I was asked by . . . One of the attorneys for the Justice Department that I write them a letter and request a civilian group be appointed by the Justice Department, I believe, or the President or somebody. And I did write a letter to him, Carl Eardley."[124]

While LBJ's memo is the first document that revealed some officials were aware that there might have been a missing autopsy photograph, even Johnson's memo isn't quite accurate. Before the Warren Commission Humes did not describe just one image that is nowhere to be found in the current inventory; he described two: a photograph of the interior of JFK's chest, and another showing the entrance wound in skull bone. Thus although they affixed their signatures attesting to the completeness of the photo file in 1966, powerful evidence suggests that Humes, Boswell and Stringer were then fully aware the declaration was not true.

Missing Chest Photographs

During Humes's testimony before the Warren Commission, he said that in order to document the path of the nonfatal bullet through a bruised area at the top of JFK's lung cavity, "Kodachrome photographs were made . . . in the interior of the President's chest." No such images are known to exist. Humes nevertheless continued to remember that he had taken these images. In 1978, the HSCA's Andy Purdy reported, "(Humes) specifically recall(ed) photographs" were taken of the President's chest: "(these photographs) do not exist."[125] Eighteen years later Humes again said much the same thing. In 1996, Humes told the ARRB under oath, "We took one of the interior of the right side of the thorax . . . and I never saw it. It never—whether it was under-exposed or over-exposed or what happened to it, I don't know."[126] Humes was not the only signatory to recall internal, chest photographs.

Another signatory to the 11/1/66 affidavit, J. Thornton Boswell, M.D., was interviewed by the HSCA in the late 1970s. The HSCA reported that Boswell "thought they photographed "'the exposed thoracic cavity and lung'" but doesn't remember ever seeing those photographs."[127] In 1996, he told the same story. ARRB general counsel T. Jeremy Gunn asked Boswell, "(A)re there any other photographs that you remember having been taken during the time of the autopsy that you don't see here?" Boswell answered, "The only one that I have a faint memory of was the anterior of the right thorax. I don't see it, and haven't (sic) when we tried to find it on previous occasions, because that was very important because it did show the extra-pleural blood clot and was very important to our positioning that wound."[128]

Similarly, chief autopsy photographer John Stringer, told both the HSCA and the ARRB that chest photographs were missing. The HSCA reported, "(John) Stringer remembers taking 'at least two exposures of the body cavity.'"[129] He swore to the ARRB that, "There were some views that we—that were taken that were missing . . . I remember (photographing) some things inside the body that weren't there."[130] Stringer also took exception to the fact that the record reflects he submitted 11 duplex film holders of undeveloped film to authorities, which should have yielded 22 images; and yet only 16 duplex images made it to the current inventory. (To the authors' knowledge, the last 11/1/66 signatory, radiologist John Ebersole, who died in September 1993,[131] was never asked about the autopsy photographs.)

The taking of interior body photographs was also recalled by another central witness, albeit one who had not signed the 11/1/66 affidavit. The HSCA reported that assistant autopsy photographer Floyd Riebe "thought he took about six pictures—'I think it was three film packs'—of internal portions of the body."[132] Riebe also gave the HSCA additional, new evidence pertaining to missing autopsy photographs. "(Floyd) Riebe said he took photographs (using) a Canon 35-mm single lens reflex and a Speedgraph (sic) lens 4 x 5."[133] There is no 35-mm film in the current inventory. Riebe repeated his claim about 35-mm film under oath to the ARRB, asserting that he'd taken six or seven 35-mm photographs with a Canon camera.[134] So besides the missing chest images Stringer took with his large format camera, there may also be 35-mm images missing.

One question naturally comes to mind: Why would witnesses who repeatedly testified the inventory of autopsy photographs was incomplete have signed the Justice Department's affidavit affirming the inventory's completeness? While it is unlikely an indisputable explanation will be found to account for the actions of all the signatories, the autopsy photographers gave the ARRB an illuminating explanation for their having signed another false affidavit about the total number of photographs taken at the autopsy. Dated 11/22/63, the ARRB excavated a second false affidavit—ARRB Exhibit #78—that specified the number of photographs that were taken on the night of the autopsy and surrendered by the photographers to the custody of Secret Service agent, Roy H. Kellerman. The affidavit was signed by John Stringer and Floyd Riebe.[135]

ARRB counsel Gunn asked Stringer: "Do you see the phrase, next to last sentence, of the document—that I'll read it to you: 'To my personal knowledge, this is the total amount of film exposed on this occasion.' Do you see that?"

Stringer: "Yes."
Gunn: "Is it your understanding that that statement is incorrect?"
Stringer: "Well, yes . . . ."

Gunn: "When you signed this document, Exhibit 78, were you intending
            to either agree or disagree with the conclusion reached in the
            second to last—next to last sentence?"
Stringer: "I told him that I disagreed with him, but they said, 'Sign it.'"
Gunn: "And who is 'they' who said, 'Sign it.'?
Stringer: "Captain Stover." (Stringer's superior, and the Commanding Of-
            ficer of U.S. Naval Medical School.)[136]

Similarly, assistant autopsy photographer, Floyd Riebe, testified that this same
            affidavit, which also bore his signature, "would be incorrect,
            yes,"[137] for it did not list the 35-mm images he said he had taken.
ARRB counsel Gunn asked him: "If this statement had been given to you to
            sign to authenticate rather than (Captain) Stover, would you have
            signed this statement?"
Riebe: "If I was ordered to, yes . . . We was shown this and told to sign it
            and that was it."[138]

Jeremy Gunn did not expound more fully on this issue with Riebe. And, alas,
though he had the opportunity to ask Drs. Humes and Boswell, and John Stringer,
why they had signed affirming the autopsy inventory was complete, he did not
do so. This, despite the fact the ARRB was already aware of the fact that Humes'
prior testimony had not been entirely truthful.

On August 2, 1998, the *Associated Press* quoted an ARRB finding: "Under
oath, Dr. Humes, finally acknowledged under persistent questioning—in testimony that differs from what he told the Warren Commission—that he had destroyed both his notes taken at the autopsy and the first draft of the autopsy
report."[139] Thus the ARRB extracted Humes' admission that he had burned *both*
a preliminary draft of the autopsy report, which he had admitted before, as well
as original autopsy notes prepared on the night of the autopsy, a fact that was
inconsistent with what he had told the Warren Commission. Besides his ARRB
admission conflicting with his 1964 testimony, it also contradicted two affidavits
he had signed shortly after the assassination. On 24 November 1963 Humes "certified" over his signature that he had "destroyed by burning certain preliminary
draft notes relating to" JFK's autopsy,[140] but that otherwise, "all working papers
associated with (JFK's autopsy) have remained in my personal custody at all
times. Autopsy notes and the holograph draft of the final report were handed to
Commanding Officer, U.S. Naval Medical School, at 1700, 24 November 1963."[141]

Humes' latter statement, repeated to the Warren Commission, was not precisely true. All "working papers" and "autopsy notes" had *not* remained with him
until he turned them over to his superior. He destroyed some of them, including
original notes he'd taken himself. But this was not an entirely new story. For
despite his Commission testimony and this affidavit averring otherwise, Humes
had previously acknowledged destroying original autopsy notes, in *JAMA*. The
explanation Humes gave—that he destroyed the bloodstained notes so they would
never become an object of morbid curiosity (because of the presence of JFK's
blood)—is unconvincing. Boswell's "face sheet," which he chose not to destroy, is
also stained with JFK's blood (Figure 4). Besides having destroyed his own autopsy notes, Humes apparently also destroyed those of his forensic consultant,
Pierre Finck, M.D.

In 1998 the *Associated Press*'s Mike Feinsilber reported that, "In an affidavit, Leonard D. Saslaw, Ph.D., a biochemist who worked at the Armed Forces Institute of Pathology in Bethesda, M.D., said that at lunch in the week following the assassination he overheard one of the autopsy doctors, Pierre Finck, 'complain that he had been unable to locate the handwritten notes that he had taken during the autopsy . . . Dr. Finck elaborated to his companions, with considerable irritation, that immediately after washing up following the autopsy, he looked for his notes, and could not find them anywhere.'" The ARRB added that, "Dr. Saslaw's main concern with what he heard Dr. Finck say is that as a scientist, he is well aware that any observations which are not written down contemporaneously, but reconstructed from memory after the fact, are not likely to be as accurate or complete as the original observations were."[142] Feinsilber also reported that, "Finck told the board he couldn't recall the lunchroom conversation."[143] Regarding the wrongly destroyed original autopsy notes and the false affidavits from JFK's pathologists, there is one question worth pondering: Would this have been a problem if JFK had been examined by civilian autopsists, that is, by men not under military command?

Missing Cranial Photographs

The other missing photographs Humes referred to in his Warren Commission testimony are at least as interesting as the missing chest photographs: images showing the entrance wound in JFK's skull bone. As Humes described them to the Warren Commission, these photographs had been taken to demonstrate the direction of the bullet's path. He said, "This (JFK's skull) wound then had the characteristics of wound of entrance from this direction through the two tables of the skull . . . and incidentally photographs illustrating this ("coning" or "beveling") phenomenon (that show the bullet's direction) from both the external surface of the skull and from the internal surface were prepared."[144]

In 1978 Humes' claim was independently corroborated by the only forensics-trained pathologist to attend JFK's autopsy, Pierre Finck, M.D. While testifying before the HSCA, he referred to some old notes he had brought along on the JFK case. In these notes, which Finck apparently prepared contemporaneously and submitted to the HSCA, he had written: "I help the Navy photographer to take photographs of the occipital wound (external and internal aspects) (sic)."[145] The purpose of such photographs, of course, was to show a forensically important feature of a bullet entrance wound: "beveling," or "coning." As with a B-B hitting a pane of glass, when a bullet goes through bone a small hole is usually left on the outside, and a larger, "beveled," crater is left on the inside. This "beveling phenomenon" is used by pathologists, though not infallibly, as an aid in determining the direction of the bullet.

Since proving the cause of death with images of the fatal would have been the central purpose to photographing the autopsy, capturing the "beveling" in JFK's skull bone would have been a routine, even elemental, kind of documentation. Suitable images would only have been taken of bone, not of soft tissue such as scalp. For "soft tissue" such as scalp will not demonstrate beveling, just as a bullet "wound" through a carpet will not show the "beveling" one would see in a "wound" through a pane of glass.

Before the HSCA in 1977, Finck described how he had directed the taking of images to specifically demonstrate how the beveling in the bone proved the bullet had entered low in JFK's skull, in occipital bone. His testimony, only released, finally, by the ARRB in 1993, shows him under siege before the HSCA's forensic consultants who were convinced there was *no* wound where Finck said it was in occipital bone. Under oath Finck insisted he directed the taking of photographs of the low wound, photographs that do not now exist.

In the following exchange, Finck was being shown the autopsy photographs before the forensics panel and asked to comment on them:

(HSCA counsel D. Andy) Purdy: "We have here a black and white blow up of that same spot (a spot on the rear of JFK's scalp he claimed was the location of the bullet's entrance—see Figure 1). You previously mentioned that your attempt here was to photograph the crater, I think was the word that you used."

Finck: "In the bone, not in the scalp, because to determine the direction of the projectile the bone is a very good source of information, so I emphasize the photographs of the crater seen from the inside the skull. What you are showing me is soft tissue wound (sic) in the scalp."

A few moments later, the following exchange occurred:

(Charles) Petty, M.D.: "If I understand you correctly, Dr. Finck, you wanted particularly to have a photograph made of the external aspect of the skull from the back to show that there was no cratering to the outside of the skull."

Finck: "Absolutely."
Petty: "Did you ever see such a photograph?"
Finck: "I don't think so and I brought with me memorandum referring to the examination of photographs in 1967 and as I can recall I never saw pictures of the outer aspect of the wound of entry in the back of the head and inner aspect in the skull in order to show a crater although I was there asking for (the photographer to take) these photographs. I don't remember seeing those photographs."

Petty: "All right. Let me ask you one other question. In order to expose that area where the wound was present in the bone, did you have to or did someone have to dissect the scalp off of the bone in order to show this?"

Finck: "Yes."
Petty: "Was this a difficult dissection and did it go very low into the head so as to expose the external aspect of the posterior cranial fascia [sic: He probably meant to say "fossa"]?"

Finck: "I don't remember the difficulty involved in separating the scalp from the skull but *this was done in order to have a clear view of the outside and inside to show the crater from the inside . . . the skull had to be separated from it in order to show in the back of the head the wound in the bone"* [146] (author's emphasis).

While no images survive in which JFK's scalp is shown reflected from the skull so as to demonstrate the skull wound [*Editor's note:* Apart from F8.], Finck wasn't the only one who remembered taking those pictures. Both autopsy photographers did, too.[147] For example, to Jeremy Gunn's question, "Did you take any photographs of the head after scalp had been pulled down or reflected," Stringer answered, "Yes."[148]

Tampered Photographs?

The ARRB interviewed the two FBI agents who were present during JFK's autopsy, Special Agents Francis X. O'Neill and James Sibert. Both had previously prepared diagrams of JFK's skull for the HSCA—only declassified by the ARRB—which depicted a rearward defect in JFK's skull (Figure 8). Interviewed by the ARRB and shown the autopsy images for the first time, both agents provided what is perhaps the most direct indictment of the extant autopsy images of JFK's skull.

ARRB counsel Gunn asked agent O'Neill: "I'd like to ask you whether that photograph (Figure 1) resembles what you saw from the back of the head at the time of the autopsy?" O'Neill: *"This looks like it's been doctored in some way*[149] . . . I specifically do not recall those—I mean, being that clean or that fixed up. To me, it looks like these pictures have been . . . It would appear to me that there was a—more of a massive wound . . . ."*[150] (author's emphasis) Similarly, Gunn asked agent Sibert, "Mr. Sibert, does that photograph correspond to your recollection of the back of President Kennedy's head?" Sibert: "Well, I don't have a recollection of it being that intact, as compared with these other pictures. I don't remember seeing anything that was like this photo . . . I don't recall anything like this at all during the autopsy. There was much—Well, the wound was more pronounced. And it looks like it could have been reconstructed or something, as compared with what my recollection was . . . ."[151] The ARRB produced an anatomical drawing that Sibert had marked denoting the right rearward location of JFK's skull wound (Figure 10).

Have Photographs Disappeared?

With so many reports of images having been taken that do not now exist, the question naturally arises: Did anyone ever see autopsy images that have since disappeared? The answer apparently is yes.

In another previously suppressed HSCA interview, former White House photographer, Robert Knudsen, who has since died, reported that he developed some negatives from JFK's autopsy, examining them in the course of his work on 23 November 1963. During the HSCA's investigation, he was shown the complete photographic inventory. Repeatedly resisting pressure to back down, Knudsen insisted that in 1963 he saw at least one image not in the inventory he was shown in 1978: an image with a metal probe (or probes) through JFK's body that entered the back at a lower position than it exited through the throat wound.[152] [Robert Karnei, M.D., a pathologist who attended the President's autopsy, gave the HSCA a similar account. The HSCA reported that, "He (Karnei) recalls them putting the probe in and taking pictures (the body was on the side at the time) (sic)."[153]] Inasmuch as Oswald is supposed to have fired from above and behind JFK, who was not leaning forward, if the back wound was indeed lower than its supposed exit mate in the throat, Oswald simply didn't do it.

There are two other witnesses who testified they saw now nonexistent photographs of JFK's head in 1963: The first was a government photographer with the United States Information Agency, Mr. Joseph O'Donnell, who was frequently detailed to the White House during the Kennedy era. Interviewed by ARRB counsel T. Jeremy Gunn, O'Donnell claimed that within a month of the assassination he was shown JFK's autopsy photographs on two occasions by his friend, White House photographer Robert Knudsen. Gunn reported that on the first occasion O'Donnell "remember(ed) a photograph of a gaping wound in the back of the head which was big enough to put a fist through, in which the image clearly showed a total absence of hair and bone, and a cavity which was the result of a lot of interior matter missing from inside the cranium."[154] On the second viewing, Knudsen showed him a photograph "in which the back of the head now looked completely intact. He (O'Donnell) said that the appearance of the hair in the 'intact back of the head' photographs was wet, clean, and freshly combed. IIis interpretation of the differences in the photographs of the President's head was to attribute the differences to the restorative work of the embalmers."[155]

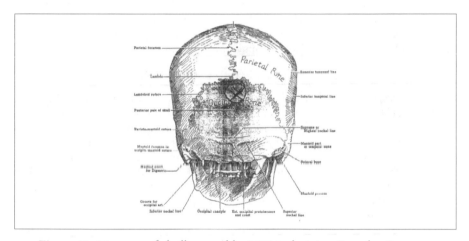

Figure 11. Diagram of skull wound by NPC technician Saundra Spencer.

Saundra Kay Spencer, a woman who developed and printed JFK autopsy images at the Naval Photographic Center (NPC) in November 1963, told the ARRB that she saw an image that revealed a hole 1 to 2 inches in diameter in the backside of JFK's skull. She located the spot on a diagram of a human skull, marking a defect that is considerably larger than, and well below, the small spot interpreted by the HSCA as the true wound of entrance.[156] (See Figure 11.) Moreover, she said that the images she developed looked nothing like those in the current inventory, but showed JFK's wounds 'cleaned up': "(N)one of the heavy damage that shows in these (the National Archives) photographs were visible in the photographs that we did."[157] Moreover, the paper on which the current photographs are printed is *not* the paper that was used by her lab in 1963, a point on which she expressed confidence because she had kept in her personal possession, and produced for the ARRB, some paper that was used at the NPC at the time she printed JFK's autopsy images.[158]

Similarly, assistant photographer Floyd Riebe told the ARRB that, in addition to now missing 35-mm images, he also took about one hundred black and white, "press pack" photographs using a large format (4 x 5) camera.[159] Shown the extant black and white images that are on thick, notched film, Riebe claimed the current images are not on the kind of film he used, which was thinner and unnotched.[160] None of the current images are on the kind of film Riebe said he had used.

After I reviewed the evidence for missing JFK autopsy photographs with Dr. Michael Baden in April, 2000, he responded that the HSCA's forensics panel had not placed much importance on missing pictures. For they had heard reports (Humes' claim in *JAMA* in 1992) that officials had confiscated the film of an unauthorized corpsman who was snapping away during JFK's autopsy. However, neither of the official photographers—Stringer and Riebe—reported that this had happened to them, and Humes knew that neither Floyd nor Reibe were the "unauthorized corpsman"; and yet it is the authorized film they said they took that can't be accounted for today. Nevertheless, the persuasive witness evidence that the ARRB compiled undermining the HSCA's autopsy conclusions is not the only reason the ARRB found to mistrust the HSCA on the autopsy evidence. It also found that the HSCA had not been entirely frank when it reported that it had authenticated JFK's autopsy photographs.

The HSCA "Authentication"

Bolstering its case that the autopsy evidence was consistent with Oswald's guilt, the HSCA announced that it had authenticated JFK's autopsy photographs. However, the HSCA publicly admitted that its authentication was not quite complete. It wrote, "Because the Department of Defense was unable to locate the camera and lens that were used to take these [autopsy] photographs, the [photographic] panel was unable to engage in an analysis similar to the one undertaken with the Oswald backyard pictures that was designed to determine whether a particular camera in issue had been used to take the photographs that were the subject of inquiry."[161]

In effect, the HSCA was saying that it was unhappy the original camera was unavailable to totally close the loop. Nevertheless, it expressed satisfaction the loop had been closed enough for confidence in the images because it had found features in the extant images that showed a kind of internal consistency one would only find in authentic images. Those consistencies, in essence, comprised the HSCA's entire case for authentication. But there was an important part of the story the HSCA didn't tell.

Luckily, the ARRB's Doug Horne did tell it, after a little excavation of once-suppressed HSCA files. It is a rather different story from the one implied by the HSCA's comment, "Because the Department of Defense was unable to locate the camera and lens that were used to take these [autopsy] photographs. . . . Regarding that sentence, Horne wrote, "By late 1997, enough related documents had been located and assembled by the authors to bring into serious doubt the accuracy of the HSCA's [statement]."[162] It was not precisely true the Department of Defense had been unable to locate the camera used to take JFK's autopsy photographs.

Apparently, the DoD *had* found the camera. The DoD had written the HSCA a letter declaring that "the only [camera] in use at the National Naval Medical Center in 1963"[163] had been sent to the HSCA for study. The HSCA, however, wasn't happy with the autopsy camera the DoD had sent. In a letter asking the Secretary of Defense to look for another one, Robert Blakey explained the problem: "[O]ur photographic experts have determined that this camera, or at least the particular lens and shutter attached to it, could not have been used to take [JFK's] autopsy pictures."[164] Whereas the HSCA publicly declared the original autopsy camera could not be located, the suppressed record suggests that in fact the correct camera had been found, but that it couldn't be matched to JFK's images.

Horne reported that Kodak, which did work for the ARRB, found no evidence the current autopsy images had been falsified. And as Horne emphasized in his memo, the HSCA's misstatement, as misleading as it is, may not be as sinister as it seems at first blush. The type of camera used was a "view" camera. It had a flat, square back that houses the film packs, and an attached bellows. Attached to the front of the bellows are an interchangeable lens and a shutter mechanism, which may be switched out for different tasks. The lens and shutter used in 1963 *may* have been replaced by the time the DoD fetched the camera for the HSCA in 1977. And so a different lens or shutter *might* explain why the camera didn't match JFK's photographs. But unfortunately there is no certainty that a different lens and shutter *do* explain the mismatch. Horne searched through the files for the tests the HSCA had conducted that proved a mismatch, but could find none. He also searched for the camera, and reported it has been lost.

So while Horne was unable to confirm an innocent explanation for the mismatch, he was unable to exclude the obvious, sinister explanation: photo tampering. The Kodak finding that the extant images reveal no tampering proves that the extant images themselves have no internal inconsistencies that would prove tampering. It cannot, however, prove that no images are missing, which in fact appears to be the case. Nor can it disprove another possibility: that the current inventory is an entirely separate set of internally consistent images, but a different set than the one that may have originally existed. So speculation that there was some kind of photographic "doctoring" is not merely the conclusion of Charles Crenshaw: it has significant support in the record. In fact, the word "doctored" was precisely the word FBI agent Francis O'Neill initially used under oath when he was first shown JFK's autopsy photographs by the ARRB.

Two Brain Examinations

On 10 November 1998, the *Washington Post* reported, "Archive photos not of JFK's brain, concludes aide to review board; staff member contends 2 different specimens were examined." The report was the first public airing of an ARRB memo advancing the "two brain" hypothesis of former Naval officer, and ARRB staffer, Doug Horne. Carefully comparing accounts of the appearance of JFK's brain on the night of the autopsy with photographs of what are said to be images of JFK's brain taken at a later, "supplemental," examination, Horne found significant discrepancies. Additional conflicts were found between credible accounts of the date when the supplemental brain examination was supposed to have been performed.

Witnesses described that a large portion of the right side of JFK's brain was absent on the night of the autopsy, and that there was damage to the cerebellum. Yet, the brain photographed during the supplemental examination reveals only a disruption of the right cerebrum with no appreciable loss of tissue, and with no loss of cerebellum. Moreover, the brain examined during the supplemental examination weighed 1500 grams, which is the upper weight limit for a complete and undamaged brain. Yet Humes told *JAMA* that 2/3s of JFK's right cerebrum had been blown away. And FBI agent O'Neill told the ARRB in 1997 that when JFK's brain was removed, "more than half of the brain was missing."[165] Shown the photos in the National Archives, O'Neill rejected them, correctly claiming, "This looks almost like a complete brain."[166]

[Author's note: Indeed, assistant autopsy photographer, Floyd Riebe, recalled things much the same way. When asked by ARRB counsel, "Did you see the brain removed from President Kennedy?" Riebe answered, "What little bit there was left, yes . . . Well, it was less than half of a brain there."[167]] *[Editor's note*: That the diagrams and photographs in the National Archives purporting to be of JFK's brain must be of the brain of someone else was the conclusion drawn by Robert B. Livingston, M.D., a world authority on the human brain. Livingston's studies are found in *Assassination Science* (1998), pp. 161—166.]

Besides O'Neill's comments and the claims of other witnesses, the photographer of record, John Stringer, rejected the authenticity of the brain photographs at the National Archives. Stringer claimed that he took images of sections of the brain, which cannot now be located, and that the images in the current file were not taken with the type of camera, or the kind of film, he had used.

Finally, whereas several lines of evidence suggest an examination of JFK's brain was performed before the body was buried on 11/25/63, contemporaneous notes of pathologist Pierre Finck, M.D., show that he was not even contacted by chief pathologist James Humes, M.D., to examine the brain until 29 November 1963. The Chief Petty Officer in charge of the lab, Chester Boyers, "told the House Assassinations Committee in 1978 that he processed brain tissue" at a time that supports Finck's recollection of a later examination, on 2 December 1963.

Conclusions

While the medical and autopsy evidence regarding Oswald's guilt should be straightforward, it is not. A huge chasm exists between (1) the credible accounts of myriad, solid witnesses and the so-called "hard" evidence, nand (2) between the examining physicians at two different locations and the autopsy photographs and X-rays. That so-called "hard evidence" has been challenged not only by work published elsewhere—for example, in the chapter by David W. Mantik, M.D., Ph.D., found in *Assassination Science* (1998)—it has also been challenged by the very autopsy witnesses one would have expected to have endorsed the evidence, by the technicians who processed that evidence, and by authorities experienced with the injuries like those JFK sustained.

The hypothesis that JFK's autopsy evidence was illegally altered is not one that the responsible skeptic grabs; rather, it is one that grabs the responsible skeptic in his search for a reasonable explanation. Because it is the simplest, and perhaps the only, way to explain the following items: why witnesses who saw the dead president overwhelmingly described an Oswald-exculpating wound in the rear of JFK's skull; why other, credible witnesses rejected the images, even calling them "doctored"—precisely because they don't show JFK's rearward skull damage; why the record reflects that more negatives were submitted by the autopsy photographers than can now be accounted for; why doctors and photographers under military command signed false affidavits and swore untruthfully; why witnesses who developed the photographs rejected the supposed authentic images as well as the film on which the current images are printed; why both of JFK's autopsy photographers and all three of his pathologists have sworn that specific autopsy photographs are missing; and perhaps also why attempts failed to match the current batch of autopsy photographs to the camera that supposedly took them, as well as why neither JFK's autopsy camera nor the tests that authenticate it match current images; or why neither the camera nor the test can be found today.

Looked at another way, assuming that JFK's death was merely what the Warren Commission said it was—a deranged act by a disgruntled loner—are there not some fantastic improbabilities that smack of a cover-up? In an innocent scenario, how likely is it that records that never threatened national security would have been suppressed from the public for over thirty years? How likely that the once suppressed records would disclose that respected, high-ranking, military physicians had knowingly signed false affidavits and given misleading testimony supporting the official verdict? That overwhelming witness testimony, some of it falsified and suppressed by the HSCA, would contradict the "hard" X-ray and photographic autopsy evidence? That ample evidence would emerge that important autopsy images are missing? That the surviving photographs don't match the credible accounts of so many witnesses, and that there is much else in the record pointing to tampering with the same surviving photographs? And, finally, in the absence of a cover-up, how likely is it that the very medical and autopsy evidence that was suppressed and falsified would so often, upon release, turn out later to have supported Oswald's innocence?

Still incomplete, though continually unfolding, the JFK medical/autopsy evidence is nothing if not fascinating and disturbing. Most of it was available in 1992 when *JAMA* set out to correct the record in the aftermath of the public outrage provoked by Oliver Stone's film *JFK*. With its legendary research capabilities, *JAMA* could have begun to unravel some of the mysteries that were only solved six years later by the efforts of the ARRB. Unfortunately, *JAMA's* editor Lundberg (who has since been fired) squandered this historic opportunity in order to pursue another goal—punishing Oliver Stone, Charles Crenshaw and anyone else who dared to travel with them.

Notes

1 Marcus Raskin, "JFK and the Culture of Violence," *American Historical Review* (April 1992), pp. 487-499; Michael Rogin, "JFK: The Movie," *American Historical Review*, (April 1992), pp. 500-505; and Robert A. Rosenstone, "JFK: Historical Fact/Historical Fiction," *American Historical Review* (April 1992), pp. 506-511.

2 Dennis Breo, "JFK's death, part II—Dallas M.D.s recall their memories," *JAMA* 267 (27 May 1992), p. 2804.

3 Charles A. Crenshaw, *JFK—Conspiracy of Silence* (1992).

4 See, for example, Ben Bradley, "Dispute on JFK assassination evidence persists," *Boston Globe*, 21 June 1981, p. A23); authors Josiah Th-

ompson (*Six Seconds in Dallas* 1967, McClelland and Perry), David Lifton (*Best Evidence* 1988, Drs. Jenkins), and Robert Groden and Harrison Livingstone, *High Treason* 1989 (Charles Baxter, M.D.). Marion Thomas Jenkins, M.D., James Carrico, M.D., Charles Baxter, M.D., Paul Peters, M.D., and Robert Shaw, M.D. had even been interviewed as a group moderated by Kevin McCarthy, a radio talk show host, on 4 June1992; see Harrison Livingstone, *Killing the Truth* (1993), p. 172 ff.

5 *JAMA* (27 May 1992), p. 2804.

6 *JAMA* (27 May 1992), p. 2805.

7 Gerald Posner, *Case Closed* (1993), p. 314)

8 *JAMA* (27 May 1992), p. 2804.

9 Lawrence Altman, "28 Years After Dallas, A Doctor Tells His Story Amid Troubling Doubts", *The New York Times* (26 May 1992), p. C3.

10 6WC40.

11 6WC32, 40, 60, 80 and 131

12 *JAMA* (27 May 1992), p. 2805.

13 Posner (1993), p. 312

14 *JAMA* (27 May 1992), p. 2805.

15 Lifton (1988), p. 704.

16 HSCA record #10010042, agency file #002086, p. 2

17 Sylvia Chase, KRON TV interview.

18 6WC53-54.

19 6WC56.

20 Lifton (1988), p. 705.

21 17WC, CE-392

22 6WC29.

23 6WC65.

24 6WC67.

25 6WC71.

26 6WC33.

27 *Report of the Warren Copmmission on the Assassination of President Kennedy* (1964), p. 523. (WR)

28 6WC41

29 WR (1964), p. 504.

30 CE-386 and CE-388.

31 7HSCA114-115.

32 7HSCA246—260.

33 7HSCA254.

34 7HSCA115: "Dr. Humes agreed that the defect was in the 'cowlick' area and not in the area of the brain tissue."

35 7HSCA115.

36 Testimony of Edgewood Arsenal's Dr. A. G. Olivier, 5WC89.

37 CE-862.

38 John Lattimer, *Kennedy and Lincoln—Medical and Ballistic Comparisons of Their Assassinations* (1980), p. 254.

39 WR (1964), pp. 501 –502.

40 Testimony of Humes and Boswell, 7HSCA253.

41 Testimony of Humes and Boswell, 7HSCA246–260.

42 Lifton (1980).

43 7HSCA37-39.

44 HSCA interview with Pierre Finck, Agency File #013617, pp. 90-91; with Robert Karnie, Agency File #002198, p. 6. The Humes source is a memo titled, "President Johnson's notes on Conversation with Acting Attorney General Ramsey Clark—January 26, 1967— 6:29 PM," obtained by Kathy Cunningham from the Lyndon B. Johnson Library.

45 Autopsy photographer John Stringer, HSCA record #180-10093-10429, agency file #002070, p. 11.

46 Stringer also in HSCA record #180-10093-10429, agency file #002070, p. 2.

47 Humes in HSCA record #180-10093-10429, agency file # 002070, p. 17.

48 Boswell in HSCA record #180-10093-10430, agency file # 002071, p. 6.

49 Robert Karnei, M.D., in HSCA, JFK Collection, RG #233, file #002198, p.5.

50 Autopsy photographer Floyd Reibe in Lifton (1980), p. 638.

51 Robert Knudsen, in HSCA agency Ffle #014028 and HSCA agency file #002198, p. 5.

52 ARRB memo entitled, "Unanswered Questions Raised by the HSCA's Analysis and Conclusions Regarding the Camera Identified by the Navy and the Department of Defense as the Camera Used at President' Kennedy's Autopsy."

53 Ibid.

54 FBI agent Francis X. O'Neill's sworn testimony before the ARRB, 12 September 1997, p. 161-162.

55 FBI agent James W. Sibert's sworn testimony before the ARRB, 11 September 1997, p. 128.

56 Kemp Clark, M.D., CE-392.

57 Robert McClelland, M D, 6H33-37

58 Charles Carrico, M.D., CE-392 and 3H361.

59 Paul Peters, M.D., 6H71.

60 Ronald Coy Jones, M.D., 6H56.

61 Marion Thomas Jenkins, M.D., CE-392.

62 Malcolm Perry, M.D., CE-392 and 17II6. See also testimony at 3II368, 372. See also 7HSCA 292-293 and 302.

63 Gene Akin, M.D., 6H65, 67.

64 Charles Rufus Baxter, M.D., CE-392. In: WR, p. 523.

65 A full compilation of the witnesses may be found at http://home.cynet.net/jfk/ag6.htm/

66 Secret Service Agent Clinton J. Hill, CE-1024.

67 James Curtis Jenkins, a Ph.D. candidate in pathology: HSCA interview with Curtis Jenkins, Jim Kelly and Andy Purdy, 29 August 1977. JFK Collection, RG 233, Document #002193, p. 4.

68 Hill in CE-1024 and 18H744.

69 Jan Gail Rudnicki in HSCA record #180-10105-10397, agency file number #014461, p.2.

70 General Philip C. Wehle, commanding officer of the military District of Washington, D. C., HSCA record #10010042, agency file # 002086, p. 2

71 Testimony of John Stringer before the ARRB.

72 Elizabeth Loftus, Eyewitness Testimony (1996), pp. 25–28.

73 Elizabeth Loftus and James M. Doyle, Eyewitness Testimony: Civil and Criminal, Second Edition (1992).

74 Television interview, Malcolm Perry, M.D., provided by David Starks. Station not identified.

75 CE-392.

76 3H368.

77 3H372.

78 7H292-293.

79 7II302 interview with Purdy 11 January 1978

80 Posner (1993), p.312.

81 ANSWERS AND DEPOSITIONS OF CHARLES BAXTER, M.D., RONALD COY JONES, M.D., ROBERT M. McCLELLAND, M.D., MALCOLM O. PERRY, M.D., PAUL C. PETERS, M.D. before the ARRB, taken on 27 August 1998 at the offices of University of Texas, Southwest Medical Center, p. 19. (Hereafter referred to as "ARRB depositions of Parkland witnesses.")

82 Ibid., p. 23.

83 Posner (1993), p. 235.

84 3WC361.

85 HSCA vol. 7:268

86 Posner (1993), p.311.

87 CE-392. In: WR, p. 532.

88 6H48.

89 6H51.

90 7HSCA286-287.

91 Posner (1993), p. 312.

92 Ibid., p.313.

93 ARRB depositions of Parkland witnesses, p. 20.

94 ARRB depositions of Parkland witnesses, p. 32.

95 Ben Bradlee, "Dispute on JFK assassination evidence persists," Boston Globe (21 June 1981), p. A-23.

96 Lifton (1988), p.704.

97   ARRB depositions of Parkland wit-
     nesses, p. 30.
98   ARRB M.D. #185. ARRB interview
     with Dr. Robert G. Grossman, 21
     March 1997.
99   CE-392. In WR, p. 520.
100 3H362
101 Harold Weisberg, *Post Mortem*
     (1975), p. 375.
102 Weisberg (1975), p.376.
103 "At the White House with Wayne
     Hawks" news conference, 22 No-
     vember 1963, 3:16 PM, CST, Dallas,
     Texas. Copy from LBJ library. The
     interview occured within 2 or 3
     hours of JFK's death.
104 Quoted in Lifton (1980), p. 56.
105 Quoted in Lifton (1980), p. 56.
106 3H378
107 3H375-376.
108 3H376.
109 WR, p. 93.
110 *Prodigy* interactive personal ser-
     vice, 14 February 1992, 7:45 AM, in
     "Arts Club" bulletin board, books-
     nonfiction. In a posting to John
     Hensley (NXVX71A) from Robert
     Artwohl (BSMK63A).
111 Including Drs. Marion.T. Jenkins,
     Malcolm Perry, Robert McClelland,
     Charles Carrico, Ronald C. Jones,
     Gene Aiken, Paul Peters, Charles R.
     Baxter, Robert Grossman, Richard
     B. Dulaney, Fouad Bashour, and
     others.
112 Loftus (1996), p. 25—26. See also
     the study to which Loftus refers,
     namely: J. Marshall, K.H. Marquis,
     S. Oskamp, "Effects of kind of ques-
     tion and atmosphere of interroga-
     tion on accuracy and completeness
     of testimony," *Harvard Law Review*,
     84 (1971), pp. 1620-1643.
113 Parkland witness Kenneth Salyer,
     M.D., for example, told the Warren
     Commission, "(JFK) had a wound
     of his right temporal region"I came
     in on the left side of him and no-
     ticed that his major wound seemed
     to be in his right temporal area"

     (6H81) But when I interviewed
     Salyer on 18 October 1993 and
     showed him copies of the authen-
     tic autopsy photographs demon-
     strating no wound behind JFK's
     right ear, Salyer said JFK's skull
     wound definitely extended behind
     JFK's ear. He also said that it ap-
     peared to him that the autopsy
     photographs had been tampered
     with. Thus Salyer confirmed the re-
     port of Robert Groden who said
     that Salyer believed the autopsy
     photographs showing an intact rear
     scalp appeared to have been tam-
     pered with.
114 7HSCA37—39.
115 Breo in *JAMA*. (27 May 1992).
116 CE-1024 (18H744).
117 HSCA record #180-10105-10397,
     agency file number #014461, p.2.
118 HSCA record #10010042, agency
     file #002086, p. 2
119 Michael Baden, M.D., may be
     reached in New York City; Cyril
     Wecht, M.D., J.D., is the coroner of
     Alleghaney County..
120 11 February 1998. ARRB memoran-
     dum to Jeremy Gunn and Tom
     Samoluk by Doug Horne entitled
     "Wrapping Up ARRB Efforts to
     'Clarify the Record' Re: The Medi-
     cal Evidence in the Assassination of
     President John F. Kennedy.'"
121 *Report of Inspection by Naval Medi-
     cal Staff on 11/1/66 at National Ar-
     chives of X-rays and Photographs of
     President John F. Kennedy*. In
     Weisberg (1975), p.573.
122 Memo from Carl W. Belcher, Chief,
     General Crimes Section, Criminal
     Division, US Dept. of Justice, 22
     November 1966. Agency:
     DOJCIVIL, Record #182-10001-
     100021
123 From a memo entitled "President
     Johnson's Notes on Conversation
     with Acting Attorney General
     Ramsey Clark—January 26, 1967—

6:29 P.M.," obtained from the Lyndon B. Johnson Library.

124 ARRB deposition of J. Thornton Boswell, 26 February 1996, p. 10.

125 HSCA record #180-10093-10429, agency file #002070, p. 17.

126 ARRB testimony of James J. Humes, 13 February 1999, p. 97.

127 A. Purdy. HSCA record #180-10093-10430, agency file #002071, p. 6

128 ARRB testimony of J. Thornton Boswell, 26 February 1996, p. 176-177.

129 HSCA record #180-10093-10429, agency file # 002070, p. 2.

130 ARRB Deposition of John T. Stringer, 16 July 1996, p. 133.

131 Obituary, *The New York Times*, 25 September 1993.

132 Lifton (1988), p.638.

133 HSCA counsel, Mark Flanagan, J.D., telephone interview with Floyd Albert   Riebe, 30 April 1978. In HSCA record #180-10105-10400, agency file #014464.

134 ARRB testimony of Floyd Albert Riebe, 7 May 1997, pp. 32-33.

135 ARRB exhibit "M.D. 78."

136 ARRB deposition of John T. Stringer, 16 July 1996, p. 136-137.

137 ARRB testimony of Floyd Albert Riebe, 7 May 1997, p. 54.

138 ARRB testimony of Floyd Albert Riebe, 7 May 1997, p. 53.

139 Mike Feinsilber, "JFK Autopsy Files Are Incomplete" *Associated Press* (2 August 1998, 11:48 a.m. EDT).

140 See "CERTIFICATE" signed by "J. J. Humes," 24 November 1963, and cosigned by George Burkley, M.D., in Weisberg (1975), p. 524.

141 Ibid., p. 525.

142 ARRB M.D. #252; ARRB contact report of interview with Dr. Leonard D. Saslaw, Ph.D., 25 April 1996.

143 Feinsilber (1998).

144 2H352.

145 HSCA record #180-10081-10347, agency file #006165, p. 8.

146 HSCA interview with Finck, pp. 90-91; agency file 013617.

147 ARRB testimony of Floyd Albert Riebe, 7 May 1997, p. 39, and ARRB deposition of John T. Stringer, 7/16/96, p. 71.)

148 IBID.

149 FBI agent, Francis X. O'Neill. Sworn testimony before the ARRB, 9/12/97, p. 158.

150 FBI agent, Francis X. O'Neill. Sworn testimony before the ARRB, 9/12/97, p. 161-162.

151 FBI agent, James W. Sibert. Sworn testimony before the ARRB, 9/11/97, p. 128.

152 HSCA agency file #014028 and HSCA agency file #002198, pp. 34-35.

153 HSCA agency file #002198, page 5.

154 ARRB interview of Joe O'Donnell, 28 February 1997, p. 2.

155 Ibid.

156 ARRB M.D. #148.

157 ARRB deposition of Saundra Kay Spencer, 7 June 1997, p. 50.

158 ARRB deposition of Saundra Kay Spencer, 7 June 1997, p. 45.

159 ARRB testimony of Floyd Albert Riebe, 7 May 1997, p. 41.

160 ARRB testimony of Floyd Albert Riebe, 7 May 1997, p. 60.

161 6HSCA226, footnote #1.

162 Memorandum for File, written by Doug Horne for the ARRB, entitled, "Unanswered Questions Raised by the HSCA's Analysis and Conclusions Regarding the Camera Identified by the Navy and the department of Defense as the Camera Used at President' Kennedy's Autopsy."

163 Ibid., p. 4.

164 Ibid.

165 *The Washington Post*, 10 November 1998, p. A-3.

166 Ibid.

167 ARRB testimony of Floyd Albert Riebe, 7 May 1997, p. 43—44.

THE UNIVERSITY OF TEXAS
SOUTHWESTERN MEDICAL SCHOOL
DALLAS

M. T. JENKINS, M.D.
PROFESSOR AND CHAIRMAN
Department of Anesthesiology

Clinical Departments of Anesthesia
PARKLAND MEMORIAL HOSPITAL
CHILDREN'S MEDICAL CENTER

November 22, 1963
1630

To: Mr. C. J. Price, Administrator
               Parkland Memorial Hospital

From: M. T. Jenkins, M.D., Professor and Chairman
               Department of Anesthesiology

Subject: Statement concerning resuscitative efforts for
               President John F. Kennedy

Upon receiving a stat alarm that this distinguished patient was being brought to
the emergency room at Parkland Memorial Hospital, I dispatched Doctors A. H.
Giesecke and Jackie H. Hunt with an anesthesia machine and resuscitative equipment
to the major surgical emergency room area, and I ran down the stairs. On my
arrival in the emergency operating room at approximately 1230 I found that Doctors
Carrico and/or Delaney had begun resuscitative efforts by introducing an orotracheal
tube, connecting it for controlled ventilation to a Bennett intermittent positive
pressure breathing apparatus. Doctors Charles Baxter, Malcolm Perry, and Robert
McClelland arrived at the same time and began a tracheostomy and started the
insertion of a right chest tube, since there was also obvious tracheal and chest
damage. Doctors Paul Peters and Kemp Clark arrived simultaneously and immediately
thereafter assisted respectively with the insertion of the right chest tube and
with manual closed chest cardiac compression to assure circulation.

For better control of artificial ventilation, I exchanged the intermittent positive
pressure breathing apparatus for an anesthesia machine and continued artificial
ventilation. Doctors Gene Akin and A. H. Giesecke assisted with the respiratory
problems incident to changing from the orotracheal tube to a tracheostomy tube, and
Doctors Hunt and Giesecke connected a cardioscope to determine cardiac activity.

During the progress of these activities, the emergency room cart was elevated at the
feet in order to provide a Trendelenburg position, a venous cutdown was performed on
the right saphenous vein, and additional fluids were begun in a vein in the left
forearm while blood was ordered from the blood bank. All of these activities were
completed by approximately 1245, at which time external cardiac massage was still
being carried out effectively by Doctor Clark as judged by a palpable peripheral
pulse. Despite these measures there was no electrocardiographic evidence of cardiac
activity.
These described resuscitative activities were indicated as of first importance,
and after they were carried out attention was turned to all other evidences of
injury. There was a great laceration on the right side of the head (temporal
and occipital), causing a great defect in the skull plate so that there was
herniation and laceration of great areas of the brain, even to the extent that
the cerebellum had protruded from the wound. There were also fragmented sections
of brain on the drapes of the emergency room cart. With the institution of
adequate cardiac compression, there was a great flow of blood from the cranial
cavity, indicating that there was much vascular damage as well as brain tissue
damage.

It is my personal feeling that all methods of resuscitation were instituted
expeditiously and efficiently. However, this cranial and intracranial damage
was of such magnitude as to cause the irreversible damage. President Kennedy
was pronounced dead at 1300.

Sincerely,

M T Jenkins

M. T. Jenkins, M.D.

*Formal report of Marian "Pepper" Jenkins, M.D., concerning the treatment of
JFK, as published in Jesse Curry's* JFK Assassination File *(1969), p. 35.*

Paradoxes of the JFK Assassination:

The Medical Evidence Decoded

David W. Mantik, M.D., Ph.D.

[*Editor's note*: After securing permission from the Kennedy attorney, Burke Marshall, Dr. Mantik visited the National Archives on at least seven occasions to review and measure the autopsy photographs, the autopsy X-rays, JFK's clothing, and the ballistic evidence. Mantik's background as a radiation oncologist (certified by the American College of Radiology), together with his Ph.D. in physics (with a thesis in X-ray scattering) from the University of Wisconsin, make him uniquely qualified to address the conundrums of this exceptional case. No other individual with such strong credentials has ever reviewed this data. For the X-ray work, in particular, a background in medical physics (with an emphasis on X-rays) is essential. These skills would not be found in the ordinary radiologist, nor would a medical physicist, by himself, be competent to address the decisive medical issues that proliferate in this case. These talents—of physician and physicist—must be combined in a single individual, as fortuitously occurs with David W. Mantik. This case has long been waiting for such a synthesis.]

> *I found the minions of the law—the agents of the FBI—to be men who proved themselves not only fully capable, but also utterly willing to manufacture evidence, to conceal crucial evidence and even to change the rules that governed life and death if, in the prosecution of the accused, it seemed expedient to do so.*
>
> —Gerry Spence

Introduction

Allegations of missing, mysterious, or even manipulated autopsy photographs, burned drafts of the autopsy report, altered X-rays, and a substituted brain are usually ascribed by the media to the conspiracy fringes. However, these admissions and intimations have recently emerged from an official review of the JFK assassination. Repeat depositions of the three autopsy pathologists and interviews with the two autopsy photographers (and many other medical personnel besides) offer fresh insights into anomalous events following 22 November 1963. In particular, a new interview with a darkroom technician who developed au-

219

topsy photographs, and new revelations from JFK's White House photographer, his family, and a close colleague, all offer further glimpses into irregular activities (related to the autopsy) immediately after the assassination.

All of these reports derive from the Congressionally mandated Assassination Records Review Board (ARRB), which was created by Congress in the surge of public interest generated by Oliver Stone's movie, *JFK*, and which ceased its operations on 30 September 1998. It is noteworthy that the ARRB itself cited ongoing doubts about the Warren Commission:

> Doubts about the Warren Commission's findings were not restricted to ordinary Americans. Well before 1978, President Johnson, Robert Kennedy, and four of the seven members of the Warren Commission all articulated, if sometimes off the record, some level of skepticism about the Commission's findings (*Final Report of the ARRB*, 1998, p. 11).

This essay focuses on the new medical evidence. Based on remarkable paradoxes in multiple areas, it is apparent that a series of extraordinary events—many illegal—occurred in the immediate aftermath of the death of JFK. This study relies partially on two essays in the present volume, one by Gary L. Aguilar, M.D., and one by Douglas P. Horne. Horne worked at the ARRB for its entire lifetime (under then-Executive Director Jeremy Gunn) and was the primary staff member (apart from Gunn) responsible for the medical evidence. Since these authors provide details not repeated here, their essays should also be read.

The Chasm that Divides the Partisans

Ever since the early years of this case, partisans have argued fiercely for their own views, some insisting that Oswald was the sole protagonist, while others insisted that a wide conspiracy implicated the CIA, the Mafia, anti-Castro Cubans, and possibly even wealthy Texas oilmen. With the passing of the years, and especially with the new releases of the ARRB, the wide chasm that divides the partisans is now easy to identify: it is the credibility of the evidence, not just the medical evidence, but also the evidence against Oswald. The present essay, however, is confined solely to the medical and scientific arena and shall say nothing useful about the Oswald evidence. [*Editor's note*: See, however, the study of Jesse Curry's *JFK Assassination File* elsewhere in this volume.] A strong argument can now be made that the medical evidence cannot be taken at face value and that prior conclusions based upon it are not reliable. In a very real sense, the discussion must begin anew, almost as if the crime had been committed last week.

In the opening quotation, Gerry Spence (*From Freedom to Slavery* 1995, p. 27) describes his own experiences with the FBI in the matter of Randy Weaver of Ruby Ridge, Idaho. The JFK case often seems hauntingly similar to Spence's own experiences. For example, in the Ruby Ridge affair Spence even notes a second "magic" bullet (1995, p. 50).

If the evidence in the JFK case is merely accepted at face value, then the conclusions are rather trivial. The rookie Scotland Yard inspector can easily solve this case—it was Oswald alone. The real challenge is to assess the credibility of the evidence. Vincent Bugliosi, [1] the former Los Angeles County prosecutor of Charles Manson (and winner of virtually all of his other cases) still maintains that Oswald did it. He is even writing a book that will attempt to prove this. I have advised him that if he ignores this fundamental issue of evidence reliability then real communication between partisans across this chasm is unlikely to be advanced.

By analogy to Gerry Spence's own experiences with the FBI, many private investigators, based on diverse lines of detailed research, believe that something is deeply, and tragically, wrong with the JFK evidence. My own analysis of the autopsy skull X-rays, based on hundreds of point-by-point measurements performed at the National Archives over multiple visits, indict the X-rays regarding several critical features—in a way that no prior investigation could do (James Fetzer, *Assassination Science* 1998, pp. 120-137). Short of X-ray alteration, these findings remain a deep, and probably insoluble, mystery, a matter to which I shall later return.

Oswald's post-mortem conviction by the Warren Commission relied rather little on the medical evidence. In their final report, the pathologists merely repeated what they had been told before the autopsy: namely that the fatal shots had come from the rear and that the *sole* assassin was already in custody. Based on the autopsy alone, they could not possibly have known who had fired the shots, nor, short of reviewing the photographic evidence from Dealey Plaza (which they did not do), could they have speculated meaningfully about the origin of the shots. This essay, being likewise largely confined to the medical evidence, can reach no meaningful conclusion about Oswald's ultimate guilt or innocence. It can, however, demonstrate in several significant ways how the medical evidence was used to frame Oswald. It can also strongly suggest that two successful shots came from the front.

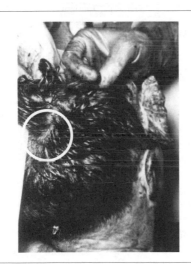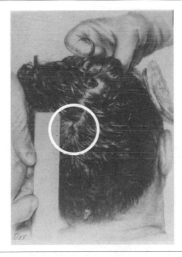

Figure 1. Posterior Head Photograph from the Autopsy. No eyewitness reported what is seen here. Eyewitnesses recalled an orange-sized hole at the low right rear. No one saw the red spot (the supposed entry wound) near the top of the ruler, and no one knew what the white spot (near the bottom, just above the hairline) represented. Ida Dox inexplicably enhanced the red spot in her drawing (right). The actual entry site is not visble; no other photgraph shows it either.

The pathologists concluded that only two shots struck JFK, both from the rear. They claimed that one struck the back of the head (just above the right hairline) and that the only other successful shot hit the upper back. They insisted on this again when interviewed by Dennis L. Breo ("JFK's death—the plain truth from the MDs who did the autopsy," *Journal of the American Medical Association*, May 1992, pp. 2794-2803). Their conclusion of two successful shots from the rear was reasserted by the House Select Committee on Assassinations (1977-1979), albeit with one highly significant change: the headshot was moved up by 10 cm so that it now coincided with the "entry" wound on the photograph (Figure 1). (*Author's note*: I shall use quotation marks around "entry," regarding this specific site, because it is not an authentic wound; the evidence for this is presented below.)

Although the House Select Committee on Assassinations (HSCA) concluded that there had been a probable conspiracy (based on acoustic data that arrived at the end of its work), in their view this additional shot from the grassy knoll had missed, thus leaving it beyond the purview of the medical evidence. The HSCA's primary conclusion of one headshot at a higher location was based critically on posterior head photographs. Although the lateral X-ray was proposed as a supporting pillar for this conclusion, I shall demonstrate later how the new evidence has shattered this pillar to bits. So, although Oswald's accusers agreed that he had hit JFK's head, they nevertheless have disagreed by ten cm (four inches) on where that bullet entered—an astonishing discrepancy of over half the width of the skull. It is as though a surgeon, operating on a melanoma of the eye, had removed the right eye instead of the left—his error in distance would have been less than that supposedly made by not one, but by three, qualified pathologists.

The ARRB

This was the state of the medical evidence when the ARRB took center stage in 1994. Contrary to prior inquiries, the ARRB was not charged with reaching any conclusions. Its mandate was merely to locate and to release evidence. Fortunately, the ARRB also deposed witnesses—those newly discovered as well as some previously deposed. It is largely these new interviews (along with some releases of previously secret interviews) that have radically altered the complexion of this case. Indeed, the weight of these new findings strongly points toward a conspiracy in the cover-up, one that involved elements of the government itself.

The ARRB, however, did not leave the impression—either in its final report (*Final Report of the Assassination Records Review Board*, US Government Printing Office, 1998), in its press releases, or in its occasional media interviews—that the medical evidence had thrown a live hand grenade into this case. In fact, rather little was said about the medical evidence. It is important to recognize, however, that there is an explanation for this peculiar silence, as Horne explains. He routinely prepared questions for the medical witnesses and assisted with the interviews and depositions. In view of the panorama of new (and often unexpected) medical evidence, of which both he and Jeremy Gunn were acutely aware, Horne proposed detailed briefings for the five Board members. According to Horne,[2] this was never done in more than a perfunctory manner. The primary reason for this disregard was that the Board had little patience with the medical evidence. As a result, they remained largely ignorant of the surprising evidence uncovered by their own staff. Their final summary, which says rather little about the medical evidence (especially those issues discussed here), bears clear witness to this state of affairs.

It should not surprise us that a Board with little medical background adopted an aloof attitude toward the medical evidence. The Board was, after all, not under any mandate to assess this evidence nor to draw any conclusions from it. Indeed, during their tenure, more progress was made in the medical evidence than in both of the preceding investigations, i.e., those performed by the Warren Commission and by the HSCA. As Harrison Livingstone has pointed out, a major reason for this improved performance was that both Gunn and Horne took seriously the possibility that the medical evidence had been altered. Furthermore, there is little doubt that serious effort is required to master the medical evidence. In fact, most Board members had full time positions elsewhere and the Board met only once or twice per month. At these meetings, there was much new evidence to review beyond the medical area. It is quite likely therefore that the Board did not have detailed knowledge of these matters.

To obtain further insight into the Board's knowledge of and attitude toward the medical evidence, I drafted a two-page questionnaire (of 25 questions) on the medical evidence. These questionnaires were sent to the former Chairman of the ARRB, John Tunheim, who agreed to act as intermediary, first by forwarding the questionnaires to the individual members and then by returning their responses to me. These questions sought to assess (to a limited degree) the Board's knowledge of and interest in the medical arena. It also directly asked them to assess the overall importance of the medical evidence for the JFK assassination. At the time of publication, some months later, no responses had been received, despite the fact that a deadline had been imposed.[3] This lack of response, from all five Board members, is, *prima facie*, a fair reflection of their attitude toward the medical evidence.

The Predicament of Prior Official Reviewers

The case made by the pathologists, based on the actual body and brain as well as authentic X-rays, rested on more solid ground than any subsequent review. These later forensic reviewers (e.g., the Clark Panel and HSCA) had no access to any of this fundamental data; the body and brain were gone—and the X-rays had been altered. Despite this patently unorthodox database—virtually no other forensic case is so limited[4]—advocates of the lone gunman theory have recited (in almost mantra-like fashion): "X forensic pathologists and Y radiologists have reviewed this material over Z years and every one of them [save for Cyril Wecht, M.D., J.D.] agrees with two shots from the rear."

The proper response to this ritual is to emphasize that it takes no great skill to reach this conclusion based on the available photographs of the back of the head—they really leave no other option. Shown these photographs, the man on the street could do just as well—and at much less expense! Even he can see the famous red spot on the photographs of the back of the head (Figure 1). But in this case, an additional question needs to be asked: if these particular pieces of photographic paper were lost, would the evidence for a high, posterior headshot then be merely paper-thin?

On the other hand, if lost photographs (which are well substantiated by the newly interviewed protagonists) that display a large hole in the back of the head were suddenly discovered—how would the argument proceed then, and what would the traditional experts then conclude? In fact, several, critical, new witnesses report having seen precisely such photographs and, as I argue in the Postscript, one of these photographs even exists in the current collection. New evidence now permits a surprisingly thorough analysis of all of these questions, as explored below.

Ultimately, the argument from the medical evidence must rely on the autopsy findings (of the body and the brain), the photographs, and the X-rays. The single gunman theory can be effectively challenged only if this database is defective. [*Editor's note*: The single gunman theory is merely an hypothesis, which appears less and less plausible with each new piece of medical or scientific evidence. It is long past time to stop denigrating proponents of conspiracy as "conspiracy theorists," as though they were devising fictions. It is the supporters of *The Warren Report* (1964) who now appear preoccupied with Procrustean fact-bending.] The primary goal of this essay is to summarize the overwhelming evidence that this is the situation that faces us today. I shall argue that none of the fundamental medical evidence—neither the brain photographs, nor the photographs of the back of the head, nor the autopsy X-rays—is entirely reliable. It is finally possible now to explain precisely how this evidence has led us astray.

Although this situation is unique in the annals of forensic medicine, nonetheless, the evidence for this view is now extremely robust, particularly with the new releases. Furthermore, due to a modest stroke of serendipity in timing, my own work with the X-rays, which was performed immediately prior to the advent of the ARRB, has now been shown to be thoroughly consistent with (and even predictive of) the ARRB's new evidence. This X-ray work led to a list of critical questions about the medical evidence—questions that were actually put to all three pathologists while under oath by the ARRB—with replies that were sometimes embarrassing (for the pathologists) and sometimes unexpected (for lone gunman advocates). [*Editor's note*: Interviews with Boswell and Humes are excerpted in Appendix F and Appendix G.]

After the medical evidence has been reviewed, one question still remains: what role did the pathologists play in this escapade? Were they merely incompetent, or did they knowingly cover-up (or even lie) at critical points along the way? The new evidence now permits us, at last, to answer these questions. The pathologists can now be seen in a new light, one that only minimally disparages their professional competence but one that exposes them to more sinister charges. Their behavior over the years is entirely consistent with this new view. In fact, my own prior perspective on them (*Assassination Science* 1998, pp. 104-107) has changed considerably over the past several years. I now believe that they were far more competent than has been supposed. The new evidence for this altered judgment is compelling. (As just one example of their competence, James J. Humes, the chief pathologist, admitted in a personal interview with Kathleen Cunningham ("'The Plain Truth' and the Autopsy of John F. Kennedy," 1995) that he had supervised the weekly brain cutting conferences at Bethesda *before the assassination*.)

Missing Photographs

The evidence for missing photographs derives from a rather long list of witnesses, including Humes, Finck, Karnei (three physicians at the autopsy), Stringer, Riebe (two autopsy photographers), Knudsen, O'Donnell (two additional photographers), and Spencer (a darkroom technician). It is not merely that one, or even two, images are missing: a wide variety of views has simply disappeared, including whole body views, a close-up of the beveled wound in the skull, the interior views of the chest cavity, the bullet entry hole over the right eye, a view of the body with the brain lying beside it, views of probes passing through the body, as well as (probably several views of) the large hole at the right rear of the head.

Why is it important to know that photographs are missing? If true, then gaping holes are immediately opened in the entire case. What if the missing photographs showed an orange-sized hole at the right rear of the head—as so many witnesses have consistently recalled? In fact, since such a photograph currently exists in the official collection (as I demonstrate in the Postscript), it is most likely that additional photographs once also showed such a large posterior hole. If such photographs once existed, then the conclusions of prior experts, over multiple investigations, become immediately irrelevant. In view of this new evidence, the posterior photographs showing the red spot (which was taken to be the skull entry wound by the HSCA, and by almost all subsequent lone gunman supporters) now lie under the deepest suspicion.

Indeed, the HSCA's conclusion of a high, posterior, skull entry rested almost solely on these posterior head photographs, which never gained the full endorsement of any of the three autopsy pathologists or, for that matter, anyone else at the autopsy either. Even the two autopsy photographers (Stringer and Riebe) and the autopsy radiologist (John Ebersole) agree with the pathologists that this red spot was not an entry wound. Furthermore, even if these peculiar photographs (of the red spot) were authentic, they still could not tell us what is most important—i.e., whether the skull underlying the scalp was intact. Until that is certain, no serious conclusions can be drawn. Yet the HSCA ignored this simple guideline and chose to declare a conclusion anyway: namely that (1) the red spot was the entry wound and (2) the skull bone at the back of the head was intact.

This is all quite simple: if photographs are missing—and there can be scant doubt of this now—then no final conclusion can be drawn about the status of the right rear skull. That question must be answered by the X-rays (discussed in a separate section below) and by the eyewitnesses. These two clues to the puzzle are completely consistent with one another, and they indicate—convincingly— that there was, indeed, a large hole at the right rear of the skull. Its variable appearance on 22 November 1963, however, proved to be a source of major confusion, as I have previously explained (*Assassination Science* 1998, pp. 331–332). Also see the notation "McC" in Figure 2C, which identifies the hinge on a posterior bone flap that occasioned much confusion. The recognition of this variable appearance of the posterior skull (depending on whether the flap was open or closed) permits this confusion finally to be laid to rest.

It might even be possible to believe in both an intact posterior scalp and a large hole in the occipital bone. Such a view strains credulity, however, in view of the major trauma to the posterior skull, as reported by so many witnesses and as

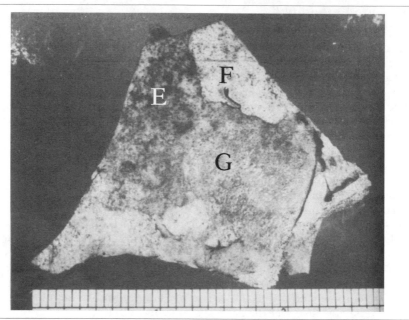

Figure 2A. *The Harper Fragment(Exterior View). In the text, this fragment is divided into three sections: (E) the left parietal bone, (F) the right parietal bone, (G) the occipital bone.*

Figure 2B. *The Harper Fragment(Interior View). Vascular markings and foramina are consistent with both parietal bone and high occipital bone.*

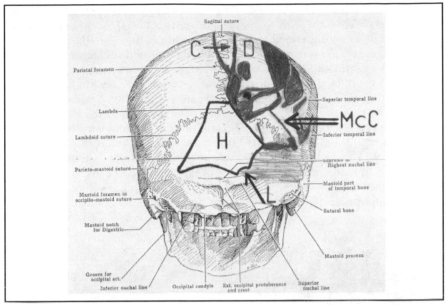

Figure 2C. The Harper Fragment as Situated in the Occiput (II). C and D are bone fragments seen on the skull X-ray and in Boswell's diagram. L is the site of lead on H. The 6.5 mm object is seen at about the 2 o'clock direction from the right upper edge of H. McC identifies the fracture line (which acted as a hinge) that McClelland described.

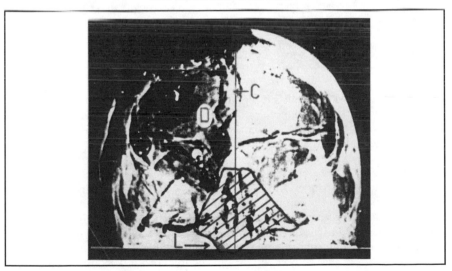

Figure 2D. The Harper Frament (oblique lines) as Placed into the Frontal Skull X-ray. The lambda point (the junction of the two lambdoid sutures and the saggital suture) lies just inferior to the upper edge of the Harper fragment. L denotes lead on the Harper Frament. The EOP lies very near the inferior edge of the black border (at the bottom of the entire image).

actually seen on the X-rays. It might even be possible to accept the intact scalp as authentic and simultaneously to interpret the red spot as a bloodspot (as Stringer suggested) or as an undefined artifact (as Dr. Humes suggested). But all of this reeks of sophistry to no useful end. That the photographic evidence was deliberately altered to mislead—in one way or another—is inescapable.

Some have argued against photographic alteration of any kind, saying either (1) that JFK's scalp in Figure 1 has merely been photographed with a toupee (even though no one recalls such an event or (2) that the back of the head in Figure 1 belongs to someone else. Consider the following argument, however, which is based on Figure 3 (the back of the torso). If the image of the scalp in Figure 1 resulted from either of the foregoing, how then did the presumably authentic image of the back in Figure 3 become attached to either (1) the toupee image of Figure 1 or to (2) the photograph of someone else's head? In either case, photographic alteration seems almost unavoidable.

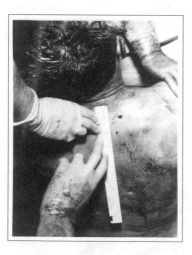

Figure 3. Official autopsy photograph of the back wound.

I would also ask which is simpler to believe: (1) that a few photographs were physically altered, or (2) that no photographs were altered, but rather that such a curiously odd set of posterior photographs naturally existed in the original set so as to lend themselves to the present deception? For option (2) to be viable, *there had to be more than one photograph that fit such a deception, and these photographs had to be consistent with one another*. When the statements of Knudsen, Karnei, Stringer, Riebe, Humes, Boswell, Finck, Spencer, and the autopsy technicians are taken into account, the first alternative appears inescapable. And when the nearly uniform statements of the Parkland Hospital personnel (who describe a large, right, posterior hole in the skull) are added to the equation, the case for photo tampering becomes virtually irrefutable.

Indeed, Spencer (the NPC darkroom technician) and Knudsen (the White House photographer) saw photographs that showed the large hole at the back of the head. Moreover, James K. Fox (the Secret Service photographer) told Mark Crouch of a burn party (on approximately 6 or 7 December 1963) at which Robert Bouck (chief of the Protective Research Section of the Secret Service) deliberately destroyed photographs and X-rays (Harrison Livingstone, *High Treason 2*

1992, pp. 322–323). Even the family of Robert Knudsen understood from Knudsen himself that such items had been destroyed. The simplest hypothesis, the one with the least clutter—although initially the most difficult psychologically—is that of photographic alteration.[5] In the end, though, it is ultimately not essential that agreement be reached on the question of how the deception occurred. It is enough to know that the photographic evidence has been deliberately manipulated to mislead—a deception that has radically altered the entire history of this case.

The Skull Wound

The official autopsy report affirms [*Editor's note*: This report appears in *Assassination Science* 1998, pp. 430–437]:

> There is a large, irregular defect of the scalp and skull on the right involving chiefly the parietal bone but extending somewhat into the temporal and occipital regions. In this region there is an actual absence of scalp and bone producing a defect which measures 13 cm in greatest diameter.

This distance of 13 cm is from front to back, as becomes apparent in Boswell's autopsy diagram (Figure 4A). Since the length of a typical skull is about 20 cm, this is truly an enormous hole, occupying well over one half its length. Furthermore, the word, "occipital," is actually employed here by Humes.

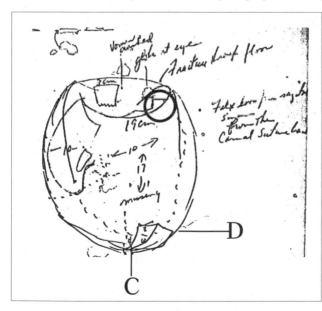

Figure 4A. *Autopsy Diagram of the Skull by Boswell. Letters C and D (added by the author) identify two bone fragments on the top-rear of the skull. Also see Figures 2C, 2D, and Appendix F.*

The notch, discussed below, is circled.

The drawing (Figure 5) that Dr. Humes supervised in preparation for the Warren Commission (actually drawn by H. A. Rydberg, a Navy artist) is consistent in size and location with Hume's written description. The hole clearly extended into the occipital area. (For comparison, see standard skull anatomy in Figure 6.) The HSCA shifted the wound out of the occipital area (thus nullifying

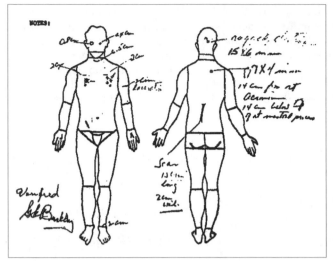

Figure 4B. *Autopsy
Diagram of the Back
by Boswell. After
Gerald Ford elevated
the back wound into
the neck (to make the
single bullet theory
possible), Boswell
agreed that he had
placed the wound too
low in this diagram.*

three autopsy pathologists, two autopsy photographers, and the sole autopsy radiologist, as well as the medical personnel) into the parietal and frontal area (Figure 7). This large displacement was based primarily on the posterior head photographs, which showed intact scalp at the rear but also (the HSCA claimed) on the skull X-rays. With this translation from the back to the top of the head, the *disagreement* with virtually all of the eyewitnesses was complete—a strange incongruity that troubled even the HSCA.

The accuracy of the photographs, most especially those of the posterior head (Figure 1), seemed suspicious when they first became public in the 1970s. The fact that not a single eyewitness—at either Parkland Hospital in Dallas or at the autopsy at the Bethesda National Naval Medical Center in Maryland—described an entry wound high on the back of the head (the red spot in the color photographs) was quite arresting. In fact, virtually every eyewitness described something quite different—not a small entry hole high on the back of the head, but rather a large (orange-sized) hole at the right rear of the head, much lower down, just above the hairline.

No such orange-sized hole is anywhere evident in the photographs. Instead, the scalp is entirely intact in this area and the hair is remarkably well groomed at exactly the same site where nearly all of the eyewitnesses recalled seeing a large hole. Such a groomed appearance is especially striking for someone who has been fatally shot in the head, whose head has literally exploded, and whose hair was not cleaned (as the questioned witnesses all agreed). The HSCA, however, hoped that it had buried this paradox:

> Drs. Ebersole [the radiologist], Finck, and Boswell offered no expla-
> nation for the upper wound [the red spot], while Dr. Humes first
> suggested that it might represent an extension of a more anterior
> scalp laceration, incident to the exit wound, in spite of the fact that
> within the photograph the margins of the wound appear to be intact
> around the entire circumference. Dr. Finck believed strongly that the
> observations of the autopsy pathologists were more valid than those

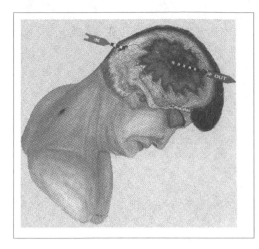

Figure 5. *Rydberg (and Humes)*
Drawing of Skull Wound for
the Warren Commission.

Figure 6. *Normal skull anatomy*
illustration by Julie Foont,
The Fundamentals of Operative
Neurosurgery *(1999)*

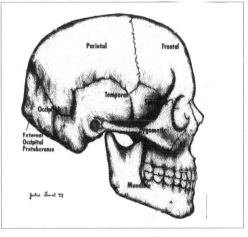

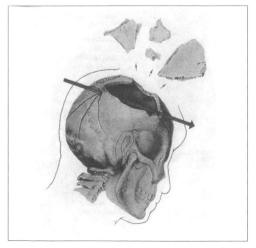

Figure 7. *Skull Wound, as*
Interpreted by the HSCA. In
disagreement with virtually every
eyewitness, the HSCA moved the
large hole from the back to the
top of the head.

of individuals who might subsequently examine photographs. (7HSCA115). [*Editor's note*: This is page 115 of Volume 7 of the 12 HSCA evidence volumes.]

The panel continued to be concerned about the persistent disparity [of four inches] between its findings and those of the autopsy pathologists and the rigid tenacity with which the prosectors maintained that the entrance wound was at or near the external occipital protuberance. Subsequently, however, in his testimony before the select committee, Dr. Humes agreed that the defect was in fact in the "cowlick" area and not in the area of the brain tissue [just above the hairline]. [*Author's note*: Humes's indisputable admission—vis-a-vis his bona fide opinion—is discussed further below.]

The HSCA concluded its findings on the large posterior hole in the skull as follows:

In disagreement with the observations of the Parkland doctors are the 26 people present at the autopsy. All of those interviewed who attended the autopsy corroborated the general location of the wounds as depicted in the photographs; none had differing accounts. . . it appears more probable that the observations of the Parkland doctors are incorrect (7HSCA 37-38).

Dr. Earl F. Rose was a member of the Forensic Pathology Panel. He had performed Oswald's autopsy, one that is widely recognized as a model, especially when compared to JFK's. Rose (7HSCA 115—the same page as the first quotation above) offered his opinion on another critical issue: the brain was not consistent with the wound described by the pathologists. In particular, the relatively intact inferior brain (Figure 8) would not have been expected, given the pathologists' low entry wound (just above the hairline). On the contrary, the under surface of the brain should have suffered major trauma from a bullet that entered just above the hairline. This conclusion by Rose was eminently sensible and, at the time, seemed to provide strong support for the HSCA's much higher entry site. In retrospect, however, it is quite certain that Rose was viewing a substitute brain, not the brain of JFK. If true, his critique would be quite beside the point.

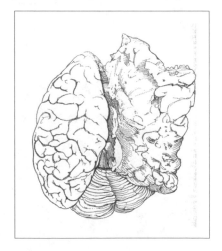

Figure 8. Drawing of the Brain as seen from above by Ida Dox for the HSCA. Based on one of several photographs at the Archives, it almost certainly represents the substituted brain. The absence of major trauma to the inferior brain is best seen at the Archives on views of the inferior surface.

(For more details on the substitute brain, see my section on the two-brain proposal or the separate paper by Horne.)

The enduring paradox about the photographs (of the back of the head) led Harrison Livingstone in 1979 (just after the HSCA's final report) to do what both the Warren Commission and the HSCA should promptly have done. In a trip paid for by Steve Parks of *The Baltimore Sun* (Robert Groden and Harrison Livingstone, *High Treason* 1980, p. 38), Livingstone traveled to Dallas and showed these images (actually copies of drawings of the back of the head, based on the work of the HSCA)—for the first time—to the Parkland medical witnesses. What he discovered was truly astonishing—the Parkland personnel radically disagreed with their authenticity. Livingstone reports:

> Since then, Livingstone, *The Baltimore Sun*, and Ben Bradlee, Jr., of *The Boston Globe*, have compiled the testimony of a number of additional witnesses, and the startling conclusion of their work is clear: *the autopsy pictures are fake*, and hold the key to the true nature of the plot which took the life of the President. (The research conducted by the *Globe* and the *Sun* was subsequently turned over to Livingstone and placed in the JFK Library in Boston.) (Groden and Livingstone 1980, p. 38.)[6]

For the 25th observance of the assassination (1988), four Parkland physicians (Robert McClelland, Richard Dulaney, Paul Peters, and Marion Jenkins) traveled to the National Archives to view the autopsy materials. On leaving, they were asked by *Nova* if their recollections disagreed with the photographs. This time many investigators expected that they would disagree, but now—another kind of surprise—these physicians seemed to imply that they had seen no discrepancies. Nonetheless, on subsequent, careful questioning, they later complained that the *Nova* program had either misquoted or misinterpreted their comments (Harrison Livingstone, *Killing the Truth* 1993, p. 305), meaning that the paradox was still alive. In particular, as Livingstone clarifies, all that these doctors had meant was that the pictures they saw in the Archives were the same as the pictures that had been publicly published.

The doctors had made no claim that the pictures accurately portrayed their recollections of 22 November 1963. Groden, subsequently, laid this matter conclusively to rest (Robert Groden, *The Killing of a President* 1993, pp. 86–88). He published photographs of these doctors, as well as similar photographs of other physician eyewitnesses and medical personnel, that show them clearly demonstrating (on their own heads) that the large hole was indeed at the right rear (and was usually quite low)—in gross disparity with the photographs.[7] [*Editor's note*: A composite of the responses of these witnesses, based on Groden (1993), may be found elsewhere in this volume.]

The virtual uniformity of their demonstrations (with the notable exception of Marion Jenkins, who changed his opinion sometime after 1978) was remarkably compelling. The paradox between the witnesses and the photographs therefore still persisted. Moreover, those physicians who had entered the National Archives had not been queried about the obvious "entry" wound in the photographs (the red spot). In fact, in their detailed medical notes of 22 November

1963, none of these doctors had mentioned such a small entry site, a truly astonishing oversight, if indeed, this "entry" site had existed at all that day.

Even Jeremy Gunn (by then an ex-Executive Director of the ARRB) commented during his deposition of five Parkland doctors on 27 August 1998, in Dallas, Texas: "In my very lay sense—and I am not a doctor—there seems to be a fair degree of coherence among the testimony that you offered about the (rearward) location of the (skull) wound." Moreover, now that the ARRB has concluded its work, we know that the witnesses still disagree—and disagree dramatically—with the photographs. Due to the efforts of Gary L. Aguilar, M.D., we now know what happened to the missing interviews with the Bethesda witnesses: they were sequestered until the year 2029.

After these interviews (and wound diagrams by the witnesses) were finally released in 1993 by the National Archives, Aguilar reviewed them, and was forced to an amazing conclusion: the HSCA's summary statement was patently wrong. In fact, *essentially all of these Bethesda witnesses agreed that there had been a large hole low on the right rear of the skull.* In 1995, Aguilar presented this startling discrepancy at a Washington, D.C., conference whose audience included Michael Baden, M.D., Chairman of the HSCA Forensic Pathology Panel and Andy Purdy, an HSCA staff member (for the medical evidence). I was also present. During this historic denouement, Baden denied any knowledge of this fundamental conflict, and Purdy denied writing the misleading conclusion.

So what had gone wrong? Although no one has yet acknowledged this egregious error—or deliberate deception—after 1 January 1979, only three individuals could have written this misleading HSCA conclusion. They were the only three staff members left: Robert Blakey, the Chief Counsel; Gary Cornwell, Deputy Chief Counsel; and Richard Billings, who had been hired to assist with the writing of the report. [8] When Aguilar queried each of them about this gross inconsistency on an absolutely pivotal facet of the case, each of these principals denied writing this statement. Seeking final confirmation on this crucial issue, I sent each of them certified letters (receiving appropriate receipts in each case), with the following responses:

(1) G. Robert Blakey—no reply;
(2) Gary Cornwell—no reply;
(3) Richard N. Billings—no reply. [9]

Two unlikely authors—since they both left the HSCA before 1 January 1979— are Andy Purdy and Mark Flanagan, who both worked with the medical witnesses. When Aguilar wrote to inquire of Flanagan, he never replied, while Andy Purdy not only denied writing the misleading summary, but also added that he was quite displeased with the misleading summary. To date, he is the only HSCA staff member to express such displeasure. This remarkable (and all too convenient) loss of memory by the probable participants—particularly on a matter of such central importance—only raises questions about the integrity (or the sincerity, or the competence) of those involved.

The pathologists themselves, although not openly describing these photographs as forgeries, have nonetheless been at some pains to intimate that something was very wrong. When asked about this flagrant "entry" wound (the red spot) high on the back of the head, Humes put the Forensic Pathology Panel on notice:

> I can assure you that as we reflected the scalp to get to this point, there was no defect corresponding to this [red spot] in the skull at any point. I don't know what that [red spot] is. It could be to me clotted blood. I don't, I just don't know what it is, but it certainly was not a wound of entrance (7HSCA 254).

Without actually labeling these photographs as forgeries, Humes could go no further without exposing the entire affair.

Pierre Finck, the third pathologist (on loan from the AFIP), when questioned by the HSCA in 1978, was somewhat more forthcoming. What was particularly striking was that (1) he specifically requested one more day with his questioners to review the photographs and (2) his testimony, like so many others, had been sealed until the year 2029. This latter decision—of what to seal and what to release—could only have been made after 1 January 1979 by the skeleton three-person HSCA staff led by Chief Counsel Robert Blakey. (The records were sequestered for 50 years, as was typical for such Congressional investigations: 1979 + 50 = 2029.)

Finck said that he did not know what either the white or the red spot were, but that the actual wound was much closer to the white spot (seen very near the hairline in Figure 1). At the autopsy, the pathologists had identified this wound by both (1) a perforating wound in the scalp and (2) a matching beveled entry site on the skull. Since Finck had previously stated that the skull entry site showed only a portion of a crater (i.e., it was not completely circumferential), the implication was obvious: bone near this site was missing (independent of the scalp's photographic appearance). By implication, based on Finck's testimony, the photograph that had played such a critical role for the HSCA was worse than useless: it not only failed to portray the actual entry hole but, even worse, it showed an entry hole that was wrong.

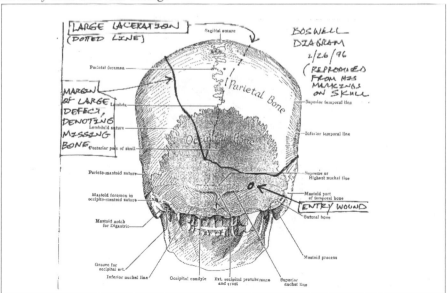

Figure 9A. Horne's rendition of Boswell's drawing of the back of the skull (#1 of 4).

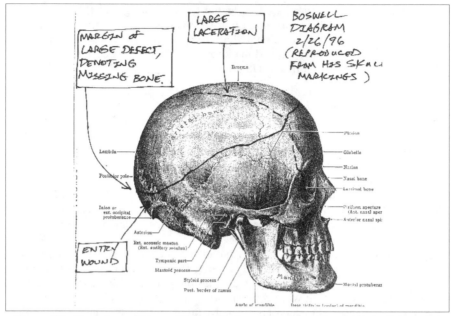

Figure 9B. Horne's rendition of Boswell's drawing of the side of the skull (#2 of 4).

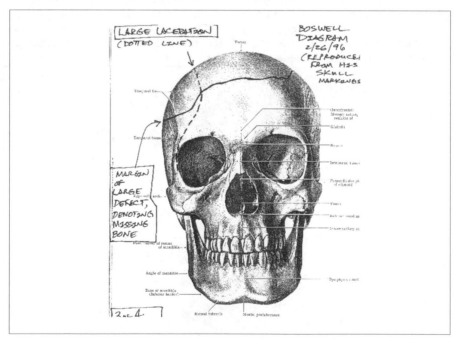

Figure 9C. Horne's rendition of Boswell's drawing of the front of the skull (#3 of 4).

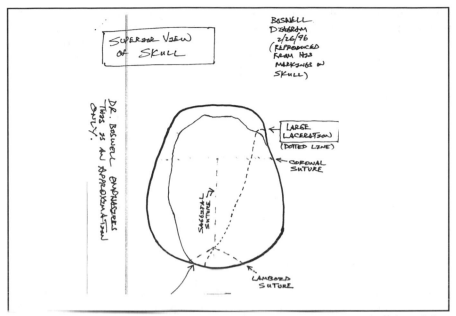

Figure 9D. Horne's rendition of Boswell's drawing of the top of the skull (#4 of 4).

Only one diagram remains from the autopsy itself: a crude sketch made by Boswell (Figure 4A) that shows a huge bone deficit, as described above (13 cm). Such a large size, by itself, would require that the large hole extend into the occipital area. In fact, Boswell clarified this for the ARRB by actually drawing this large hole on a skull. (Figure 9 is Horne's 2D reproduction of Boswell's drawing on a 3D skull.) In this sketch, a large hole does in fact extend far into the occiput, well into the region where the scalp appears to be intact in the photograph.

Although Humes, in his ARRB testimony, stated, for the very first time, that the occipital bone was intact under the scalp—saying that the entry hole was completely circumferential—that is not at all what he had stated previously. In fact, like both Boswell and Finck, he had previously reported that the entry wound was only partially circumferential, meaning that some bone was necessarily missing under the visible scalp in the famous photograph. By telling this unexpectedly new story to the ARRB, Humes contradicted both (1) his own Warren Commission diagram and also (2) the actual word "occipital" in the official autopsy report that he himself had written.

In summary, then, none of the three pathologists could explain (1) why the scalp (at the right rear) appeared so intact in the photograph (despite the absence of cleaning, on which they agreed), or (2) what the red spot represented, or (3) what the white spot represented, or (4) why the supposed entry site was not centered in the photograph. In fact, in view of all of these points the photographs (of the back of the head) actually served no purpose at all. Worse than that, though, these photographs were misleading, and showed an "entry wound" that no one could recall. Although Boswell did not recall the red spot, nor could he see (in the photograph) the actual entry wound, when asked by the ARRB if the photograph had been altered, he evaded the question. Instead, he merely suggested that, on technical grounds, he doubted that a photograph could be so altered. The primary question—of whether the photographs actually looked altered—remained forever unanswered. This question was not put to Humes. [*Editor's note*: See the diagram of different descriptions of the head wound—at Parkland, at Bethesda, and by the HSCA—elsewhere in this volume.]

The three pathologists were hardly alone in their skeptical opinions of these (back of the head) photographs. When John T. Stringer, the chief autopsy photographer, was deposed, he also agreed that the entry site had been low on the back of the head—and that it was not the red spot in the photographs. I personally interviewed the one autopsy physician, John Ebersole, in my own specialty (radiation oncology). He, too, concurred with the low entry site. In fact, it is quite striking that no one at the autopsy (or at Parkland, either, for that matter) ever recalled the red spot. It was this site on which the HSCA and all subsequent, lone assassin advocates have established their case. This point is so critical that it needs to be restated: *the most critical piece of evidence for the HSCA's case—the red spot—was never reported by any witness, at either Parkland or at Bethesda. The HSCA literally based its case on a piece of paper.*

In view of the HSCA's misleading summary statement (7HSCA37-38, cited above), this now known *consistency* between the Parkland and the Bethesda witnesses (that there had been a large hole at the right rear) was quite unanticipated. Aguilar then displayed these (approximately 40) witness statements in a remarkable table (see Aguilar's article). Of these, all but one witness agreed that there had been a large hole at the right rear of the skull. (The one exception recalled a similar wound, but on the left side.) Faced with this astounding near unanimity between Dallas and Bethesda, advocates of authenticity (of the posterior head photographs) now had only one recourse, and they repeated it almost as a mystic incantation—eyewitnesses are not reliable! Of course, even these devotees could say nothing at all about the status of the posterior skull, which was, after all, the primary issue—the problem was that the scalp covered the area of the skull in question. The proper conclusion of the HSCA regarding the status of the *skull* should have been agnosticism, but they willingly crossed this line.

To this now hoary myth of eyewitness unreliability, the work of Marshall, et al., has given us a wholly new perspective. The eyewitness evidence from this study is presented in detail elsewhere. [*Editor's note*: See Dr. Mantik's essay on the Zapruder film in Part V.] Although eyewitnesses may be unreliable when asked to recall (especially much later, as in criminal trials) specific details of a complex sequence of events, or the exact features of a stranger's face only briefly glimpsed (such as those witnesses who thought they saw Oswald on November 22), under the right circumstances they can be remarkably accurate. These requirements are straightforward: the events in question must be simple and salient, and the events must be promptly recalled. When these conditions are met, eyewitnesses are often 90% accurate, and sometimes even 98% accurate, as the Marshall study showed. And when many witnesses independently recall such an event in just the same way, such as a hole in the back of the head, then the final conclusion is as certain as most events in life can be.

As Aguilar has often emphasized in his public presentations, if these witnesses had made merely random errors of recall, then the entries in his table should be randomly scattered between the two columns. Obviously, they are not—the witnesses are in remarkable agreement that there was a large hole at the right rear of the head (and that it was closer to the bottom than to the top of the head). When it is further recalled that many of these witnesses were trained professionals, physicians accustomed to seeing daily trauma in the ER (including the chief of neurosurgery whose observations of the brain were critical to resuscitation efforts), and that they all recalled the posterior head in the same way, the evidence for such a large hole begins to seem incontrovertible. It surely cannot be argued that this large hole was not both simple and salient. Furthermore, the *contemporaneous* notes of the Parkland physicians were published in *The Warren Report*, and are still easily obtainable at most local bookstores and libraries. Their depictions in these notes are undeniable. [*Editor's note*: Curiously, many of these published notes were handwritten, making them difficult to read, which may now be understandable. See *The Warren Report* 1964, pp. 485-491.]

Those who argue that these photographs of the *scalp* accurately portray the posterior *skull* (two clearly different anatomic areas, for which two different sets of data are required) have necessarily insisted that the physicians, since they were primarily trying to save a life, were too hurried to make accurate observations. However, both Drs. Giesecke and McClelland give the lie to this version—they recall using a flashlight to peer inside the skull for some time. McClelland described the back of the head in some detail:

> As I took the position at the head of the table. . . I was in such a position that I could very closely examine the head wound, and I noted that the right posterior portion of the skull had been blasted. It had been shattered, apparently, by the force of the shot so that the parietal bone was protruded up through the scalp and seemed to be fractured almost along its posterior half, as well as some of the occipital bone being fractured in its lateral half, and this sprung open the bones that I mentioned in such a way that you could actually look down into the skull cavity itself, and see that probably a third or so, at least, of the brain tissue, posterior cerebral tissue and some of the cerebellar tissue had been blasted out (6H33). [*Editor's note*: This is page 33 of Volume 6 of the 26 volumes of the *Warren Commission Hearings*.]

McClelland's description is remarkably consistent with the X-rays, as I explain below. It also explains why the Zapruder film shows no obvious hole in the back of the head after the final headshot (traditionally, at about frame 313), which I have previously discussed (*Assassination Science* 1998, pp. 263–342).

On another occasion, after noting that one-third of the brain had been blasted out, McClelland added the following comments:

> . . . there was not only a horrible gaping wound but that it was (sic) a cavity that extended down into the head. And as I stood there holding the retractor, I was looking down into it all the time. I was no

more than eighteen inches away from the wound all the time, standing just above it, which was ten to fifteen minutes at the least. And
during that time I had a continuing impression of that gaping cavity.
And during that time I had a strong impression that a portion of
what appeared to be the cerebellum fell backward through the wound
onto the scalp and hair that was hanging back from the head. . . .
There was a great deal of matted hair and blood around the edges of
[the wound]. . . . At the National Archives [for the *Nova* show] it was
my assumption—and it was just an assumption—that there was
enough of the flap left to pull up over the back portion of the wound
and to hide the. . . wound. . . . One might be led to believe that this
was intact head back here. That's not the case. It wasn't. The skull
was missing underneath the scalp (Livingstone 1992, pp. 288-289).

When the ARRB interviewed (21 March 1997) a second neurosurgeon, Dr. Robert G. Grossman, who had assisted in Trauma Room One, he also recalled that
he and Kemp Clark (chief of neurosurgery) had to lift the head in order to see the
large hole, which clearly implied that it was not at the top of the head where the
HSCA had placed it. His more detailed anatomic description confirmed a low,
right, posterior hole in the skull, so low that the cerebellum could be seen.

These photographs (of the back of the head) are, at the very least, not an
accurate portrayal of the real condition of the head. Several witnesses—Riebe,
O'Neill, Kenneth Salyer, M.D., Fouad Bashour, M.D., Jackie Hansen Hunt, M.D.,
as well as several Bethesda medical personnel—have either disagreed forcefully
with the official photographs or have overtly charged photographic alteration.

This section is appropriately closed with a list of physicians who, at
some time, stated that the photograph of the back of the head was (at least)
distinctly different from what they had seen at Parkland:

Kemp Clark	Marion Jenkins	Jackie Hunt	Malcolm Perry
Joe Goldstrich	Jim Carrico	Ronald Jones	Robert McClelland
Gene Akin	Paul Peters	Charles Baxter	Charles Crenshaw
Richard Dulaney	Fouad Bashour	Kenneth Salyer	Adolph Giesecke.

In case the reader is waiting for a companion list—those who saw this photograph and immediately recognized it as authentic—there is none. *No Parkland
physician, on first seeing the posterior photograph of the head, recognized that image as authentic!*

The Autopsy Photographs

If these eyewitnesses to the state of JFK's head are correct, how then are
these photographs to be explained? It is here that the ARRB's new evidence is
particularly arresting. The ARRB discovered witnesses previously unknown to
the public who provide remarkable substantiation, each in his or her own way
(and with no apparent personal agendas), for either highly misleading photographs or possibly even for photographic alteration. Although they suggest no
reasons for such alteration, their evidence, when taken collectively, is unprec-
edented in the annals of forensic science.

Saundra Spencer, NPC photo technician

Saundra Spencer, a photographic technician who worked at the secretive Naval Photographic Center (NPC) in Anacostia, Maryland, recalled, under oath, that she had processed and handled JFK autopsy films.[10] A Secret Service agent, whom she thought was James K. Fox, had brought to her about four or five duplex film holders (containing eight to ten individual films) for processing, probably on Sunday morning, November 24. *It is critical to note that these were color negatives, not transparencies.* She is sure of this because her division did not handle color transparencies.

Three features immediately leap out as anomalous in her account—(1) the use of Anacostia, when Bethesda had its own photo lab and where autopsy photographers always did their own processing; (2) the rather limited number of films (far too few to represent the entire autopsy); and (3) the presence of color negatives, rather than color transparencies. According to Stringer, the autopsy photographer, the *only* color photographs exposed were color transparencies, *not* color negatives. Furthermore, only color transparencies exist in the Archives today—there are *no* color negatives.

What Spencer added next was even more striking. She had retained, and brought with her to the deposition, a photograph of JFK that had been developed about ten days before the assassination. It had been taken at an event that she was able to identify and to date. *By comparing the identifying marks on this film to the autopsy films, she was able to conclude that she had developed none of the extant autopsy films.* In addition, after reviewing the autopsy films, she stated that none of the *images* were like those she had developed and printed. (She had printed at least one view of the face, so she was sure that it was JFK.)

She recalled that the images she had seen in 1963 were clean and free of blood, not at all like other autopsies she had seen. This blood-free characteristic is similar to the extant posterior head photographs (Figure 1) but not like the blood-spattered untidiness that virtually all of the eyewitnesses have recalled. There were no measuring devices, as she would ordinarily have expected, and no identification tags. She saw a small throat wound, about the diameter of a thumb or a finger, about half an inch across, by her description (much smaller than that seen in the extant autopsy photographs). Most important of all, however, she saw a photograph of the back of the head with a 2 or 2 1/2-inch hole—just about where all of the eyewitnesses placed it.

Robert Knudsen, White House photographer

Robert Knudsen was deposed by the HSCA, but, since he died in 1989, he could not be deposed by the ARRB. For the HSCA, he recalled seeing photographs with multiple probes in the body, showing the points of entry and exit, with the point in the back lower than the point in the front, an obvious violation of the single bullet theory (SBT). Knudsen was one of several witnesses who recalled probes in the body (including several witnesses who saw them in photographs). Such probes were also described in a CBS memorandum (10 January 1967) from Robert Richter to Les Midgley,[11] in which a conversation with Humes himself was recalled by Jim Snyder of the CBS bureau in Washington, D.C. Snyder went to the same church as Humes, but also knew Humes's boss, who lived right across the street from Snyder. Humes implied that one X-ray, apparently with a probe in it, would answer many questions about the [supposed] bullet trajectory from the back to the throat.

The Knudsen family added further, astonishing details when interviewed by the ARRB. Mr. Knudsen had told his wife that the Secret Service had destroyed autopsy films. He had also told her that he knew who was probably responsible for the disappearance of some of the autopsy films, but that he was not going to stick his neck out because he had a family to protect. [12] Secret Service agent, James K. Fox, had also told Mark Crouch a similar story about destruction of autopsy photographs and X-rays (Livingstone 1992, p. 245). Mrs. Knudsen telephoned a former Navy colleague who recalled one photograph that showed the back of the head "blown out." On follow-up, she confirmed that this was indeed the back (not the top) of the head.

Shortly after her husband had testified to the HSCA, moreover, there had been a burglary of her own house; she still wondered if there was a connection. All available family members agreed that Mr. Knudsen had photographed the autopsy and that it was the hardest thing he had ever had to do. Furthermore, he had told them that he was the only one in the morgue with a camera. (Paradoxically, however, no one actually in the morgue recalls his presence.) All three interviewed family members did not see him at home for three days after he left to meet Air Force One at Andrews Air Force Base.

After his HSCA appearance, he told his family that four or five pictures that he was shown were not consistent with the autopsy—and that one of the photographs had been altered. His son, Bob, said, "hair had been drawn in," on one photograph to conceal a missing portion of the top-back of the head.

All three family members agreed that Mr. Knudsen had appeared before an official government body in 1988, about six months before he died in January 1989. They all believed that he had testified on Capitol Hill, and that it may have been a Congressional inquiry. All were unanimous that he had returned from this encounter feeling very disturbed, saying that four photographs were missing and one was badly altered. Mrs. Knudsen actually used the phrase, "severely altered," several times. She confirmed that the photographs he saw in 1988 were not consistent with what he had seen at the autopsy. He had also added that the details in the background of the room were wrong (the autopsy medical personnel agree with this). He concluded that this encounter had been a waste of time, because as soon as he would answer a question he would immediately be challenged and contradicted by those who had already reached their own (different) conclusions.

Joe O'Donnell, USIA photographer

Joe O'Donnell, friend and occasional colleague of Robert Knudsen, was deposed by the ARRB. Within a short time after the assassination—in fact on two different occasions—Knudsen had shown him autopsy photographs. On the first of these, he saw a hole (about the size of a grapefruit) in the back of the head, about two inches above the hairline. This hole penetrated the skull and was very deep. Another photograph showed a hole in the forehead, above the right eye; this wound was round and about 3/8 inch in diameter.

On the second occasion the back of the head was intact and the hair was neatly combed, looking slightly damp or wet (reminiscent of Figure 1). On this second occasion, the wound over the right eye had disappeared. He also recalled an image of JFK lying on his back, with a metal probe emerging from his right side (no probes are visible in the current collection).

During a second interview, he again recalled a gaping wound at the right rear of the head, big enough to put his fist through; there was a total absence of hair and bone. He repeated that there was an apparent entry hole above the right eye, which he interpreted as the bullet that had caused the large hole at the right rear of the head. (This photograph no longer exists.)

He also recalled showing the Zapruder film to Jackie Kennedy, who said that she never wanted to see it again. O'Donnell interpreted this to mean that he was to remove the headshot images—so he took out about ten feet! He believes that this was the original film. The reason he is certain that this was the original film (I listened to this repeatedly on the audiotape) is that the Zapruder film that he has since seen (on multiple occasions on television) is quite unlike the one that he saw. He specifically mentioned a very obvious halo around JFK's head after a headshot that he no longer sees on the current film. [13]

Robert Karnei, M.D.

Karnei, a pathology resident at Bethesda (and later chief at the AFIP), would have performed the autopsy had it been a routine one. He recalls repeated attempts by Finck to probe the wound in the right shoulder. One of his certain memories is that photographs were taken of the probe in the wound (no such photograph exists). He recalled that Humes twice had asked for permission to enlarge the scope of the autopsy, first for the chest, then later for the abdomen. (Humes has adamantly claimed that he was solely in charge.) Karnei said that the control at the autopsy was so tight that he was surprised that the pathologists were allowed to take their notes out of the morgue. (Finck never did find his—see Aguilar's essay.) He recalled that the embalmers were putting some wax into a tear or a laceration near the eye. (This may be corroboration for a shot to the right temple/forehead. An embalmer, Tom Robinson, has also recalled his work at this site; his recollections are introduced later.) Karnei had heard a story that Dr. Humes had called Dallas to talk to a surgeon later in the evening, *before the body left the morgue*, from which they had learned that the tracheotomy had been made through a bullet wound in the throat. (The pathologists, especially Humes, have claimed that they were entirely ignorant of this wound until the following day, Saturday, 23 November.)

John Stringer, the Photographer

Stringer admitted that, contrary to his usual practice, most photographs taken on 22 November 1963 had no identification cards. He had used a large format, Graphic View camera, which required duplex film holders. He listened to a tape recording he had made with David Lifton in 1972, in which he located the large head wound at the rear. With the ARRB, however, he claimed that the back of the head photograph was authentic and that his earlier recording with Lifton was wrong. Despite using the word "occiput" in the Lifton interview, he was now unable to explain why he had used that word!

Despite seeing no new physical evidence, he had changed his mind about the location of the large hole. After seeing the posterior photograph, he no longer believed that the large hole was at the back of the head. Nonetheless, he did not accept the red spot as an entry hole, claiming instead that it was an insignificant blood clot. Although he saw, in the photograph, that the scalp was entirely intact, he nonetheless insisted that the bone beneath it was disrupted, but he was uncertain about whether all of the occipital bone was present.

He recalled taking photographs of the skull interior, which he no longer saw in the collection. Most importantly, however, he recalled photographing the brain and brain sections. *None of these photographs exist today, as he was able to prove by examining the type of film used for the extant photographs; the film he had used was a different type.*

When asked about the document that he had signed (which said that all of the photographs were present), he said that he knew the document was false, but that he had been ordered to sign it. He agreed with the pathologists about the location of the skull entry hole, which was near the white spot. He concluded by saying that a shot to the back from above and behind would not fit with the wounds he saw, *a statement that is in obvious contradiction to the SBT.*

John W. Sibert, FBI note taker

Sibert recalled for the ARRB that the massive skull wound was at rear and that the hair was all matted, blood-soaked, and stuck together. The wound in the back was well below the shoulders, even below the scapula. The largest metal fragment in the skull was behind the right frontal sinus (not at the back of the skull, where the 6.5 mm object is located today on the skull X-rays). Like O'Neill, he still recalled that Humes had described surgery to the head (consistent with Lifton's thesis that the body had been altered). Furthermore, he recalled that Humes had never retracted that statement at the autopsy. He recalled a chrome probe placed into the back wound. Very near the end of the autopsy, Humes had concluded that the back bullet had fallen out during cardiac resuscitation. Like virtually everyone else who was asked, he did not recall the stirrup under JFK's head. Most importantly, the photograph of the back of the head did not look at all like what he saw at the autopsy. He even questioned whether the skull had been reconstructed (no one at the autopsy saw any reconstruction). On the contrary, just where the scalp is entirely intact in the photograph, he had seen a large wound at the autopsy. Like O'Neill, he disputed many significant points in Specter's statement to the Warren Commission (related to their own FBI report about the autopsy). He concluded by admitting that he was unsure about conspiracy, but that he was certain about one thing—the SBT could not possibly be true, because he saw exactly how low the back wound had been.

Francis X. O'Neill, FBI note taker

During the evening of the assassination, O'Neill interviewed Roy Kellerman (who had occupied the right front seat of the limousine). Kellerman was certain that he heard JFK speak after the first shot, meaning that the bullet could not have passed through his throat. (This would invalidate the SBT, since that bullet would have rendered JFK speechless.) He severely criticized Specter for ignoring this part of his report (which is understandable since Specter wanted no contradictions to his SBT). He regarded Specter as a flunky for the Warren Commission. He was extremely surprised that the Warren Commission had interviewed neither him nor Sibert. Furthermore, their FBI report of the autopsy had been left out of both *The Warren Report* as well as the 26 volumes of the *Hearings*. He also recalled that the back wound was at least two inches down from the shoulder.

He recalled that much of the brain was missing, definitely inconsistent with the brain images in the Archives, which he was shown. His best estimate was that more than one half of the brain was missing. As further confirmation of this, he recalled seeing a great deal of brain tissue on the jackets of Kellerman and Greer. [*Author's note*: The extant brain photographs, which I have seen on multiple visits, show rather little brain tissue missing.] He recalled looking at the X-rays as long as the pathologists did, and he did not recall the 6.5 mm object. Perhaps even more importantly, however, he did not recall any discussion of such an object at the autopsy.

He severely disagreed with Boswell's upward relocation of the back wound in 1977; in fact, he ridiculed Boswell for changing this location. [*Author's note*: Boswell had disagreed with his own autopsy diagram! He had probably been enticed to do so in order to support the SBT, which was *de rigueur* by then.] He recalled that the brain was weighed! [*Author's note*: The pathologists have never actually denied this—they have simply claimed not to know why the weight was missing from the record.] Like everyone else who was asked, he did not recall the stirrup under the head either. He remarked that the eyes were open at the autopsy, but in the photographs the appearance of the eyes was not consistent. At one point, he described the back of the head photographs as "doctored," although later he seemed to want to retract this. In any case, the photographs looked nothing like the head at the autopsy. He specifically did not recall the hair as being so clean.

Weighing the Evidence

If this case were straightforward, none of these recollections should exist. By themselves, these accounts of Spencer, Knudsen (and his family), O'Donnell, Karnei, Stringer, Sibert, and O'Neill provide striking evidence for photographic alteration. However, the narrative does not end there. In view of *the now conspicuous agreement* between witnesses at Parkland and Bethesda (that there was a large occipital hole) and the relentless disagreement of the pathologists with the HSCA (about the level of the rear entry wound in the head), the statements (many under oath) of these newly found witnesses greatly increases the probability of photographic alteration and calls into question the accuracy of the extant photographs (of the back of the head).

Since these photographs do not accurately portray the wounds, that, by itself, is quite enough to severely challenge the conclusions of prior investigations. The extant autopsy photographs have been described—even within the ARRB—as doing more to conceal than to reveal the actual nature of the skull wounds. Moreover, because the pathologists have repeatedly insisted that they carefully documented all of the critical features with photographs (they had stated to *JAMA*[14] that these wounds were obvious), the conclusion is inescapable—*the photographic collection has been deliberately manipulated to mislead.*

The presence of a left lateral skull photograph, and the simultaneous *absence* of the potentially much more pertinent right lateral, suggests deliberate culling of the collection. Furthermore, Earl McDonald, an autopsy photographer trained by Stringer, described how photographs were usually taken—with stepwise closer views and with thorough labeling. This was, in fact, Stringer's usual practice, according to McDonald, but none of these features are seen in the present collection. Suspicions are only aroused when it is recalled that Stringer was known to be a very meticulous and widely respected photographer.

If the photographs had shown the true state of JFK's head, according to the witnesses who saw such *photographs* of a large hole (to say nothing of the many witnesses who saw the actual hole), it is highly unlikely that the HSCA would have concluded that the fatal shot had come from the rear. In fact, the exact opposite is far more likely—faced with such a large hole in the back of the head and with no apparent entry site for a posterior bullet, they would have concluded that JFK had been shot from the front. In view of the statements of far too many witnesses—Humes, Boswell, Karnei, Stringer, Riebe, Knudsen, O'Donnell, and Spencer—critical photographs are indeed missing. Furthermore, Saundra Spencer, Robert Knudsen, and Joe O'Donnell specifically recalled seeing—and handling—photographs that did show a large hole at the rear.

Not a single eyewitness—at either Parkland or at Bethesda (certainly not the pathologists)—has endorsed the red spot as an "entry" site—surely a unique state of affairs. How is it possible for literally *no one* to have seen an entry site that Humes (according to *JAMA*) found "blatantly" obvious? On the contrary, the fact that the true entry wound is not visible at all strongly suggests that something is profoundly wrong with this picture. Moreover, all medical witnesses at the autopsy who have expressed an opinion—including all three pathologists, the radiologist, and the two medical photographers—have endorsed a much lower entry wound, just above the hairline at the right rear of the head.

An entirely independent kind of evidence for photo-alteration is contained in the remarkably wide range of witnesses who did not see the stirrup (under the head) at the autopsy, but rather saw a block or chock under the head. These include the autopsy technicians, the FBI note takers, the photographers, and the embalmers. McDonald, who photographed the ARRB board members and who also worked at the morgue after 1963, recalled that he had never seen such a device used at a Bethesda autopsy. The autopsy personnel agreed with this. [*Editor's note*: Harrison Livingstone had made this point in 1992.]

The invisibility in the photographs of this lower entry wound, and the protests of the pathologists that it was originally obvious, only add to the probability that the photographic collection has been deliberately manipulated so as to eliminate this entry site. However, the matter does not end there. Even if this lower site were accepted, it would lead to impossible dilemmas for lone gunman advocates. The trail of metallic debris, lying more than 10 cm higher on the skull X-ray, would then immediately demand a second headshot, a conclusion that would deliver a mortal blow to the lone gunman theory. But for any conspirator who wished to change the verdict of history, such photographic manipulation would have provided an easy solution.

Moving the headshot up by 10 cm immediately circumvented the embarrassingly low entry site proposed by the pathologists, thus avoiding the insoluble dilemma of a second headshot. The difficulties of this new proposal, however, are discussed extensively below. Because they did not review the X-rays, this discrepancy—between the high bullet trail and the low entry site—did not trouble the Warren Commission. It first surfaced with the Clark Panel in 1968, when the X-rays were reviewed, and the problem persisted with the HSCA, which spent a good deal of time with the X-rays and much time trying to purge history of this alarming paradox. Nonetheless, the pathologists have stubbornly persisted, insisting that they got it right at the autopsy, seemingly unconcerned with the insoluble dilemmas that they generated by their stubbornness. This apparent lack of concern, however, came back to haunt them when they were deposed by the ARRB. (See the depositions of Drs. Boswell and Humes in the addenda.)

Dr. Boswell sketched the location of the large hole at the rear of the head on a skull for the ARRB. Douglas P. Horne has transcribed these as accurately as possible onto 2D views from several directions (Figure 9). These images speak for themselves: the large hole clearly extended deep into the occipital area. During my two conversations with Ebersole, after he described the entry wound just above the posterior hairline, I asked him where the large hole began. In remarkable agreement with Boswell's recent sketch (and also in agreement with Boswell's autopsy diagram), Ebersole located it at about one inch from the entry hole— *clearly in the occiput*. A detailed optical density study of this same area on the frontal skull X-ray is also consistent with this conclusion. Finally, Finck, in his "Personal notes on the Assassination of President Kennedy" (1 February 1965) to his AFIP superior, Brig. Gen. J. M. Blumberg, clearly stated that the wound did extend into both the frontal and the occipital areas.

Although a large hole was present at the right rear of the skull at both Parkland and at Bethesda, another question can be asked (as Lifton has done for decades): were the wounds the same at both hospitals? In their ARRB interviews, Sibert and O'Neill still insisted that Humes had asked about surgery to the head—and had never retracted this question while at the autopsy. Furthermore, the ARRB queried several Parkland witnesses about the V-shaped wound in the right forehead and none recalled this. Parkland physicians who have denied seeing such a V-shaped wound include Jackie Hunt, Ronald Jones, Malcolm Perry, Paul Peters, Don Curtis, Richard Dulaney, and Adolph Giesecke. This "wound" is visible in the photograph of the throat wound (Figure 16), but a better view is the Groden superior profile (Livingstone 1992, photographs between pp. 432-433). The ARRB even asked Humes if he had made such an incision—but he denied it. This mysterious wound strongly supports Lifton's thesis that the body was altered between Dallas and Bethesda. Furthermore, witnesses such as Robinson (discussed elsewhere here), recalled seeing multiple, small, metal fragments in a container at the autopsy, reportedly taken from JFK. These fragments, of course, are no longer in evidence. For detailed photographs of partial bullets said to be from JFK, see Livingstone (1998, p. 562). Lifton has advanced other compelling arguments for such an illegal interception of the body between Dallas and Bethesda, which are not addressed here.

Conclusions: The Skull Wounds

1. Not a single witness—at either Parkland or at Bethesda—ever reported the red spot seen in the posterior photograph of the head (Figure 1), the same site that the HSCA selected for the entry wound. Furthermore, the pathologists have stubbornly refused to authenticate this site, saying that it was far too high. Therefore, whether this red spot was subsequently inserted into the photographs (in the darkroom) or was rather some bizarre artifact, this "entry wound" is irrelevant to the case.

2. Virtually all witnesses recalled a large hole at the right rear of the skull, where the photographs show only well combed, slightly wet, hair, with intact scalp. In fact, no Parkland physician, on first seeing these photographs, recognized them as authentic. Indeed, if the entire collection had been rephotographed, such alteration might not be detectable by photographic experts.

3. The skull sketch (Figure 5) that Humes prepared for the Warren Commission (with Harold A. Rydberg as artist) showed the large hole extending far posteriorly, into the occiput just as the pathologists and virtually all of the eyewitnesses have reported. The X-rays are also consistent with this interpretation, particularly when it is recognized that a flap of bone at the rear of the skull could move in and out like a trap door, so that the back of the skull could take on varying appearances, depending on exactly how far this bone flap had swung open. This bone flap was actually described by McClelland, and can be seen on the frontal X-ray, where the hinge appears as a complete fracture line (see McC in Figure 2C). [*Editor's note*: For more discussion of this issue, see *Assassination Science* 1998, pp. 331-332.]

4. The location and size of the scalp defect is less certain. No additional photographs exist to resolve this issue. I tend to side with the morticians, who, because of the nature of their work, would have known the real state of affairs. They report that the scalp could not be closed in this area. In his ARRB deposition, Humes also recalled that several centimeters of posterior scalp remained open. Since no scalp fragments were later recovered, this seems a reasonable conclusion.

5. By utilizing the skull X-rays, the previously mysterious F8 photograph (see the Postscript) can now be interpreted as the back of the head. This should be no surprise because the pathologists' initial inventories actually described this view as posterior skull. This analysis is consistent with the eyewitnesses—and is also remarkably consistent with the X-rays.

6. The above interpretation of F8, in turn, suggests a site of origin for the Harper fragment (Figures 2A-2D), an unexpected bonus not likely to result from a false interpretation of F8. When the Harper fragment is placed into this site, an astonishing event occurs. The *Dallas* pathologists (who actually called it occipital bone) identified a probable lead deposit on this bone. After my placement of the Harper fragment, this site of lead lay eerily close to the *Bethesda* pathologists' rear entry wound.

7. In agreement with Lifton's thesis, the body was probably altered between Dallas and Bethesda. The bizarre tracheotomy seen at Bethesda seems to me the strongest argument for such unlawful activity, but the evidence from the head is also persuasive, as discussed above.

Did a Bullet Strike the Skull from the Right Front?

At the news conference at Parkland Hospital immediately after the assassination, Malcolm Kilduff, the assistant press secretary (Pierre Salinger was over the Pacific with several cabinet members, leaving Hawaii for Japan), was asked about the cause of death. He stated: "Dr. Burkley told me, it is a simple matter . . . of a bullet right through the head." The striking feature of his response, however, was the non-verbal portion: as he made this statement, he pointed toward his right forehead, *indicating the entry site*. A photograph (Figure 10) captured this gesture at the critical moment. A follow-up question asked: "Can you say where the bullet entered his head, Mac?" To this Kilduff replied: "It is my understanding that it entered in the temple, the right temple." Later that day, Chet Huntley repeated this: "President Kennedy, we are now informed, was shot in the right temple. 'It was a simple matter of a bullet right through the head,' said Dr. George Burkley, the White House medical officer" (Vincent Palamara, *JFK: The Medical Evidence Reference* 1998, p. 44).

Figure 10. White House acting press secretary, Malcolm Kilduff, points to his right temple in response to a reporter's question as to where the President was hit.

Others corroborate this location, such as Seth Kantor (20H353),[15] a Scripps-Howard reporter whose notes stated: "intered (sic) right temple." Charles Crenshaw, M.D.,[16] one of the treating physicians in Trauma Room One, demonstrated on live television for Geraldo Rivera ("Now It Can Be Told," 2 April 1992) just where this shot entered: near the hairline, just above the lateral border of the right eye socket. [*Editor's Note*: This video clip is included in my video, "*JFK: The Assassination, The Cover-up, and Beyond*." (See p. 468 below.)]

David Stewart, a physician not called before the Warren Commission, perhaps because he had given public talks about the frontal shots, had been present for the treatment of all three of JFK, Connally, and Oswald. When asked about the fatal shot to JFK, Stewart responded:

> Yes, sir. This was the finding of all the physicians who were in attendance. There was a small wound in the left front[17] of the President's head and there was a quite massive wound of exit at the right backside of the head and it was felt by all of the physicians at the time to be a wound of entry which went in the front. . . (Harold Weisberg, *Post-Mortem* 1969, pp. 60-61).

Other Parkland physicians who clearly support a frontal headshot include Robert McClelland, Ronald Jones, Donald Seldin, and Gene Akin (Vincent Palamara, *JFK: The Medical Evidence Reference* 1998).

Tom Robinson, the funeral home employee who restored JFK's head, described a wound, about 1/4 inch across, above the right eye, near the hairline, where he had to place wax to disguise it. He added that this wound was so close to the hairline that the hair could easily cover it, which may explain why more witnesses did not see it. And Joe O'Donnell, who viewed autopsy photographs within the first week, witnessed an obvious wound above the right eye *in a photograph*, which he interpreted as the entry for the bullet that had caused the large hole at the right rear.

But the most objective evidence for precisely such a frontal shot lies on the skull X-rays. It should first be noted that the trail of debris obviously does not match a bullet entry near the external occipital protuberance (EOP), the site preferred by the pathologists. Essentially no one, save for the three pathologists (and the photographers and the radiologist), believed in a single headshot that entered at such a low site. (My own view is that one headshot did enter near the EOP, just as the pathologists said, but that there was also a subsequent, frontal shot.) Instead current, lone gunman advocates now necessarily support the HSCA's much higher entry wound (the red spot).

But this does not work, either. First, the lateral X-ray (Figure 11) shows the 6.5 mm fragment lying one centimeter below the "entry" site (which lies where the skull has been fractured), but the trail of debris is noticeably higher than even this "entry" site—and even higher than the 6.5 mm object. No lone gunman supporter has ever explained this discrepancy: it is simply ignored. Even worse, though, the Warren Commission claimed (17H257) that the nose and tail of this bullet were found inside the limousine, meaning that this supposed bullet cross section must have come from *inside* the bullet (sic). Although no ballistics expert has ever seen a cross section from the outside of a bullet deposited at an entry site, this did not deter the Warren Commission. In fact, what they accepted was even more incredible than this—they concluded that this cross-section lay one centimeter *inferior* to the entry site! By doing so they surpassed all prior cases on two separate features at once. (See Bonar Menninger and Howard Donahue, *Mortal Error*, 1992, p. 68.)

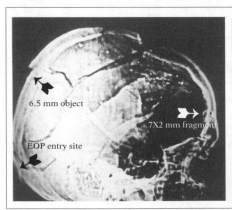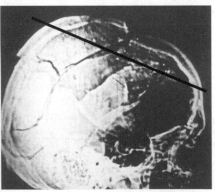

Figure 11A. Lateral autopsy X-ray. Note the trail of metallic debris across the top of the skull, at least 10 cm above the occipital wound that the pathologists identified.

Figure 11B. Lateral autopsy X-ray, showing direction of X-ray beam used for frontal X-ray.

Although no proposed, posterior entry site matches this trail of metallic debris, on the other hand, a bullet that entered the right forehead, near the hairline, directly over the outer edge of the right eye socket, would match this bullet trail with remarkable precision. Furthermore, a close look at the frontal view on the diagram that Boswell drew for the ARRB (Figure 9C) shows a notch in the frontal bone at just this site (where the bullet entered). As further confirmation that this notch is no accident, examine Boswell's sketch from the night of the autopsy (Figure 4A). The notch is also there!

When I examined the frontal X-ray, I used a bright light to highlight the outside of the skull. I could then easily see the top edge of the remaining frontal bone (high in the forehead). Furthermore, with the optical densitometer, I measured the transmission of light above and below this edge over a long distance. The area above the (supposed) bone edge was darker (and the optical density values higher), implying less bone, whereas the area below it was lighter (the optical density values were lower), which implied residual frontal bone. These measurements therefore verified what I had seen with my naked eyes with the bright light—I had identified the edge of the frontal bone. I could now trace the remaining frontal bone with good accuracy. This sketch is shown in Figure 12— the same sketch that was published in 1995 (Livingstone 1995, p. 101), well *before* Boswell made his sketch for the ARRB. The same notch is also shown in my X-ray based sketch. This notch is therefore a critical piece of evidence: the frontal bullet knocked out a small fragment of bone here.

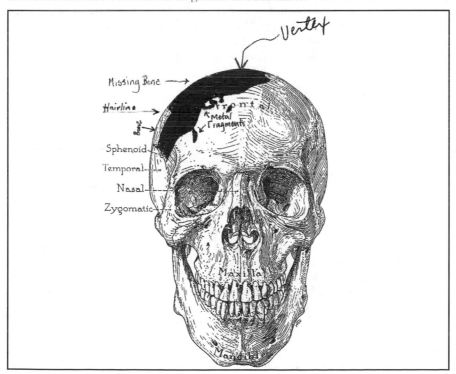

Figure 12. Residual frontal bone: Mantik's analysis of the skull

In summary, the X-rays, especially in conjunction with Boswell's sketches, provide powerful confirmation of a shot from the front. Five lines of evidence support a such a frontal shot, near the hairline, above the outer border of the right orbit: (1) a wound was seen in the scalp (attested to by Kilduff, Crenshaw, Stewart, McClelland, Akin, Kantor, O'Donnell); (2) the notch in the frontal bone was still recalled by Boswell for the ARRB, (3) the notch is actually seen on the X-rays, (4) the trail of metallic debris on the X-rays is more consistent with such a frontal shot than with it is with any posterior shot proposed to date; and (5) close examination of fragments in this debris strongly suggests that, overall, the larger ones are located closer to the rear. This would be expected for a shot from the front (but not for a shot from the rear)—because the larger ones initially contained more energy (energy is proportional to mass), they should have traveled farther.

One other point should be emphasized, Boswell's *unprompted* recall of this notch (in his diagram for the ARRB), especially after so many years, raises question of whether he understood at the autopsy itself just what this site represented. As noted above, Joe O'Donnell recalled for the ARRB an apparent bullet would in the scalp at just this site. If such a wound was so obvious in the photograph that O'Donnell saw, then there is surely a good chance that Boswell also saw it at the autopsy and understood all too well what it meant—i.e., a second headshot. Unfortunately, this question was never put to any of the pathologists—or to any other eyewitness, for that matter—not even by the ARRB.

One more question should be asked. Where could a frontal shot—to the right forehead/temple—have originated? The traditional answer of the grassy knoll does not fit well, because such a trajectory should have traversed the left brain. (Whether a shot missed from the grassy knoll is a separate issue, not discussed here, because it is outside the purview of the medical evidence.) However, a shot from the north storm drain *at the top of the overpass* is far more feasible (Grant Leitma, "Where Did the Front Shot Come From?", *Fourth Decade*, November 1993, p. 31). For such a bullet to exit through the right rear of the skull, however, an additional sideways deflection on striking the skull would appear necessary. Such a deflection may be reasonable, however, especially since the skull surface is sloping where this bullet entered, and this slope would lend itself to such a sideways deflection.

The Back Wound

It was Commission member Gerald Ford who initially elevated this wound to the back of the neck—in order to salvage the SBT. (See *Assassination Science* 1998, p. 177.) Supporting a wound in the back of the torso (rather than the back of the neck) were the following: the pathologists' official autopsy report, the Sibert and O'Neill report, Boswell's autopsy diagram, the autopsy photographs, and the eyewitnesses. All of these agreed that the back wound (Figure 2) was in the back of the torso, not the back of the neck. The one exception to this remarkable agreement is Boswell's second opinion: after he was asked to reconsider his original autopsy drawing (Figure 4B), he agreed to elevate the back wound. By doing so, he denied the accuracy of his own autopsy diagram! On seeing this change, Francis O'Neill, one of the FBI agents at the autopsy, ridiculed Boswell for this convenient after-the-fact change of mind. It should also be noted that Admiral Burkley initialed Boswell's diagram as approved (see his signature in Figure 4B), so if Boswell indeed had grossly misrepresented the back wound in his own diagram, then Burkley, too, had been gravely mistaken. That both physicians would have made such a grievous error seems unlikely. When Boswell was first questioned by the ARRB, he first said that this wound lay at a cervical level, but when shown the autopsy photograph he opted for T2!

Admiral George Burkley's death certificate (dated 23 November 1963) placed this wound at T3 (the third thoracic vertebra). Burkley's choice of T3 raises a serious question. It is not likely that he would merely have glanced at the body and made this correlation by himself. More likely, he obtained this information from the pathologists, either at the autopsy, or during the next day when the autopsy report was being written. Ebersole, in my conversation with him, actually placed the wound at T4. Ebersole's comments must be taken seriously because his specialty (like mine) was radiation oncology. This is the sole specialty in which correlation of internal anatomy with external anatomy is essential—if this is not done correctly, the tumor will be missed by the therapeutic X-ray beam. The levels of T3 and T4, although noticeably lower than the top of the scapula, do receive surprising support from other sources. Of these sources, the shirt and coat are the most intriguing. According to Robert Frazier of the FBI (*The Warren Report* 1964, p. 92), the hole in the shirt was 5 3/8 inches (13.65 cm) below the top of the collar; the hole in the coat was 5 3/4 inches (13.8 cm) below the top of the collar. My own measurements at the Archives agreed closely with these. An excellent photograph of the shirt can be seen in Weisberg's *Post-Mortem* (1975, p. 597); for the coat, see Livingstone (1998, pp. 24-25) or Groden (1993, p. 78). While at the Archives I had a 6' 4" live, male model (S. M.) put the coat on. I was struck at how low this hole actually was—by both palpation and visual inspection, the hole was about 10 cm (four inches) *below the scapular spine*! There is a horizontal seam in the coat across the top of the back; I could feel the top of the scapula at 2–3 cm above the seam, whereas the hole lay an additional 7–8 cm below the seam. Additional evidence for such a low back wound has been previously compiled. (See *Assassination Science* 1998, pp. 110–111.) If this evidence is correct, then the photograph of the back wound has been altered.

Several witnesses, however, including Humes, place the back wound much higher than this—at the top of the scapula—which would be consistent with the photograph (Figure 2). To correlate this level with a particular vertebral body, normal anatomy is shown in Figure 13. In this photograph, the top of the scapula would lie between T1 and T2. Standard anatomy textbooks place the scapular spine (the visible horizontal portion near the top) at about T2 (Carmine Clemente, *Anatomy, A Regional Atlas of the Human Body* 1987, Figure 140). Anatomy textbooks (Clemente 1987, Figure 591, and J. C. Boileau Grant, *Grant's Atlas of Anatomy* 1972, Figure 458), place the 3rd or 4th tracheal ring (the level of the throat wound)[18] at about C7. So even when coupled with a back wound at the higher level of T1 or T2, however, the level of C7 for the throat wound is devastating to the SBT—the back wound is then obviously lower than the throat wound! For these two wounds to connect, Oswald would have had to shoot from the trunk of the limousine. It is not difficult to imagine why Ford felt compelled to give the SBT a modest assist. The upward direction (from back to front) of a line connecting the back wound to the throat wound was apparently demonstrated by transit probes at the autopsy—for which photographs no longer exist, but which so many observers recall. So even if the photographs of the back wound are accepted as authentic (and the wound were at T1 or at T2), there is still a very serious problem for the SBT. However, if the evidence listed above for an even lower back wound (i.e., T3 or T4) were correct, then the SBT would be flagrantly ridiculous.

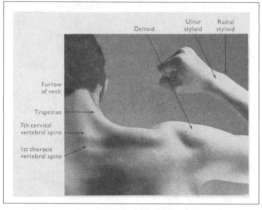

Figure 13. Normal anatomy of the back (D. W. McKears and R. H. Owen, Surface Anatomy for Radiographers *(1979), p. 41).*

The above arguments apply within a vertical plane, but equally powerful arguments against the SBT apply within a horizontal plane. The first individual to recognize this paradox was John Nichols, M.D., a pathologist at the University of Kansas (John Nichols, "The Wounding of Governor John Connally of Texas," *The Maryland State Medical Journal*, October 1977). He drew a model cross section of anatomy, and concluded that a bullet fired from the lateral angle of the sniper's nest simply could not exit at the midline of the throat without striking bone. And since the X-rays at this level show at most minor trauma to the transverse process of T1, this trajectory could be ruled out, according to Nichols.

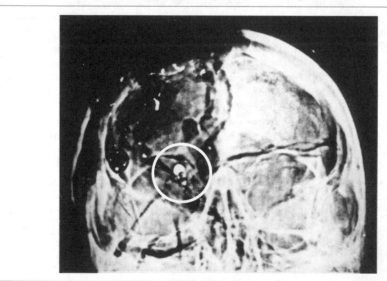

Figure 14. Frontal Autopsy X-ray. The largest "metal" fragment, a 6.5 mm object (circled) that lies inside the right orbit was added later in the darkroom.

The ideal test would be a CT scan of JFK's body, but CTs were not yet available. A set of frontal and lateral X-rays might have done almost as well, but no lateral autopsy X-ray exists. So I did the next best thing. I took detailed measurements from the frontal X-rays (at the Archives) through the upper back and lower neck. Then I located a real CT scan of a patient similar in overall size to JFK. When these measurements were integrated with this CT scan, it was obvious that the HSCA trajectory was highly unlikely. [*Editor's note*: This experiment is reproduced elsewhere in this volume.]

If the bullet had transited at mid-T1 or above it would have struck bone (the lateral processes of the vertebrae) and caused major fractures (that are clearly not seen on the chest X-ray). On the other hand, if it had transited at a lower level, it would have passed through the lung, causing air to escape into the chest cavity (i.e., a pneumothorax). Although the pathologists saw a bruise at the top of the lung, they saw no penetrating wound in the lung itself. The bullet, therefore, did not pass through the lung. Additional arguments against the SBT, based on the location of the back wound at five centimeters from midline, have previously been described (*Assassination Science* 1998, pp. 102-103), and will not be repeated here. In summary, then, powerful arguments, in both the vertical and horizontal planes show how the SBT violates both common sense as well as basic anatomy. These issues were never addressed, let alone explored, by the Warren Commission, or even by the HSCA.

What caused the (non-penetrating) back wound? There is fairly compelling evidence that it was either the first shot fired, or the first shot to hit JFK. Roy Kellerman (Palamara 1998, pp. 105-108) recalls that when he turned around he saw JFK put his hand up (on his back) and that he also heard JFK say: "My God, I am hit!" O'Neill included this comment by Kellerman in his FBI report. He later recognized how important it was because it violated the SBT. O'Neill therefore considered this to be a crucial remark by JFK. The whereabouts of this bullet—or whether it was ever recovered—is still debated. Years later a sabot was found on the roof of an adjacent office building (Sloan 1993, pp. 111-112), thus raising the possibility that an attempt had been made (with an underpowered round) to plant a Mannlicher-Carcano bullet on JFK. Other possible causes for the back wound include: (1) shrapnel from a bullet that struck the street or sidewalk, (2) a piece of the pavement that was launched by a bullet that struck the street or the sidewalk (Palamara 1998, pp. 213-214), or (3) a bullet that first struck the seat back of the limousine and then shattered or exploded. (Ed O'Hagen is currently doing a photographic analysis of this latter possibility, while Roy Schaeffer had previously pointed out a possible bullet hole in the seat back (behind JFK) in photographs taken of the limousine at the White House garage.) If the spectroscopic evidence is accepted, then (1) the projectile that entered the back was metallic (copper residue was found on the clothing) and (2) the projectile that entered the throat was not metallic (no copper residue was found on the clothing).

According to *The Warren Report*, the nose and tail of this bullet were found inside the limousine; therefore this cross section must have come from *inside the bullet*, which is an undeniably preposterous proposal. The situation is even worse than this, however. One of the bullet fragments found in the limousine (and still in the Archives) has its copper jacket peeled back by almost 180 degrees. How this could happen, merely by striking skull, is almost miraculous. On the other hand, if the bullet had first struck pavement, then such a peeling back might occur, but that would mean one additional bullet. The Commission could consider none of these options because any one of them would have meant conspiracy (too many bullets).

The Throat Wound

Malcolm Perry, M.D., the ENT surgeon at Parkland, thrice described this small, smooth, round wound as an entry wound during the press conference at Parkland on 22 November 1963. (See *Assassination Science* 1998, Appendix C.) Within the week after the assassination, virtually all of the Parkland doctors agreed that this had been an entrance wound. Margaret Henchcliffe (6H141-143), one of the E.R. nurses, said that she had never seen an exit wound that looked like this. However, according to Charles Crenshaw, M.D., after a visit by the Secret Service following the assassination, the doctors seldom discussed the assassination among themselves. Moreover, their testimony before the Warren Commission changed drastically, even though they had seen no new evidence with their own eyes.

At the autopsy, the pathologists did not describe this wound, even though Perry maintained that he had left the wound "inviolate," i.e., still readily visible. It seems quite certain now that this ignorance of the bullet wound by the pathologists was merely feigned, because the pathologists knew that the lone assassin theory was in vogue and that such an obvious entry wound would contradict it. Also, even if they had wanted to connect an entering bullet from the back to the throat wound (as a supposed exit site), they knew well enough (from everything they had seen at the autopsy) that the back wound was far too low for this to work.

Humes claimed that he first learned of the throat wound from Perry, when they spoke by telephone after 8 AM Saturday morning, November 23. It is curious, however, that Perry, in his subsequent Commission testimony (6H16), seemed uncertain about the timing of this call, first recalling that it was Friday afternoon! It was only after he was prompted that he agreed to the Saturday morning scenario. Perry may also have been subjected to pressure to change his conclusion about a bullet entry into the throat. Graduate student James Gouchenaur (HSCA File # 180-10109), on 1 June 1977, recalled a conversation with Secret Service agent Elmer Moore, who expressed remorse for badgering Perry into changing his testimony about the entrance wound in the throat. Audrey Bell also told Livingstone that Perry had received calls during the night from Bethesda (Livingstone 1995, p. 192).

The list of autopsy witnesses who knew of the throat wound is surprisingly long and has been meticulously assembled by Kathy Cunningham, L.P.N. Now, however, after Boswell's admission to the ARRB that he did know of this projectile wound while at the autopsy (it is clear that he was not merely referring to the tracheotomy), the evidence of all of these witnesses is scarcely needed anymore.

Based on a telephone call during the autopsy, Ebersole, the radiologist, told me (see Appendix E) that the projectile wound to the throat was already known at the autopsy. It is noteworthy that tissue samples were taken of the tracheotomy wound, a procedure that makes no sense at all for a simple tracheotomy.

Many witnesses have described seeing probes in the body during the autopsy (or sometimes in photographs of the body), and that these probes passed through the tracheotomy. For a simple tracheotomy to be probed also makes no sense, but if a bullet wound were located there, then both a probe and tissue samples would make sense. I shall say no more about this feigned ignorance of the pathologists, because the evidence contrary to this charade is now simply overwhelming.

Instead, the relevant question is: what caused the wound and where did the bullet go (if there was one)? The traditional critic's scenario for why the X-rays showed no metal debris (in the throat) is that the bullet (or fragments) was removed surreptitiously. That the tracheotomy wound changed dramatically between Parkland and Bethesda seems likely. When first asked about this by David Lifton, Perry replied that the tracheotomy was only about 2-3 cm across, but when pushed on this question, Perry successively increased the width until now he seems unwilling to deny that the gaping, irregular wound in the photographs is entirely his work (Lifton 1988, Chapter 11). In his Afterward, Lifton listed medical eyewitnesses from Parkland who agreed that the tracheotomy wound was not at all what they remembered (others could now be added). Perry's own, initial, surprised reaction on seeing the photograph of his (supposed) tracheotomy is especially noteworthy (see Lifton's Afterward). Now, however, he seems not to care anymore, as he wrote to James H. Fetzer (16 February 1998):

> I don't wish to relive that tragic weekend, and I avoid reading about it (sic). . . . I don't believe there is credible evidence of a "cover-up," nor does anyone I know think so. . . . Most of us view the conspiracy theories as mainly self-serving, usually based on distortions and selected interviews with people who had little or nothing to do with the actual events, and invariably coupled with an ignorance of medicine and trauma. I find that I really don't care anymore because I know what the truth is and that's sufficient.

Charles Crenshaw has strongly insisted that the tracheotomy at Parkland was much smaller, not at all like the one in the photographs. (Boswell's autopsy diagram clearly states the diameter as 6.5 cm; see Figure 4B.) Crenshaw also reminded the ARRB that the flange on the tube was 5 cm, and that the wound was—it almost necessarily had to be—smaller than that. David Lifton's own research (1988, Chapter 11) has suggested that the flange was even smaller than this, possibly 4 cm or even as small as 3 cm.[18] The wound in the photographs is certainly much larger than that. For the Commission, Humes even described it as large as 7 to 8 cm, although for *JAMA* he described it as only half that size.

A new witness to this question has recently emerged, someone who was in Trauma Room One, a medical student at the time, Joe D. Goldstrich, M.D.,[19] more recently from San Diego, California. When he was asked about this specifically (Sloan 1993, p. 89), he recalled his initial impressions on seeing the autopsy photographs: confusion and consternation. He said: "The whole front of his neck was wide open. It had simply been filleted." Ebersole also expressed to me his near horror at seeing such a large and irregular tracheotomy.

The widened and ragged appearance at the autopsy of this supposed mere incision strongly suggests that the tracheotomy was enlarged, perhaps during a search for bullets or for metal debris prior to the autopsy. There is, however, no certain way of knowing what, if anything, was found. Curiously, Livingstone (1998, p. 562) reproduced detailed photographs (including some documentation for them) of partial bullets said to have been removed from JFK. Nothing is said, however, about whether these were from the skull or from the throat.

The primary argument against such a frontal bullet to the throat is the minimal trauma seen in the spine (on the X-rays), as well as the absence of a corresponding exit wound in the back. Although there is a probable (tiny) fracture to the right lateral process of T1 on the X-rays, that is all. It is not even certain whether this fracture was present before the shooting. The direction of such a proposed shot also poses serious difficulties—the autopsy evidence strongly suggests that it was traveling diagonally from left to right, consistent with a shot from the left front. Even worse, though, its remarkably limited range is puzzling, because most ordinary bullets would, without striking bone, easily have passed through the chest and exited from the back. This one apparently did not.

As I contemplated this paradox some years ago, I realized that any radiolucent object (i.e., something invisible on the X-rays) would be consistent with all of the evidence. And then I wondered, if there really had been a complete hole in the windshield (Larry Sneed, *No More Silence* 1998, pp. 147–148), was it possible that *a fragment of glass* had caused the throat wound? It met all of the requirements: it was radiolucent, it had a limited range, the pathologists (probably) would not have seen it, and, furthermore, the bullet might even have come from the right front. In particular, a spray of glass particles, diverging in a cone (even from a right front shot) might have permitted some of them to strike JFK in a left to right direction. [20]

A close examination of the Altgens photograph (taken at about Zapruder frame 255) shows that a path from the windshield to JFK's throat was entirely unobstructed. This seemed an uncanny corroboration for this proposal. Furthermore, some versions of this photograph show a mark (resembling a spiral nebula with a dark hole in the center) in the windshield that could be a through and through hole. [*Editor's note*: Roy Schaeffer detected this feature in this photograph (*Assassination Science* 1998, pp. 143-144). Schaeffer has also summarized his conclusions in an unpublished manuscript, *The Slaying of Camelot*.] It was only recently, however, on re-reading the comments of Tom Robinson (from Gawler's funeral home), that I became conscious of possible additional evidence for this proposal.

Robinson described three tiny holes in the right cheek, near the right eye. I had previously ignored these, because I could not relate them to anything else. The reason that Robinson recalled these at all is because the fixative solution was leaking from them. Such wounds could hardly have been caused by debris coming from inside the cheek: the distance from sites of major trauma in the brain was too remote. Furthermore, bone would have obstructed such a path from the brain. Instead, something must have struck JFK's cheek from the outside. But no other limousine occupants had suffered similar injuries, so why just JFK?

If tiny fragments of glass had been emitted in a small cone of scattering (a small cone is the likely scenario, because of the bullet's initial high speed), then it is possible that JFK, *and no one else*, would have been hit. This conclusion is based on JFK's position in the Altgens photograph, and also on the presumed angle of incidence of the bullet. Douglas Weldon, J.D., has recently informed me that he is aware of further, current research by John Ritchson on this very question. [*Editor's note*: Weldon reviews windshield evidence elsewhere in this volume, listing several, independent witnesses who recalled a through and through hole in the windshield.]

Moreover, witnesses to the windshield hole (Palamara 1998, p. 63) often described a specific and consistent site that matches the site seen in the Altgens photograph. In the present volume, Weldon introduces the Ford Motor Company employee (whose audiotape I have heard) who saw the windshield—and the hole—before the windshield was destroyed. Based on his inspection, this employee concluded that the shot had come from the front. As further corroboration of his veracity (he was not versed in the assassination literature), he placed the hole at the proper site. Weldon also reviews the seemingly inconsistent testimony of government employees who examined the windshield at different times—which suggests that they were examining different windshields. Robert Livingston, M.D., has advised me (and others, too) that when he worked at the National Institutes of Health in 1963, he had heard of orders for multiple windshields. Like Weldon, he, too, has wondered if the original windshield was (illicitly) substituted. [*Editor's note*: See *Assassination Science* 1998, pp. 165-166.] The windshield currently stored in the Archives does not contain a through and through hole.

Weldon lists several witnesses who recalled a shot from the left front, probably from the storm drain on the south overpass. At present, that drain has been covered over, but in 1963 it was open. Its location mirrors a similar drain site on the north overpass, the one that I have proposed for the origin of the shot to the right forehead. Furthermore, Weldon adds that the image in the Cancellare photograph seems to show someone holding a rifle at this site. None of this information ever came to the attention of any government inquiry.

Weldon's proposal has more than one attractive feature. First, it may explain the odd, almost unique, fireworks-like sound of the first shot that so many witnesses recalled. Weldon has learned that a shot passing through a windshield sounds just like fireworks going off. Furthermore, such a shot would have the proper left to right trajectory, although it could still not explain the limited range of such a bullet, as implied by the autopsy findings. In addition, if a shooter really had fired from the left front it might explain the odd reports of several witnesses who described a left temple entry wound. These include physicians McClelland, Jenkins, Giesecke, the priest Oscar Huber, photographers Altgens and Similas, and recently, Hugh Huggins (aka Hugh Howell)—Robert Kennedy's emissary to the autopsy (Sloan 1993, p. 183). One more witness is Lito Puerto, a neurosurgery resident under Kemp Clark (Palamara 1998, p. 75). For a discussion of the left entry wound, see Lifton (1988, pp. 45-47).

Crenshaw had recalled that the left temple, after removal of a blood clot, had shown no underlying wound. I had found this to be persuasive evidence against such a left temple shot and had therefore discarded this possibility. But now I am less certain. On the other hand, knowing how easy it is to reverse left for right (as I have done many times in this case—as also did Robert Blakey, on national television), I naturally wonder if some of these witnesses merely reversed left for right and that most of them had actually seen a shot to the right temple/forehead.

Such a shot from the left front, however, might explain marks found on the north sidewalk along Elm Street, as Weldon notes. A successful shot to the left temple would actually match the large hole at the right rear better than a shot from the right front, although the metallic debris on the X-rays would still strongly support a right frontal shot. But perhaps the question should be changed. Is it possible that yet a third shot struck JFK's head? It is difficult for me to believe that three shots struck the head in such a short time interval, but I admit that, with the available evidence, I cannot totally rule out this possibility. If the current X-rays could be thoroughly scanned in great detail, it is possible that a third shot could be excluded or perhaps even confirmed.

For the throat wound, therefore, some uncertainties remain. Was it caused by a bullet (of remarkably limited range) or instead by a glass fragment? Was this shot fired from the left front (consistent with the observed trajectory), or from the right front (which might have ejected a glass fragment with the required trajectory, the observed short range and the requisite invisibility to X-rays)? It is not likely, short of exhumation, which might or might not be sufficient, that these issues can ever be entirely resolved.

There is one final question, however. If a glass fragment caused the wound, then where did the bullet go? There are two possibilities: either (1) it struck somewhere inside the limousine (either staying inside or possibly exiting) or (2) it struck somewhere outside the limousine. The available evidence may be consistent with either interpretation. Many witnesses, reported by the Warren Commission (also see Menninger 1992, pp. 68-74, for a discussion of such ricochet bullets and the witnesses who saw them), either saw or heard bullets strike the street and the surrounding turf, some in front of the limousine and some in back.[21] The Commission ignored these witnesses, but their testimonies were nonetheless included in the volumes of its *Hearings*.

Alternately, the bullet could have struck inside the limousine. Roy Schaeffer, using an enlargement of a photograph of the inside of the limousine (taken at the White House garage), believes that he has identified a bullet hole in the rear seat, near Jackie's right elbow. Could this hole conceivably represent a frontal shot that was deflected after striking the windshield?

Whether such a bullet stayed inside the limousine or exited and (possibly) struck the street remains uncertain. What is known, without any doubt, is that the Secret Service was astonishingly protective of the limousine in Dallas after the shooting. Several witnesses even saw them tear the film from a young boy's movie camera after he had photographed the limousine interior at Parkland Hospital. The premature disappearance of the limousine, in the immediately subsequent days (as discussed by Weldon), is also suspicious. It would seem that a more determined attempt was made to destroy evidence than to preserve it. If the limousine did contain evidence of conspiracy (either from bullet holes in the upholstery or even in the windshield, or from physical bullets or fragments), then such efforts would have been expedient (as part of the cover-up).

The Brain(s)

Initially, I did not know whether the skull contained any brain tissue at all at the autopsy, partly because of the comments of several autopsy personnel, but also because of surprising evidence that the skull may have been (illegally) explored before the autopsy (Lifton 1988). After reflecting on this question, however, I eventually recognized that the X-rays might hold the answer. In due course I was able to address this question both by means of an experiment and also by repeated measurements of optical density (OD) performed on the X-rays at the National Archives. The conclusions were quite straightforward: (1) there really is a brain within the skull as seen on the X-rays; (2) it is totally incompatible with the photographs of the brain (I have repeatedly viewed these photographs myself—even using a stereo viewer—at the National Archives); and (3) the amount of residual brain, along a measured line of sight, varies in different parts of the X-rays from as low as 25% to as high as 90%, but on the right side (which shows the least brain tissue) is often between 30 and 60%.

The most surprising result, though, was the loss of brain tissue on the left side (only 2/3 to 3/4 remains), and the virtually total absence of brain in a large bilateral area at the front—the large void that Humes describes in his excerpted testimony (see the addendum). In addition, I was able to demonstrate that the area of the right cerebellum showed only about 25-30% of the expected amount for a totally intact brain, thus confirming the descriptions of the Dallas physicians that this area had been severely traumatized. These X-ray observations of the cerebellum also disagreed radically with the photographs, which showed an almost normal cerebellum. In the laboratory, using a real skull and simulated brain material (used in departments of radiation oncology), I was able to explore these issues in more detail and at some leisure. By taking X-rays of skulls variously filled with simulated brain tissue, and then taking measurements on these X-rays, the resulting OD data provided strong confirmation for the conclusions I had reached from the extant JFK X-rays.

While at the National Archives, I answered one additional question: was it possible that much of the brain was actually present, but had been displaced to the outside of the skull? By passing a bright light over the entire circumference of the skull, I was able to see even small amounts of soft tissue that would otherwise have been invisible. Since, except for scalp, I saw essentially no such soft tissue here, the conclusion was obvious—the missing brain was not outside of the skull. During his ARRB interview, Humes also agreed that brain was not visible outside of the skull. Therefore, the chief paradox persisted: a truly huge amount of brain was missing, in gross contradiction with the photographs of the brain. I could only conclude that the brain photographs were not those of JFK. Indeed, after examining all of the eyewitness evidence—from Parkland and from Bethesda—and surveying the publicly available image of the brain, Robert B. Livingston, M.D., a world authority on the brain and founder of the Department of Neuroscience at UC-San Diego, came to the same conclusion. (See *Assassination Science* 1998, pp. 161-166).

Although Livingstone (1995, p. 261) had proposed that the brain had been switched, what no one had yet considered—perhaps because it seemed so disgraceful—was the possibility that there had been two different brain examinations, of two different brains, on two different occasions. However, on reviewing the new evidence uncovered by the ARRB and integrating this with previously available information, Douglas P. Horne, Senior Military Analyst for the ARRB, proposed precisely that. He assembled a large number of disparate pieces of evidence, all of which were strikingly consistent with this proposal. He offered three separate lines of evidence for his stunning conclusion: (1) timeline conflicts, (2) the visible appearance of the brain at the two different dates, and (3) discrepancies in the film and photographic techniques employed. [*Editor's note*: Horne's study may be found elsewhere in this volume.]

Evidence from the X-rays that I had obtained prior to the activities of the ARRB constituted yet a fourth pillar for this surprising discovery. In view of Horne's accessible study (in this volume), I present here only the tables (Tables 1-4) that summarize all of this evidence. When viewed in this fashion, the case for two brains is quite remarkable. It is difficult, in retrospect, to imagine an alternate explanation that can reasonably explain so many odd details.

Table 1: Timeline Conflicts

Evidence for an early brain exam (c. 11/25/63)

Boswell to HSCA: the exam was 2-3 days after 11/22
Stringer to HSCA: the exam was 2-3 days after 11/22
Boswell: Finck was absent
Stringer: Finck was absent, but Boswell and Humes were present
Boyers to HSCA: body tissues processed by 11/24
Benson to HSCA: more tissue processed on 11/25
Boswell to ARRB: all tissue slides examined by 11/24
Humes to JAMA: RFK wanted brain buried with body (interment was 11/25)

Evidence for a later brain exam (c. 12/2/63)

Finck's written report to Gen. Blumberg— notified on 11/29 re. a later exam
Finck to ARRB: exam could not have occurred in 2-3 days
Boyers to HSCA: 6 paraffin blocks, 8 sections processed on 12/2 (brain tissue)
Clossen typed report closer to 12/2 than to 11/25
Humes to Specter: all 3 pathologists at brain exam (stated with B&F present)
Hand written date on final report is 12/6

It should also be noted that Humes initially told the ARRB that the brain examination occurred 1-2 days after 11/22/63 (which seems far too early, since brains usually require 10-14 days to fix in formalin). But, as the deposition proceeded, Humes kept moving the date farther away from 11/22. Horne observed that Humes's attitude during this discussion was both defensive and flippant.

Table 2: The Appearance of the Brains at the Examinations

Appearance at the Earlier Exam (c. 11/25/63)

Humes to *JAMA*: 2/3 of right cerebrum missing
Boswell to HSCA: brain too torn up to show a track
All 3 pathologists saw an entry wound near the EOP
    (which would imply cerebellar trauma)
X-rays show 30–35 tiny metal particles

Appearance at the Later Exam (c. 12/2/63)

Finck to Blumberg: brain surface looked different from 11/22
Brain mass: 1500 gm (inconsistent with major tissue loss)
Photographs: most of brain present
Robert Kischner, M.D., to ARRB: brain in photo was fixed for 2 weeks
Boyers to HSCA: he saw a bullet track, para-saggital laceration described
Parasaggital laceration 4–5 cm inferior to vertex, no cerebellar trauma
Finck's personal notes: no metal fragments
Humes: he does not note any metal fragments either

Table 3: Conflicts in Film and Photographic Techniques

Photographic Evidence at the Earlier Exam (c. 11/25/63)

Stringer to ARRB: photos of sections, including sections on a light box
Stringer to ARRB: no views of the inferior (basilar) surface
Stringer to ARRB (re. B&W): negatives on Kodak portrait pan in duplex
        holders (no numbers on film)
Stringer to ARRB (re. color): Kodak Ectachrome positive transparencies

Photographic Evidence at the Later Exam (c. 12/2/63)

Photographs: no sections in official record
Humes and Boswell: no sections taken
Humes and Finck: describe basilar views
Photographs: basilar views in the official record
Archives negatives: on Ansco film from a numbered 12-pack
Archives films: on Ansco film (with notches), per Stringer

Richard Davis, a neuropathologist at the AFIP, could think of no reason for ever
omitting brain sections in a gunshot wound case. (He was not asked if a cover-up
might be one reason). Boswell told the ARRB the same thing, but could not
explain why this fundamental rule had (apparently) been violated in the case of
JFK.

Table 4: The Skull X-rays vs. the Brain Photographs

Skull X-rays (11/22/63)

Lateral X-ray: black bifrontal area—implies brain missing on both
        left and right in a large area
Lateral X-ray: black bifrontal area—implies 1/4 to 1/3, at least, of
        total brain (in addition, more brain is missing from other
        parts of the X-ray)
Frontal X-ray: right infra-orbital transverse black band shows only
        30% of total brain at the level of the cerebellum
Frontal X-ray: just below this, 80% of the brain is present
Frontal X-ray: fracture line above left orbit shows only 60–65%
        of total brain

Brain Photographs (c. 12/2/63)

Left brain intact
Right brain mostly intact
Minimal cerebellar trauma
Bifrontal areas mostly intact

The point of Table 4 is to illustrate the impossible conflicts between the X-rays (taken at the original autopsy) versus the photographs (most likely taken on about Monday, 2 December 1963) of what must be two different brains. These discrepancies, especially in both frontal areas, are otherwise impossible to resolve. The case for conspiracy could be solidly based on this single discrepancy alone.

During his deposition before the ARRB, Humes came very close to revealing the truth about the brain (while viewing a photograph of it), as shown in the following monologue:

> Boy, I have trouble with this. I don't know which end is up. What happened here? Looking at this photograph, which is labeled #46, the structure which is on the right side of the brain appears to be intact—the cerebrum intact—and that's not right, because it was not. And, and (sic) the structure which is all distorted (pause), let me see (pause), well (pause), well, I guess this, this (sic) is the left side of the brain, more or less intact.

The Skull X-Rays

In their autopsy report, the pathologists described the trail of metallic debris as beginning near their proposed entry site (near the EOP) and extending to just above the right eye (*Assassination Science* 1998, pp. 430-437). The FBI report of Sibert and O'Neill (Warren Commission Document CD-7, reproduced by Josiah Thompson, *Six Seconds in Dallas* 1967, Appendix G), which they compiled as eyewitnesses at the autopsy, placed the largest metal fragment above the right eye and the next largest at the rear of the skull. The pathologists' report does not provide any detailed description of these metal fragments.

The 6.5 mm "Metal" Object

In 1968, a panel of physicians appointed by then Attorney General Ramsey Clark described, for the first time in history, a 6.5 mm "metal" cross section of a bullet fragment (see Figure 14) that lay at the rear of the skull. I have used quotation marks around the word "metal" because its authenticity is dubious. The evidence for this conclusion has previously been described. [*Editor's note*: See *Assassination Science* 1998, pp. 120-137.] The evidence for forgery is based upon hundreds of point-like measurements of optical density on the X-rays at the National Archives. Optical density is merely a quantitative means of representing the lightness or darkness of a given point on the X-ray film.

The reasons for my conclusion that this object could not have been on the original X-rays, aside from its striking historical absence, were eightfold, as follows.

1.   On the lateral X-ray, the transparency of the 6.5 mm object is much less (less light gets through) than for a real 6.5 mm metal slice from an actual

Mannlicher-Carcano bullet (as I showed by X-raying a section from such a bullet taped to a real human skull). In other words, a real 6.5 mm piece of metal looks much lighter than the object on the lateral X-ray.

2.   On the frontal view, a superposition of images *inside* this 6.5 mm object can be seen with the naked (myopic) eye; a small hand held magnifying lens works well, too. The original bullet fragment described by Sibert and O'Neill can be seen inside (partially overlapping) the 6.5 mm object. The 6.5 mm object itself is a phantom that was later introduced in a darkroom laboratory. Such phantom effects have been described in books on special effects in photography, as I discussed in my earlier study (*Assassination Science* 1998, pp. 120-137).

3.   On the frontal X-ray, a transmission scan (taken at intervals of 0.1 mm) of the 6.5 mm object, is entirely consistent with the impression offered by the naked (myopic) eye—most of the metal lies on the right side of the object. (Right and left are oriented with respect to JFK's skull.) It represents the authentic shrapnel described by Sibert and O'Neill.

4.   On the lateral X-ray, the transmission measurements (actually OD data) imply more metal at the bottom of this 6.5 mm object than at the center. To the naked eye (see Figure 14), however, on the frontal X-ray a sector at 4 to 6 o'clock is missing, so the data (from the lateral X-ray) should have shown *less* metal at the bottom. On the frontal X-ray, however, I could actually see with my myopic eyes the original, small piece of shrapnel that was originally located there (described by Sibert and O'Neill). What I saw with my naked eyes was totally consistent with the OD data. The *authentic* shrapnel was thicker at the bottom than at the top.

5.   The teeth are easily visible at the Archives, although they do not appear in any publicly available images. On the frontal X-ray, the 6.5 mm object is very transparent—very definitely lighter (from front to back) than all of the dental amalgams superimposed on one another. This was repeatedly confirmed with OD measurements. This implies that the front-to-back thickness of this 6.5 mm object should be greater than all of the dental amalgams (mercury and silver) stacked on top of one other. In fact, the measurements imply that the front-to-back thickness of this 6.5 mm object should be nearly 10 times larger than it actually is on the lateral X-ray!

6.   On the lateral X-ray, the transmission measurements imply that the 6.5 mm object is much thinner (from left to right) than one dental amalgam. This is to be expected since the lateral measurements of transparency provide an authentic estimate of this object while the frontal view has been altered. Furthermore, we already know that the left-to-right thickness of the authentic shrapnel on the original X-ray (as seen with the naked eye and as reported by Sibert and O'Neill) was only 2-3 mm across. All of this data is consistent.

7.   On the lateral X-ray, the transmission of this 6.5 mm object and the transmission of the 7 x 2 mm object (above the right eye) are similar, as they should be for fragments of about the same authentic thickness (about 2 mm). This is consistent with the FBI report, but it is wholly inconsistent with the visible (and inauthentic) 6.5 mm object on the frontal view—because the forgers increased its width in the darkroom.

8. On the frontal view, the 6.5 mm object is astonishingly thicker from front to back (by the transmission measurements) than the 7 x 2 mm fragment, even though the naked eye can see (on the lateral X-ray) that they are actually about the same thickness. This is because, on the frontal view, the forgers overexposed the 6.5 mm object in the darkroom.

In summary: (1) this evidence is self-consistent, (2) it is consistent with Sibert and O'Neill, and (3) it is consistent with the historical record—from which this 6.5 mm object was totally absent until 1968, five years after the autopsy. In my prior essay, I described how easy it would have been in 1963 to add a phantom object of this kind to an X-ray. On modern duplicating X-ray film, I also found this rather simple do to in the darkroom. For example, a real scissors was placed over the original X-ray film in the darkroom. The scissors blocked out the light and resulted in a dark image of a scissors on the copy film. Then shrapnel was added by placing a cardboard template with holes over the first X-ray film. Where the light passed through the holes the image became lighter on the copy film. In another case, my daughter's plastic template for a pterosaur was superimposed in the darkroom over a real skull X-ray film (see p. 432 below).

Since the publication of my prior essay, Larry Sturdivan, the HSCA ballistics expert, has also stated his unequivocal opinion that this 6.5 mm cross-section cannot possibly represent a piece of metal. In an e-mail conversation with Stuart Wexler, Sturdivan responded as follows (9 March 1998), regarding the 6.5 mm object:

> I'm not sure just what that 6.5 mm fragment is. One thing I'm sure it is NOT is a cross-section from the interior of a bullet. I have seen literally thousands of bullets, deformed and undeformed, after penetrating tissue and tissue simulants. Some were bent, some torn in two or more pieces, but to have a cross-section sheared out is physically impossible. That fragment has a lot of mystery associated with it. Some have said it was a piece of the jacket, sheared off by the bone and left on the outside of the skull. I've never seen a perfectly round piece of bullet jacket in any wound. Furthermore, the fragment seems to have greater optical density thin-face on [the frontal X-ray] than it does edge-wise [the lateral X-ray]. . . . The only thing I can think is that it is an artifact.

The sole purpose of taking X-rays at the autopsy was to locate—and then to remove (for forensic purposes)—bullets, or large bullet fragments. That this (apparently largest) object in the X-rays was neither described nor removed at the autopsy has been simply inexplicable. In view of the mysterious absence of this 6.5 mm object from the historical record (until 1968), it would seem inevitable that the pathologists should have clarified this central issue as soon as possible. Nonetheless, the question remained unasked and unresolved, both by the HSCA and then later by *JAMA*. It was finally asked by the ARRB, when all three pathologists, under oath, finally came face to face with this unique paradox. Their independent answers were at times both astonishing and embarrassing for them. Excerpts of Boswell's and Humes' depositions may be found in Appendix F and Appendix G.

In these new depositions, all three pathologists denied seeing the 6.5 mm object at the autopsy. Boswell and Humes, in particular, were quite emphatic that they had not seen it, and that they had not removed anything of that size. Ebersole's comments to me also agreed with them. Humes, like Sturdivan, raised the possibility that it may have been an artifact. My response to this is straightforward. Until Humes knew otherwise at the autopsy, it was clearly his responsibility to remove any large object that looked even remotely like a bullet fragment. There is absolutely nothing in the historical record to suggest any discussion about an artifact on the X-ray films during the autopsy. No pathologist— nor Ebersole, nor any autopsy personnel—has ever suggested or even hinted at such a possibility. Nor has any official investigation ever intimated that this 6.5 mm object might be an artifact. That it was a random artifact (as Sturdivan wants to believe) is most unlikely—after all, *the images of the 6.5 mm object are spatially compatible on the two views* (the frontal and the lateral). How likely is it that a supposedly random artifact would have agreed in this striking fashion? The only sensible explanation is that it is indeed an artifact—but one intelligently placed at exactly the right site.

This entire subject lies well outside of the official record. If Humes indeed had seen this object on the autopsy X-rays *while at the autopsy*—even if he thought it was an artifact—he was under the greatest obligation to describe and discuss it or, better yet, simply to search that portion of the skull to confirm whether or not a bullet fragment was there. Not finding it, he could then have concluded that it was an artifact. But nothing like this exists in the record: nothing like this ever happened. Sibert and O'Neill describe nothing of this sort in their FBI report, nor does the autopsy report, nor do the pathologists in their ARRB depositions (or in any prior deposition), nor do any other Bethesda witnesses recall any discussion of such an object.

Instead, there is only an eerie silence, exactly what would be expected if this object had been added later (in the darkroom) as I have proposed. In fact, as I have previously explained, this was really quite simple to do. Contemporaneous radiology textbooks (e.g., John B. Cahoon, Jr., *Formulating X-ray Techniques* 1961) contain detailed recipes that were routinely used in that era for the copying of X-ray films. That these led to copies with remarkably good fidelity is also stated in the textbooks of that era—an original and a copy published side by side can be impossible to distinguish, as even the above author noted (p. 42).

The Trail of Metallic Debris on the Lateral X-ray

Humes and Boswell had great trouble with the trail of metallic debris as well (Figure 11). [*Editor's note:* See the discussion of Smoking Gun #4 in the Prologue.] In the autopsy report, it is described as extending from the EOP (the entry site for their posterior skull bullet) to a site above the right frontal sinus. Unfortunately for them, the trail of debris lies 10 cm higher at the back of the head—an extraordinary paradox that I have pointed out on numerous occasions (e.g., Letter to the Editor, *Vanity Fair*, February 1995, p. 34), but which neither the HSCA nor *JAMA* ever seemed curious about. (Cornwell's account is one exception). It is here, more than anywhere else, that Humes has tipped his hand. Shortly before he was asked about this trail in his ARRB testimony, Humes had laid claim to a good memory (supposedly demonstrated by his recall of three late arriving bone fragments). Furthermore, he wrote the autopsy report within 24 hours of the event itself, so that he had no excuse for not recalling this trail correctly. Moreover, it is the only such trail on the X-rays and necessarily must relate closely to the path of a projectile. There can therefore be no excuse for mislocating this trail, especially by more than half the width of the skull. Finally, Humes was aware of this trail at the autopsy, while *simultaneously* observing his EOP entry site. These were not sequential events. (See the addenda for the astonishing responses of both Humes and Boswell to questions about this trail.)

Ebersole's role in altering the X-rays is suspicious. He was called to the White House by the Secret Service on Saturday, 23 November (according to Custer, the X-ray technologist). Immediately after this (again according to Custer)—that same Saturday morning—Ebersole directed Custer in the taking of X-rays of skull fragments and bullet fragments taped to skull fragments. I believe, like Custer, that these were initial, exploratory steps in the alteration of the autopsy X-rays. Sometime later, most likely within the first month, but probably even earlier, Ebersole, in a bizarre episode involving "Aunt Margaret's skirts" (HSCA Record No. 180-10102-010409), was recalled to the White House to review the skull X-rays. This is when he drew the straight pencil lines on the skull X-rays (that are still there). The cover story for this visit is that his input was being requested for a bust of JFK, unabashedly based upon a skull that was quite thoroughly shattered. Most likely, however, he was simply being monitored for his reaction to the (now altered) X-rays.

It is noteworthy that the Secret Service was involved in this caper, just as they were also involved in the processing and development (and probable alteration) of the autopsy photographs. The chief of the Secret Service, James J. Rowley, apparently was a friend of J. Edgar Hoover and had briefly served in the FBI (under Hoover). Rowley was also the first person to shake LBJ's hand when he stepped off the plane at Andrews Air Force Base. Rowley continued to serve in the Johnson administration, as did both Admiral Burkley and Robert Knudsen, both of whom worked directly out of the White House.

The Burned Drafts

Humes finally admitted to *JAMA* that he had prepared a diagram at the autopsy, a diagram that never surfaced anywhere. This is in striking agreement with Boswell's comments to Josiah Thompson: "Yes, I'm sure there was another sheet, which had that measurement on it, and which had height, weight [perhaps even the missing fresh brain weight], and some other information. I'm sure of it" (Lifton 1988, Chapter 18). Humes had also informed *JAMA* and the HSCA (7HSCA257) that he faithfully copied everything that he had burned in his fireplace; if so, where is this diagram? Humes repeatedly regaled the Warren Commission and the HSCA with his anecdote about burning his autopsy notes: he did not want them to become an object of veneration, as he thought he had seen occur in the case of Lincoln's chair at the Henry Ford Museum in Dearborn, Michigan. In his ARRB deposition of Humes, Jeremy Gunn sets out, with remarkable tenacity—and to Humes's considerable exacerbation—to clarify this record, as follows.

Gunn: How many pages of notes did you take, approximately?

Humes: Oh, I can't tell you now. Maybe two or three. . . . [None of these have ever appeared in any official record.]

Gunn: Have you ever observed that [Boswell's autopsy diagram] appears to have bloodstains on it as well?

Humes: Yes, I do notice it now. . . .

Gunn: Did you ever have any concern about the President's blood being on the document that's now marked Exhibit 1?

Humes: I can't recall, to tell you the truth. . . .

Gunn: I'd like to show you the testimony that you offered before the Warren Commission. . . . I'd like you to take a look at pages 372 to the top of 373, and then I'll ask you a question. . . . Mr. Specter asked [a] question. . . . "Answer [by Humes]: In the privacy of my own home, early in the morning of Sunday, November 24, I made a draft of this report, which I later revised and of which this represents the revision. That draft I personally burned in the fireplace of my recreation room." . . . Does that help refresh your recollection of what was burned in your home?

Humes: Whatever I had, as far as I know, what was burned was everything exclusive of the finished draft that you have. . . .

Gunn: My question [is] whether it was a draft of the report that was burned or whether it was handwritten notes.

Humes: It was handwritten notes and the first draft that was burned.

Gunn: Do you mean to use the expression "handwritten notes" as being the equivalent of draft of the report?

Humes: I don't know. Again, it's a hair-splitting affair that I can't understand. Everything that I personally prepared until I got to the status of the handwritten document that later was transcribed was destroyed. You can call it anything you want, whether it was the notes or what, I don't know. But whatever I had, I didn't want anything else to remain, period.

Gunn: . . . Now, again, the question would be: Did you copy the notes so that you would have a version of the notes without the blood on them but still notes rather than a draft report?

Humes: Yes, precisely. Yes. And from that I made a first draft, and then I destroyed the first draft and the notes. [This is the great admission—for the first time in thirty three years, Humes finally admits to burning more than one item.]

Gunn: So there were, then, two sorts of documents that were burned: one the draft notes, and, two, a draft report?

Humes: Right. . . .

Gunn: Why did you burn the draft report as opposed to the draft notes?

Humes: I don't recall. I don't know. There was no reason—see, we're splitting hairs here, and I'll tell you, it's getting to me a little bit, as you may be able to detect. The only thing I wanted to finish to hand over to whomever, in this case, Admiral Burkley, was my completed version. . . .

Gunn: When I first asked the question, you explained that the reason that you had destroyed it was that it had the blood of the President on it.

Humes: Right.

Gunn: The draft report, of course, would not have had the blood of—
Humes: Well, it may have had errors in spelling or I don't know what was the
             matter with it, or whether I even ever did that. I don't know. I can't
             recall. I absolutely can't recall, and I apologize for that. But that's the
             way the cookie crumbles. I didn't want anything to remain that some
             squirrel would grab on and make whatever use that they might. . . .

Although Humes goes on to insist that the final draft differed in no significant way from the earlier draft, the Sibert and O'Neill report is quite different
from the final autopsy report. Their FBI report was based on notes taken at the
autopsy; furthermore, these two men had stayed until the official autopsy was
over. Most likely, based on their report, *JAMA* had reported on 4 January 1964
that a bullet had been removed from deep in JFK's right shoulder. [Note again,
contrary to Gerald Ford's interference, that the neck was not the site of the wound,
even in this early report.] As late as 26 January 1964, *The New York Times* also
reported that a bullet had lodged in JFK's right shoulder. A similar report appeared in *The Washington Post* of 18 December 1963. The *Post* reaffirmed its
report several years later, on 29 May 1966, even recalling that the initial story
had been confirmed with the FBI before publication. The only possible conclusion from all of this is that Humes drastically revised his conclusions after the
FBI had left, which was after the autopsy had officially concluded. Humes has
always attributed this change to learning (supposedly on Saturday morning, after speaking to Dr. Perry in Dallas) that the tracheotomy had been performed
through the bullet wound. However, the autopsy witnesses, who saw a probe
pass through the tracheotomy site, leave little doubt that this explanation is dis-
ingenuous.

If the first draft did differ from the final version, what items might have
changed? There are many possibilities. The first draft may have contained (1)
the fresh brain weight; (2) a description of a residual brain so shattered and so
small that no possible trail could be seen (quite different from the brain photographs in the Archives), which would hardly have been consistent with a single
headshot; (3) a description of seriously disrupted cerebellum, which would have
corroborated the reports of the Parkland doctors and would have implied a large
occipital skull wound (hardly consistent with the photographs that show an intact scalp and the red spot); (4) an accurate description of the trail of metallic
debris, going across the *top* of the skull, where it would have been grossly inconsistent with the much lower occipital entry wound that the pathologists discovered on the inner skull surface; (5) a forthcoming description of the large hole at
the rear of the skull, as opposed to the (probably deliberately) imprecise wording
of the autopsy report; (6) a description of their attempts to find a bullet path
between the back wound and the throat wound (which would obviously have
implied knowledge of the bullet wound in the throat); (7) a transit wound, determined by through and through probes (and also by an abrasion collar), that
went *upward* from back to front, in striking disagreement with the SBT; (8) a
frontal wound in the high, right, forehead/temple near the hairline, where the
frontal bullet probably entered (see the section on the frontal headshot). Since
Humes expired in 1999, we will probably never know how these different drafts
evolved. In some ways, though, it no longer matters, because so many other
clues now exist to the actual state of affairs at the autopsy. Humes's state of mind

on that particular weekend is no longer material to the medical evidence, although I shall comment below on the pathologists' behavior, insofar as it affords liberty for speculation on their impact on other medical aspects of the case.

The Autopsy Protocol: Is It Authentic?

Is the current autopsy protocol (CE-387) the same as the one that was signed on Sunday, November 24? Although at first sight this question seems radical, it has previously been discussed by Lifton (1988, chapters 17 and 18) and was again raised by Douglas P. Horne at the ARRB ("Chain-of-Custody Discrepancy Regarding Original Copy of JFK Autopsy Protocol, 2 August 1996). Lifton had obtained, under the Freedom of Information Act, a Secret Service memorandum (dated 12 February 1969) of a meeting that included Secret Service Inspector Kelley. As Harry R. Van Cleve, Jr., of the General Services Administration explained, although the Secret Service had transferred autopsy items 1 through 9 to the Kennedy family on 26 April 1965, they, in turn, had not transferred all of these items to the Archives. In particular, important autopsy materials from 9 were missing; this had been discovered on 29 October 1966, at the time of the original donation. These items included tissue slides and a stainless steel container (most likely a brain). But Kelley noted yet another problem: item 9 had also included the original autopsy protocol and seven copies! These, too, were gone. But the problem was even stranger than this: on 3 October 1967 (*the following year*) the Secret Service sent the (supposed) original autopsy protocol to the Archives! Even more interesting was that James J. Rowley, *Chief of the Secret Service*, signed out this transfer. Horne even discovered a receipt dated the next day, which was signed for by an Archives official named Simmons. As Kelley wrote: "This could raise the question about two original autopsy protocols. We, of course, were unable to resolve this discrepancy since we do not have access to the paper referred to in Dr. Burkley's inventory. We can speculate. . . ." As Lifton concludes, this matter was never resolved.

Horne's memo notes several other serious problems. The (supposed) original protocol transferred by the Burkley inventory reads: ". . . An original signed by Dr. Humes, pathologist." However, the extant protocol (CE-387; see *Assassination Science* 1998, pp. 430-437) is signed by *all three pathologists*. Horne adds that this apparent discrepancy is especially peculiar because the inventory is, in all respects, quite precise. (*Author's note*: these problems are thoroughly confounded by the absence of a typewritten date on both the extant autopsy protocol and on the supplementary examination of the brain. Were these omissions deliberate?)

Horne then lists one of the great lingering mysteries about the medical evidence, a transcript from an Executive Session of the Warren Commission (27 January 1964), quoting J. Lee Rankin, the Chief Counsel:

> We have an explanation there in the autopsy that probably a fragment came out the front of the neck, but with the elevation the shot must have come from, and the angle, it seems quite apparent now, since we have the picture of where the bullet entered in the back, that the bullet entered below the shoulder blade to the right of the backbone, which is below the place where the picture shows the bullet came out in the

neckband of the shirt in front, and the bullet, according to the autopsy didn't strike any bone at all. . . (Weisberg 1975, p. 307).

Since no known version of an autopsy report—not CE-387, nor the Sibert and O'Neill report, nor any subsequent FBI report, nor even the official (Bethesda) autopsy report—describes a *fragment* emerging from the throat, *this is a completely inexplicable mystery, still unresolved to this very day.*

Horne also notes that Burkley's death certificate, completed on 23 November 1963 (Saturday), describes the back wound at the level of T3. It seems unlikely that Burkley, without consultation, would have reached such a detailed anatomic conclusion. The obvious question is: did Burkley obtain this from an earlier version of the autopsy protocol, one that has since vanished?

Horne adds that an FBI summary report (9 December 1963) concluded that a bullet had lodged in JFK's back. This may have served as the source for the various media (and *JAMA*) reports with the same information. The extant protocol (CE-387) was not formally transmitted to the FBI until 23 December 1963. Therefore, time was available for changes in the protocol—changes of which the FBI might have remained ignorant.

Horne believes it likely that the autopsy protocol was revised between 24 November and 11 December 1963. This would explain (1) the media reports of a bullet in the back, (2) the FBI reports, including that of Sibert and O'Neill, that differed from the extant protocol, (3) the strange content of the extant protocol, and (4) the appearance, probably on 11 December, of Secret Service agents (including Elmer Moore) at Parkland Hospital. Their apparent purpose was to show the (extant) protocol to the Parkland physicians, to get them to agree to the official story. Horne also notes that the viewing of the Zapruder film in this critical interval may have raised insoluble timing problems: the throat wound clearly could not have occurred at the same time as the headshot. Horne concludes with one strange fact: the first known media report of a transiting bullet (one that exited the throat) appeared in the *Dallas Times-Herald* on 12 December 1963, just one day after the Secret Service visit to Dallas!

For this scenario to work, Horne notes that the original protocol (presumably dated November 24) had to be suppressed, and then later replaced by one written shortly afterward. He speculates that this substitution could have occurred during the transfer from Burkley/Secret Service to the Kennedy family in April 1965. The Navy letters of transmittal (24 November) and the receipts (24 and 25 November) could have remained in place even though the autopsy protocol was no longer the same. Only Burkley and a few Secret Service officials need have been privy to this deception.

Horne notes that Humes and Boswell persistently claimed that *there was only one autopsy protocol* and Humes claimed that it was signed on Sunday, November 24. If the above arguments are correct, however, then both Humes and Boswell have committed perjury.

The remaining mystery is how Rankin saw a copy of the earlier protocol. Careful reading of the transcript does not prove that Rankin actually held such a copy in his hands at that moment. Perhaps, by accident, he had seen one of the copies of the original. What is known is that the extant protocol (CE-387) was transmitted by the Secret Service to the Warren Commission on 20 December 1963. Therefore, since the Commission already had this protocol on 27 January

1964 (the date of the Executive Session), another mystery is why Rankin was not quoting from it rather than from some other version.

The following items are also suspicious: (1) none of the seven copies exists today, (2) Humes's handwritten protocol (Weisberg 1975, pp. 509–523) does not contain a date, (3) the extant protocol was not publicly available until it appeared in *The Warren Report*, (4) Boswell's diagram did not appear in *The Warren Report*, and (5) the Sibert and O'Neill report was omitted from *The Warren Report*.

Rankin's quote raises another question: was the back wound truly *below the shoulder blade*? Rankin specifically refers to a "picture" as his reason for so describing it. If it was that low, it would be consistent with the above discussion of a wound at T3 (Berkley's death certificate) or T4 (Ebersole's description to me). Such a low site would also be consistent with other evidence (*Assassination Science* 1998, pp. 110-111), most especially with the holes in the coat and shirt. If that were the true location, it would mean that the photograph of the back (Figure 2) was altered to elevate the wound, but it would also suggest that Rankin himself was complicit in later accepting the SBT in face of a back wound that he knew was too low (as he himself stated in the above quote).

The role of Admiral George Gregory Burkley in all of this is most curious. Although initially he was quite emphatic that there had been no conspiracy, in 1982 he told Henry Hurt (*Reasonable Doubt* 1985, p. 49) that he did believe in a conspiracy. He had previously admitted similar sentiments on tape (Oral History, JFK Library, 17 October 1967); when asked about the number of bullets that had entered JFK's body, he responded: "I would not care to be quoted on that." Burkley's attorney, William F. Illig, also told Chief Counsel Richard A. Sprague (Palamara 1998, p. 46) that Burkley had entertained the possibility of conspiracy. According to Illig, Burkley did not even rule out the possibility of two headshots. It is curious, but true, that Burkley did not testify before the Warren Commission, despite the fact that he was the only physician present at both Parkland and at Bethesda. When David Lifton tried to interview him, he refused to cooperate (Lifton 1988, pp. 401-402). James Folliard ("Blaming the Victims: Kennedy Family Control over the Bethesda Autopsy," *The Fourth Decade*, May 1995, p. 5) extensively explored Burkley's role at the autopsy. According to *The New York Times* (11 January 1969), Burkley remained LBJ's personal physician from 12:30 PM, 22 November 1963 until January 1969, when Johnson retired. If I could choose one witness to depose under oath it would be George Burkley. Unfortunately, Burkley died before the ARRB legislation was passed, thus leaving many interesting questions unasked. His daughter, Nancy Denlea, refused to donate his personal papers to the ARRB.

Altered Photographs: How Was It Done?

[*Author's note*: Although this section is necessarily speculative, what I propose here seems the simplest explanation for the current evidence. Nonetheless, new evidence could modify this proposal, which reflects the fallibillity of scientific reasoning. The available evidence is clearly incomplete.]

The images that Spencer saw are a key to the puzzle. There are too many odd features in her recollection—the photo collection was too limited, the images were on color negatives (instead of on transparencies), and the wrong lab was used. The central clue lies in the nature of the images: they are almost bloodless, which is oddly similar to the extant views of the back of the head. Spencer's activity at the Anacostia lab was probably an intermediate step in the alteration process. Although at least one photograph showed JFK's face, this view might have been included merely to misdirect Spencer into believing that the entire set of photographs that she saw was authentic.

The fact that they were on color negatives is *prima facie* proof that they were not originals. That Spencer saw autopsy photographs only once is also evidence that this entire operation (of film alteration, in my view) was compartmentalized. As further evidence, Knudsen and Fox both recall that they traveled more than once to Anacostia, on errands with these photographs, while Spencer—by her own testimony—was involved only once. Furthermore, Spencer's recollection of the date of her work differs from that of Knudsen and Fox.

An additional clue is the presence of a *small* throat wound, only about half an inch across (according to Spencer). This image can only be of someone else's throat or possibly a photographic alteration of an original autopsy photograph. But why would this have been included in the set at all?

If the tracheotomy had been altered (e.g., in a search for a bullet), then the inclusion of a small throat wound in the set (perhaps designed to mimic the throat wound in Dallas) would have permitted the subsequent *photographic restoration* of the throat wound to its Parkland Hospital status. That this was ultimately not done, of course, is a separate issue; perhaps the forgers decided that

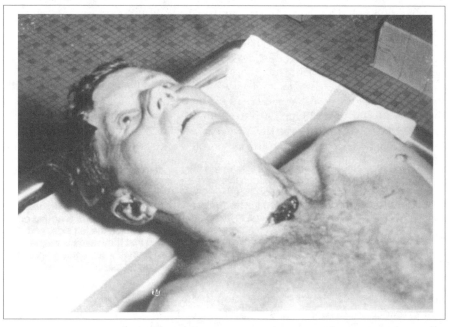

Figure 15. Photograph of the Throat Wound. Malcolm Perry, who performed the tracheotomy, was never asked to demonstrate his technique by submitting a photographic collection of his own work.

such a transformation was too risky, especially since so many individuals had seen a much larger, and much more irregular, wound at the autopsy (Figure 15).

What were the prior and subsequent steps in this process and where did they occur? Although this cannot be answered with certainty, the preparation of composite photographs may have involved processes such as soft matte insertions (Groden 1993, p. 85). The existence of color negatives (as seen by Spencer) is proof that the original color transparencies had already been re-photographed, probably with a view to forming composites as the next step. Spencer may also have seen photographs of another body, as suggested by the small tracheotomy wound.

Although an image of someone else's hair could have been used to cover the large hole in the posterior head, another possibility is the use of (the image of) the left side of JFK's own posterior scalp (by turning the negative over in a double exposure), so as to cover the wound on the right—assuming that an appropriate image existed in the original collection. Once these composite photographs were deemed satisfactory, then the images had to be converted, once again, to color transparency format, which is what currently exists in the Archives. No existing evidence pinpoints where this work was done, other than the frequent visits to the NPC.

An official statement (HSCA Record # 180-10109-10368), signed in February 1967 (three years and three months after the event) by Roy Kellerman, Robert Bouck, Edith Duncan, James K. Fox, and Thomas Kelly, attempts to reconstruct the whereabouts of the autopsy films. Bouck gave the films to Fox on November 27 (Wednesday) and then Fox took them to NPC that same day. B&W negatives were developed, and *color positives* were made from the colored film. Color transparencies are not mentioned. Lt. V. Madonia did the processing and development. Fox then returned these materials to Bouck at about 2:30 pm the same day. Several days later, Fox made B&W prints at the SS lab (in the Old Executive Office Building, which could only handle B&W). On about December 9 (Monday), Fox took the color positives to NPC and made color prints. These were returned to Bouck by 6 pm the same day.

What is curious about this sequence is that both Spencer and Knudsen are missing and that Spencer did not see autopsy photographs on any of the cited dates. Furthermore, Spencer handled color negatives, not transparencies. In addition, Madonia had independently claimed he could not have done this work since he was the supervisor and his laboratory skills had atrophied. So what can be concluded? Most likely, the procedures followed were more complex than most participants recognized, or perhaps memories had faded in the rather long interval. Nonetheless, one person is present in all of these stories—it is James K. Fox, the Secret Service photographer. It is likely that (under Bouck's direction) he played the major role, at least as a liaison. Whether he actually constructed composite photographs, however, we cannot determine based on the available evidence.

It is likely, however (since he processed JFK films, probably on several occasions), that he understood the whole sequence of events. If Fox knew, then Bouck (his immediate superior) and James J. Rowley (Chief of the Secret Service) should also have known. Beyond that it is impossible to see with any clarity into the hierarchy. (Rowley's superior was the Secretary of the Treasury, Douglas Dillon.)

The witnesses tell us that the NPC could have handled all of the photographic formats discussed. We do not know, however, whether work was done at some other government lab (possibly motivated by the enhanced secrecy offered by compartmentalization). The Knudsen family does recall occasional encounters over the years with other government photographers. Although it is likely that the secretive NSA had extensive photographic facilities at that time, there is no evidence to suggest their involvement. On the other hand, both James Fetzer and I have received anonymous letters claiming that the AFIP was involved, but this has never been pursued. At the present time, nothing in the record indicates that the films went anywhere but the NPC and the Secret Service laboratory (in the Executive Office Building). In fact, in an ARRB interview, Velma Reumann (Vogler) recalled:

> . . . a strong, independent recollection of NPC personnel boxing up all photographic materials . . . related to the assassination on the orders of Robert Kennedy and sending them to the Smithsonian Museum for permanent storage sometime within 6 months or so after the assassination. . . . She said she was certain of this because she, herself, was required to call an official at the Smithsonian to discuss the imminent transfer, and recalls the individual to whom she spoke was as surprised by the selection of the Smithsonian as she was. (Also see Livingstone 1998, pp. 441–442.)

Any list of prime suspects (whether witting or unwitting) for the alteration of the photographs must include Robert Knudsen. He told his family (who apparently believed him) that he had photographed the autopsy, a story that was almost certainly false, in any literal interpretation, because no one recalls his presence at the autopsy. Why he found it necessary to recount this misleading story to his family (and to maintain it until death) is curious, but it is also a clue—particularly since one personal trait that his wife voluntarily recalled was his honesty. She also recalled that he was quite reliable about keeping secrets, voluntarily adding that sometimes military people must "take secrets to the grave" with them, especially when ordered to do so. It should be noted that Knudsen *implied* to the HSCA that he first encountered the photographs on the morning after the assassination, when Burkley handed them over in a paper bag. But even though he was quite certainly not at the autopsy, Knudsen also recalled that he had been up all night! Was Knudsen already working with the photographs, perhaps even during the autopsy, thus lending some truth to the story that he told his family? Curiously, the *Associated Press* ran a story (31 July 1998) by Deb Riechman:

> New testimony released Friday about the autopsy on John F. Kennedy says a second set of pictures were (sic) taken of Kennedy's wounds— pictures never made public. The existence of additional photographs— believed taken by Robert L. Knudsen during or after the autopsy . . . raised new questions . . . . But the new evidence sheds no light on the whereabouts of the second set of pictures.

George Lardner (*The Washington Post*, 2 August 1998) also reported on photographs believed to have been taken at Bethesda by Robert Knudsen. Perhaps Knudsen did photograph the autopsy, after all, by the indirect process of taking pictures of autopsy pictures. This, by itself though, would be an odd state of affairs, which no investigation ever addressed. Within a few days of the assassination, according to Joe O'Donnell (Knudsen's colleague), Knudsen showed him photographs that first showed a hole at the right rear of the head, and then, several days later in a similar view, the hole was gone. This disclosure by Knudsen inevitably suggests some knowledge of abnormal activities; furthermore, given the unavoidable compartmentalization of such nefarious behavior (assuming that it actually occurred), Knudsen's knowledge of it is striking. Either he, or someone very close to him, had to be involved.

Given his ability to keep a secret (according to his wife), it is difficult to believe that he would have chosen this moment to give away someone else's secret, especially for such a highly covert project. More likely, he himself had performed, or had assisted in, these very alterations. As the White House photographer, Knudsen clearly possessed darkroom skills—in his own HSCA testimony he recounts processing films at Anacostia during the initial weekend. Furthermore, his position as White House photographer had two important advantages for conspirators: (1) his subsequent loyalty (and silence) could easily be monitored by powerful figures close to the White House, and (2) he had access to, and often used, the White House section of the secretive Naval Photographic Center at Anacostia.

Was Knudsen asked to re-photograph the autopsy photographs, perhaps after being given a cover story, one that he either believed, or decided that he must accept (e.g., perhaps that the Kennedy family needed a sanitized version of the autopsy)? If so, he might even have claimed some innocence in the matter, particularly if he did not know how the photographs would later be used. Perhaps guilt and exasperation, which were recalled by his wife, later emerged at the 1988 hearing, as he became fully aware of how his own work had contributed to the cover up. The only other known candidates for an alteration role are James K. Fox (Secret Service photographer) and Vincent Madonia (supervisor of the NPC color laboratory). Knudsen's possession of original and altered photographs within the first week, his curious busyness during the first night, and his own self-admitted hectic schedule, provide some corroboration for such illicit activity. When his subsequent, official appearance in 1988 and the earlier burglary at his home (shortly after his HSCA deposition) are added to the riddle, his own participation becomes even more suspect. That he never confessed to his family that he had really not photographed the autopsy only adds to the suspicious character of his story.

In his own interview, Madonia also recalled being extremely busy for the first three days (precisely the time interval described by Knudsen), beginning, strangely enough, *the very evening of the autopsy*. He also recalled additional, smaller projects over the succeeding days. Although Knudsen described Madonia's personal processing and development of some of the autopsy photographs on one occasion, Madonia implied that he (Madonia) was primarily a supervisor during these busy days and that he probably could not even have functioned well in the darkroom. If true, he would be left mostly outside the net of conspiracy. (I have listened to his deposition on audiotapes and that is my impression from the tapes as well.)

Knudsen also recalled for the HSCA that he saw photographs that showed probes in JFK's back. But if he was not at the autopsy, how could he have seen such probes—unless he saw *photographs* with probes? And if he saw such photographs, why were they made available to him, particularly since he played no official role in the autopsy? Why was his presence necessary at all when he and Fox took the duplex holders to Anacostia? Wasn't one courier enough on such a busy weekend? Given the corroboration of such probes by many witnesses—Karnei, O'Donnell, Sibert, O'Neill, autopsy technicians, and others—it is likely that Knudsen did see such probes. If so, these photographs have disappeared. Moreover, if his recall of the probes were wrong, why would so many other witnesses all invent the same odd story of seeing such probes?

Douglas Horne was present when Kodak digitized the autopsy photographs for the ARRB in Rochester, NY. He recalls that a careful examination of the posterior head photographs was made, with the specific purpose of identifying matte insert lines or any other evidence of photographic alteration, but no evidence was seen. However, a complete re-photographing of all autopsy photographs could make it difficult to detect such alteration. Perhaps this task was what kept Knudsen so busy, particularly if composite photographs had to be made. The fact that multiple trips to Anacostia did occur, over several days, is consistent with such a step-by-step process—perhaps even requiring several revisions until the end product was satisfactory—and then, finally, re-shooting the entire set.

An additional possibility is that some negatives were deliberately turned over in the dark room during the preparation of prints. (Liz Snyder first proposed this possibility to me in February 2000, in Monterey, California.) This process would have reversed left for right. For example, if an intact, left, rear scalp had existed in the original collection, then such manipulation might have restored the right scalp. Furthermore, if the left back had been substituted for the right back (Figure 3), then a fake wound could more easily have been superimposed onto the back. Figure 3 does display several odd features: (1) the ruler is not aligned with the spine, (2) although the letters and numbers are not reversed on the ruler, a drug (Tuinal) is advertised, (3) the pair of hands on the ruler cannot belong to the same person (the right hand is on top and the left hand is on the bottom), (4) the hand on the top of the right shoulder is a right hand (rather than the expected left hand), (5) there is a small dark area adjacent to the fourth finger of the left hand, (6) across the midline from this latter site, almost at the mirror image site, is another dark area, and (7) the site of the wound, based on the pathologists' actual measurements, has previously been displayed on this same photograph (*Assassination Science* 1998, p. 444—see the circled X). Also see nurse Diana Bowren's location of the back wound in Livingstone (1993, photograph opposite p. 368).

This photograph raises numerous questions, as follows. (1) Were parts of this image reversed? (2) Why is a Bethesda ruler not being used (John Stringer, the photographer, said that it was)? (3) Was the real wound located near the left fourth finger—or possibly even at the mirror image site on the right? (4) Was the ruler (and perhaps also the hands) later added to the photograph? (5) What actual purpose is served by the ruler in its present odd location? (6) Is the wound in the photograph really as far as 5 cm from the midline (as officially reported)? [*Author's note:* James Thornton, M.D., a surgeon, has recently begun exploring the possibility that some photographs have been partly or completely reversed. It is curious that no one heretofore has examined this possibility.]

The autopsy camera is yet another unexpected paradox. The HSCA concluded that the only camera that the Navy could produce for the HSCA investigation—a camera that the Navy, in fact, considered to be the actual autopsy camera—could not have been used for taking the extant autopsy photographs! [*Editor's note*: Gary Aguilar, M.D., elsewhere in this volume, discusses this point.] Consider, however, that if all of the photographs had been re-shot, it would explain not one, but two, mysteries: (1) why the photographs do not match the camera (they may have matched a different camera, possibly the Nikon used by Knudsen, an issue no one ever explored), and (2) why photographic alteration has been so difficult to detect.

If Knudsen had participated in this affair, who would have issued his orders? In his HSCA interview, he recalled following orders issued by Admiral Burkley, who, like Knudsen, was a Navy man. Several autopsy witnesses describe Burkley as controlling the autopsy itself. In oral interviews at the JFK Library in Boston, Burkley agreed that this was his role. If true, might he also have played a role in the alteration of the autopsy photographs? Since he was JFK's personal physician that weekend (Kathleen Cunningham, however, has noted that Janet Travell was listed as the official White House physician), since he had completed a death certificate for JFK, and because he was the only individual present both at Parkland and at Bethesda, his unaccountable absence from the Warren Commission witness list remains quite inexplicable.

The recent interviews and releases by the ARRB have thoroughly altered our view of the medical evidence. It is no longer good enough merely to point to the back of the head photograph and conclude (as prior, official reviews have done) that the headshot came from the rear and that the posterior skull was intact. Let us be honest about this: medical experts are not even required. Even the man in the street can guess that this red spot is supposed to be a wound—and probably even a wound of entry! But there has always been a problem with this convenient solution to the crime of the century—the three pathologists have persistently disagreed with this conclusion. Not only have they disagreed, but they have disagreed vigorously. I suspect that they were right, that a bullet really did enter at the EOP, but that it was not the only headshot. In conclusion, with the introduction of the new witnesses suspicions about the accuracy—and even the authenticity—of the posterior head photographs have deepened considerably.

The Harper Bone Fragment [22]

At 5:30 pm, Saturday, November 23, a pre-med student, Billy Harper, found a fragment of skull bone (7HSCA123-124) on the grass south of Elm Street, not too far from where Jean Hill had been standing. (The exact site is not well defined, however.) Harper took it to his uncle, Jack C. Harper, M.D., who in turn showed it to A.B. Cairns, the chief pathologist at Methodist Hospital. A total of three Dallas pathologists examined the bone and they identified the site of origin as the occiput. (On 22 November 1992, on a Palm Springs radio talk show, I helped to interview one of these pathologists, Dr. Gerhard Noteboom, who reaffirmed that conclusion; he also recalled the lead deposit on the fragment.) The bone was then shipped to Admiral Burkley, who, in turn, gave it to the FBI, where it was lost. Fortunately, photographs were taken in Dallas (Figure 2A and Figure 2B). A ruler on the photograph permits an estimate of size: it is about 7 x 5.5 cm, and trapezoidal in shape.

Joe Riley, Ph.D., a neuroanatomist (formerly in academia), places this bone into the parietal area (Joe Riley, "Anatomy of the Harper Fragment," *JFK Deep Politics Quarterly*, April 1996). Riley and I have exchanged many (mostly e-mail) comments about this fragment. Although we succeeded modestly in reducing our disagreements, nonetheless, we still remained far apart, with Riley continuing to favor a parietal origin, while I favored an occipital origin. Having great respect for Riley's expertise, I put this question aside for several years. But, as I continued to review the X-rays, the mystery photograph F8 (the Postscript), the statements of the Dallas pathologists and the Bethesda pathologists, and the fragment itself, I remained convinced that it was (mostly) of occipital origin. I believe that Riley has overlooked much valuable evidence, and that his objections can be effectively countered. The employment of the X-rays and the proper orientation of photgraph F8 (see below) are a powerful combination that should not be overlooked, especially when coupled with information on the bone itself.

If I understand him correctly, Riley has primarily argued that the Harper fragment cannot be from the low occiput, as Groden shows it (1993, p. 83). In fact, I agree with Riley on this point because the fragment is actually (mostly) from the high occiput, but it includes a small portion of adjacent parietal bone as well—on both sides of midline. The exterior surface appears to show the junction of three suture lines. If this is true (Riley does not agree), then this bone should be fairly easy to place: there are few skull sites with such a trifurcate junction. One of them is the lambda point, the junction of the parietal and occipital bones, right at midline. Now it seemed to me that the shortest of these lines (the one going straight up to the top edge in the photograph) was the midsaggital suture, and the two lines going off to either side of this were the lambdoid sutures. But Riley argued that one of these was a fracture line, not a suture line, an issue that simply cannot be resolved with finality from a 2D image. I argued, however, that it was odd that such a fracture line was not apparent on the inside of the bone. Furthermore, it seemed to me that the supposed fracture line contained too many fine twists and turns. It looked much more like a suture line, unlike other real fracture lines that I could see on the X-rays or, for that matter, on the edge of the Harper fragment itself.

I had thought that Riley's fracture line was supposed to lie between sections F and G in Figure 2A, because it contained the smallest number of fine twists and turns. However, I was stunned when I saw that J. Lawrence Angel, Curator of Physical Anthropology at the Smithsonian, who was consulted by the HSCA about its significance, had totally ignored the line between sections E and F (without any explanation), which assuredly contains many tight curves, as one would expect for an authentic suture line. But then I realized why Angel had made this mistake. He had probably been misled by the faulty HSCA diagram (Figure 7) that showed no hole at the back of the skull. Since he had already placed the large, late arriving fragment anterior to the coronal suture (which may be correct), he had only one other site left, the gap in the parietal bone, which is where he put it.

The entire bone segment F (the upper right portion of the fragment as viewed from the exterior) appears whiter because it has little blood on it, whereas the two adjacent segments are bloodstained. It would appear that suture lines act as a barrier to the spreading of blood. I accidentally discovered evidence for this when I was doing skull experiments with simulated brain material, I noticed that the dye in this material leaked from the inside of the skull to the outside, right along the suture lines, but only along such lines. In other words, these suture lines acted like miniature sinks, thus stopping blood from crossing over. An explanation therefore exists for why segment F might have remained unstained.

Both Angel and Riley argued for a parietal site based on the vascular grooves (curvilinear indentations) and the foramina (perforating holes for small vessels) on the inside surface. But I found it easy to demonstrate exactly these same features in the *upper occipital bone* on two genuine human skulls that I owned, and I could easily see them in multiple anatomy textbooks, extending over many decades, so I did not consider these arguments to be decisive. Moreover, the direction of the vascular grooves, although consistent with a parietal site, was also surprisingly consistent with an upper occipital site, which was also not hard to demonstrate. I could easily see these on my skulls (the grooves did go in the right direction) and it was not hard to find photographs in texts that were equally supportive. (I doubt that Angel ever did this exercise, since he automatically ruled out the back of the head, nor do I really know if Riley performed this exercise for the *upper occiput*, since he seemed so focused on the lower occiput.)

When I examined the triangular area of missing bone (see the small white triangle in the figure in the Postscript), near the low midline, on photo F8, I remembered that I had seen this empty triangle before on the X-rays. (Although I did not mention it in the Postscript, this argument, too, helped to persuade me of the correct orientation of F8.) I already knew, from naked eye viewing (with very myopic eyes, the best kind for the job) and from detailed OD measurements, that bone was absent in just this same triangular area on the frontal X-ray (approximately inside the lower left nose). I had not gone looking for this; I merely happened one day to notice it while at the Archives. Since no one had reported such missing bone from the left side of the skull, I was surprised and decided to explore it further with more OD measurements. Since I now knew the orientation of F8 and its dimensions (there is a ruler on F8) and because I could correlate identical objects on F8 with the photographs and because I already knew the dimensions on the skull (from my own measurements at the Archives), I could now estimate the size of this empty triangle on F8.

It was probably some time later, when I returned to this jigsaw puzzle, trying to imagine where the Harper fragment might fit into the skull. When I did, I realized that its left edge (on the exterior view) might fit into the empty triangle. In fact, it seemed to fit extremely well, so I proceeded to the other borders. In particular, I wanted to know how far it would extend towards the right, because the pathologists had placed their entry hole to the right of midline. As I measured this distance on F8 and compared it to the well-defined distance along the bottom edge of the Harper fragment, I realized that the right edge of the Harper fragment lay very close to the pathologists' EOP entry hole. But then it really hit me: after all of this, I had quite unexpectedly placed the lead debris (on the Harper fragment, described by the Dallas pathologists as possibly from a bullet, and still visible in the photograph) almost exactly where the Bethesda pathologists had said the bullet entered. I stared, almost too shocked to believe it. I returned to the X-rays looking for possible contradictions and found none. I reviewed all of the borders, to be sure that the X-rays permitted such a place-ment—and they did! In addition, the lambdoid sutures, one on each side of the skull, as examined on both the lateral and frontal X-rays, are also remarkably consistent with this interpretation.

The Harper fragment (H) is shown situated in the occiput in Figure 2C. Let-ters C and D identify bone fragments. Letter L denotes the site of lead on H. The 6.5 mm object is shown at about the 2 o'clock direction from the right upper edge of H; it also lies directly inferior to the letter D. The letters McC (for McClelland) identify the fracture that functioned as a hinge for a bone flap that could swing either open or closed. This movement has been the cause of much confusion about the status of the occiput: when the flap was open (as at Parkland) it produced an orange sized hole at the right rear, but when closed (as on the frontal X-ray) it seemed that there was no major hole at the right rear. I have named this hinge after McClelland, who actually described the bone flap. This fracture is also visible on the frontal X-ray. The area inferior to this flap is not well seen on the X-rays (it is obscured by overlying bone), but the OD measure-ments suggest that some bone is missing below this flap. This would be consis-tent with the eyewitnesses' recall of an orange-sized hole at this site. The semicir-cular notch, located on line BA and just inferior to letter C, is where Baden placed the exit wound.

The Harper fragment (H) is placed into the frontal skull X-ray in Figure 2D. In this figure the lambda point (the junction of the two lambdoid sutures and the saggital suture) lies slightly inferior to the top of the Harper fragment. Most of the lambdoid sutures can be seen on the frontal and lateral X-rays, at sites that are consistent with this interpretation. Furthermore, where these sutures are missing is exactly where the Harper fragment (not present at the autopsy) fits into the skull. Optical density measurements confirm that bone is indeed miss-ing where the Harper fragment has been placed here. Baden's semicircular notch is not visible here, but must lie between bone fragment C and the top of the Harper fragment. The letter L denotes lead on the Harper fragment. Regarding Baden's notch, Roger McCarthy of Failure Analysis Associates has shown that beveling can occur from a gunshot even without an exit or an entrance wound as the direct cause (Livingstone 1995, p. 313).

This is the simplest, and the most complete, integration of all of the known evidence. Furthermore, after looking at genuine human skulls and textbooks, I see no real problem with the evidence on the bone itself, from either the inside or the outside. Finally, though, I would emphasize that, like the certainty of the three autopsy pathologists about the site of the entry wound, we should also take seriously the word of three Dallas pathologists who actually saw the real 3D bone. They all agreed that it was occipital, which is probably the best evidence we shall ever get on this question. I have merely found the only reasonable place at the back of the skull where it could possibly fit. Such a conclusion is, inciden-tally, yet one more proof that bone was indeed missing from the back of the head, as if more proof were really required on this point.

Neutron Activation Analysis (NAA)

Having once taught a course in nuclear physics (1971-72) while on the Michi-gan physics faculty I was naturally captivated by the statement that NAA had confirmed the SBT. I had even watched Robert Blakey declare on national television that NAA was the lynchpin of the SBT theory—for anyone who had the wherewithal to understand it. Since I thought that such a statement might include me, I determined to look into it. Several months later, when I finally obtained access to the NAA data in the HSCA volumes (at UC-San Diego, while on vacation), I was surprised, on even a first reading, at how unconvincing it seemed.

This was a critical moment for me, a time when the lone assassin theory began to disintegrate; if a supposedly final, and indisputable, proof from nuclear physics was so feeble, I could only imagine that other proofs of the lone assassin theory would be even more unreliable. Later, I had the pleasure of reading a detailed critique by Wallace Milam, which only further undermined the NAA evidence. More recently, a Stanford physicist, Art Snyder, Ph.D., has been exploring the statistics of NAA for these metal fragments in further detail. Just several months ago, I listened with gratification as Snyder explained his arguments in a lecture. By all reasonable measures, based first on the work of Milam, and now on the work of Snyder, the NAA does not support the SBT. Nor does it support conspiracy though: it is simply inconclusive, actually almost useless. I am hopeful that Snyder will eventually publish his work so that Blakey can explain his "lynchpin" one more time for us.

The Behavior of the Pathologists

The bedrock of the case against the pathologists is the trail of metallic debris, especially as seen on the lateral X-ray. This trail, lying high on the skull, must surely be related to a projectile passing nearby. Its great distance (actually more than 10 cm) from the pathologists' entry site (near the EOP) is impossible to reconcile with a single shot at the EOP. Since the pathologists saw this trail at the autopsy, while they *simultaneously* identified an EOP entry, they must have known, and understood all too well, exactly what it meant—a second shot to the head. Writing the official autopsy report within 24 hours, Humes certainly knew well enough where this trail lay, specifically that it lay nowhere near his EOP entry site. This is not a matter of professional competence or training—it requires only an elementary education, at best. I know for certain (because I tested him) that my now ninth grade son (who hopes some day to become a forensic scientist), given the information about the bullet trail and the EOP entry site, could have done better than this: he quickly recognized that this data set implied a second shot.

This was the moment of truth for James J. Humes. He could have described the trail correctly, which would always thereafter have invited the question of a second headshot (using exactly the argument that Cornwell had invoked). But he chose instead to follow the clear directions that he had received as the autopsy began (the sole gunman had shot from the rear and was already in custody). Because he chose to support the lone gunman theory, he had no choice but to displace this trail downwards by a huge distance. Because he did not have to review the autopsy X-rays, or even the photographs, for the Warren Commission, no questions were asked at that time about his dangerous maneuver.

When he next saw the X-rays, with the Clark Panel in 1967, he must surely have seen the curious 6.5 mm object (for the first time) and he was probably immediately suspicious. His comments were not recorded during this panel, however, but an official opportunity arose with the HSCA. Here, however, despite several opportunities to describe the unanticipated materialization of this object, he made no attempt to do so. Instead, he chose to agree with Cornwell that he had made a grievous error, an apology that he totally ignored when he next had a chance—during his *JAMA* interview.

The photographs of the posterior head also offered an opportunity to raise questions of authenticity, particularly with respect to the red spot. Moreover, in excerpts from his ARRB testimony (Appendix G) Humes actually stated that, even after all reconstruction attempts, the scalp remained open for several centimeters. Yet, even the briefest glance at Figure 1 reveals the paradox: the scalp is completely closed and the hair is all well manicured, not at all open by the several centimeters that Humes recalled. Humes was not directly asked to explain this obvious discrepancy, but he must surely have been aware of it.

The brain weight is yet another paradox. Standard textbooks give the upper limit of normal for the adult male brain at about 1400 grams. (I understand that Oliver Cromwell's was much larger, but he was not Jack Kennedy.) Yet Boswell during his ARRB interview admitted that 1/3 of the *total brain* was missing and Humes during his *JAMA* interview (1992, p. 2798) maintained that 2/3 of the right cerebrum was gone; this is also a huge percentage of the total. Although they both unabashedly insisted that they saw no inconsistency with the recorded brain weight of 1500 grams, they offered no rational explanation either. This is not the behavior of reasonable men, yet their entire careers bear clear testimony to their otherwise rational, and widely respected, professional behavior. It is only here in the JFK case that they *seem* to have lost their way.

The unexplained, even (*apparently*) egregious, omission of the fresh brain weight is beyond comprehension. Neither of them had any explanation for this. But Boswell's comments to Lifton (cited above) provide the answer. Almost certainly they had measured it, but the results (perhaps on Humes's lost notes and diagrams) had disappeared. Whether Humes immediately knew that this recorded brain weight had to be lost, or whether he only recognized it later, cannot be known, but ultimately it does not matter. The fact is that Humes's notes and diagrams did disappear, meaning that the fresh brain weight could never be used as an indisputable proof that a different brain had later been examined. If the real brain was buried with the body (on Monday, 25 November)—as Humes claimed was planned in advance—he may have been aware of this possible snafu well before he submitted his final draft on Sunday, 24 November, and therefore might already have destroyed his notes and diagrams. His admissions to the ARRB seem consistent with exactly this behavior.

The entry wound in the right forehead is yet another issue. Given the trail of bullet debris on the X-rays, and an entry wound in the forehead (seen by O'Donnell in a photograph, and by others on the body), is it possible that the pathologists really did not know? Boswell's unexpected recall (35 years later) of the notch in the right forehead bone speaks volumes. Furthermore, Tom Robinson's unprompted recall of placing wax into just such a hole only increases the probability that the pathologists had feigned ignorance of this site. Even Karnei, who was only occasionally present at the autopsy, recalled this reconstruction work in the right forehead by Robinson, so how could the three principal pathologists have missed it?

Regarding their professed ignorance of the projectile wound to the throat, they stand on dangerously thin ice. Even Ebersole (in his conversation with me) recalled a telephone conversation with Dallas, from which they learned of this wound *before the autopsy was over*. Ebersole even recalled that certain logical consequences followed from this bit of intelligence: he stopped taking X-rays, because now the mystery (of the exit for the back wound) was solved. Kathy Cunningham's meticulous accounting of the many in the morgue who did know of this wound provides essentially irrefutable proof that the pathologists really did know. Moreover, Robert Livingston, M.D., then the Scientific Director of two NIH institutes (across the street from the Bethesda National Naval Medical Center) and who had extensive experience with gunshot wounds while serving in the Pacific [23], clearly described the throat wound directly to Humes by telephone just before the autopsy. Livingston had heard about the throat wound but was naturally puzzled because Oswald had supposedly fired from the rear. He therefore emphasized to Humes the importance of a careful dissection of the neck. [*Editor's note*: See *Assassination Science* 1998, pp. 161-163.] Livingston later recounted this episode *under oath* during Crenshaw's defamation suit against *JAMA*.

The pathologists' biopsies of the tracheotomy edges and the passing of probes through a supposedly *simple tracheotomy* make no sense at all, unless they either knew, or at least suspected, that a projectile had passed through the throat. Finally and remarkably, during his ARRB testimony, Boswell himself shamelessly admitted that he knew of the projectile wound in the throat while still at the autopsy, thus agreeing with one other autopsy physician, John Ebersole. In fact, only three years after the assassination, Boswell had told *The Baltimore Sun* (Richard H. Levine, 25 November 1966, front page article) that, before the autopsy began, the pathologists had been apprised of JFK's wounds and what had been done to him at Parkland. In particular, Boswell said: " We concluded that night that the bullet had, in fact, entered the back of the neck, traversed the neck and exited anteriorly." Yet, even after all of this, it must be emphasized that a bullet wound to the throat is *completely absent* from the official report until the day after the autopsy. There can be only one intelligible explanation: they understood all too well that such a small, smooth wound to the throat, honestly described, would immediately be recognized as an entrance wound. Furthermore, they also understood that, after all of their probing (especially through the tracheotomy), if this wound were connected to the back wound, it could not be reconciled with a shot from the so-called sniper's nest. [24]

In his refusal to discuss JFK's adrenals, Humes had already displayed his willingness to conceal information, even after it had become almost common knowledge that JFK had Addison's disease. Even in front of his own forensic colleagues on the HSCA Forensic Pathology Panel, he refused all comment. [25] But we have learned more about Humes from the episode of the burned documents. We now know that he was quite willing to leave—or even to create—a misleading impression if it served his purpose. The preposterous story of the bloody, burned autopsy notes (which disguised the additional burning of the first draft) proves that he was willing to put out cover stories for his own actions.

If Humes and Boswell participated in the charade of a two-brain examination, in the process duping their associate Pierre Finck, they have indeed opened themselves to the most serious of charges. (It is an astonishing irony that another associate, the radiologist Ebersole, in turn probably duped them—by altering the X-rays.) By doing so, they not only covered up the most critical evidence, but they also abused the trust of an associate. The evidence that this dishonorable behavior occurred is, unfortunately, very powerful.

As Stringer so clearly stated, when ordered by Captain Stover (of Bethesda) to sign the Naval medical affirmation of 1 November 1966, he signed it—even though he knew it to be false. Can there be any doubt that the physicians, too, were placed under similar pressures to comply? Even Finck, in his testimony at the Garrison trial, admitted, under oath, that Humes was following orders during the autopsy and that he was not autonomous. Humes himself, on other occasions, clearly submitted to the wishes of Admiral Burkley: Humes granted his request for the prompt return of the brain, so that it could (presumably) be buried with the body, and Humes, by his own description, delivered all of the biological materials to Burkley.

In his ARRB deposition, Humes even suggested that he was writing the autopsy report for Burkley. Furthermore, Burkley's rank of Admiral placed him near the top of the military hierarchy, probably second (in this situation) only to the Surgeon General of the Navy, Admiral Edward Kenney, who was also at the autopsy. Humes's background in the military, and also his commitment to the Church, had provided ideal training for his role as obedient disciple. From the very outset, he must have seen the lay of the green. (Humes used a golfing metaphor to close his own testimony.) The pathologists had been told, before the autopsy began, that the sole suspect was already in custody, that he had fired from the rear, and that their job as pathologists was simple—they just had to find the bullet. [26]

Even Finck, in more private moments, has expressed his own indignation at the entire affair. The overheard conversation at the AFIP cafeteria (see Aguilar's essay), which was recalled for the ARRB by biochemist Leonard Saslaw, is quite telling: Finck bitterly complained about the immediate disappearance of his autopsy notes—which he apparently never recovered—while he was still in the morgue. Cyril Wecht, M.D., J.D., personally encountered Finck at breakfast in February 1965, at the Drake Hotel in Chicago during their specialty meetings. Although he disclosed nothing specific, Finck was still ruminating about the autopsy, implying that he wished he could recount what had really happened, with the clear insinuation that the most extraordinary events had occurred.

On 29-31 January 1968, a Special Forces captain, John McCarthy, was convicted of murder in South Vietnam, in a case in which Pierre Finck participated in a cover-up (17 August 1995 interview with McCarthy by Jim DiEugenio). Finck controlled a file that contained exculpatory evidence, but whose existence he denied. In March 1970, just after McCarthy had been released from Leavenworth on military "bail," his attorney, Steward Davis, was having coffee in a Pentagon cafeteria, when a lawyer from the forensic pathology department approached him. This lawyer then escorted Davis to Finck's office, where he was shown the "nonexistent" file. He was told that a copy machine was just down the hall, and Davis was left alone. Inside the file was the recantation (of August 1968) of Captain Richard Mason, the expert witness who had testified against McCarthy (and who had remained in the courtroom after his testimony!).

Also included were letters from Finck (who was Mason's superior) to Mason suggesting that he get on board (with the .38 theory), and another letter, congratulating him on his recantation. The FBI file of 9 February 1968, with exculpatory evidence, was also present. Davis was therefore certain that both the FBI and Finck knew that exculpatory evidence existed and that nothing had been done about it. DiEugenio implies that the Pentagon was eager to convict a Special Forces man because they (the Pentagon) were not in charge of Special Forces operations. (McCarthy recalls outright glee within the Pentagon at the prospect of a court martial for a Special Forces captain in a case of premeditated murder.) My point in presenting this episode is to show that, like Humes (and probably like Boswell), Finck, too, could be persuaded to follow questionable directives from his superiors.

When Humes was interviewed by Paul Hoch, immediately after an appearance before the HSCA, he stated:

> I wish they'd asked some more questions. . . . I was surprised at the Committee members. . . . They sort of had a golden opportunity, you know. I was there, but they didn't choose to—and it didn't bother me one way or the other: whatever pleased them, pleased me (Lifton 1988, Chapter 24).

Gary Cornwell (the Deputy Chief Counsel for the HSCA), based on his own experiences, has described Humes's acquiescence to demands of authority (*Real Answers* 1998, pp. 71-74). Cornwell had decided (and apparently still believes) that Humes had not intentionally misreported the autopsy, but that he was merely incompetent. Based on this, he planned to confront Humes with the lateral X-ray evidence that shows the bullet trail lying nearer to the top of the skull than to the bottom. Cornwell understood well enough that, on national television, he could administer the *coup de grace* to Humes, so that Humes would have no choice but to admit his (supposed) *faux pas* in placing the entry wound far too low.

Cornwell, celebrating his unassailable strategy in advance, tipped his hand to a member of the Forensic Pathology Panel. This specialist, readily understanding the power of Cornwell's argument and its inevitable success, tried to dissuade him, on the basis that Humes was a respectable professional who should not be so manhandled. There the matter was dropped, but the next day, just before the session was to open, this same pathologist, acting now as a messenger from Humes, reported that Humes was now willing to confess to error in his autopsy report! Cornwell therefore met privately with Humes and confirmed that this was indeed true. As I observed on videotape (supplied by Wallace Milam), Humes thereupon did exactly that: he pointed to the much higher site on the lateral X-ray as the entry, thus nullifying his own autopsy report and also the entry site that he had previously drawn on a skull for the HSCA. Cornwell concludes by commending Humes for admitting his past mistakes.

But then later Cornwell offers his own confession (pp. 188-189):

> But I admit that I have not closely followed, much less been actively involved in, all of the continuing research and evaluation of "newly discovered" evidence. . . .

Even though Cornwell's book was published in 1998 (the same year that the ARRB *concluded* its work) there is no mention of the ARRB's existence, or of its over 60,000 newly released documents. Nor is there any mention of the *JAMA* articles (of 1992) in which Humes totally ignores his HSCA testimony (the one that had so pleased Cornwell) and in which he once again reverts to the low entry site! But my point is mainly about Humes, not about Cornwell. Humes was quite agreeable to changing his testimony under pressure—even though his conversion was obviously not authentic—nor was it long lasting. How likely is it then, that when under even greater pressure (such as at the autopsy), Humes would somehow have resisted such pressure and stoutly reported only the facts, without a trace of deviousness?

Unquestionably, the pathologists were under enormous pressure, the kind that most ordinary individuals never encounter. Their careers could well have been permanently jeopardized. From the comfort of a recliner nearly forty years later, it is all too easy to judge them by our own standards. They had been driven into an impossible *cul de sac*— whether to obey their own internal ethics, morality, and honesty (and to let the facts fall where they may) or to conform to the rigid, authoritarian structure that had nurtured and protected them for so many years. But this same structure now would tolerate only one answer: the lone assassin. We can only dream of the conflicts that seethed in their own conscious (and subconscious) minds, nor can we know with certainty how they resolved these issues for themselves as the years passed.

Like most of us, however, it is probable that, once a decision had been reached, second thoughts were few. Most likely, these became increasingly fewer as the years passed. Furthermore, as psychologists know so well, when something is believed for long enough, it begins to take on the texture of truth. So it is even possible, after a while, that the pathologists began to believe that only two shots had been fired from the rear. As memory experts know from countless experiences, the human mind is incredibly flexible, quite capable of adding hues and textures, not originally present, to the silver screens of human memory, especially as time overtakes us all.

Nevertheless, I still have some doubts about this scenario. Why, for example, did the pathologists take so long to agree to be interviewed by *JAMA*—by a fellow pathologist (George Lundberg, M.D.) no less, a former military man, and a friend of one of them (Humes)? Why did they dodge the press conference that Lundberg had to manage by himself in front of the AMA logo? Why did they not simply volunteer to come to the ARRB rather than actually requiring the delivery (for Humes and Boswell) of a subpoena for their final bow? Let me be quite honest. I suspect that they had not totally forgotten, that they really did recall some of the things they had done, and that such memories were still too sensitive to be publicly exposed. But perhaps I am wrong. About such things we can only speculate. But I still wonder.

Whenever possible, the pathologists told the truth, as they did regarding the EOP entry site. For this fact, their innate adamancy and professionalism rose to the fore. Their refusal to accept the red spot as an entry wound, their refusal to recognize the 6.5 mm object as present on the original frontal X-ray, and their insistence that they had taken photographs no longer in evidence—all of these attest to their honesty and competence.

But there is another side, too. Boswell agreed to elevate the back wound to comply with the SBT; Humes moved the metallic debris downward by over 10 cm (and ignored this obvious evidence for a second headshot); neither of them were willing to impeach the photographs of the back of the head (showing an impossibly intact scalp); Humes burned his first draft (or drafts) and put out a ridiculous cover story; Humes refused to be forthright with respect to the adrenals; all of them pretended, at least for awhile, that the throat wound was invisible at the autopsy; all ignored the evidence for a frontal headshot; Humes successively changed his opinion about the SBT (finally accepting it); he successively changed the width of the tracheotomy; and Humes (alone) even once agreed that the posterior entry wound lay high on the skull.

When the pathologists behaved irregularly, it was not out of malice or of caprice nor usually from incompetence, but because they had been boxed into a corner, where they really had little choice, either because of external constraints placed upon them, or because of internal constraints due to decisions they themselves had already made about the facts of the case. Having walked so far down this road, it was unlikely that they could ever, even to themselves, admit—or perhaps even recall, had they wished—the path that had carried them to their final destination. Their responses before the ARRB, as shown so clearly in the excerpts presented in the addenda, are more than sufficient proof of the state of their minds. It is unlikely that a frank confession of their misdeeds, as some of their critics would have desired, would ever have been forthcoming. We must instead be content with our present knowledge of what actually transpired during those critical hours and days, knowledge that is much fuller today than it was even five years ago.

Indeed, several other odd events are consistent with the above interpretation. During the Garrison trial, when Finck seemed to be saying a bit too much (as Boswell actually stated in his own ARRD deposition), Boswell was rushed to New Orleans to back Finck up as needed (or perhaps even to contradict him), but he was never called to the stand. It is certainly intriguing that Boswell was invited to supervise the autopsy of Martin Luther King, Jr. (recounted in Boswell's ARRB deposition), an invitation he declined. Humes's involvement in LBJ's benign biopsy is also curious; some cynics have wondered if Humes's involvement was a reward for his work in the JFK matter.

A final comment seems appropriate. These Bethesda doctors are not the only physicians to adjust their sails to the political winds. The physicians at Parkland are hardly blameless, either. Recall that, although they initially agreed that shots had been fired from the front, when they testified before the Warren Commission, their stories changed. In fact, as Crenshaw reports (Palamara 1998, p. 31), following the visit of the Secret Service, which included a briefing about the official autopsy results, almost all talk among the physicians about the autopsy came to a halt. Most notably, Malcolm Perry, who had thrice described the throat wound as an entry wound during his press conference, later did a complete about face, now agreeing (despite seeing no objective new evidence) that it was an exit wound, after all. (Regarding Perry's quite different private comments, see the "Afterward" in Lifton (1988).)

So powerful was the social pressure over this issue, that several of the Parkland doctors, who had so clearly described cerebellum as extruding from the head wound (these summaries are actually in *The Warren Report*, many in the doctors' own handwriting), later changed their story and said that the cerebellum was now safely back inside the skull, even though, in the interim, they had seen no new physical evidence. When *JAMA* published its pathetic attempt to whitewash the government's account, his former colleagues convicted Crenshaw of publicity seeking, even though they agreed with Crenshaw about the wounds. [27] Crenshaw's colleagues had merely raised their fingers into the political breezes, to see which way the winds were blowing. They clearly did not wish to tack into any stormy seas.

That the physicians at both Bethesda and Parkland succumbed to authority should not have surprised us. As Robert Proctor recounted ("Racial Hygiene: The Collaboration of Medicine in Nazism," in *Medicine, Ethics and the Third Reich*, ed. John J. Michalczyk, 1994, p. 36), 3000 doctors (6% of the profession) joined the National Socialist Physicians' League by January 1933—*before* Hitler rose to power! Proctor states: "In fact, doctors joined the Nazi party earlier and in greater numbers than any other professional group. By 1942, more than 38,000 doctors had joined the Nazi party, representing about half of all doctors in the country."

F. A. Hayek (*The Road to Serfdom* 1944, reprinted 1994, p. 209) also comments on this all-too-predictable behavior: "The way in which . . . with few exceptions, her [Germany's] scholars and scientists put themselves readily at the service of the new rulers is one of the most depressing and shameful spectacles in the whole history of the rise of National Socialism. It is well known that particularly the scientists and engineers, who had so loudly proclaimed to be the leaders on the march to a new and better world, submitted more readily than almost any other class to the new tyranny." Hayek also cites R. A. Brady (*The Spirit and Structure of German Fascism*) as concluding that the scientist is perhaps the most easily used and "coordinated" of all specialists in modern society. Was G. Robert Blakey aware of these behavior patterns when he took control of the HSCA and promptly (and intensively) began to employ precisely these specialists?

A Summary of the Medical Evidence

1. Two headshots were fired, the first striking JFK low on the right rear, in agreement with the pathologists; the second struck later from the front, at the hairline, just above the outer border of the right eye socket. To be consistent with the metallic trail on the lateral skull X-ray, this must have occurred when JFK's head was erect, such as in Zapruder frame 321. This latter shot did not originate from the grassy knoll, but may have been fired from the storm drain on the north overpass, where so many bystanders gathered immediately afterwards.

2. The trail of metallic debris on the X-rays is consistent with this second headshot.

3. The 6.5 mm "metallic" object was later added to the frontal X-ray. Actually, a fresh X-ray film was double exposed in the darkroom, first with the image of the original X-ray and then with the 6.5 mm object. This resulted in an undetectably altered, new frontal X-ray. The original X-ray was then either deliberately lost or destroyed. This curious 6.5 mm object, being identical to the caliber of the Mannlicher-Carcano, was then used to tie Oswald to the crime.

4. A large orange-sized hole was present at the right rear of the skull, consistent with the exit of the frontal bullet.

5. Something struck the back (probably from the first shot fired), but did not penetrate. Besides a bullet, other possible projectiles include shrapnel, or even a piece of the street or sidewalk.

6. A projectile entered the throat, but did not exit. The nature of this projectile is still debated, with some (e.g., Lifton) arguing that it was a bullet that was (illegally) extracted before the autopsy, while I have here proposed a second possible projectile, namely, a glass fragment from the windshield. The available evidence does not permit a final choice. That the tracheotomy wound was enlarged, during a surreptitious search for such a projectile, is likely. Evidence also suggests that the head wounds were altered, probably in a search for bullets or bullet fragments.

7. Critical photographs were removed from the original autopsy collection, mostly those of the large posterior hole. Although it is not essential to an overall view of this case, I have concluded that photographs were altered, mostly to hide the large exit wound at the rear. In addition, the body itself (and at least one photograph seen by Joe O'Donnell) did show a right forehead/temple bullet entry. All of this evidence, if it ever existed, has long since been deeply buried, with the exception of the X-rays, which still contain surprising evidence for precisely such a frontal shot.

8. A second brain was substituted for the genuine brain. At the time of the official brain exam (of this different brain), the real brain may already have been buried with the body, although its actual whereabouts cannot be known with certainty (except perhaps by the Kennedy family).

9. The pathologists told the truth, insofar as they could, so long as it did not damage the lone assassin theory. What they themselves actually believed probably lies beyond our knowledge, but this no longer matters. When they could not tell the truth without traumatizing the lone assassin theory, they sometimes had no choice but to lie and to cover-up. I have tried, not always successfully, to sympathize with their almost unimaginable plight.

10. High government officials had to approve, and probably to transmit, orders for alteration of critical forensic evidence, e.g., photographs, X-rays, and the physical evidence. The Secret Service, led by James J. Rowley, held the critical autopsy materials. Possibly a small number of critically placed individuals tacitly understood what needed to be done, and few words were ever actually exchanged. Persons who might have warranted a grand jury investigation were (a) Robert Knudsen, White House photographer; (b) James J. Rowley, Chief of the Secret Service; and (c) Admiral (Dr.) George Burkley. It is interesting that all three (a) worked out of the White House, (b) retained their jobs during the LBJ administration (in which loyalty mattered), and (c) like LBJ, believed in a JFK conspiracy.

11. The effort to manipulate the physical evidence could easily constitute an entirely separate essay. The actual appearance of the largest metal fragment removed from the skull (still housed at the Archives, as CE-483, where I have examined it) compared to its supposed identical, but obviously different, appearance on the skull X-rays is merely one issue.

12. All of the official government inquires were hamstrung by the manipulated medical evidence, by the misrepresentations of the pathologists, and by these agencies' own surprising, and (apparently) naïve, lack of suspicion. Given the state of the medical evidence, the (apparently) sincere testimony of many experts was not necessarily wrong—it was merely irrelevant.

13. The efforts of political bodies of inquiry that are beholden to others (e.g., the Challenger disaster—see Richard P. Feynman, *What Do You Care What Other People Think?* (1988), not discussed here, is a remarkable example of this class) are inevitably emasculated by often-conflicting lines of loyalty. The exertions of the ARRB, which was not really an inquiry at all, but only an information gathering adventure, was, in many respects, a superior model for future panels. This board was beholden to no other entity (or individual). Although criticisms have inevitably been leveled at it—both by some of its staff and by those of us who mostly just observed—it is likely that its private citizens merely tried to do their best. It may be difficult to do better than that. It is possible, however, that future inquiries could build on this model. Perhaps the process should be divided into two stages: (1) the collecting of all possibly relevant evidence (modeled after the ARRB), and (2) a subsequent panel, totally unrelated to the first, that actually makes decisions based upon all of the evidence (perhaps even employing a jury of ordinary citizens, when that is appropriate). This suggestion is somewhat analogous to grand jury proceedings (at the first level), and the subsequent actual trial (at the second level), although for grand juries, and the actual trial, the same individuals may be involved at both levels.

Postscript: The Mystery Photograph F8

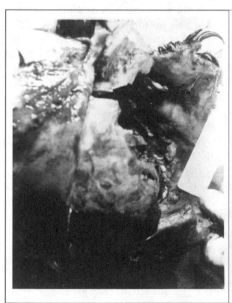 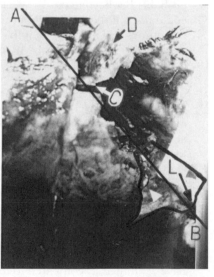

The mysterious skull photograph F8.   Mantik's analysis of photograph F8.

Autopsy photograph F8 (the label derives from the list of Fox photographs) has generated endless controversy. This view has been exceptionally difficult to orient, even for the pathologists. Line BA was interpreted by Michael Baden, M.D., of the HSCA as passing from left to right, with the visible bone lying immediately anterior to the coronal suture. In fact, point B lies deep in the occiput, while point A is situated toward the front of the skull. Line BA divides the skull into left and right. Point L identifies the lead deposit on the Harper fragment; its location on the skull is remarkably consistent with the pathologists' skull entry site. The small white triangle identifies a triangle discussed in the text. The black circumferential perimeter outlines the site of origin of the Harper fragment. Letters C and D identify small bone fragments that are also identified in Figures 4A and 7. In F8 the Harper fragment appears distorted because of the perspective offered by the camera. Beyond point A (in the photographs at the Archives) a tangential view of the chest and abdomen (with fat pads folded back) can be seen. I determined this by stereo viewing of two, nearly identical, color photographs of F8.

In this section I present proof that this photograph (B&W #17, #18 and color #44, #45 in the current collection) shows the posterior skull. Even Robert McClelland, M.D., insisted, after his visit to the Archives, that the collection included a view of the large hole as seen at Parkland Hospital. It must have been F8. During their initial inventory review (signed on 10 November 1966), the pathologists labeled this as a posterior view: "Missile Wound of Entrance in Posterior Skull, Following Reflection of Scalp." Furthermore, in his ARRB deposition (reported to me by Douglas Horne), Humes located the entry wound (in the posterior skull) toward the bottom of this photograph (as oriented here). This agrees with my interpretation, but disagrees with Baden, who described it more as a view from the left side. At their ARRB depositions, none of the pathologists could orient this photograph. However, when the X-rays are used in conjunction with the photograph, then its orientation becomes unambiguous, as I describe here in stepwise fashion.

1. Note the remaining frontal bone (Figure 12), as determined from the frontal skull X-ray. This is consistent with Boswell's drawing at the autopsy (Figure 4A) and also with his drawing for the ARRB, as rendered by Horne (Figure 9A–D). Note that the upper edge of the remaining frontal bone lies close to the hairline. Although not shown here, these drawings are also consistent with the drawings of Angel, the physical anthropologist, who served as an expert witness for the HSCA (7HSCA228-230). Giesecke (6H74) is one Parkland physician who did describe the large skull defect as extending from the occiput to the browline, in remarkable agreement with Boswell.

2. On the lateral skull X-ray (Figure 11B), I have indicated, with a line passing through the metallic debris, how the X-ray beam would have transited the skull when the frontal X-ray was taken. For confirmation of this X-ray trajectory note that (a) on the frontal X-ray (Figure 14) the metallic debris is closely bunched from top to bottom, as would be expected if the X-ray beam were traveling nearly parallel to this debris, (b) the transverse fracture just above the left eye (on the right side of the page) corresponds to the discontinuity at the rear of the lateral X-ray, and (c) the 7 x 2 mm metal fragment lies

well above the right eye socket on both views. (There is additional evidence
for this conclusion not given here.)

3. On the frontal X-ray, all of the bone is absent just above the trail of metallic
    debris.

4. In the HSCA interpretation of F8 (I have watched Baden demonstrate this
    on television), the segment BA runs from left to right across the skull at the
    coronal suture; therefore, according to the photograph, almost all of the
    bone anterior to this line segment was intact. This conclusion made some
    sense, because the largest, late arriving bone fragment had a suture line at
    one edge, which the HSCA took to be the coronal suture. Angel agreed that
    this was the coronal suture, but he placed this bone fragment anterior to the
    coronal suture, whereas Baden (in an unintended confirmation of the con-
    fusion that reigned over this issue) placed it *posterior* to the coronal suture!
    What convinced Baden was the semicircular notch (just below the letter C
    in the photograph) at the edge of the bone, which he took to be the exit site
    for the posterior bullet. Furthermore, this largest, late arriving bone frag-
    ment showed (on its X-ray image) multiple, tiny, metal particles, strongly
    suggestive of an exit site, meaning that it had to fit next to the notch (in
    Baden's view). The largest bone fragment can probably be placed anterior to
    the coronal suture (as Angel did), thus still permitting the actual exit site to
    lie at or near the coronal suture. (The X-rays leave an irresolvable ambiguity
    about the orientation of the bone fragments: it is impossible to distinguish
    inside from outside—and, strangely enough, the pathologists said nothing
    to clarify this. No photographs were taken either.)

5. Notice, however, that we have now arrived at a *reductio ad absurdum*—there
    is a fatal contradiction in Baden's interpretation: from the X-rays, we know
    that bone must be missing all the way forward to the hairline, but Baden has
    just told us that it is present all the way back to the coronal suture! (On the
    lateral X-ray, this is where the skull is fractured at the skull vertex.) If the
    bone really were present to the coronal suture, then, on the frontal X-ray, we
    would see bone right at the very top on the right side of the skull, just as it is
    present on the left side. We can be certain of this because we know (from
    step 1) what the beam's eye view is, i.e., we know the direction that the X-ray
    beam traveled at the top of the skull during the taking of the frontal X-ray.
    Therefore, Baden's orientation of F8 is certainly wrong.

6. On the other hand, if F8 is the back of the head, then the line segment BA is
    the midsaggital line. There is further confirmation that this is correct. While
    at the Archives, I viewed this photograph and its near twin (most views are
    pairs, taken with the camera slightly displaced in successive views) with a
    stereo viewer, which, for this view, is particularly illuminating. The bone
    surface (left of midline) was quite rounded, as would be expected for the
    occiput. In addition, the fractured bone islands at the right front (labeled C
    and D) could now be appreciated in 3D. After some staring, I realized that
    there were only two, and that they corresponded to the two bone islands on
    the frontal X-ray (also labeled C and D). Their sizes, shapes, and locations
    all fit perfectly. But one additional feature surprised me. In the color photo-
    graphs at the Archives, there was more to see beyond the top edge of the film
    than is visible here. I finally realized that I was looking tangentially across

the chest and abdomen. I could actually see a nipple (extending out into space in 3D) and—the biggest surprise—I could see fat pads folded back from the abdominal incision.

7. There is a specimen bottle at the bottom left of this photograph (not well seen here), which seemed to suggest that Baden might have been right after all. However, now that I knew where parts of the body were located, I could conclude that the head had merely been rotated into a nonstandard orientation, no doubt to better expose the large, occipital hole for the camera, and that the specimen jar posed no special problem in interpretation.

8. Having concluded that the large defect extended all the way to the anterior hairline, Boswell's 13 cm measurement for the large hole fits better than it would for an anterior border at the coronal suture. This is further confirmation of my conclusion.

9. When questioned about this notch (on the bone edge) in F8 by the HSCA, Humes (7HSCA249) did not hesitate to say that the notch was *not* in the frontal bone, thus disagreeing with Baden's orientation!

10. In conclusion, the orientation described here is consistent with the historical orientation, with the X-rays, with Humes's comment about the notch, with Boswell's two drawings (one at the autopsy and one for the ARRB), and even with Angel's drawings—but not with Baden's orientation. From this photograph, we can be certain that the back of the head was blown out— quite dramatically, in fact—just like all of the witnesses said. It is very difficult to escape the conclusion that a frontal headshot led to this injury. This deduction, of course, also corroborates the recollections of all of those new and old witnesses who saw autopsy photographs with such a massive defect, which, in turn, means that other photographs really have disappeared.

Acknowledgments

Harry Livingstone and David Lifton are justifiably recognized as primary trailblazers in the medical evidence. Their books served as invaluable guides during the period of my initiation. I later had the pleasure of meeting and collaborating with both. By responding promptly to my initial letter of inquiry, Cyril Wecht, M.D., J.D., greatly encouraged my initial ideas; he has continued to be a bastion of support. An unintended consequence of JAMA's sorry attempt at journalism was my introduction to Gary Aguilar, M.D. and to James Fetzer. I owe much to both. My seemingly inevitable and uncanny agreement with Wallace Milam, on almost every issue, was a source of great encouragement. Kathy Cunningham often served as an inexhaustible resource, not just for me, but also for many others. I am also indebted to Roy Schaeffer and Milicent Cranor for sharing their insights with me. These, and many others beside, have made my own work possible. For their contributions to the cause of truth, I hold them all in high regard—they have served their country well.

Notes

1. Spence (for the defense) and Vincent Bugliosi (for the prosecution) opposed one another in the television production, *On Trial: Lee Harvey Oswald* (London Weekend Television) and shown on *Showtime* (1986).

2   This is based on a personal conversation with Douglas Horne (and Patricia L. James, M.D.) at the San Francisco airport on 12 March 2000.

3   Since I had set a deadline of 15 April 2000, I called Tunheim's office on 26 April. I was informed that the questionnaires had indeed been mailed out (on about 20 March 2000) but that no replies had been received. When this book went in press in June, still no responses had been received.

4   The traditional approach is well demonstrated in Cyril Wecht, *Grave Secrets: A Leading Forensic Expert Reveals the Startling Truth About O.J. Simpson, David Koresh, Vincent Foster, and Other Sensational Cases* (1996).

5   Perhaps because I have established that the X-rays have been altered, it is easier for me to surmount the emotional and psychological hurdles that obstruct belief in photographic alteration. There is nothing like personal experience to open one's eyes.

6   David Lifton has advised me that he first saw prints of the autopsy photographs in spring 1981, when he went with Mark Crouch to visit James K. Fox. Lifton obtained prints in December 1982 from Crouch, who had made copies from Fox's set. In that same month, and in January 1983, Lifton became the first person to show actual prints of the autopsy photographs to the Parkland medical personnel. As before, the images surprised them. Lifton has recounted his own experiences in the Afterword to *Best Evidence* (1988, p. 703). Malcolm Perry's surprised reaction to the tracheotomy makes for especially interesting reading.

7   Groden (1993, pp. 83-84) illustrates the large hole. Although this is fairly accurate, the X-rays show that the large hole extends anteriorly to the hairline. A drawing of the posterior skull by autopsy lab technician, Paul O'Connor, is surprisingly accurate (Groden 1993, p. 87).

8   Blakey and Billings later wrote a conspiracy book in which they implicated the Mafia (G. Robert Blakey and Richard Billings, *Fatal Hour: the Contract, the Killing, the Cover-up* 1981). Cornwell also authored a conspiracy book (*Real Answers* 1998).

9   Addresses and phone numbers are in my files.

10   Livingstone (*High Treason* 1998, pp. 501-536) reprinted Spencer's complete transcript. Livingstone also summarized the new medical evidence (pp. 403-543), a synopsis that was very useful for my own synthesis.

11   Roger Feinman, a former employee of CBS, graciously supplied this information. This CBS documentary of 25, 26, 27, 28 June 1967, with Walter Cronkite narrating, was critiqued in Josiah Thompson, *Six Seconds in Dallas* (1967).

12   After listening to these interviews on audiotape, I was struck by how often, and with what great emphasis, all three family members stated that their father was highly secretive about anything related to the autopsy. For example, none of them knew for certain where he had gone to testify in 1988, and, although they seemed to understand that he did not accept *The Warren Report*, he had actually never stated his opinion directly. They clearly understood that he wanted to avoid any public discussion of this entire issue.

13   I am not at all persuaded, based merely on his description, that he saw the original film. What is more likely is that he saw a copy of the original that was distinctly different from any extant copy.

14   Dennis Breo, *JAMA* (27 May 1992), pp. 2794–2807.

15   Seth Kantor was a friend of Jack Ruby. He recalled seeing Ruby at Parkland Hospital shortly after the shooting, but the Warren Commission chose not to believe him. Kantor later published his own account of these events (Seth Kantor, *Who Was Jack Ruby* 1978), in which he described Ruby's ties to the FBI, the CIA, and to organized crime.

16   Charles Crenshaw, *Conspiracy of Silence* (1992); also see *Assassination Science* (1998), pp. 37–60.

17   It is probable that Stewart, like so many others in this case (including Robert Blakey, on a national talk show), has reversed left for right. Although this cannot now be known with certainty, Crenshaw's recollection of a right frontal entry wound would seem consistent with this interpretation. That Stewart, after discussing this issue with the other Parkland doctors, would still speak out publicly—some time later—on this matter is surely a demonstration, at the very least, of his true convictions.

18   For a detailed chronology of the tracheal wound and its varying descriptions over the years, see Lifton (1988, chapter 11). Lifton also notes that Baxter, at Parkland, placed the incision at the second ring (6H42), while the autopsy report placed it at the third and fourth rings.

[19]   His closest boyhood friend was Henry Zapruder, son of Abraham Zapruder.

[20]   See Vincent DiMaio, *Gunshot Wounds* (1985), pp. 80–85, and especially J. Thornton, "The Effects of Tempered Glass on Bullet Trajectory," *AFTE Journal* 15 (July 1983), p. 29.

[21]   For the behaviour of ricochet bullets, see DiMaio (1985), pp. 88–92.

[22]   See the discussion of the Harper fragment in Palamara 1998, pp. 74–75.

[23]   Livingston and I have since become good friends, visiting at one another's homes—even taking a trip together—and he has consistently repeated this same story. It is certainly in character for him to have involved himself in such a matter. His prior presidency of Physicians for Social Responsibility (an organization that won a Nobel Peace Prize) speaks volumes about his willingness to take unusual responsibility upon himself.

[24]   Since the throat wound so obviously arose from a frontal projectile, I had predicted that *JAMA* would not have the courage to describe the physical characteristics of the throat wound, but that, instead, they would merely employ innuendo to impugn physicians such as Charles Crenshaw for saying that it was an entry wound. Unfortunately, I was right. As a result, *JAMA* later paid Crenshaw $213,000 in a legal settlement—a quite avoidable public relations *faux pas*. Astonishingly enough, the editors of my own journal lacked the courage even to admit their error to a fellow physician, Charles Crenshaw (*Assassination Science* 1998, pp. 37–60). As an AMA member, I felt that my professional dues had been abused during this disgraceful escapade. I later resigned from the AMA, in protest over its unethical behavior.

[25]   I discussed Humes's willingness to follow authority—and to do so with surprising tenacity (a trait I could not relate to)—with a close friend who is a Catholic, a Notre Dame graduate, and a university affiliated psychiatrist. He explained to me that Humes's military background, his training as a Catholic, and his continued activity in the Church (even on Saturday morning, 23 November), provided perfect training for his obedience to authority figures. Gary Cornwell's book offers further insight into this side of Humes; for Cornwell's story, see my analysis of the pathologists' characters.

[26]   If they were really faced with a 6.5 mm bullet cross section (on the frontal X-ray), obeying their orders should have been simple—they had only to extract this object. That they so obviously failed even to search for this 6.5 mm object is striking.

[27]   When five Parkland doctors were deposed by the ARRB, Jeremy Gunn made exactly this point—the doctors really did agree about the wounds, after all.

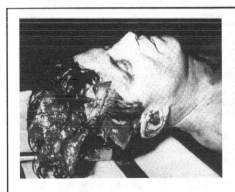

[Editor's note: During the deposition (Appendix G), Gunn asks Humes whether the hair was cleaned before photographs were taken, because some of the alleged autopsy photographs (above) are inconsistent with others of the back of the head. They can't all be authentic, but—like most of the evidence in this case—they can all be faked. For those who are familiar with the evidence and are not cognitively impaired, this case bristles with smoking guns. (See Robert Groden, The Killing of a President *1993, pp. 82–85.)]*

THE CONSPIRACY THEORIES

The official version of the murder—lone nut #1 shoots JFK, gets shot by lone nut #2—seems improbable. Competing theories have problems, too.

THE SCENARIO	WHAT'S THE PLOT?	WHAT'S THE HITCH?
❶ The Ultimate "Black Op" (The CIA did it.)	The CIA (or a few rogue agents) feared JFK would sell out to the Reds—and dismember the agency itself. And CIA types knew how to do hits on the qt. Oswald, an ex-defector, could have been a CIA recruit. Or perhaps just a "patsy," maneuvered into place to cover for sharpshooters elsewhere in Dealey Plaza.	Oswald was no hit man, and making him a patsy would have taken great logistical legerde-main. Then how to silence the real hit persons? Hit *them*?
❷ The Ultimate Mob Hit (The Mafia did it.)	What would happen to *you* if you hired the mob to do your murders, shtupped a mob-connected gadabout—*and* cracked down on organized crime? Oswald was a mob guy's nephew; Ruby had scary mob acquaintances. Small-timers, both; but some don might have thought their obscurity meant deniability.	Would *truly* wiseguys take the suicidal risk of whacking a presi-dent? How did they arm-twist Ruby into hitting Oswald? How did they know *he* wouldn't talk?
❸ Cuban Caper I (Anti-Castro exiles did it.)	Anti-Castro exiles felt Kennedy hung them out to dry during the abortive CIA-sponsored Bay of Pigs invasion. The supposedly pro-Castro Oswald used a New Orleans address occupied by anti-Castro activists; odd, yes? And Ruby had been in Cuba, visiting a mob chum who later became an anti-Castroite.	Would Cuban exiles have trust-ed the Anglo commie Oswald? Or, if he was a patsy, could they have set up this more elaborate plot unhelped and undetected?
❹ Cuban Caper II (Castro did it.)	Castro was well aware of American plots to assassinate him; no less a conspiracy theorist than Lyndon Johnson suspected Castro had ordered Kennedy killed in retaliation. Oswald, a self-pro-claimed Marxist and Castro supporter, had visited the Cuban Embassy in Mexico City two months before the assassination.	Castro has said ordering the hit would have been stupid. He *would* say that. But it would have been stupid—even if the too-traceable Oswald hadn't done it.
❺ Mission From Moscow (The KGB did it.)	Oswald also visited the Soviet Embassy in Mexico, where he met with a KGB official known to be involved in "wet affairs"—i.e., sabotage and assassinations. After defecting to the Soviet Union in 1959, Oswald—or, more baroquely, an Oswald double—may have come back to the United States a programmed assassin.	Wet Affairs Rule One: Don't meet programmed assassins in the embassy. And why risk nu-clear war to replace a young hard-liner with an old one?
❻ Coup D'Etat (Lyndon Johnson, the Joint Chiefs, the intelligence community and the military industrial complex did it.)	This is less a theory than filmmaker Oliver Stone's countermyth of recent American history: the establishment bad guys wanted JFK dead so the war machine could run riot in Vietnam and weapons makers could get rich. Well? It all happened, didn't it?	With so many people ready to help—from hit squad to autopsy team to Warren Commission—why a Rube Goldberg scheme in view of a plazaful of witnesses?
❼ Honey, I Shot the President I (A Secret Service Agent did it, by accident.)	Maryland ballistics expert Howard Donahue argues that JFK was accidentally shot in the head by a Secret Service agent in the follow-up car; his AR-15 supposedly went off when he picked it up in response to Oswald's shots. In the echo chamber of Dealey Plaza, the agent himself may not have known he'd fired.	None of the nine other passen-gers ever reported hearing a gun go off in the follow-up car. (The agent in question, understand-ably, wouldn't talk to Donahue.)
❽ Honey, I Shot the President II (Oswald did it, but he was shooting at John Connally.)	Marina Oswald testified that she thought her husband may have been shooting at John Connally, not JFK. Why? Oswald felt Connally, former navy secretary, had brushed off his attempts to upgrade his Marine Corps discharge. And a Dallas lawyer said he overheard Oswald plotting Connally's murder with Jack Ruby.	For someone *not* shooting at the president, Oswald—or who-ever—did a deadly efficient job. Supposedly he wasn't much of a marksman, but was he this bad?

A summary of assassination theories published in Newsweek
(22 November 1993).

[Editor's note: *Neither the Mafia, pro- or anti-Castro Cubans, or the KGB could have extended their reach into Bethesda Naval Hospital to fabricate X-rays, substituted another brain for that of JFK, or subjected the Zapruder film to extensive alteration. While evidence suggests that the Mafia and the CIA were indeed involved in the assassination, the only hypothesis that appears to withstand the impact of these new findings is that of a large-scale conspiracy along the lines of Scenario 6. From this perspective, Oliver Stone's film,* JFK, *appears to have provided the most accurate, complete, and comprehensive portrayal of what actually happened in Dealey Plaza that has ever been presented to the American people though the mass media.*]

Part IV

Evidence of a Government Cover-Up:
Two Different Brain Specimens in President Kennedy's Autopsy

Douglas P. Horne

[*Editor's note*: Douglas P. Horne served as an officer in the United States Navy long before assuming the duties of Senior Analyst for Military Records for the Assassination Records Review Board (ARRB). In this stunning study, he explains how new information that the ARRB acquired—including interviews with the autopsy pathologists—lead him to the discovery that two brain examinations had been conducted subsequent to 22 November 1963, which involved two different brains. Anyone who has ever wondered whether new discoveries are still possible should find this report fascinating. Horne has earned the nation's admiration and gratitude for the intelligence and courage that he has displayed in bringing these remarkable findings to the attention of the American people.]

On 9 November 1998 the Associated Press ran a national wire story written by Deb Riechmann that was based on my ARRB staff memo concerning events related to the post-autopsy handling of President Kennedy's brain. This story appeared virtually intact in *The New York Times* the next day, and was subsequently published in numerous papers all over the nation in varying formats and lengths. On November 10th, *The Washington Post* published a similar (but expanded) story written by staff writer George Lardner, discussing the conclusions in my 32-page ARRB staff memo about the patterns in the official record that strongly suggest two different brain specimens were examined by the government's Navy pathologists following their 22 November 1963 autopsy on the body of President John F. Kennedy. [*Editor's note:* See *Probe* (May-June 2000), pp. 16–26.]

My "Memorandum for the Record"—in reality an analytical research paper—posits: (1) that while the first brain examined was actually the real brain of the deceased President, evidence of this examination has been suppressed; (2) that the images of the second brain specimen examined have been falsely represented

299

for years—since at least April 26, 1965 when they were transferred from USSS custody to the custody of the Kennedy family—to have been "President Kennedy's brain;" and (3) that the evidence of this examination (i.e., the photographs in the National Archives) do not depict the true condition of President Kennedy's brain following his autopsy because they are *not images of his brain—rather, they are images of a different brain*. [*Editor's note*: This conclusion was drawn independently by Robert B. Livingston, M.D., a world authority on the human brain and corroborated by the X-ray studies of David Mantik, M.D., Ph.D., both published in *Assassination Science* (1998).]

In the *The Washington Post* article, I was accurately quoted as saying that I was "90-95 per cent" certain that the brain photographs in the National Archives among the Kennedy Deed-of-Gift autopsy materials were not of President Kennedy's brain. I can tell you now that I was being conservative when I made that statement. As far as I am concerned, there *were* two different specimens examined. It would appear that Navy pathologists Drs. Humes and Boswell executed this charade (although at whose behest and for what reasons we can only speculate). I am convinced that Army pathologist Dr. Pierre Finck, the third of the three autopsy prosectors, was the poor "dupe" upon whom this incredibly brazen hoax was perpetrated.

However, it wasn't just Dr. Finck who was victimized. Additional victims have included every official investigation that has relied upon the brain photographs in the National Archives as "official evidence" in the assassination. This includes the Clark Panel in 1968, the Rockefeller Commission in 1975, and the HSCA in 1977 and 1978. Other victims include the Parkland Hospital treating physicians (whose credibility has been repeatedly challenged because the pattern of brain damage in these photographs conflicts with the damage to the skull and brain they remember seeing during the President's treatment in Dallas). Ultimately, of course, the real victims are the American people, who have been deceived and had their true history denied them.

In the AP wire story by Deb Riechmann, former ARRB General Counsel and Head of Staff Research and Analysis (and later Staff Executive Director) Jeremy Gunn was quoted as saying the following about the hypothesis in my memo: "There are questions about the supplemental brain exam and the photos that were taken. There are inconsistencies in the testimony of the autopsy doctors about when that exam took place. These are serious issues. The records are now out there for the public to evaluate." The next day George Lardner, Jr. of the *The Washington Post* quoted Jeremy Gunn as saying he thought it "highly plausible" that there were two different brain exams following the autopsy. Read this article and decide for yourself. Remember what the fictional character Sherlock Holmes once said (paraphrasing): "Once you have eliminated the impossible, whatever you have left, no matter how incredible it may seem, is the truth." I never dreamed when I joined the Review Board staff that I would develop such a "radical" hypothesis or commit it to writing; it was 100% evidence-driven, I can assure you, and was not conceived out of any preexisting theories or hypotheses.

It still surprises me that no one in the independent JFK research community postulated this series of events prior to the release of my memo to the public in November 1998. [*Editor's note*: The conclusion of Robert B. Livingston, M.D., was in fact presented to the public during a press conference held in New York

City on 18 November 1993, but was not reported to the American public, as *Assassination Science* (1998), pp. 141-166, explains.] The patterns in the evidence had been public since the summer of 1993 when the HSCA's internal records were released in compliance with the JFK Records Act. The ARRB's medical evidence reinvestigation (or rather, "clarification effort") only confirmed and strengthened the validity of the preexisting pattern that was already present in the documentary record. All of the records the HSCA collected that allowed me to build the two-brain hypothesis are present in HSCA staff interviews of medical witnesses *that were sealed for fifty years after the HSCA ceased operations*.

Robert Blakey has often tried to use the justification that sealing records of investigations for 50 years was, and is, "normal Congressional practice." This flimsy excuse does not withstand even the most cursory examination. Why? Because *selected* interview transcripts and interview summaries (e.g., the transcript of Humes and Boswell in Closed Session before the Forensic Pathology Panel in 1977; the transcript of Humes before the Committee in Open Session in 1978; and transcripts or summaries of staff interviews of Parkland physicians Jenkins, Carrico and Perry) *were published* in Volume 7 of the HSCA report. However, staff summary reports of interviews with Dr. Boswell, autopsy photographer John Stringer, Navy Chief Petty Officer Chester Boyers, and Navy civilian employee Leland Benson—all of which close the circle of evidence that indicates there two brain specimens examined after the autopsy—were sealed in 1979 for 50 years and liberated only by the JFK Act in 1993, instead of in the year 2029, as intended by Robert Blakey.

Other key medical evidence documents—none of which contained classified material—that were sealed for 50 years in 1979 by the HSCA included staff interview summaries of autopsy technicians, Paul O'Connor and James Jenkins, third year resident, Dr. Robert Karnei, and the key sworn testimonies of Army autopsy prosector Dr. Pierre Finck, autopsy radiologist, Dr. John Ebersole, and White House photographer, Robert L. Knudsen. *Someone on the staff of the HSCA had to make those decisions on what to publish, and what to "bury" by sequestration for 50 years*. Former HSCA staff member, Andy Purdy, denied to ARRB staff members during a January 1996 interview that he had anything to do with the decisions regarding which items to publish and which items to place under seal. In fact, he said he had always assumed that *all* of the medical evidence transcripts and interview reports would be published, and felt it was "wrong" that they were not. Purdy told the ARRB that the last of the regular HSCA staff (except Blakey and Cornwell) was let go by 31 December 1978.

The record shows that the HSCA report was written by Staff Director and Chief Counsel Robert Blakey, Deputy Counsel Gary Cornwell, and Richard Billings, who previously worked for *Life* magazine (and spearheaded its short-lived, aborted 1966 reinvestigation of the assassination). (Billings and Blakey co-authored a book immediately after the HSCA report was published [*Editor's note*: entitled *Fatal Hour: The Assassination of President Kennedy by Organized Crime* (1981)] that blamed the President's murder on the Mafia—a finding that Andy Purdy vehemently opposed during his discussions with the ARRB staff in January of 1996.) The HSCA Final Report and accompanying 12 volumes of evidence were published in March of 1979, three months after the last of the regular staff was let go.

If Purdy was telling the truth when he said he was not involved in the decisions about which interviews and transcripts would be sealed (i.e., suppressed),
then the field is narrowed to the three people mentioned above. If the suppressed
HSCA medical witness interview reports prepared by its own staff had not been
opened in 1993 in response to the JFK Act, there would be no "two brain exam
hypothesis" to discuss today. Thank you, Oliver Stone, for upsetting the members of Congress with your film to the point where they decided, thirteen years
later, to release their own sealed files.

Provided below, in greatly abbreviated form, is a summation of the evidence
for two separate brain examinations following President Kennedy's autopsy, followed by some closing commentary that speculates about why anyone would
have orchestrated such a dangerous charade—what in my opinion constituted
possible criminal activity: obstruction of justice. [*Author's note*: My original research memo was first published on 28 August 1996; two interim revisions were
published on 25 and 27 March of 1997; and the Final Revision was published on
2 June 1998. Anyone interested in precise citations, dates, and page numbers of
source material should consult the 32-page memo. That information is omitted
here due to space limitations and for the sake of readability.]

**In summary, three different sets of indicia, or patterns in the evidence,
support the hypothesis that two different brain specimens were examined
subsequent to the autopsy on the body of President John F. Kennedy. They
are:**

(a) conflicting evidence of the timing of the brain exam(s);

**(b) conflicting evidence as to the type of film, and photographic techniques,
used to photograph the brain(s); and**

**(c) conflicting evidence regarding the appearance of the brain at autopsy
versus the appearance of the brain in the photographs at the Archives.**

One person who formerly held a very high post on the Review Board staff has
said repeatedly to me that he could just as easily have come up with an alternate
explanation for the evidence that I cite (other than positing two separate brain
examinations), but to my knowledge he never has. Nevertheless, in his opinion
the conflicts in the evidence in which I see distinct patterns are all just a "meaningless soup." My response to this argument is that rather than forming a "jumble"
or "meaningless muddle," as one would expect if the conflicts in the evidence
were simply the result of random error, it is my contention that when the medical witnesses' statements and testimony are studied on a broad canvas, or with a
wide-angle lens, as they should be, the evidence for these two separate events is
so strong that the two-brain-exam hypothesis literally jumps out and almost hits
one between the eyes. To me, concluding that two different brain specimens
were examined is as obvious (and dramatic) as seeing the precipitate magically
falling out of a solution for the first time in a high school chemistry class. I hope
the reader shares my excitement as you study the evidence summarized below.

Timeline Evidence for Two Separate Events:

Examination Number One:

- Dr. Boswell told the HSCA that the brain was examined 2 or 3 days after the
  autopsy, and also told the ARRB the same thing, finally concluding that oc-

curred on Monday, 25 November 1963. Boswell did not list Dr. Finck as among those present to either the HSCA or the ARRB, and told the ARRB he didn't think Pierre Finck was present.

- Autopsy photographer John Stringer also told the HSCA that he photographed the brain at a brain exam conducted 2 or 3 days after the autopsy, and likewise told the ARRB it was examined 2 or 3 days after the autopsy, and on a workday, in the morning. Stringer told the ARRB in an unsworn interview that he did not believe Finck was present and, during his ARRB deposition, did not independently recall Finck being at the brain exam when he listed those that he remembered as present. Thus, Stringer and Boswell together have very consistently established that the first brain examination occurred 2 or 3 days after the autopsy, most likely 3 days later, on Monday, 25 November 1963.

- Navy (Bethesda) civilian employee Leland Benson told the HSCA that he went home for the weekend on Friday, 22 November 1963 before President Kennedy's autopsy and returned to work on Monday, 25 November 1963. He said that on the morning of Monday, November 25th he processed tissue from President Kennedy that was delivered to him with a route slip. Since Chief Chester Boyers told the HSCA he finished processing all tissue from the autopsy on the body on Sunday, November 24th, and since Dr. Boswell similarly told the ARRB that he finished examining all of the tissue slides from the autopsy on November 24th, it is reasonable to speculate that Leland Benson processed *brain tissue* following the supplemental examination of President Kennedy's brain Monday morning.

Examination Number Two:

- U.S. Army pathologist Dr. Pierre Finck wrote a report about his participation in the JFK autopsy for his superior, General Blumberg, dated 1 February 1965, in which he recorded that Dr. Humes had called him about the need to examine the brain on 29 November 1963. In his report, Finck continued, writing that he had subsequently (exact date unknown) examined the brain along with Drs. Humes and Boswell, and a Navy photographer. It is widely accepted that Finck's date is accurate, because he kept diaries. Many years later, Dr. Finck testified to the ARRB that the brain exam he attended could *not* have been 2 or 3 days after the autopsy; he said that was "too soon." Thus, 31 years later, he corroborated the accuracy of what he wrote in the Blumberg report, and in doing so, indirectly supported the claims of others that he was not present at the "early" brain exam.

- Navy Chief Petty Officer Chester Boyers told the HSCA that he prepared six paraffin blocks and eight sections of brain tissue on 2 December 1963. Oddly, but fortunately, there are *two* HSCA interview reports (Agency File Numbers 014462 and 013614) prepared by Mark Flanagan about this *one* interview. I only became aware of the second one recently, when Dr. Gary Aguilar made it available to me. The "second" report (013614) is significant, because in it Flanagan writes that Boyers made notes recording what actions he took shortly after the events took place, on 22-24 November and 2 December 1963, respectively. Therefore, Chief Boyers' recollections in this HSCA interview are just as reliable as Dr. Finck's in the Blumberg report, since like Finck, he too made contemporaneous written records of events. The recollections of Boyers and Finck together constitute a very definite and very reliable window for the second brain exam: sometime between 29 November and 2 December 1963, inclusive.

The Shifting Recollections of James J. Humes

Dr. Humes, the chief prosecutor at the autopsy, is all over the calendar on when "the brain exam" took place. The conflicts in his testimony may be intentional, and meant to obfuscate, but I think it is more likely that he has trapped himself with conflicting statements over the years and has no choice but to do a dance from "left foot to right foot," like a man on a hot plate. I believe Dr. Humes is on a hot plate of his own making. Consider the following:

- Humes told Arlen Specter under oath in 1964 that the supplementary autopsy report was "prepared some days after the examination [on the body]. This delay [was] necessitated by, primarily, our desire to have the brain better fixed with formaldehyde before we proceeded further with the examination of the brain." The document under discussion is CE-391, the supplementary autopsy report, dated 12/6/63 (two weeks after the assassination); but the date is handwritten, and not typed like the rest of the report. Therefore, the meaning of the handwritten date is unknown. Arlen Specter never asked Humes when the brain examination was conducted, and never asked him why there was a handwritten date on a typewritten report, or what significance the date had. This behavior, for an experienced and competent big-city district attorney, is most curious. Any recent graduate fresh out of law school would have "laid the proper foundation" for that document by asking those questions.

- Humes told Specter under oath during this same testimony that he, Boswell, and Finck examined the brain. Finck and Boswell were both in the room during his testimony to Specter. (This is clear contextually from the follow-on questions asked of Boswell and Finck the same day.)

- In contrast, Humes told *JAMA* in 1992 (and repeated to the ARRB under oath) that Rear Admiral Burkley told him Robert Kennedy wanted the brain interred with the President's body—thus implying that it was examined prior to the funeral on Monday afternoon, 25 November 1963. Our present-day knowledge of the contents of the Blumberg report—of a brain examination attended by Finck, Humes and Boswell well after the funeral—makes this "problematic," to say the least.

- When ARRB General Counsel Jeremy Gunn first asked Humes whether the brain exam happened within one or two days after the autopsy, Humes said yes. But the more he was asked about the timeline during his ARRB deposition, the more distance Humes placed between that event and the autopsy; his testimony kept shifting. Furthermore, his attitude about timeline questions was defensive, and his responses flippant in tone. Eventually Humes modified his original answer to say that the brain exam may have taken place two or three days after Sunday, November 24th, nicely splitting the difference between what I am convinced were two separate events.

Could a Brain Have Been Sectioned After only Two-and-One-Half Days of Fixation?

The answer is, "Yes," but only if the brain was perfused. Dr. Dick Davis, acting Chief of Neuropathology at the AFIP in November 1963, told the ARRB that at Bethesda in those days, a combination of exfusion (soaking in solution) and infusion (injected drip), called "perfusion," was used to fix brains. Davis said that a brain fixed by perfusion could be ready for cutting as early as 2 to 3 days after autopsy, instead of the normal 10-14 day delay required by exfusion (soaking). If one carefully reads the HSCA summary of its interview with Navy autopsy technician James Jenkins, and then studies the ARRB testimony of Drs. Humes and Boswell, it is clear that President Kenndy's brain was fixed by perfusion technique and therefore could have been "cut" within 2 or 3 days of its removal at autopsy.

Recollections of Film Used (and Angles Shot) Do Not Match Film in the Archives:

- John Stringer told the ARRB in both an unsworn interview and again during his deposition that he photographed the brain as it was being serially sectioned, yet there are no photographs of serial sections among the brain photos at the Archives.
- John Stringer testified persuasively to the ARRB that he only photographed the intact, fixed brain (prior to sectioning) from above, and that he did not shoot basilar views (i.e., of the underside of the brain), yet approximately one half of the brain photographs at the Archives are basilar views. In the Blumberg report, Dr. Finck states that both superior and inferior views of the brain he examined were photographed. To me, this discrepancy indicates that John Stringer was not the photographer at the event Dr. Finck attended. This interpretation was lent credence by John Stringer following his ARRB deposition, when he told me, in the lobby of the National Archives, that Dr. Finck was not present at the brain exam he attended.
- John Stringer testified to the ARRB that the black-and-white negatives he shot of the brain were exposed on un-numbered Kodak portrait pan film in duplex film holders, yet the black-and-white negatives at the Archives were exposed on Ansco film from a numbered 12-shot film pack. [*Author's note:* Unlike film in duplex holders, film in a film pack contains numbered frames, and is also much thinner than the relatively thick film substrate manufactured for duplex holders.]
- John Stringer testified to the ARRB that the color films he shot of the brain were Kodak Ektachrome color positive transparencies, yet when he examined the color positive transparency images of the brain at the Archives, he testified that the notches on the color film indicated that it was not Ektachrome film, and he offered his opinion that these color positive transparencies of a brain may also be on Ansco brand film.

Appearance of the Brain at Autopsy Conflicts with the Brain
Photos at National Archives:

- In his 1 February 1965 report to General Blumberg, Dr. Finck wrote this
  about the appearance of the brain at the supplementary brain examination:
  "The convolutions of the brain are flat and the sulci are narrow, but this is
  interpreted as a fixation artefact because the change was not observed at the
  time of autopsy." Dr. Finck is clearly stating here, in an official report to an
  Army General only 14 months after the autopsy, *that the brain examined looked
  different at the supplementary exam than it did at the autopsy*. I cannot over-
  emphasize how important this is, in light of the strong independent timeline
  evidence of a second exam, with Dr. Finck in attendance, sometime between
  29 November and 2 December 1963. Dr. Finck apparently assumes that the
  brain is President Kennedy's—who would assume otherwise under normal
  circumstances?—and is then left with only one logical conclusion: it looks
  different as a result of "fixation artefacts." But in light of the above evidence,
  doesn't Occam's Razor compel us to reevaluate Dr. Finck's conclusion? [*Editor's
  note*: The author refers to the methodological principle that simpler explanations are always preferable to more complex explanations, as long as they are
  adequate to the evidence.] In my view, it is much more likely that the brain
  observed by Finck at the supplementary exam looked different than it did at
  autopsy simply because it *was* a different brain.
- Former Gawler's Funeral Home mortician Tom Robinson told the ARRB that
  after removal at autopsy, the portion of President Kennedy's brain that was
  missing was the portion "in the back," and placed his hand on the posterior
  portion of his own head when he made this statement.
- Former FBI Special Agent Francis X. O'Neill, Jr. testified to the ARRB that
  more than half of President Kennedy's brain was missing at autopsy, and said
  that his recollection of the damage was inconsistent with the damage shown
  by the brain photographs at the Archives. He said that he remembered the
  back portion of the brain was the biggest portion missing (gesturing with his
  hand to the right rear of his own head, behind his right ear, so that there was
  no doubt about what he meant).
- The brain weight of 1500 grams (which actually exceeds the weight of the
  average normal male brain) recorded by Finck in the Blumberg report, and
  by Humes in the supplemental autopsy report, is totally inconsistent with a
  brain more than half-gone at autopsy when it was removed. [*Editor's note*:
  Robert B. Livingston, M.D., has advised me that an average normal adult
  human brain weighs between 1350 and 1400 grams.]
- ARRB medical consultant Dr. Robert Kirschner told the ARRB that the brain
  imaged in the Archives photographs appears very well fixed, as if it had been
  in formaldehyde at least two weeks. That judgment is most inconsistent with
  the brain in the images having been examined on Monday morning, 25 November 1963, two-and-one-half days after the autopsy on the body.

The implications of the five points above are that the first brain examined
(by Humes, Boswell and Stringer) was President Kennedy's brain, and that the
second specimen examined (by Humes, Boswell, Finck, and an unknown photographer) was someone else's. It seems likely that the first brain *was* serially

sectioned and the second specimen was *not* serially sectioned, and in contrast only had small pieces of tissue removed from it. [*Author's note*: in opposition to Stringer's strong recollections to the ARRB, on two occasions, that he photographed individual serial sections on a light box, Drs. Humes and Boswell have always maintained that only small sections, or slivers, were removed from the brain and that it was *not* serially sectioned so as to "preserve the specimen." Presumably, Stringer is describing the authentic specimen, and Humes and Boswell are describing the second, fraudulent specimen.]

It is interesting to note that in the Blumberg Report, Finck writes that he requested a neuropathologist from the AFIP be present at the brain exam, but that Humes refused. Humes, by his own admission, also decided not to serially section the brain. Former AFIP acting Chief of Neuropathology Dr. Dick Davis— a former acquaintance of Dr. Boswell's—told the ARRB that he could conceive of *no circumstances* (his emphasis) in which a brain damaged by gunshot would not be serially sectioned following autopsy. Well, I can conceive of one circumstance: if it is not the authentic specimen taken from the deceased and had been damaged by cutting rather than by gunshot, then those involved in such a charade would certainly *not serially section* the specimen and would keep a neuropathologist out of the room *at all costs*. And that, apparently, is what happened when Humes, Boswell, and Finck met to examine "someone else's brain" sometime between 29 November and 2 December 1963.

Of course, it was surely represented to Dr. Finck (dishonestly) by Drs. Humes and Boswell as "President Kennedy's brain"; but was Dr. Finck fooled? One wonders if he had suspicions that something was wrong. His signature is not present on the supplementary autopsy report, which is signed only by Dr. Humes. Why? Did he refuse to sign? Or was it rewritten, without his knowledge, after he and Boswell signed it? He certainly recorded for posterity, in the Blumberg Report, the different appearance of the brain he examined at the supplementary (brain) autopsy from the brain he examined during the autopsy on the body.

During his ARRB deposition John Stringer testified he only recalled Navy pathologists Humes, Boswell, and himself at "the" brain exam. After his ARRB deposition, when I asked him the direct question Jeremy Gunn failed to ask under oath: "Was Dr. Finck present at the brain exam [meaning the brain exam Stringer attended, the first one]?" Stringer answered, with a wry smile on his face, and a twinkle in his eyes: "No, I don't think they wanted him there; he caused too much trouble at the autopsy." And then his ride appeared out in front of Archives II in College Park, Maryland, and he drove off without me getting a chance to ask him what he meant by *that*.

Wait a minute! "He caused too much trouble at the autopsy?" *Whatever* that meant, if it were an opinion shared by Humes and Boswell, that might well explain why Finck did not meet with Humes and Boswell on Saturday, November 23rd to review the first draft of the autopsy report, and why he was likewise not invited to the examination of the authentic brain, on Monday, November 25th.

So why would anyone do such a thing? I think the answers are simple:

- The real brain, examined on or about Monday, 25 November 1963, constituted unassailable evidence of a shot from the front, and was incompatible with the "cover story" of a lone shooter from behind. Sectioning it confirmed this. It was politically incorrect, and was just plain dangerous, *period*.

- Admiral Burkley's demand that the examination be conducted quickly so it could be buried with the body, per Robert Kennedy's wishes, was simply a stratagem to get the brain away from Humes and Boswell; it was an excuse used by him to get custody of the best evidence in the murder of the President. It may or may not have been buried with the President on 25 November 1963; we simply do not know.

- The condition of the real brain was consistent with the reports of the Dallas doctors, who said President Kennedy had an exit wound in the right rear of his head, from which damaged cerebral and cerebellar tissue extruded. Allowing it to remain in evidence would have confirmed that the President was shot from the front, and would have made it impossible to sell the "cover story" to the American people.

- Removing the real brain from evidence and substituting photographs of another brain, with intact cerebellar hemispheres, and with a pattern of damage roughly consistent with a shooter from above and behind, would support the "cover story" that a lone man in a building shot a man in a car from above and behind. It also had the added benefit that *it could also be used to discredit the testimony and observations of the Dallas doctors.*

Although not the subject of this essay, I believe, as does David Lifton, that the widely divergent descriptions of the wounds on President Kennedy's body, as seen in Dallas at Parkland Hospital on the one hand, and as seen later that day at the National Naval Medical Center at Bethesda, Maryland, on the other hand, together constitute *prima facie* proof that President Kennedy's body was altered—tampered with—prior to the commencement of the Navy autopsy, presumably to remove evidence (i.e., bullets or bullet fragments) inconsistent with the lone-assassin-from-behind cover story. [*Editor's note*: See, for example, David Lifton, *Best Evidence* (1980).] The very nature of this gross tampering—butchery, actually—enlarged the head wound to four or five times its original size, expanding the damage to include the top and right side of the skull. Therefore, retention of the authentic brain, showing exit damage only to the rear of that organ, and likely containing gross evidence of rather sloppy post-mortem cutting (evidence of tampering), could not be allowed.

The authentic brain would not only have corroborated the observations of the Dallas doctors, but would have been most inconsistent with the enlarged head wound seen and documented at Bethesda. Thus, a substitution was imperative. This was certainly realized almost immediately, which explains: (1) why Dr. Finck, who caused "too much trouble at the autopsy," was not invited to the examination of the authentic brain, and (2) why Dr. Burkley forcefully demanded it be returned "so it could be buried with the body." The genius of the charade we are discussing here is that the substitution of a second, fraudulent brain specimen with a different pattern of damage actually lent legitimacy to the false pattern of wounding on President Kennedy's body recorded at Bethesda and provided the primary means by which all future investigations would be deceived.

Furthermore, using Dr. Finck as a witness to the examination of a fraudulent specimen placed him in the unenviable category of a dupe, in which he could, if needed, provide the ultimate "verification" that "Yes, indeed, these photographs represent the brain as I saw it at the supplemental examination," or words to that effect. Why include Dr. Finck in a charade if there was some danger that he might insist on a neuropathologist, or notice that Specimen #2 looked different than the real brain? Because to *exclude* him may have been considered even more dangerous. It might have looked suspicious if one of three prosectors at the autopsy had been excluded from the supplemental brain examination.

After all, this was the death of the President. It had to be properly documented. Given this, it continues to seem peculiar to me that whereas all three prosectors attended a supplementary brain exam, only Dr. Humes signed CE-391, the supplementary autopsy report. Why? Perhaps Dr. Finck "caused too much trouble" at the second brain exam, just as Stringer said he did at the autopsy. His insistence that a neuropathologist be present, and his observation that the brain looked different at the supplemental exam than it did at autopsy, make one wonder whether those who invited him to this exercise later wished they had not done so.

Dr. Finck, it has become clear, decided to have a massive "memory lapse" by the time of his ARRB deposition. In contrast to the fierce lion portrayed in the JAMA article in October of 1992, the Dr. Finck deposed by the ARRB had clearly become a timid, confused pussycat. He remembered more about how he spent his summers in the late 1930s, and about what he was doing when he arrived in America in 1952 than he did about the autopsy he performed on President Kennedy in 1963. Jeremy Gunn and I found the transformation from the lion who growled at Dennis Breo of *JAMA* to the kitten deposed by the ARRB remarkable. But then Mr. Breo didn't really know the evidence in the case, and Finck was not under oath during the *JAMA* interview, as he was with the ARRB.

Motivation

What would cause Drs. Humes and Boswell to participate in the false examination of a "second" brain? I certainly do not view them as masterminds of any plot. But I do view them as men following orders from superiors. What excuse or reasons were they given? "National Security"? The prevention of "World War III"? No doubt something like that. But whatever their motivations, there is persuasive evidence that they were co-opted commencing the night of the autopsy, and continuing on through the examination of a second brain specimen sometime between 29 November—2 December 1963. This troubling pattern continued into November 1966 during the cataloging of the autopsy photographs and x-rays, and finally into January 1967 with the preparation of the so-called "Military Review" of the autopsy report.

Humes and Boswell have been backpedaling ever since, giving conflicting and unsatisfactory answers to serious questions about the evidence—answers that should be more or less the same, but unaccountably are not. Finck, who tenaciously battled with the HSCA's forensic pathology panel over the location of the entrance wound in the head, left America and eventually returned to his native Switzerland to retire in seclusion. Humes and Boswell bonded closely while in the Navy (despite very different personalities) and maintain a close relationship to this day. They visit each other a couple of times a year, often enough to call each other "bridge partners," yet they cannot get their stories straight about what happened at President Kennedy's autopsy.

The documentary record of two post-autopsy brain examinations, which strongly suggests that two different specimens were examined, is an irrefutable indication that something was terribly amiss during the two weeks following the President's death. The most obvious implication is that the official story (of a lone assassin from behind shooting the President) is probably not true, since it appears to be supported primarily by the condition of a fraudulent specimen at the second brain examination. This specimen is inconsistent with the now-documented condition of President Kennedy's brain at the autopsy on his body and, presumably, at the first brain examination on Monday morning, 25 November 1963, as well.

Of those living today, I suspect only Drs. Humes and Boswell know the real story of who ordered them to examine a second specimen, suppress the evidence of the first specimen examined, and what reasons they were given. Unfortunately, they have chosen not to reveal these secrets, even under oath, apparently preferring the severe criticism they have received over the years for their supposed incompetence, to the alternative of opening up a Pandora's Box at this stage in their lives that would lead to endless questions and heightened controversy. [*Editor's note:* Humes has died since this piece was written.]

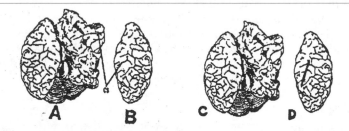

A. HSCA exhibit F-302. Drawing made from photograph of brain illustrating subcortical damage.
B. Mirror image drawing of left hemisphere in Figure A. Distortion due to damage and/or post-fixation artifact is minimal.
C. HSCA exhibit F-302 (again). Drawing made from photograph of brain to show subcortical damage.
D. Mirror image drawing of left hemisphere in Figure A. Black line illustrates schematically the direct cortical damage predicted based upon skull X-rays, which Dr. Mantik has now demonstrated to be composites.

This is the superior view of "a brain" represented by the photographs in the national Archives. This image is of the specimen at the second brain exam, and cannot be the brain of President John. F. Kennedy.

[Editor's note: *These figures are from Joseph N. Riley, Ph.D., "The Head Wounds of John Kennedy,"* The Third Decade *(March 1993), pp. 1-15, as it appears in a statement by Robert B. Livingston,* Assassination Science *(1998), p. 165.*]

Interviews with Former NPIC Employees:
The Zapruder Film in November 1963

Douglas P. Horne

[*Editor's note*: In June and July of 1997, the ARRB interviewed two former CIA employees of the NPIC (National Photographic Interpretation Center), Homer McMahon and Bennett Hunter, who were involved in processing a movie of the death of JFK the weekend of the assassination. As Douglas Horne observes in a memorandum not included here, the Secret Service agent who couriered this film— which appears to have been the original "out of camera" film taken by Abraham Zapruder—to the NPIC told them that the film was developed by Kodak at Rochester, NY, contrary to the existing documentary record, which indicates that the film and three copies were processed in Dallas, TX. These reports are as astonishing and revealing as those concerning the occurrence of two brain examinations and the existence of two brains, which once again demonstrates that the ARRB has produced far more than its share of "smoking guns."]

CALL REPORT: PUBLIC

Document's Author: Douglas Horne/ARRB   Date Created: 06/12/97

The Players
Who called whom?   Dave Montague and Douglas Horne called Homer A. McMahon of
                     Witnesses/Consultants

Description of the Call
Date::   06/12/97
Subject: **Dave Montague and Douglas Horne Called Homer A. McMahon (Modified on June
           13, 1997)**

Summary of the Call:
[See Contact Profile for details on how this individual was located.]

   Dave Montague located Mr. McMahon and initiated telephonic contact on June 9, 1997; I was invited to participate in the interview as the staff member most interested in, and most familiar with, the NPIC working notes of their analysis of the Zapruder film.
   The following is a summary of the independent recollections of Mr. McMahon made during ARRB's cursory, initial assessment interview. Comments are not verbatim unless in quotations:

-He was the Head of NPIC's color lab in 1963. At that time NPIC was no longer in NW Washington above Steuart Motors (where it was during the Cuban Missile Crisis), but had relocated to BLDG 213 in the Washington Navy Yard, following a quick 90-day renovation of a warehouse with no windows directed by Robert Kennedy. McMahon was careful to clarify that he was an employee of NPIC in 1963, not the CIA, and that the CIA only "paid his salary."

-McMahon did recall the Zapruder film analysis in some detail, and confirmed ARRB's understanding that the analysis (of which frames in which shots struck occupants of the limousine) was performed at the request of the Secret Service. He recalled that a Secret Service agent named "Bill Smith" personally brought the film over to NPIC, and that the personnel involved in the analysis were himself (McMahon), Bill Smith of the USSS, and a third person whose name McMahon would not reveal to us during the interview "because he is still current."

-TIMING: McMahon thought that the analysis had occurred only "1 or 2 days" after the assassination; he also recalled that there was a great sense of urgency regarding the desired product, and that he had to "work all night long" to complete the required work (described below). At one point he said he thought he had gone into work about 1 A.M. to commence the analysis; later he corrected himself and said that perhaps it was more like 8 P.M., but that in any case he was sure that the work occurred after normal working hours, required him to return to work, and that the analysis went on all night long.

-McMahon never used the name Zapruder film during the interview; he repeatedly referred to the film in question as an "amateur movie" of the assassination brought to NPIC by the Secret Service.

-PROVENANCE OF THE FILM: McMahon stated that Secret Service agent Bill Smith claimed he had personally picked up the film from the amateur who had exposed it, had flown it to Rochester for developing, and had then couriered it to Washington, DC to NPIC for analysis and for the creation of photographic briefing boards, using still photographic prints enlarged from selected individual frames of the movie. After twice mentioning Rochester as the site where the film was developed, Dave Montague (in an attempt to specify whether McMahon was referring to R.I.T., or Kodak) asked whether he meant Kodak, and McMahon emphatically said "I mean Kodak at Rochester." I asked him how firm he was that this is what the Secret Service agent told him, and he said he was "absolutely certain."

-REASONS FOR ANALYSIS AT NPIC VICE ANOTHER LOCATION: McMahon said that USSS agent Bill Smith told him the reason the film had been couriered to NPIC was because NPIC had special, state-of-the-art enlarging equipment which Kodak did not have at Rochester. McMahon said that after the analysis of where shots occurred on the film was completed, many frames were selected ("perhaps as many as 40, but not more than about 40") for reproduction as photographic prints, and that NPIC's special "10-20-40 enlarger" was used to magnify each desired image frame "40 times its original size for the manufacture of internegatives." McMahon said that the internegatives were then used for the production of multiple color prints of each selected frame. He said that the color lab at NPIC where he worked did not prepare the actual briefing boards, but that he assumed the briefing boards were prepared somewhere else at NPIC, in some other department.

-In response to clarification questions by Horne, McMahon said that *at no time was the amateur movie copied as a motion picture film* ,and that the only photographic work done at NPIC was to make color prints. He could not remember whether the prints were 5" X 7" format, or 8" X 10" format.

-Horne asked whether he was working with the original film or a copy, and McMahon stated with some certainty that he was "sure we had the original film." Horne asked why, and he said that he was sure it was the original because it was Kodachrome, and because it was a "double 8" movie. Horne asked him to clarify whether the home movie was slit or unslit, and McMahon said that he was pretty sure the film was UNSLIT, because "we had to flip it over to see the image on the other side in the correct orientation." He said that the movie was placed in an optical printer, in which the selected frames were then magnified to 40 times their original size for the production of internegatives. He said a "liquid gate" process was used (on the home movie frames) to produce the internegatives.

-Prior to the production of internegatives and color prints for briefing boards, he said he recalled an analysis "to determine where the 3 shots hit." He said he would not share the results of the analysis with us on the telephone. The film was projected as a motion picture 4 or 5 times during the analysis phase, for purposes of determining "where the 3 shots hit."

-At this point Horne informed Mr. McMahon that CIA's HRG had deposited a surviving briefing board and the original working notes in the JFK Collection in 1993 for access by the public, and that they were not classified. Montague promised to send McMahon an information package explaining the JFK Act and the Review Board's mandate, and Horne and Montague asked Mr. McMahon is he would be willing to submit to a formal, in-depth, recorded interview at Archives II with the briefing board and the working notes available to him during the interview. He agreed.

-McMahon explained that the working notes were "prepared jointly by the 3 of us working on the project that night." END

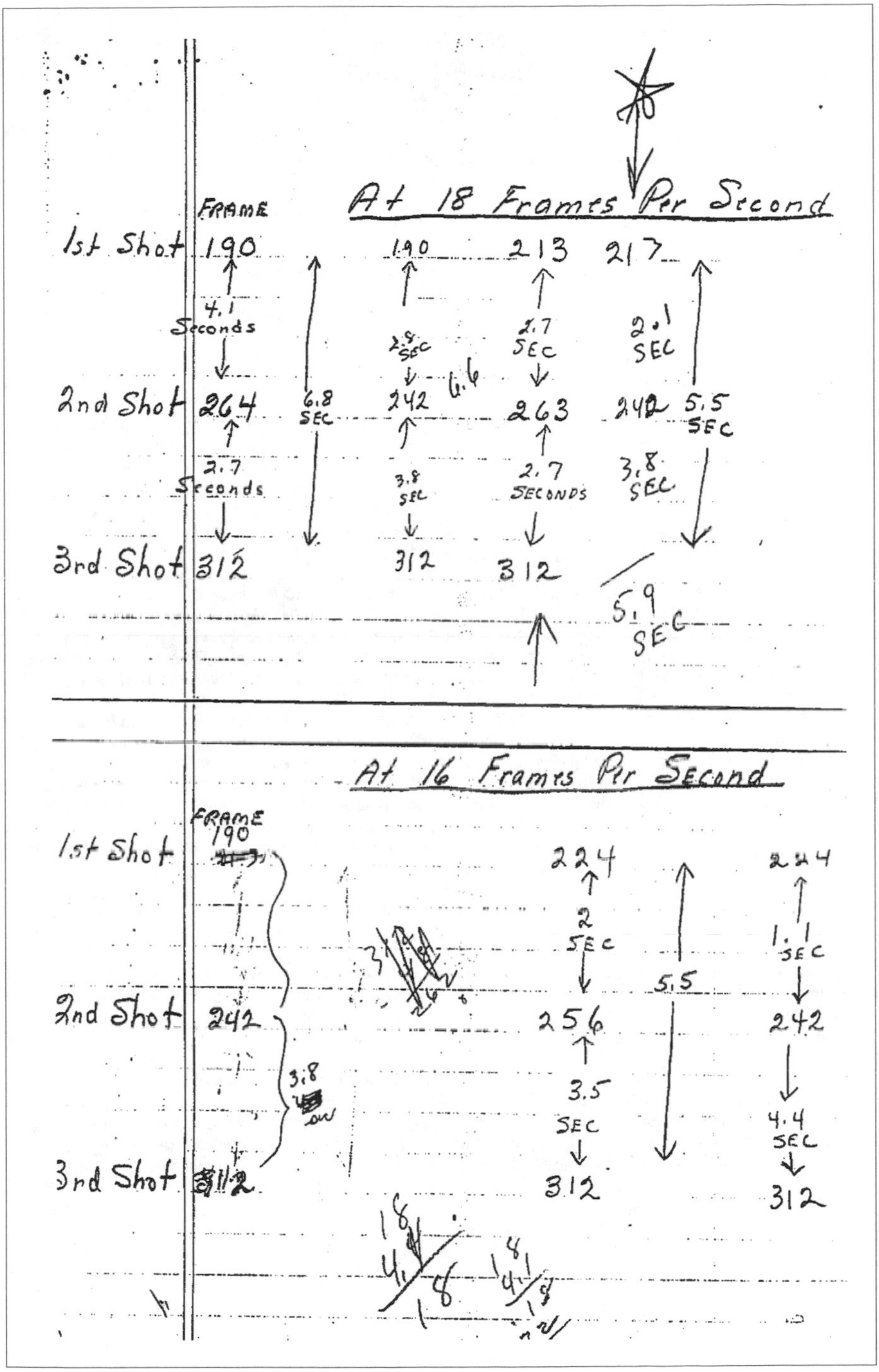

(Undated) NPIC working notes for preparing a "briefing board"

MEETING REPORT

Document's Author: Douglas Horne/ARRB   **Date Created:** 06/18/97

Meeting Logistics

Date:	06/17/97
Agecny Name:	CIA
Attendees:	Morgan Bennett Hunter (Ben Hunter) was interviewed by Doug Horne, Jeremy Gunn, Dave Montague, and Michelle Combs
Topic:	ARRB Staff Interviewed Ben Hunter (Grammatical Edits Made on June 19, 1997) (Final Edit Made June 20, 1997)

Summary of the Meeting

ARRB staff interviewed Ben Hunter on June 17, 1997. The interview was arranged by HRG at ARRB's request. Mr. Hunter had remarked to his wife (an HRG employee), during C-Span coverage of the Review Board's Zapruder film public hearing, that he had worked on an analysis of the film at NPIC in 1963 shortly after the assassination. His wife relayed that fact, and the name of his supervisor at NPIC (who also worked on the Z-film analysis), Mr. Homer A. McMahon, to the ARRB via Barry Harrelson at HRG. Previous to this interview, ARRB staff had conducted a brief initial assessment interview of Mr. McMahon on the telephone.

Mr. Hunter was on active duty in the USAF prior to working for NPIC (National Photo Interpretation Center). While in the Air Force as an enlisted man (at Offut Air Force Base in Nebraska, at SAC Headquarters), he received photographic training and worked on "special processing" programs, which he explained were aerial and early satellite photography (reconnaissance) products. He said he was offered a job at NPIC before he left the Air Force. He said he left the Air Force on 30 November 1962, started working at NPIC (then located at 5th and K Streets in the Steuart Ford dealership building in NW Washington) on 17 December 1962, and helped NPIC move to its new quarters at BLDG 213 in the Washington Navy Yard on January 1, 1963. He said that he worked on the same kind of aerial/satellite reconnaissance products at NPIC as he did in the Air Force; he specifically mentioned that NPIC had the capability to handle 70 mm KH4 film, and 9.5" U-2 KHB film. He said that the majority of his experience in the Air Force was with B & W film, because all of the reconnaissance film in those days was B & W. He said that he assisted Homer McMahon in establishing the Color Lab at NPIC sometime during 1963, after working 6-9 months in the B & W section at NPIC; he said Homer McMahon was the head of the new color lab and was his supervisor. Just prior to leaving the Air Force, and just after joining NPIC, Mr. Hunter said he did a lot of work on reconnaissance photography of surveillance of Cuba during, and following, the Cuban Missile Crisis. He said much of the work was follow-up photography to ensure that the Soviet missiles really had left Cuba.

Mr. Hunter said he did participate in an NPIC event involving the Zapruder film in 1963, but cautioned at the beginning of the interview that his memory of this event was "extremely fuzzy," and told us repeatedly that Mr. Homer McMahon's memory was probably much better than his. Listed below is a summary of the essential pieces of information he passed to us during the interview:

-He recalled that he and Homer McMahon worked with the Zapruder film very shortly after the assassination in 1963, just 2 or 3 days afterwards. At another point he said it may have been the next day (Saturday) or Sunday, November 24, and that he thought it was prior to the funeral of President Kennedy. He recalled that no one else from NPIC (other than he and Homer McMahon) was in the building, which means it was almost certainly the weekend of the assassination; he also recalled that he had to drive in from home to do this job, and that he was not already at work when the project was assigned.

-He recalled that a "Captain Sands" delivered the home movie of the assassination to him and Homer McMahon; he thought Sands (a person in civilian clothes whom was simply addressed as "Captain") was probably with the CIA Office of Security, or perhaps was the NPIC Head of Security, but could not be sure today. He said that another person may have been present, or arrived with Sands, but could not remember much about that. Later in the interview, when he was asked whether he remembered any Secret Service involvement, he said that our question did ring a bell with him, and that yes, he did believe there may have been a Secret Service employee present. He said that the others (Sands, the person with Sands, and McMahon) were already present when he arrived. He said Sands remained "close by," observing the work, while he and McMahon handled and worked with the Zapruder film.

-He said Sands directed that he and McMahon not talk about their work that night with anyone, not even anyone else at NPIC, and that if people were to press him on it, they were to be directed to call Captain Sands. In fact, when he put in for overtime for the Zapruder film work, Hunter said he would not tell the Head of the Photographic Lab the reason, the person became upset, and he had to direct that supervisor to call Captain Sands for an explanation.

-The Zapruder film was not copied as a motion picture; in fact, Hunter said that NPIC did not have that capability for color movies, since they were in the business of still, B & W reconnaissance photography for the most part. He said that the assigned task was to analyze (i.e., locate on the film) where occupants of the limousine were wounded, including "studying frames leading up to shots," and then produce color prints from appropriate frames just prior to shots, and also frames showing shots impacting limousine occupants. He recalled laying the home movie out on a light table and using a loupe to examine individual frames. He could not recall whether they received any instructions as to number of shots, or any guidance as to where to look in the film.

-He recalled making internegatives from about 8 total selected frames from the movie, and then making multiple (number uncertain) 8" X 10" or 9" X 9" color prints from the internegatives. The machine used for manufacture of the internegatives was a "10 X 20 X 40 enlarger." He said that on initial attempts, the internegative size was 8" X 10", but that later the size of the internegs was "cut down." By this he did not mean cropped, but that the final internegs used were smaller than the initial size of 8" X 10". He said that the process of selecting frames of interest, and the production of the internegatives, took a minimum of 1 to 2 hours, and perhaps a maximum of 3 to 4 hours to accomplish.

-He did not personally participate in the making of any briefing boards, although he said he would not be surprised to find out that someone else at NPIC may have.

-His memories of film content were limited to seeing a skull explosion, bone fragments, and Jackie Kennedy crawling on the trunk of the car. Apparently to those involved that night the film was only referred to as a "home movie," but he seemed convinced that it was the Zapruder film based on subsequent viewings of it over the years in documentaries. He had no independent recollection of which way the President's head moved (forwards or backwards) from his memories of work that night. He recalled that there were 2 or 3 frames showing the "head explosion," which he alternatively described as "a cloud of material surrounding President Kennedy's head."

-His impression is that the film was probably in 16 mm format, but was **not** of an unslit double-8 mm film. It was his strong impression that they were working with the original, but when asked whether there were images present between the sprocket holes, he said that it was his reasonably strong impression today that there were no such images present between the sprocket holes in the film he examined at NPIC. At one point he described the film as "not high resolution."

-All materials created or used had to be turned in to Sands upon completion of their work: the motion picture film itself; finished prints (of approximately 8 views); test prints (made for the purpose of determining color balance); test internegatives; and the final internegatives used to make the prints.

-As he talked during the interview, his estimates of the amount of time involved to do this work expanded, to the point where by the end of the interview, he was convinced that the entire job probably took a minimum of between 5-7 hours to accomplish. Before talking with us about the details of the process, he said he would initially have estimated only 2-3 hours of work. He recalled that the work started during the daytime, and ended during the night-time.

-When asked, he said he did recall counting frame numbers (i.e., counting off the location of selected frames) on the movie film.

-When asked if he or his co-worker McMahon made any notes, he said that he had no specific recollection of having done so, but that if they did, the notes were probably related to color correction (i.e., use of filters).

-EXAMINATION OF NPIC WORKING NOTES: The NPIC working notes, released twice in response to FOIA lawsuits as "CIA document 450," are numbered today as RIF # 1993.07.22.08:41:07:620600, Agency File number 80T01357A, JFK Box # JFK39. The original working notes were placed in the JFK Collection at NARA in 1993 by the CIA's HRG, along with one surviving briefing board (which consists of 4 panels). The briefing board is also in JFK Box # "JFK39," which is one large flat containing the four briefing board panels (RIF # 1993.07.21.15:48:04:930600) and the original working notes from NPIC. This interview was conducted at a CIA office space, not at Archives II in College Park. Consequently, ARRB staff had a good photocopy of the working notes with them, but not the briefing board.

-Comments of Mr. Hunter during examination of the NPIC working notes are summarized below:

----He recognized his handwriting on only one page: the handwritten page which describes the organization of the briefing board panels; and on this page, he only recognized two words (the column headers "Print #" and "Frame #") as being written in his hand. He said the remainder of the writing on this half-page was not his. He did not remember seeing the page before, or witnessing its creation, or writing on it--he simply recognized the writing for two of the column headers as his.
----He did not recognize any of the other pages in the NPIC working notes, nor did he think that such activity (e.g., 3 different shot scenarios, and calculation of seconds between shots at two different camera speeds) took place during the night he and Mr. McMahon performed their work. He was of the belief that the activity described in the NPIC working notes occurred during a second event at NPIC, one which occurred after the work done by he and Mr. McMahon.
----He said that to him, the kind of analysis represented by the NPIC notes looked like it may have been done by mensuration experts at NPIC, and said that if this were the case, he would think that candidates for this kind of analysis would be either Todd Augustine, Allan Gill, or Steve Clark.
----He said that he could recall no discussion of the film speed of the camera which took the assassination movie (whereas in the notes, both a 16 FPS, and an 18 FPS, timing scenario for shots is laboriously computed in longhand).
----He said at one point that "I think this was done again" during the tenure of the Warren Commission
----Even after viewing the NPIC notes referring to three sets each of 28 individual selected frames, he did not waver from his opinion that only about 8 frames were selected for reproduction that night by he and Mr. McMahon.

Mr. Gunn asked Mr. Hunter to review his pay stubs from 1963 to see if he could determine, from overtime records, the timing of this event. Mr. Hunter agreed.

At the conclusion of the interview Mr. Hunter expressed a desire to get together with Mr. McMahon and talk about these events from 1963. We asked him to defer until after we had formally interviewed Mr. McMahon, in person. Jeremy Gunn then suggested that on the day we schedule a formal McMahon interview at NARA, that we invite Mr. Hunter the same day so that following the McMahon interview, both men could view the briefing board and original notes together and share their impressions with each other. Mr. Hunter said he liked that idea. END

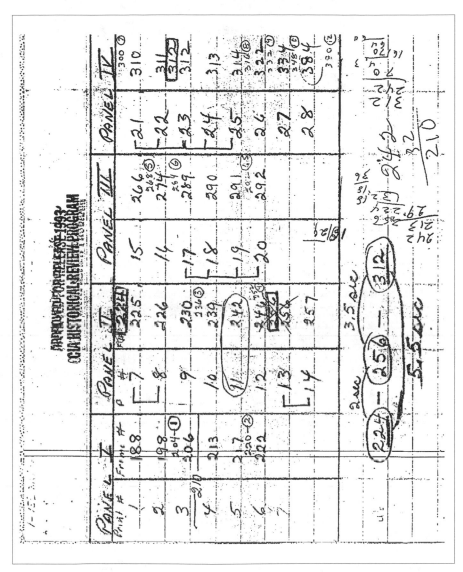

(Undated) NPIC working notes for preparing a "briefing board"

CALL REPORT

Document's Author: Douglas Horne/ARRB   **Date Created:** 06/26/97

The Players

Who called whom?   Douglas Horne called Morgan Bennett Hunter (Ben Hunter) of CIA

Description of the Call

Date: 06/26/97
Subject: Doug Horne Called Ben Hunter

Summary of the Call:

I spoke briefly with Ben Hunter to say that the July 2, 1997 interview of Mr. McMahon had been cancelled (at his--Ben Hunter's--request) and that Mr. McMahon had rejected the tentative rescheduled interview date of July 11 (for the same reason Hunter had been unavailable on July 2--vacation). I told him there was no scheduled date now for our interview with Homer McMahon, and that my instructions were to interview Homer McMahon as soon as practical, at a time convenient to Mr. McMahon. I told him that if he (Ben Hunter) was available at that time, we would include him; otherwise, we would schedule a second viewing of the briefing board panels for him subsequent to the McMahon interview.

Following discussion of these logistical details, Mr. Hunter said that he had been thinking about the events at NPIC which he discussed with us, and wished to amend his previous comments as follows:
-He said he now recalls that a Secret Service agent did deliver the materials to NPIC;
-He said he now believes it was the Secret Service agent who said "don't discuss this with anyone, and if people persist in knowing what you were doing, refer them to Captain Sands;"
-He said he now is fairly certain that Captain Sands was a high-ranking employee in NPIC's management structure, possibly the second or third highest ranking member of the organization. He does still recall that Sands was present during the NPIC event he discussed with us--the manufacture of internegatives and prints from selected frames of the Zapruder film.

Mr. Hunter said that he still wants to talk with Homer McMahon, even if they cannot view the photographic briefing board panels together due to schedule conflicts. I told him this was fine, but that we wanted to interview Mr. McMahon first, and promised to pass McMahon's telephone number to him *after* ARRB had concluded its discussions with McMahon. END

PANEL I		PANEL II		PANEL III		PANEL IV	
Print No.	Frame No.	Print No.	Frame No.	Print No.	Frame No.	Print No.	Frame No.
1	188	7	225	15	266	21	310
2	198	8	226	16	274	22	311
3	206	9	230	17	289	23	312
4	213	10	239	18	290	24	313
5	217	11	242	19	291	25	314
6	222	12	246	20	292	26	322
		13	256			27	334
		14	257			28	384

(Undated) NPIC typed summary for preparing a "briefing board"

MEETING REPORT

Document's Author: Douglas Horne/ARRB   **Date Created:** 07/15/97

Meeting Logistics

Date: 07/14/97
Agecny Name: Witnesses/Consultants
Attendees: Homer McMahon, Jeremy Gunn, Doug Horne, Michelle Combs, and Marie Fagnant
Topic: **ARRB Interviewed Homer McMahon**

Summary of the Meeting

ARRB staff followed up its June 9, 1997 telephonic initial assessment interview of Mr. McMahon with an in-depth, in-person interview at Archives II during which the original working notes from NPIC and a surviving photographic briefing board could be used as exhibits to test the recollections of the witness. The interview was audiotaped; therefore, this meeting report will only recount substantive highlights of the interview.   (All statements which read as if they were "facts" are actually Mr. McMahon's recounting of events as he remembers them in 1997.)

Mr. McMahon was manager of the NPIC (National Photo Interpretation Center) color lab in 1963. About two days after the assassination of President Kennedy, but before the funeral took place, a Secret Service agent named "Bill Smith" delivered an amateur film of the assassination to NPIC and requested that color prints be made of frames believed associated with wounding ("frames in which shots occurred"), for purposes of assembling a briefing board. Mr. Smith did not explain who the briefing boards would be for, or who would be briefed. The only persons who witnessed this activity (which McMahon described as an "all night job") were USSS agent Smith, Homer McMahon, and Ben Hunter (McMahon's assistant). Although no materials produced were stamped with classification markings, Smith told McMahon that the subject matter was to be treated as "above top secret;" McMahon said that not even his supervisor was allowed to know what he had worked on, nor was his supervisor allowed to participate. Smith told McMahon that he had personally picked up the film (in an undeveloped condition from the man who exposed it) in Dallas, flown it to Rochester, N.Y. (where it was developed by Kodak), and then flown it down to NPIC in Washington so that enlargements of selected frames could be made on NPIC's state-of-the-art equipment.

After the film (either an unslit original or possibly a duplicate) was viewed more than once on a 16 mm projector in a briefing room at NPIC, the original (a double-8 mm unslit original) was placed in a 10X20X40 precision enlarger, and 5" X 7" format internegatives were made from selected frames. A full-immersion "wet gate" or liquid gate process was used on the original film to reduce refractivity of the film and maximize the optical quality of the internegatives. Subsequently, three each 5" X 7" contact prints were made from the internegatives. He recalled that a minimum of 20, and a maximum of 40 frames were duplicated via internegatives and prints. All prints, internegatives, and scraps were turned over to Bill Smith at the conclusion of the work. Some working notes were created on a yellow legal pad, and they were turned over also. At the conclusion of the work, McMahon said he knew that briefing boards were going to be constructed at NPIC from the prints, but he did not participate in that, and did not know who did. McMahon stated definitively that at no point did NPIC reproduce the assassination movie (the Zapruder film) as a motion picture; all NPIC did was produce internegatives and color prints of selected still frames.

Although the process of selecting which frames depicted events surrounding the wounding of limousine occupants (Kennedy and Connally) was a "joint process," McMahon said his opinion, which was that President Kennedy was shot 6 to 8 times from at least three directions, was ultimately ignored, and the opinion of USSS agent Smith, that there were 3 shots from behind from the Book Depository, ultimately was employed in selecting frames in the movie for reproduction.   At one point he said "you can't fight city hall," and then reminded us that his job was to produce internegatives and photographs, not to do analysis. He said that it was clear that the Secret Service agent had previously viewed the film and already had opinions about which frames depicted woundings.

At one point in the interview, Mr. McMahon described in some detail various health-related memory problems which he claims to suffer from. Details are on the tape.

Toward the end of the interview, McMahon was shown the NPIC working notes and the surviving briefing board (there are four panels), which are both in the JFK Collection in flat # 90A.

NPIC Working Notes: McMahon recognized the half-sized sheet of yellow legal paper containing a handwritten description of briefing board panel contents, and on its reverse side containing a description of the work performed that night and how long each step took, as being written in his own handwriting (and partially in Ben Hunter's). He said that three other full-length yellow legal pad pages of notes (containing three possible 3-shot scenarios, a 16 FPS and 18 FPS timing analysis, and additional timing computations) were not in his handwriting, and were not made by him or previously seen by him.

Briefing Board Panels (4): McMahon looked at the 28 photographs on all four briefing board panels, and said that he had made all of them; he also said that some were missing. I asked him which types of images that he had produced he thought were missing, and he said he thought motorcade images from prior to frame 188 (i.e., earlier in the motorcade, before the limousine disappeared behind the roadsign) were the photographs he produced which were not on the briefing board panels. He said it looked to him like the prints he had produced had been trimmed, i.e., made smaller. END

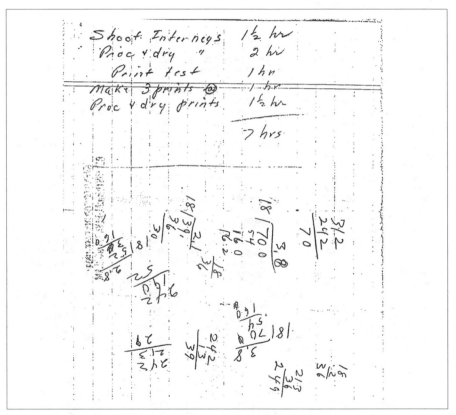

(Undated) NPIC notes related to processing of home movie frames

[Editor's note*: In a memorandum not included here, Douglas Horne reports that, based upon his interviews with Homer McMahon and Bennett Hunter, it became evident that the types of processing mentioned here ("shoot internegs . . . print test . . . make three prints @") refers to the production of still frames,* "with the manufacture of greatly magnified individual 8 mm movie frames as internegatives as the intermediate step in this process" *in preparing three briefing boards with the same 28 still frames apiece rather than to the reproduction of the film as a motion picture (original emphasis).]*

MEETING REPORT

Document's Author: Douglas Horne/ARRB   **Date Created:** 08/14/97

Meeting Logistics

Date:	08/14/97
Agency Name:	CIA
Attendees:	Morgan Bennett ("Ben") Hunter, Homer McMahon (Retired NPIC), Doug Horne(ARRB) , and Jim Goslee (ARRB)
Topic:	**Processing of Zapruder Film by NPIC in 1963 (Revised August 15, 1997)**

Summary of the Meeting

Jim Goslee and I met this date with Bennett Hunter at the National Archives in order to show him the surviving NPIC briefing boards (and associated original NPIC working notes) made from blowups of individual frames from the Zapruder film. When ARRB staff interviewed Mr. Hunter on June 17, 1997, we promised him that we would show him the NPIC briefing boards at Archives II; this meeting was the delivery on that promise. Mr. Hunter brought Homer McMahon, his former supervisor at NPIC (and the person who worked with him on the Zapruder film project) with him to this meeting. [ARRB had previously interviewed Mr. McMahon at Archives II and shown him the briefing boards and original working notes on July 14, 1997.]

Mr. Hunter and Mr. McMahon examined the 4 NPIC briefing board panels (Hunter for the first time, and McMahon for the second time), and the original NPIC working notes, both of which can be found in flat # 90A.

Mr. Hunter confirmed unequivocally that this *was* the material that he and Homer McMahon copied the weekend of the assassination. I asked him if he now recalled making more than 8 prints, and he said no--that he still recalled making only about 8 prints--but reiterated again that the prints on the briefing boards are the same work material/subject matter he and Homer printed that night at NPIC in November 1963.

I asked both men if they still recalled that their event occurred prior to the President's funeral, and they both emphatically said yes. Mr. McMahon said he believes they performed their work the night of the same day the President was assassinated, and Bennett Hunter said he was of the opinion they did their work on the second night after the assassination (i.e., Saturday night).

At one point Mr. McMahon said "I know who [at NPIC] made the briefing boards, but I'm not going to tell you." Later in our meeting I asked him if he would reconsider his decision not to reveal the identity of the person whom he believed made the briefing boards, and he said he would not, explaining that the person may still be "current." He did state that the Secret Service agent took the materials to this person and stayed with the NPIC employee who made the briefing boards during that process.

Both men examined the NPIC working notes again (the originals from flat # 90A), and both agreed that the only page they saw the night of their work was the half-sheet of yellow legal paper, which contains an itemization on its "reverse" side of various steps in the developing process for the internegatives and still prints, and the times required to perform each step. Homer McMahon stated that on the reverse side where the entry "print test" is found, the print test consisted of making one 8" X 10" print, and one 5" X 7" print. (The 8" X 10" print from the print test can be found today in flat # 90A.) McMahon confirmed that on the "front" side of this scrap of paper, he did not recognize the information regarding the briefing board panels as his handwriting, but *did* recognize the arithmetic calculations at the bottom of the page as being in his own hand. Bennett Hunter recognized two words at the top of columns one and two of this page ("print #" and "frame #") as being in his own handwriting, but no others. Both men agreed that none of the long sheets of yellow legal paper which are part of the NPIC working notes were seen or produced by them in November 1963. They both felt, following discussion, that some of the photogrammetry experts at

NPIC in 1963 probably produced those notes regarding the 3 different shot-scenarios, film speed, seconds between shots, etc.

Homer McMahon remembered again that the Secret Service agent stated definitively that the assassination movie was developed in Rochester, and that copies of it were made in Rochester also, and that he personally watched one of those copies projected at least 10 times that night prior to making the internegatives of selected frames. Mr. Hunter agreed that it seemed very likely to him that the copies of the motion picture film would "probably have been made at Rochester," but did not independently recall that himself.

Homer McMahon recalled that Captain Sands was a Navy Captain who was one of the duty officers at NPIC; Bennett Hunter never did recall the name "Bill Smith" (the Secret Service agent remembered by McMahon), even after discussing the matter with McMahon.

Bennett Hunter suggested we contact Dick Stowe (formerly of Kodak) to inquire about possible developing of the Zapruder film at Rochester. He also reiterated (from our first interview with him) that Mr. Steve Clark of the CIA (now Deputy Director of OIT) may know who produced the 3 long yellow legal pages of notes.

Bennett Hunter asked for a copy of our tape of the Homer McMahon interview, and I promised to provide him with one. END

(An edited version of) CE-902.

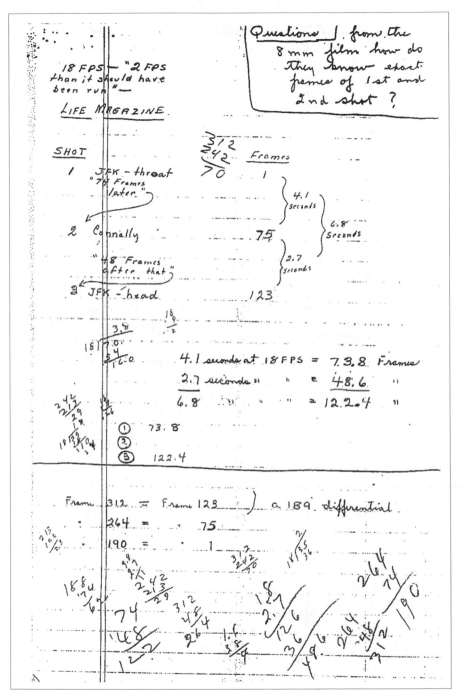

(Undated) NPIC working notes related to a shot sequence analysis published in Life.

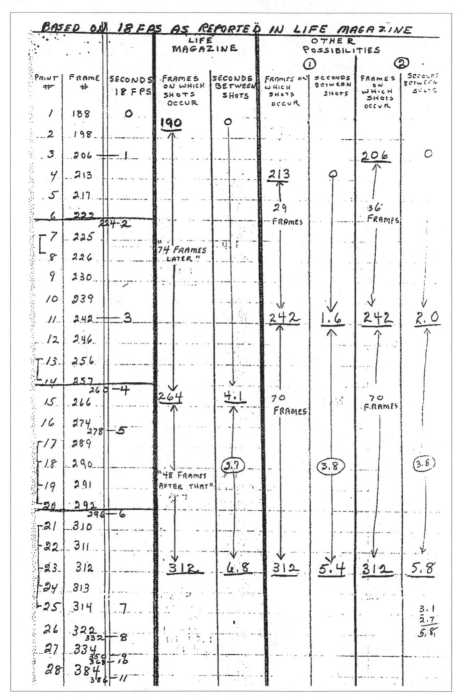

(Undated) NPIC working notes related to a shot sequence analysis published in Life.

Editor's note:

Pedestal as a key to JFK cover-up

Jack White, renowned researcher of JFK photo evidence, stands by the Dealey Plaza pedestal from which Abraham Zapruder presumably filmed the assassination of JFK. White, who has studied the murder since 1963, was a photo consultant to the HSCA in 1977-78. Illustrating some of his most important discoveries, he demonstrates here how this pedestal played a pivotal role in many photos and films of this tragic event. His studies are useful in exposing image alteration by government custodians in their effort to distort the evidence and subvert our ability to discover the truth.

James H. Fetzer, Ph.D.

The Great Zapruder Film Hoax
and other photographic frauds perpetrated by the U.S. government

Jack White

The official story goes like this. At noon on 22 November 1963, Dallas dress manufacturer Abraham Zapruder and his secretary stood on the above pedestal and took the most famous film of all time, the Zapruder movie of the assassination of President John F. Kennedy.

But that position appears to be difficult to defend. On the pages that follow, I will prove:

- that the Zapruder film, the Nix film, and other photos of the murder have been altered;
- that the Zapruder film itself may have not been taken by Abraham Zapruder;
- that a handful of surviving unaltered photographs provide proof of alteration;
- that in the Zapruder film as it exists today, people who were present at the time are no longer present; people who were not present at the time are present; the sun changes its position in the sky and casts false shadows; people remain mysteriously motionless when they should be moving; small people grow tall and tall people shrink; people make impossibly rapid movements; signboards and lampposts reposition themselves; on and on—impressive evidence of alteration that emerges from the extant photographic record.

Let us begin with an unheralded photograph by Charles Bronson, who was standing on another pedestal across the plaza. It was examined by the FBI but was not regarded as evidentially significant, perhaps because it was blurry on its right side and dark on its left. But the FBI ignored details of Zapruder and his secretary, Marilyn Sitzman, which can be brought out by expert photographic techniques. See "The Zapruder Waltz" next.

1

Who shot the alleged Zapruder film of the assassination?

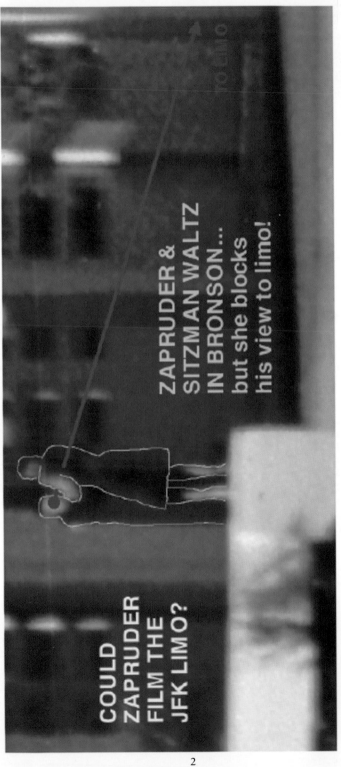

COULD ZAPRUDER FILM THE JFK LIMO?

ZAPRUDER & SITZMAN WALTZ IN BRONSON... but she blocks his view to limo!

to limo

Abraham Zapruder, with his secretary Marilyn Sitzman, allegedly photographed the JFK assassination while standing on a pedestal in Dealey Plaza. But did he? Recently analyzed evidence shows not only that Zapruder could not have filmed "the Z-film", as it is known, but that this film and several other movies and photos of the assassination have been fabricated, altered, or faked to conceal evidence of the crime. Above is an image derived from a slide taken by Charles Bronson. Previously unpublished, it shows that Zapruder's line of sight to the JFK limousine was blocked by Sitzman who seemingly abruptly positions herself east of Zapruder. Moreover, if all these photos were authentic, then, as I have shown below, in a period of less than six secs, Zapruder and Sitzman would have moved completely around the small pedestal in a manner that I call "The Zapruder Waltz". These images display motions that the couple could not have made and make it virtually impossible for Zapruder to have shot the film that bears his name.

The Zapruder Waltz: 2 images below are genuine, 3 are tampered alterations. Which are which?

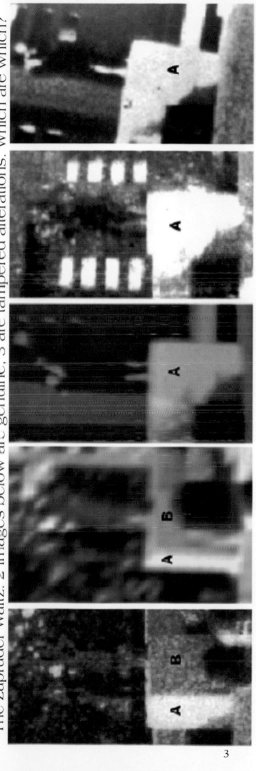

Betzner + .874 sec

From Houston and Elm, Hugh Betzner shot a photo from which this image is cropped. A very short Zapruder stands beside a very tall Sitzman, diagonally across the small rectangle. The "A" side of the cube faces south to Elm Street; the "B" side faces east to the TSBD. A large purse is in front of Sitzman's feet. Zapruder appears about 9 inches shorter than Sitzman. [Altered]

= Willis + .153 sec

From almost the same location as Betzner, Phil Willis shot a photo from which this image is cropped. It seems to show almost the same image only .874 sec later. Though blurry, it is essentially the same pose as Betzner, with a tall Sitzman and a short Zapruder. No camera is clearly evident in either photo. Relatives of Sitzman say she was 5'10" tall. Zapruder relatives say he was also 5'10" tall. [Altered]

= Bronson + 4.48 sec

From a pedestal at Houston and Main, Charles Bronson shot the slide from which this image is cropped. Note that side "A" of the pedestal faces directly toward him. Only .153 sec after the Willis photo, Sitzman has whirled around to the front of the pedestal, Zapruder being now to the rear. Her purse is now behind her feet and her back is to the motorcade. She wears a dark dress with light sleeves. [Genuine]

= Moorman + .17 sec

From the opposite side of Elm Street, Mary Moorman shot a Polaroid photo from which this image is cropped. The hatless, short Zapruder has the camera about a foot from his face and pointed toward the ground. In 4.48 secs, short Zapruder has changed positions with tall Sitzman: The purse is now to the front of the pedestal. Zapruder's knees sag. From her lower viewpoint, Moorman captures sky through the pergola windows. [Genuine]

= Nix (5.67 secs.)

From the sidewalk just below Bronson, Orville Nix shot a movie from which this frame has been taken. From a line of sight like Moorman's, it clearly shows a taller Zapruder with hat and camera. In only .17 sec, Zapruder and Sitzman have changed positions entirely. Compare this view with Bronson. The viewpoint is the same, but positions are reversed. In 5.67 secs, the couple waltzed around the pedestal. [Altered]

3

The Street People and the Silver Trailer Van "Magic Act"

From his pedestal, Zapruder filmed some magic acts that rival David Copperfield in their legerdemain. Along the north curb of Elm, the Z-film shows a group of spectators who stand single-file at the curb, almost totally motionless for about a minute without changing their positions. They are seen in the first 131 frames of the film as the 3 lead motorcycles turn, the lead police car rounds the corner and leaves the visual field, and the JFK limo suddenly appears well-down Elm. Another group of Street People are seen standing in the Elm crosswalk at the intersection of Elm and Houston. All of them remain virtually motionless. Moreover, they all appear to be Caucasian, although other photos show many blacks in both of these groups.

I decided to compare Zapruder frames like the above to other photos taken of the same scene at the same time. At the left is a photo by AP photographer James Altgens from the corner of Main and Houston. At the right is a photo taken by Jim Towner from the corner of Elm and Houston. As you can see from the comparisons below, *none* of the persons in the Elm crosswalk in Zapruder can be seen in Altgens. And the Silver Trailer Van so prominent in Towner is not conspicuous in Zapruder.

4

A large silver trailer van is seen in Towner (above), just behind a white laundry truck. In Zapruder (below), the laundry truck is seen through tree leaves, but the silver trailer van is not visible behind it. In my opinion, the bright reflectivity of the aluminum should have made the van obvious even in shadows. The Towner photo, which clearly shows both the laundry truck and the large trailer van, is unaltered. The Zapruder film shows the laundry truck but not the van. Why?

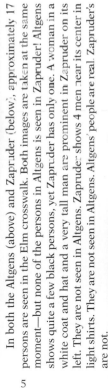

In both the Altgens (above) and Zapruder (below), approximately 17 persons are seen in the Elm crosswalk. Both images are taken at the same moment—but none of the persons in Altgens is seen in Zapruder! Altgens shows quite a few black persons, yet Zapruder has only one. A woman in a white coat and hat and a very tall man are prominent in Zapruder on its left. They are not seen in Altgens. Zapruder shows 4 men near its center in light shirts. They are not seen in Altgens. Altgens' people are real. Zapruder's are not.

5

Moorman Polaroid photo contains absolute proof of Zapruder film tampering

Because it was an instant photo that was copied and widely published within hours of the assassination, the Moorman Polaroid is guaranteed to be an authentic image. In 1982, I photographically reproduced a high-quality copy from the Moorman, which yielded a recognizable image of an apparent rifleman in a police uniform behind the wooden fence on the grassy knoll. Here is a hand-tinted color version of the Polaroid. It shows this person, dubbed "Badgeman", and two other persons: a soldier named Gordon Arnold, who was film-ing the motorcade from the knoll, and another man behind the fence wearing a T-shirt and a construc-tion helmet. A billow of smoke obscures the chin and rifle of Badgeman. It was been ascertained that the Moorman was taken at about the very same time as Zapruder frame 315, assuming the Z-film is genuine. Then someone—possibly Badgeman—fired his shot a split second before frame 313, which records the head shot. But the Z-film does not appear to be genuine.

Since the Moorman is genuine, I decided to use it as a control to test the authentic-ity of the Zapruder film. To do this, it was essential to establish the exact position where she stood for the correct line-of-sight exposed in the image. I discovered a point within the photo that aligned 2 widely disparate points that established that unique line-of-sight. At the left is a graphic image of the points of reference I aligned, which are easily located in the plaza. Two edges of the window openings in the rear of the paragola (A and B) in the photo exactly coincide with the top and south edge of the pedestal (C and D). As you can see, the angles AB and CD form a large cross (+), which is readily perceived across Elm where Moorman stood to take her picture.

Where was Mary standing when she took the photo?

Both Mary Moorman and her friend Jean Hill have always cc that they stepped off the curb into the street to take this photo. (Jean was processing the film as Mary shot the pictures.) This puzzled me, since the Zapruder film shows them on the grass about 2 feet south of the curb. Either Mary and Jean are wrong, or the Zapruder film is wrong. At the right, we seen Jean (in the red coat) and Mary at the time the photo was taken as seen from Zapruder's pedestal. They are obviously on the grass. From the line-of-sight internal to the photo, it is possible to ascertain whether Mary was on the grass or standing in the street, as she and Jean have claimed.

On the grass

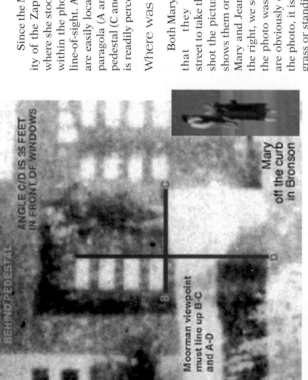

ANGLE A/B IS 54 FEET BEHIND PEDESTAL

ANGLE C/D IS 35 FEET IN FRONT OF WINDOWS

Moorman viewpoint must line up B-C and A-D

Mary off the curb in Bronson

Mary and Jean were not on the grass; therefore, the Zapruder film is faked

I knew that Mary was approximately 5'2" tall. I prepared a stake to drive into the turf to represent Mary as seen in the Z-film. I went to Dealey Plaza with stake, hammer, tape measure, and camera to locate her position and the camera's line-of-sight. My experiment is recorded below.

Left: Orange cross locates Moorman line of sight on my stake, only 44.5" above the grass.

Below: Multiple overlay of 3 photos to scale shows actual height and location of Moorman lens (A) and Zapruder's depiction (Z) in relation to the limo in frame 312. Note that Zapruder's Mary is about 1 foot too high and 6 feet too far east to be on the line-of-sight of her photo.

Right: Street surface just off the curb is about 1 foot lower than position on the grass, proving that Mary stepped off the curb to take the photo. Thus, the Z-film is faked

Street about 12 inches lower than where Moorman was standing.

Moorman height 62"

Lens line of sight

Lens height is 44.5 inches from Moorman feet

Moorman standing 2 feet from curb

Z-312 overlaid over limo photo in reconstruction location, with red dot marking Moorman lens location.

This also showed that in Zapruder, Mary and the limo are about 6 feet too far east.

Photo overlay of actual lens location which I found to be about a foot lower.

LENS HEIGHTS

312

Z   A

7

The Nix film, Arnold film, and Oliver film: more destruction of photo evidence

The Zapruder film was not the only film altered or destroyed as evidence. Five other photographers with 8mm movie cameras filmed part or all of the Elm Street murder: In addition to Abraham Zapruder on the pedestal, there were Marie Muchmore from the Houston Street monument, Orville Nix from the sidewalk at Main and Houston, Charles Bronson on a pedestal just above Nix, Beverly Oliver on the grassy infield on the south side of Elm, and Gordon Arnold on the grassy knoll just southwest of Zapruder's pedestal.

A Nix frame taken at almost the same instant as the Moorman frame at left.

A Muchmore frame showing Mary and Jean Hill, as Clint Hill sprints to the JFK limo.

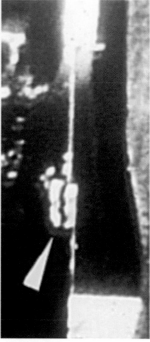

OLIVER

Beverly Oliver is seen in Muchmore filming the limo. The FBI confiscated her film.

Charles Bronson shot this slide, then switched to his movie camera for a very brief film.

The Nix film (2 frames below) is very crudely retouched. Yellow pointers indicate the edge of an area blacked-in. The (disputed) image of a possible shooter behind the top of a car also appears to be added.

Soldier Gordon Arnold, using his mother's new 8mm camera, planned to film the motorcade from atop the Triple Underpass, but a man in a suit stopped him. He found a spot at the top of the grassy knoll behind the concrete wall, which had a good view, and began to film as the limo appeared. His perspective was similar to Abraham Zapruder's. Almost immediately after the shots, one of which passed by his ear, a crying "policeman" with dirty fingernails came from behind the fence and, at gunpoint, confiscated his film.

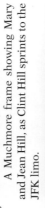

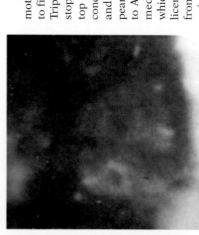

In a late Nix frame, this area is still blacked in, but the person behind the car has now disappeared and "windows" apparently from a railway passenger car have been added.

A documentary film maker tried to convince Beverly Oliver that the frame at left below is a frame from her confiscated film and that it shows one of the assassins leaning on the car top. This issue was addressed by the HSCA in 1978, which drew the conclusion that the image was not that of a person. My personal opinion is that it is an artifact of other retouching, which blacked in other areas at the top of the knoll.

Known to be Nix frame

Said to be Oliver frrame

Blue sky should be visible in Nix

Nix frames (lower left) show black sky behind tree ard pergola. All other photos of this area show blue sky through the tree leaves and behind the pergola. What was being hidden?

The Stemmons sign in Zapruder makes dramatic changes in size and location

This base photo was taken from the Zapruder pedestal on Monday after the assassination by the DPD. I decided to test Z-frame overlays against it.

I have superimposed frame Z-34 and Z-194 over the base photo, which was taken by the Dallas police. All are to the exact same scale, as noted in the box to the left. Z-34 fits exactly. Z-194 shows the dramatic extent of enlargement of features of the photo. The Stemmons sign is now much bigger and in a different location. Enlargement increases gradually to a maximum with respect to background features as shown below.

1. Thornton sign aligns in both Z-34 and DPD photo.
2. Lamppost aligns in both photos.
3. Background building aligns in both photos.
4. Purse & Company building aligns in both photos.
5. Records Building aligns in both Z-34 and background.
6. In Z-194, it is scaled exactly the same as in Z-34; yet hole in wall is aligned on west end, but is too long on the opposite end, indicating that Z-194 has been enlarged.

Yellow curb strips in "the kill zone" provide an exact scale for Z frame match

The Z-film shows several short stripes of yellow paint on the south curb of Elm. Years later, remnants of the stripes still identify their location. I went to the plaza and taped yellow poster board on the curb to exactly coincide with these stripes. I then photographed them from the Zapruder pedestal (photo at lower left, with Z-357 overlaid) so that the curb strip is overlaid with the same size and position. With the stripe exactly the same in both images, it is obvious that the green infield grass in the Z-frame extends well across Main Street (green lines). James Altgens standing at the curb is also noticeably larger than he should be. The background from the curb upward has been greatly enlarged through magnification.

The following page displays another illustration of this process of magnification, which makes Toni Foster, the young lady running across the grass, appear to be nearly 7' tall, when she was actually only 5'2" tall. This specific editing may have been intended to remove indications of the limo stop reported by many eyewitnesses.

Toni Foster
Giant Running
Woman

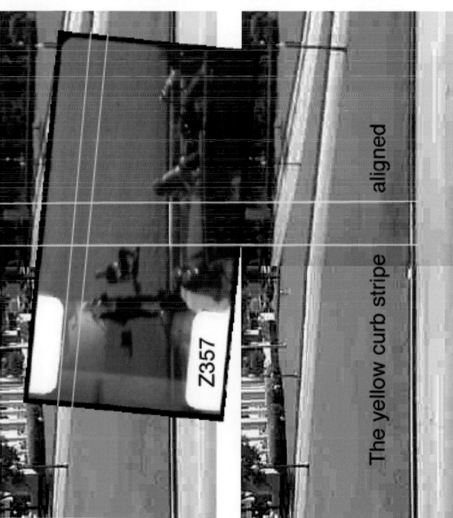

Z357

The yellow curb stripe   aligned

People grow, people shrink, people appear, people disappear in Zapruder's film

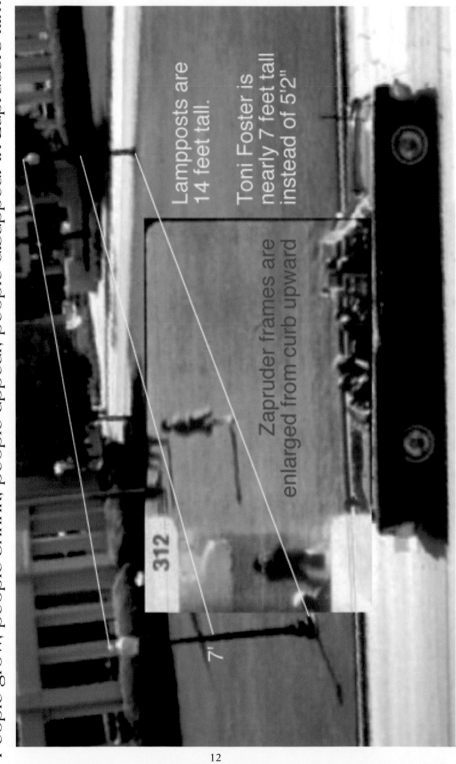

Lampposts are 14 feet tall.

Toni Foster is nearly 7 feet tall instead of 5'2"

Zapruder frames are enlarged from curb upward

312

7'

Above. Toni Foster, 5'2" tall, is seen running across the plaza grass, as she appears in several Z-frames. Prior to her identification, she was known only as "Runningwoman". When Z-312 is overlaid in relation to her position, she is (purely coincidentally) exactly between 2 lampposts, which are 14' high. Her height in the film thus has to be nearly 7'.

Zapruder makes this man disappear on the next page

Pickupman

Earlier I showed how the group of people (left) in the Elm-Houston crosswalk do not correspond to the same group photographed at the same time by Altgens. It seems farfetched to imagine that a new group would appear and the old group disappear merely by this change in perspective. This appears inexplicable if the photos are authentic.

Z-233 (lower left) shows a group of persons on the sidewalk beyond a row of nine apertures in the wall. In November 1999, while taking photos from the pedestal, I took a photo of the same area. Here it and the Z-frame are to the same scale. I noticed that my photo included a row of 3 parking meters along the curb, which are normally about 5' high. Here they are about even with the tops of parked cars. In the Zapruder frame, the group of about 6 persons is shorter than the orange line demarcating the tops of the meters, which means they are all shorter than 5' tall. Coupled with the substitution of people in the Elm crosswalk, many of the spectators along the motorcade route as shown in "the Zapruder film" must be fabrications, whose precise purpose is obscure.

The short Parking Meter People

Orange lines indicate the height of the parking meters along the Houston Street curb.

z404

z411

Pickupman appears, truck changes in Cancellare

Within 20 secs of the shooting, Frank Cancellare of *Life* magazine took the above photo. Note the Newmans are still on the ground. Circled is a pickup truck on Commerce Street. When enlarged, we see the truck seems to have a man with his left hand on some other cargo in its truckbed. Compare the enhancement (below) that shows other cargo in the truckbed. It is definitely an uncovered truckbed with a man and some cargo. The man is much too short to be standing in the street. When compared to Z-404 and Z-411 just 20 secs earlier (right), however, the truck has a covered bed, no cargo, and no man in back.

Z-404 and Z-411 are only about 2/5 sec apart. In that brief time span:

A. a lamppost shadow appears;
B. an open truckbed is covered;
C. the truckbed gains a bright side rail;
D. a large truck suddenly appears, moving in the next lane. In Cancellare, the truck can be seen 2 car lengths farther east, enough for about 20 secs to have lapsed.

Contrast enhancement showing large box behind truck cab and something in the rear, which Pickupman holds.

Zapruder makes sun move backward in the sky!

Many shadows in the Z-film are suspect. After checking with a London astronomer for accuracy, I took the photo of the same lamppost in Z-414 (inset below) at 12:30 P.M. on 11-22-99. It yields an image from the Zapruder pedestal that is 113 degrees from the Main Street curb. The shadow of the same lamppost in the same location in Z-414 is 133 degrees from the same curb. If this Z-frame is a true photo of a true shadow, then it had to have been taken about 30 minutes earlier, when the sun was further east, to account for this 20 degree discrepancy, suggesting an earlier film shoot.

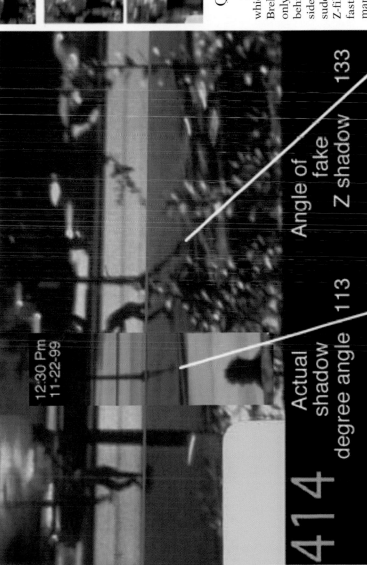

12:30 Pm
11-22-99

414

Actual shadow degree angle 113

Angle of fake Z shadow 133

Quick Brehm and son

Robin DeLoria make this comparison, which shows that, in only 1 sec, Charles Brehm claps his hands 4 times—and in only 4 frames. Brehm's son appears from behind his dad to a position standing beside him. This is only one of example of sudden movements by many people in the Z-film that appear to occur impossibly fast. Other researchers have identified many others.

In Zapruder and Nix, people come and people go

Zapruder

Nix enlarged

369

Nix

5-year old Jeff Franzen (1) was taken to see the motorcade by his father (2) and his mother (3), just as Z-369 portrays them (top left). Next to the Franzen family stands an unidentified man (4), all by himself. No one else is seen in this frame. Notice that Mrs. Franzen is holding her husband's left hand, while he has his right hand atop Jeff's head. The blond Mrs. Franzen has a purse at her left elbow and wears a tight-fitting skirt. The unidentified man has on dark pants and a light sweater. I located a good Nix frame taken at almost the same instant (bottom). The positions of Jackie and of Clint Hill are very similar. In the enlarged inset (top right), Mr. Franzen still has his right hand on Jeff's head, but Mrs. Franzen has completely disappeared. The unidentified man is still in position. Now a woman companion (5) has materialized and is embracing his left shoulder. She seems to be wearing an orange headscarf and a black topcoat, which flares at the bottom. Nobody like this woman is seen anywhere in Zapruder. And what has happened to Mrs. Franzen? Nix is wrong or Zapruder is wrong: they can't both be right.

When the Zapruder film was first published in *The Warren Report* (1964), it was taken to be the definitive depiction of what happened and a precise clock of the assassination. With the passage of time, more and more anomalies have been discovered. As I have shown on these pages, we now know something we didn't know then: the film is a fake.

15 May 2000

16

Paradoxes of the JFK Assassination:
The Zapruder Film Controversy

David W. Mantik, M.D., Ph.D.

[*Editor's note*: In this essay, David W. Mantik, M.D., Ph.D., who has undertaken the most extensive and detailed studies of its internal content and other properties—including comparisons of the film to other copies, of the film to other photographs and films, and of the film to eyewitness reports—in the history of the study of the assassination of JFK, provides a framework for understanding and exploring the questions raised by the lack of authenticity of the film, which has been extensively edited using highly sophisticated techniques. Those who wish to pursue this issue in greater detail should see the studies on this topic in *Assassination Science* (1998), which includes Mantik's transformational work.]

> *It is misleading to claim that scientific advances and scholarly experiments can cause all photo fakes to be unmasked. Questions about authenticity remain. Many photos that once were considered genuine have recently been determined to be faked. The authenticity of some is still being debated. . . .*
>
> —Dino Brugioni

A Visit to the South: Does History Repeat?

A regal couple traveled to the south of their own realm where they were intensely disliked by many. They were feted at a state dinner. An open motorcade was held for them in the morning. Surprisingly, the crowds were large and friendly. Suddenly, a bomb was thrown at them. It exploded behind the car and several were injured. The motorcade stopped momentarily, and then continued on to the Town Hall. After a brief reception there, the husband decided to visit the hospital to see those who had been injured. Unfortunately, the motorcade took the wrong route so the governor shouted at the driver to stop and turn around. As soon as the car stopped, the assassin, who stood within ten feet, fired several shots, one striking the husband and one the wife. The royal couple remained frozen and upright. Then the car leaped forward and the wife plunged backward against her husband. Both were soon dead. The date was Sunday, 28 June 1914.

It was the feast of St. Vitus, a Serbian national holiday that celebrated two major Serbian battles—symbols of Serbian independence. The city was Sarajevo, Bosnia. The husband was Archduke Franz Ferdinand, heir to the Austrian throne. The assassin was a high school student, Gavrilo Princip, a Bosnian conspirator who lost his arm in the resulting melee and who died a few years later of TB. His name meant "Bringer of Tidings." This event precipitated World War I.

Based on the sources cited below, the conspiracy was organized in Belgrade by the Black Hand with the connivance of Serbs in position of power—army officers and government officials, including frontier authorities. The Austro-Hungarian government suspected this and the Austrian authorities found evidence to prove most of this although they knew nothing of the Black Hand and mistakenly suspected the Narodna Obrana. In 1925 a Serbian politician, Jovanovich, who had been Minister of Education in the Serbian Cabinet, casually mentioned that the Cabinet knew of the plot and discussed it in May or early June. He recalled details of its organization. Although a colleague denied this, his denials were unsupported and Jovanovich's story was probably true. [*Author's note*: Sources included (1) Francis Whiting Halsey, *The Literary Digest: History of the World War* (1919), (2) Emil Ludwig, *July 1914* (1929), (3) S.L.A. Marshall, *The American Heritage History of World War I* (1964), (4) Laurence Lafore, *The Long Fuse: An Interpretation of the Origins of World War I* (1965), and (5) Lee Davis, *Assassination: 20 Assassinations That Changed History* (1993).]

Does History Repeat? Some Analogies

The JFK and Ferdinand assassinations contain remarkable similarities; in both cases, the following statements can be made.

- The southern region was disaffected with the central government.
- The wife accompanied her husband.
- Murder occurred during a motorcade.
- Security was limited during the motorcade, despite rumors of possible assassination attempts. Ferdinand ridiculed an offer from Count Harrach to stand on the left footboard beside him. In Sarajevo, as in Dealey Plaza, the streets were unguarded.
- The motorcade stopped momentarily after the first loud sound and after the governor's shout.
- The governor turned around to look at the victim after the initial shooting.
- The fatal shot occurred either at or very close to the time that the vehicle stopped.
- Two or three shots were usually reported.
- The victim sat erect when the fatal shot hit.
- Death followed quickly.
- Evidence of a government conspiracy later emerged.
- Eyewitnesses were the source of the early reports.

My purpose in presenting this historical summary is not simply to note the existence of a conspiracy—moreover a probable government conspiracy in both cases—nor merely to draw engaging historical analogies, but, more importantly, to emphasize how the Zapruder film has affected our view of the JFK murder, in a manner that photography could not do for the Sarajevo assassination.

[*Author's note*: To avoid confusion between the out-of-camera original film and the current film in the Archives—which are not identical, in my view—I shall use the term "extant" to describe the film currently held by the Archives.]

Without the Zapruder film, we would be forced to rely on the reports of eyewitnesses. Their descriptions have been included in the above summary—even when they disagreed with the Zapruder film. For example, witnesses who described the movement of the limousine almost uniformly recalled a limousine stop (albeit a very brief one) in Dealey Plaza—in direct contradiction to the extant Zapruder film. And those who described the position of JFK's head at the instant of the final headshot almost always reported that he was erect—also in distinct disagreement with the extant film. This particular issue has previously been discussed in some detail (*Assassination Science* 1998, pp. 273-274 and pp. 286-292).

The witnesses also disagree sharply with the extant film regarding the movement of JFK's head. They describe a slumping forward (probably on two successive occasions), including a *forward* slump immediately after the fatal headshot, the same moment when the film shows a violent *backward* snap of the head. It is also noteworthy that an early observer of the film (Zapruder's partner, Erwin Swartz) failed to describe a head snap, and that both Dan Rather and Deke DeLoach (Cartha DeLoach, *Hoover's FBI: The Inside Story by Hoover's Trusted Lieutenant* 1995, p. 139) describe JFK going *forward* after the fatal head shot. DeLoach describes seeing the film on the evening of the assassination and Rather saw it within several days. None of these three described what is seen on the extant film—the head snap, which is at once both obvious and stunning.

If the Zapruder film is authentic, and yet displays such profound disagreement with the eyewitnesses (who speak with almost one voice), then deeply troubling questions arise about any historical event not recorded by a motion picture camera—even in those cases in which the eyewitnesses agree. If such radical cynicism about historical events is justified, then all historians should be put on notice that almost nothing in history can be certain—since eyewitnesses, no matter how high their level of agreement, would be essentially useless.

By way of illustration, without a confirmatory movie film of the Sarajevo assassination, we could not be certain how many shots were fired, what the governor did or said during the motorcade, where the victims were struck by bullets, or even what route was taken. Nevertheless, most of this information is recorded—and recorded consistently—in the early news bulletins (see the sources cited above) even though there are no photographs. The early newspaper articles are also in surprising agreement about the day's events. This agreement is sustained in subsequent books over a long time interval; those cited above range from 1919 to 1993.

If the extant Zapruder film is authentic—and the witnesses therefore so uniformly wrong—we ought to seriously doubt these Sarajevo witnesses, and all of the accounts based on them. If we adopted this extreme distrust of eyewitnesses, then all historical events before 1888 (Edison's Kinetograph) must be inherently not just unreliable but, in fact, flagrantly unreliable. Historians have rarely espoused such radical cynicism about what can be known (Edward Hallett Carr, *What is History? The George Macaulay Trevelyan Lectures* 1965, pp. 3-35). Although history is filled with cases in which the facts are uncertain, this very uncertainty, especially when the facts are critical, is usually acknowledged explicitly by historians rather than silently concealed.

Although historians do sometimes disagree vigorously about the facts, such as the murder of Adolph Hitler by his own staff (Hugh Thomas, *The Murder of Adolph Hitler: The Truth about the Bodies in the Bunker* 1995), often the facts are not in dispute and yet there is disagreement about the interpretation of events. Henry Steele Commager (*The Nature and the Study of History* 1965, pp. 59-60) has described how views of Southern reconstruction changed dramatically between the early twentieth century and the post World War II era, becoming less harsh in the latter period. Likewise, C. Vann Woodward, former Sterling Professor of History at Yale, has concluded (*Thinking Back: The Perils of Writing History* 1986, p. 112): "I doubt that revisionist scholarship has been more active in any field of American or Southern history than it has in Reconstruction historiography during the last generation."

Another example in which the facts are quite clear but the interpretation is in some doubt is the death of Meriwether Lewis: was he robbed and murdered as he slept alone in a cabin in central Tennessee while en route to Monticello? Or did he shoot himself during a severe depression (perhaps while deranged after weeks of serious drinking), once in the head and once in the chest, slash himself with his razor, and then [tongue-in-cheek] steal his own gold watch and money? (Willard Sterne Randall, *Thomas Jefferson, A Life* 1993, p. 571.)

Advocates of Zapruder film authenticity seem oblivious to the logic of their own views. By ignoring the surprising agreement (actually, near unanimity) of the JFK witnesses, they must logically maintain an extremely pessimistic view of what can be known in history, a view not commonly embraced by professional historians (Robin Winks, editor, *The Historian as Detective: Essays on Evidence* 1968; David Hackett Fischer, *Historians' Fallacies: Toward a Logic of Historical Thought* 1970).

In fact, this radical distrust of eyewitnesses—even when they strongly agree—is so extreme that it frankly borders on historical nihilism. Such a view is close to that of the logical positivist, Ayer, who wondered (A. J. Ayer, *Philosophical Essays* 1965, p. 168): ". . . whether we have sufficient ground for accepting any statement at all about the past, whether we are even justified in our belief that there has been a past." During his lifetime, Ayer won rather few followers; even fewer remain today (Ernst Breisach, *Historiography* 1983, p. 331).

[*Editor's note*: Frames of the Zapruder film may be viewed in books such as (1) Robert Groden, *The Killing of a President* (1993), (2) Richard Trask, *Pictures of the Pain* (1994), (3) Noel Twyman, *Bloody Treason* (1997), and (4) Stewart Galanor, *Cover-Up* (1998).]

Assassination Records Review Board (ARRB)

As a result of Oliver Stone's movie, *JFK*, the Assassination Records Review Board (ARRB) was established by Congress in 1992 and was signed into law by George Bush on 26 October 1992. Board members were nominated by Bill Clinton by September 1993 and sworn in on 11 April 1994. Congress finally appropriated funds by 1 October 1994. The ARRB submitted its final report on 30 September 1998 (*Final Report of the Assassination Records Review Board*, 1998).

Due to the efforts of the ARRB, several controversial issues related to the Zapruder film have been resolved, or at least partially resolved. The work of Roland Zavada, a retired Kodak engineer with special expertise in film production (who was re-hired by Kodak to perform work for the ARRB), has contributed to several new insights.

The dark intersprocket area. When the movie is projected the image between the sprocket holes is not seen on the screen. The image in this intersprocket area can, however, be examined manually, frame-by-frame. Much of this area is then seen to be darker than the central (projected) image, particularly after about Z-235. Zavada shot film through several cameras of the same model as Zapruder's and discovered that a dark region was commonly seen over most of this intersprocket area. This dark intersprocket area occurred repeatedly with several cameras and was similar to Zapruder frames after about Z-235. Independently, Brian Edwards and Phil Giuliano performed similar simulations with identical model Bell & Howell cameras in Dealey Plaza. They have shared their films with me and frame-by-frame analysis has shown similar results in these films. (Zapruder used a Bell & Howell Model 414 PD Director Series movie camera; P = power zoom; D = dual electric eye.)

Zavada concluded that the claw was responsible for this dark intersprocket area. The claw advances the film, frame by frame. It moves downward when the shutter is closed, then moves upward when the shutter is open; during this exposure the claw casts a partial shadow on the intersprocket area, enough to cause the darkening seen in the intersprocket images. Although this explanation has been touted by some as proof, in and of itself, of authenticity, in fact, such an image could persist even after film alteration. This could occur, for example, if the original frames had first been magnified and then re-shot through the same camera. If the new frames had been magnified enough, the intersprocket area could be entirely eliminated— by excluding it from the captured image of the new film. Of course, all of the new frames would be magnified, but if this were done in a continuous manner it would be difficult to detect such uniform magnification. Furthermore, if all of the new frames had been shot through the same camera, then the resulting intersprocket images would again exhibit a dark area— just like the initial generation. (Oddly enough, Zapruder's camera was not returned to him from the FBI until several months after the assassination. Is it possible that it was used in the process of alteration?)

Or, if a different camera had copied the identical field of view but did not itself produce a claw shadow, then the new film would still exhibit a dark area in the intersprocket area (from the first generation film). This could be achieved, for example, by manual copying in a single frame mode (each frame would be advanced manually), in which case a claw would not be necessary. A more detailed discussion of this problem, including useful images, may be found at Anthony Marsh's web site: www.boston.quik.com/amarsh/.

In any case, the dark area in the intersprocket image need not be a direct byproduct of reframing; the claw movement most likely causes it. What is less clear though is why this dark area is difficult to see in frames before about Z-235. Its absence is especially obvious in the *Life* issue of 25 November 1966. Zavada did not address this paradox.

The ghost image inferior to the upper sprocket hole. In frames beginning at about Z-310, in the upper one third of the intersprocket area, there is a superimposed image of the front portion of a motorcycle. Why such a superposition occurs only at the time of the fatal head shot and nowhere else is peculiar. Zavada examined this image, found that it could be simulated in his laboratory experiments, and concluded that it was a double exposure from an adjacent frame. For example, during exposure of the (arbitrary) first frame, the lower portion of the field of view for that frame extends into the upper portion of the second (still unexposed) frame. This occurs because a hole in the aperture plate (for the claw mechanism) permits light to shine onto a small portion of the *second frame*. Only when the shutter is again opened is the full image for the second frame exposed.

However, this ghost image (from the first frame) can only be seen when the primary image in the second frame is dark. If the primary image in the second frame is too light the ghost image is difficult to detect against such a light background. Such double exposures were also seen in the Edwards and Giuliano films; often these ghost images did not display discrete objects but were simply lighter patches with well-defined borders. This area of overlap was reproduced at about the same site and with approximately the same size as the ghost images seen in the Zapruder film, thus confirming Zavada's hypothesis.

Although Zavada seemed satisfied with his explanation, it still appears to fall short of full clarification. Zavada repeatedly advised us that his primary task was to address technical issues. It was not his mandate to analyze the actual content of the images, e.g., he did not ask whether animation specialists had been at work on certain frames, or whether the content of one frame was consistent with that of other frames.

Another line of evidence is the quality of the central image in the (arbitrary) first frame compared to the ghost image in the second frame. According to Zavada, they were formed at the same instant, and should therefore display similar features. But this is not always the case: e.g., the central image in Z-319 is obviously blurred, whereas the ghost image in Z-320 is distinctly sharper. Since both images were formed at the same instant, according to Zavada, why do they show such different tracking characteristics? Again, Zavada offered no explanation.

Motorcycle fender movement. I have previously summarized (Fetzer 1998, p. 312) how the motorcycle fender in the intersprocket image bounces up and down in a highly erratic fashion between Z-312 and Z-331. Using an EKG caliper, I measured from the top of the fender to the sprocket hole and displayed this data in a table. An even more remarkable impression is possible by means of the CD version of the Z film, as prepared by MPI. By zooming in on this intersprocket area while the film is running, the remarkably artificial movements can be appreciated by the human eye.

Occasional doubled images. Poor tracking of a moving vehicle within a single frame can result in image doubling of background objects such a pedestrians. Such poor tracking also causes blurring of the moving vehicle. Frames immediately before and after such an event usually do not display such image doubling, so the tracking error must be very brief. Although none of Zavada's shots on Elm Street produced a double image,[1] such events were occasionally seen in the simulated films of Edwards and Giuliano.

Limousine magnification and the grassy background opposite Zapruder. The Edwards and Giuliano simulations show limousine magnifications similar to the Zapruder film at about Z-313, i.e., the length of the limousine occupies about the same fraction of the entire frame width in both cases. These simulations also suggest that Main St. (beyond the top of these frames) probably lies outside the field of view—as is also the case in the Zapruder film. Whether the magnification in the Zapruder film changes (it should not) between the Stemmons freeway sign and the fatal head shot, however, may need further study.

It is also possible that some frames in the interval between the sign and Z-313 are composites—i.e., normal foreground magnification and increased background magnification. In some of these frames there is little in the background to help decide this question. This question recurs below; Moorman's location in the Zapruder film, in particular, is most likely due to a composite image.

The Legal Status of Photographic Evidence

Milicent Cranor reminds us that, because of the possibilities of photographic tampering, eyewitnesses have legal priority over photographic evidence (*Assassination Science* 1998, p. 265). Such evidence cannot be accepted in court until eyewitnesses have vouched for it (*McCormick on Evidence*, 3rd ed., 1984, Section 214). Nonetheless, scores of lawyers in past government investigations of the JFK murder chose to ignore this rule. Eyewitnesses were regularly accused of seeing or hearing events that (supposedly) could not be true because they were inconsistent with the official conclusions. A search throughout the many volumes of the Warren Commission and the House Select Committee on Assassinations (HSCA) reveals no reference to this fundamental principle.

The Chief Arguments for Authenticity

The chain of possession. Josiah Thompson summarized this argument during a debate at the JFK Lancer Conference in November 1998. [*Editor's note:* His talk was later reprinted as "Why the Zapruder Film *Is* Authentic," *JFK Deep Politics Quarterly* (April 1999).] Thompson's argument is that the film was always accounted for and could not have journeyed anywhere for alteration.

Recent releases by the ARRB, however, suggest otherwise. The Homer McMahon interviews, in particular, suggest a broken chain of possession. [*Editor's note:* See the NPIC reports by Douglas Horne elsewhere in this volume.] McMahon was head of the color lab at the National Photographic Interpretation Center (NPIC) in 1963. He describes receiving the film (without a doubt, the Zapruder film) from a Secret Service agent who had flown it to Rochester for development before bringing it to the NPIC. McMahon's recollections were corroborated by one of his assistants, Bennett Hunter, who was also interviewed by the ARRB.

As best these two could recall, they received the film on the weekend immediately after the assassination (almost certainly before the funeral). McMahon recalls seeing the film projected at least 10 times that night. It was his opinion, based on this viewing, that JFK was shot 6 to 8 times from at least three directions, but the Secret Service agent told McMahon that there were just three shots, and that these all came from the Book Depository. McMahon and his assistant were told to keep their work secret and were prohibited even from telling their supervisors (who were not present).

The chain of possession argument relies critically on the memories of those who handled the film that day. Those skeptics who disparage the recollections of the Dealey Plaza witnesses nonetheless insist that the memories of the film handlers that day were flawless. Why those who handled the film that day can be trusted, while those who witnessed the assassination are not credible, is known only to disciples of film authenticity. Besides this reliance on the memory of the film handlers, however, the chain of evidence argument relies on sworn affidavits—to the effect that only three copies of the film were made at the Jamieson laboratory on 22 November 1963.

For the credibility of these affidavits[2] ultimate reliance must be placed on human honesty—there is no movie film that documents the preparation of only three copies of the film. How do we know that the affidavits were honest, or even that the signatories were actually in a position to witness everything they claimed to see? Is it even possible that the affidavits were deliberately prepared—possibly at the suggestion of the Secret Service—merely to cover up the existence of additional copies? Paul Rothermel, head of security for H. L. Hunt (Twyman 1997, p. 552; Harrison Livingstone, *Killing the Truth* 1993, p. 522 and p. 533) has long claimed that he received a copy of the film on the day of the assassination.

More recently, William Reymond, a French journalist, claims to have seen a different film in France, which may be either Hunt's copy or a descendant of it. Was the original switched at the Jamieson laboratory for a copy and then given to the Secret Service for transportation to Rochester that same evening? Was Zapruder merely given a copy when he thought he had the original? If so, how would he have known the difference? The fact is that no documentary evidence, nor anyone's memory, can settle a question of this nature.

My purpose here is merely to emphasize that the chain of possession argument, like all historical issues, ultimately relies on human memory and human honesty. Wherever either of these is in doubt, the chain of possession argument fails. And these recent claims—by McMahon, by Hunter, and by Reymond—do raise questions about the chain of possession, questions that could not be raised just a few years ago. I would conclude, at the very least, that arguments for film authenticity require much more than a simple chain of possession argument to make their case.

If the film was altered, why leave in evidence that suggests a frontal shot? I have previously addressed this entirely sensible objection in some detail (*Assassination Science* 1998, p. 272), but it still provokes discussion and emotion, so several more comments may be useful. Based on a careful review of the eyewitnesses, JFK most likely slumped forward twice, once after the throat shot, and then immediately after the fatal headshot (a motion not seen in the extant film). Between these two events, it is most likely that Jackie (slowly) lifted JFK to an erect position so that she could examine his face closely. In Erwin Swartz's interview with Noel Twyman, this is exactly what he described in the film that initial weekend. It seems likely that this upward movement, in a later version of the film (unnaturally accelerated by excised frames), has come to be seen as the head snap.

If the limousine really did stop, what other options did the editors have? They could simply have left JFK leaning forward for the entire sequence, thus retaining only one episode of slumping forward. This would mean that his position would have changed little even after the fatal headshot. Such a choice would, however, have the distinct disadvantage of being rather too simple a sequence to coincide with the memory of any observer and would therefore have raised suspicions merely because of its odd simplicity. Once this option was excluded any other choice required that JFK come erect again—at one speed or another.

If the original speed of JFK's slow upward movement (i.e., no frame excision) were kept, then the limousine stop (or near stop) would still be visible. To eliminate the limousine stop, editing within frames would have been required. JFK's slow upward movement would have to be retained in most (or all) frames but the limousine movement would have to be altered. This would require composite frames, frames in which JFK's actions would be continuous but in which the limousine movement was accelerated by the editing process. This would have been no small task and would, in addition, have carried an associated risk of detection. Much easier than the composition of new frames would have been the simple excision of unaltered frames (at regular intervals) in order to hide the limousine stop. (Such frame excision might also have erased evidence for backward flying debris from the headshot.) Such frame excision would, of course, have accelerated JFK's backward movement—which is now seen as the head snap.

Wesley Liebeler, assistant counsel for the Warren Commission, recalled that the Warren Commission never paid much attention to the head snap. Furthermore, the film was hidden from public view until 1975 (twelve years later) and even then no official permission was granted to Geraldo Rivera for his public showing. Such reticence suggests that the editors were not eager to share their product with the public. Perhaps there was a genuine fear that the head snap would suggest a frontal shot—but because the editors were assured that the public would not see it, they may have decided that nothing further was necessary.

In conclusion, without knowing what the original film actually showed, we can only speculate on the difficulties faced by the forgers. Those who emphasize the self-defeating result of the head snap (as suggesting a shot from the front) must ask themselves what technical problems the forgers faced and also whether they were told that the public would not see the film. So long as these answers remain unknown, not too much emphasis can be placed on the head snap as a proof of authenticity. This is particularly so since the head snap was not spontaneously reported either by Dealey Plaza witnesses, or by early viewers of the film—such as Swartz, Rather, and DeLoach. Finally, the reversal of the critical frames Z-314 and Z-315, when published by the Warren Commission, does suggest that the head snap was a concern even in 1964.

The final headshot most likely struck when JFK was sitting erect. This is based both on eyewitness testimony and on the lateral skull X-rays. The trail of metallic debris actually rises from front to back within the skull, a most unlikely trajectory for a frontal shot that occurred with JFK's head tilted forward as seen in Z-312. Supporters of two immediately successive headshots (at Z-312 and at Z-313, approximately) have never seriously faced this objection. On the contrary, the X-rays argue strongly for a headshot while JFK was sitting erect (or nearly erect) such as near the end of the head snap (at Z-321 in the extant film). Furthermore, those eyewitnesses who comment at all on this issue, especially the

Secret Service agents who rode in the follow-up car, also recall that JFK was erect at the moment of the final headshot.

My own interpretation of all of the evidence is that JFK was hit first in the head from the rear while slumped forward such as in Z-312, then struck in the head for a second time (but from the front) while sitting erect. Such a posterior headshot has been strongly supported by the pathologists for over 35 years but they persistently ignored evidence for the second headshot. Only the second headshot produced a spray of blood; not enough blood could have accumulated before the first shot to give rise to such a visible spray. The bloody spray now seen at Z-313 was probably imported from the image of the second headshot (which is no longer seen in the film).

Technical challenges. It has been argued that (1) there was insufficient time for a tedious and lengthy editing task, (2) no optical printers existed for enlarging 8 mm film and no precedent existed for such manipulation with 8 mm film, (3) the available light sources were too weak to enlarge an 8 mm film, (4) the multiple generations required for such a process—first enlargement from 8 mm, then film alteration, and then reduction again to 8 mm—would have yielded too much contrast build-up through multiple generations of copying, especially for a final copy on Kodachrome II, and (5) available film was not fast enough for such enlargement. These are all serious objections, some of which admittedly cannot be answered easily or with finality.

(1) Regarding the length of time required for the final product, my own view is that the editing went on for a long while. After the initial weekend, there is no record of a screening again until 25 February 1964. This provides a rather long time interval (two months) for completion of the alterations. It is not likely that the work was completed overnight, or even within a few days. It is even possible that no alteration was done within the first few days. Only several frames were published in *Life* magazine within the early weeks. These must have been retained unchanged, but most frames were not published at all in these early issues of *Life*.

(2) We know from the testimony of Moses Weitzman, who for some time employed Robert Groden, that optical printers existed (at least by the late 1960s) that could enlarge 8 mm film. We also know now, contrary to Robert Groden's earlier protestations, that such a process could have captured the intersprocket image. To clinch this argument, the "home movie" portion of the Zapruder film—a known copy (not the original)—does contain intersprocket images (although seriously degraded), thus proving that the intersprocket image could be copied. Although there may have been no precedent for enlargement of 8 mm film, the commercial firms in existence (Bob Colburn, Moses Weizman) were able to perform such enlargements, some of which were done for *Life* magazine within a few days; these latter may have been done by Colburn (Twyman 1997, p. 56).

(3) Regarding the strength of available light sources, Homer McMahon told the ARRB that he produced 8x10 still enlargements of single frames. It was apparently routine for NPIC to perform such blowups from very small negatives. If sufficiently powerful light sources were not available on standard optical or contact printers, is it possible that NPIC equipment (or similar equipment) was used for such blowups? Is it even possible that some of

these 8x10 frames created by McMahon were employed in the process of alteration? If so, construction of a custom optical (or contact) printer, used in a manual frame-by-frame mode, may have been required. It should also be recalled that the work required on the Zapruder film (about 25 seconds) is worlds away from a full Hollywood feature such as *Mary Poppins* (1964); for the extant Zapruder film, fewer than 500 frames exist, and many of these may have needed no alteration at all. Finally, Zavada's report (Study 3, p. 5) states that a 150-300 watt lamp was used on the Bell & Howell Model J printer (presumably used to make the first day copies). But this could be customized for higher output in order to increase printing speeds. If so, then perhaps its light output could also have been adjusted when working with 8 mm film.

(4) From his own experiments, Zavada reported that copying showed "tremendously effective retention of resolution" through three generations of contact printing (using modern film and chemicals), although tones were off by the third generation. He also noted that the first 60 batches of Kodachrome II (from 1961—the batch used by Zapruder) had lower contrast and longer exposure latitude than later batches. This would have increased the possibility of copying in 1963 without building up excess contrast. Furthermore, the chemicals used at that time (not available at present) would have contributed to increased fidelity during copying. In other words, both the film and chemicals used in 1963 would have increased the probability of copying through multiple generations without detection. Zavada concluded (R. J. Zavada, "JFK Photographic Evidence," September 1998, p. 25): "The 1963 film process combination had a greater opportunity to yield good quality than our practical test. The Secret Service copies attest to this fact. One of our limitations was that the Kodak Qualex Laboratory ceased processing Kodachrome Movie film in 1997, requiring us to use a test process yielding slightly different toe characteristics." [*Author's note:* The word "toe" here refers to the left side of the characteristic curve of the film.]

(5) Although there is merit to the argument that available film was not fast enough (for enlarging 8 mm film), what is not known is whether commercial printers were actually used. For example, if custom printers (perhaps in a manual mode) had been used with potent light sources (such as those employed by McMahon to produce the NPIC prints), then the argument becomes moot—in this manual mode, longer exposure times could compensate for film speeds that were too slow.

Only after a good deal of effort did I discover that copying X-rays in 1963 was entirely different from today (*Assassination Science* 1998, pp. 120-137). In particular, the available film in 1963 made it quite easy to alter X-rays—and to do so without detection. Is it conceivable that the technical factors for Kodachrome II (both film and available chemicals) in 1963 made alteration easier then than it would be now? Zavada's statement implies that the answer is certainly yes. What is less certain is whether these factors were sufficiently different to make it fully feasible (as it was for the X-rays). In face of the current absence of 1963 film and chemicals, this question may never be answered.

Several observers have suggested that Kodachrome II film is distinctive and can be recognized at a glance by an expert. But others—Jamieson among them (and Jack White, too)—say that it is not that simple, that a side-by-side comparison of the two would be required. In this case, of course, that is not possible: the out-of-camera film appears to be missing. The next best comparison would be the original home movie (taken on the same roll of film by Zapruder) vs. the extant film now stored in the National Archives. Unfortunately, and despite the efforts of the ARRB, the original home movie segment has never been located. If this were ever located, this comparison—using a full battery of chemical and physical tests—could put the question of authenticity finally to bed.

Psychological issues: altering the film for a cover-up is too great a risk for any reasonable person to take. Since this is a psychological argument no final answer is possible, but many lines of evidence suggest otherwise. What if this rational person were ordered to alter frames? To raise the ante, what if he were not told the significance of the particular step he was asked to perform, or perhaps was given a cover story that seemed credible? Then what would he do? Would our rational man decline to do such work, merely because he vaguely suspected foul play? And what would he do if his career were at risk?

Similar issues arise in the case of the photographs taken by the Dallas police of the Oswald evidence. John Armstrong has made a powerful case that these photographs were extensively altered. Why would anyone do this when they faced a serious risk if caught? This JFK case also contains convincing evidence of altered documents (items that emerged from the FBI). The paper bag that supposedly surrounded Oswald's rifle is a case in point: one FBI document reports that it matched the paper at the Book Depository while another reports the exact opposite. Logically, at least one of these is a probable forgery. So the same question arises: why would someone take this risk? Although the question cannot be answered specifically in these cases, it is nonetheless apparent that someone did take just such a risk.

The autopsy photographs and X-rays raise identical issues. Based on the recent ARRB interviews, both with the pathologists and with newly discovered witnesses, the evidence for photographic alteration is now very difficult to ignore. My own work on the X-rays (*Assassination Science* 1998, pp. 120-137), which was reviewed without suggested changes by Kodak's Director of Medical Physics, is still a powerful indictment of the X-rays. The ARRB directed precise questions about the X-rays at pathologists Humes and Boswell while they viewed them; their answers provide astonishing corroboration (often at great personal embarrassment for them) for X-ray alteration, just as I had predicted based on my own studies of the X-rays.

So the question is similar: if government employees were willing to alter autopsy X-rays and photographs, willing to alter Oswald evidence photographs and related documents, why would they be unwilling to alter a movie film? Particularly if provided with a cover story, would they truly choose this moment to dig their feet into some vaguely defined ethical ground? What is particularly ironic about this argument is that some individuals who advance it actually believe that the photographs and/or X-rays were altered, or that the Oswald evidence has been forged. Such a view is not logically consistent.

Secrecy of this sort is impossible; someone would have told by now. This statement assumes that no one has told, but that is probably not true. I have previously described a personal encounter (*Assassination Science* 1998, p. 341) in which a purported former CIA employee claimed contemporaneous knowledge of film alteration. His name is Oswald LeWinter and his association with the CIA was reported in 1998, both in American tabloids and in respectable European newspapers, regarding documents that may be germane to Princess Diana's death.[3] I have also received a handwritten note from someone who claims to know the perpetrators' identities; the names of several suspects were even listed. [*Editor's note*: I received similar correspondence, which I forwarded to the Department of Justice. For my efforts, I received a form letter in reply.]

This information was also forwarded to Douglas P. Horne at the ARRB. Based on a telephone call, he suspected that this trail led nowhere. Whether this is sufficient follow-up I do not know. More recently, the French journalist, William Reymond, has seen a clearly different version of the film in France. What is striking is his description of specific motorcade events that are not seen in the extant film (such as the turn at Houston and Elm), and the fact that eyewitnesses had previously reported these same events. Since Reymond apparently had not known about the eyewitness reports, his screening of this film becomes even more meaningful. All of these events at least raise doubts about whether the secrets have been kept.

The larger question, though, is whether major secrets can be kept for long intervals of time. Many lines of evidence suggest that this is not only possible, but for bureaucracies, is surprisingly common (John Ralston Paul, *Voltaire's Bastards* 1992). Gary L. Aguilar, M.D., has recently reminded us that Daniel Ellsberg, who released the Pentagon Papers, recalls that in 1964 at least 100 people knew the same information that he disclosed in 1971, yet no one said anything about it before he did ("Ellsberg Remembers," *The Nation* (27 May 1997), p. 7).

On the morning that the first nuclear bomb was exploded in the New Mexico desert in 1945, Mrs. Leslie Groves received a telephone call. The caller suggested that she listen to the radio during the day since one of her family members would be in the news. Not knowing what to expect, and not even knowing which family member was meant, she was shocked to learn that her husband, General Leslie Groves, had been the military director of the Manhattan Project. Many others at Los Alamos, to say nothing of family and friends, honored this same state of secrecy. Neither the public nor the media knew any significant details of this project during the several years that it continued, or if they did know, they also kept the secret.

Former Secretary of Energy Hazel O'Leary tried (irresponsibly) to take credit for exposing the (unethical, by today's standards) radiation experiments that began in the 1940s. However, it was only through the persistent and courageous work of Eileen Welsome of *The Albuquerque Tribune* that this matter came to light (Eileen Welsome, *The Plutonium Files*, 1999). My files contain numerous examples of medical misbehavior over several decades—about which no one ever said anything for many years. Without Welsome we may never have learned about the radiation experiments either. Furthermore, these experiments were performed at blue ribbon universities and institutions. In each of these cases the secret was kept for many years, and often kept by many.

Walter Goodman ("Mass Media: The Generation of the Lie," *All Honorable Men* 1963, Chapter 4) recalls the TV quiz shows of that era. Congressional hearings were conducted and participants (at all levels) were questioned under oath. New York County District Attorney Frank Hogan (interim HSCA Chief Counsel Robert Tanenbaum later worked in the same office) reported that of 150 contestants on *Tic-Tac-Dough* and *Twenty-One*, no fewer than 100 had lied about getting answers. Would we have known any of this without Herbert Stempel? Could we even—especially during that era—have believed it? Nor can it be said that disclosure was inevitable, since the shows were losing popularity and their long-term survival was becoming less certain.

Eyewitnesses are unreliable. This claim has been repeated so often that scarcely anyone dares question it. Although the statement is often true there are, in fact, important exceptions. I have always granted the obvious: eyewitnesses are not very good at identifying a human face only briefly glimpsed (e.g., purported witnesses to Oswald sightings such as Howard Brennan and Helen Markham), nor are they reliable at recalling a complex sequence of events. The human brain is simply not programmed for such tasks. On the other hand, when a simple and important event occurs, humans can be quite remarkable for recalling it with consistency and with accuracy. In the heat of debate, it is precisely this fact that is forgotten.

As a physician who specializes in the treatment of cancer, I routinely take medical histories from patients and family members. If there is one thing I have learned in medicine over the decades it is simply to listen and let the patient tell his own story. Almost always, by the time he has finished, the diagnosis is obvious. If humans are so unreliable as eyewitnesses, then how is it that they can be so reliable, and so consistent, when telling their own stories? The answer is simple: they really do recall these medical events, events that are usually uncomplicated and that are also very important to them. If eyewitnesses were so unreliable, then a patient's diagnosis should not typically be evident after a brief medical history but, in fact, it is.

As a sports fan, I occasionally reminisce about major sports events with friends or family. During these conversations I have never encountered an occasion where the precise details of what happened became a major issue—the kind that would send us scurrying to the sports history books or to a video replay. On the contrary, for an event that was significant for both of us, the facts were never in doubt; the conversation instead centered on what happened before and after the main event, but especially on the significance of the event. How is it possible that we could so easily agree on the central facts if eyewitnesses have such poor recall for events? The fact is that they don't, at least not for events that are reasonably simple and that are also significant in some way to the viewer.

The Lincoln assassination has long held interesting parallels to the Kennedy assassination (Richard Belzer, *UFOs, JFK, and Elvis* 1999, p. 92). In this case, the events at Ford's Theater, the pursuit of Booth, his capture, the subsequent hanging of conspirators—various authors mostly agree upon these primary details. And such agreement has persisted for many years, despite the absence of photographs of these events (aside from the hangings). How is this possible if eyewitnesses are so unreliable? Or are we merely simpletons to believe these tales?

Another striking example of eyewitness credibility has recently reached the media. During this very weekend (14-16 May 1999) the descendants of Sally Hemings have been invited to join Thomas Jefferson's descendants at a Monticello reunion.[4] This event, which would have been miraculous only several years ago, has arisen due to DNA comparisons between a living descendent of Sally Heming's youngest son, Eston, and five acknowledged Jefferson family descendants ("Jefferson fathered slave's last child," *Nature* 396: 27; November 5, 1998). The same Y-chromosome markers were found in each. This has led most scholars, even former skeptics, to concede that Jefferson had a sexual relationship with Sally Hemings.

This is an astounding turnabout for professional historians, almost none of whom had taken this relationship seriously. Dumas Malone, who spent 40 years writing a multi-volume biography (*Jefferson, the Virginian* 1948), had previously denounced this story as "filth" and "virtually unthinkable in a man of Jefferson's moral standards." Willard Sterne Randall (1993) called the story "one of America's most durable myths, unproven and unprovable." How Randall knew this story to be a myth if it could not be proved—or correspondingly disproved—he was too arrogant to explain. Jefferson's most recent biographer, Joseph J. Ellis, also originally rejected this liaison.

That these respected biographers could all reach the same wrong conclusion was possible at least partly because they all ignored a long standing oral tradition within the Hemings clan that Jefferson was indeed the father of some, if not all, of Sally's children. How many of these authors interviewed any of Sally's descendants, examined their photographs, or tried to trace the story in any way? Randall's biography does not even mention such possible avenues of research. This episode of gross ignorance also reminds us of the danger of believing authorities when evidence is lacking, no matter how often they speak, no matter their credentials, and no matter how many of them line up in a row. In this case their personal biases overcame their professional training as historians.

Eyewitnesses in the Professional Literature. Is there any evidence in the professional literature regarding witness reliability for items that are relatively simple and salient? For this answer, we turn to a remarkable publication. Elizabeth Loftus has summarized this paper (*Eyewitness Testimony* 1996, p. 25); ironically, the dust jacket of her book questions the reliability of eyewitnesses. Contrary to the dust jacket, however, the original University of Michigan paper by Marshall, Marquis, and Oskamp (*Harvard Law Review* 84: 1620 (1971)) makes a startlingly powerful case for eyewitness reliability—providing that certain conditions are met.

Marshall et al. showed a two-minute, home made, color movie film with sound to 151 "witnesses." Within minutes of their viewing they gave a "free report," during which the interrogator said almost nothing. In individual interviews held in private rooms they were asked to be as accurate and complete as possible, with the understanding that the interviewer had not seen the movie. After this, they were examined using one of four types of questions: (1) open-ended with moderate guidance, (2) open-ended with high guidance, (3) structured, multiple choice questions, and (4) structured leading questions. In addition, half of the witnesses encountered a supportive atmosphere whereas the other half met a hostile atmosphere. To assess salience of specific items, a second group (high school students and members of the survey staff) were asked to recall as many as possible of the 900 items in the movie; if more than 50% of these viewers reported a particular item it was labeled highly salient. The conclusions of this study are as follows.

The first surprise was that the experimental atmosphere, whether hostile or supportive, had no important effect on either the accuracy or completeness of the testimony. In the free report format, the accuracy of the witnesses was never less than 95% for any degree of salience, and it was 99% for highly salient items. And for these items, it made little difference how the questions were asked: the accuracy ranged from 96 to 99%.

The free report format yielded the lowest completeness—70% for highly salient items. For these items, higher levels of completeness were found for moderate guidance (84%), high guidance (88%), multiple choice (98%), and leading (98%) questions. The greater the salience, the less was the effect of different types of interrogation on accuracy. Also, as salience increased there was only a small increase in completeness. The authors note that the trade-off between accuracy and completeness was much less than expected; in fact, coverage could increase a great deal while accuracy declined only slightly.

Accuracy and completeness were also assessed by type of item: person, action, sound, and object. In the free report, accuracy for sounds was 92%, while the other formats ranged from 78% to 90%. For actions—the most pertinent item for the JFK motorcade—accuracy remained high with moderate guidance (97%) or even with high guidance (94%). For actions, completeness was as follows: free report (28%), moderate guidance (38%), high guidance (42%), multiple choice (86%), and leading (87%). These researchers concluded: "Our witnesses were able to testify with impressive ability. For instance, those confronted with leading interrogation in a challenging atmosphere testified with approximately 83% accuracy and 84% coverage."

The astonishing reliability of these witnesses is quite remarkable: it is totally contrary to the traditional view of eyewitness unreliability. What made these witnesses so reliable? The authors note that an immediate interview is different from the usual courtroom situation, which often occurs months or even years after the event. This promptness, no doubt, improved the performances of the witnesses. The authors also add, however, that salience is a major factor and they emphasize that prior studies had often investigated nonsalient items.[5]

What relevance does this have for the JFK assassination? It is highly relevant. Many of these witnesses recalled the motorcade events, not months or years later, but within a brief period, sometimes even within minutes—just as in the experiment. Even more importantly though, they described salient actions—such as whether or not the motorcade stopped, or which direction JFK moved in the limousine at certain critical moments. And, finally, they described items that were rather simple—easily within the ability of the human brain to recall without great difficulty.

In fact, the events seen in the two-minute movie in the experiment were distinctly more complex than a simple question of whether the motorcade stopped, or whether JFK moved forward or backward with the final headshot. Therefore, contrary to what adherents of film authenticity have claimed, the Marshall experiment has shown convincingly that eyewitnesses (and ear witnesses, too) can accurately recall simple and important events. This Marshall study has taught us that a blanket statement of eyewitness unreliability is simple minded—we must instead ask what is being demanded of our witnesses. When the items are simple and salient—and recall is prompt—they can do remarkably well.

The Chief Arguments Against Authenticity

Time constraints prohibit a review of much germane evidence against authenticity that has accumulated during the past several years. I have selected the arguments presented here based on my perception of their strength as well on as my familiarity with them. Other critics of the film would doubtless have a somewhat different list.

The Dealey Plaza witnesses. (*Assassination Science* 1998, pp. 273–275). In my prior essay I listed ten witnesses (of many eligible candidates) who reported a limousine stop. For this effort I was primarily criticized for using an indirect quote for Chaney (instead of a direct one). In reply, I would ask a more direct question: what did the ten closest witnesses report? First, did they describe the movement at all? Then secondly, what did they see? It is quite striking that each of these ten witnesses did describe what the limousine was doing; this would not have been expected if the limousine had traveled at a nearly uniform speed—as the Zapruder film suggests. This uniformity of the *closest witnesses* is also remarkable though because many Dealey Plaza witnesses are not known to have commented on the limousine. These latter, however, were uniformly farther from the limousine, some much farther away, and might therefore not have paid as close attention to the limousine as the closest witnesses.

But all ten of the closest witnesses did comment quite explicitly—and they all saw it either stop, or nearly stop. Their comments show no equivocation. These witnesses (in no particular order) and their statements follow. The Newmans are counted only once.

- Bobby Hargis: "At that time [just before a shot to the head] the Presidential car slowed down. I heard somebody say, 'Get going.' I felt blood hit me in the face and the Presidential car stopped immediately after that" (6H294). ". . . I felt blood hit me in the face, and the Presidential car stopped immediately after that and stayed stopped about half a second, then took off at a high rate of speed." (Trask 1994, p. 209, who quotes from an interview with *The Dallas Times Herald*.)

- B. J. Martin: He saw the limousine stop". . . just for a moment." (Newcomb and Adams, *Murder from Within* 1974, unpublished, p. 71.)

- Douglas Jackson: ". . . the car just all but stopped. . . just a moment." (Newcomb and Adams 1974, p. 71.)

- James Chaney: ". . . from the time the first shot rang out, the car stopped completely, pulled to the left and stopped" (2H44-45, 3H266). Marrion Baker, his fellow officer, attributed this quotation to Chaney. Mark Lane confirmed that Chaney had indeed said this (2H45) and Lane then added ". . . [it] seemed to be so generally conceded by almost everyone that the automobile came to—almost came to a complete halt after the first shot—did not quite stop, but almost did."

- Bill Newman: "I believe Kennedy's car came to a full stop after the final shot." (Bill Sloan, *Breaking the Silence* 1993, p. 169.) ". . . I've maintained that they stopped. I still say they did. It was only a momentary stop, but. . ." (Newcomb and Adams 1974, p. 96, who cite an interview by Mary Woodward in the *Dallas Morning News*, 11/23/63; also see Jim Marrs, *Crossfire* 1989, p. 70.)

- Mary Moorman: "She recalls that the President's automobile was moving at the time she took the second picture, and when she heard the shots, and has the impression that the car either stopped momentarily or hesitated and then drove off in a hurry." (22H838-839; Harold Weisberg, *Photographic Whitewash* 1967, p. 160.)
- Jean Hill: ". . . the motorcade came almost to a halt at the time the shots rang out. . . . It [the limousine] was just almost stopped" (6H208-209).
- Charles Brehm: ". . . between the first and second shots the President's car only seemed to move some 10 or 12 feet. It seemed. . . that the automobile almost came to a halt after the first shot. . . " (22H837-838).
- Alan Smith: "The car was ten feet from me when a bullet hit the President in the forehead. . . the car went about five feet and stopped." (Newcomb and Adams 1974, p. 71, who cite *The Chicago Tribune*, 11/23/63, p. 9.)
- Mary Woodward: "Apparently the driver and occupants of the President's car had the same impression because instead of speeding up, the car came to a halt after the first shot." (2H43; *Dallas Morning News*, 11/23/63; also see Marrs 1989, p. 28.)

That all of these closest witnesses comment at all on the limousine movement—independent of the type of movement—is, by itself, extraordinary. In view of Marshall, these witnesses clearly considered the limousine movement to be a salient feature of the entire event. This is totally contrary to what devotees of film authenticity would have us believe about the motion of the limousine. Furthermore, the witnesses' actual words leave no room for a slight deceleration. Instead, they uniformly described a dramatic deceleration, and for many of them it was a literal stop. Furthermore, all four of the closest motorcyclists agreed that the limousine stopped; since they were riding immediately beside the limousine and trying to mimic its speed, they, of all people, should be reliable witnesses.

If witnesses can indeed recall simple and important events, this surely must be one of them. Why would all ten closest witnesses recall the same event—in the same way—unless that was really what had happened? And why would all four of the closest motorcyclists invent such a stop if none existed? Readers who have watched the extant Zapruder film might ask themselves: would they have commented at all on the limousine speed? If so, what would they have said? Would they have reported either a stop (most unlikely) or even a near stop (unlikely)?

There are many more witnesses to the stop than those listed above ("59 Witnesses: Delay on Elm Street," *The Dealey Plaza Echo 3/2*, July 1999, Vince Palamara, pp. 1-7). [*Editor's note*: This study appears elsewhere in this volume.] In fact, virtually every witness who commented on the limousine movement recalled a stop or a near stop. Moreover, this stop was widely taken for granted at the time; it was reported contemporaneously in the media (*Newsweek*, 2 December 1963, p. 2 and *Time*, 29 November 1963, p. 23), by later biographers (*UPI's Four Days* 1964; William Manchester, *The Death of a President* 1967; Jim Bishop, *The Day Kennedy Was Shot* 1968)—and, much later, even by the media's current hero of lone assassin aficionados, Gerald Posner, who describes the limousine stop as follows: "Incredibly, Greer sensing that something was wrong in the back of the car, slowed the vehicle to almost a standstill" (*Case Closed* 1993, p. 234). How

Posner squares this astonishing statement with his presumed acceptance of the film he does not bother to explain.

The head snap was spontaneously described neither by the Dealey Plaza witnesses nor by early viewers of the film. In the recent past, moreover, the jet effect as an explanation for the head snap has been fully discredited in independent experiments performed by Arthur Snyder, Ph.D. and Doug DeSalles, M.D. It can no longer be offered as a viable explanation for the head snap. In addition, a long list of arguments against that particular explanation has been previously recounted (*Assassination Science* 1998, pp. 279–284). The other explanation offered by Warren Commission supporters—the neuromuscular reaction—has never received any credible support from appropriate experts in the neurosciences. The many arguments against it are also recounted in *Assassination Science* (1998, pp. 279-284). Nothing new has emerged to resuscitate this idea. Jackie's simultaneous head snap (originally noted by Itek; see *Assassination Science* 1998, p. 283) remains a mystery as well—unless film alteration is accepted. In summary, none of the traditional explanations can account for the head snap. By itself, this argument alone requires that film alteration be taken seriously.

The traditional Warren Commission critic, for years, has taken the head snap as an obvious proof of a frontal shot. Itek originally pointed out, however, that this simply could not work, mainly because it is not a simple matter of transferring energy from the bullet to the motion of the head. The problem is that JFK's head (and upper torso, too) must be lifted substantially against gravity. This requires a great deal of energy—energy that is no longer available for the kinetic energy of the head. These calculations demonstrate that the energy left over cannot reproduce the head snap of the Zapruder film.

I found this to be true even after I revised some of Itek's anatomic values. [*Editor's note*: This is one of many manifestations of the importance of the author's expertise in both medicine and physics.] Unfortunately, no one else, to my knowledge, has corroborated these calculations, even after all of these years. In summary, then, these arguments about the head snap leave believers of film authenticity in a very difficult position. They are left with no explanation for the most remarkable feature of the film—the head snap.

Many witnesses describe an erect posture at the instant of the final headshot, after which JFK is commonly described as slumping forward. Such witnesses, mostly Secret Service agents in the follow-up car, are Swartz, Ault, Hargis, Hickey, Kinney, Landis (*Assassination Science* 1998, pp. 289–290). These descriptions of erect posture are totally inconsistent with the Zapruder film, in which the (single) headshot occurs when JFK is slumped forward and to the left. But when the question is raised (as it rarely is) about what posture the witnesses saw at the moment of the headshot, none of them describe JFK as slumped over. This issue—so striking when it is considered—has received almost no discussion whatsoever.

Those witnesses who do describe JFK's position at the moment of the headshot describe him as sitting erect. And most of these then go on to describe how JFK next slumped forward (probably for a second time). How is it possible for such a simple—and memorable—event to be remembered so incorrectly (if authenticity devotees are correct) by so many relevant witnesses, especially in view of Marshall's research? This simple recollection should not tax the abilities of human memory, nor is it so inconsequential that it would be forgotten. In fact, it is just the kind of incident—one with simple actions and salient events according to Marshall—that witnesses would recall. In fact witnesses do recall these events with remarkable consistency. If there were no Zapruder film, how would the assassination be described in history books? It is likely that the Zapruder version would be unknown.

The early reenactments. I will say rather little here about the first two reenactments, for which I previously cited (*Assassination Science* 1998, pp. 305-308) the meticulous articles by Daryll Weatherly (*The Investigator*, Winter 1994-95, p. 6) and Chuck Marler (*Assassination Science* 1998, pp. 249-261). Their work has, unfortunately, received little attention—but also little criticism. The point is simple—these reenactments as well as associated documents and eyewitness statements—place the final head shot (the second, in my view) about 30 to 40 feet further down Elm Street than Z-313. Warren Commission data tables actually place the final shot at 294 ft from the "sniper's" window, not the 265 ft that corresponds to Z-313. This greater distance of about 294 ft was actually identified in a photograph (Figure 1) printed in *Newsweek* (pp. 74-75) as recently as 22 November 1993. In summary, the data tables, documents, and figures from these early reenactments remain powerful corroboration for the alteration of the film. The evidence is so powerful, in fact, that proponents of authenticity usually ignore it. There is little else for them to do.

Inconsistencies with other photographic evidence. This substantial area can be addressed only briefly here. Jack White has discovered new—and astonishingly robust—evidence, based on a simple reenactment he performed in Dealey Plaza. In the famous Moorman Polaroid, taken immediately after a headshot, Jack noticed the geometric pattern in the background arcade over JFK's head. He also noticed Zapruder's pedestal in the foreground and he recognized that, by lining up both of these features, it was possible to locate Moorman (actually Moorman's eye) very precisely at the moment she took her picture. Although her distance from the arcade remained uncertain, her lateral and vertical position could be determined quite exactly. [*Editor's note*: White's newer discoveries, some quite surprising, appear elsewhere in this volume.]

When I attempted to reproduce this I was astonished. As I lined up one corner of the pedestal with a chosen point on the background arcade, I could immediately see that this technique was exquisitely sensitive to even slight head movements. The smallest movement of my head put it out of alignment. So I lined it up precisely and then placed a knife in the ground to mark the exact lateral position. Then I moved a short distance away, and without looking at the ground, attempted to reproduce what I had just done. To my amazement, I could do this repeatedly to within an inch, just as Jack had implied. Next I looked at the vertical location. It was immediately obvious that I had to crouch far down in the grass in order to reproduce the image seen in the Moorman photo. I stepped onto the street immediately adjacent to the curb—and discovered that I still had to crouch quite a lot.

On a subsequent visit, I was able to use as a model a young woman who was only slightly taller than Moorman. When standing on the grass south of Elm St. (Figure 2), she had to crouch a good deal in order for her eye to reproduce the background alignment of the Moorman photo. Next she stepped onto the street;

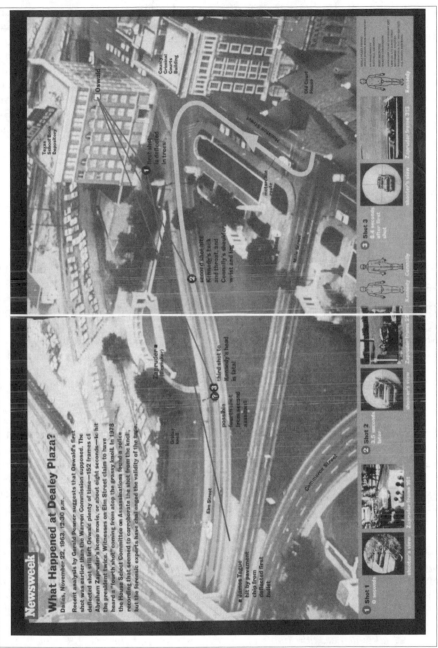

Figure 1. This astonishing photograph, from Newsweek (22 November 1993), shows the final headshot at 30-40 feet further down Elm Street than frame Z-313 (the supposed final headshot). This downhill location is strongly suggested by early reenactments as well as data tables and documents, all of which the Warren Commission ignored.

even here she had to crouch a bit (Figure 3). Jack White has determined that several, if not many, layers of blacktop have been added to Elm Street since 1963, thus raising it by several inches. These successive layers were obvious to me, too, when I looked for them. Now here is the paradox: the Zapruder film shows Moorman standing upright on the grass during her photo, with the camera held to her eye. Based on our reenactments this was impossible—she should have been crouching, in a rather obvious fashion, or the camera should have been held well below eye level. Jack was able to explain this however. By Moorman's own account, she was not standing on the grass when she took this photo—she was on the street.

In 1963, Mary Ann Moorman Krahmer was interviewed by KRLD; Debra Conway supplied the interview.

Moorman: Uh, just immediately before the presidential car came into view, we were, you know, there was just tremendous excitement. And my friend who was with me, we were right ready to take the picture. And she's not timid. She, as the car approached us, she did holler for the president, "Mr. President, look this way!" And I'd stepped out off the curb into the street to take the picture. And snapped it immediately. And that evidently was the first shot. You know, I could hear the sound. And . . .

Jones: Now when you heard the sound, did you immediately think 'rifle shot?'

Moorman: Oh no. A firecracker, maybe. There was another one just immediately following which I still thought was a firecracker. And then I stepped back up on to the grassy area. I guess just, people were falling around us, you know. Knowing something was wrong. I certainly didn't know what was wrong.

These are Moorman's own words—she stepped into the street to take her Polaroid picture. As if for emphasis, she also recalls not just stepping back onto the grass, but precisely when she did so. In fact, based on our reenactments and without the additional layers of blacktop, it is likely that Moorman could have stood erect in the street, with the camera to her eye, while taking the photo, just as she recalled. It is unusual in this JFK case to make a prediction, and then later to have it verified so precisely by a statement directly from the mouth of the pertinent witness.

So what happened to Moorman in the Zapruder film? When these composite Zapruder frames were formed, the composition experts placed her on the grass, instead of in the street. Whether they moved her laterally (and, if so, why) is still an open question. In any case, this evidence is powerful and direct confirmation that at least several composite frames were made. Anyone can go into Dealey Plaza and check this out independently, as I was able to do in a few seconds. To my knowledge, this argument remains unrefuted. (See Figures 2 and 3.)

Internal evidence: film maps of the extant film and the two SS copies. The following new information derives from an ARRB memorandum (dated 9 April 1997) by Douglas Horne—and also from observations made at the National Archives by Harry Livingstone[6] and Doug Mizzer. In the chain-of-custody affidavits that were signed in Dallas after the assassination, a Kodak laboratory official

Figure 2. This shows how Mary Moorman would have had to stoop during her famous photograph if the Zapruder film were authentic and she was standing on the grass.

Figure 3. Where Moorman actually stood, by her own words, although the road has been repaved multiple times in the interval. Without these additional layers, she could probably have stood erect, with the camera to her eye, just as she is shown in the Zapruder film.

identified the out-of-camera film as perforated by the number 0183 (which was placed at the time of development). Unfortunately, the exact site of this perforation on the film was not identified in the affidavit. The extant film (i.e., the purported original film currently in the National Archives) does not contain any perforated number. But since this number 0183 was photographically copied (or printed) onto Secret Service (SS) copies #1 and 2 *following* the home movie segment, this seemed to imply that 0183 originally was punched only after the home movie segment. If true, then the absence of 0183 from the extant film (which shows only the motorcade) would be expected. According to Zavada, standard Kodak practice was to punch this processing number after the last image on the second side. If this practice had been followed with the Zapruder film, then a 0183 should have appeared after the motorcade side. None of the remaining numbers (the image of 0183, the punched 0186) coincide with this practice. A review of the intact *original* home movie side might prove enlightening; unfortunately, it remains unlocated.

The chain-of-custody affidavits (for reasons unknown) do not mention serial number 0184, which remains a mystery—because it has never been located and because the Kodak lab has no record of any roll of film that would correspond to it (critics have suggested that this was the Hunt copy). They do state that the numbers 0185, 0186, and 0187 were punched (one per copy) through the three copies made at the Jamieson laboratory on 22 November 1963. While SS copy #1 has no perforated number in it, SS copy #2 does have the number 0186 perforated through its black leader. This is the only perforated number currently present in any of the two SS copies, or the extant film.

In SS copy #2, this perforated number (0186) precedes the first portion of the motorcade segment. Curiously though, the number 0186, while physically continuous with the beginning of the motorcade segment, is separated from the actual motorcade images by a photographically copied (i.e., printed) splice. This image of a splice occurs only 12-1/4 inches after a physical splice (according to Livingstone's film map—Zavada's report does not contain this information). This photographic splice suggests that a physical splice was present (for reasons unknown) in the source material—supposedly the original film. This enigma is only exacerbated by the knowledge that the original was processed intact without removing the four-foot leader, as the Zavada report reminds us. *This expected four-foot leader is seen neither in the extant film nor in SS #2.* Instead the extant film contains three (sic) separate leaders each followed by a splice, after which the motorcade begins. This motorcade sequence includes 6' 3" of images and 2'7" of black film, with no splice between them. These distances obviously cannot explain the 12-1/4" interval seen on SS #2. Since SS #2 has earmarks of authenticity (e.g., 0186 punched through it, loading fog, and the pre-motorcade images), we would expect to see an image of the four-foot leader. None is seen, however, which suggests either that (1) the Zavada report is wrong about the leader, or (2) SS #2 is not a first day copy—despite its apparently authenticating features.

Thus, while the presence of the perforated number 0186 on SS #2 is consistent with the chain-of-custody affidavits, the presence of the photographically printed splice raises questions about the source film: was the source film really the out-of-camera original? If so, why did this source film contain a physical splice? If so, how and why did it get there? Or was the source film not the out-of-camera original?

Because film is unavoidably exposed to light when it is loaded into a camera, all developed film should contain loading fog, but none is seen before the motorcade sequence in the extant film. However, examination of SS copies #1 and #2 reveals an explanation for this: most (all but a few frames) of the pre-motorcade segment (a green chair and three bystanders in Dealey Plaza) that is seen in both SS copies is absent from the extant film. Thus, no loading fog is present in the extant film because the pre-motorcade segment is missing—it appears to have been cut off.

On SS #2, the second portion of the motorcade has been separated from the first portion and actually precedes it in the present configuration. Between these two segments lie four physical splices and three sections of leader. The reason for this odd arrangement is unknown.[7] Because of the dense concentration of information in these paragraphs, I have assembled the following table. The LMH copy (the *Life* copy), supposed by Zavada to be a first day copy, is included in this table, based on a recent report by Zavada (see the Addendum):

Evidence Item	SS #1	SS #2	LMH Copy	Extant Film
perforated number	no	0186 (a)	no	no (e)
initial fog	yes (b)	yes (c)	no (d)	no (e)
terminal fog	yes (f)	yes (f)	yes (f)	no (e)
image of 0183	yes (g)	yes (g)	yes (g)	N/A (h)

Table 1. The Film Maps

In the following, the letters "a" through "h" correlate with the above table.

(a) The perforated number 0186 is separated from the motorcade by a photographic splice, thus suggesting that a physical splice existed (for reasons unknown) in the source film (supposedly the original). The perforated number 0186 lies at the *beginning of the motorcade side*, an obvious inconsistency with the image of 0183, which lies at the *end of the home movie side*.

(b) Initial fog is separated from the motorcade by a physical splice. Therefore earmarks of authenticity are not available. On the home movie side (for SS #1, SS #2, and LMH), no initial fog is seen—this portion has probably been cut off in each of the three copies.

(c) Initial fog is followed by the pre-motorcade images (the green chair and three bystanders) and then the motorcade. Except for the photographic splice this sequence seems normal. An additional inconsistency, however, is the absence of an image of a four-foot leader; Zavada clearly states that this leader was not removed from the out-of-camera film before it was copied on the first day. If a four-foot leader was attached to the original film while it was copied, where is its image on the copy? Zavada does not address this additional conundrum.

(d) Nothing before Z-214 exists in this copy.

(e) Both the initial and terminal portions have been removed from the extant film.

(f) Terminal fog follows the home movie segment.

(g) The photographic image of 0183 follows the terminal fog on the home movie side.
(h) This entry does not apply to the extant film, which should contain a punched number 0183 but no image of a number; an image of 0183 would only be expected in subsequent generations.

If the extant film and the two SS copies were authentic there should be no oddities in the above table. In fact there are many, as listed here.

(1) Uninterrupted (i.e., no physical or photographic splices) loading fog does not precede the motorcade segment in SS #1, SS #2, or in the extant film.
(2) In SS #2, fogged film and a perforated number 0186 are both present, which would ordinarily be earmarks of authenticity. However, a photographic splice is present where none should exist. Furthermore, an image of the four-foot leader (which was attached to the original film, according to Zavada) is missing. In addition, because this is the sole, normal, fogged sequence on any of the films, another question may be raised: rather than representing an image of fog from the original film, was this fog on SS #1 caused by light striking SS # 1 directly? If so, this fog would provide no support for authenticity at all.
(3) No perforated processing number (0183, 0185, 0186, 0187) is continuous (i.e., no intervening physical or photographic splices) with the motorcade in any of the three copies or in the extant film..
(4) Although the perforated number 0186 appears at the *beginning* of the motorcade side, the photographic image of 0183 appears at the *end* of the home movie side—in SS #1, SS #2, and LMH.
(5) The Zavada report states that the perforated number (e.g., 0183)—or its photographic image—would ordinarily appear after the last image of the second side (the motorcade side). In fact, it appears at the *end* of the last image on the first side (the home movie side).

Internal evidence: in the Zapruder film, the intersprocket images extend to the left edge.[8] Zavada shot film through identical model cameras, using his wife as a model (see Zavada, page 33 of part 4, particularly Figure 4-26), and found that the intersprocket image did not extend nearly to the left edge. What is particularly relevant here is that Zavada's test camera was set on full telephoto—the same setting that Zapruder used throughout the motorcade. Most importantly, this particular photograph of Mrs. Zavada, standing in front of a garage door, was taken in full sunlight. The sequence that immediately follows shows a light colored garage door in the immediate background—fully illuminated by sunlight. Such full illumination is critical because it increases the penetration of the image into the intersprocket area (as Zavada determined).

Why is it so critical that Zavada's intersprocket image does not extend all the way to the edge? Because the intersprocket images in the extant Zapruder film extend much farther—nearly to the very edge. An excellent example is frame Z-312, in which Jean Hill can be seen at the very edge—in clear disagreement with Zavada's simulation. This discrepancy between the Zapruder film and Zavada's simulation is consistent with the suggestion that some frames (at least) in the extant film have resulted from re-shooting—by using a magnified original as the image source. In particular, it would be possible to magnify the original image just enough so that the intersprocket image (from the original film) remained just outside of the captured image for the new film. As a result, of course, all objects in the new frame would be larger than they were in the original. If a composite image were formed, however, then some objects could have been returned to their original size (or any size desired by these specialists).

Such a re-shooting has the distinct merit of overcoming one major, and possibly otherwise insurmountable hurdle—the elimination of the telltale edge prints on the left side of the original film. Two such overlapping sets of edge prints—as a copy would otherwise unavoidably contain—would be *prima facie* proof that the altered film was a copy. These edge prints are placed at the time of manufacture and inevitably show up after development on all film.

But even more evidence exists on this score. When Zavada shot additional film of a gray wall through an identical model camera (again at full telephoto), this time using graduated f-stop settings, he found once again that the intersprocket images extended only partially to the left, not as far as in the extant Zapruder film (see Zavada's report, page 34 of part 4, including Figure 4-27). Zavada also determined that the penetration of the image into the intersprocket area depended on the aperture of the camera— i.e., on how wide open the iris was. The smaller the aperture (or the brighter the ambient light), the greater was the penetration.

Yet even Zavada (part 4, page 35) acknowledged: "Overexposure will show an increase in image penetration and *extreme overexposure* [emphasis added] can produce full penetration is possible (sic)." It hardly needs to be said—and no one has claimed—that Zapruder's film shows such extreme overexposure (it does not). Despite this, however, the Zapruder film does show intersprocket images going to the edge of the film, in clear disagreement with Zavada's simulation. This evidence, therefore, constitutes compelling—and independent—evidence of film alteration. It would seem either that Zavada missed the significance of this evidence or that he was reluctant to address it.

Internal evidence: first frame overexposure (this issue was first raised by Doug Mizzer). Zavada addressed this issue by using several Bell & Howell cameras of the same model as Zapruder's camera. When the camera is stopped and then restarted it takes a finite amount of time for the motor to get up to normal speed. This, in turn, means that for a brief interval the frames will advance slower than normally. Because the frames are advancing slower, the exposure time will be longer for these frames and the images will appear lighter than usual (overexposure). At three separate occasions during the home movie sequence (supposedly on the same film as the motorcade sequence) this actually occurs, and at each occasion such overexposure is visible.

However, on the one occasion when the camera apparently stops during the motorcade (just before the limousine appears) an overexposure is not visible. This inconsistency is remarkable and should normally have raised the question of whether the camera actually did stop, or whether the effect is absent because frames had been excised at this juncture. However, Zavada gives no hint of recognizing this central question of authenticity. He recognizes that there is no overexposure when the limousine appears, but he makes no attempt to explain it. (In his research, to give him some credit, however, he finds that not all tested Bell & Howell cameras showed this overexposure effect.)

Internal evidence: the differences among the three supposed copies of the film made by Jamieson on 22 November 1963. Two of these supposed copies are now held by the National Archives and listed as Secret Service copies # 1 and 2. I had previously described (*Assassination Science* 1998, p. 325) the differences in density between these two copies: Secret Service copy #1 is much darker than copy #2. Zavada confirmed this observation and tried to explain it. He proposed that exposure bracketing—different exposures for each of the three copies—was used by Jamieson as a technique to assure that at least one of the three copies would show good fidelity.

There are two problems with this explanation: (1) the density difference between the two Secret Service copies is too large for such bracketing (this is actually stated in the Zavada report), and (2) there is no documentation that such bracketing was done. In fact, the exact opposite is the case: Jamieson seemed quite sure that such exposure bracketing was not done—he recalled that the same printer light and filter pack were used for all three copies.

Greer's rapid head turn. This has been summarized well by Noel Twyman (*Bloody Treason 1997*). The driver's turn is far too rapid. Furthermore, as Twyman notes, the absence of blurring during such a rapid turn is often overlooked. Such absent blurring is, by itself, a powerful indictment of the film. All of this remains unexplained.

Toni Foster's peculiar stop: Z-321 to Z-322. Foster is the pedestrian in the background grass. Her lateral separation from the adjacent (ghost) motorcycle image is constant between these two frames. Because the camera is tracking the limousine, her image should undergo a regular and steadily growing displacement from the motorcycle image. It is obvious from preceding and following frames that this is exactly what happens—but it does not happen for these two frames. It is also apparent from nearby frames that Foster is not jumping to and fro within single frame intervals, so as to appear stationary between these two frames (1/18 second), a physical impossibility in any case.

For all nearby frames, the motorcycle, the limousine, and other objects advance uniformly across the field of view, as they should—but Foster remains quite stuck for these two frames. She retains almost exactly the same lateral position. To the tracking camera she seems to stop within 1/18 second, and then immediately to resume her regular frame-to-frame displacement within the next 1/18-second. This physical impossibility cries out for an explanation, but none has been forthcoming from devotees of authenticity.

The trail of debris on the skull X-ray. This trail is totally *inconsistent* with a frontal head shot at Z-312 or Z-313. When JFK's head is tilted far forward, a shot from the knoll or from the storm drain on the north overpass (the latter is more likely) could not produce a bullet trail that rises from front to back with respect to the skull while JFK is tilted so far forward. Rather, such a shot should descend with respect to the skull (from front to back)—in radical disagreement with the trail seen on the lateral skull X-ray. Only when the head is tilted back (e.g., at Z-321) could such a frontal shot produce such a trail. Obstinate adherents of the frontal shot (at about Z-313) as an explanation for the head snap prefer to ignore this paradox from the X-rays, just as they ignore the Itek arguments against a frontal shot as an explanation for the head snap.

Blur analysis by Weatherly. Daryll Weatherly notes that many frames show a seemingly impossible paradox between the camera tracking as predicted by (1) the image content at the right side of two successive frames and (2) the image clarity actually seen on the second of these frames. ("A New Look at the 'Film of the Century'," Harrison Livingstone, *Killing Kennedy* 1995, Appendix.) These paradoxes exist for both moving and stationary objects. Not only are the predictions of image clarity often wrong, but also sometimes they are exactly opposite to what is seen. Such paradoxes recur in many, many Zapruder frames but were not seen in the Giuliano and Edwards simulations in Dealey Plaza during my brief review. Aside from the proposal of film alteration, these blur analysis paradoxes remain unexplained. Zavada did not address this issue; for him, this required an analysis of film content, a subject that lay outside his technically limited mandate. My own analysis of many additional frames (unpublished) also frequently yields startling discrepancies. This is true for blurring seen both horizontally and vertically. One of Weatherly's examples is discussed next.

The right edge of the image is the same in Z-302 and Z-303; also, the highlights on the roll bar in both images are well defined, although they are somewhat sharper in the latter frame. These observations are consistent—they both indicate that the camera was tracking well. Therefore all moving objects (the limousine and motorcycle) should be well defined, which is the case. All is well so far. It should also be noted, however, that the background figures in the grass are also well defined in Z-303. Between Z-303 and Z-304 the camera falls slightly behind the limousine: in Z-304, more of the front of the limousine has been cut off. Therefore the tracking is not accurate—the camera has slowed down slightly. Since the camera is moving more slowly now, the background (stationary) observers should be seen more clearly (the camera is moving slower with respect to them than in the prior frame). But what is seen is not consistent with this—in fact, the background observers are obviously much less clear in Z-304 than in Z-303. No logical explanation has been offered for such singular features.

What Other Proofs of Inauthenticity Might Be Possible?

One possible proof would be the discovery of a film that shows (or even suggests) the leftover work of the forgers. There may actually be a candidate for this role—the odd 8 mm film given to me by David Lifton (*Assassination Science* 1998, pp. 321). Although this film, of uncertain ancestry, employs only frames from the extant film, many show a superposition of images or other odd features. For example, when Clint Hill tries to climb onto the back of the limousine, the curb can be seen through his leg. It is particularly striking that the manufacturing date of this film, based on the symbols in the edge prints, is 1941, 1961, or 1981.

The possibility that this film is left over from the actual forgery is conceivable for two reasons: (1) it is an 8 mm film and (2) the film could well have been manufactured in 1961, the same date as the extant film (both contain two triangles that identify the date of manufacture). Proponents of authenticity have argued that it was difficult—perhaps even impossible—for alterations to be made to an 8 mm film. But here is just such a film—it is in 8 mm format and it does contain irrefutable anomalies that may be proof of alteration. Furthermore, the film was almost certainly manufactured in 1961, so this copy could have been prepared as early as 1963. That this copy was made soon after the assassination is also supported by the manufacturer's date code (the year was 1963) on SS #1, SS #2 and the LMH copy. Why would the date code of 1961 on this odd film *precede* the date on the Secret Service copies (especially if they really were first day copies)? On the other hand, if Lifton's copy were produced in 1981 (the next consistent date code) or later, what purpose would be served by making such an odd copy at such a late date?

Discovery of a film that shows more frames than the extant film (Assassination Science 1998, pp. 298-300). A surprising number of individuals claim to have seen just such a film. The Zavada report itself, indirectly, raises this very question. Early on 23 November 1963, two FBI agents came to Kodak to view the film for about one hour. They counted frames, cursed the sign, and exclaimed when bullets (plural) impacted between JFK's flinches. Such precision, even to the point of counting frames, is certainly not simple based on the extant film. To complete all of this in one hour, using the extant film, would actually be a remarkable achievement. If they truly succeeded in this on the original film, then the subsequent jiggle analyses would have been unnecessary—one could instead simply have counted JFK's flinches. Such an achievement raises the possibility that they were viewing a different film. One of the Kodak staff members, interviewed for the Zavada report, also recalled that he (and Zapruder, too) could see three distinct jumps by JFK, from which they concluded that at least three shots had been fired. That conclusion would be very difficult to draw from the extant film. Furthermore, three successful shots—and one missed shot (that hit James Tague)—would immediately require a second gunman. If three shots were indeed seen in the original, then that, by itself, may have been sufficient reason for the forgers to alter the film.

More recently, several additional witnesses (including Joe O'Donnell—see my essay, "The Medical Evidence Decoded") have recalled a different film. Three times over 25 years, Rich Della Rosa has seen a different film; he describes this film as being of high quality. He saw Greer make a wide turn onto Elm Street, an event not seen on the extant film. He also saw the limousine stop briefly on Elm Street, an event not seen today. It is remarkable that William Reymond also saw these same events in the film that he recently saw in France.

Finally, Scott Myers has also seen a film that is distinctly different from the extant film and which may have been the same version that Della Rosa (and possibly Reymond) saw. This has led to a peculiar situation in which a small number of individuals know from personal experience that the extant film has been altered, but devotees of authenticity obviously do not regard these individuals as credible—but no one has explained why they are not credible.

Epilogue

Like most concerned citizens, I, too, find it difficult at times to believe, at a deep emotional level, that anyone would deliberately and illegally falsify a movie film of such significance. Unfortunately, this issue cannot be decided by emotion alone—precedence must be given to the evidence. Just as most of our media now find it easier to ignore the enormous weight of evidence for conspiracy in the JFK assassination, some of our fellow critics now find it easier to believe in a more limited conspiracy—one that was too conservative to alter a movie film. But if the extant film is authentic, why then has so much suspicious evidence accumulated to the contrary? If the extant film were genuine, almost none of the evidence discussed here should exist.

As a specific example, in the Zapruder film why doesn't Moorman appear in the street where she must have stood—based both on the evidence of her own Polaroid and on her own recollections? Why does Foster stop so abruptly at Z-321 and then resume her regular displacement so quickly again? Why do the first two reenactments disagree so radically with the extant film? Why do various observers, over many years, report seeing a different film, starting as early as 22 November 1963—with Deke DeLoach of all people? Why do the Dealey Plaza witnesses (including the ten closest) disagree so fundamentally with the film? Why does Weatherly's blur analysis yield so much contradictory information? Why is the traditional critic's frontal head shot at about Z-313 in such arresting disagreement with the trail of metal debris on the lateral X-ray film?

For all of these questions, and many more besides, there are no easy answers—except that of film alteration. Although the easy road is to circumnavigate this mountain of evidence, the honest approach is to sift and weigh the evidence as a whole. And if we still cannot agree after all of this, then perhaps a re-reading of Ronald White's essay, "Apologists and Critics of the Lone Gunman Theory: Assassination Science and Experts in Post-Modern America," (*Assassination Science* 1998, pp. 377-410) will assist us at least in understanding the chasm that divides the "realists," like myself, who consider the authenticity of the film to be a theory that has been falsified, from the "relativists," like Josiah Thompson, who consider the theory to be a paradigm laden with anomalies, burdened but unbroken.

Acknowledgments

I am indebted to our editor, Jim Fetzer, for constantly encouraging my research and specifically for arranging a conference at the University of Minnesota where I presented an earlier version of this study. Special thanks must also go to Doug Horne, David Lifton, Jack White, Noel Twyman, Doug Mizzer, Harry Livingstone, Phil Giuliano, Roy Schaeffer, Milicent Cranor, and Brian Edwards for their inestimable contributions to this cause. I apologize in advance to those I should have mentioned but have failed to recognize—it was not deliberate. A surprising number of unnamed—but very interested—private investigators have contributed both stimulating ideas and clues.

I am often plied with tantalizing hints that time constraints prohibit me from pursuing as thoroughly as I would wish. I hope that these investigators will understand that my sometimes-slow responses do not reflect a lack of interest. If anything, the opposite is typically true—I wish that I had more time for them. So I strongly encourage them to pursue their original ideas vigorously. Eventually, I believe, the growing trove of evidence will persuade most serious students that the Zapruder film has indeed been altered.

Addendum: LMH "First Day Copy"

In 1999, Roland J. Zavada examined the LMH Co. "First Day Copy" (hereafter described as LMHFDC) and published a report: "Addendum to Technical Report #318420P: Analysis of Selected Motion Picture Photographic Evidence." In this report Zavada claims that the third copy made by Jamieson on 22 November 1963 is the LMH copy (also known as the *Life* copy). In an unrelated matter, but still one of great interest, Zavada also reports (letter to Douglas P. Horne, 14 March 2000) that the Zapruder family transferred their copyright and complete inventory of films to the Sixth Floor Museum in Dallas.

Zavada's chief new finding is that the optical density of LMHFDC lies between SS #1 (a dark copy) and SS #2 (a light copy). New measurements show that the LMHFDC density is closer to SS #2, and Zavada advances technical arguments for why this is a reasonable expectation, *although he did not predict it*. He claims that this result proves that Jamieson bracketed the printing exposure level in order to achieve at least one good copy. Critics, on the other hand, might well argue that, since Jamieson had initially denied that such bracketing was done, these new results only constitute further proof that the bracketing of these films (SS #1, SS #2, LMHFDC) was done at a later date and at some other site. In other words, since Jamieson reportedly did not use bracketing, he could not have made these copies.

LMHFDC begins at about Z-214, when the limousine is near the Stemmons freeway sign. Therefore, nothing can be said about initial loading fog or the perforated number supposedly placed during developing. However, as in SS #1 and SS #2, terminal fog, and then an image of 0183, appears after the final image (of a scene) on the home movie side.

Zavada again claims (as he did in his initial September 1998 report) that the septum line is characteristic of the Jamieson printer. He also adds that the line is the same in each of SS #1, SS #2, and LMHFDC. In his September 1998 report, however, Zavada had stated: "I'm sure the reader is aware that our attempt to exactly replicate the 1963 JAMIESON [printer to] produce [a] septum line has not been successful." (What he should have said is that his attempt to match the septum line on the *home movie sequence* was not successful—he merely assumes that these copies were made on the Jamieson printer, but this is exactly what is being questioned.) Doug Mizzer (in a memo to Harry Livingstone) summarized this evidence: the septum line on the SS copies is about 0.036 inches wide, whereas the line on the filmstrip cited by Zavada and that produced on the Bell & Howell Model J Printer in 1959 was only 0.020 to 0.025 inches wide—a large, and easily visible, difference. This means that Jamieson's printer might very well not have made these purported first day copies.

This question of the septum line is not trivial. It is Zavada's hypothesis that the intersprocket images on the home movie side were produced by a separate light source *that also produced the septum line*. But if the septum line is not authentic, then Zavada's explanation for the intersprocket images (on the home movie side) is also in doubt. In fact, Zavada reports on his trial with an old Model J printer that used an independent tungsten lamp. He concludes: "A trial print was made to determine the extent and penetration of the light along the perforation edge [intersprocket area] of the film. The results showed that although edge illumination was achieved, no light penetrated between the perforations."

To make the above negative result even worse, Jamieson quotes Robert Colley (Jamieson letter of 21 October 1997 to Zavada), a printer operator who was actually in the lab on 22 November: ". . . in order to retain the original edge numbers, the B-Wind originals were printed FULL APERATURE [sic] (pix and sound area) from TAILS." Despite this clear statement, however, Zavada concludes exactly the opposite (Study 3, p. 3): ". . . the initial belief that the prints were printed 'full aperture,' picture plus sound, also proved incorrect based on the examination of the images of the resulting prints." In my view, this is a perfect example of circular reasoning—the question is whether the copies in question are indeed first day copies, but Zavada merely assumes that they are, and then proceeds to draw conclusions based on his *assumption*.

Based on the above data, Doug Mizzer argues that because the SS copies do have edge printing, then, if they were made on the Jamieson printer, they should not have a septum line (on the home movie side). Therefore, since both SS copies do have a septum line and edge printing, they could not have been made on Jamieson's printer. The reverse statement is this (quoting Mizzer): ". . . if the copies were made on Jamieson's printer in the pix only mode, there would be a septum line on both sides of the film [i.e., the motorcade side, too], but there would be NO EDGE PRINTING." (*Author's note*: In fact, both sides contain edge printing and the motorcade side in the SS copies has no septum line.)

To further confound matters, Zavada received a letter from Herb Farmer (1 August 1998) of the USC School of Cinema and Television. Farmer, who had four old Model J's, stated: "None of our model J printers have had any modification for edge marking printing at the picture printing aperture." Furthermore, he then added: "If I were faced with the original printing problem, I would probably have printed the film on the model J with the printing aperture wide open which would expose everything from the inside edge of the sprocket hole on the printing sprocket side to the opposite edge of the film (the picture and track area)." In other words, both Robert Colley and Herb Farmer have implied that the motorcade side (for the first day copies) should contain intersprocket images—but, in fact, *none are seen*.

In view of all of the above, many of Zavada's conclusions must remain in grave doubt. Unfortunately, he seemed quite unable to conceive of the possibility that the present three copies are not Jamieson copies. Instead, he obviously preferred to accept what he had been told—namely that these three are authentic first day copies. There is a distinct sense of *deja vu* here—this is the same mental state that so hampered prior investigations of the medical evidence. (See my essay, "The Medical Evidence Decoded," elsewhere in this volume.)

Notes

The opening quotation for this essay is from the Preface to Dino A. Brugioni, *Photofakery: The History and Techniques of Photographic Deception and Manipulation* (1999). Brugioni, a founder of the CIA's National Photographic Interpretation Center (NPIC), examines many methods for faking and detecting faked photographs.

1   In a letter to me (26 February 2000) Douglas P. Horne noted that Zavada actually had not seen any such double images during his shooting experiments in Dealey Plaza.

2   Regarding such written affirmations, four autopsy personnel (Humes, Boswell, Ebersole, and Stringer) signed a document entitled, "Report of inspection by naval medical staff on November 1, 1996, at the National Archives of X-rays and photographs of autopsy of President John F. Kennedy." Nonetheless, subsequent comments by several of these signatories made it clear that the clos-

ing assurances in this document were false: contrary to their statements, not all of the autopsy photographs were included in the collection. Therefore, there already exists in this JFK case a demonstration of how little reliance can be placed on written affirmations prepared by attorneys for the signature of others.

3   Among LeWinter's many escapades in the world of intelligence, his role in William Casey's meetings in Paris (October 1980) are particularly well documented. A short biography is also cited. See Gary Sick, *October Surprise* 1991, pp. 149-150. Sick served on the National Security Council staff under Presidents Ford, Carter, and Reagan. A second book that lists many of LeWinter's adventures (see the index) is Rodney Stich, *Defrauding America: Encyclopedia of Secret Operations by the CIA, DIA, and other Covert Agencies* 1998.

4   Subsequently, the foundation that owns Monticello also acknowledged that Jefferson was the father of one, if not all six, of Sally's children (*San Bernardino County Sun*, 27 January 2000, p. A11).

5   Even the ARRB, in its final report, disparaged eyewitness testimony in general. In particular, their report seems to mock a Parkland physician for describing Jackie as dressed in white (instead of pink)—surely a nonsalient item!

6   Livingstone has recently published a series of five articles ("The Zapruder Film: A Study in Deception," *The Fourth Decade*, May 1999 through January 2000). Livingstone's energy and passion have greatly advanced the discussion of Zapruder film authenticity. His work also initially ignited my own interest in this complex issue.

7   Douglas P. Horne has reviewed the factual content of the preceding paragraphs (regarding the film maps) and has confirmed their accuracy.

8   Since I had missed the full implications of this issue in my initial reading of the Zavada report, I am greatly indebted to Douglas Horne for bringing it to my attention again.

[*Author's note:* I also spoke by telephone, and sent a certified letter, to the Department of Justice before they paid $16,000,000 for the film (which price did not include the copyright). My letter strongly recommended one simple test: just shoot some film through Zapruder's camera. DoJ never responded to my letter and this undemanding test has never been done. In a subsequent letter, I suggested that the Zapruder family should be required to refund the purchase price if the film were ever proven to be altered. DoJ did not respond to this letter, either.]

[*Editor's note*: Mantik's letter to DoJ, which appears on the following page, was one of a series of communications between the editor, David W. Mantik, and Jack White with Leslie Batchelor, Assistant Deputy Attorney General, who was representing the ARRB in negotiations over compensation for the government taking possession of the Zapruder film as an "assassination document." The question of authenticity not only affects the film's value as an historical artifact but even extends to the question of copyright, since presumably the copyright privilege would attach only to the original "out of camera" version shot by Abraham Zapruder on 22 November 1963 and not to any subsequently altered version. (See Appendix B.)]

August 14, 1998

Ms. Leslie Batchelor
Civil Division
Department of Justice, Room 3736
950 Pennsylvania Avenue, NW
Washington, DC 20530

Re: Authenticity of the Zapruder film

Dear Ms. Batchelor:

Thank you for your courteous response to me today on the telephone.

I think no one in the JFK assassination research community could ask for much more than a film (or films) shot through the *original* Zapruder camera. Such an experiment has already been done within the past year with a virtually identical camera-- with nearly the same serial number. I have seen these films. This experiment has succeeded only in raising even more questions. It is critical that this experiment be repeated with the *original* camera, which, I am told, has been on display at the Sixth Floor Museum in Dallas, Texas.

There has been serious speculation that the images on the extant Zapruder film have been magnified in the process of alteration and therefore cannot be the original. I have personally calculated the expected angle of view from the known optical parameters of this camera. Using known sized objects in the actual field of view (e.g., the limousine, the background buildings) it is also possible to calculate the angle of view that is actually seen in the film. The disagreement between these two numbers is larger than I would expect at the full zoom (telephoto) setting that Zapruder said he used. And if the camera had actually been set at less than full zoom, the mismatch is even worse. The direction of this disagreement does suggest that the extant images are too large, as has been implied previously. Furthermore, I did not find this problem for the Nix film.

It is absolutely critical that the actual angle of view be determined for the original camera when set at full zoom. This will be trivial for any expert to do. I suggest, however, that one simple additional step be taken. To satisfy the critics, some well known object should be filmed from a well known position (e.g. the Lincoln Memorial as seen from the Washington Monument). This will allow anyone afterwards to do their own measurements of size and distance and to calculate the angle of view, which can then be compared to the actual film. If these simple steps are taken, they will go a long way toward satisfying the questions of many chronic students of this case.

My understanding is that the Assassination Records and Review Board has been reluctant to engage in investigations of this type, apparently interpreting such steps as beyond their charter. However, I note that the FBI will soon be examining material found on one of the bullets discovered in JFK's limousine. That is obviously an investigation, so, if that can be justified, then surely shooting film through the *original* Zapruder camera can also be justified.

Thank you again for your attention to this matter. I am very pleased that you are positioned to assist in a matter that is so central to our national history.

Sincerely yours,

David W. Mantik, M.D., Ph.D. (Physics)

Letter of 14 August 1998 from David W. Mantik, M.D., Ph.D., to Leslie Batchelor, Assistant Deputy Attorney General, proposing that the authenticity of the film be tested by taking new images with the original camera, which might serve to settle many important questions. The Department of Justice, however, declined to accept this recommendation and, as a consequence, these questions remain unsettled.

Date: Thu, 03 Sep 1998 16:11:05 -0500

To: Ms. Leslie Batchelor US Department of Justice

Dear Ms. Batchelor:

Let me introduce myself. I am Jack White, historical researcher of the JFK case for 35 years. My specialties are the JFK photographic evidence and the identity of Lee Harvey Oswald. I was a photographic consultant to the House Select Committee on Assassinations in the late 70s.

Dr. James Fetzer has asked me to send you on a regular basis the results of ongoing studies of the Z film and the MPI video for consideration in the Justice Department assessment of the Zapruder film. This is an ongoing study by Dr. Fetzer, Dr. David Mantik, me, and about a half dozen other qualified researchers. This is message number 1.

I will be sending you additional email messages the next few days or weeks, covering the following:

1. A listing of possible anomalies observed in the film.

2. A listing of possible anomalies observed in the MPI video/DVD version.

3. Various graphic depictions of anomalies as computer attachments. I am attaching to this message one of the graphics which I believe clearly shows tampering. Please respond by email as soon as possible IF you receive this graphic. Many of my explanations will depend on your ability to receive photos on your computer screen, so I need to know as soon as possible so I may proceed.

Please let me know by return email if you receive the attachment. It is a photo I took in Dealey Plaza in July from the Z pedestal. Overlaid is Z frame 304, showing Jean Hill and Mary Moorman in their exact position and sized as closely as possible to actuality. Clearly the Z frame shows much more area than is seen from the Z viewpoint. I plan to reshoot the July scene with far greater accuracy, using an 8-foot pole marked in feet for exact scale. I will describe each graphic I send, and will answer any questions which may occur to you.

I have many VERY CONVINCING exhibits indicating tampering.

After I hear back from you I will start sending study results.

Cordially,

Jack White

An email of 3 September 1998 from Jack White to Leslie Batchelor, Assisstant Deputy Attorney General, volunteering to submit evidence of alteration of the original Zapruder film at her request. He recieved no response from the Department of Justice in this matter.

Part VI

Jesse Curry's
JFK Assassination File
Could Oswald Have Been Convicted?

James H. Fetzer, Ph.D.

[*Editor's note*: Jesse Curry's *JFK Assassination File* (1969), the existence of which I learned from John Hamilton, J.D., provides ample evidence to exonerate Oswald of the assassination of JFK. Without any doubt, given the evidence available here, any reasonably competent defense attorney could have gained an acquittal; indeed, he almost certainly could have forestalled an indictment. This probably explains why Oswald was denied the right to legal representation, a blatant violation of his Constitutional guarantees, even though he repeatedly requested representation.]

Among the important players during President John F. Kennedy's visit to Dallas on 22 November 1963 was Chief of Police Jesse E. Curry, who had joined the department on 1 May 1936 and retired on 10 March 1966. He was uniquely situated to influence and (even) control many events associated with the assassination, including the conduct of the motorcade, its route and its security, the search for the killer, the apprehension and interrogation of Lee Harvey Oswald, and his transfer from city to county custody, during which Oswald in turn was assassinated by Jack Ruby. After his retirement, former Chief Curry would publish his own *JFK Assassination File* (1969), a 135-page paperback book that was sold exclusively in 7-11 Stores across the United States in limited numbers.

This slender, relatively obscure, volume has several fascinating features. Divided into seven chapters ("A Turbulent City," "The Security Planning," "The Fatal Motorcade," "The School Book Depository," "Lee Harvey Oswald," "Assassination Evidence," and "The Oswald Killing"), it includes an assembly of photographs, documents, and records, 65 of which are identified as "exhibits" and assigned numbers, as a judicial proceeding in a court of law would require. As Jesse Curry himself explains at the conclusion of Chapter 1, he has attempted to present a first-person account based upon his own personal experience:

From the documents and evidence in my file I have attempted to present an objective historical reconstruction of the investigation. This is not an attempt to present a new theory about what happened at the assassination. It does not attempt to support any existing theory or validate the findings of *The Warren Comission Report*. . . . Unanswered questions and puzzling evidence are not buried in irrelevant facts or answered by theories and conjecture. The events and evidence must be allowed to speak for themselves, and people must form their own conclusions (Curry 1969, p. 8).

These are admirable sentiments, worthy of emulation. However, it is difficult to imagine why he would have bothered to go to this much trouble unless he harbored reservations of his own about the conduct of the inquiry and the guilt of the accused. The evidence he presents suggests that Lee Oswald could never have been convicted of this crime.

My USMC Background

Commissioned an officer in the United States Marine Corps upon my graduation from Princeton University in June 1962, by November 1963, I was a 2nd Lieutenant serving as Fire Direction Officer of the Mortar Battery/1st Battalion/ 12th Marines/3rd Marine Division, which was based in Okinawa. My unit had recently been moved out to cover the evacuation of American civilians, were it to prove necessary, in the aftermath of the assassinations of Ngo Dinh Diem and his brother, Ngo Dinh Nhu. But things cooled down enough that this measure was not needed, and we were sent to Taiwan instead.

Anchored out in Kaohsiung Harbor aboard the LPH Iwo Jima, I was awakened by the Officer of the Deck, Fred Rentschler, my Executive Officer, who informed me that the President had been shot in Dallas. The time was around 3:30 AM, which corresponded to around 1:30 PM in Texas. He awakened me again about an hour later to tell me that a communist had done it, which even then seemed to me to be pretty fast work. I do not recall strong sentiments being expressed by the officers and men at the time, but the Marine Corps was the most professional and the least political of the services.

Recruit Training

By June 1964, I had returned to the states and been assigned as a Series Commander at the Recruit Depot in San Diego. (This is the same place and rifle range, Edson Range, where Oswald had been trained.) In that capacity, I supervised teams of drill instructors as we took groups of recruits through training cycles. My principal responsibility was to make sure the DIs did not kill any of the recruits. When I first arrived, we had the capacity to train 8,000 recruits on 11 week cycles but, the following year, it fell to me to revise the program to train 16,000 on 8 week cycles. By June 1966, I held the rank of Captain but resigned to pursue a Ph.D. in the philosophy of science at Indiana University.

The book that captivated my interest at the time was *Six Seconds in Dallas* (1967), in part because its author, Josiah Thompson, was a professor of philosophy. I found his presentation compelling and began to study the case. I would guess that, from 1967 until 1981, I thought about the death of Jack Kennedy virtually every night, attempting to sort out some connection between Dallas, the CIA and the Mafia. I can still recall the shiver I experienced when I read the entries in *Who's Who* (circa 1964) for Charles and Earle Cabell, which I have reproduced in *Assassination Science* (1998).

The Office of Naval Intelligence

The hypothesis that Lee Harvey Oswald was responsible for the death of JFK is more than faintly ridiculous. Oswald's history with the Marines strongly suggests that he was recruited early by the Office of Naval Intelligence. An oficer knows everything there is to know about his men, and, if Oswald was studying Russian (including an apparent stint at the Monterey School) and if he was stationed at Atsugi (the most secure base in our military arsenal at the time), it was official business. Indeed, his intelligence connections have been thoroughly documented by Philip Melanson, *Spy Saga* (1990). [*Editor's note*: See also John Newman, *Oswald and the CIA* (1995), Noel Twyman, *Bloody Treason* (1997), Michael Calder, *JFK vs. CIA* (1998), and James Bamford, *Body of Secrets* (2001), which illuminates the origins of the assassination with our own Joint Chiefs of Staff.]

Oswald's DD 1173 (Curry 1969, p. 109)

The strongest confirmation that Oswald was working for naval intelligence may be his DD 1173—N 4,271,617—a form of identification only issued for those injured on active duty to insure their medical coverage or for civilian employees overseas who needed military ID. (Similar ID was carried by Francis Gary Powers, U-2 pilot and CIA contract agent downed in the Soviet Union.) Issued 11 September 1959 and in his possession at the time of his arrest, it was nearly obliterated when it was finally released by the FBI in December 1966. But photographs may be found in Ray and Mary LaFontaine, *Oswald Talked*, (1996) and in Jesse Curry's *Assassination File* (1969).

Too Little Ability, Too Few Rounds

Moreover, Lee Oswald had neither the ability nor the opportunity to assassinate the President in Dealey Plaza. Although he qualified with a 212/250 in 1957, he seems to have failed to qualify in 1958 and barely qualified with a 191/250 in 1959. That his best score was as a recruit is unsurprising, since that is the period of most intense instruction. His training was with an M-1, which is semi-automatic, rather than with a single-shot, bolt-action weapon, such as the Mannlicher-Carcano. Oswald was not trained to use a telescopic sight, to shoot at moving targets, or to fire from tall buildings.

Among the more fascinating of recent discoveries has been that of Noel Twyman, who has observed that only two spent shell casings were recovered from the alleged assassin's lair. [*Editor's note*: See Robert Groden, *The Search for Lee Harvey Oswald* (1995), p. 166.] In *Bloody Treason* (1997), he reprints an evidence photograph showing two spent and one unspent shells. Similar photographs may be found in Gary Shaw's *Cover-Up* (1976) and, significantly, also in Jesse Curry's *Assassination File* (1969), a copy of which I have reproduced below. Curry also included an FBI report dated 23 November 1963 that is signed by J. Edgar Hoover listing two spent cartridge casings and one unspent cartridge. If there were only two spent cartridges, then *The Warren Report* (1964) must be wrong.

Magic Bullets and Paper Bags

The two spent shell casings are marked "1," while the single unspent cartridge is marked "6." Other interesting items include "3," which Curry describes as "A metal fragment from the arm of Governor Connally," a description the FBI report confirms. According to the single bullet theory, it would have to be from CE-399, which is the alleged "magic bullet." Since CE-399 is not missing nearly enough metal—indeed, it is nearly pristine apart from some lengthwise distortion—this "evidence photograph" proves that CE-399 could not have been the "magic bullet" that hit President Kennedy and Governor Connally, which destroys the single bullet theory at a single bound.

The paper bag marked "7," moreover, is supposed to be the wrapping in which Oswald had brought his Mannlicher-Carcano into the Texas School Book Depository. Anyone who has dealt with weapons of this kind, no matter whether rifles or carbines, knows they can be both oily and awkward. If this bag had been used to carry a rifle or carbine—no matter whether assembled or not—it would have been oily or torn. (Try this as an experiment.) If it was not used by anyone to carry a rifle or carbine anywhere, it surely was not used by Oswald to carry his assembled or disassembled Mannlicher-Carcano into the building.

Wrong Kind of Rifle, Wrong Kind of Rounds

For reasons I do not pretend to fathom, Josiah Thompson has been spending time lately trying to convince Noel that there really *were* three spent cartridge casings from scratch. A third—crimped—cartridge casing of dubious origin was indeed later produced. Even if he were right about that (and these photographs and reports undermine his position), the bullets themselves contradict the autopsy evidence, especially X-rays that display a trail of metallic debris in the President's brain. These are standard military full-metal jacketed bullets that are designed to wound or kill, but not to tear or maim. They are not exploding bullets of a kind that could have distributed metal debris through a brain.

That those who conspired to frame him had to have been unfamiliar with this carbine has also been substantiated by many other sources, including Harold Weisberg, *Whitewash* (1965), Peter Model and Robert Groden, *JFK: The Case for Conspiracy* (1976), and Robert Groden and Harrison Livingstone, *High Treason* (1989), who have observed that the Mannlicher-Carcano, with a muzzle velocity of about 2,000 fps, does not qualify as a high-velocity weapon. Since the death certificate, the autopsy report, and *The Warren Report* (1964) agree that JFK was

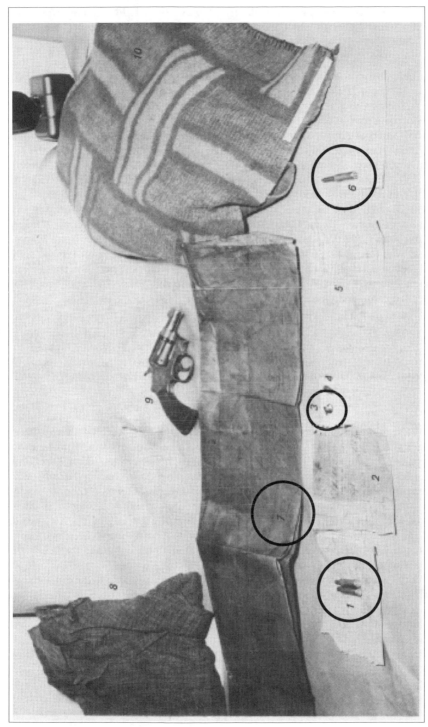

The Evidence Photo (Curry 1969, p. 88). Circle 1. The two spent 6.5mm cartridge casings. Circle 3. The large metal fragment removed from Governor Connally. Circle 6. The unspent 6.5mm cartridge. Circle 7. The wrapping paper Oswald is alleged to have used.

killed by high-velocity bullets, evidently he was not killed by bullets fired from
the Mannlicher-Carcano, as I also observed in the Prologue.

An Absence of Opportunity

In his chronology for 22 November 1963 elsewhere in this volume, Ira David
Wood III records that at least three different Book Depository employees reported seeing Oswald in or around the second floor lunchroom before the assassination over and beyond the motorcycle patrolman and the supervisor who confronted him there immediately after. At 11:50 AM, William Shelley saw him when
he (Shelley) came down to eat lunch; at Noon, Eddie Piper saw him on the first
floor, when he (Oswald) told him he was going up to eat; at 12:15 PM, Carolyn
Arnold observed him sitting in the lunch room; and, at 12:25 PM, she saw him
again, but on the first floor near the front door of the building.

Some of these witnesses would later hesitate to confirm their initial reports
after encounters with the FBI, but that does not alter their significance. Indeed,
no later than 12:32 PM, Oswald was confronted by motorcycle patrolman Marrion
Baker, who found him in the second floor lunchroom and held him in the sights
of his revolver until he was assured by Roy Truly, Oswald's supervisor, that Oswald
was an employee. Baker stated later that the man did not seem out of breath but
appeared calm. As related in *The Warren Report* (1964), pp. 141-142:

> Truly said of Oswald: "He didn't seem to be excited or overly afraid or any-
> thing. He might have been a bit startled, like I might have been if somebody
> had confronted me. But I cannot recall any change of expression of any kind
> on his face." Truly thought that the officer's gun appeared to be almost touch-
> ing the middle portion of Oswald's body.

Posnerian Implausibilities

These and other anomalies are treated as though they were virtues by Gerald
Posner, *Case Closed* (1993), who reports the Warren Commission's finding that it
was *possible* to get from the sixth floor to the lunchroom in less than 90 seconds,
while dismissing the eyewitness testimony that placed him on the first or second
floor! Similarly, he treats the weapon's low muzzle velocity as though it made it
more likely for a bullet to pass through two bodies without damaging itself, ignoring the impossibility of low-velocity bullets inflicting high-velocity wounds!
And, as *Assassination Science* (1998) explains, the computer reconstruction he
cites completely disregards powerful evidence of an entry wound to the President's
throat and another to his right temple.

That Oswald was reputed to have been drinking a Coke at the time he was
confronted—as Posner himself presupposes in a diagram of his purported movements immediately after the assassination (Posner 1993, pp. 480-481)—has struck
me as rich with commercial possibilities. What does the successful marksman
who has just assassinated the most powerful man in the world want to do first?
Hurry across a warehouse floor, ditch his trusty Mannlicher-Carcano, rush down
four flights of stairs and head into a lunchroom—for what purpose? Why, to
have a Coke! Just imagine Oswald with his carbine in one hand and bottle of
Coke in the other. I guess things *really do go better* with Coke. (His adrenaline
would have been pumping so hard he couldn't even get coins into a machine!)

Rush to Judgment

Toward the conclusion of his little book, Curry explains that, even though Oswald was being portrayed all over the world as the man who had killed the President in Dallas, "The Dallas Police Department did not assume that Oswald was guilty and suspend the investigation. . . . Other suspects were still being sought, and Oswald's associates were very carefully being screened to determine if a conspiracy was behind the assassination" (Curry 1969, p. 121). Once again, however, Curry's sentiments are contradicted by the evidence. Even before the President had been buried, the District Attorney, Henry Wade, was declaring that Oswald was guilty of the crime, "to a moral certainty and beyond a reasonable doubt."

Arrest Report on Lee Harvey Oswald (Curry 1969, p. 79)

It would have been a practical impossibility at this point in time to have investigated all of Oswald's friends and acquaintances from his service in the Marine Corps, his pseudo-defection to the Soviet Union, his resurfacing in New Orleans, and his new life in Dallas. In fact, Oswald was only formally charged with the murder of President Kennedy at 1:30 AM on Saturday morning, during a highly irregular proceeding and without any legal representation. Any pretense of investigative integrity and objectivity, however, is completely shattered by the contents of Oswald's "Arrest Report," which was filled out at 1:40 PM on 22 November 1963, including the following specification of arrest details: "This man shot and killed President John F. Kennedy and Police Officer J. D. Tippit. He also shot and wounded Governor John Connally" (Curry 1969, p. 79).

The Negative Paraffin Test

Curry also includes a copy of the paraffin test on Oswald, which indicated that nitrates were present on his hands but were not present on his right cheek. According to the caption Curry added to the report, the nitrate patterns on his hands was consistent with the allegation that he fired the revolver that killed Officer Tippit. But, as any avid TV watcher knows, they are also consistent with the handling of printing ink instead, as would be expected of someone who handled boxes in a book depository. Since the paraffin test taken of the right side of his face did not reveal nitrates and no test was taken of the left side, these results offered no evidence of his having fired a rifle or a carbine. [*Editor's note:* See Harold Weisberg, *Never Again* (1998), pp. 335-337.]

Paraffin test results of 22 November 1963 (Curry 1969, p. 86).

The Patsy

Oswald repeatedly asserted that he was a "patsy," a designated fall-guy who takes the rap while the real culprits escape unscathed. When he was shown the backyard photograph that would later be published on the cover of *Life* (21 February 1964) and used to convict him in the mind of the public, he asserted that that was his head pasted onto someone else's body. [*Editor's note*: That Oswald was right has now been proven beyond a reasonable doubt. See, for example, *Assassination Science* (1998), p. 84 and pp. 206-208.] He also remarked that now everyone would know who he was, not boastfully but with distress, as though his cover identity had been blown.

It may be worth noting that a character in Oliver Stone's film, *JFK*, identified only as "Colonel X," was a real officer by the name of Fletcher Prouty, who never met with Jim Garrison in Washington, D.C., but who was a liaison between the White House, the Pentagon, and the CIA on matters of national security. Just prior to the President's visit to Texas, he was sent to the South Pole for ceremonial reasons. During a stopover in Christchurch, New Zealand, on 23 November 1963, he read an account of the assassination, roughly at the same time the suspect was being charged. On an inside page of the paper was a portrait-quality photograph of Lee Oswald, whose exact source remains unknown. That was pretty fast work. [*Editor's note*: It appears to be the "Moscow defection photo" that ran in many American papers in 1959. See, for example, Groden (1995), pp. 40-41.]

Photograph from the Christchurch, New Zealand "Star" (23 November 1963).

[*Editor's note*: LBJ was actually sworn in as the 36th President. This photograph could most appropriately be entitled, "A Portrait of the Patsy as a Young Man".]

The Truth is Not Enough

In spite of overwhelming evidence of cover-up and conspiracy in the death of JFK, there are discouraging signs. In August 1975, Geraldo Rivera featured Robert Groden and Dick Gregory as guests and showed a copy of the Zapruder film to the American public, which helped contribute to the creation of the HSCA. In August 1999, however, he featured Gerald Posner and Gary Mack, proclaiming his agreement with Posner that the Warren Commission got everything wrong—*except* that JFK was killed by a lone, demented gunman named Lee Harvey Oswald! But if the Warren Commission relied upon false premises, then how can Geraldo possibly know that its conclusion is true?

The Warren Commission was never even able to ascertain a motive for why Oswald would have wanted to kill the President. According to his wife, Marina, for example, Lee admired JFK and what he was doing for the country. The genius of depicting him as a lone, *demented* gunman, therefore, attends the lack of responsibility that implies: if he was irrational, there is no point searching for a rational motive for his deed! *The Warren Report* (1964) is surely the greatest fraud ever perpetrated on the American people. But whether average citizens will ever learn the truth about their history, I fear, hangs upon two slender reeds: our nation's historians and the Fourth Estate.

[Editor's note: *Our nation's newspaper of record,* The New York Times, *has frequently ignored or suppressed new developments in the study of the assassination of our 35th President, preferring to uncritically reaffirm the indefensible tenets of* The Warren Report *(1964). The publication of this story was therefore somewhat of a surprise. A discussion of the failure of our national media to cover this case may be found in* Assassination Science *(1998).]*

Papers Highlight Discrepancies In Autopsy of Kennedy's Brain

WASHINGTON, Nov. 9 (AP) — Documents on the assassination of John F. Kennedy released today raise questions about autopsy work on the President's brain and underline unresolved discrepancies.

The documents, 400,000 pages being made public at the National Archives, were compiled by the Assassination Records Review Board, an independent panel set up by Congress to collect and release material related to Kennedy's death.

In the board's effort to expand and clarify the record, details surfaced suggesting that two brain examinations may have been conducted at the Naval Medical Center in Bethesda, Md., raising questions about the authenticity of the brain examined.

Also unresolved were discrepancies between how doctors at Parkland Hospital in Dallas described the head injury immediately after the shooting and how it was later described by pathologists in Bethesda.

Although the Warren Commission concluded that there was a single assassin, the matter has been hotly debated for 35 years. The board studied old testimony and medical evidence and reinterviewed witnesses.

Jeremy Gunn, executive director of the board, which ended its work in September, said: "There are questions about the supplemental brain exam and the photos that were taken. There are inconsistencies in the testimony of the autopsy doctors about when that exam took place."

Three military pathologists agreed that they conducted an autopsy of Kennedy's entire body at Bethesda immediately after it was flown back from Dallas. But they offer questions about recollections about the timing of a subsequent examination of the brain.

Two doctors, J. Thornton Boswell and James Humes, told the review board that the brain examination occurred two or three days after the death. Dr. Humes told the Warren Commission that he, Dr. Boswell and a third pathologist, Dr. Pierre Finck, were present when the brain was examined. But when he testified to the review board in 1996, Dr. Humes did not list Dr. Finck among those present. Dr. Boswell maintains that Dr. Finck was not there.

But Dr. Finck says the brain examination occurred later. In a memorandum he wrote to his commanding officer 14 months after the assassination, Dr. Finck said Dr. Humes did not call him until Nov. 29, 1963 — seven days after Kennedy was killed — to say it was time to examine the brain. Dr. Finck wrote that all three pathologists examined the brain together and that "color and black-and-white photographs are taken by the U.S. Navy photographer."

The conflicting testimony caused Douglas Horne, chief analyst for military records, to conclude that two separate brain examinations might have been conducted, "contrary to the official record as it has been presented to the American people."

In a telephone interview, Dr. Boswell said the only photographs of the brain were taken at the autopsy.

The New York Times *(10 November 1998)*

Paradoxes of the JFK Assassination:
The Silence of the Historians

David W. Mantik, M.D., Ph.D.

[*Editor's note*: In this essay, David W. Mantik, M.D., Ph.D., the most qualified student to ever study the death of JFK, reflects upon the apparent incapacity, unwillingness, or even cowardice of professional historians to come to grips with what, given its domestic and international consequences, surely qualifies as among the most important events in recent American history, perhaps even in recent world history. Another essay that should be read on this subject is Ronald F White, Ph.D., "Apologists and Critics of the Lone Gunman Theory: Assassination Science and Experts in Post-Modern America," *Assassination Science* (1998).]

> *The most dangerous and vicious of all forgeries are those committed in behalf of a cause—the cause of a nation, of an institution, or of a leader— and intended to bring about a permanent falsification of history.*
> —Allan Nevins[1]

Between 1994 and 1998, the Assassination Records Review Board (ARRB) processed for release approximately 60,000 JFK assassination documents. Its staff also conducted new depositions and interviews with many medical witnesses, some completely new to the case. This wide panorama of fresh sources amassed a compelling case for a post-assassination cover-up in the medical evidence, an area heretofore almost totally ignored by historians. Inasmuch as the assassination is a major event of the twentieth century, and may well represent a turning point in American history, it is incumbent upon historians to understand and explain this event—as well as those that surround it. To date, however, a deafening silence has reigned on these matters, as historians have preferred to tolerate the harvest of *The Warren Report* rather than to cultivate their own fields.

Possibly inquisitive historians, naturally enough, have no craving to be tainted as balmy by the media paintbrushes, as well might befall them were they to admit publicly to such curiosity. The plain fact, though, is that this controversial issue frightens historians: most genuinely fear for their own professional prestige, and many fear subconsciously at what would gaze back at them from the subterranean depths of this case were they to peer too intently into the well of history. Given the unique nature of these events, and their profound impact on America, this fear is understandable. Ultimately, however, these issues must be faced honestly and responsibly. It is no longer sufficient merely to quote a lawyer turned journalist on these serious questions, nor can the matter be left to the most amateur of professions—the media.

Given the manipulation of the autopsy materials (which were controlled by the Secret Service), the post-assassination cover-up necessarily required the assistance of key government personnel, probably at a high level, possibly even the highest. The growing body of evidence for this conclusion is now simply too great to ignore. Heretofore, the historians' tacitly donned mantle of innocence radiated an aura of genteel credibility, but that mantle has become threadbare. If historians continue to deny the deceitful reality underlying the post-assassination cover-up, they, too, risk becoming accessories after the fact. The bar of history is even now calling them to the stand. The time for a response has come.

Introduction[2]

In the summer of 1993, shortly before a visit to the Hearst Castle in San Simeon, I was called to consult on Patricia Lake, an elderly patient with lung cancer. She communicated to me a goal that no other patient—before or since—has ever disclosed: she was writing an autobiography that she hoped to turn into a movie or a play. From a colleague, I soon learned that she was the only child of Marion Davies and William Randolph Hearst (1863-1951), the newspaper magnate and jingoist for the Spanish-American War, who had been immortalized by Orson Welles in the movie, *Citizen Kane* (1941). The striking fact, though, is that Patricia Lake had lived most of her life without knowing who her true father and mother were, which was why she had started writing her autobiography so late. This extraordinary story was recounted in her obituary (*The Los Angeles Times* 31 October 1993, p. 14).

Like my patient who had a secret personal history, countries also have hidden histories, as David W. Belin learned with some distaste in 1975, when he served as Executive Director of the Rockefeller Commission. On 22 December 1974, Seymour Hersh had written a front-page story for *The New York Times* that alleged illegal CIA activities in the US. The next month, President Gerald Ford chose Nelson Rockefeller to lead an investigation of the CIA. Belin, a former counsel to the Warren Commission, was selected by Ford[3] (who had also served on the Warren Commission) to be its Executive Director. During his tenure, Belin learned about the "family jewels," a secret record of CIA activities.[4] He would later write:

> The family jewels contained references to CIA consideration of plots to assassinate Cuban premier Fidel Castro, Dominican Republic dictator Rafael Trujillo, and possibly Premier Patrice Lumumba of the Congo. (Belin, *Final Disclosure* 1988, p. 93)

Ford subsequently initiated new legislation that made it illegal for an American to "... engage in, or conspire to engage in, political assassination" (Belin 1988, p. 128). A similar law was passed (regarding the assassination of US presidents) after the death of JFK. Prior to his murder, it was not federal crime to kill a US president. When a Pandora's box such as this is opened, life becomes unpredictable; the publication of these revelations altered most Americans' view of their own history, particularly since these discoveries came close upon the heels of the Watergate fiasco. Now that another treasure trove has been opened—the new JFK documents and interviews released by the Assassination Records Review Board (ARRB)—our view of American history must inevitably change once again.

The Hidden History of the JFK Assassination

For nearly four decades, historians have chosen to hide from the thorny issues posed by the JFK assassination. Their silence—actually a near abdication[5]—has permitted the media to set the agenda for one of the major events of the twentieth century. When forced to offer an opinion on this matter, historians have chosen, with few exceptions, to recite the Warren Commission version at face value. Given this straitjacket, they have therefore assumed that Oswald did it. That era of innocence has been dying for some time, however, and, by any reasonable measure, is now irrevocably moribund.

Historians are faced with a troubling new challenge—how to write an accurate and responsible history of 22 November 1963, one that takes into account a great deal of new evidence, but also one that cannot avoid turning previous views thoroughly upside down. Since he also served as a board member for the ARRB, Henry F. Graff, Emeritus Professor of History at Columbia University, is a particularly illustrative example of this dying paradigm. Graff chose a remarkably hagiographic title for his high school textbook in American history, in which he stated unequivocally: "He [Oswald] denied any knowledge of the shootings, but the evidence against him was overwhelming" (Graff, *America: the Glorious Republic* 1988, p. 787).[6]

A similar attitude toward Oswald was portrayed in an early post-assassination textbook:

> [JFK] was shot in the head by an assassin, Lee Harvey Oswald. . . [who] had fired upon the President with a rifle from the window of a distant warehouse. No one actually saw him pull the trigger. He was apprehended largely because, in his demented state, he killed a policeman later in the day. . .. He denied his guilt, but a mass of evidence connected him with the crime. . ... foreign countries [were convinced] that some nefarious conspiracy lay at the root of the tragedy. Oswald, the argument ran, was a pawn, his murder designed to keep him from exposing the masterminds who had engineered the assassination. *No shred of evidence supported this theory*. (John A. Garraty, *The American Nation: A History of the United States* 1966, emphasis added)

A later textbook opened the door to conspiracy just a crack: "However, many questions remained unanswered. Private citizens have launched their own investigations. Many still believe that Oswald was part of a conspiracy. Still, no convincing evidence exists" (Thomas V. DiBacco, *History of the United States* 1991, pp. 698–699). A fourth text pushed the door open just a bit more: "In subsequent years, however, questions arose about the assassination; and new investigations—including one commissioned by a committee of the House of Representatives in 1979[7]—cast doubt on the Warren Commission's findings" (Carol Berkin, *A History of the United States: American Voices* 1992, p. 790).

Historians' Fear of "Inarticulate Unpopularity"

The historians' fear of ridicule has surely been a dominant motive for their silence. Merely by waving their denigrating paintbrushes over all lone gunman critics, the media has succeeded in painting any potentially curious historian into a corner where he can expect to be labeled as either a "conspiracy theorist" or an "assassination buff." This is a patently absurd situation, inasmuch as historians who study the Lincoln assassination[8] are never called "conspiracy theorists," and those who study the Garfield or McKinley assassinations are not called "assassination buffs." It is only about the Kennedy assassination[9] that the media have persisted in launching these *ad hominem* attacks.[10]

Moreover, those who favor the single gunman theory are not correspondingly called "lone gunman theorists" nor are they (Gerald Posner, for example) ever called "assassination buffs." This campaign of denigration has been entirely one-sided and it has been very powerful—essentially cutting off all intelligent debate. It is rare in contemporary American society to see an issue so censored—by both the political right and the political left—that snide remarks are often deemed acceptable.[11] Let us be quite honest about this: because of the media's predictable fusillade of tar and feathers, historians are visibly embarrassed at the mere mention of the JFK assassination. This embarrassment is often covered up with curious knowing asides, as if only the *cognoscenti* could understand what all the smirking was about.

Regarding this fear of ridicule, Thomas Spencer Jerome has captured the problem exceptionally well:

> [The historian] finds furthermore that there are various sorts of obligations laid upon him to refrain from truth-telling under diverse penalties. He is a member of a state, a church, a party, a class, a clique, a family, and in all these relations he is virtually obliged to see things as they are not, and to speak that which is false, under penalties varying from execution down to mere inarticulate unpopularity, most difficult to be borne. ("The Case of the Eyewitnesses," in Robin Winks, editor, *The Historian as Detective: Essays on Evidence*, 1968, p. 190)[12]

Here is the heart of the matter. It is not that historians (or their *de facto* stage managers —in this case, the media) have settled on the lone gunman theory after a thorough review of the evidence. Merely listening to one of them for several minutes is often sufficient to reveal his (or her) primitive grasp of the case. In fact, the real problem lies elsewhere. It is this man's (or woman's) fear of embarrassment before his (or her) peers—the dreaded "inarticulate unpopularity," described by Jerome, that has led to the historians' present tongue-tied silence. The media have been able to abort nearly any serious discussion merely by *ad hominem* attacks, no matter the expertise of the lone assassin critic in question. They have argued by not arguing. They have won by not fighting. It would be difficult to find a better illustration of the dictum, "who controls the present controls the past" (George Orwell, *Nineteen Eighty Four* 1949, p. 32).

The Power of the Media

The power of the media has served its masters well; with one exception, no well-known historian has yet publicly entertained an alternate scenario in the JFK assassination. That exception is Michael R. Beschloss:

> Richard Helms found Lyndon Johnson distracted well into 1964 by his worry that Kennedy had been assassinated by conspiracy. As Helms recalled, the Agency was "very helpful to Johnson on this" and met the new President's request for an independent CIA study. Motion pictures of the Dallas motorcade and autopsy photographs were sent over to the Agency. (Beschloss, *The Crisis Years: Kennedy and Khrushchev, 1960-1963* 1991, p. 682)

Why the American public was expected to believe the lone assassin theory of *The Warren Report* (September 1964), when LBJ himself did not, has never been explained, nor have the contents or conclusions of this CIA study ever been released to the public. Beschloss concludes, "We will probably never know beyond a shadow of a doubt who caused John Kennedy to be murdered and why" (Beschloss 1991, p. 687).

Dissenting from this conspiracy view and probably speaking for most historians, Stephen Ambrose[13] praised Gerald Posner's much-ballyhooed book, *Case Closed* (1991):

> Posner has done a great service, in the process proving that a single researcher, working alone, is always preferable to a committee. This is a model of historical research. It should be required reading for anyone reviewing any book on the Kennedy assassination. Beyond the outstanding job of research, Posner is a dramatic storyteller. The recreation of Oswald's, and Jack Ruby's, personalities is wonderfully well done. This case has indeed been closed by Mr. Posner's work.

However, several sources patently admired by Posner—those whom he actually cites—have not been kind to Posner, as can be seen from the following three examples:

(1) Robert Blakey, Chief Counsel for the House Select Committee on Assassinations (HSCA), regarding Posner's *Case Closed*, wrote: "Posner often distorts the evidence by selective citation and by striking omissions. . . he picks and chooses his witnesses on the basis of their consistency with the thesis he wants to prove." ("The Mafia and JFK's Murder—Thirty years later, the question remains: Did Oswald act alone?" *The Washington Post National Weekly Edition*, 15-21 November 1993, p. 23.)

(2) Historian David Wrone (of the University of Wisconsin-Stevens Point) stated in a peer reviewed journal: ". . . his book is so theory driven, so rife with speculation, and so frequently unable to conform his text with the factual content in his sources that it stands as one of the stellar instances of irresponsible publishing on this subject. Massive numbers of factual errors suffuse his book, which make it a veritable minefield" (*Journal of Southern History* 61 (February 1995), p. 186).[14]

(3) Roger McCarthy, President of Failure Analysis Associates (FaAA), the company that provided the scientific material for the mock trial of Oswald performed by the American Bar Association in 1992, executed a sworn affidavit
stating that (1) Posner had requested his company's prosecution material
but not the defense's material, that (2) Posner failed to declare in his book
that FaAA had also prepared a case for the defense, that (3) the jury, after
hearing both sides, could not reach a verdict, and that (4) Posner failed to
acknowledge the role of the American Bar Association in the trial. Finally,
McCarthy added that during Posner's early television interviews, he left the
clear impression that the prosecution work in question had been done at his
(Posner's) specific request and he did not acknowledge the role of FaAA.
(See Addendum 1.)[15]

Both Ambrose (in history) and I (in physics) completed our doctoral work at
the University of Wisconsin. We were both born and raised in Wisconsin (see
Ambrose, *Comrades* 1999). I had hoped, partly for these reasons, to be able to
open a conversation with him, but all of my correspondence has been met with
silence. In this, he is probably no different from his colleagues. Jacob Cohen[16]
has responded similarly to my attempts to engage him in dialogue. Moreover,
when I submitted a letter to the editor in response to Max Holland, "The
Docudrama That is JFK," *The Nation* (7 December 1998), it was ignored. Holland offered no informal response either, but Arthur Schlesinger, Jr., who is often
cited in Holland's article, after reading my letter, offered his opinion that I might
reasonably have expected at least a personal reply from Holland. (See Addendum 2.)

But this silence over Dealey Plaza cannot last forever. Inevitably, this deliberate evasion must break down; even now, it can be maintained only by ignoring a
treasure trove of new evidence. Some day a (probably young) historian will catch
the sunlight glistening from this newly found repository, will gradually recognize its worth, and begin to turn it over, piece by piece. After he has done so, the
weight of the evidence will force his colleagues to follow, albeit with some heavy
foot dragging. After the prolonged silence of the historians, this pioneering historian will recognize the impossible paradoxes and contaminated evidence in
this case, and will thereby forever alter all subsequent discussion. But so long as
historians accept the evidence at face value, our history books will continue to
mislead yet more generations of school children, as I unfortunately discovered
last year in the case of my own daughter, who was in the fifth grade at the time,
where she heard a talk that incriminated Oswald as the lone gunman.

The Misleading Medical Evidence[17]

Powerful evidence now exists for forgery or, at the very least, a highly deceptive depiction of the most critical forensic evidence. This includes misleading or
seriously altered autopsy photographs, forged skull X-rays, and the substitution
of a different brain. Compared to this seemingly-radical interpretation, however,
all other explanations pale in explanatory power, so much so that they strain
credulity far more.

The evidence for forgery within the X-rays is particularly strong. My quantitative measurements of the skull X-rays at the National Archives (using, for the first

time, an optical densitometer) have been presented in multiple graphs (*Assassination Science* 1998, pp. 120–137). By eight distinct and consistent lines of evidence, these objective and reproducible data led to a clear cut prediction, namely: that the largest metal-like object (6.5 mm across and nearly round) on the *extant* skull X-rays was not present on the *original* X-rays. Astonishingly enough, this is entirely consistent with the historical record, since no one at the autopsy ever reported such an object. (As in the case of other forged evidence, foul play was suspected early on by Harrison Livingston, *High Treason* 1989, p. 81.)

A short time later, quite independently of my own work, Larry Sturdivan, the ballistics expert for the HSCA, also concluded—based on his ballistics expertise—that this same bullet-like image could not possibly represent a real bullet fragment. (He is quoted in the companion medical essay.) Therefore, two separate lines of evidence from two quite different disciplines agreed that something was very wrong with these X-rays. To put this question finally to bed, I asked the ARRB to interrogate all three pathologists about this most flagrant—and noteworthy—object on the X-rays. *Under oath*, not one of the three could recall seeing this object on the X-rays during the evening of the autopsy, despite the fact that the primary purpose of the X-rays was to locate and remove precisely such major pieces of forensic evidence.

Moreover, when I asked him about this object, John Ebersole, the radiologist, abruptly and forever terminated our entire conversation. Quite independent of possibly imperfect human memories, no such object had been removed during the autopsy, as I could judge for myself at the National Archives. The two fragments removed during the autopsy are still housed there (CE-843). Neither are remotely like the 6.5mm object; both are much smaller. Nor can studies performed on them in the interval explain this enormous discrepancy. The negative responses from the three pathologists—as well as fragment evidence in the National Archives—therefore led directly to two major conclusions: (1) my hypothesis that this 6.5 mm bullet-like object was not visible on the original X-rays was validated,[18] and (2) a critical prop for the HSCA's high bullet entry (on the back of the head) was abruptly shattered.[19]

After all of this, the only residual evidence for a shot to the top rear of the head was photographic. At this critical juncture none of the three pathologists could be called upon to resuscitate the HSCA's hypothesis of a single successful assassin. That was because each of them had strongly disagreed with the HSCA's proposal of a shot high to the back of the head, as the HSCA itself embarrassingly understood (and admitted in print) during its own investigation in 1977-78 (7 HSCA 115). Moreover, the ARRB discovered previously buried information about the autopsy camera. The HSCA had actually examined the only camera that could have been used to take the autopsy photographs, and had found that it did not match the current films in the Archives. The HSCA then buried its own discovery.

But now the tension heightened, for these photographs, too, were called into question on yet other grounds. The ARRB heard from *several, independent,* new witnesses who had seen (and handled) actual autopsy photographs that no longer exist. Other evidence makes it painfully clear that multiple autopsy photographs are indeed missing, photographs that undeniably conflict with the extant photographs (of the back of the head) and that also bear directly on the question of a frontal head shot. As a result, the accuracy (possibly even the authenticity) of the existing photographs (of the back of the head) has fallen under the deepest suspicion. Since the now-dubious shot to the (high) back of the head was the *sine qua non* for the HSCA's sole successful gunman (apart from a second gunman who missed)—and for virtually all subsequent lone gunman theories—the case for the lone assassin has been severely, if not irreparably, damaged. [*Author's note*: These issues are all discussed in much greater detail in the companion medical essay, where I introduce further evidence from the X-rays and even from the pathologists themselves, which corroborates all of the above statements.][20]

The evidence for substitution of a different brain is also remarkably strong, based on a myriad of disparate, but consistent, pieces of data compiled by Douglas Horne of the ARRB (and supported by Jeremy Gunn, the Executive Director). Furthermore, my direct comparison of the skull X-rays (using quantitative data) to the brain photographs (work I had actually completed prior to the ARRB), has provided ideal corroboration for Horne's proposal of two separate brain examinations of two different brains on two different dates. [*Editor's note*: Horne's study and Mantik's medical essay appear elsewhere in this volume.]

By all that is reasonable, these new discoveries ought to reverse the judgment of history. Heretofore, dozens of experts who never saw the body itself, on seeing the posterior head photographs, have had no choice but to conclude that JFK was shot in the head from the rear. Virtually all the eyewitnesses, on the other hand, dispute the photographs of the back of the head. If these images have been fabricated (or even merely designed to mislead), as now seems indisputable, then the fundamental question stands open, almost as if the murder had occurred only yesterday. And the evidence presented in the companion medical essay—derived from an astonishing variety of sources—makes precisely such a case for falsification or, at the very least, for intentional obfuscation. Moreover, if Oswald really did it by himself, as the offical accounts proclaim, why were such extensive—and dangerous—projects of alteration undertaken at all? Why would it have been necessary to frame a guilty man?

This essay, based solely as it is on the medical evidence, can say nothing about whether Oswald pulled a trigger on that sunny November day. It can, however, conclude that the photographs of the posterior scalp have been critically manipulated; that the X-rays of the head have been critically altered; and that the brain was replaced following its removal from the skull at the original autopsy. The purpose of all this activity must have been to tie the alleged assassin to a posterior headshot. After all, the forged 6.5 mm fragment (on the X-ray) had been placed at the back of the skull to match Oswald's location—and the Mannlicher-Carcano does fire 6.5 mm caliber bullets. Moreover, these deceptions could have had no other objective than to mislead and confuse subsequent investigations. That information, by itself, goes some way toward deciding just what Oswald may, or may not, have been doing on that particular Friday in November.

As Allan Nevins stated (in the opening quotation), the most vicious forgeries are those committed in behalf of a cause, specifically those that are intended to bring about a permanent falsification of history. The forgeries (or, at least, gross deceptions) in this case clearly fall into the category that Nevins described; in fact, it is likely that they are the best possible demonstration in history of what he had in mind. Since the result of the forgeries was to implicate a single gunman (Oswald) and thereby to exclude all other suspects, they have, in effect, altered history. If there was a conspiracy to assassinate JFK, then all of those involved have been given a pass to freedom, merely by virtue of the altered medical evidence. And if the conspiracy was a domestic one, especially if it involved elements of the American government, then surely it ought to be a matter of interest to American historians.

If the photographs and X-rays were altered, who did it? And who substituted a different brain for the real one? Surely not the Mafia, who could not have gained access to such guarded items. Nor, for similar reasons, could the anti-Castro Cubans, or the Texas oilmen, or any other non-government group hijack such physical evidence. Only key individuals of the American government (the Secret Service, in particular) had access to these critical items. By itself, this conclusion forces us to take yet another look at the situation. Were key individuals, probably high level government officials, accessories after the fact? Yet it is inescapable. No one, save critically placed government officials, could have permitted this alteration to occur. Indeed, to minimize the risk of subsequent leaks, it is likely that individuals within the government performed the very deceptions in question, even though collaboration with individuals outside the government cannot be excluded, based merely on the present discussion.

John Kaplan (Winks 1968, p. 402) has disparaged the Warren Commission critics (Mark Lane, in particular) because they attacked the lone gunman theory on one isolated issue after another, rather than offering a single coherent critical theory. But what would Kaplan say now? Kaplan's request, although initially a severe challenge to the critics, was intrinsically reasonable. Kaplan had concluded: "It has only rarely been argued that . . . the physical exhibits were altered" (Winks 1968, p. 373). He would not now be able to make that statement. In fact, precisely the opposite is true. It is now possible to construct a kind of unified field theory of the medical evidence in the JFK assassination—the medical evidence is simply not trustworthy. This is just the kind of self-consistent counter-case that Kaplan had demanded. If the medical evidence—the most fundamental evidence in the entire case—has been altered, then this proposal of highly misleading, or even altered, evidence is exactly the type of coherent criticism that Kaplan had required—though perhaps not exactly what he had desired.

The Great Divide

The great divide that separates the partisans in this case is now complete. Those who accept the medical evidence at face value stand on one side, while those who hold suspect most of the medical evidence stand on the opposite side of a yawning chasm. Kaplan, like most of his contemporaries—whether critics or loyalists—could not have foreseen this outcome. Too much information still lay hidden at that early date. By analogy, Arthur Schlesinger, Jr. ("The Problem of Hope," reprinted in Winks 1968, p. 533), has commented on how difficult it would have been in early 1940 for a futurist to forecast the next three American presidents. He would hardly have named the first of these as an obscure senator from Missouri, who anticipated an election loss to the Missouri governor in the 1940 Democratic primaries. Nor would he have considered an unknown lieutenant colonel in the US Army. Nor, finally, would he ever have considered a young man still at Harvard as the third.

As historians begin to review the evidence for a post-assassination cover-up in the medical evidence—one that can no longer be written off as merely benign—they will face major obstacles. Much of this evidence, by its very nature, is medical and scientific and therefore lies outside the customary domain of historians. To analyze it, they must master some basic concepts in anatomy, ballistics, forensic science, radiology, and even some basic physics.[21] To ignore these areas will result in their being entirely at the mercy of the traditional experts, a situation that has already persisted far too long. It is long past time for these authorities to have the last word; each wave of new information in this case has successively shown the reigning authorities to be, not so much wrong, as merely irrelevant.

When close examination of the primary evidence in a case proves it to have been so fundamentally flawed, it is unreasonable to expect traditional experts to be of much value. After all, their life long habit has been to accept these data at face value and then to use their specialized training to make acceptable inferences. Forensic pathologists rarely review cases without the body and the related physical evidence. But that is exactly what happened in the several official reviews of this case—no body, no brain, or even tissue slides were available. The evidence for a single posterior headshot rested almost solely on photographs, and to a lesser extent on X-rays, the same photographs and X-rays that have now been challenged on nearly every imaginable ground and that have also raised serious questions (such as the location of the wounds) in the minds of all three autopsy pathologists.

The Predicament of the Forensic Experts

During a four-hour meeting in Monterey, California, on 19 February 2000 (attended by several independent investigators, including a private detective[22]), I obtained responses to several critical questions, specifically and independently, both from Cyril H. Wecht, M.D., J.D., and from Michael M. Baden, M.D. Both had previously served on the HSCA Forensic Pathology Panel, which Baden chaired. Both men are internationally respected in forensic science; many readers will recall seeing Baden on the stand during the O.J. Simpson trial.[23] Their responses are contained in the following statements. To review a case based solely on photographic and X-ray evidence—without the body or the brain—as was repeatedly done in this case, is distinctly unusual in forensic pathology. Furthermore, these experts do not receive special training in the identification of altered photographs or of altered X-rays, nor are they typically asked to determine whether a brain is authentic (by DNA analysis, for example) before deriving conclusions from it.

In any case, for the subsequent forensic reviews of the JFK evidence, the brain, which is the most important evidence of all, had been missing since at least October 1966. In summary, doubts about authenticity are almost inconceivable during the lifetime of an ordinary forensic specialist. But for the JFK case, these issues of authenticity are absolutely central. In fact, it is quite probable that there is no other case as extreme as this in the annals of forensic medicine. A modern democracy has never had to confront a potentially explosive situation quite like this before. I have described what havoc a much simpler case of forged documents played in the national history of France (Addendum 3).

So historians, to their enormous discomfiture, confront a truly alien situation; they must not only become familiar with fields quite foreign to their training, but, in order to recognize forgeries, they must, in a sense, become even more expert than the experts themselves. It is surely no small surprise that no well-known historian has stepped forward to volunteer for such a daunting task. Much easier, and much more common, has been the path of authors such as John Kaplan, Professor at the Stanford University Law School, who accepted the evidence in this case at face value ("The Case of the Grassy Knoll: the Romance of Conspiracy," in Winks 1968, pp. 371–419). Although Kaplan's article is inevitably dated (written years before the HSCA), it is still an instructive example. Out of curiosity, I carefully combed his essay for items in dispute at present. Confining myself strictly to the medical and scientific evidence (although many Oswald evidence items are also in dispute), I counted no fewer than twenty to thirty medical statements—depending on the selection criteria employed—which have no credibility today. In view of this, it is scarcely a surprise that agreement has been impossible to obtain in this case. Kaplan and I would not even know where to begin a conversation.

Historical Analogies: Revised Verdicts

History has generously provided analogous cases in which new evidence has dramatically reversed the earlier verdict of history. Previous authors[24] have cited the French character assassination of Alfred Dreyfus (between 1894 and 1906) for its similarity to the JFK assassination. Indeed, because of its many lessons, I have summarized this case in Addendum 3. Based on forged documents, Dreyfus was convicted of passing French military secrets to the Germans. The most obvious feature of both controversies was their stubborn unwillingness to die. Each was a chronic, festering wound in the body politic, though the Dreyfus affair was settled much more quickly.

The three successive Dreyfus trials are paralleled by the three American inquiries into Kennedy's murder: the Warren Commission, the House Select Committee on Assassinations (HSCA), and the ARRB.[25] In the Dreyfus case there was a proven patsy, while in the JFK case, Oswald claimed to be a patsy, a claim that is accepted by many independent investigators today. The silencing of witnesses in the JFK case (often at perspicuous moments) was paralleled by the silencing of Picquart. Furthermore, just as Oswald was probably framed[26] by (or at the behest of) government agents, so also government operatives framed Dreyfus.

In both cases, the resistance of the governments to opening their secret files was exceptional. This astonishing tenacity—even after 35 years in the JFK matter—persisted during the ARRB's attempts to obtain records, first by the CIA and the FBI,[27] but later by the US Air Force, the Secret Service, the President's Foreign Intelligence Advisory Board, and the Office of Naval Intelligence (ONI).[28] [*Editor's note:* The Secret Service even destroyed Presidential protection survey reports *after the ARRB requested them; see the Proluge,* "Smoking Gun #14".] Some investigators believe that Oswald had worked for ONI; that ONI was extremely interested in Oswald is not in doubt.[29] In the French case, public sentiment against the Jews deflected suspicion from the real offenders, whereas, in the American case, public fear of communism threw suspicion upon Oswald. Dreyfus was convicted without due process of law (his attorney could not see the evidence), whereas Oswald had no effective legal representation, and was ultimately convicted (after his death) by the Warren Commission's prosecutorial brief.

Another such example is the affair of the destroyer USS *Maddox* in the Gulf of Tonkin (1964), which led to what was, in effect, an American declaration of war on Vietnam.[30] It was only later widely recognized that no shots had been fired at the *Maddox*, and that the radar operators had panicked after seeing ghosts on their screens. Kenneth Davis quotes Stanley Karnow (*Vietnam: A History* 1983): "Even Johnson privately expressed doubts only a few days after the second attack supposedly took place, confiding to an aide, 'Hell, those dumb stupid sailors were just shooting at flying fish.'" (Davis, *Don't Know Much About History* 1995, p. 371). It was eventually discovered that the Tonkin Gulf resolution itself had been prepared two months *before* the *Maddox* affair (Davis 1995, p. 371; Howard Zinn, *A People's History of the United States* 1999, pp. 476–477). As Walt Rostow admitted after the Congressional vote on the resolution, "We don't know what happened, but it had the desired result" (Davis 1995, p. 372).

A third example of the power of new evidence—scientific in this case—is the Sally Hemings affair. For nearly two centuries, historians flatly denied that Thomas Jefferson could have engaged in an affair with a slave. Dumas Malone, who spent forty years writing a multivolume biography, had even denounced this story as "filth" and "virtually unthinkable in a man of Jefferson's moral standards" (Malone, *Jefferson, the Virginian*, 1948). But new evidence ("Jefferson fathered slave's last child," *Nature* 396: 27; 5 November 1998) has led to a dramatically different view, even by mainstream historians. That this turnabout could occur after totally opposite statements from the authorities shows once again the fallibility of historians, or for that matter, any human disagreement in which the evidence is limited.

Even physicists have had to recant some theories of their own in the face of new evidence, while Stephen Jay Gould regales us with stories of paleontologists who still find surprises in the fossil record. An example is the recent discovery that bees appeared at least 100 million years before flowering plants (*Dinosaur in a Haystack* 1995. p. 105). In history, especially, new evidence may emerge at any time, but particularly so on matters within the memory of those still living, and such evidence may totally reverse the previous judgments of history. The limited view of the past still available to us in surviving documents, recollections, artifacts, and inscriptions has been strongly emphasized by historians Carl L. Becker ("What is Evidence? The Relativist View—'Everyman His Own Historian,'" in Winks 1968, pp. 6-7) and R. G. Collingwood ("The Pleasures of Doubt: Re-enacting the Crime—'The Limits of Historical Knowledge,'" in Winks 1968, pp. 514–517).

A fourth example—one that again demonstrates the power of collective human memory (analogous to Thomas Jefferson's black descendants)—was presented on public television by *Nova* (WGBN of Boston) on 23 February 2000: "Are the Lembas of southern Africa one of the 'The Lost Tribes of Israel'?" New DNA analysis has demonstrated that males from Jewish families named Cohen (or Cohane), by Jewish tradition descended from the priestly line of Aaron (the brother of Moses), have a greater than 50% incidence of a particular Y-chromosome marker (the Cohen modal haplotype) that only 10% of the general Jewish male population possesses. The black Lemba tribe of Zimbabwe, a tribe with long traditions as Jews (proscription of pork, circumcision, yarmulkes, prayer shawls, Semitic names, and ritual slaughter with knives that boys keep for life-long use) also demonstrate about the same 10% incidence of these same Y-chromosome markers as layman (non-Cohen) Jews, a figure that is much higher than for non-Jewish groups. Particularly striking, though, was the unusually high (nearly 50%) incidence of the Cohen model haplotype in an elite subclan of the Lemba, known as the Buba. This new scientific evidence requires a reassessment of these traditional—and initially incredible—claims of the Lemba as descendents of the lost tribes. (Lemba traditions also recall that their ancestors founded the "Great Zimbabwe," built between the thirteenth and fifteenth centuries A.D.) These new scientific data provide more support for the validity of collective human memory and also furnish additional support for the reliability of eyewitnesses' recall of specific kinds of events. In a more general sense, though, this episode raises questions about the possible historical roots of other so-called myths. Other examples of myths turning into reality include the work of Heinrich Schliemann (Troy), Sir Leonard Wooley (Ur), and Sir Arthur Evans (Minos).

New evidence from World War II, for example, includes the probable murder of Hitler by his own staff (Hugh Thomas,[31] *The Murder of Adolph Hitler: the Truth about the Bodies in the Bunker* 1995) and FDR's foreknowledge (and perhaps even deliberate provocation) of the Japanese attack on Pearl Harbor (Robert Stinnett, *Day of Deceit* 2000).[32] The latter is based on numerous, recently released documents under the Freedom of Information Act that Stinnett dug out, and also by new interviews that he conducted with still-living protagonists in this matter. If the JFK controversy is considered to be long-lived, though, then it might usefully be compared to the Pearl Harbor controversy, which has already occasioned nine official investigations. Although the final judgment of history is still open on these issues from World War II, this new information will require further serious debate and has the potential again to alter our view of history.

In the realm of literature, Richard Altick ("The Scholar Adventurers," 1950, reprinted in Winks 1968, pp. 108-126) has reminded us of how much new material has emerged in the history of English literature and in the biographies of many of its principals, even in the recent past. In this sense, the past, at least as we view it from the present, is not fixed but rather is ever changing. In fact, the closer to the present an event lies, the more likely it is to change (in interpretation, and even in its basic facts) at some future date. Furthermore, the full implications of a given event may take years, decades, or even longer, to be fully evident. The American Declaration of Independence (whose writing Jefferson deemed less important at the time than his work on the Virginia constitution) is surely a good example of this, its full implications becoming clear only as the decades passed. Consider, for example, the Confederacy's view of this document during the Civil War. These may well be reasons why standard textbooks ignore so much recent American history, an issue that is discussed immediately below.

My former field of physics is crammed with similar examples of new evidence that overturned old theories. For example, classical physics had predicted that the electromagnetic radiation emitted by a black body (an object that absorbs all of the radiation that strikes it) would be infinite at higher frequencies, an absurd result that was appropriately dubbed the "ultraviolet catastrophe." This seemingly simple phenomenon could not be explained by classical physics.

A thoroughly radical revolution, quantum physics, was initiated in October 1900 by Max Planck when he derived the correct formula for this effect. It still remains curious that such a seemingly simple effect was the catalyst for twentieth century physics.

A Black Hole in Twentieth Century History

Any future historian who risks discussing the assassination, or any of the issues that surround it, without mastering the core evidence of the assassination—including these issues of authenticity—will hazard gross error and distortion. Yet these events are essential to our understanding of 20th Century; lists of the century's major events typically include the JFK assassination. If this is indeed a major event, but our history textbooks will not offer even a reasoned hypothesis on who killed an American President, then what purpose do they serve? And if assassination related issues are simply avoided, even including those related to the proximate causes of the war in Vietnam, then a black hole has invaded our own history.

For example, both John M. Newman (Newman, *JFK and Vietnam: Deception, Intrigue, and the Struggle for Power* 1992) and Robert McNamara (McNamara, *In Retrospect: The Tragedy and Lessons of Vietnam* 1995, pp. 95–96) argue strongly that JFK would not have involved the US in such a war. Even John Connally, one of LBJ's oldest and closest friends, supports this interpretation (Connally, *In History's Shadow: An American Odyssey* 1993 p. 358). Comments by Arthur Schlesinger, Jr. (in Robert Brent Toplin, ed., "Nixon," *Oliver Stones' USA: Film, History, and Controversy)* and documents released by the ARRB also support this conclusion (*Probe*, March/April 1998).[33] Finally, a new book by David Kaiser (*American Tragedy: Kennedy, Johnson, and the Origins of the Vietnam War*, 2000) describes the war as a pivotal event in American history and as the greatest policy miscalculation in the history of American foreign relations. Kaiser also emphasizes that JFK, often alone, resisted the policies he had inherited from Eisenhower and that he especially resisted involvement in Southeast Asia. This evasion of the JFK assassination, and its aftermath, by historians cannot last forever. Like the physical universe, history also abhors a vacuum.

James Loewen (*Lies My Teacher Told Me* 1995, pp. 233–247) has pointed out the distinction made by many African societies between the remote past (the zamani) and the recent past (the sasha). The former lies beyond the memory of anyone still alive, whereas the latter lies within the memory of the living. One of Loewen's charges is that history textbooks, in general, leave a huge gap in the recent past. Loewen suggests that the authors simply lack the courage to discuss controversial subjects—subjects on which their adult readers, who lived through the events, might well have strong views of their own. For the JFK assassination, this concern is more powerful than for any other subject; in fact, not even Loewen discusses it! In another history book that is somewhat outside the mainstream (Davis 1995, pp. 364–367), supporters of the lone gunman theory are given serious credibility, while critics are given, at most, a demeaning pat on the rear. Yet another history tome that is somewhat off the beaten path (Howard Zinn, *A People's History of the United States* 1999) solves this entire problem with ease. Although Zinn[34] provides a refreshing review of too often neglected, albeit important, events in American history, when it comes to the JFK assassination—one of the twentieth century's major events and one of history's greatest mysteries—the admirable Zinn opts for total silence.

The Law of Facts and Frameworks

C. S. Lewis[35] relates the tale of the woman who saw a ghost but who still refused to believe in the immortal soul (*Miracles: A Preliminary Study* 1947, p. 7). Arnold Toynbee (*A Study of History* 1973, p. 486) has articulated a similar concept: "Facts, then, cannot come into existence without the good offices of an hypothesis." These two British authors have proposed the same idea: if one's worldview does not have room for a specific concept then the evidence for that concept remains invisible. This same theme runs through several works in historiography such as those by Barbara Tuchman (*Practicing History: Selected Essays* 1982, pp. 13–32), Ernst Breisart (*Historiography: Ancient, Medieval and Modern*, 1983 pp. 326–336), and David Hackett Fischer (*Historians' Fallacies: Toward a Logic of Historical Thought* 1970, p. 4).

Fischer describes this issue as the Baconian fallacy, to wit, the idea that an historian can work without preconceived hypotheses: "He is supposed to go a-wandering in the dark forest of the past, gathering facts like nuts and berries, until he has enough to make a general truth."[36] For the most definitive statement of this principle, however, I can do no better than to quote Carl Becker:

> Left to themselves, the facts do not speak; left to themselves they do not exist, not really, since for all practical purposes there is no fact until someone affirms it. The least the historian can do with any historical fact is to select and affirm it. To select and affirm even the simplest complex of facts is to give them a certain place in a certain pattern of ideas, and this alone is sufficient to give them a special meaning. . . . It is thus not the undiscriminated fact, but the perceiving mind of the historian that speaks ("What is Evidence?" in Winks 1968, pp. 18–19).

Preceding Lewis, Toynbee, Fischer, and Becker in identifying this logical concept, though, were two other giants of intellectual history, Charles Darwin and Immanuel Kant. Stephen Jay Gould quotes Darwin as follows:

> About thirty years ago there was much talk that geologists ought only to observe and not theorize; and I well remember someone saying that at this rate a man might as well go into a gravel pit and count the pebbles and describe the colors. How odd it is that anyone should not see that all observation must be for or against some view if it is to be of any service! (Gould 1995, p. 148)

Even before Darwin's quotation, Kant, in a famous quip cited by Gould (p. 148), noted that concepts without percepts are empty, whereas percepts without concepts are blind. I have therefore re-labeled this fundamental insight as "The Law of Facts and Frameworks." All of these writers have recognized the same idea, namely: that information cannot function as evidence when it lies beyond a conceptual framework.

If data speak most clearly when they lie within a specific framework (and are correspondingly silent when they do not), then the example par excellence—of how to employ highly selected data and simultaneously to disregard all discordant data—must be *The Warren Report*. As a corollary, data that did not lie within the framework of the Commission's preordained conclusions were buried. Such data must now, almost literally, be dug up from the ground to see the light of day. My companion medical essay provides an alternative model, one that encompasses a much greater range of evidence in this case. Long silent data ignored by the Commission (often without explanation) begin, at last, to find their voices.

The Death Throes of *The Warren Report*

Regarding the death throes of old theories, such as (in my view) *The Warren Report*, Gould has offered a deep insight:

> We say, in our mythology, that old theories die when new observations derail them. But too often—I would say usually—theories act as straitjackets to channel observations toward their support and to forestall potentially refuting data. Such theories cannot be rejected from within,[37] for we will not conceptualize the disproving observations. . . . We escape by importing a new theory and by making the different kinds of observations that any novel outlook must suggest. (Gould 1995, p. 151)

Gould then illustrates his insight with Luis and Walter Alvarez's[38] proposal (1979) that an asteroid or comet caused the mass extinction that killed the dinosaurs. As Gould notes, this proposal has won increasing support in the intervening two decades.

Warren Commission supporters have generously illustrated Gould's concept of a theory in decline—these devotees have been remarkably creative at bending any disagreeable fact to fit the framework of *The Warren Report*. Blakey and Wrone (cited above) have caustically assented to this conclusion, viewing these writers as tied up in straitjackets. The critiques by Weisberg and Scott (also cited below)—and of other authors not cited here—illustrate many more examples of such Procrustean fact-bending. Even worse, though, sometimes these disciples are so committed to their hypothesis that evidence that grossly violates their worldview cannot even be seen, such as when Posner describes the limousine stop, a conclusion that would immediately prove alteration of the Zapruder film (Posner 1993, p. 234).[39] Most assuredly, this conclusion would be quickly denied—with revulsion—by Posner himself, were it brought to his attention.

The JFK assassination may also be the best historical example of disparate facts that make no sense at all within a particular logical structure (the one erected by the Warren Commission), but which suddenly become luminous when seen through the lens of an alternate hypothesis. Examples are the bullets that several witnesses either saw or heard strike Elm Street. Their reports are included in the Warren Commission's 26 volumes of supporting evidence, but are totally ignored and never explained in the 888-page report itself. Other examples are the 6.5 mm "bullet" cross section at the back of the head on the JFK skull X-rays, an object that no one reported until 1968, or the very long list of apparently disparate facts that suddenly fell into place when Douglas P. Horne proposed two separate examinations of two different brains on two different dates.[40] The explanatory power of the new paradigm is striking, embarrassingly so when compared to the old one (*The Warren Report*). The number of old, previously ignored, facts that suddenly come alive, like Pinocchio, is astonishing. The examples cited in this paragraph are merely a small cross section of the entire case.

The reverse situation—that of a previously missing concept (and the supporting facts that were overlooked)—is Jared Diamond's recent Pulitzer Prize winning opus, *Guns, Germs, and Steel* (1997) in which he brilliantly proposes a general theory, based largely on evolutionary biology, of the rise and fall of human societies. The facts that support his proposal have been known for some time, but the disparate nature of the evidence—much of it lying outside of the traditional boundaries of historical research—meant that these facts were invisible until the proper hypothesis was advanced.

Detective fiction provides many similar illustrations: the critical forensic facts cannot be recognized until the correct hypothesis is advanced (R. G. Collingwood, "Who Killed John Doe? The Problem of Testimony—from *The Idea of History*," in Winks 1968, pp. 39–60). In a very real sense, Toynbee is correct: if facts have no meaning within a larger context, there is a sense in which these facts do not exist at all. Until they fall into place within a logical structure (a theory or hypothesis) they have no life of their own and eventually they may disappear completely.

Historians will have trouble with this case for the above reasons as well—there is simply no historical precedent of this magnitude, i.e., a case in which so much of the physical evidence has either been altered or deliberately made deceptive. Although cases of forged documents, occasionally of forged physical evidence, or even of photographs,[41] can be cited, there is no comparable case in which such extensive suspicion is warranted, let alone proved. In this sense, too, historians will be entering strange waters. They will find themselves almost rudderless. If this were some obscure area of history it would be one matter, but this is different; like downtown Manhattan, the entire area has already been thoroughly explored—and staked out. Historians are much more accustomed to entering a virgin terra incognito where their footsteps are the only fresh ones (or nearly the only fresh ones). How different this will be for them; it is likely that this thought, too, has frightened them from entering the fray. Scores of self-designated experts lurk behind the nearest shrubs with glee, eagerly hoping to throw daggers into the backs of these newly arriving historians or to catch them in some unsuspecting trap. Such a stimulating setting will seem like an extraterrestrial encounter to the historian, who is, more often than not, a civilized explorer, not an adventurer into well traveled territories that contain heavily armed and warring factions.

The End of Silence?

Perhaps, though, this ancient glacier of silence (about the post-assassination cover-up) is beginning to melt a bit. For his recent book, Michael Parenti (*History as Mystery* 2000), drawing extensively from the synthesis of Gary L. Aguilar, M.D., has described the misrepresentations of Gerald Posner. (See also Harrison Livingston, *Killing Kennedy* 1995, Chapter 7.) That this discussion occurs in a book that is not solely devoted to the JFK assassination is also a good sign. Here-

tofore, virtually all discussions of the JFK murder have occurred in a kind of
vacuum, almost as if the events had transpired on Mars. But the more the assassination and the attendant cover-up are seen as merely another chapter in American history, the better we shall all understand it, not to mention related historical events, and the more likely it is to appear in standard history textbooks. By
writing about it in this fashion, Parenti has done us a great service.

Historian David Wrone has also entered the arena. He has written about the
Zapruder film ("The Zapruder Film. A Brief History with Comments," 1997) and
co-authored *The Assassination of JFK: Comprehensive Historical and Legal Bibliography* (1980). He has also described the waywardness of Gerald Posner. Regarding Posner's misdeeds, in particular, the media have been astonishingly silent. But this is not hard to understand. Since the death of David Belin, a fervent
believer in the lone gunman theory, the media, like the ancient Philistines, have
had no comparable champion to match up against the Davids (there are literally
many) on the other side in this case.

Michael L. Kurtz, a professor of history at Southeastern Louisiana University, has taught a course on the assassination for several decades, and has published peer-reviewd articles, such as "The Assassination of John F. Kennedy: A
Historical Perspective," *The Historian* 45 (1992), pp. 1–19, as well as a thought-
ful and detailed book in several editions (*Crime of the Century: the Kennedy Assassination from a Historian's Perspective* 1993). Kurtz himself is also proof that
the medical and scientific evidence is well within the grasp of the historian who
makes a serious effort to master it. His book also provides a great deal of historical background for the probable forces at work in the assassination. His book
deserves to be widely read by historians.

Three more books should be added to this short list: (1) Henry Hurt, *Reasonable Doubt: An Investigation into the Assassination of John F. Kennedy* (1985); (2)
John Newman, *Oswald and the CIA* (1995); and (3) Peter Dale Scott, *Deep Politics
and the Death of JFK* (1993).[42] Although Hurt initially expected to find convincing evidence that Oswald had acted alone, his research forced him to conclude
that the evidence actually pointed away from Oswald. He now believes that the
assassination led to a pervasive transfer of power and brought about profound
changes in America.

Newman is both an historian[43] and a twenty-year former military intelligence
officer with the National Security Agency. He employs new interviews with highly
placed officials and newly released documents to show Oswald through the eyes
of the intelligence community. The Oswald connection takes Newman into the
agency's most secret elements, including the Soviet Russia Division, Angleton's
ultra-secret Counterintelligence Special Investigation Group, and the Special
Affairs Staff's anti-Cuban operations.

Scott, a former Canadian diplomat and current professor of English at UC
Berkeley, believes that JFK's death was not just an isolated case, but was rather a
symptom of hidden and deeper processes in domestic and international policies.
He goes on to identify the "structural defects" within the US government that
first permitted the crime to occur and then to go unpunished. He argues that the
JFK assassination has enduring relevance even today because these deep structural defects have still not been corrected. Mainstream historians never cite any
of these books, if they have even read them.

On the Predictability of History

A traditional view has it that history cannot be predicted (Barbara Tuchman, *Practicing History: Selected Essays* 1981, p. 249), that historians find it difficult enough to explain events after the fact, let alone before it. Jared Diamond, however, has challenged that view, at least for certain situations. He has amassed an amazing quantity and variety of evidence, largely from evolutionary biology, to explain the fates of human societies, beginning with the rise of agriculture in the Fertile Crescent. He has furthermore challenged historians to ". . . develop human history as a science, on a par with the acknowledged historical sciences such as astronomy, geology, and evolutionary biology." (*Guns, Germs, and Steel* 1997, p. 408). At the same time, however, Diamond acknowledges that individual events—and their subsequent impact on history—cannot be predicted.

For example, if Churchill had been killed as a pedestrian in 1931 by a New York taxi driver (Robert Cowley, Editor, *What If: the World's Foremost Military Historians Imagine What Might Have Been* 1999, pp. 306–307) or if Hitler had been killed during a 1930 traffic accident (Diamond 1997, pp. 419–420), history would have followed a different path. Similarly, if the peace loving Kaiser Frederick III of Prussia had not smoked cigars[44] (Alfred Jay Bollet, "Smoking and Cancer in the 19th Century," *Resident and Staff Physician*, August 1997, pp. 45–47) he might have ruled longer than 99 days in 1888, thus preventing his arrogant and militaristic son, Kaiser Wilhelm II, from aggravating tensions before World War I. Curiously, Wilhelm II had his own encounter with a cigar in 1889 (the year of Hitler's birth), when Annie Oakley came to Berlin. Annie was stunned when the Kaiser publicly volunteered to puff on a cigar while she shot it with her Colt. Not daring to risk a major loss of face, and wishing that she had had less alcohol the night before, she took aim and blew his ashes away (Cowley 1999, pp. 290-291). After World War I began, Annie began to realize that she had made a mistake; after the war was over she wrote to the Kaiser, asking for a second shot, but he never replied!

My own analogy is that evolutionary biology, which Diamond used to make his astonishing predictions, is like statistical mechanics. Based on physical interactions among large numbers of submicroscopic particles, powerful predictions can be made, but about a unique atom or an individual molecule—like a single human being—nothing useful can be predicted. Likewise, if Diamond is correct, successful predictions are sometimes possible for selected human societies, just as they are for large collections of particles.

For the prediction of post-assassination cover-ups, however, by analogy to individual atoms and molecules, the historian is quite helpless, unless he just happens to interview one of the perpetrators at the right moment and this individual is willing to talk! For the JFK assassination, no one (possibly excepting the initial perpetrators) could have predicted the turns and twists through which this case would pass before finally reaching its present denouement. It is only within the past several years, and especially since the new releases by the ARRB, that the contours of this unique case have arisen, like the Sphinx, from the sands of history.

It may be, however, that Diamond would wish to suggest more work for the historians—for example, that certain historical milieus predict for certain outcomes. At the time of the JFK assassination, for example, the climate in America was one of fear of international communism; in retrospect, the moral environment within the government condoned the overthrow of foreign leaders, or even their assassination; and the intelligence establishment was becoming autonomous. Regarding this last point, Arthur Krock,[45] the Washington correspondent for *The New York Times*, had written:

> The CIA's growth was "likened to a malignancy" which even the "very high official was not sure even the White House could control. . . any longer. . . .. If the United States ever experiences [an attempt at a coup to overthrow the Government] (sic) it will come from the CIA and not the Pentagon." The agency "represents a tremendous power and total unaccountability to anyone." ("In the Nation: The Intra-Administration War in Viet Nam," 3 October 1963, p. 34.)

Does a constellation of symptoms such as this, perhaps with several others added to the mix, predict that a nation is ripe for either an assassination or some other major violation of its traditional ethical norms? Not being a historian, it is not my place to make this argument, but perhaps historians should examine such issues.[46]

The Fallacy of Moral Superiority

The French have long been famous for their Gallic sense of superiority, which they so disastrously demonstrated during the Franco-Prussian war—by wearing their traditional *pantaloons rouge* (for the last time). Fischer (1970, p. 6) reviews the work of the distinguished French historian, Fustel de Coulanges (1830-1889), whose students applauded him after a lecture, to which he responded with the famous line: "Do not applaud me. It is not I who speaks to you, but history which speaks through my mouth." According to Fischer, Fustel was convinced that he had diminished the national French bias that had so marred the writing of his chauvinistic colleagues—but (according to Fischer) he had merely disguised it. In his major work, written immediately after the Franco-Prussian war, his (Fustel's) main point was to minimize the Teutonic influence that other scholars had discovered in the development of French and English institutions.

But just as Fischer named a historical disease (Carr's disease) after an English scholar, so also Germany does not escape his sarcasm. He censures German historicism (Fischer 1970, p. 156), especially the "nasty idea that whatever was becoming, is right." Given this view, he notes that Germany's downward descent into Nazism was a natural evolution. But Fischer does not stop there—he aims a barb at the more modern notion of "Top Nations," of whom the US is now foremost:

> Something of the fallacy of ethical historicism appears in the absurd and dangerous idea that America's rise to power and prosperity is a measure of its moral excellence—that the history of the Republic can be seen, in short, as a system of morality. How many of us have not, at some time, silently slipped into this error.[47]

Indeed, the adjective, "glorious," in the title of Graff's history text—*America: The Glorious Republic*—is an illustration of this error. A prior expression of this superior American attitude was manifest destiny (Norman Graebner, editor, *Manifest Destiny* 1968), an attitude usually attributed to the 1840s, but which was presaged by the European-American treatment of its native peoples almost as soon as Columbus met the Arawaks, carried on at Acoma, New Mexico (1599), continued by slave trading Pilgrims of New England, maintained during the Pequot War of 1636-37, and particularly polished during the subjugation of the civilized Cherokees by Andrew Jackson and Chief Justice John Marshall (Loewen 1995, pp. 91–129).

The 1840s saw the annexation of California and the western territories after the Mexican-American War, a war opposed by Abraham Lincoln (then in Congress) and by Henry David Thoreau. This expansionist attitude culminated with American tacit assent to the overthrow of Queen Liliuokalani of Hawaii in 1893 (followed by American annexation), and the (still controversial) sinking of the *Maine* in Havana harbor (February 1898), which ignited the Spanish-American War.[48] This latter led directly to the Philippine incursion, including massive American strikes against civilians, while Filipinos fought back against America's unwanted hegemony, in the process killing 5000 Americans, an episode all but forgotten by Americans today. All of these episodes personify the American arrogance of power—an arrogance that derived at least in part from America's fundamental presumption of moral superiority. More recent American excursions, partly based on this same historical tradition, include Vietnam, Guatemala, Costa Rica, Iraq, Grenada, Africa, Cuba, the Balkans, and others all too familiar.

The JFK assassination is yet one more example of America's sense of moral superiority. In Europe, especially, this tragedy was immediately recognized as a probable conspiracy; indeed, a domestic conspiracy was quickly suspected. Two of the most outspoken of these foreign observers were Hugh Trevor-Roper and Bertrand Russell, certainly no dim intellectual lights. [*Editors's note:* Russell's essay on this subject appears elsewhere in this volume.] Meanwhile in France, Leo Sauvage, a reporter for *Le Figaro*, published *The Oswald Affair* in March 1965, only six months after *The Warren Report*. (In fact, Sauvage had completed his book a year earlier, but his New York publisher reneged on its signed contract after *The Warren Report* was published.) Europeans have a much longer sense of history, having seen all too many powerful leaders toppled in one country after another, often by conspiracy.[49]

If the American media are to be believed, only in America do such things *not* happen. In fact, this attitude toward the JFK assassination is one of the best examples of America's sense of moral superiority,[50] an attitude held primarily now by the ruling elite, and often seen at both the left and right ends of the political spectrum. Thomas Sowell has captured the sense of moral superiority felt by the left:

> What a vision may offer, and what the prevailing vision of our time emphatically *does* offer, is a special state of grace for those who believe in it. Those who accept this vision are deemed to be not merely factually correct but morally on a higher plane. Put differently, those who disagree with the prevailing vision are seen as be-

ing not merely in error, but in sin. (*The Vision of the Anointed* 1995, pp. 1–6)

Joseph Epstein adds: "Disagree with someone on the left and he is more likely to think you selfish, a sell-out, insensitive, possibly evil" ("True Virtue," *New York Times Magazine*, 24 November 1985, p. 95). On the other hand, the deep-rooted moral superiority felt by the right against the left scarcely needs to be noted. Gary North summarizes this position:

They [the conspirators of the left] "breathe together" against God and God's law, and also against all those who are faithful to God. . . . Thus, the conspirators are at war against Western Civilization. It outrages them. (Larry Abraham, *Call It Conspiracy* 1985, p. xi)

The plebeians are expected to accept the pronouncements of the anointed—namely that America has been granted a special exemption from the devious misdeeds of other nations—such that the conspiracies of other countries cannot possibly infect America. A short list of such foreign examples (in modern times) includes the unsuccessful attempts on Hitler and DeGaulle, and the successful assassinations of Rajiv Gandhi, Anwar Sadat, Luis Colosio,[51] and Salvadore Allende. The plot against FDR[52] and the assassination attempt on Truman[53] are, of course, never mentioned. Ironically, this iconoclastic attitude persists despite the fact that America is one of the easiest places in the world to be murdered. Moreover, this fallacy of American moral superiority is ridiculed by the rest of the world.

The notion that America is stamped from a special mold—one that imparts a nearly indestructible guarantee against political assassinations on its own turf—is perceived as preposterous elsewhere. This parochial attitude among Americans has recently leaped to the fore again—in archeology of all places. As the JFK assassination did for its warring factions, so also the question of the earliest known New World sites of humans has recently raised the emotions of archeologists around the world (to a fever pitch in some places) and has deeply divided them. Americans insist that their sites in North America (usually with Clovis, New Mexico, brands of stone tools) are the oldest, while specialists in Europe tend to side with South American researchers who claim distinctly older sites on their own continent.

The Responsibility of Historians

Becker suggested (Winks 1968, p. 7): "History is the memory of things said and done," while Carr stated: "History is the record of what happened." If these are reasonable definitions, then history cannot be the story of what did *not* occur. Such accounts do not belong in the nonfiction section of our libraries, but should be consigned to the fiction section, as some wags have proposed for *The Warren Report*. Winks has also noted: "There have always been many historians who were more concerned that truth should be on their side than that they should be on the side of truth"—a dictum that might reasonably have been applied to Gerald Ford at the moment that he elevated JFK's back wound into the neck (in order to resuscitate the single bullet theory)—without any supporting medical data and without prior consent from the pathologists.

Fischer (1970, p. 315) affirms that a primary purpose of historical scholarship is to help a people (or a nation) achieve self-knowledge, in the way that a psychoanalyst seeks to help a patient. Surely part of that goal is the stripping away of unrealistic illusions. But what shall we say about those historians, such as those whom Winks cites above, who do not try to strip away our national illusions? If these illusions persist, how then shall we address the pervasive and deeply structural problems of America—for example, illusions about the morality of our involvement in certain foreign wars and in many foreign interventions, illusions about our treatment of native Americans and of our black citizens, illusions about our treatment of our underclass in general, illusions about the myth of upward mobility, and illusions about the pervasive nature of bribery and corruption at most levels of American society?

If historians will not address the JFK assassination, not only do they abort the self-understanding that Fischer had wanted for them, but something even more significant follows. According to Henry Hurt, *Reasonable Doubt* (1985), a pervasive transfer of power occurred after the assassination, while Peter Dale Scott, *Deep Politics and the Death of JFK* (1993), advises us that these deep "structural defects" still persist within the American government. John Newman, *JFK and Vietnam* (1992), makes a powerful case that the US could have escaped the war in Vietnam had JFK not been killed. All of these are deeply serious charges—charges that historians have largely ignored. By preserving their silence, historians risk becoming culpable in these charges. Such culpability, if granted, would go well beyond a mere evasion of self-understanding.

If key individuals in the US government, including some in very high positions, participated in the subsequent cover-up (in altering the medical evidence, for example)—then these silent historians have, in effect, functioned as accessories after the fact. This is a very serious charge, but the historians' abandonment of this matter can hardly lead to any other conclusion. A defense for their past behavior, however, may reasonably be offered, one to which I am not unsympathetic. Previously, the available information for conspiracy, though strong, was still growing and the pronouncements of the media made it difficult for historians to part company from *The Warren Report*. But that era is long gone. It is now time for historians to distance themselves from the journalists, and from the remainder of the media, as well.

The journalists—in fact, the entire media—must relinquish their stranglehold on this case. Regarding these primary guardians of the lone gunman theory, Barbie Zelizer[54] has indicted them:

> . . . journalism has not required the trappings of professionalism: many journalists do not readily read journalism textbooks, attend journalism schools, or enroll in training programs (J. Johnstone, E. Slawski, and W. Bowman, *The News People* 1976). Codes of journalistic behavior are not written down, codes of ethics remain largely nonexistent, and most journalists reject licensing procedures (Clement Jones, *Mass Media Codes of Ethics and Councils* 1980; Robert Schmuhl, *The Responsibilities of Journalism* 1984). Journalists are also indifferent to professional associations, and the largest professional association—the Society of Professional Journalists/Sigma Chi—claims as members only 17% of American journalists. Jour-

nalists act as members of a professional association in only a limited sense. (*Covering the Body: The Kennedy Assassination, the Media, and the Shaping of Collective Memory* 1992, p. 6)

Ronald F. White[55], who holds a Ph.D. in history, concurs with this narrow view of journalism as a profession:

> . . . by Kuhnian standards, journalism does not necessarily possess the institutional foundations necessary for the cultivation of expertise. . . . Even more serious is the fact that journalism lacks a subject matter upon which expertise can be attributed. *(Assassination Science* 1998, p. 403)

The role of the media in contemporary American society has been well summarized by Paul Weaver:

> The media are less a window on reality than a stage on which officials and journalists perform self-scripted, self-serving fictions. ("Selling the Story," *The York Times,* 29 July 1994, p. A13)

Two other authors on my bookshelves who are extremely critical of the role of the media in contemporary American society are (1) Pulitzer Prize winning author, Ben H. Bagdikian (*The Media Monopoly* 1992) and (2) Noam Chomsky (*Necessary Illusions: Thought Control in Democratic Societies* 1989). Bagdikian has warned about the chilling effects of corporate ownership and mass advertising, while Chomsky argues that the press no longer serve as advocates of free speech and democracy but rather are the servants of the moneyed corporations. Most importantly, for our understanding of media coverage of the JFK assassination (in my view), Chomsky claims that journalists entering the system cannot make their way unless they conform to these ideological pressures. [*Editor's note*: Yet Chomsky persists in regarding conspiracy theories as romantic illusions in the case of JFK, which allows him as well to disregard the serious obligations that an understanding of this event poses.]

The judgments of the media about the JFK case—almost the sole opinions currently accepted on the American scene—implicitly include conclusions on highly technical and professional subjects, including anatomy, medicine, radiology, ballistics, forensic science, trajectories, neutron activation analysis and more. When have journalists mastered all of this expertise? Furthermore, what knowledge do journalists have of altered or misleading photographs, forged X-rays, and substituted brains? Have any of them read any of the thousands of pages of new releases from the ARRB, or even *The Warren Report* itself, let alone the twelve HSCA volumes? These critical questions cannot simply be left to one of the most amateur of professions in America[56]—but for nearly forty years that is precisely what has happened. On the contrary, historians, who belong to a long-standing profession with an authentic knowledge base, must now begin their own research. They can no longer rely on amateurs. Amateur hour is over.

After all, on what other historical matter would historians offer obeisance to the media? For example, would Stephen Ambrose have permitted Dan Rather (a frequent commentator on the JFK assassination) to set the agenda for his compelling account of D-Day or for his engaging chronicle of Lewis and Clark? Or would David Herbert Donald have allowed even Walter Cronkite (a pundit on Oswald's supposedly miraculous hit) to outline his insightful biography of Lincoln? These are transparently absurd notions, even for historians, yet this is exactly what has happened in the JFK assassination. These remarkable new ARRB revelations—particularly in the medical evidence, but also those that pertain to Oswald—now leave historians with no legitimate excuses. These matters lie beyond the capability of anchormen on the evening news, to say nothing of the common journalist. It is time for the JFK assassination to be taken seriously by historians. One of the greatest events of the 20th century deserves more than snide remarks and sly snickers, or the culpable acquiescence of portentous silence. Historians have some serious work to do.

Historians: Detectives or Pedagogues?

After I had written the above passage, I began to browse through my personal collection of history books looking for further historical insights into this case. Within a few seconds, to my complete amazement, my eyes alighted upon several paragraphs by Herbert Butterfield in a paperback that I had purchased before the assassination. I was astonished by how perfectly Butterfield had captured the essence of the historians' present plight. It was as though he had seen into the future and had written these words explicitly for the present essay—and especially to describe the workings of the Warren Commission. The words are timeless, though they were first delivered at the request of the Divinity Faculty at the University of Cambridge in Michaelmas term 1948, as follows:

> The only appropriate analogy to the authentic work of historical reconstruction is the case of the detective working out the solution of a crime problem in a conventional work of fiction. At the first stage you have the stupid inspector from Scotland Yard who sees all the obvious clues, falls into all the traps, makes all the common sense inferences, and lo! the criminal is self-evident. The whole story of the crime in fact is immediately made clear to us; there is a plausible role in that story for each of the characters concerned; the solution satisfies the mind, or at any rate the mind at a given level; and indeed for this poor Scotland Yard inspector one would say that the study of history ought to be the easiest occupation in the world. Detective stories may not in other ways be true, but it is the case in human affairs that the same set of clues, envisaged at a higher level of thought, with or without additional evidence—the same set of clues reshaped into a new synthesis by a Sherlock Holmes[57]—may produce a new map of the whole affair, an utterly unexpected story to narrate,[58] and possibly even a criminal where in the first place we had never thought to look for one. And the same thing is liable to happen when an historical episode is reconsidered and reconstructed after, say, a century of learned controversy.

> In other words, the development of the scientific method in nineteenth century historiography did not merely mean that this or that fact could be corrected, or the story told in greater detail, or the narrative amended at marginal points. It meant that total reconstructions proved to be necessary, as in the detective stories, where

a single new fact might turn out to be a pivotal one; and what had been thought to be an accident might transform itself into an entirely different story of murder.[59] In these circumstances, evidence, which had seemed to mean one thing, might prove to be capable of an entirely different construction.[60] (Herbert Butterfield, *Christianity and History* 1960, pp. 25–27)

Besides the almost frightening prescience and pertinence of these insights for this case, there was another striking feature of these words for me. Butterfield had captured the essence of my own experience. How often—over many years and often deep into the night—had I wrestled with these discordant and prickly facts. At rare intervals, after puzzling over clues that simply would not fit, I would be granted a new hint (perhaps from a colleague who did not appreciate its value) or I might stumble around a corner and unexpectedly alight upon a new vantage point. On these occasions, I would quickly run back to the primary evidence yet one more time to test a new hypothesis. And sometimes—unexpectedly, and to my great amazement—the pieces finally fit, and I could only wonder how I had missed that particular insight for so long. The fact though is that this case has been so utterly muddled from the beginning (because of the misleading evidence) that it was possible to take only one small step at a time—for fear of shortly ending up in a ditch or in a blind alley. I would like to believe that my missteps over the years now permit me—when the cobblestones on the path fit together like old friends—to jog on ahead at times as I survey new evidence.

I cannot leave Butterfield behind though without also offering his opinion on the authors of history textbooks—comments that are directly relevant to our present predicament. These lines appear on Butterfield's very next page:

If historical education gets into the hands of heavy pedagogues, who teach a hard story in a rigid framework and expect it to be memorized, then new depths of unimaginativeness will have been reached, not possible of attainment without an education in history. If men at twenty learn to see events of history in a certain framework, and learn that framework so thoroughly that it remains on their minds in after-years—if they learn it without acquiring imagination and elasticity of mind—then we can say. . . , that by the study of history, a merely probable national disaster can be converted into a one hundred per cent certainty.

That is exactly what has happened in this case. Whereas initially even the media had some doubt[61] about Oswald's guilt, there is now none at all—a one hundred per cent certainty now reigns among the mainstream media and among mainstream historians.[62] Particularly illuminating is the case of one eastern historian, whose early essays seemed to appreciate some paradoxes in this case. His more recent attitude, on the other hand, has been strident and mocking—a contrast to his initial outlook. He has forgotten how, as a younger man, he himself felt about the fundamental uncertainties in this case. In his now hardened position, he is the model of the historian whose mental elasticity has vanished and whose framework has long since been frozen in concrete. For such elasticity of thought, our only hope would now appear to be a new generation of historians whose eyes have not yet been covered by "the hands of heavy pedagogues." This is not necessarily a severe criticism of this historian, nor is he especially unusual; even Einstein could never accept the full implications of quantum theory. Ironically, it was not for his new theory of relativity, but as a reward for his 1905 groundbreaking work on the photoelectric effect (in quantum mechanics) that he won a Nobel Prize in physics.

Epilogue

Two books from an earlier period of my life are particularly interesting for the light that they shed on a superficially innocent time, but one that, in fact, had a more ominous underlying reality: (1) Fred J. Cook,[63] *The Corrupted Land: the Social Morality of Modern America* (1966), and (2) Walter Goodman, *All Honorable Men: Corruption and Compromise in American Life* (1963). Both volumes review the quiz shows of that era. This sorry episode of American history provides a profound, even frightening, insight into the morality of the common man.

In addition, Richard N. Goodwin (the husband of the LBJ biographer, Doris Kearns Goodwin), has described his personal conversations, as a Congressional investigator, with Herbie Stempel and with Charles Van Doren. Goodwin recalls a single, chilling episode (regarding a quiz show participant) that may shed more light on the probable state of mind of the post-assassination accomplices in the JFK murder than any other incident I have ever known:

> A young, impoverished, poorly briefed, Greenwich Village poet realized, in the middle of his appearance, that he was being asked the identical questions put to him during an earlier private session with a producer. On air, watched by millions of people, he felt compelled to answer, but immediately afterward he accused the production team of fraud and angrily refused to return for his next appearance. He wanted no part of their phony quiz show. The producers were stunned. And they had a right to be. For in my entire investigation, I found no other individual who refused to participate. A man of principle, or a fool [ed.—literally, a Village idiot], he alone sailed against the wind. I don't even remember his name, but I owe him a debt of gratitude, living proof that at least one man could cling to moral principle amid the wonderland of fantasy and greed. (Richard N. Goodwin, *Remembering America* 1988, pp. 58-59)

What can we expect next in the JFK case? If one thing is certain, it is that the media will not inform the public. Their recent behavior—after a jury reached a conspiracy verdict in the assassination of Martin Luther King, Jr.—only clinches the point. This somewhat surprising verdict received only scant mention in the media. America's newspaper of record, *The New York Times* (10 December 1999), buried it deep inside that day's edition—on page 25—while the front page carried a story about a new weight loss method used by Chinese women. In the JFK case, a major breakthrough would be just one American history textbook that merely mentioned the possibility of a post-assassination cover-up in the medical evidence. Given the past record of the publishers, though, that is not likely to occur anytime soon.

Nor does the publishers' primary motive of profit provide grounds for optimism. Most likely this troubling new view of history will unfold in books and articles of limited circulation. Eventually, a critical mass of published material will accumulate, sufficient to bring about a thorough transformation of the textbooks and even (this will surely be the last step) the recognition by the media that something went thoroughly wrong in America, not just on 22 November 1963, but also in the tragic days that followed. Perhaps I can even hope that some day my grandchildren, as yet unborn, will no longer be required to listen to such myths in school, but may instead learn authentic American history from those troubling days and nights. I would not even mind if other similar myths were barred from the classroom. Perhaps I, too, am not yet too old to dream.

Addendum 1: The Roger McCarthy Affidavit

I, Roger L. McCarthy, having been duly sworn, declare as follows:

1. I am Chief Executive Officer of Failure Analysis, Associates, Inc., (FaAA) which is headquartered in Menlo Park California. FaAA, founded in 1967, is the largest engineering firm in the nation dedicated primarily to the analysis and prevention of failures of an engineering or scientific nature. FaAA is a wholly owned subsidiary and the largest operating unit of The Failure Group, Inc., (Failure). Failure employs almost 500 full time staff, including almost 300 degreed professionals, more than 90 of whom hold doctorates in their fields. We maintain nine offices in the U.S., three in Europe, and one in Canada. I am also Chief Executive Officer of The Failure Group, Inc. The Failure Group, Incorporated is a publicly traded company on the NASDAQ exchange, under the symbol "FAIL."

2. I hold five academic degrees: 1) A Bachelor of Arts in Philosophy from the University of Michigan, 2) A Bachelor of Science in Mechanical Engineering from the University of Michigan, 3) An S.M. degree in Mechanical Engineering from the Massachusetts Institute of Technology, 4) The professional degree of Mechanical Engineer (Mech. E.) from the Massachusetts Institute of Technology, and 5) A Ph.D. in Mechanical Engineering from the Massachusetts Institute of Technology (MIT). I graduated from the University of Michigan Phi Beta Kappa, Summa Cum Laude, the Outstanding Undergraduate in Mechanical Engineering in 1972, and a National Science Foundation Fellow.

3. I am a Registered Professional Mechanical Engineer in the states of California (#M20040) and Arizona (#13684). I have authored several dozen scientific papers, and currently serve on the Visiting Committee of MIT's Mechanical Engineering Department. In 1992 I was appointed by President Bush to two year term on the President's Commission on the National Medal of Science. I have attached my current resume with a listing of my publications as exhibit 1.

4. In early 1992 Failure Analysis Associates, Inc. (FaAA) was approached by the representatives of the American Bar Association (ABA) to assist in putting together a "courtroom of the 21st century" instructional session, in the form of a mock trial, for the Annual ABA meeting, which was to be held that summer in San Francisco, California. FaAA was involved in the process of selecting the topic of the trial, which was eventually decided to be the trial of Lee Harvey Oswald for first degree murder for the assassination of President John. F. Kennedy in Dallas in 1963. To simplify the task in coordinating the extensive computer analysis and evidence, FaAA agreed to provide the expert witness analysis, and the testifying experts themselves, for both the prosecution and defense. Separate teams were assembled to assist each side.

5. While FaAA was not funded for the investigation or evidence developed for either side, we applied the best techniques available to some, but certainly not all, of the questions that have remained concerning the assassination, and Lee Harvey Oswald's role in it. The "Courtroom of the 21st Century" theme required the most modern

computerized animation and video presentation. There was not a conclusion reached by FaAA as a company concerning the issues of the assassination. Each of our teams did its best within the factual, time and resource constraints to assist the two eminent trial lawyer teams to resolve the key issues for their respective sides. In the end, after two days of trial, the mock jury, selected by the jury analysis firm DecisionQuest, was split 7 for conviction and 5 for acquittal of Lee Harvey Oswald on the first degree murder charge.

6. Each of our teams sought to find sufficient information in the extensive investigation records of the Warren Commission, and the House Select Committee proceedings, that, when combined with the unparalleled technical analysis skills of our organization, would produce incontrovertible scientific findings that would resolve some of the outstanding issues one way or another. I believe the jury's inability to resolve Oswald's guilt in light of FaAA's investigation, and state-of-the-art visualization, stems from the fact that 1) FaAA did not have the time or resources to completely analyze the whole investigatory record, and 2) there are gaps in the factual record that our analysis was unable to bridge. For example, if the National Archives could locate the brain of President Kennedy, which was sent to them and not buried with his body, we believe the direction of the fatal bullet could be incontrovertibly resolved.

7. Subsequent to our presentation one Gerald Posner contacted Dr. Robert Piziali, the leader of the prosecution team, and requested copies of the prosecution material, but not defense material, which we provided. Eventually Random House published a book by Mr. Posner entitled *Case Closed*. While Mr. Posner acknowledges in the book the material from Failure Analysis Associates he does not mention or acknowledge the ABA, or mention or acknowledge that there was additional material prepared by FaAA for the defense. Incredibly, Mr. Posner makes no mention of the fact that the mock jury that heard and saw the technical material that he believes is so persuasive and "closed" the case, but which also saw the FaAA material prepared for the defense, could not reach a verdict.

8. In early televised interviews of Mr. Posner that were witnessed by FaAA staff, Mr. Posner made no attempt to correct any supposition by a questioner that the FaAA analytical work was performed at his request for him, and certainly left quite the opposite impression.

Further the affiant sayth not.

This affidavit was signed by Roger L. McCarthy and notarized on 6 December 1993.

Addendum 2: My Response to Max Holland

In *The Nation* (7 December 1998) Max Holland claimed that there was only an armful of books of lasting value on the assassination, which he listed. Given Holland's bias, it was hardly surprising that none of these books makes a serious case for conspiracy. Each book, in my view, either is seriously flawed (Holland even admits this about one), riddled with errors of fact, or grossly biased. All are now hopelessly out of date. Serious—even devastating—critiques of these books have appeared elsewhere; it is outside the scope of this essay to itemize these critiques. Surprisingly, though, during Holland's rather long discussion, he scarcely mentioned the medical evidence—the primarily decisive evidence—so I thought it wise to remind him of this. My letter appears below. It was never published and Holland has never acknowledged it. A friendly note from Arthur Schlesinger, Jr., suggested that a reply from Holland, even if informal, would have been appropriate. To date only silence has reigned. Such silence, particularly when preceded by embarrassing, but authentic, questions about this case, has become the signature trademark of the historians (and the journalists, too).

13 December 1998

Letters to the Editor, *The Nation*
13 Irving Place
New York, New York 10003

Re: "The Docudrama That Is JFK" by Max Holland

Dear Editor:

Mr. Holland's (JFK) opus meanders intoxicatingly from piccolo to contra bassoon but only fleetingly sounds the leitmotiv of the assassination. For those who are not tonally deaf, that central theme is heard in the medical evidence.

From the new medical depositions taken by the Assassination Records Review Board (ARRB), we now know that the only recognized autopsy photographer, John Stringer, did not take the autopsy photographs of the brain. A memorandum issued by the ARRB strongly suggests that two different brains were autopsied and that the brain photographs in the National Archives most likely are not those of JFK. My personal, detailed studies of the autopsy skull X-rays, including an original use of optical densitometry, show virtually no brain tissue in a fist-sized area at the front of the skull, just where the photographs (paradoxically) show nearly intact brain. My measurements are not only consistent with the conclusions of the ARRB, but actually anticipated them by several years.

The shot (or shots) to the head pose even worse conundrums for Holland. If he agrees with the pathologists that JFK was struck low on the right rear of the skull, he then has no explanation for the obvious trail of metallic debris that lies more than 4 inches higher. Alternately, if he concludes that a bullet entered much higher, he must then believe that all three qualified pathologists were wrong by 4 inches, and that an absurdly unique event occurred in the history of ballistics—namely that an internal 6.5 mm cross section of a bullet was sliced out and then migrated 1 cm lower and stayed there. In addition, and after all this, he must also believe that the trail of metallic debris still lies well above his proposed entry site. No ballistics expert has ever testified to seeing so much nonsense from one bullet.

Even worse for Holland, just within the past year, Larry Sturdivan, the ballistics expert for the 1977–78 Congressional investigation, has insisted that this 6.5 mm cross section cannot represent a metallic fragment at all—thus crippling the central basis for the conclusions reached in prior official inquiries. My own research on the X-rays over the past 5 years (performed at the National Archives and now published in *Assassination Science*, edited by James Fetzer) agrees with Sturdivan that this object cannot be a real piece of metal. I have, in addition, shown how simple it was in that era deliberately to manufacture an altered X-ray with a 6.5 mm metallic image added to it (so that Oswald's rifle would be incriminated). Finally, at my request the ARRB specifically asked each of the autopsy pathologists under oath if they recalled seeing this flagrantly obvious, 6.5 mm object on the X-rays during the autopsy. Just as I had predicted, none of them could recall this artifact—one that my 7-year-old (nonradiologist) son instantly spotted on the extant anterior skull X-ray.

It is past time for Holland to transport his opus from the baroque era into the modern era. The new themes composed by the ARRB must now be played for a younger audience whose ear canals are not yet encrusted by decades of earwax. The baroque era is over.

Sincerely yours,

David W. Mantik, M.D., Ph.D.
Assoc. Prof. of Radiation Sciences, School of Medicine,
Loma Linda University, Loma Linda, CA
Ph.D., Physics, University of Wisconsin, 1967
M.D., University of Michigan, 1976
Board Certified by the American College of Radiology, 1980

Addendum 3: The Dreyfus Affair

On 9 October 1859, Alfred Dreyfus was born into a prosperous Jewish family in Mulhausen, Upper Alsace, France. Following the unification efforts of Otto von Bismarck, the Germans took possession of the provinces of Alsace and Lorraine after the Franco-Prussian War of 1870. In 1874, Dreyfus left Alsace to live in France. He became a French army officer at age 21 and by 1894 (age 34) he was assigned to the general staff. Although the French feared Germany, hope of recovering the lost provinces was still high; the French looked to the army for leadership, contrasting the officers to the politicians who were too often seen as corrupt and ineffective.

In September 1894, a memorandum ("bordereau") was found in the wastebasket of the German military attaché in Paris. It was an unsigned letter promising information about secret military matters. Because his handwriting was similar to the memorandum—and also possibly because he was a Jew[64] and had lived in Alsace, where he still had connections—Dreyfus was arrested on 15 October 1894.

Despite his claims of innocence, Dreyfus was convicted by a court martial which met in secret. He was deported to Devil's Island in French Guiana. At the trial, his own lawyer was not permitted to see the evidence against him.

The attitude of French high society toward this case is apparent from its veneration of General August Mercier, the Minister of War (in 1894), who had first ordered the arrest. At parties of the *haut monde*, ladies rose to their feet when Mercier entered the room.

In May 1896, new evidence suggested that another French officer, Major Marie Charles Esterhazy, was communicating with the German military attache. The counterespionage unit had a new head, Lt. Col. Georges Picquart, who found that Esterhazy's handwriting was a remarkable match to that of the memorandum. Rather than investigating further, however, Picquart's superiors reassigned him to Tunisia on a dangerous expedition to silence him, but not before he had confided his discovery to a legal advisor.

Alfred's brother, Mathieu, then took up the cause. By October 1897, Esterhazy's name was mentioned publicly and a trial seemed inevitable. Military officials, however, resisted this attempt; more incriminating material was probably added to the secret file against Dreyfus during this time and, in January 1898, Esterhazy was acquitted during a court marital held behind closed doors.

Emilie Zola, the great novelist, then immediately published a newspaper article entitled "J'accuse" ("I accuse") which charged the authorities with conspiring to imprison an innocent man and also to permit a guilty man to remain free, an action that astonished the world. Queen Victoria was stupefied, and negative reactions arrived from around the world, including Berlin, Chicago, and Melbourne. Zola was shortly thereafter convicted of libel and had to flee the country. Many thought that a Jewish conspiracy was out to humiliate the French army, while others thought that the military was arrogant, evading an admission of error and resisting civil authority. The Catholic Church opposed a retrial, thus reviving the old issue of separation of church and state.

On 31 August 1898, Major Hubert J. Henry, an intelligence officer, committed suicide while under arrest at Mont Valerien, but not before admitting that he had forged one of the secret Dreyfus documents. Esterhazy promptly fled France and Dreyfus was returned to Rennes for a new trial, which began on 7 August 1899 (one year after the suicide). Dreyfus, although his innocence was now scarcely in doubt, was again found guilty—but under extenuating circumstances—and he was persuaded to accept a pardon from the French President.

In 1904, more forgeries were discovered in the files and on 12 July 1906, the Cour du Cassation, after a lengthy review, declared unanimously that Dreyfus had been innocent all along—and reinstated him in the army. Esterhazy and Henry were now considered to be the true culprits, who had supplied secrets to the Germans. They had used anti-Semitic sentiment to throw suspicion on Dreyfus—who was thereafter awarded the Legion of Honor.

Picquart was also restored to the army—with a rank of general of the brigade—and within three months Clemenceau appointed him minister of war. And Zola, whose letter had been so critical in the whole process, was given a last resting place in the Pantheon on 4 June 1908. During the procession to the Pantheon, a journalist, Gregori, twice shot at Dreyfus, causing a minor injury to his forearm. He was later acquitted of a murder charge, his plea being that he had merely intended a "demonstration."

The Dreyfus affair had been a French nightmare for twelve years. An unintended consequence was the official separation of church and state. Dreyfus went on to serve in World War I, retiring as a lieutenant colonel. On July 12, 1935, at the age of 74, he died in Paris. Today his statue still stands in Paris at Boulevard Raspail and Boulevard Montparnasse near the Luxembourg Gardens and the great Balzac by Rodin.

Dreyfus sources

1. *The Encyclopedia Britanica* (sic), 11th edition, volume 2, pp. 143-145 (1910). Cambridge, England.
2. *The Encyclopedia Britanica* (sic), 11th edition, volume 8, p. 579 (1910). Cambridge, England.
3. *The Proud Tower, A Portrait of the World Before the War: 1890-1914*, Barbara Tuchman (1966). The Macmillan Company, New York, New York.
4. *The Dreyfus Case*, Louis Snyder (1973). Rutgers University Press.
5. *The Diary of Captain A.F. Dreyfus*, Beekman (1977); a reprint of the 1901 edition.
6. *The Affair*, Jean-Denis Bredin; tr. by Jeffrey Mehlman (1986). Braziller.
7. *The Dreyfus Affair: Art, Truth, and Justice*, Norman Kleeblart, ed. (1987). University of California Press.
8. *Encyclopedia Americana*, volume 9, p. 395-396 (1997). Grolier, Inc., Danbury, CT.

Addendum 4: Conspiracies

The Social Contract is nothing more or less than a vast conspiracy of human beings to lie to and humbug themselves and one another for the general Good. Lies are the mortar that bind the savage individual man into the social masonry.

—Herbert G. Wells

Conspire: *L. conspirare, to breathe together.* 1. to plan and act together secretly, esp. in order to commit a crime.

Foreign (20th century)

Franz Ferdinand	Rajiv Gandhi	Louis Mountbatten
Czar Nicholas II	Adolf Hitler	Rafael Trujillo
Salvadore Allende	Charles DeGaulle	Benigno Aquino
Anwar Sadat	Luis Colosio	Leon Trotsky
Ngo Dinh Diem	Rene Schneider	Pancho Villa
Ngo Dinh Nhu	Jacobo Arbenz	Grigorii Rasputin
Mohammed Mossadegh	Fidel Castro	Walter Reuther [65]
Patrice Lumumba	Malcolm X	Pope John Paul II [66]

Fraser: British History [67]

Stephen (1135-54): attacked in battle by his own wife and his wife's uncle.

Henry II (1154-89): Thomas a Becket is assassinated.

Richard I (1189-99): Richard and King Philip of France defeat Richard's father, Henry II, in battle, after which Henry II dies.

John (1199-1216): he betrays his father, Henry II, in his last days, then battles his brother, Richard, in a clash over Aquitaine.

Henry III (1216-72): overthrown in battle at Lewes by Simon de Monfort.

Edward I (1272-1307): William Wallace leads Scots in revolt & victory at Stirling Bridge.

Edward II (1307-27): Edward's best friend, Gaviston, is captured and murdered by his enemies. The King's first cousin, Thomas of Lancaster, plots against him. After defeat of English at Bannockburn, Thomas controls the strings. Later, his Queen, and her consort, invade England, and the King retires. His jailers later thrust a red-hot spit into his bowels, in order not to leave a mark on him.

Richard II (1377-99): revolt of peasants led by Wat Tyler. Gloucester, Arundel, the Earl of Warwick lead attack against the King. The Merciless Parliament of 1388 leads a full-scale attack on the King's household. Bolingbroke sails from Boulogne and Richard's troops desert. Richard is later secretly murdered in Pontefract Castle, leaving Bolingbroke (Henry IV) haunted by guilt.

Henry IV: (1399-1413): see prior paragraph.

Henry VI (1422–71): York's oldest son enters London in triumph, while the King and Queen escape over the border to Scotland. Henry regains the throne nine years later, but then loses it again and spends his last years as a wandering fugitive. He is eventually executed.

Edward IV (1461-83): Warwick leads a revolt against the King.

Richard III 1483-85): Buckingham, with the assistance of the Woodvilles and the exiled Henry Tudor, revolts against the King. Henry wins the final battle and Richard's dead body is thrown over a packhorse for burial.

Henry VIII (1509-47): Norfolk and Gardiner conspire against Essex.

Charles I (1625-49): He loses his head in the Revolution, making a short king even shorter.

Charles II (1660-85): Coleman and the Jesuits are killed in the matter of the Popish plot. The word, "cabal," enters the English language.

James II (1685-88): William of Orange lands in England and displaces the King, who was allowed to hunt and philander until a stroke took him away at age 66. Perhaps he had the better of the deal, after all.

George I (1714-27): South Sea bubble leads to huge financial losses for some. Walpole becomes England's first prime minister. A succession of Jacobite plots follow—most notably one led by Bishop Attbury's conspiracy.

George III (1760-1820): Americans conspire against Parliament and Crown. The King is also the target of several assassination attempts. Mother Nature, via porphyria, conspires against the King

George IV (1910-36): forged Zinoviev letter leads to downfall of government.

George VI (1936-52): Real Indians, led by Gandhi, conspire against British rule.

Elizabeth II (1952-): death of Princess Diana (?)[68]

Addendum 5. Believers in a JFK Assassination Conspiracy

Lyndon Baines Johnson, President of the United States[69]
Richard M. Nixon, President of the United States[70]
John B. Connally, Governor of Texas[71]
J. Edgar Hoover, Director of the FBI
Clyde Tolson, Associate Director of the FBI[72]
Cartha DeLoach, Assistant Director of the FBI
William Sullivan, FBI Domestic Intelligence Chief
John McCone, Director of the CIA
David Atlee Phillips, CIA disinformation specialist
    (Chief of Covert Actions, Mexico City, 1963)
Stanley Watson, CIA, Chief of Station
The Kennedy family[73]
Admiral (Dr.) George Burkley, White House physician
James J. Rowley, Chief of the Secret Service[74]
Robert Knudsen, White House photographer (who saw autopsy photos)
Jesse Curry, Chief of Police,[75] Dallas Police Department
Roy Kellerman (heard JFK speak after supposed magic bullet)
William Greer (the driver of the Lincoln limousine)
Abraham Bolden, Secret Service, White House detail & Chicago office
John Norris, Secret Service (worked for LBJ; researched case for decades)
Evelyn Lincoln, JFK's secretary
Abraham Zapruder, most famous home movie photographer in history
James Tague, struck by a bullet fragment in Dealey Plaza
Hugh Huggins, CIA operative, conducted private investigation for RFK
Sen. Richard Russell, member of the Warren Commission
John J. McCloy, member of the Warren Commission
Bertrand Russell, British mathematician and philosopher
Hugh Trevor-Roper, Regius Professor of Modern History at Oxford University
Michael Foot, British MP
Senator Richard Schweiker, assassinations subcommittee (Church Committee)
Tip O'Neill, Speaker of the House (he assumed JFK's congressional seat)
Rep. Henry Gonzalez (introduced bill to establish HSCA)
Rep. Don Edwards, chaired HSCA hearings (former FBI agent)
Frank Ragano, attorney for Trafficante, Marcello, Hoffa
Marty Underwood, advance man for Dallas trip
Riders in follow-up car: JFK aides Kenny O'Donnell and Dave Powers
Sam Kinney, Secret Service driver of follow-up car
Paul Landis, passenger in Secret Service follow-up car
John Marshall, Secret Service
John Norris, Secret Service
H. L. Hunt, right-wing oil baron
John Curington, H.L. Hunt's top aide
Bill Alexander, Assistant Dallas District Attorney
Robert Blakey, Chief Counsel for the HSCA
Robert Tanenbaum, Chief Counsel for the HSCA

Richard A. Sprague, Chief Counsel for the HSCA
Gary Cornwell, Deputy Chief Counsel for the HSCA
Parkland doctors: McClelland, Crenshaw, Stewart, Seldin, Goldstrich, Zedlitz,
    Jones, Akin, and others
Bethesda witnesses: virtually all of the paramedical personnel
All of the jurors in Garrison's trial of Clay Shaw[76]
Bobby Hargis, Dealey Plaza motorcycle man
Mary Woodward, *Dallas Morning News* (and eyewitness in Dealey Plaza)
Maurice G. Marineau, Secret Service, Chicago office
Most of the American public
Most of the world's citizens

Acknowledgments

Gary L. Aguilar has contributed greatly to this piece with several critical suggestions. Michael Parenti's bibliography on historiography was a passport to new lands for me. John Newman, Douglas Horne, Roger Peterson, Jim DiEugenio, Dennis Bartholomew, Walt Brown, Michael Kurtz, Patricia L. James, Harry Livingstone, and John and Sherry Szabo have all provided useful reviews and vital suggestions.

It is especially gratifying to thank my own son, Christopher (now 14), for his unique insights. I especially recall our discussion over dinner in San Diego, after viewing the film, *1984*. In addition, we have had pleasant discussions about many books cited here that he has also read. I also thank my daughter, Meredith (now 12), and my wife, Patricia, for tolerating my preoccupation with this case.

Notes

1   "The Case of the Cheating Documents: False Authority and the Problem of Surmise," *The Gateway to History* (1938). Nevins wrote the Foreword to John F. Kennedy, *Profiles in Courage* (1956).

2   For a deeper understanding of this article, the companion medical essay (which also appears in this volume) is required reading: David W. Mantik, M.D., Ph.D., "Paradoxes of the JFK Autopsy: The Medical Evidence Decoded."

3   In a curious coincidence, Ford, Belin, and I all earned professional degrees from the University of Michigan. Even more curiously, Ford (the last surviving member of the Warren Commission) and I have both chosen to live in the same desert community, within walking distance of one another.

4   On 2 November 1975, Ford fired William E. Colby, CIA Director, who had disclosed the family jewels. The next day the Church Committee considered a letter from Ford demanding that its assassination report be held secret (Daniel Schorr, *Clearing the Air* 1977, p. 159).

5   After I had used the word "abdication," I discovered that Max Holland ("Making Sense of the Assassination," *Reviews in American History* 22: 191–209 (1994)) had preceded me with this descriptor. Holland also agrees that historians have steered well clear of this controversy. Historian Michael Kurtz has also observed: "However, few journalists and virtually no scholars have conducted any serious research into the assassination, and their criticisms of the advocates of a conspiracy have generally assumed the guise of name-calling and innuendo rather than legitimate scholarly dissent," in Robert Brent Toplin, ed., "Oliver Stone, *JFK*, and History," *Oliver Stone's USA: Film, History, and Controversy* (2000), p. 173.

6   Graff was nominated for the ARRB by the White House staff. That anyone with such an outspoken and longstanding bias against Oswald was chosen for the ARRB is strik-

ing. During the lifetime of the ARRB, at its final press conference, and during an interview with Dan Rather on the 35th observance, Graff repeatedly insisted that his attitude toward Oswald had not changed. Several other board members, particularly Kermit Hall, followed his example, noting their persistent support for the lone assassin theory. Curiously, however, these members never discussed the medical evidence with the media. Both Graff and Hall are former Army intelligence officers and Graff has long been a member of the Council on Foreign Relations. Although Graff was conspicuous during ARRB media events, he was noticeably absent from public (working) meetings of the ARRB, so much so that rumors began to circulate about his health. Regarding Hall, when he was an administrator at the University of Tulsa, he gave the game away when he fell into a trap laid for him by fellow Oklahoma resident, John Armstrong. For more details on these matters see Jim DiEugenio, "Media Watch: Graff & Posner Spin the Final Report," *Probe* (January-February, 1999).

[7] Although the House Select Committee on Assassinations (HSCA) issued its report in 1979, it was actually established by Congress in 1976. Graff (1988, p. 793) made the same error.

[8] William A. Tidwell, *Come Retribution: the Confederate Secret Service and the Assassination of Lincoln* (1988), makes a compelling case for the complicity of the Confederacy in the plot to kidnap Lincoln.

[9] An occasional exception is the Martin Luther King, Jr., assassination, which a jury recently found to be a conspiracy (*The New York Times*, December 10, 1999, p. 25).

[10] David Hackett Fischer has critiqued such *ad hominem* attacks: "But an *ad hominem* debate is unlike tennis in one respect—it is a match which everybody loses: players, referees, spectators and all" (*Historians' Fallacies: Toward a Logic of Historical Thought*, 1970, p. 293). Also see *The American Historical Review* 73: 996,1710 (1968).

[11] Examples of this genre are (1) Jacob Cohen, "Yes, Oswald Alone Killed Kennedy," *Commentary*, June 1992; (2) Nick Gerlich, "Tragedy on Elm Street: Facts and Fictions in the JFK Assassination," *Skeptic*, Volume 6, Number 4, 1998; (3) Max Holland, "The Docudrama That Is JFK," *The Nation*, December 7, 1998.

[12] The problem noted by Jerome is, unfortunately, not confined to historians—it infests our entire culture, as John Ralston Saul has observed : ". . . never have so few people been willing to speak out on important questions. Their fear is tied not to physical threats, but to standing apart from fellow experts or risking a career or entering an area of nonexpertise. Not since the etiquette-ridden courts of the eighteenth century has public debate been so locked into fixed positions, fixed formulas and fixed elites expert in rhetoric" (*Voltaire's Bastards: the Dictatorship of Reason in the West* 1992, p. 29).

[13] Despite their opposite views of the JFK assassination, Ambrose has offered glowing dust cover reviews for both Posner and Beschloss. Also see Stephen Ambrose, "Writers on the Grassy Knoll: A Reader's Guide," *New York Times Book Review*, 2 February 1992, pp. 23-25.

[14] My own impression of Posner is similar to Wrone's: *Case Closed* is the only book I have ever stopped reading because I came to doubt the integrity of its author.

[15] Several other writers have offered devastating critiques of Posner. Two major examples are (1) Harold Weisberg, *Case Open: The Omissions, Distortions and Falsifications of Case Closed* (1994); and, (2) Peter Dale Scott, "Case Closed? Or Oswald Framed? A Review of Gerald Posner, *Case Closed*: Lee Harvey Oswald and the Assassination of JFK," Peter Dale Scott (1993). The media have steadfastly ignored these critiques.

[16] For further insight into Cohen's role, see E. Martin Schotz, *History Will Not Absolve Us: Orwellian Control, Public Denial, and the Murder of President Kennedy* (1996), pp. 226–229. Schotz is a psychiatrist.

[17] Earlier writers on the medical evidence were David Lifton (*Best Evidence* 1980) and Harrison Livingstone (*High Treason* 1989—co-authored with Robert Groden; *High*

Treason 2 1992; *Killing the Truth*, 1993; and *Killing Kennedy* 1995). I owe both a personal debt of gratitude for their pioneering research and for their generous assistance.

18   By way of explanation, I have described—and have easily been able to reproduce—how this bullet-like image was a subsequent double exposure, superimposed (in the darkroom) onto the now lost original X-ray during the production of the (one) remaining frontal skull X-ray. There is surprising eyewitness support for this activity, so that the time of this forgery can be dated with some certainty. There is reason to believe that the photographic manipulations occurred at about the same time.

19   In a suspiciously conspicuous oversight, the HSCA never identified the proposed entry site for this bullet on the frontal skull X-ray. In retrospect, the reason for this is obvious—there is no visible entry site. This conclusion was verified by precise optical density measurements (of the area in question) at the National Archives.

20   The pathologists' alternate proposal (for a headshot from a sole assassin) is even more absurd—so flagrantly absurd, in fact, that current lone gunman advocates have long since abandoned it. The disproof of the pathologists' proposal is embarrassingly simple, as is demonstrated in the companion medical essay.

21   Douglas P. Horne (ARRB staff member) and Jeremy Gunn (Executive Director), who deposed the medical witnesses, have proved that this is nonetheless possible. Though they arrived with no specific medical training, their work, by far, surpassed that of their predecessors on the HSCA and on the Warren Commission.

22   This was Josiah Thompson, well known for his early work on the case (*Six Seconds in Dallas*, 1967).

23   Baden has recalled his own professional experiences (*Confessions of a Medical Examiner* 1989), while Cyril Wecht has also described his adventures (*Grave Secrets: A Leading Forensic Expert Reveals the Startling Truth About O.J. Simpson, David Koresh, Vincent Foster, and Other Sensational Cases* 1996).

24   After I had summarized the Dreyfus case, I discovered that other writers had noted this analogy before me. Examples are (1) Leo Sauvage, *The Oswald Affair: An Examination of the Contradictions and Omissions of the Warren Report* 1966, pp. 330-331; (2) Art and Margaret Snyder, "Case Still Open: Skepticism and the Assassination of JFK," *Skeptic*, Volume 6, No. 4, 1998; and (3) E. Martin Schotz 1996, p. 247.

25   This pales, however, in comparison to the nine official investigations of the Japanese attack on Pearl Harbor (Robert Stinnett, *Day of Deceit: the Truth about FDR and Pearl Harbor* 2000).

26   The medical evidence for this frame-up is summarized in the companion essay cited in footnote 2.

27   *Probe* (July 22, 1995 and September 22, 1995), front-page articles.

28   Douglas P. Horne volunteered this information in a letter to me (February 26, 2000); Horne served as Chief Analyst for Military Records while at the ARRB. Most of this information is also contained in the *Final Report of the Assassination Records Review Board* (US Government Printing Office, 1998), although a close reading is required to arrive at the same conclusion.

29   For ONI references, see the index in John Newman, *Oswald and the CIA* 1995.

30   America's last declaration of war was in 1941, immediately after Pearl Harbor—now 59 years ago.

31   The dust cover describes Thomas as an internationally respected surgeon who is also an authority on gunshot wounds and their forensic interpretation. He is the author of *The Murder of Rudolph Hess*, which exposed critical evidence about the Spandau prisoner.

32   Charles Beard, who wrote one of the most famous monographs in American history (*An Economic Interpretation of the Constitution* 1913), also charged that FDR and his accomplices had secretly manipulated American policy to bring about World War II

(Charles Beard, *President Roosevelt and the Coming of the War 1941: A Study in Appearances and Realities* 1948). Beard would undoubtedly find some vindication in Stinnett's new book.

[33] The ARRB released a highly pertinent document—regarding the SECDEF conference of 6 May 1963, held in Hawaii, during which McNamara met with top military brass at CINPAC HQ in Camp Smith. The withdrawal of 1000 US troops by December 1963 was specifically advised—and endorsed by McNamara. Furthermore, McNamara subsequently advised that this phase-out program was too slow. Also see Jim DiEugenio, "The Review Board Releases JFK Vietnam Documents," *Probe*, January-February, 1998 and Jim DiEugenio, "McNamara's Secret," *Probe*, March/April 2000.

[34] Schotz (1996, p. 249) has described Zinn's previous interest in the JFK case.

[35] C.S. Lewis, and Aldous Huxley, too, died on 22 November 1963.

[36] This theme is also reviewed by Peter Novick (*That Noble Dream: the "Objectivity Question" and the American Historical Profession* 1988, pp. 33-37), who notes that it is actually the vulgarizations of Francis Bacon's work that are the chief concern in this context. To Novick's credit, he also uses the same quote from Darwin that appears immediately below.

[37] Michael Baden, M.D., apparently still accepts the authenticity of the autopsy photographs, despite all of the evidence that has accumulated against them. I suspect that his view of the autopsy X-rays is similar. Jim DiEugenio reminds us (*Probe*, July/August 1996 and November/December 1998), however, that when Baden served under Chief Counsel Robert Tanenbaum, who favored conspiracy, Baden seemed open to the possibility of conspiracy, but when Robert Blakey replaced Tanenbaum, Baden became a supporter of the single gunman theory. During a telephone conversation with me (7 April 2000), Tanenbaum confirmed that Baden had indeed initially been open to the possibility of conspiracy. Tanenbaum also confirmed to me a remarkable confession by Dan Rather in 1993 (DiEugenio, *Probe*, January-February, 1999, p. 3): "We really blew it on the Kennedy assassination." According to Tanenbaum, Rather had admitted what he has never hinted at on television—namely that the journalists' investigation of the JFK assassination has been inadequate. Like Robert Blakey, Tanenbaum, too, is still a believer in conspiracy; he has even written a fictionalized account of his experiences while on the HSCA (*Corruption of Blood*, 1995).

[38] Luis Alvarez, the Nobel Prize winning physicist, proposed the jet effect as an explanation for JFK's head snap (seen in the Zapruder film); this time, however, Alvarez was wrong. See the next footnote.

[39] David W. Mantik, "Paradoxes of the JFK Assassination: The Zapruder Film Controversy," in this volume.

[40] George Lardner, Jr, "Archive Photos Not of JFK's Brain, Concludes Aide to Review Board; Staff Member Concludes 2 Different Specimens Were Examined," *Washington Post*, 10 November 1998; Deb Riechmann, "Newly Released JFK Documents Raise Questions About Medical Evidence," *Associated Press*, 9 November 1998.

[41] On the very day that I wrote this paragraph, the front page of the *Los Angeles Times* quoted Rafael Perez, who described multiple shootings in which LA police officers doctored photographs of shooting scenes to conceal their mistakes. In one case, ketchup was splattered around to mimic blood, according to the transcripts (*Los Angeles Times*, 15 February 2000). Also see *Time* (6 March 2000) pp. 30–34.

[42] Max Holland ("Making Sense of the Assassination," *Reviews in American History* 22: 191–209 (1994)) reminds his readers that Scott's book, published by the University of California Press, was approved for publication by twenty UC professors, including four senior historians.

[43] Newman holds a Ph.D. in history from George Washington University and is Associate Professor of History at the University of Maryland.

44   Long before Europeans smoked cigars, Columbus found the Arawaks smoking them. In 1555, for the first time, tobacco arrived in Spain and, three years later, the Portuguese introduced Europeans to snuff (Davis 1990, p. 4). Little did Columbus know that he was sowing one seed (tobacco) in preparation for World War I. Besides Kaiser Frederick III, it is likely that two American presidents died as a result of cigar smoking: U.S. Grant, who was given fine cigars after an early Civil War victory, and Grover Cleveland, who developed a cancer of the palate (Bollet 1997, pp. 45–47).

45   Since 1935, Krock had been a family intimate of Joseph P. Kennedy, who was the US Ambassador to the court of St. James before World War II. Krock assisted JFK (Thomas C. Reeves, *A Question of Character, A Life of John F. Kennedy* 1991, p. 49) in the writing of his 150 page undergraduate thesis: *Why England Slept*, which was submitted on 15 March 1940. JFK's father purchased 30,000 to 40,000 copies to help make the book a best seller. In view of Krock's assistance, and JFK's cultivation of journalists in general, was the "very high official," whom Krock cites, actually JFK himself?

46   A similar question is raised by Fischer (1970, p. 315), who suggests that history can be useful for questions of an "if, then" sort. He wonders what conditions have made social stability, social freedom, and social equality maximally coexistent, and then suggests that it may be time for more historians to address such problems.

47   Fischer offers the delightful and pertinent tale of the character in an English academic novel who answers the phone with the line: "History speaking!"

48   Admiral Dewey, after his victory at Manila Bay, was quoted as saying (Louis A. Coolidge, *An Old-Fashioned Senator: Orville H. Platt* 1910, p. 302): "If I were a religious man, and I hope I am, I should say that the hand of God was in it." Richard Hofstadter (*The Paranoid Style in American Politics* 1965, p. 176) quotes the *Christian and Missionary Alliance* as saying that the victory "read almost like the stories of the ancient battles of the Lord in the times of Joshua, David, and Jehosophat (sic)."

49   I have just finished reading *The Lives of the Kings and Queens of England* (Antonia Fraser 2000). Although I knew many of these stories before, to be reminded once again of so many sordid events (often internecine conspiracies) still provoked a certain degree of shock, especially as I contemplated events in America. See Addendum 4.

50   Since Hofstadter, apparently based on a unique source that he has never disclosed, already knew that the JFK assassination was not a conspiracy, he was able to conclude (Hofstadter 1965, pp. 6–7): "One need only think of the response to President Kennedy's assassination in Europe to be reminded that Americans have no monopoly of the gift for paranoid improvisation."

51   Alex Cox, "The Colosio Assassination," *Probe*, January/February 2000.

52   A U.S. House committee, chaired by John McCormack and Samuel Dickstein, stated in its final report that it found credible evidence of a plot to overthrow the American government with a military coup (*US House of Representatives, Public Statement of Special Committee on Un-American Activities*, Seventy-third Congress, Second Session, 24 November 1934). Also see Barbara LaMonica, "The Attempted Coup Against FDR," *Probe*, March/April, 1999 and Oliver Stone, "On Nixon and *JFK*," in Toplin 2000, pp. 289-290. The most detailed monograph, however, is by Jules Archer (*The Plot to Seize the White House* 1973). Archer recounts how the plotters tried unsuccessfully to enlist two-time medal of honor winner, ex-Marine, Major General Smedley Darlington Butler in the plot that he helped to expose. Archer also interviewed McCormack (who was once Speaker of the House). McCormack still had no question but that Butler's testimony had been entirely credible; moreover, McCormack believed that if Butler had cooperated, the plot might have succeeded. I would emphasize that Butler's name is difficult to find in the indices of history textbooks—or even in the memories of American historians.

53 Alfred Steinberg, *The Man from Missouri: the Life and Times of Harry S. Truman* 1962, pp. 390–391.

54 Zelizer was an Assistant Professor of Rhetoric and Communication at Temple University. She is currently at the University of Pennsylvania.

55 White is an Associate Professor at the College of Mount St. Joseph in Cincinnati, and holds a Ph.D. in history from the University of Kentucky

56 Although the vast majority of the media still believes that Oswald did it, this is not the first time that they have played the roles of lemmings. In the summer of 1948, reporters were about 8-1 in their belief that Dewey would win the election (Steinberg 1962, p. 328). The Chicago *Tribune*'s headline, DEWEY DEFEATS TRUMAN, is still a classic in American history. Curiously, Dewey's running mate was Earl Warren; their campaign manager was Allen Dulles, who would become another member of the Warren Commission.

.57 Immediately after the assassination, J. Edgar Hoover also invoked the image of Sherlock Holmes. When Thomas Mann, the US ambassador to Mexico, promptly began to investigate the supposed Oswald visits to the Mexican embassy (apparently because Mann suspected an Oswald double—an issue that is still very much on the front burner today), Hoover told him bluntly, in a note from SOG, to stop trying to play Sherlock Holmes—and Mann unfortunately obliged.

58 Max Planck's discovery of the formula for black body radiation is the perfect illustration of such a radical revolution.

59 At some risk of badgering the reader, I shall point out that the Scotland Yard inspector plays the role of the Warren Commission; Oswald, however, does not play the role of the criminal in question. Finally, the "entirely different story of murder" implies suspects other than Oswald.

60 Fischer (1970, p. 5) concurs with this view of history. He uses the analogy of a master architect who draws a sketch in the sand (e.g., for pyramids), following which laborers cut their stones to fit this monument. But then another architect arrives on the scene and he says that pyramids are out and obelisks are in. Unfortunately, however, most of the old stones are unusable for this purpose. *The Warren Report* (and its so-called facts) is an analogue to the pyramid (and its unusable stones), whereas the obelisk (a monument to conspiracy) must be largely constructed with new stones (i.e., new evidence).

61 The cover of *Life* (25 November 1966) read: "Did Oswald Act Alone? A Matter of Reasonable Doubt." The article itself concluded that the case should be reopened.

62 Even Barbara Tuchman fell into this trap; without any discussion, and with no analysis, she unequivocally named Oswald as JFK's murderer (Tuchman 1981, p. 255). A more recent, and more egregious, example is Paul Johnson (*A History of the American People* 1997), whose work, like Tuchman's, I generally admire. He claims (pp. 868–869): "In more than thirty years since the crime took place, however, no further evidence of any significance has emerged, and virtually all historians now accept that Oswald alone was responsible." What is so ironic about this statement is that its immediate source (citation 64) is not an historian, after all, but rather a lawyer turned journalist (Posner). For the tens of thousands of historians who are caricaturized by this statement, not a single historian is actually cited. An even worse irony is that, only two footnotes earlier (citation 62), a genuine historian is cited—it is Beschloss, who believes in conspiracy, but Johnson does not inform his readers of Beschloss's belief. Johnson also ignores the work of Kurtz, Newman, Wrone, Hurt, Scott, Weisberg, and all other serious writers. To complete the debacle, Johnson also overlooks the ARRB, which had actually begun its real work by early 1995, whereas Johnson's book was not published until 1997.

63 It is probably no accident that Cook was one of the earliest critics of *The Warren Report*; see Schotz (1996, pp. 217–233) for Cook's illuminating anecdotes about his encounters in this case.

[64] On 25 April 1895, the "Jewish Peril" had been violently debated in the Chamber of Deputies; at the same time, the Rothschild bank in Paris had also been bombed.

[65] Robert F. Kennedy, *The Enemy Within* (1960).

[66] Claire Sterling, *The Time of the Assassins: Anatomy of an Investigation* (1983).

[67] Antonia Fraser, *The Lives of the Kings and Queens of England* (2000).

[68] To my amateur historian's mind, it would appear that the rise of Parliamentary government, and the subsequent decline of royal power, correlates with a decrease in conspiracies against the king, especially those triggered by intrafamilial feuds. A statistical analysis of this question would be welcome.

[69] Harrison E. Livingstone, *High Treason* (1989), pp. 8, 68, 344, and 422.

[70] In his series of television interviews with David Frost, Nixon, seemingly without thinking, referred to JFK's conspirators *in the plural*—before quickly and consciously reversing himself.

[71] Although Connally has given verbal assent to *The Warren Report*, he has said much indirectly to malign it. He and Nellie both told the Commission that their own recollection of the shots did not support the SBT—and that, furthermore, they could never be persuaded to believe it. At the instant of shooting, he said, "My God, *they're* going to get us all." As an inpatient at Parkland, he said: "*They* also got the President." Finally, just before he died, he was quoted in *Time* (28 June 1993): "Here we are, I thought, 30 years later, still speculating about what did or did not happen. And no one will ever know the complete truth."

[72] Internal FBI memorandum, 4 April 1967.

[73] Seymour Hersh, *The Dark Side of Camelot* 1997, p. 451. "He [Robert Kennedy] and Jacqueline Kennedy were convinced that the president had been struck down not by communists, as J. Edgar Hoover and many others believed, but by a domestic conspiracy. . . ." Although Hersh is probably wrong about Hoover's true opinion, it is nonetheless striking that he lists Hoover, whose massive FBI tomes provided the basis for *The Warren Report*, as a believer in conspiracy.

[74] James Hepburn, *Farewell America* (1968), p. 59.

[75] F. Peter Model and Robert J. Groden, *JFK: the Case for Conspiracy* (1976), p. 53.

[76] Oliver Stone, "On Nixon and JFK," in Toplin (2000), p. 277.

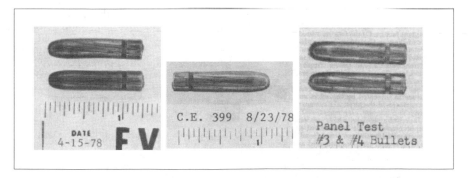

CE-399 and four FBI and HSCA test rounds that never hit anything.

[Editor's note: CE-399 is the bullet that is alleged to have passed through the President's neck, exited his throat, entered Connally's back (shattering a rib), exited his chest, impacted his right wrist, and embedded itself in his left thigh. Now you know why they call it "the magic bullet".]

Soviets Knew Date of Cuba Attack

By Vernon Loeb
Washington Post Staff Writer
Saturday, April 29, 2000: A04

Shortly after the failed Bay of Pigs invasion of Cuba in 1961, a top CIA official told an investigative commission that the Soviet Union had somehow learned the exact date of the amphibious landing in advance, according to a newly declassified version of the commission's final report. Moreover, the CIA apparently had known of the leak to the Soviets--and went ahead with the invasion anyway.

In an effort to oust Fidel Castro, the CIA organized and trained a force of about 1,400 Cuban exiles and launched the invasion on April 17, 1961. Castro's soldiers easily repelled the landing force in less than 72 hours, killing 200 rebels and capturing 1,197 others in what became one of the worst foreign policy blunders of the Cold War.

The investigative commission, chaired by Gen. Maxwell Taylor, was established almost immediately and held a series of secret hearings at the Pentagon before sending a sharply critical report to President Kennedy in June 1961.

While portions of the Taylor Commission's report were made public on two previous occasions, in 1977 and 1986, many pages had been blacked out for security reasons by the CIA. The newly declassified version, in contrast, is nearly free of deletions and contains a wealth of new detail.

The National Archives released the document late Wednesday to the nonprofit National Security Archive, where senior analyst Peter Kornbluh has been working for years to prod the government to release all classified documents on the Bay of Pigs.

. . . . .

Documents found in Soviet archives previously indicated that the Russians had learned some details of the operation in advance, but the Taylor Commission report shows for the first time that the CIA knew about the leak and proceeded with the invasion nevertheless.

The revelation came in testimony before the Taylor Commission--blacked out in previous releases of the report--by Jacob D. Esterline, the CIA operations official who headed the task force responsible for coordinating the invasion.

"There was some indication that the Soviets somewhere around the 9th [of April] had gotten the date of the 17th," Esterline testified. "But there was no indication at any time that they had any idea where the operation was going to take place."

How the leak occurred is still a mystery.

In extremely candid testimony, Esterline called Tony Varona, one of two Cuban exile leaders working closely with the agency, "an ignoramus of the worst sort" who had "no conception whatsoever of security."

Referring to Varona and his cohorts, Esterline complained, "I've never encountered a group of people that were so incapable of keeping a secret."

For this reason, he explained, CIA planners told none of the Cuban participants when the invasion would actually take place until a briefing on April 12. Since the Soviets had by then already obtained the date, either through a source or a communication intercept, "we were able to isolate the fact that the leak could not have been Cuban," Esterline said.

Kornbluh said there is no indication that Esterline or anyone else at the CIA warned President Kennedy of the leak before the invasion took place.

. . . . .

Most of the on-line text of an article from The Washington Post

[Editor's note: *An agency capable of this magnitude of treachery was capable of planning and executing the assassination of a President of the United States who had threatened "to shatter it into a thousand pieces". If historians are now able to reassess responsibility for the failure of the Bay of Pigs invasion, perhaps they can find it within themselves to reassess responsibility for the death of the President who authorized it.*]

Epilogue

16 Questions on the Assassination

Bertrand Russell

[*Editor's note*: Bertrand Russell, one of the most distinguished minds of the 20th century, was quite disturbed by the assassination of JFK and its aftermath, especially the feeble evidence advanced against the alleged assassin. His "16 Questions" are worth considering even today, especially in light of what we know now. This essay, which was written prior to publication of *The Warren Report*, reflects how quickly a keen mind can discern deception, even without the benefit of daily exposure to the American press. In retrospect, that might have been a distinct advantage. It may not take a genius to understand what happened to JFK, but this essay demonstrates that it doesn't hurt.]

The official version of the assassination of President Kennedy has been so riddled with contradictions that it has been abandoned and rewritten no less than three times. Blatant fabrications have received very widespread coverage by the mass media, but denials of these same lies have gone unpublished. Photographs, evidence and affidavits have been doctored out of recognition. Some of the most important aspects of the case against Lee Harvey Oswald have been completely blacked out. Meanwhile the FBI, the police and the Secret Service has tried to silence key witnesses or instruct them what evidence to give. Others involved have disappeared or died in extraordinary circumstances.

It is facts such as these that demand attention, and which the Warren Commission should have regarded as vital. Although I am writing before the publication of the Warren Commission's report, leaks to the press have made much of its contents predictable. Because of the high office of its members and the fact of its establishment by President Johnson, the Commission has been widely regarded as a body of holy men appointed to pronounce the Truth. An impartial examination of the composition and conduct of the Commission suggests quite otherwise.

The Warren Commission has been utterly unrepresentative of the American people. It consisted of two Democrats, Senator Russell of Georgia and Congressman Boggs of Louisiana, both of whose racist views have brought shame on the United States; two Republicans, Senator Cooper of Kentucky and Congressman

Gerald R. Ford of Michigan, the latter of whom is leader of his local Goldwater movement, a former member of the FBI and is known in Washington as the spokesman for that institution; Allen Dulles, former director of the CIA; and Mr. McCloy, who has been referred to as the spokesman for the business community. Leadership of the filibuster in the Senate against the Civil Rights Bill prevented Senator Russell attending a single hearing during this period. The Chief Justice of the United States Supreme Court, Earl Warren, who rightly commands respect, was finally persuaded, much against his will, to preside over the Commission, and it was his involvement above all else that helped lend the Commission an aura of legality and authority. Yet many of its members were also members of those very groups which have done so much to distort and suppress the facts about the assassination. Because of their connection with the Government, not one member would have been permitted under American law to serve on a jury had Oswald faced trial. It is small wonder that the Chief Justice himself remarked: 'You may never know all of the facts in your life time." Here, then, is my first question: *Why were all the members of the Warren Commission closely connected with the U.S. Government?*

If the composition of the Commission was suspect, its conduct confirmed one's worse fears. No counsel was permitted to act for Oswald, so that cross-examination was barred. Later, under pressure, the Commission appointed the President of the American Bar Association, Walter Craig, one of the leaders of the Goldwater movement in Arizona, to represent Oswald. To my knowledge he did not attend a single hearing, but satisfied himself with representation by observers. In the name of national security, the Commission's hearings were held in secret, thereby continuing the policy which has marked the entire course of the case. This prompts my second question: *If, as we are told, Oswald was the lone assassin, where is the issue of national security*? Indeed, precisely the same question must be put here as was posed in France during the Dreyfus case: *If the Government is so certain of its case, why has it conducted all its enquiries in the strictest secrecy?*

At the outset the Commission appointed six panels through which it would conduct its enquiry. They considered: (1) What did Oswald do on November 22, 1963? (2) What was Oswald's background? (3) What did Oswald do in the U.S. Marine Corps, and in the Soviet Union? (4) How did Ruby kill Oswald? (5) What is Ruby's background? (6) What efforts were taken to protect the President on November 22? This raises my fourth question: *Why did the Warren Commission not establish a panel to deal with the question of who killed President Kennedy?*

All the evidence given to the Commission has been classified "Top Secret," including even a request that hearings be held in public. Despite this the Commission itself leaked much of the evidence to the press, though only if the evidence tended to prove Oswald was the lone assassin. Thus Chief Justice Warren held a press conference after Oswald's wife Marina, had testified, he said, that she believed her husband was the assassin. Before Oswald's brother Robert, testified, he gained the Commission's agreement never to comment on what he said. After he had testified for two days, Allen Dulles remained in the hearing room and several members of the press entered. The next day the newspapers were full of stories that "a member of the Commission" had told the press that Robert Oswald had just testified that he believed that his brother was an agent of the Soviet Union. Robert Oswald was outraged by this, and said that he could not remain silent while lies were told about his testimony. He had never said this and he had never believed it. All that he had told the Commission was that he believed his brother was in no way involved in the assassination.

The methods adopted by the Commission have indeed been deplorable, but it is important to challenge the entire role of the Warren Commission. It stated that it would not conduct its own investigation, but rely instead on the existing governmental agencies—the FBI, the Secret Service and the Dallas police. Confidence in the Warren Commission thus presupposes confidence in these three institutions. *Why have so many liberals abandoned their own responsibility to a Commission whose circumstances they refuse to examine?*

It is known that the strictest and most elaborate security precautions ever taken for a President of the United States were ordered for November 22 in Dallas. The city had a reputation for violence and was the home of some of the most extreme right-wing fanatics in America. Mr. and Mrs. Lyndon Johnson had been assailed there in 1960 when he was a candidate for the Vice-Presidency. Adlai Stevenson had been physically attacked when he spoke in the city only a month before Kennedy's visit. On the morning of November 22, the Dallas *Morning News* carried a full-page advertisement associating the President with communism. The city was covered with posters showing the President's picture and headed "Wanted for Treason." The Dallas list of subversives comprised 23 names, of which Oswald's was the first. All of them were followed that day, except Oswald. *Why did the authorities follow as potential assassins every single person who had ever spoken out publicly in favour of desegregation of the public school system in Dallas, and fail to observe Oswald's entry into the book depository building while allegedly carrying a rifle over four feet long?*

The President's route for his drive through Dallas was widely known and was printed in the Dallas *Morning News* on November 22. At the last minute the Secret Service changed a small part of their plans so that the President left Main Street and turned into Houston and Elm Streets. This alteration took the President past the book depository building from which it is alleged that Oswald shot him. How Oswald is supposed to have known of this change has never been explained. *Why was the President's route changed at the last minute to take him past Oswald's place of work?*

After the assassination and Oswald's arrest, judgement was pronounced swiftly: Oswald was the assassin, and he had acted alone. No attempt was made to arrest others, no road blocks were set up round the area, and every piece of evidence which tended to incriminate Oswald was announced to the press by the Dallas District Attorney, Mr. Wade. In such a way millions of people were prejudiced against Oswald before there was any opportunity for him to be brought to trial. The first theory announced by the authorities was that the President's car was in Houston Street, approaching the book depository building, when Oswald opened fire. When available photographs and eyewitnesses had shown this to be quite untrue, the theory was abandoned and a new one formulated which placed the vehicle in its correct position.

Meanwhile, however, DA Wade had announced that three days after Oswald's room in Dallas had been searched, a map had been found there on which the book depository building had been circled and dotted lines drawn from the building to a vehicle on Houston Street. After the first theory was proved false, the Associated Press put out the following story on November 27: "Dallas authorities announced today that there never was a map. Any reference to the map was a mistake."

The second theory correctly placed the President's car on Elm Street, 50 to 75 yards past the book depository, but had to contend with the difficulty that the President was shot from the front, in the throat. How did Oswald manage to shoot the President in the front from behind? The FBI held a series of background briefing sessions for *Life* magazine, which in its issue of December 6 explained that the President had turned completely round just at the time he was shot. This, too, was soon shown to be entirely false. It was denied by several witnesses and films, and the previous issue of *Life* itself had shown the President looking forward as he was hit. Theory number two was abandoned.

In order to retain the basis of all official thinking, that Oswald was the lone assassin, it now became necessary to construct a third theory with the medical evidence altered to fit it. For the first month no Secret Service agent had ever spoken to the three doctors who had tried to save Kennedy's life in the Parkland Memorial Hospital. Now two agents spent three hours with the doctors and persuaded them that they were all misinformed: the entrance wound in the President's throat had been an exit wound, and the bullet had not ranged down towards the lungs. Asked by the press how they could have been so mistaken, Dr. McClelland advanced two reasons: they had not seen the autopsy report—and they had not known that Oswald was behind the President. The autopsy report, they had been told by the Secret Service, showed that Kennedy had been shot from behind. The agents, however, had refused to show the report to the doctors, who were entirely dependent upon the word of the Secret Service for this suggestion. The doctors made it clear that they were not permitted to discuss the case. The third theory, with the medical evidence rewritten, remains the basis of the case against Oswald. *Why has the medical evidence concerning the President's death been altered out of recognition?*

Although Oswald is alleged to have shot the President from behind, there are many witnesses who are confident that the shots came from the front. Among them are two reporters from the Fort Worth *Star Telegram*, four from the Dallas *Morning News*, and two people who were standing in front of the book depository building itself, the director of the book depository and the vice-president of the firm. It appears that only two people immediately entered the building, the director, Mr. Roy S. Truly, and a Dallas police officer, Seymour Weitzman. Both thought that the shots had come from in front of the President's vehicle. On first running in that direction, Weitzman was informed by "someone" that he thought the shots had come from the building, so he rushed back there. Truly entered with him in order to assist with his knowledge of the building. Mr. Jesse Curry, however, the Chief of Police in Dallas, has stated that he was immediately convinced that the shots came from the building. If anyone else believes this, he has been reluctant to say so to date. It is also known that the first bulletin to go out on Dallas police radios stated that "the shots came from a triple overpass in front of the presidential automobile." In addition, there is the consideration that after the first shot the vehicle was brought almost to a halt by the trained Secret Service driver, an unlikely response if the shots had indeed come from behind. Certainly Mr. Roy Kellerman, who was in charge of the Secret Service operation in Dallas that day, and traveled in the presidential car, looked to the front as the shots were fired. The Secret Service have removed all the evidence from the car, so it is no longer possible to examine the broken windscreen. *What is the evidence to substantiate the allegation that the President was shot from behind?*

Photographs taken at the scene of the crime could be most helpful. One young lady standing just to the left of the presidential car as the shots were fired took photographs of the vehicle just before and during the shooting, and was thus able to get into her picture the entire front of the book depository building. Two FBI agents immediately took the film from her and have refused to this day to permit her to see the photographs which she took. *Why has the FBI refused to publish what could be the most reliable piece of evidence in the whole case?*

In this connection it is noteworthy also that it is impossible to obtain the originals of photographs of the various alleged murder weapons. When *Time* magazine published a photograph of Oswald's arrest—the only one ever seen— the entire background was blacked out for reasons which have never been explained. It is difficult to recall an occasion for so much falsification of photographs as has happened in the Oswald case.

The affidavit by police officer Weitzman, who entered the book depository building, stated that he found the alleged murder rifle on the sixth floor. (It was at first announced that the rifle had been found on the fifth floor, but this was soon altered.) It was a German 7.65mm. Mauser. Later the following day, the FBI issued its first proclamation. Oswald had purchased in March 1963 an Italian 6.5mm. carbine. DA Wade immediately altered the nationality and size of his weapon to conform to the FBI statement.

Several photographs have been published of the alleged murder weapon. On February 21, *Life* magazine carried on its cover a picture of "Lee Oswald with the weapon he used to kill President Kennedy and Officer Tippit." On page 80, *Life* explained that the photograph was taken during March or April of 1963. According to the FBI, Oswald purchased his pistol in September 1963. *The New York Times* carried a picture of the alleged murder weapon being taken by police into the Dallas police station. The rifle is quite different. Experts have stated that it would be impossible to pull the trigger on the rifle in *Life's* picture. *The New York Times* also carried the same photograph as *Life*, but left out the telescopic sights. On March 2, *Newsweek* used the same photograph but painted in an entirely new rifle. Then on April 13, the Latin American edition of *Life* carried the same picture on its cover as the US edition had on February 21, but in the same issue on page 18 it had the same picture with the rifle altered. *How is it that millions of people have been misled by complete forgeries in the press?*

Another falsehood concerning the shooting was a story circulated by the Associated Press on November 23 from Los Angeles. This reported Oswald's former superior officer in the Marine Corps as saying that Oswald was a crack shot and a hot-head. The story was published everywhere. Three hours later AP sent out a correction deleting the entire story from Los Angeles. The officer had checked his records and it had turned out that he was talking about another man. He had never known Oswald. To my knowledge this correction has yet to be published by a single major publication.

The Dallas police took a paraffin test of Oswald's face and hands to try to establish that he had fired a weapon on November 22. The Chief of the Dallas Police, Jesse Curry, announced on November 23 that the results of the test "proves Oswald is the assassin." The Director of the FBI in the Dallas-Fort Worth area in charge of the investigation stated: "I have seen the paraffin test. The paraffin test proves that Oswald had nitrates and gun-powder on his hands and face. It proves he fired a rifle on November 22." Not only does this unreliable test not prove any such thing, it was later discovered that the test on Oswald's face was in fact negative, suggesting that it was unlikely he fired a rifle that day. *Why was the result of the paraffin test altered before being announced by the authorities?* [*Editor's note:* For more discussion of the paraffin test, see page 368 above.]

Oswald, it will be recalled, was originally arrested and charged with the murder of Patrolman Tippit. Tippit was killed at 1:06 p.m. on November 22 by a man who first engaged him in conversation, then caused him to get out of the stationary police car in which he was sitting and shot him with a pistol. Miss Helen L. Markham, who states that she is the sole eye-witness to this crime, gave the Dallas police a description of the assailant. After signing her affidavit, she was instructed by the FBI, the Secret Service and many police officers that she was not permitted to discuss the case with anyone. The affidavit's only description of the killer was that he was a "young white man." Miss Markham later revealed that the killer had run right up to her and past her, brandishing the pistol, and she repeated the description of the murderer which she had given to the police. He was, she said, "short, heavy and had bushy hair." (The police description of Oswald was that he was of average height, or a little taller, was slim and had receding fair hair.) Miss Markham's affidavit is the entire case against Oswald for the murder of Patrolmen Tippit, yet District Attorney Wade asserted: "We have more evidence to prove Oswald killed Tippit than we have to show he killed the President." The case against Oswald for the murder of Tippit, he continued, was an absolutely strong case. *Why was the only description of Tippit's killer deliberately omitted by the police from the affidavit of the sole eye-witness?*

Oswald's description was broadcast by the Dallas police only 12 minutes after the President was shot. This raises one of the most extraordinary questions ever posed in a murder case: *Why was Oswald's description in connection with the murder of Patrolman Tippit broadcast over Dallas police radio at 12:43 p.m. on November 22, when Tippit was not shot until 1:06 p.m.?*

According to Mr. Bob Considine, writing in the New York *Journal American*, there had been another person who had heard the shots that were fired at Tippit. Warren Reynolds had heard shooting in the street from a nearby room and had rushed to the window to see the murderer run off. Reynolds himself was later shot through the head by a rifleman. A man was arrested for this crime but produced an alibi. His girl-friend, Betty Mooney McDonald, told the police she had been with him at the time Reynolds was shot. The Dallas police immediately dropped the charges against him, even before Reynolds had time to recover consciousness and attempt to identify his assailant. The man at once disappeared, and two days later the Dallas police arrested Betty Mooney McDonald on a minor charge and it was announced that she had hanged herself in the police cell. She had been a striptease artist in Jack Ruby's nightclub, according to Mr. Considine.

Another witness to receive extraordinary treatment in the Oswald case was his wife, Marina. She was taken to the jail while her husband was still alive and shown a rifle by Chief of Police Jesse Curry. Asked if it was Oswald's, she replied that she believed Oswald had a rifle but that it didn't look like that. She and her mother-in-law were in great danger following the assassination because of the threat of public revenge on them. At this time they were unable to obtain a single police officer to protect them. Immediately Oswald was killed, however, the Secret Service illegally held both women against their will. After three days they were separated and Marina has never again been accessible to the public. Held in custody for nine weeks and questioned almost daily by the FBI and Secret Service, she finally testified to the Warren Commission and, according to Earl Warren, said that she believed her husband was the assassin. The Chief Justice added that the next day they intended to show Mrs. Oswald the murder weapon and the Commission was fairly confident that she would identify it as her husband's. The following day Earl Warren announced that this had indeed happened. Mrs. Oswald is still in the custody of the Secret Service. To isolate a witness for nine weeks and to subject her to repeated questioning by the Secret Service in this manner is reminiscent of police behaviour other countries, where it is called brain-washing. *How was it possible for Earl Warren to forecast that Marina Oswald's evidence would be exactly the reverse of what she had previously believed?*

After Ruby had killed Oswald, DA Wade made a statement about Oswald's movements following the assassination. He explained that Oswald had taken a bus, but he described the point at which Oswald had entered the vehicle as seven blocks away from the point located by the bus driver in his affidavit. Oswald, Wade continued, then took a taxi driven by a Darryll Click, who had signed an affidavit. An enquiry at the City Transportation Company revealed that no such taxi driver had ever existed in Dallas. Presented with this evidence, Wade altered the driver's name to William Wahley. Wade has been DA in Dallas for 14 years and before that was an FBI agent. *How does a District Attorney of Wade's great experience account for all the extraordinary changes in evidence and testimony which he has announced during the Oswald case?*

These are only a few of the questions raised by the official versions of the assassination and by the way in which the entire case against Oswald has been conducted. Sixteen questions are no substitute for a full examination of all the factors in this case, but I hope that they indicate the importance of such an investigation. I am indebted to Mr. Mark Lane, the New York criminal lawyer who was appointed Counsel for Oswald by his mother, for much of the information in this article. Mr. Lane's enquiries, which are continuing, deserve widespread support. A Citizen's Committee of Inquiry has been established in New York for such a purpose, and comparable committees are being set up in Europe.

In Britain I invited people eminent in the intellectual life of the country to join a "Who Killed Kennedy Committee," which at the moment of writing consists of the following people: Mr. John Arden, playwright; Mrs. Carolyn Wedgwood Benn, from Cincinnati, wife of Anthony Wedgwood Benn, MP; Lord Boyd-Orr, former director-general of the UN Food and Agricultural Organisation and a Nobel Peace Prize winner; Mr. John Calder, publisher; Professor William Empsom, Professor of English Literature at Sheffield University; Mr. Michael Foot, Member of Parliament; Mr. Kingsley Martin, former editor of the *New Statesman*; Sir Compton Mackenzie, writer; Mr. J. B. Priestley, playwright and author; Sir Herbert Read, art critic; Mr. Tony Richardson, firm director; Dr. Mervyn Stockwood, Bishop of Southwark; Professor Hugh Trevor-Roper, Regius Professor of Modern History at Oxford University; Mr. Kenneth Tynan, Literary Manager of the National Theatre; and myself.

We view the problem with the utmost seriousness. US Embassies have long ago reported to Washington world-wide disbelief in the official charges against Oswald, but this has never been reflected by the American press. No US television programme or mass circulation newspaper has challenged the permanent basis of all the allegations—that Oswald was the assassin, and that he acted alone. It is a task which is left to the American people.

Secret Service agent with bucket and sponge washing brains and blood from the limousine at Parkland. (See Richard Trask, Pictures of the Pain *(1994), p. 41.)*

Appendix A:

A Precis of
Assassination Science (1998)

James H. Fetzer, Ph.D.

[*Editor's note*: Although *Murder in Dealey Plaza* (2000) appears after and stands as a sequel to *Assassination Science* (1998), in many respects, it serves as an introduction to the kinds of studies that were presented in the earlier volume. Because many of them are technical and scientific in character—including, especially, the optical densitometry studies of the autopsy X-rays undertaken by David W. Mantik, M.D., Ph.D.—some readers may appreciate having a synopsis of the contents of that book, which includes studies by eleven contributors. Charles Crenshaw, M.D.; Bradley Kizzia, J.D.; David W. Mantik, M.D., Ph.D.; Robert B. Livingston, M.D., Jack White, Ron Hepler, Mike Pincher, J.D. and Roy Schaeffer, Chuck Marler, Ronald F. White, Ph.D., and myself.]

Assassination Science provides a collection of studies by physicians, scientists, and other serious students that is intended to place the investigation of the death of JFK on an objective and scientific foundation. The contributors are among the best-qualified individuals to ever examine the medical and the photographic evidence in this case, including a world authority on the human brain who is also an expert on wound ballistics, a physician with a Ph.D. in physics who is also board certified in radiation oncology, a philosopher who is an expert on critical thinking and a former Marine Corps officer, a physician who attended both the dying President and Lee Harvey Oswald at Parkland Hospital, a leading expert on the photographic evidence who served as a special advisor to the House Select Committee on Assassinations (HSCA), and other highly-qualified students of the assassination of JFK.

Assassination Science is distinctive among works on the assassination of President Kennedy for several reasons. First, it is the only collaborative study that brings together the original work of physicians, scientists, and other serious students: there are eleven contributors, rather than only one. Thus, readers have the benefit of exposure to the research efforts of multiple investigators who set forth their findings in clear and accessible language. Second, it includes the most important studies of the medical evidence since the publication of David Lifton's *Best Evidence* in 1980 and the most important studies of the Zapruder film ever presented. These results completely undermine previous investigations of the death of JFK, including especially the official government inquiries of the Warren Commission and of the HSCA.

Third, it provides the only comprehensive and detailed critique and response to a series of articles published in the *Journal of the American Medical Association (JAMA)* in 1992-93. [*Editor's note:* An exception is Harold Weisberg, *Never Again* (1995).] These articles, which were based upon interviews with the physicians who performed the autopsy at Bethesda Naval Hospital, were hyped by the Editor-in-Chief of *JAMA*, George Lundberg, M.D., who proclaimed that they were being welcomed into the "peer reviewed" literature on the assassination, in spite of the fact that they had not been refereed by experts on the crime and Lundberg knew that at the time. Nevertheless, they received enormous attention by the national press, even though they were based upon the selection and elimination of evidence to provide a biased report in support of a predetermined conclusion.

Fourth, it reports and explains the most important scientific findings in the history of the study of the assassination of John Fitzgerald Kennedy, which include:

- the discovery that some autopsy X-rays have been fabricated to conceal a massive blow-out to the back of the head caused by a shot from the front;
- the discovery that other autopsy X-rays have been altered by the superposition of a 6.5 mm metal object that was not present on the original X-rays;
- the discovery that diagrams and photographs that are supposed to be of the brain of JFK must be of the brain of someone other than John Kennedy;
- the discovery that the President alone was hit by at least four shots: one to his throat (fired from in front), one to his back (fired from behind) and two to his head (fired from behind and from the front);
- the discovery that the official "magic bullet" theory cannot possibly be true;
- the discovery that an absolute minimum of at least six shots were fired in Dealey Plaza during the assassination;
- the discovery that the Zapruder film of the assassination, which has been viewed as the nearest thing to "absolute truth" by some, has been extensively edited using highly sophisticated techniques;
- the discovery that Lee Harvey Oswald appears to have been framed using manufactured evidence, including the back-yard photographs;
- the discovery that the Warren Commission inquiry was a political charade featuring —a phoney bullet —a phoney limo —phoney wounds.

Fifth, it reports and records repeated efforts to bring these discoveries to the attention of the American people, including a national press conference held in New York City on 18 November 1993, which explained many of these findings and how they were discovered, but which the nation's newspapers have yet to print; strenuous and repeated attempts by telephone, letter, and fax to convince the American Broadcast Network (including Nightline and ABC WORLD NEWS WITH PETER JENNINGS) to cover this story that were without success; repeated efforts to inform the nation's leading newspaper, *The New York Times*, that its coverage of the assassination, including book reviews and even obituaries, was biased and irresponsible, but which *The Times* has chosen to completely ignore.

Sixth, it reports and records repeated and strenuous efforts to bring these new findings and discoveries, which completely undermine previous investigations by the federal government, to the attention of the Department of Justice.

The correspondence between James H. Fetzer, Ph.D., and Mary Spearing, Chief of the General Litigation and Legal Advice Section, provides a case study of the difficulties encountered in the pursuit of justice in a bureaucracy. In spite of his best efforts, Fetzer was unable to convince the Justice Department that the new findings concerning the fabrication of the X-rays and the substitution of diagrams and of photographs dictate a reinterpretation of the evidence in this case, even though previous government inquiries took for granted that this evidence was authentic.

Seventh, it reports and records sustained efforts by American citizens to contribute their time and their talents to clarifying the nature of what has previously been assumed to be the "best evidence" in this case in an effort to bring closure to the American people. The members of this group, including distinguished scientists and recognized authorities within their respective fields, have sought to fill' the vacuum created by the failure of the government to adequately investigate the assassination and to compensate for the dismal record of the press by reporting new discoveries that appear to demonstrate conclusively that there was a large-scale conspiracy and cover-up by the government in the death of JFK.

The studies published here are thus intended to convey at least three general lessons. One, that even journals as prestigious as *JAMA* are not immune from political abuse, indications of which abound with respect to its coverage of the medical evidence in this case. Two, that new discoveries, including scientific findings of fundamental importance, continue to be made, supporting the possibility that truth is not beyond our grasp. Three, that journals, newspapers, and agencies on which we all depend do not always serve the people's interests. The pursuit of truth, the protection of justice, and the preservation of democratic institutions require eternal vigilance. As long as we are ignorant, we are not free.

Article from The New York Times
(4 August 1999), p. A1.

[Editor's note: *In spite of repeated efforts by David W. Mantik, M.D., Ph.D., Jack White, and myself— and no doubt by others as well— to inform the Department of Justice of extensive evidence that the extant Zapruder film is not the out-of-camera original but had been faked, the government went forward with its acquisition at taxpayers expense. (See Appendix B and the communications from Mantik and White elsewhere in this volume).*]

GOVERNMENT TOLD TO PAY $16 MILLION FOR ZAPRUDER FILM

RECORD FOR U.S. ARTIFACT

Arbitrators Set Reimbursement for One-of-a-Kind Strip on Kennedy Assassination

By DAVID JOHNSTON

WASHINGTON, Aug. 3 — A divided Federal arbitration panel announced today that the Government must pay the heirs of Abraham Zapruder $16 million for his film of President John F. Kennedy's assassination, the highest price ever paid for a historical American artifact.

Appendix B:

Letter to Leslie Batchelor of 25 August 1998

James H. Fetzer, Ph.D.

[*Editor's note*: When David W. Mantik, M.D., Ph.D., Jack White, and I discovered that the ARRB was planning to secure permanent possession of the Zapruder film as an "assassination record," but that negotiations over compensation were being handled by the Department of Justice, we were concerned that no one in the Department involved in this matter might be in a position to understand the kinds of issues involved in assessing the authenticity of the film. When I learned that Leslie Batchelor, an Assistant Deputy Attorney General, had been designated for this role, we tried to bring her "up to speed" on the issues, but the course of events would show that our faxes, phone calls, cards and letters were to no avail. An arbitration board ultimately fixed the sum at $16 million.]

25 August 1998

Ms. Leslie Batchelor
Civil Division
U.S. Department of Justice
950 Pennsylvania Avenue (Room 3736)
Washington, D.C. 20530

Re: The Fabrication of Evidence in the Assassination of President John Kennedy

Dear Ms. Batchelor,

Your letter of 14 August 1998 concerning the film of the assassination of President Kennedy that was taken by Abraham Zapruder in response to my letter of 20 July 1998, has both surprised and disappointed me. In this letter, you assert that "independent experts have examined the Film and have concluded that it is the out-of-camera original film taken by Abraham Zapruder on 22 November 1963." You also suggest that "the Department of Justice will make every effort to ensure that the cost of obtaining the Film [by compensating his family for taking it into governmental possession] is reasonable." Your remarks raise very serious questions in my mind about your competence to assess the logical, empirical, scientific, and (even) legal issues involved here.

(1) LEGAL ISSUES:

How can the Civil Division have settled the question of authenticity when the FBI is investigating the question of tampering with the film? Your letter appears to be inconsistent with one I have received from John E. Collingwood, Assistant Director of the Office of Public and Congressional Affairs, of 29 July 1998, in response to my letter to Attorney General Janet Reno of 5 July 1998, in which I conveyed information about the identity of individuals who might have been involved in the editing and alteration of the Zapruder film together with supporting evidence. (A copy of my letter to Janet Reno was included in my letter to you.) Since the FBI investigates "all credible information" in this case and is investigating this issue, how can this question have been settled?

(2) LOGICAL ISSUES:

How can independent experts have possibly established that the currently available film is "the out-of-camera original taken by Abraham Zapruder on 22 November 1963"? The film is "authentic" in the appropriate sense only if its individual frames--of which there are 486--have not been altered and the sequence of frames is identical with the sequence Zapruder originally filmed on 22 November 1963. From a logical point of view, the hypothesis that the film is authentic has the character of a generalization that, IN EVERY RESPECT, the film has not been altered or edited. Have these "experts" studied each of the 486 frames to insure that none of them has been altered? And how could they possibly know that not even one frame has been removed from the film?

(3) SCIENTIFIC ISSUES:

Are your "experts" aware of previous work on the film by [highly qualified] students of the assassination? Without knowing what hypotheses are under consideration, it is virtually impossible to conduct experiments, observations, and measurements that are relevant to determining the truth or the falsity of any hypothesis; indeed, evidence is only relevant in relation to specific hypotheses, where the presence or absence of specific evidence increase or decreases the likelihood that that hypothesis is true. Have the experts you are using in this case been presented with copies of studies such as those identified below in order to know the kinds of anomalies that have previously been detected? Otherwise, it is logically absurd to maintain, as you have done in your letter, that they have established that the available film is unaltered and unedited.

(4) EMPIRICAL ISSUES:

Have these "experts" examined the findings of previous studies of the film that provide one indication after another of film alteration or editing in order to "explain them away"? These important studies, which I have sent to you, include the blur analysis of Daryll Weatherly published in KILLING KENNEDY (1995), the major study of the film by David W. Mantik, M.D., Ph.D., published in ASSASSI-NATION SCIENCE (1998), the report of findings from a recent visit to the National Archives by Harrison Livingstone published in THE FOURTH DECADE (1998), and more recent work by Mantik, Doug Mizzer and David Lifton, and by Mantik and Jack White that has appeared in electronic discussions. Unless your experts have investigated and explained their findings, the conclusion that the available film is indeed the out-of-camera original cannot possibly be justified.

(5) SCIENTIFIC ISSUES:

What is the source of the materials that are being subjected to analysis by your "experts"? Multiple copies originally made by the FBI and by the Secret Service are stored in the National Archives. These copies, however, do not appear to have the same features or properties from copy to copy, as David Mantik has explained (ASSASSINATION SCIENCE, pp. 323-338; summary, p. 338). Have your "experts" compared these copies to determine why they differ with respect to their features or properties? The original was recently subjected to "digital enhancement" by MPI of Chicago, which might be thought to provide the best available copy for study. But Michael Parks has discovered that some of its frames are reversed (Z-331 and Z-332) and that other frames have been removed (Z-341 and Z-350)! So which version of the film has been subjected to study?

(6) EMPIRICAL ISSUES:

Have the "experts" consulted in this case reviewed the eyewitness testimony in this case? Eyewitness after eyewitness reported that the driver of the limousine either slowed substantially or brought the vehicle to a complete stop: "When the shots were fired, it [the car] stopped" (Earle Brown 6H233); "The [limo] stopped immediately after that and stayed stopped for about half a second, then took off . . . ." (Bobby Hargis 6H294); "The President's driver slammed on the brakes—after the third shot" (Robert MacNeill, *The Way We Were*, 1963); and similar testimony from more than a dozen eyewitnesses, including the four motorcycle patrolmen who were riding with the limousine, which has been summarized by Mantik (ASSASSINATION SCIENCE pp. 273-275). If the eyewitnesses are correct, the currently available film cannot be authentic and must have been severely edited.

(7) LEGAL ISSUES:

How can the authenticity of the film be established independently of the eyewitness testimony in this case? According to MCCORMICK ON EVIDENCE, 3rd edition (1984), Section 214, concerning photographs and sound recordings, "The principle on which photographs are most commonly admitted into evidence is the same as that underlying the admission of illustrative drawings, maps, and diagrams. Under this theory, a photograph is viewed merely as a graphic portrayal of oral testimony, and becomes admissible only when a witness has testified that it is a correct and accurate representation of the relevant facts personally observed by the witness." As I observed in ASSASSINATION SCIENCE, p. 210, the practice of the Warren Commission and apologists for its findings appears to be the opposite, where photographs and films--including fabricated X-rays--have been used to discount eyewitness testimony. That practice must not be allowed to continue in this case.

(8) LOGICAL ISSUES:

The conclusion that the currently available film is "the out-of-camera original taken by Abraham Zapruder" on 22 November 1963 would be justifiable only if the issues that have been raised above have been investigated and resolved. If the only studies that have been undertaken have focused on a few frames of the film without considering the findings that have been described in this letter, then it should be obvious to every American that the Department of Justice has been taken in by fallacious reasoning that does not withstand critical scrutiny. Clearly, the examination of a few selected aspects of the film could support, at best, a conclusion that nothing inconsistent with the film's authenticity has been discovered. But that is a far different matter, from a logical point of view, than concluding that the film is authentic. The degree of support for authenticity is a function of the degree of competeness with which these issues have been investigated and resolved.

It should also be apparent that the question of compensation and the question of authenticity are intimately interrelated, where the compenation that is due to the Zapruder family would be powerfully affected by determination that the film is not "the out-of-camera original" that was taken in Dealey Plaza on 22 November 1963. As I have explained above, an enormous amount of available evidence (to be found in sources such as those that I have cited above) establishes--beyond a reasonable doubt, in my judgment--that the Zapruder film has been extensively edited/altered using highly sophisticated techniques. Much of this evidence has appeared in ASSASSINATION SCIENCE (1998), which presents the most extensive studies of the film currently to be found within the public domain. No one should remotely imagine that authenticity can be settled without resolving these matters.

Unless your "experts" have resolved these matters, therefore, your conclusions are indefensible. Without resolving them, it would be impossible to conclude that the film is the "out-of-camera original" on suitable logical, evidential and scientific grounds. Without suitable grounds for settling the question of the authenticity of the film, the question of compensation cannot be properly addressed. The Department of Justice, at this point in time, has been sufficiently apprised to know the considerations that matter in this case. It is all-too-apparent that, if compensation is now settled without properly resolving these issues, then the Department of Justice will appear to be participating in concealing evidence of conspiracy and coverup in the assassination of John F. Kennedy, which is an appalling legacy of shame. We are entitled to have a Department of Justice that promotes the cause of justice.

Yours truly,

James H. Fetzer
McKnight Professor

c: Same as letter of 5 July 1998

Appendix C:

FBI Protective Research Report
of 27 Novermber 1963

Form No. 1488 (Revised)
MEMORANDUM REPORT
    (7-1-50)

~ CD-80

UNITED STATES SECRET SERVICE
TREASURY DEPARTMENT

ORIGIN White House Detail OFFICE   Washington, D.C.   FILE NO. CO-2-34,030

TYPE OF CASE	STATUS	TITLE OR CAPTION
Protective Research	Closed	Assassination of President John F. Kennedy

INVESTIGATION MADE AT	PERIOD COVERED	
Washington, D.C.	November 22-23, 1963	

INVESTIGATION MADE BY
SAIC Harry W. Geiglein
SA Charles E. Taylor, Jr.

DETAILS

SYNOPSIS

This report relates to the measures employed to effect security of the President's car, 100-X, and the follow-up car, 679-X, on return from Dallas, Texas, following the assassination of President Kennedy.

DETAILS OF INVESTIGATION

This investigation was initiated on November 22, 1963, following receipt of instructions from ASAIC Floyd M. Boring, White House Detail, that steps be taken to effect security of the President's car (100-X) and the follow-up car (679-X) on their return from Dallas, Texas. President John F. Kennedy occupied the rear seat of SS-100-X when he was assassinated, and SS-679-X was directly behind the Presidential limousine at the time of the assassination. These two vehicles were driven to Love Field, Dallas, Texas, for immediate transportation to Andrews Air Force Base, Washington, D.C.

Following the arrival of President Lyndon B. Johnson and the remains of President Kennedy at Andrews Air Force Base, the reporting Special Agents conferred with Captain Milton B. Hartenblower, Duty Operations Officer, and Lt. Colonel Robert Best, Provost Marshal, Andrews Air Force Base, to arrange for landing instructions of the Air Force cargo plane transporting the subject vehicles and to escort these vehicles from Andrews Air Force Base. Also, arrangements were made with the U. S. Park Police for motorcycle escort of these automobiles to the White House Garage.

310

DISTRIBUTION	COPIES	REPORT MADE BY	DATE
Chief	Orig. & 2 cc	SPECIAL AGENT C. E. Taylor, Jr.	11/27/63
Washington	2 cc	APPROVED	11/27/63
		SPECIAL AGENT IN CHARGE Harry W. Geiglein	

(CONTINUE ON PLAIN PAPER)   U. S. GOVERNMENT PRINTING OFFICE   16-61509-2

CO-2-34,030
Page 2

At 8:00 P.M. on November 22, 1963, SS-100-X and SS-679-X
arrived at Andrews Air Force Base on Air Force Cargo Plane No.
612373 (C-130-E), which plane was assigned to the 76th Air
Transport Squadron from Charleston Air Force Base and piloted
by Captain Thomason. The plane was taxied to a point just off
of Runway 1028, approximately 100 yards from the Control Tower
at Andrews AFB, and a security cordon was placed around the
aircraft while these vehicles were being unloaded.

On the plane accompanying these vehicles were Special Agents
Kinney and Hickey.

The Presidential vehicles were driven under escort to the
White House Garage at 22nd and M Streets, N.W., Washington, D.C.,
arriving at approximately 9:00 P.M. SS-100-X was driven by
SA Kinney, accompanied by SA Taylor, and SS-679-X was driven by
SA Hickey, accompanied by Special Agents Keiser and Brett.

On arrival, SS-100-X was backed into the designated parking
bin and SS-679-X was parked a few feet away. A plastic cover
was placed over SS-100-X and it was secured. The follow-up car,
SS-679-X, was locked and secured. Special Agents Keiser, Brett,
and the reporting Special Agent effected security, assisted by
White House Policemen Snyder and Rubenstal.

At 10:10 P.M., Deputy Chief Paterni, ASAIC Boring, and
representatives from Dr. Burkley's office at the White House,
William Martinell and Thomas Mills, inspected SS-100-X.

At 12:01 A.M., November 23, 1963, the security detail was
relieved by Special Agents Paraschos and Kennedy and White House
Policeman J. W. Edwards.

At 1:00 A.M., as per arrangements by Deputy Chief Paterni,
a team of FBI Agents examined the Presidential limousine. This
team was comprised of Orrin H. Bartlett, Charles L. Killian,
Cortlandt Cunningham, Robert A. Frazer, and Walter E. Frazer.
                                                    THOMAS

Mr. Orrin Bartlett drove the Presidential vehicle out of
the bin. The team of FBI Agents, assisted by the Secret Service
Agents on duty, removed the leatherette convertible top and the
plexi-glass bubbletop; also, the molding strips that secure the
floor matting, and the rear seat. What appeared to be bullet
fragments were removed from the windshield and the floor rug in
the rear of the car.

310

CO-2-34,030
Page 3

The two blankets on the left and right rear doors were removed, inspected, and returned to the vehicle. The trunk of the vehicle was opened and the contents examined, and nothing was removed. A meticulous examination was made of the back seat of the car and the floor rug, and no evidence was found. In addition, of particular note was the small hole just left of center in the windshield from which what appeared to be bullet fragments were removed. The team of agents also noted that the chrome molding strip above the windshield, inside the car, just right of center, was dented. The FBI Agents stated that this dent was made by the bullet fragment which was found imbedded in the front cushion.

During the course of this examination, a number of color photos were taken by this search team. They concluded their examination at 4:30 A.M. and the car was reassembled and put back in the storage bin.

At 8:00 A.M. on November 23, the security detail was relieved by Special Agents Hancock and Davis and White House Policeman J. C. Rowe. SA Gonzalez relieved SA Hancock at Noon and at 4:00 P.M., Messrs, Fox and Norton, Protective Research Section, photographed the Presidential limousine. At 4:30 P.M., SA Gonzalez contacted SAIC Bouck and Deputy Chief Paterni and, at their request, the flowers, torn pieces of paper, and other miscellaneous debris were removed from the floor of the rear of the car (SS-100-X) and taken to the Washington Field Office. At that time, the special detail securing the Presidential limousine and the follow-up car was discontinued.

DISPOSITION

This case is closed with the submission of this report.

310

CET:mkd

Appendix D:

Ford Motor Company Intra-Company Communication of 18 December 1963

Ford Motor Company   Washington Office
Intra-Company Communication   December 18, 1963

TO: R.W. Markley, Jr.
FROM: F. Vaughn Ferguson
Re: Changes in White House "Bubbletop"

On November 23rd, the day following the President's assassination, I went to the White House garage in response to a telephone call to my home from the Secret Service. When I arrived about 10:00 a.m., the White House "Bubbletop" was in a stall in the garage with two Secret Service men detailed to guard it. A canvas cover was over the unit. I was permitted only to see the windshield of the car and then only after the guards had received permission from higher ranking Secret Service personnel. Examination of the windshield disclosed no perforation, but substantial cracks radiating a couple of inches from the center of the windshield at a point directly beneath the mirror. I was at the garage only about one hour that day, but while I was there Morgan Geis contacted the Secret Service and told them to have me make arrangements to replace the windshield.

The following day, when I returned to the garage, the unit was no longer under guard. The Secret Service had cleaned the leather upholstery the day before, but underneath the upholstery buttons dried blood was still in evidence. On my own initiative, I pulled up these upholstery buttons and with a knife removed the caked blood around them. At this time, there was a heavy odor of dried blood still noticeable. There was a large blood spot on the floor covering which the Secret Service had not been able to remove, but I did nothing further about it that day.

In response to my call of November 25, personnel from Arlington Glass came to the White House garage that same day to replace the windshield. The Arlington Glass personnel advised Morgan Geis and me that removal would cause additional damage to the windshield but Geis told them to go ahead and remove it anyway. The Arlington Glass personnel did remove it by putting their feet against the inside of the windshield and pushing it out. In doing so, additional cracks formed (downward to the bottom of the windshield). A Mr. Davis of the Secret Service then took the windshield and put it in the stockroom under lock and key and I have not seen it since.

That same day, November 25, I tried to clean the blood spot on the carpet with only moderate success. Late that afternoon I called Hess and Eisenhardt who agreed to send new carpeting including masking and binding. It was also that day that Morgan Geis called my attention to a dent in the chrome topping of the windshield at a point just above the rear view mirror and asked why I hadn't fixed it while I was at it. I told him that my experience with chrome had been that in trying to remove a dent of that size lead only to additional marks that further marred the trim. In addition, the dent is not visible when the top is on the unit.

On November 26th, late in the afternoon after I had left, the carpet masking and binding arrived at the garage from Hess and Eisenhardt. When I got to the garage on the 27th and

was told that the carpeting material was in, I contacted Morgan Geis who arranged with the White House upholstery man to receive the metal piece containing the carpet, remove the old carpeting, replace it with the new carpet, and return the piece to me for reinstallation in the "Bubbletop." This upholsterer did not complete the job until late Friday afternoon the 29th.

On the morning of December 2nd, the re-carpeted piece was delivered to me by a Secret Service agent named Davis and I then reinstalled it. Also on the 2nd of December I noticed that the two lap robes had a few blood spots on them, but, more than that, were soiled from handling and required cleaning. The White House chauffeurs were detailed to take the lap robes to Fort Myer for cleaning. These persons remained with the lap robes until they were cleaned and returned the same day.

I think this represents a complete account of changes made in the "Bubbletop" since November 22.

F.V. Ferguson

Using modern duplicating X-ray film, a real scissors was placed over the original X-ray film in the darkroom. The scissors blocked out the light and resulted in a dark image of a scissors on the copy film. Then shrapnel was added by placing a cardboard template with holes over the first X-ray film.

Where the light passed through the holes, the image became lighter on the copy film.

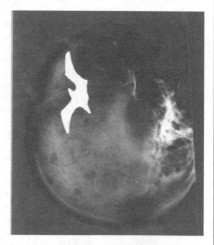

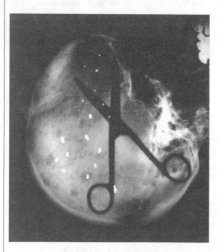

In another case, my daughter's plastic template for a pterosaur was superimposed in the darkroom over a real skull X-ray film (see p. 266 above).

Examples of X-ray Fabrication by David W. Mantik, M.D., Ph.D.

Appendix E:

Conversation with John Ebersole, M.D.
of 2 December 1992

Transcribed by David W. Mantik, M.D., Ph.D.

[*Editor's note*: John Ebersole, M.D., was the Navy medical officer in charge of radiology during the autopsy of JFK, though the actual X-rays were taken by Jerrol Custer, an enlisted medical technician. Having discovered that the X-rays have been fabricated by imposing a patch over a massive blow-out in the back of the skull (in the case of the lateral) and by adding a 6.5 mm metallic object (in the case of the anterior/posterior), David W. Mantik, M.D., Ph.D., was eager to discuss the X-rays with Ebersole. Fortunately, Ebersole was willing to talk with him—up to a point—and Mantik has transcribed their extremely interesting conversation, which occurred but a few months prior to Ebersole's death.]

On 2 November 1992, in response to my letter to John Ebersole, the autopsy radiologist, Ebersole phoned me at my office and we discussed the JFK autopsy for about 10 to 15 minutes, at most. I promised that I would phone him back, which I did on 2 December 1992 (at his home). This second conversation was recorded; the entire conversation is transcribed here. I donated a copy of this tape to the ARRB.

Female voice (Mrs. Ebersole?): Hello.

Mantik: Hi. This is Dr. Mantik calling for Dr. Ebersole.

Female voice: Just a moment, please. (Pause)

Ebersole: Hello.

Mantik: Hi. This is Dr. Mantik.

Ebersole: Yeah.

Mantik: I'm sorry I haven't had a chance to call sooner. We've gotten really busy out here.

Ebersole: Uh-huh.

Mantik: All these snowbirds keep coming over here and trying to see us. You probably never had that problem over there. [*Mantik note:* Ebersole and I shared the same specialty of radiation oncology. He was practicing in Lancaster, PA, at that time.]

Ebersole: No.

Mantik: Yeah. Well, I thought I'd follow up on my letter and see if there was a chance that we could get together sometime soon.

Ebersole: Ah, I don't think so. I would really like to drop this whole subject.

Mantik: Oh, I'm a little surprised. OK.

Ebersole: Yeah, I think everything you need to know is contained in the two articles in *JAMA*, the articles by Boswell and Hume (sic) and the one by Finck. [*Mantik note:* These were actually written by Dennis Breo.]

Mantik: OK, OK, so you basically support what they said there?

Ebersole:	Yeah, absolutely, across the board. I think they've got everything there. After all, they are pathologists, and they were carrying out the specialty of pathology. As a radiologist, I was there only to help them, not to perform the thing. But I don't, I don't really care to carry this on, you know, any further.
Mantik:	Oh, OK, I—
Ebersole:	Everything's been said that's—
Mantik:	I understand then.
Ebersole:	—been said. Ah, unfortunately, I wish Jim and J. Boswell had published much earlier.
Mantik:	Oh, it would have been wonderful. I've always wanted to talk to somebody who was there. That's why I was so excited about being able to talk to you a little bit.
Ebersole:	I would think that I would have very little to add, if any, really nothing to add to what you can get from those articles.
Mantik:	Uh-hmm. So your impression, too, when you saw that head wound was that the shot was from the back.
Ebersole:	Oh yes.
Mantik:	Yeah.
Ebersole:	Back and above.
Mantik:	Back and above, uh-huh. And the back wound—
Ebersole:	I had Pierre Finck as an instructor at AFIP.
Mantik:	Did you?
Ebersole:	And he was, you know, adamant about that, because [garbled] was always on the side of the wound of entrance.
Mantik:	So when you looked at the back of the head, what did you see there?
Ebersole:	Saw a wound—
Mantik:	Yeah.
Ebersole:	—saw a big wound.
Mantik:	It was pretty big on the back?
Ebersole:	Well, the exit (sic) wound was big. They—it had chopped up the skull.
Mantik:	Yeah, in the occipital—
Ebersole:	The wound was a single beveled wound.
Mantik:	If you looked at him from the back, like if he was standing in front of you, could you see the big exit wound?
Ebersole:	Yeah.
Mantik:	Uh-hmm.
Ebersole:	Sure.
Mantik:	How wide was it? That's what I've always wanted to ask somebody.
Ebersole:	Ah, I can't remember.
Mantik:	You just don't remember. The other thing you mentioned last time, about the back wound, was about T4? That about right?
Ebersole:	Ah, T4, yeah.
Mantik:	Yeah. Did you use a radio-opaque marker to identify that?
Ebersole:	No.
Mantik:	Oh, just clinical—
Ebersole:	That was a clinical impression.
Mantik:	—a clinical observation. About the level of the scapular spine, or so?
Ebersole:	Yeah.
Mantik:	Yeah. That sounds about what I would have guessed from that, too. So, oh, I know, there was one question I was really hoping I could ask you. You say that there were five or six skull X-rays that were taken? [*Mantik note:* The official collection contains only three; Ebersole had recalled five or six in our first telephone conversation, also. Curiously enough, this is also the (independent) rec-

ollection of Jerrol Custer, the technologist. He has confirmed that to me directly.]

Ebersole: Yeah.

Mantik: Ah, do you remember if any X-rays were taken right after they removed the brain from the skull?

Ebersole: No, I don't.

Mantik: Just don't remember.

Ebersole: —don't remember, and I doubt if any were.

Mantik: Uh-hmm.

Ebersole: X—rays were taken, in general, whole body X-rays were taken before the autopsy—

Mantik: Um-hmm.

Ebersole: —you know, right away.

Mantik: Right, that's what I understood.

Ebersole: And a chest was taken again after the autopsy was complete.

Mantik: Right, OK. The head wasn't manipulated at all between, I mean, just, even moving it up in any direction, like when you put the cassette in there behind, there was not much movement of the head, was there?

Ebersole: Umm, there was the usual movement—

Mantik: Nothing unusual.

Ebersole: —lateral position versus the AP.

Mantik: Yeah, no major movement of fragments or tissue?

Ebersole: No.

Mantik: Yeah, that's what I wanted to know. Yeah, that's what I assumed. You didn't take any X-rays of bullet fragments that night or the next day, did you?

Ebersole: I took an X-ray of a large bone fragment that was sent up from Dallas.

Mantik: That was on the evening of the 22nd?

Ebersole: Yeah.

Mantik: And anything the next day, at all, that happened?

Ebersole: What's that?

Mantik: Did anything happen at all the next day?

Ebersole: [Slight pause] No, not really.

Mantik: Nothing at all, no more X-rays?

Ebersole: [*Mantik note:* Inaudible; my impression at the time was that he had clearly implied that the answer was, "No."]

Mantik: Did you use some metal on the skull for magnification? Do you remember that?

Ebersole: No, did not. [*Mantik note:* There is a visible metal strip that Custer, the technologist, recalled, but it does not contain identifiable marks that could be used for determining magnification.]

Mantik: Did not use any, huh?

Ebersole: Did not.

Mantik: And you saw—

Ebersole: —and that presented a problem because I could not remember the type of the— source to film distance, and so on. [*Mantik note:* He is describing his later trip to the White House to review the X-rays, in which the question of magnification arose. This odd escapade is described in my essay in *Assassination Science*.]

Mantik: You saw the posterior wound in the skull yourself?

Ebersole: Yes.

Mantik: Yeah, so you could see the beveling yourself, or was that the pathologists' impression?

Ebersole: You could feel it.

Mantik: You could actually feel it?

Ebersole: Oh, yeah.

Mantik: Yeah. OK. The thing that puzzled me about that, you know, was that Boswell said in his testimony that they got these three [bone] fragments late in the autopsy and then they put this back together, and it was only then that he could see that entrance wound, and that's caused a lot of—

Ebersole: —could have been.

Mantik: Yeah, that's caused a lot of confusion. So you think that could have happened that way then?

Ebersole: Ah, could have.

Mantik: Yeah, OK. Jeez—

Ebersole: I don't remember after what—

Mantik: That's, that's what I keep saying to myself: gee, why, why didn't somebody write this all down within a year or two?

Ebersole: Humes had his notes [*Mantik note:* which have never appeared anywhere in the record], and ah—

Mantik: Yeah, did he take notes at the autopsy?

Ebersole: Yes.

Mantik: Yeah, did he have a diagram there, too?

Ebersole: I don't know, I—

Mantik: —don't know, huh? (Pause) Hmm, do you have any photographs of these X-rays yet?

Ebersole: No.

Mantik: So you don't even have those, huh?

Ebersole: They were turned over immediately after processing, turned immediately over to Secret Service.

Mantik: Uh-hmm. Uh-hmm.

Ebersole: Or what I assumed to have been Secret Service.

Mantik: Interesting. You saw the tracheostomy, too, didn't you?

Ebersole: (pause) I saw, yeah.

Mantik: What did that actually look like? There seem to be some differing opinions on that.

Ebersole: Well, it looked like an explosive (sic) type of wound, with lipping, ah, but clean, you know, we assumed that it was a surgical wound.

Mantik: Looked like a scalpel incision?

Ebersole: Yeah.

Mantik: Uh-huh. Was it the size you would expect for a tracheostomy?

Ebersole: Yeah, except it was, you know, too transverse. I wouldn't want to do a tracheotomy like that (said with some feeling).

Mantik: Um-hmm. OK, that's an interesting comment. Was it open when you first saw it, or was it sutured?

Ebersole: It was open.

Mantik: It was open, not sutured. Uh-hmm. OK. Fascinating. Burkley was there, too, at the autopsy, wasn't he? (Pause) Admiral Burkley?

Ebersole: I don't remember—

Mantik: —don't remember him.

Ebersole: I don't remember him being there.

Mantik: Let me tell you what puzzles me about him. He was the only doctor who was at Dallas and also at the autopsy and he certainly must have known about that anterior neck wound, and I just can't understand why he didn't tell Humes about that.

Ebersole: I don't, frankly—I don't remember his being there.

Mantik: You don't actually remember him—

Ebersole: I wouldn't say he wasn't—

Mantik: OK.

Ebersole:	—but I don't remember his being there.
Mantik:	Yeah.
Ebersole:	And it was, oh, 10:30 at night before we got the communication from Dallas— [*Mantik note:* Ebersole had told me during our first conversation that they had learned about the throat wound from Dallas that night. In prior conversations, he had also stated that he had learned of the projectile wound to the throat during the autopsy—that, in fact, he had stopped taking X-rays after that intelligence had arrived, because the mystery of the exit wound—corresponding to the back entrance wound—was solved.]
Mantik:	Uh-hmm. Uh-hmm.
Ebersole:	I think Burkley may well have been with the President's wife.
Mantik:	Yeah, that could be, couldn't it? Your job was mainly to look for the bullets, as I understand it, on the X-rays?
Ebersole:	Yes, because for a while everyone, investigating officers and so on, felt there was an entry wound, i.e., in the back, and no exit wound—
Mantik:	Sure.
Ebersole:	—ah, but that was later proven to be wrong.
Mantik:	Yeah, so you, ah, you really didn't see any big fragments on the X-ray, then, I gather—on the skull X-ray?
Ebersole:	Any what?
Mantik:	Did you see any big bullet fragments at all on the skull X-ray?
Ebersole:	No. No.
Mantik:	Nothing, nothing big at all?
Ebersole:	The bullet did a typical thing, it smashed into, ah, you know, ah, hundreds of pieces—
Mantik:	Uh-hmm. Uh-hmm.
Ebersole:	—once inside the skull.
Mantik:	Yeah. Where, where was that track? That was the other curious thing, I wasn't quite sure.
Ebersole:	Oh, roughly, it was from the occiput up forward. [*Mantik note:* This is also what Humes said in his official report, but the trail is actually more than 10 cm higher than this on the X-rays. Ebersole recalled drawing straight lines on the X-rays with a pencil during his visit to the White House. While at the National Archives, I was able to confirm that these two pencil lines are still present—and that they are located on only one side of the lateral X-ray film. In other words, the current X-rays are not copies of those that Ebersole saw at the White House; such copies would not show pencil markings on only one side. We can be confident, therefore, that the current X-rays are the same ones that Ebersole viewed at the White House. An entirely separate question, though, is whether the current X-rays are identical to those at the autopsy. In this very interview, Ebersole denies seeing any large metal-like fragments on the X-rays, but that cannot be true of the current X-rays. Since the 6.5 mm object is a (nearly complete) cross section of a (purported Mannlicher-Carcano) bullet, it must considered to be a large fragment. The eyewitness evidence suggests that the X-rays were altered promptly after the assassination (similar to the photographs). Most likely, Ebersole was recalled to the White House for the sole purpose of verifying that he would not dispute the altered X-rays. The cover story—of needing measurements for a bust—is absurd; pre-mortem X-rays existed for this purpose, as if anyone would ever use X-rays at all for such a purpose.]
Mantik:	From the external occipital protuberance?
Ebersole:	Yeah.
Mantik:	It was down that far, huh?
Ebersole:	Well, I don't want to say that for sure.

Mantik: OK.

Ebersole: It was, basically, from occiput, looking at the lateral view, as I remember, from occiput up toward the right forehead.

Mantik: Yeah, yeah, that's what Humes said, too, exactly what he said.

Ebersole: In fact, there was a little ecchymoses over the right, ah, right eye.

Mantik: Uh-hmm, yeah, I remember his saying that, too.

Ebersole: Otherwise, everything was intact, except for the tremendous wound.

Mantik: Yeah, now that big wound that we mentioned before, that went well behind the ear, didn't it?

Ebersole: Yeah.

Mantik: Over the parietal, parietal area behind the ear, didn't it?

Ebersole: —(garbled) it was multi-wound fragments.

Mantik: Uh-hmm, was that very close to that entry wound? Do you remember? (Pause) The big one and the little one?

Ebersole: Yeah, it was fairly close. Its most posterior margin was probably oh two, two and a half centimeters lateral to the entry wound. [*Mantik note:* This is a critical observation; he has just placed the large hole directly in the occipital bone—just where the photograph shows well-groomed hair.]

Mantik: Oh, OK, that's interesting, yeah. Would it be close to the lambdoid suture—the junction of the occiput and parietal bones?

Ebersole: I wouldn't want to say.

Mantik: Just not sure about that one. Yeah, fascinating. Boy, I wish you guys had all written a book about this. This would have been fascinating.

Ebersole: Yeah, what fascinates me is why people are so fascinated by it.

Mantik: Because there are so many contradictory pieces of evidence. It's like a murder mystery.

Ebersole: Yeah, you can find that in the Borden case, in the Lindberg case, doctor, you can find it in any one of hundreds of criminal cases. [*Mantik note:* If I recall correctly, Ebersole had taken courses on writing detective stories and actually did write these as a hobby. I have never tried to determine if he was published.]

Mantik: Yeah, well, maybe you're right, yeah.

Ebersole: Why this particular thing should become an obsession with people, I have no idea.

Mantik: Uh-huh.

Ebersole: It was a nut who decided to kill a man, and you can do it.

Mantik: Uh-hmm. Uh-hmm. Now, that wound, that big wound we were talking about, would that have gone far enough back, in the back of the head that you could even have seen the cerebellum?

Ebersole: I, I wouldn't want to say. I could not identify any cerebellum as such from what I saw.

Mantik: But the hole itself, would it have been low enough to see it?

Ebersole: I, I don't know. I don't want to say.

Mantik: OK.

Ebersole: That would have to be from the photographs, I would think, the stuff that's in the Archives.

Mantik: Oh yeah, you saw the photographs, didn't you?

Ebersole: Not entirely, no.

Mantik: Oh, I'm surprised; I'd thought you'd have seen those. You don't remember those, then?

Ebersole: No, I knew John who took the photographs, an excellent civilian—

Mantik: Yeah, John Stringer, yeah.

Ebersole: —but I didn't see the finished product.

Mantik: You never saw those. I thought you might have seen those, ah, when you went back there to testify.

Ebersole: No, and I went back to test the X-rays were, in fact, the X-rays taken. [*Mantik note:* This curious episode is recounted in my essay in *Assassination Science.*]

Mantik: Yeah, what did you think about that?

Ebersole: Hell, they were the X-rays I took.

Mantik: Yeah, OK. But you know what puzzles me about that, that uhm—?

Ebersole: A lot of things puzzle you, doctor.

Mantik: —that, that Clark Panel report saw that 6.5 mm fragment.

Ebersole: Yeah (change in tone of voice—almost like resignation, then a pause). Well, I tell you, I, ah, I don't know if you realize it or not, but I have a bronchogenic carcinoma with a metastases to the cerebellum. [*Mantik note:* I have always found it striking that Ebersole chose this particular question at which to stop the interview. The question remained, of course, forever unanswered. The list of suspects for X-ray alteration is very short, with Ebersole at the top of the list. His activities in the radiology department, on Saturday, November 23rd (as recalled by Custer, the technologist) as well as Ebersole's subsequent, curious visit to the White House (to view the X-rays), is consistent with such illegal behavior.]

Mantik: Oh, gosh. [*Mantik note:* At our national, specialty meetings in San Diego (between these two telephone calls), I had learned from a Pennsylvania technologist that Ebersole was receiving radiation treatment for lung cancer, but I had not known that he had developed brain metastases.]

Ebersole: And I'm not doing well at all.

Mantik: Oh, jeez.

Ebersole: And I would really like to close out this discussion.

Mantik: Oh, we can stop anytime you like.

Ebersole: OK.

Mantik: Surely. Listen, thank you so much.

Ebersole: I know. Bye.

Mantik: Bye.

[*Mantik note:* Ebersole died several months later. I believe that I was the last person to interview him about his role at the JFK autopsy.]

Doctors Affirm Kennedy Autopsy Report

By LAWRENCE K. ALTMAN

Breaking a 28-year silence, the two pathologists who performed the autopsy on President John F. Kennedy have affirmed their original findings that he was hit by only two bullets, fired from above and behind, and that one of them caused the massive head wound that killed him.

And five doctors who attended the President in the emergency room of a Dallas hospital said they observed nothing while treating him that contradicts the pathologists' findings. They also criticized another doctor in the emergency room that day, one whose new book asserts a conspiracy to cover up evidence that the President was shot from the front, not the back.

Dennis L. Breo

Drs. James J. Humes, left, and J. Thornton Boswell, who performed the autopsy on John F. Kennedy, broke a 28-year silence.

A front page story in The New York Times *(20 May 1992) featuring a photograph of James J. Humes, M.D., and J. Thornton Boswell, M.D.*

Appendix F:

Deposition of J. Thornton Boswell, M.D.,
before the AARB on 26 February 1996

Edited by David W. Mantik, M.D., Ph.D.

[*Editor's note*: Although he was not a forensic pathologist and had never performed an autopsy on on a gunshot victim before, J. Thornton Boswell, M.D.,
was one of the three pathologists who conducted the autopsy on President John
Fitzgerald Kennedy. When it became evident that he would be deposed by the
ARRB, Gary Aguilar, M.D., David W. Mantik, M.D., Ph.D., and others suggested
some of the questions that might be asked of him. As it happened, he was deposed by Jeremy Gunn, who asked many of the questions that Aguilar, Mantik,
and others had proposed, with some rather surprising results. For discussion,
see the studies by Aguilar and Mantik elsewhere in this volume.]

Jeremy Gunn, with Douglas P. Horne in attendance, deposed J. Thornton
Boswell, assistant JFK pathologist, on 26 February 1996. The following are excerpts from his deposition. Gunn begins by asking about the throat wound.

Gunn:	When you referred to the wound in the anterior neck, what was your first impression?
Boswell:	...oh, we thought they had done a tracheotomy, and whether or not that was a bullet wound, we weren't sure, initially. It was after we found the entrance wound [*Mantik note:* he probably means the back wound] and then the blood external to the pleura [inside the chest] that we had a track, and that proved to be the exit wound; but it was so distorted by the incision, initially we just assumed it to be a tracheotomy.
Gunn:	Did you reach the conclusion that there had been a transit wound through the neck during the course of the autopsy itself?
Boswell:	Oh, yes. [*Mantik note:* This is truly arresting—because it conflicts so grossly with what all the pathologists have said over all these years, but also be- cause the FBI report knows nothing about this. Boswell here is contradict- ing the entire story told by the pathologists over many decades. It is impos- sible to know if he has simply forgotten the official cover story and these are now his (possibly) honest recollections. In any case, his statements are totally unexpected.]
Gunn (p. 44):	...Do you recall ... thinking ... that ... that the anterior neck ... may have been a wound of some sort?
Boswell:	I think it was pretty obvious ... that it was a tracheotomy wound. Then, as the evening progressed, the question became whether it was both an exit wound and a tracheotomy wound, because right in the middle there was what appeared to be the exit wound through which they had cut.... [*Mantik note:* Again, this is a striking admission—totally at odds with the story that Humes told until his death in 1999, and that the other pathologists sup-

ported. Humes always insisted that he knew nothing about a projectile wound in the throat until he spoke to Dr. Perry (who had performed the tracheotomy) on Saturday morning. How Boswell can admit to seeing this projectile wound at the autopsy only demonstrates his remarkable flexibility of mind.]

Gunn (p. 49): Do you remember whether the fresh brain was weighed?

Boswell: I doubt that it was weighed…. Well, I shouldn't say that. It was formalin fixed. We floated them in formalin and a piece of cloth, and it was taken, and it probably was weighed. Why the weight is not down here, I do not know. [*Mantik note:* Boswell is here referring to his own autopsy diagram. Humes has admitted that he had one, too, but that he (most likely) burned it. It is quite possible that Humes's (never officially seen) diagram contained the fresh brain weight. The reason that the fresh brain weight was destined for the dustbin becomes obvious in Horne's article about the two brains.]

Gunn: Wouldn't it be a fairly important thing to weigh if there were a gunshot wound to the head?

Boswell: Especially with some of it missing, that's true…. We had a neuropathologist from the AFIP that came over, and we took it out of the formalin after it was fixed a couple of days—in fact, on Monday…. [*Mantik note:* This date becomes critical in Horne's proposal of two separate brain examinations. Boswell's memory here, too, must be wrong. There is no record of any AFIP pathologist ever examining the brain; Richard Davis, the primary candidate from the AFIP, has denied this.] But we elected not to cut the brain because the trauma was evident on the surface [*Mantik note:* this must be the brain in the extant photographs—it does show an obvious track on the surface] without having to cut it, and we thought that it might be important to preserve…. And we put it back in the formalin, and it was delivered to Admiral Burkley in a bucket…and then we never saw it again.

Gunn: When was it delivered to Admiral Burkley?

Boswell: I believe it was on Monday, but I'm not sure, because we wrote up an addendum to the autopsy, I think on Monday, after we had examined the brain. And I had read the slides on Sunday, so…. and I think [Humes] took the slides with the brain and the addendum to Admiral Burkley on Monday. But I'm not absolutely sure. I'll rely on Jim's memory for that. [*Mantik note:* This date becomes important in the two-brain scenario.]

Gunn (p. 90): …what portions of the scalp were missing when you first began the autopsy?

Boswell: Actually, very little…. The morticians were able to cover this defect completely by using some sort of plastic to cover the brain cavity, because there wasn't much bone to replace the brain cavity. But they were able to use his scalp to almost completely close the wound. [Humes also agrees with this, although he admits that the scalp actually could not be completely closed. Based upon all of the evidence, the scalp was almost all there—but not enough to close it. Therefore, the posterior scalp photographs (since they show entirely intact scalp—contrary to what both pathologists recalled) cannot be authentic.]

Gunn: So it would be fair to say that, although there was a very large piece of skull missing, there was very little scalp missing.

Boswell: Right.

Gunn (p. 123): Was a [microscopic] section made of the wound of entrance on the neck or back?

Boswell: Both. [*Mantik note:* This is yet one more confirmation of the pathologists' knowledge at the autopsy of the bullet wound in the throat. There would be no reason to take tissue from a simple tracheotomy incision. Cyril Wecht, M.D., J.D. (telephone conversation of 4-19-00) agrees that no forensic pathologist would sample an uncomplicated tracheotomy incision.]

Gunn later quizzes him on the location of the back wound.

Boswell (p. 155): Well, it's certainly not as low as T4 [the fourth thoracic vertebra]. I would say at the lowest it might be T2. I would say around T2. [Even this is much too low for the SBT.]

Gunn (p. 190): And approximately what percentage of President Kennedy's brain had been destroyed or removed?

Boswell: ...Less than a third.

Gunn: A third of the right hemisphere or a third of the total?

Boswell: A third of the total.

Gunn (p. 193): Was it possible to determine the course of the bullet through the skull by an examination of the brain?

Boswell: Not of the brain. It was a little bit easier by examination of the skull, but the right hemisphere of the brain is just so torn up, and there's no way of determining a track. [*Mantik note:* The drawings of the brain (Figure 8) suggest a fairly obvious track. At this moment, however, Boswell is recalling the authentic brain. Just about a half page above this Boswell has stated the opposite, namely that the trauma was evident on the surface. He cannot have it both ways for a single brain. But both were true for him, because he saw two quite different brains at two different dates.]

Gunn next begins to quiz him on the 6.5 mm object on the frontal X-ray.

Gunn: Let me draw your attention to a white semicircular marking in what appears to be in the right orbit.... Do you know what that object is?

Boswell: No.

Gunn: Do you know whether that is an artifact...as part...of the developing process or whether that is a missile fragment?

Boswell: No, I can't tell you that. I don't remember the interpretation. I see a lot of metallic looking debris, X-ray-opaque material, at the site of the injury. [*Mantik note:* This statement is strange, because this debris is more than 10 cm above the occipital entry site that the pathologists cited for the bullet entry. It is nowhere near the "site of injury" that they described.] And I remember that there were a lot of fragments around the right eye, and the rest of these could be from bullet fragments as well. I'm not sure—we found a couple of very minute metal fragments, but I do not relate them to the X-ray (sic). [*Mantik note:* Boswell has evaded the question that Gunn asked, so Gunn tries again.]

Gunn: Can you relate that, again, apparently large [6.5 mm] object to any of the fragments that you removed?

Boswell: No. We did not find one that large. I'm sure of that.... [*Mantik note:* With this admission, Boswell confirmed my proposal that this object was not on the frontal X-ray during the autopsy. Neither Humes nor Finck could recall it, either. Quite strikingly, when I asked the autopsy radiologist, Ebersole (Appendix E) about it, he abruptly, and forever, stopped the conversation. How likely is it that all three pathologists, the radiologist, and all of the other autopsy personnel, too, could have missed this most important object at the autopsy? I have seen no reasonable answer to this question in the vast assassination literature, and I predict that there will never be one— simply because this object was not there. Furthermore, anyone who accepts this conclusion (that it was not there) immediately concurs that there was a post-assassination cover-up of considerable magnitude—so that this is extremely hazardous terrain for lone assassin advocates.]

Gunn (p. 204):   Are the minute fragments referenced in the autopsy protocol [the official report] those fragments that go along the top of the [frontal X-ray]?

Boswell: Right.

Gunn: And I would just note that it says that, "They're aligned corresponding with the line joining the above described small occipital wound [the EOP wound] and the right supraorbital ridge [the bony ridge above the right eye]." To me, it appears as if the line does not correspond with an entrance wound, but would be elsewhere. [*Mantik note:* "Elsewhere" is 10 cm away.]

Boswell: Is that from the autopsy?

Gunn: This is the autopsy protocol…. But the question for you is:Is what you are seeing on the [lateral] X-ray itself what is being referred to in the portion of the autopsy protocol that I just quoted?

Boswell: Right. Although I interpret it differently now [*Mantik note:* by more than four inches] than whoever (sic) did that. I see the line here, but it doesn't connect with the wound of entry, although they (sic) say it does there. And apparently we (sic) gave this to the cops [FBI], O'Neill and Sibert.

Gunn (p. 206):   Was there any other X-ray that you now recall having seen that showed a line of metallic fragments connecting to the small wound of entry?

Boswell: Not of the head.

Gunn: Is the fragment trail that you see… does that correspond to what you saw on the night of the autopsy, as best you recall?

Boswell: Yes. [*Mantik note:* So Boswell, like Humes, can offer no explanation for this egregious misrepresentation of the medical evidence—the deliberate displacement of the bullet trail by four inches. This is so gross, in fact, that Boswell has attempted to distance himself from it by saying that "they" did it. He implies it is Humes's fault, yet, at the same time, he claims—again like Humes—that the X-rays are authentic. He cannot have it both ways.]

Gunn: OK. I think that's it for the X-rays.

After Boswell explains that he was asked to supervise the autopsy on Martin Luther King, Jr., which he declined to do, Gunn returns to the entry wound at the back of the head.

Gunn: Did you understand or did you ever come to believe that the Clark Panel located the entrance wound at a point superior [at the red spot] to where you had identified the entrance wound in the autopsy protocol?

Boswell: I never believed this. I think Jim [Humes] at one point came to believe this, because he testified before the House commission (sic) to that effect. [*Mantik note:* I have verified the truth of this statement about Humes; when Humes stood before an enormous blow-up of the lateral skull X-ray before the HSCA, he pointed directly at the higher entry site—the one that the Clark panel, and the HSCA, too, had selected. Wallace Milam gave me a videotape of this interrogation, so I am now certain that—on this sole occasion-Humes really did point at the upper site (near the red spot). Without this videotape, there would have been lingering doubt.]

The deposition closes with Boswell drawing, albeit very reluctantly, on a model skull, to illustrate the large hole in the skull. I present and discuss this drawing (as copied by Douglas Horne from the ARRB skull) in the X-ray section of my medical essay above. It is consistent with the X-rays, and, even more remarkably, it is consistent with the eyewitnesses. It is, however, in gross disagreement with the intact scalp seen on the back of the head (Figure 1). This drawing by Boswell is an extraordinary and permanent contribution to the entire case, and finally puts many critical issues to bed.

Appendix G:

Deposition of James J. Humes, M.D., before the AARB on 13 February 1996

Edited by David W. Mantik, M.D., Ph.D.

[*Editor's note*: Although he was not a forensic pathologist and had never performed an autopsy on a gunshot victim before, James J. Humes, M.D., was selected to head the team of three pathologists who conducted the autopsy on President John Fitzgerald Kennedy. When it became evident that he would be deposed by the ARRB, Gary Aguilar, M.D., David W. Mantik, M.D., Ph.D., and others suggested some of the questions that might be asked of him. As it happened, he was deposed by Jeremy Gunn, who asked many of the questions that Aguilar, Mantik, and others had proposed, with some rather surprising results. For discussion, see the studies by Aguilar and Mantik elsewhere in this volume.]

Chief Pathologist James J. Humes was deposed on 13 February 1996. The transcript is 250 pages long; only selected portions are reproduced here. The questioner was Jeremy Gunn, with Douglas P. Horne in attendance. The brain is the first topic presented here.

Gunn (p. 74): Was the fresh brain weighed?

Humes: I don't recall. I don't recall. It's as simple as that. [*Mantik note:* FBI agent O'Neill, who took notes at the autopsy, recalls that it was weighed. Boswell, independently, once admitted that he, too, recalled this event (cited in my medical essay above). It may have appeared on Humes's notes, which never appeared in any official record.]

Gunn: Would it be standard practice for a gunshot wound in the head to have the brain weighed?

Humes: Yeah, we weigh it with a gunshot wound.... Normally we weigh the brain when we remove it. I can't recall why—I don't know, one, whether it was weighed or not, or two, why it doesn't show here. I have no explanation for that....

Gunn: OK. For the thyroid over on the right column.... There's no weight there....

Humes: It probably wasn't removed. I don't know. Let me go back for one minute. I was told to find out what killed the man. My focus was on his wounds. I didn't approach it like it was a medical death due to some disease [*Mantik note:* a curious comment since JFK was rumored to have had Addison's disease, a diagnosis which might have been determined at the autopsy] or whatever. I was focusing primarily and almost exclusively on the wounds. So I don't know. I don't know if I weighed the thyroid or not....

Gunn: And there was a gunshot wound to the neck, wasn't there?

Humes: ... There was a bullet wound in the back above the scapula. [*Mantik note:* This is a long distance from the neck, to where Gerald Ford elevated it-- without any medical or forensic input.]

Gunn next introduces the [woefully inadequate] autopsy diagram, prepared by Boswell. Gunn has just asked about the meaning of the mysterious number 10 on the diagram. [We must remember that Humes's diagram—which he admitted to *JAMA* that he had made—and Finck's, too (see Slauson's comments on what happened to Finck's in the essay by Gary Aguilar, M.D., elsewhere in this volume), have never been made public. In Boswell's defense, it is possible that one or both of these lost diagrams were more complete and more comprehensible—but were lost because they were not consistent with the single assassin theory.]

Humes (p. 87): ...but your guess is as good as mine, to tell you the truth.

Gunn: Up at the top of the skull, there is..., I assume 3 centimeters. Do you see that?

Humes: Yes.

Gunn: Do you have any knowledge about what that would mean?

Humes: I certainly don't....

Gunn then asks Humes about the fracture lines in the skull.

Humes: ...I didn't detail all those for the reasons that I stated in the protocol [the autopsy report]. They're going this way and they're going that way, and, you know, that's the way it goes (sic)....

Gunn: ...there are numbers written at the bottom, a 4, a 3 over a 6. Do you see those?

Humes: Yeah.

Gunn: Do you know what those signify?

Humes: No....

Gunn (p. 89):   Was scalp missing? ....

Humes: There was some scalp missing, but we were able to pretty much close the scalp, skin, when we finished everything....

Gunn: So there was no scalp that came to the autopsy room? [*Mantik note:* The absence of such late arriving scalp is confirmation that Humes is probably right, that most of the scalp was there, although several centimeters may have been missing, as he soon recalls.]

Humes: No....

Gunn: When the embalming process was completed, approximately how much scalp was missing?

Humes: Oh, I don't know. Maybe three or four centimeters, something like that. Not much.... [*Mantik note:* Without seeming to be conscious of it, Humes is telling us quite directly that the photographs of the back of the head cannot be accurate. This is because they show the entire scalp present— none at all is missing.]

Gunn: Approximately where was the missing scalp as of the time that the embalming process was completed?

Humes: You got me (sic)....

Gunn moves on to the X-rays.

Gunn (p. 100): So all of the X-rays of the cranium were taken before...any metal fragments were removed?

Humes: Exactly.

Gunn: Do you have any recollection now about the shapes of the fragments that
                 were removed?
Humes: They were small and irregular. That's all I can tell you.
Gunn: Long and sliver like or roundish or—any recollection?
Humes: Flat, irregular, two or three millimeters [*Mantik note:* The suspicious object
                 on the frontal X-ray is 6.5 mm and almost circular; it is hardly irregular.]

Gunn (p. 107) then returns to the brain.

Humes: …But the brain was damaged, and it didn't lend itself well to infusing it like
                 we normally do. So we placed it in a very generous quantity of 10% forma-
                 lin…. [*Mantik note:* The elimination of perfusion, which Humes clearly
                 implies here, means that the brain would gain rather little additional mass
                 during the fixation process. Therefore, the argument of some that the large
                 brain mass of 1500 gm due to fixation becomes quite untenable.]
Gunn (p. 110):   And the whole circumference of the entry wound was visible without any
                 reconstruction of the skull?
Humes: Oh, yeah, sure. [*Mantik note:* No one else has ever said this, nor had Humes
                 ever said this before! Such a central finding is conspicuously absent from
                 the autopsy report--and from all other comments by each of the three pa-
                 thologists. This conclusion is also not supported by the X-rays nor by the
                 prior reviews of any other specialist. Furthermore, such a circumferential
                 hole, if present, surely ought to be visible somewhere in the photographic
                 collection, but it is not. Despite Humes's apparent certainty about this ques-
                 tion, his statement is categorically wrong. This comment by him is simply
                 inexplicable.]
Gunn: In which bone was the entrance wound?
Humes: Occipital bone….

Gunn then turns to the back wound.

Gunn (p. 141):   You see that Dr. Burkley identifies [*Mantik note:* in the death certificate
                 that he prepared as JFK's physician] the posterior back [wound] at about
                 the level of the third thoracic vertebra?
Humes: Yes.
Gunn: Was that correct? [*Mantik note:* This is critical to the SBT--it should be
                 much higher in order to sustain the SBT.]
Humes: I don't know (sic). I didn't measure from which vertebra it was (sic). It's
                 sometimes hard to decide which vertebra, to tell you the truth, by palpa-
                 tion. Maybe you can do it accurately because the first and second—did I
                 say third? Oh, he says third thoracic. I think that's much lower than it actu-
                 ally was. I think it's much lower than it actually—you have seven cervical
                 vertebrae. I don't know. I mean, he's got a right to say anything he wants,
                 but I never saw it before, and I don't have an opinion about it (sic). [*Mantik
                 note:* If it really was the first or second vertebra, Humes, by his own words
                 here, has no excuse for not documenting this, since T1 and T2 can usually
                 be identified without much difficulty. The HSCA chose T1. It probably was
                 no higher than T1 or T2, but it may have been lower.]
Gunn: Did you ever discuss which vertebra—?
Humes: I never discussed anything about it with George Burkley, period, or any-
                 body else. I mean, with all due respect, you seem to have come to me from
                 left field (sic). You know, I just—they're not things which I'm aware of (sic)….

Gunn then asks about the date of the brain examination.

Humes (p. 146): I don't know, Monday or Tuesday [November 25 or 26], or some day at the
                 beginning of the week….

Gunn:	Earlier in the deposition today, you made reference to a sectioning of the brain. If I understood correctly, that took place one or two days afterwards.
Humes:	Yeah. [*Mantik note:* This is an astonishing confession, since there are no photographs of such sections, even though Stringer recalls taking them. In fact, until this moment, the pathologists had officially insisted that the brain was not sectioned. In view of Douglas Horne's proposal of two separate brain examinations (on two different dates with two different brains), it is quite certain that Humes is here recalling the one occasion at which the authentic brain actually was sectioned, but for which no official records remain.]
Gunn:	Did that happen within one or two days after?
Humes:	Yes, shortly after. I can't tell you what day now. [*Mantik note:* There is no documentary evidence for this early date, but Humes is recalling the examination of JFK's brain on (probably) the morning of the funeral (Monday), whereas the substitute brain, described in the official report, was examined about a week later (possibly on another Monday). This chronology fits with all of the evidence; see Horne's article for more on these issues. These apparent slips of memory by Humes actually provide further corroboration for Horne's proposal.]

Gunn refuses to abandon this issue and he asks Humes again for the date.

Humes (p. 149):	A couple of days after Sunday [November 24], after they were delivered. I don't know. In that week some day. I don't really know. It didn't seem to be important to me at the time, and still doesn't, quite candidly (sic). [*Mantik note:* Anyone who wanted to know where the brain went would take great exception to this eccentric—or possibly feigned—lack of interest by Humes. If the brain had been buried with the body on Monday, November 25, then any examination after this could not be of JFK's brain, despite Humes's indifference. That such a misleading, later examination occurred is Douglas Horne's (highly probable) proposal.]
Gunn:	Did you ask [Admiral Burkley] or wonder how they would be able to inter the brain if the President had already been buried?
Humes:	No, I didn't worry about it one way or another (sic)....

In view of the great paradoxes about the back of the head photograph (Figure 1), Gunn next wants to know if the hair was cleaned before the photographs were taken.

Gunn (p. 156):	No cleaning, no combing of the hair or anything or that sort?
Humes:	No, no, no, no, no....

Gunn later returns to the question of whether any occipital bone was missing.

Gunn (p. 171):	So on the scalp of President Kennedy here, still in View No. 4 [see Figure 1], that underneath the scalp the bone was all intact with the exception of the puncture wound—
Humes:	Yeah.... [*Mantik note:* This is flagrantly at odds with the X-rays, and even with Humes's own diagram for the Warren Commission (Figure 5), and even with Humes's own autopsy report. Once again, Humes is behaving in a totally incomprehensible fashion.]

Gunn then turns to the "entry" wound on the posterior head photograph (Figure 1 of my medical essay above); he is inquiring about the red spot, high on the back of the head.

Gunn (p. 177):	Dr. Humes, are you able to identify what you have described previously as an entrance wound in the posterior skull of President Kennedy on photographs in View 6?

Humes: This is the same problem I had at the [HSCA] committee hearings…. I had difficulty trying to see which was which among these things, between here and there (sic).… I mean, they threw these up on a great big screen and said which is what, and I really had difficulty. I couldn't be sure. I'm disappointed. I was disappointed in that regard. I still have trouble with it.

Gunn: Are you able to identify on View 6 the entrance wound?

Humes: Not with certainty, I'm sorry to tell you.

Gunn next refers to the small white spot just above the hairline (Figure 1 of my medical essay above) on the right rear of the skull. This is more than 10 cm below the red spot.

Gunn (p. 180):   . . . is that where you now would identify what you believe to be the entrance wound in the skull?

Humes: I cannot flat-footedly say that. I have trouble with it. The head is turned toward one side [*Mantik note:* only slightly, not enough to matter]. I don't know. It's very difficult. Very difficult. It's an educated guess, to be perfectly honest.

Gunn: For that marking that is towards the bottom near the hairline [the white spot], what is your best understanding of what that designates?

Humes: I don't have the foggiest idea (sic). See what's important is where is the wound in the bone. You can't tell from these pictures. [*Mantik note:* Humes is right—it is the bone that really matters; unfortunately for Humes, and for history, too, no unambiguous photographs of this bone exist. However, see my discussion in the medical evidence Postscript, in which precisely such a photograph, from the current official set, is identified.]

Gunn (p. 181):   Did you have any difficulty identifying the scalp entry wound during the time of the autopsy?

Humes: No, I didn't at the time of the autopsy…. [*Mantik note:* This is one of the most damning statements of his testimony. He had already made the same statement to *JAMA*. No doubt, the three pathologists could identify the wound, both in the skull and in the scalp. However, the only obvious wound in the photographs (the red spot) was not seen by anyone at either Parkland or at Bethesda. The three pathologists (and the two photographers and the radiologist, too) certainly did not give any importance to the red spot, unequivocally denying that it represented an entry site. The only individuals to give any importance to it had not seen the body.]

Gunn next turns to my questions about the metal fragments. They begin by looking at the frontal X-ray.

Gunn (p. 183):   Could you examine the B&W photographs and see if they help?

Humes: They don't help me. You can't even see any wound in the upper area of this (sic)….

Gunn then turns to the mysterious skull photograph F8. See the Postscript to my medical essay, where, with the assistance of the X-rays, I demonstrate that this is the sole remaining photograph that does indeed show the authentic large hole at the right rear of the skull. Recall also that Robert McClelland, M.D., after returning from the Archives, volunteered that the current collection does contain such a photograph. F8 is the one. Once this is granted, then such a large hole immediately implies a frontal headshot. It is hardly surprising, therefore, that, for the cover-up, additional photographs (which would have properly oriented this wound, have been deliberately lost).

Gunn (p. 185):   The first question for you would be whether you can orient those photos so as to describe what is being represented in the photographs.

Humes: Boy, it's difficult. I can't. I just can't put them together. I can't tell you what—
Gunn: Can you identify whether that is even posterior or frontal or parietal?
Humes: No, I can't....

Humes's troubles don't stop there—he has the same problems with the brain photographs, as follows.

Gunn (p. 203): ...If you can just look at the basilar view [from underneath] of the brain, if you could describe what that view shows....

Humes: Boy, I have trouble with this. I don't know which end is up (sic). I don't know what happened here.... [*Mantik note:* Having seen these at the Archives, I know that this is really not so difficult as Humes implies.]

Gunn (p. 213): Did you notice that what at least appears to be a radio-opaque fragment during the autopsy [the mysterious 6.5 mm object]?

Humes: Well, I told you we ...retrieved one or two, and—of course, you get distortion in the X-ray as far as size goes. [*Mantik note:* That is not true in this case; there is actually very little image magnification, as I have determined from detailed measurements on the X-rays at the Archives; Humes is merely buying time for his answer here.] The ones we retrieved I didn't think were of the same size as this would lead you to believe. [*Mantik note:* That is certainly true of those metal fragments now in the Archives, as I discovered when I examined them. The most striking finding is actually the discrepancy in shape (of these metal fragments in the Archives) when compared to the fragments seen in the X-rays: the larger one is not 7x2 mm, as seen above the right frontal sinus in the X-rays, nor does it look like the 6.5 mm object, but (in the Archives collection) it is rather pancake shaped and much smaller (c. 2x3x2 mm). None of the tests performed on this object should have changed its shape. This paradoxical shape, by itself, is a bizarre situation and has never been examined or discussed by any official body.]

Gunn: Did you think they were larger or smaller?

Humes: Smaller. Smaller; considerably smaller.... But I don't remember retrieving anything of this size. [*Mantik note:* This confession was the best possible confirmation of my X-ray work. Humes has no memory of the 6.5 mm object—the same one that I concluded was actually not on the X-ray during the autopsy. The other two pathologists agreed, and the radiologist, when asked this question, abruptly terminated the entire conversation, which was never resumed. *The entire purpose of the X-rays was to locate such metal objects.* The invisibility of this object to the pathologists, and to all other autopsy observers, as well—and its absence from the forensic record—is surely one of the deepest mysteries of this entire case. I believe that this mystery has now been solved with the proposal of selectively (and critically) altered X-rays—i.e., the 6.5 mm object was superimposed on the original X-ray by a simple dark room technique which I have both discussed and demonstrated. In 1963, this was surprisingly easy to do; my prior essay (*Assassination Science*, 1998, pp. 120-137) even cites recipes from contemporaneous textbooks that could have been employed in precisely such an undertaking. I have been able, using current duplicating film, to produce astonishing figures, such as a scissors (made of air) lying entirely inside a skull, or a pterodactyl flying around inside a human skull. I have shown these actual composite X-rays (not just pictures of them) at public lectures. For an early description of my work, see Anthony and Robbyn Summers, "The Ghosts of November," *Vanity Fair* (December 1994), p. 97.]

Gunn: Well, that was going to be a question, whether you had identified that as a possible fragment and then removed it?

Humes: Truthfully, I don't remember anything that size when I looked at these films. They all were more of the size of these others. [Notice that he does not claim a loss of memory about this object. He clearly implies that he does remember—and that it simply was not there.]

Gunn: What we're referring to is a fragment that appears to be semicircular.

Humes: Yeah…

Gunn then asks about the dark frontal area on the lateral skull X-ray (Figure 11A–B of my medical essay), an area that appears to contain almost no tissue at all, despite that fact that the body and brain photographs suggest little or no missing tissue at this same site.

Humes (p. 216): What seems to be the frontal portion of it. I don't understand why that is [so dark]. You'd have to have some radiologist tell me about that (sic). I can't make that out…. I don't understand this great void there [the dark area at the front]. I don't know what that's all about.

Gunn (p. 218): I had another question for you about the lateral X-ray…. And that is whether you can identify the particles that you made reference to before and where they appear in this photograph. [*Mantik note:* He is asking about the trail of metallic debris (see Figure 11A–B of my medical essay).]

Humes: Well, you see, there's nothing in this projection [the lateral view] that appears to be of the size of the one that appeared to be above and behind the eye [the 6.5 mm object] on the other one [the frontal view]. But that could be positional or the other thing is an artifact (sic). I don't know what…. [*Mantik note:* Actually the object at the rear of the lateral skull—that should correspond to the 6.5 mm object—is quite easy to see on the X-rays in the Archives. It was even described by Sibert and O'Neill in their FBI report. It spatially correlates with the 6.5 mm object on the frontal X-ray. It is the right size--almost exactly 6.5 mm high. These comments by Humes are simply inexplicable. I do not know whether he is being deliberately obtuse or whether he truly does not understand the X-rays.]

Gunn: Do those metal fragments—or do those radio-opaque objects help you in any way identify entrance or exit wounds?

Humes: No. No, they really don't.

Gunn: Is there any relationship or correlation between those metal fragments and the bullet wound?

Humes: Not that I can make out at all, no. They seem to be random. [*Mantik note:* Most likely, they represent the trail of a frontal bullet, as is discussed elsewhere in my medical essay.]

Gunn: OK. Dr. Humes, I'd like to show you…the autopsy [report], and ask if you would read the paragraph on page 4…. [*Mantik note:* This is about the bone fragments that were received late in the autopsy from Dallas.]

Humes: …And then we got these [bone] fragments, at one margin of it there's something that seemed to match up with that fragment that was still in the skull. My memory's pretty good (sic). I said we had three. That's what we have, I guess. I described several metallic fragments along the line [on the lateral X-ray] … joining the occipital wound with the right supraorbital ridge [above the right eye]….

Gunn (p. 221): Could you point out for me [on the lateral X-ray] where the minute particles of metal in the bone are in relationship to the small occipital wound and the right supraorbital ridge?

Humes: Well, they don't relate at all in this picture, as far as I'm concerned.

Gunn: "This picture" being [the lateral X-ray]?

Humes: Yeah. I don't know where I got that, but there's—the occipital wound would never be up that high…. There's nothing up there (sic)….

Gunn (p. 222): Do you see any fragments that correspond with a small occipital wound?

Humes:	No. [*Mantik note:* I have confirmed this on the X-rays in the Archives; there is no metallic debris near the low occipital site that the pathologists identify as the entry site—although that does not necessarily disqualify it as an entry site.]
Gunn:	Do you recall having seen an X-ray previously that had fragments corresponding to a small occipital wound?
Humes:	Well, I reported that I did, so I must have (sic). But I don't see it now (sic).... All I know is that I wrote it down. I didn't write it down out of whole cloth (sic). I wrote down what I saw. [*Mantik note:* No X-ray of JFK shows such a trail near the occipital entry site. This reply by Humes is preposterous. On one hand, he claims that the X-rays are authentic, but, on the other hand, he says that, in 1963, he actually saw a metallic trail extending from low on the skull—near his entry site—to the supraorbital area. This is sheer, unassailable nonsense, and Humes must surely know it. Gunn probably took this line of questioning as far as he could go. Any further questions, I am told by Douglas Horne, might have propelled Humes straight out of the room. Humes has been caught in the fundamental lie of the X-rays. For those who like smoking guns, this is as close as anything gets in this case.]
Gunn:	Does that raise any question in your mind about the authenticity of the X-ray that you're looking at now in terms of being an X-ray of President Kennedy?
Humes:	Well, there's aspects of it I don't understand. I don't understand this big void up—maybe a radiologist could explain it. I don't know what this big ... [dark area at the front of the lateral X-ray] that takes up half of the skull here, I don't understand that.
Gunn:	Do you remember seeing that on the night of the autopsy?
Humes:	No, I don't.... [*Mantik note:* Nonetheless, he has still claimed that the X-rays are authentic.]

Gunn soon after wants to know whether Humes ever met President Johnson.

Humes (p. 236):	I met with President Johnson, but not in any way connected with this. In fact, I'm wearing a pair of cuff links that he gave me today. I was able to report to him that the nodule we took out of his larynx was benign, and he was very happy.
Gunn:	I can imagine. I would be, too. You don't wish your cuff links to be part of the exhibit (sic)—
Humes:	Oh, I think we ought to just take that out of the report, if you don't mind. I shouldn't have mentioned it, I suppose. But not everybody has a pair of these presidential cuff links (sic).

Before closing the deposition, Gunn asks the one question that should routinely be asked of all witnesses, but which, given the straitjacket donned by the legal set, was almost never asked by the Warren Commission or by the HSCA.

Gunn (p. 236):	...[can you] think of any additional information that would ... help provide a better understanding of either what happened during the autopsy or the wounds that were inflicted on President Kennedy?
Humes:	I have trouble conjuring up—I wish that the photographs were more graphic and more specifically helpful than they are. I'm disappointed by that, and I didn't find that out with certainty, really, until I got to that House Select Committee hearing. I had difficulty. There were a lot of people around, and they were showing and throwing these up, and I really didn't have the time that I had even today. I was even more confused at that point. But, you know, that's spilled milk....

Gunn: Are there any additional comments that you'd like to make? I told you I'd
                   give you that opportunity.
Humes: No. I'm still somewhat vague on the precise bottom line of all your efforts
                   to do these things…. But if you ask a person enough questions often enough,
                   you're going to confuse themselves sooner or later and not say the same
                   thing twice…so I'm concerned that we've got so much information put
                   together that we—well, there's an expression in golf. You get paralysis of
                   analysis. You know, you get more information than you can usefully put
                   together. But that's for your—I mean, that's for you to decide, not me. I
                   can't tell.

A summary of Humes's testimony. Besides reading this transcript, I have listened to
the actual tape of this deposition (and many others described in my medical essay).
What struck me (and what is not evident in the transcript) is how quickly, and how
unhesitatingly, Humes affirmed the authenticity of both the X-rays and the photographs
(of both the brain and the body). Yet he cannot identify several critical features in the
posterior head photograph (such as his supposedly obvious entry wound that did not
require any shaving of the head, as he stated to *JAMA*), nor can he orient either the brain
photographs or the mystery F8 photograph of the skull, nor does he understand (or
even recall) the large dark area at the front of the lateral skull X-ray, nor can he (even
remotely) explain why the trail of bullet debris disagrees by four inches with his official
report, nor can he explain why the most important object on the extant X-rays—the
largest "metal" fragment—was neither seen nor removed during the autopsy. After all of
this (apparent) ineptitude, and despite forthrightly (and often) admitting confusion and
uncertainty during his interrogation, he nonetheless insists that there is one point about
which he is still certain--the photographs and the X-rays are authentic. As the deposition with Humes closed, he avowed that he would rather not undergo such questioning
every day. As I pondered this, I could not but think of Lyndon Johnson's first address to
Congress (27 November 1963): "All I have I would have given gladly not to be standing
here today."

Article from The New York Times
(1 August 1998, p. A9)

[Editor's note*: If the official
government account is correct,
why then has so much of the
evidence in this case been altered,
created, or destroyed? The simplest
explanation for government
involvement in the cover-up, after
all, is government involvement in
the crime. Indeed, when systematically applied to alternative
theories, government involvement
is the only hypothesis that can
adequately explain what we now
know about the death of JFK.*]

(August 28, 89
*Second Set of Photos
Of Kennedy Autopsy*

WASHINGTON, July 31 (AP) —
According to testimony released today about the autopsy on President
John F. Kennedy, a second set of
photographs, in addition to the set at
the National Archives, was taken of
Kennedy's wounds. The second set of
photographs was never made public
and its whereabouts is not known.

The second set is believed to have
been taken by a White House photographer, Robert L. Knudsen, during or
after the autopsy, at the National
Naval Medical Center in Bethesda,
Md. Its existence raises new questions about how the autopsy was conducted, a subject of intense debate
for 35 years.

[The Warren Commission and The Warren Report*] both ignored
or suppressed what was opposed to the predetermined
conclusion that Oswald alone was the assassin.*

*This meant that the destruction, alteration and
manipulation of evidence had to be "overlooked."*
It was.
*This meant that impossible testimony from
preposterous witnesses had to be credited.*
It was.
This meant that invalid reconstructions had to be made.
They were.
*This meant that valuable evidence available
to the Commission had to be avoided.*
It was.

*This meant that the incontrovertible proofs in the
photographs had to be replaced by elaborate and invalid
reenactments which, in turn, had to be based upon inaccuracies,
misinformation and misrepresentation,
which is what was done.*

—Harold Weisberg

Index

A

a fragment of glass 258
a sabot found 255
A/P cranial X-ray 254
ABC News ix
Abt, John 117
Adams, Bill 164
Adams, Perry 172
Adams, Victoria 44, 45, 46
additional bullets found 76-77
additional frames 354-355
admissibility of films and photographs 331
adrenal insufficiency 61
affidavit, Roger McCarthy 398
AFIP (Armed Forces Institute of Pathology) 206
Aguilar, Gary 7-9, 64, 152, 175, 220, 234, 239, 243, 279, 286, 295, 303, 337, 387, 405, 440, 444, 445, 466
Akin, Gene 56, 60, 150, 180, 197, 199, 240, 249, 252, 298
Aldredge, Eugene 152
Alexander, William 69, 80, 101
Allende, Salvadore 392
Allman, Pierce 51
altered medical evidence 376-380, passim
Altgens photograph 151, 148-149, 169, 258
Altgens photograph 34-35, passim
Altgens, James 28, 34, 35, 123, 152, 259, Insert-4, Insert-5
Altick, Richard 383
Altman, Lawrence K. 439
Alvarez, Luis 386, 408
Alvarez, Walter 386
AM/LASH 20
AMA (American Medical Association) 175, 177
Ambrose, Stephen 375, 376, 394, 406
American Medical Association (AMA) 175, 177
ammunition clip 81-82
Andrews, Dean 172
Angel, J. Lawrence 294, 280-281
Angleton, James Jesus 388
anti-Castro Cubans 13, 161, 167, 379
Applin, George 89
AR-15 43
Aragon, Ernest 165
Arce, Danny 19, 34
Archer, Jules 409
Arden, John 419
Armed Forces Institute of Pathology (AFIP) 206, 243
Armstong, Andrew 87
Armstrong, John 336, 406
Arnett, Charles 35
Arnold film Insert-8
Arnold, Carolyn 27, 28, 28, 29, 366
Arnold, Gordon 41, Insert-6
ARRB 1, 2, 175, 371, 432, 222-223
ARRB as a model for future inquiries 292
arrest report on Lee Harvey Oswald 367-368
Artwohl, Robert 196
Ashby, Bill 137
assassination buffs 374
Assassination Records Review Board (ARRB) x
Assassination Science ix, 421-423, passim
Atkins, Thomas 34
Ault, C. 343
Aunt Margaret's skirts 268
autopsy at Bethesda 112-113
autopsy camera 278
autopsy protocol revised 272
axis of debris 7, passim
Ayer, A. J. 328

B

Babuska lady 45
back wound 252, 253, 434, 442, 446, passim
back wound, photograph of 228
background magnification 330
backyard photograph 369, 417, 432
backyard photographs 104, 116
Bacon, Francis 408
Baconian fallacy 385
Baden, Michael 182, 188, 200, 210, 234, 293-295, 380, 407-408
Badgeman Insert-6
Bagdikian, Ben H. 394
Bakeman, George 112
Baker, Bobby 17
Baker, Marrion 33, 37, 40, 46, 121, 172, 341, 366
Baker, Mrs. Donald 59
Ball, George 103
Barbee specimen 76
Barbee, William 76
Barker, Eddie 52
Barnes, Pete 110
Barnes, W. E. 72, 79
Bartholomew, Dennis 405
Bartholomew, Richard 57
Bartlett, Orrin H. 135, 429
Bashour, Fouad 56, 177, 199, 240, 240
Baskin, Robert 123
Batchelor, Leslie 358-360, 424
Baughman, Chief 162-163
Baxter, Charles 56, 60, 150, 176-181, 190, 192, 197, 199, 240, 297, 298
Bay of Pigs 412
Beard, Charles 407
Beauboeuf, Alvin 53
Becker, Carl 382, 385, 385, 392
Behn, Jerry 62, 85, 159, 160-164, 167, 168, 169
Belcher, Carl W. 202
believers in JFK assassination conspiracy 404
Belin, David 372, 388, 405
Belknap, Jerry B. 29
Bell, Audrey 174, 179, 256
Belmont, Alan 85, 114
Belzer, Richard 338
Benavides, Domingo 73, 78, 91
Benn, Anthony Wedgwood 419
Benn, Mrs. Carolyn Wedgwood 419
Bennett, Glen 26, 37, 60, 122, 167
Benson, Leland 301, 303
Bentley, Paul 72, 92
Berger, Andy 96
Berkley, George G. 273
Beschloss, Michael 375, 406, 410
Betzner, Hugh 125, Insert-3
Betzner, Hugh, Jr. 39
beveling 435, 206-207
Billings, Richard N. 234, 296, 301
Bishop, Jim 42, 99, 102, 137, 159, 173
Bishop, William 68
Blakey, Robert 200, 211, 234, 235, 282-283, 290, 296-297, 301, 375, 386, 404, 408
Bledsoe, Mary 53, 58, 90
blob 10
Blumberg, J. M. 247, 303, 306
blur analysis 353, 355
Bobby Baker scandal 94
body alteration 308
body alteration thesis 244, 247
body unlawfully removed 96
body was altered 248

N

O

T

U

Acknowledgments

The incentive for this volume came from the release of more than 60,000 documents and records by the Assassination Records Review Board (ARRB), which was motivated by the surge of public interest stimulated by Oliver Stone's film, *JFK*. I and all other students of the assassination of John F. Kennedy are therefore indebted to Oliver Stone and to the ARRB for their contributions to the public record. Many of the contributors partipated in a conference, The Death of JFK, held on the Twin Cities campus of the University of Minnesota, 14–16 May 1998, which I organized and moderated. Reflecting on these new developments led me to consider how they might be presented to a wider audience. If there ever were valid excuses for ignorance, real or feigned, in this matter of moment, they no longer obtain. As Jefferson observed, as long as we are ignorant, we are not free.

As a great admirer of Bertrand Russell, not least for his willingness to engage in issues of public debate, it is an honor to republish his "16 Questions on the Assassination", *The Autobiography of Bertrand Russell, 1944-67* (London: George Allen and Unwin, Ltd., 1969), pp. 197-204, by permission of Taylor & Francis. Vincent Palamara, "59 Witnesses: Delay on Elm Street", *The Dealey Plaza Echo* 3 (July 1999), pp. 1–7, and portions of James H. Fetzer, "Where were you when JFK was shot?", *The Dealey Plaza Echo* 3 (November 1999), pp. 26–29, which have been incorporated into "Jesse Curry's *JFK Assassination File*", appear by permission of Ian Griggs, Editor. Douglas P. Horne, "Evidence of a Government Cover-Up: Two Different Specimens in President Kennedy's Autopsy," *Kennedy Assasssination Chronicles* 4 (1998), appears by permission of Debra Conway, JFK Lancer Publications & Productions.

I am grateful to David W. Mantik, M.D., Ph.D., Gary Aguilar, M.D., Ira David Wood, III, Douglas Weldon, J.D., Vincent Palamara, Douglas P. Horne, and Jack White for their excellent contributions. Towner frames by permission of Tina Towner Barnes. Each of the authors retains copyright of his work as follows:

"'Smoking Guns' in the Death of JFK" © 2000 James H. Fetzer
"22 November 1963: A Chronology" © 2000 Ira David Wood III
"59 Witnesses: Delay on Elm Street" © 2000 Vincent Palamara
"The Kennedy Limousine: Dallas 1963" © 2000 Douglas Weldon
"The Secret Service: On the Job in Dallas" © 2000 Vincent Palamara
"The Converging Medical Case for Conspiracy in the Death of JFK"
    © 2000 Gary Aguilar
"Paradoxes of the JFK Assassination: The Medical Evidence Decoded"
    © 2000 David W. Mantik
"Evidence of a Government Cover-Up: Two Different Brain Specimens in President Kennedy's Autopsy" © 2000 Douglas P. Horne
"The Great Zapruder Film Hoax" (color photo insert) © 2000 Jack White
"Paradoxes of the JFK Assassination: The Zapruder Film Controversy"
    © 2000 David W. Mantik
"Jesse Curry's *JFK Assassination File*: Could Oswald Have Been Convicted?"
    © 2000 James H. Fetzer
"Paradoxes of the JFK Assassination: The Silence of the Historians"
    © 2000 David W. Mantik

Contributors

GARY L. AGUILAR, M.D., of San Francisco, CA. An opthalmologist specializing in plastic and reconstructive surgery, he is also Assistant Clinical Professor of Opthalmology at Stanford University and the University of California, San Francisco. He has lectured extensively on the assassination of JFK and has a special interest in the medical evidence, on which he is a leading authority, including especially eyewitness reports from Parkland Memorial Hospital and Bethesda Medical Center.

JAMES H. FETZER, Ph.D., of Duluth, MN. McKnight University Professor of Philosophy at the University of Minnesota, where he teaches on its Duluth campus, he received his A.B. *magna cum laude* from Princeton and his Ph.D. in the history and philosophy of science at Indiana. He has published 20 books and more than 100 articles in philosophy of science and on the theoretical foundations of computer science, artifical intelligence, and cognitive science. He edited *Assassination Science* (1998).

DOUGLAS P. HORNE of Falls Church, VA. A *cum laude* graduate of Ohio State University with a B.A. in history, he has studied the assassination of JFK since 1966. He served as a surface warfare officer in the U.S. Navy from 1975-85, then served another ten years as Operations Manager at a naval field office in Pearl Harbor. He left this position and relocated to Washington, D.C., in 1995 to accept an appointment with the Military Records Team on the staff of the ARRB, where he subsequently became Senior Analyst for Military Records.

DAVID W. MANTIK, M.D., Ph.D., of Rancho Mirage, CA. He received his Ph.D. in physics from Wisconsin and his M.D. from the University of Michigan. A Board Certified Radiation Oncologist, he has done pioneering work studying the autopsy X-rays with densitometry, a type of investigation never before performed, and has conducted the most extensive studies of the Zapruder film ever undertaken. His important studies of the X-rays and of the alteration of the film appear in *Assassination Science* (1998).

VINCENT PALAMARA of Pittsburgh, PA. A graduate of Duquesne University, he has investigated Secret Service aspects of the death of JFK since 1988 and is now widely recognized as the leading expert on this subject. His first book, *The Third Alternative—Survivors Guilt: The Secret Service and the JFK Murder*, has been very well received. In addition to his articles in assassination research journals, he has completed a second book, *JFK: The Medical Evidence Reference*, which is also viewed as a valuable resource.

BERTRAND RUSSELL (1872-1970), among the most prominent philosophers of the 20th century, published more than 100 books during his long and distinguished career. He held a wide variety of positions at Cambridge University and elsewhere, displaying an unusual concern for contemporary affairs that set him apart from most of his academic colleagues. Some of his most important work was on the foundations of logic, mathematics, and the theory of knowledge. He received the Nobel Prize for literature in 1950.

JACK WHITE of Fort Worth, TX. A leading expert on photographic aspects of the assassination of JFK, he produced *The Continuing Inquiry* for the celebrated investigator, Penn Jones, with whom he worked for three years. He served as an advisor on photographic evidence for the House Select Committee on Assassinations during its reinvestigation of 1977-78 and for Oliver Stone in producing his motion picture, *JFK*. He has prepared a special color-photo section on the alteration of the Zapruder film for this volume.

DOUGLAS WELDON, J.D., of Kalamazoo, MI. An attorney for the County of Kalamazoo Circuit Court and Adjunct Professor for Western Michigan University's Department of Criminal Justice and its Graduate Department of Educational Leadership, he received his J.D. from Thomas M. Cooley Law School, a Master's degree in Educational Leadership from Western Michigan University, and a degree in Political Science and Sociology from Olivet College. He has undertaken extensive investigations of the Presidential Lincoln limousine.

IRA DAVID WOOD, III, of Raleigh, NC. A native of North Carolina, he is an award-winning director, actor, and playwright, who became a student of the death of JFK while contemplating a dramatic work on the assassination. The outcome has been a chronology of events for 22 November 1963, which he still considers to be an on-going "work in progress" now of nearly ten years standing. A graduate of the North Carolina School of the Arts, he is the founder, and Executive Director, of Theatre In The Park in Raleigh, NC.